Beginning Android 4
Games Development

Mario Zechner
Robert Green

Apress®

Beginning Android 4 Games Development

Copyright © 2011 by Mario Zechner and Robert Green

ISBN-13 (pbk): 978-1-4302-3987-1

ISBN-13 (electronic): 978-1-4302-3988-8

President and Publisher: Paul Manning
Lead Editor: Steve Anglin
Development Editor: Gary Schwartz
Editorial Board: Steve Anglin, Mark Beckner, Ewan Buckingham, Gary Cornell,
    Morgan Engel, Jonathan Gennick, Jonathan Hassell, Robert Hutchinson,
    Michelle Lowman, James Markham, Matthew Moodie, Jeff Olson, Jeffrey Pepper,
    Douglas Pundick, Ben Renow-Clarke, Dominic Shakeshaft, Gwenan Spearing,
    Matt Wade, Tom Welsh
Coordinating Editor: Adam Heath
Copy Editor: Chandra Clarke
Compositor: MacPS, LLC
Indexer: BIM Indexing & Proofreading Services
Artist: SPi Global
Cover Designer: Anna Ishchenko

Distributed to the book trade worldwide by Springer Science+Business Media, LLC., 233 Spring Street, 6th Floor, New York, NY 10013. Phone 1-800-SPRINGER, fax (201) 348-4505, e-mail orders-ny@springer-sbm.com, or visit www.springeronline.com.

For information on translations, please e-mail rights@apress.com, or visit www.apress.com.

Apress and friends of ED books may be purchased in bulk for academic, corporate, or promotional use. eBook versions and licenses are also available for most titles. For more information, reference our Special Bulk Sales–eBook Licensing web page at www.apress.com/bulk-sales.

Any source code or other supplementary materials referenced by the author in this text is available to readers at www.apress.com. For detailed information about how to locate your book's source code, go to http://www.apress.com/source-code/.

Dedicated to our idols, fans, families, and loved ones

Contents at a Glance

Contents

About the Authors

 **Mario Zechner** is a software engineer in R&D by day, and an enthusiastic game developer by night, publishing under the name of Badlogic Games. He developed the game Newton for Android, and Quantum for Windows, Linux, and Mac OSX, besides a ton of prototypes and small-scale games. He's currently working on an open source cross-platform solution for game development called libgdx. In addition to his coding activities, he actively writes tutorials and articles on game development, which are freely available on the Web and specifically his blog (http://www.badlogicgames.com).

 **Robert Green** is the founder of the game studio Battery Powered Games in Portland, Oregon. He has developed nine Android games including Deadly Chambers, Antigen, Wixel, Light Racer, and Light Racer 3D. Before diving full-time into mobile video game development and publishing, Robert worked for software companies in Minneapolis and Chicago, including IBM Interactive. Robert's current focus is on cross-platform game development and high-performance mobile gaming. Robert often updates his personal blog with game programming tidbits at http://www.rbgrn.net.

Acknowledgments

We would like to thank the Apress team that made this book possible in the first place. Specifically we'd like to thank Candace English and Adam Heath, our awesome coordinating editors, who never got tired answering all of our silly questions; Matthew Moodie for helping us structure the sections and giving invaluable hints and suggestions to make this book a whole lot better; and Damon Larson and James Compton, for being the brave souls that had to correct all of our grammar errors. Thanks guys, it's been a pleasure working with you.

Special thanks to all of our friends around the globe who gave us ideas, feedback, and comfort. This goes specifically to Nathan Sweet, Dave Clayton, Dave Fraska, Moritz Post, Ryan Foss, Bill Nagel, Zach Wendt, Scott Lembke, Christoph Widulle, and Tony Wang, the coding ninjas working with me on libgdx; John Phil and Ali Mosavian, long-time coding buddies from Sweden; and Roman Kern and Markus Muhr, whom Mario has had the pleasure to work with at his day job.

Rob would like to thank his wife, Holly, for all of her patience and understanding throughout not just this book but his game development career. Without her, he wouldn't have been able to make it this far. He would also like to thank his parents for bringing home that KayPro II in the 80s, buying him his 486 in 1993 and allowing him to chase that lifelong curiosity that is technology and software.

Last, but certainly not least, Mario would like to thank his love, Stefanie, who put up with all the long nights alone in bed, as well as his grumpiness. Luipo!

—Mario and Rob

Introduction

Hi there, and welcome to the world of Android game development. You came here to learn about game development on Android, and we hope to be the people who enable you to realize your ideas.

Together we'll cover quite a range of materials and topics: Android basics, audio and graphics programming, a little math and physics, and a scary thing called OpenGL ES. Based on all this knowledge, we'll develop three different games, one even being 3D.

Game programming can be easy if you know what you're doing. Therefore, we've tried to present the material in a way that not only gives you helpful code snippets to reuse, but actually shows you the big picture of game development. Understanding the underlying principles is the key to tackling ever more complex game ideas. You'll not only be able to write games similar to the ones developed over the course of this book, but you'll also be equipped with enough knowledge to go to the Web or the bookstore and take on new areas of game development on your own.

A Word About the Target Audience

This book is aimed first and foremost at complete beginners in game programming. You don't need any prior knowledge on the subject matter; We'll walk you through all the basics. However, we need to assume a little knowledge on your end about Java. If you feel rusty on the matter, we'd suggest refreshing your memory by reading the online edition of *Thinking in Java*, by Bruce Eckel (Prentice Hall, 2006), an excellent introductory text on the programming language. Other than that, there are no other requirements. No prior exposure to Android or Eclipse is necessary!

This book is also aimed at the intermediate-level game programmer that wants to get her hands dirty with Android. While some of the material may be old news for you, there are still a lot of tips and hints contained that should make reading this book worthwhile. Android is a strange beast at times, and this book should be considered your battle guide.

How This Book Is Organized

This book takes an iterative approach in that we'll slowly but surely work our way from the absolute basics to the esoteric heights of hardware-accelerated game programming goodness. Over the course of the chapters, we'll build up a reusable code base, so we'd suggest going through the chapters in sequence. Of course, more experienced readers canskip certain sections they feel confident with. Just make sure to read through the code listings of sections you skim over, so you will understand how the classes and interfaces are used in subsequent, more advanced sections.

Getting the Source Code

This book is fully self-contained; all the code necessary to run the examples and games is included. However, copying the listings from the book to Eclipse is error prone, and games do not consist of code alone, but also have assets that you can't easily copy out of the book. Also, the process of copying code from the book's text to Eclipse can introduce errors. We took great care to ensure that all the listings in this book are error free, but the gremlins are always hard at work.

To make this a smooth ride, we created a Google Code project that offers you the following:

- The complete source code and assets, licensed under the GPL version 3, available from the project's Subversion repository.

- A quickstart guide showing you how to import the projects into Eclipse in textual form, and a video demonstration for the same.

- An issue tracker that allows you to report any errors you find, either in the book itself or in the code accompanying the book. Once you file an issue in the issue tracker, we can incorporate any fixes in the Subversion repository. This way, you'll always have an up-to-date, (hopefully) error-free version of this book's code from which other readers can benefit as well.

- A discussion group that is free for everybody to join and discuss the contents of the book. We'll be on there as well, of course.

For each chapter that contains code, there's an equivalent Eclipse project in the Subversion repository. The projects do not depend on each other, as we'll iteratively improve some of the framework classes over the course of the book. Therefore, each project stands on its own. The code for both Chapters 5 and 6 is contained in the ch06-mrnom project.

The Google Code project can be found at http://code.google.com/p/beginning-android-games.

Chapter 1

Android, the New Kid on the Block

As kids of the early nineties, we naturally grew up with our trusty Nintendo Game Boys and Sega Game Gears. We spent countless hours helping Mario rescue the princess, getting the highest score in Tetris, and racing our friends in Super RC Pro-Am via Link Cable. We took these awesome pieces of hardware with us everywhere we could. Our passion for games made us want to create our own worlds and share them with our friends. We started programming on the PC, but soon realized that we couldn't transfer our little masterpieces to the available portable game consoles. As we continued being enthusiastic programmers, over time our interest in actually playing video games faded. Besides, our Game Boys eventually broke...

Fast forward to 2011. Smartphones have become the new mobile gaming platforms of this era, competing with classic, dedicated handheld systems such as the Nintendo DS and the PlayStation PSP. This development renewed our interest, and we started investigating which mobile platforms would be suitable for our development needs. Apple's iOS seemed like a good candidate for our game coding skills. However, we quickly realized that the system was not open, that we'd be able to share our work with others only if Apple allowed it, and that we'd need a Mac in order to develop for the iOS. And then we found Android.

We immediately fell in love. Android's development environment works on all the major platforms—no strings attached. It has a vibrant developer community, happy to help you with any problem you encounter, as well as offering comprehensive documentation. You can share your games with anyone without having to pay a fee to do so, and if you want to monetize your work, you can easily publish your latest and greatest innovation to a global market with millions of users in a matter of minutes.

The only thing left was to figure out how to write games for Android, and how to transfer our PC game development knowledge to this new system. In the following chapters, we want to share our experience with you and get you started with Android game development. Of course, this is partly a selfish plan: we want to have more games to play on the go!

Let's start by getting to know our new friend, Android.

A Brief History of Android

Android was first seen publicly in 2005, when Google acquired a small startup called Android Inc. This fueled speculation that Google was interested in entering the mobile device space. In 2008, the release of version 1.0 of Android put an end to all speculation, and Android went on to become the new challenger on the mobile market. Since then, Android has been battling it out with already-established platforms, such as iOS (then called iPhone OS) and BlackBerry OS. Android's growth has been phenomenal, as it has captured more and more market share every year. While the future of mobile technology is always changing, one thing is certain: Android is here to stay.

Because Android is open source, there is a low barrier of entry for handset manufacturers using the new platform. They can produce devices for all price segments, modifying Android itself to accommodate the processing power of a specific device. Android is therefore not limited to high-end devices, but can also be deployed in low-cost devices, thus reaching a wider audience.

A crucial ingredient for Android's success was the formation of the Open Handset Alliance (OHA) in late 2007. The OHA includes companies such as HTC, Qualcomm, Motorola, and NVIDIA, which all collaborate to develop open standards for mobile devices. Although Android's code is developed primarily by Google, all the OHA members contribute to its source code in one form or another.

Android itself is a mobile operating system and platform based on the Linux kernel version 2.6, and it is freely available for commercial and noncommercial use. Many members of the OHA build custom versions of Android with modified user interfaces (UIs) for their devices, such as HTC's Sense and Motorola's MOTOBLUR. The open-source nature of Android also enables hobbyists to create and distribute their own versions. These are usually called *mods*, *firmware*, or *roms*. The most prominent rom at the time of this writing was developed by a fellow known as Cyanogen, and it aims to bring the newest and best improvements to all sorts of Android devices.

Since its release in 2008, Android has received seven version updates, all code-named after desserts (with the exception of Android 1.1, which is irrelevant nowadays). Each version of the Android platform has added new functionality that is relevant, in one way or another, for game developers. Version 1.5 (Cupcake) added support for including native libraries in Android applications, which were previously restricted to being written in pure Java. Native code can be very beneficial in situations where performance is of utmost concern. Version 1.6 (Donut) introduced support for different screen resolutions. We will revisit that development a couple of times in this book because it has some impact on how we approach writing games for Android. With version 2.0 (Éclair) came support for multi-touch screens, and version 2.2 (Froyo) added just-in-time (JIT) compilation to the Dalvik virtual machine (VM), the software that powers all the Java applications on Android. JIT speeds up the execution of Android applications considerably—depending on the scenario, up to a factor of five. Version 2.3, called Gingerbread, added a new concurrent garbage collector to the Dalvik VM. Early in 2011,

Android spun off a tablet version called Honeycomb, which took on the version number 3.0. Honeycomb contained more significant application programming interface (API) changes than any other single Android released to date. By version 3.1, Honeycomb added extensive support for splitting up and managing a large, high-resolution tablet screen. It added more PC-like features, such as USB host support and support for USB peripherals, including keyboards, mice, and joysticks. The only problem with this release was that it was only targeted at tablets. The small-screen/smartphone version of Android was stuck with 2.3. Enter Android 4.0 AKA Ice Cream Sandwich (ICS), which is the result of merging Honeycomb (3.1) and Gingerbread (2.3) into a common set of features that works well on both tablets and phones.

ICS was a huge boost for end-users, adding a number of improvements to the Android user interface and built in applications such as the browser, email clients, and photo services. Among other things for developers, ICS merges in Honeycomb UI APIs which bring large-screen features to phones. ICS also merges in Honeycomb's USB periphery support, which gives manufacturers the option of supporting keyboards and joysticks. As for new APIs, ICS adds a few such as the Social API which provides a unified store for contacts, profile data, status updates, and photos. Fortunately for Android game developers, ICS at its core maintains good backward compatibility, ensuring that a properly constructed game will remain well-compatible with older versions like Cupcake and Eclair.

Fragmentation

The great flexibility of Android comes at a price: companies that opt to develop their own UIs have to play catch-up with the fast pace at which new versions of Android are released. This can lead to handsets no more than a few months old becoming outdated, as carriers and handset manufacturers refuse to create updates that incorporate the improvements of new Android versions. A result of this process is the big bogeyman called *fragmentation*.

Fragmentation has many faces. To the end user, it means being unable to install and use certain applications and features due to being stuck with an old Android version. For developers, it means that some care has to be taken when creating applications that should work on all versions of Android. While applications written for earlier versions of Android will usually run fine on newer ones, the reverse is not true. Some features added to newer Android versions are, of course, not available on older versions, such as multi-touch support. Developers are thus forced to create separate code paths for different versions of Android.

In 2011, many prominent Android device manufacturers agreed to support the latest Android OS for a device lifetime of 18 months. This may not seem like a long time, but it's a big step in helping to cut down on fragmentation. It also means that new features of Android, such as the new APIs in Ice Cream Sandwich, become available on more phones, much faster. Still, there will always be a significant portion of the market that is running older Android versions. If the developers of a game want mass market acceptance, the game will need to run on no fewer than six different versions of Android, spread across 400+ devices (and counting!).

But fear not. Although this sounds terrifying, it turns out that the measures that have to be taken to accommodate multiple versions of Android are minimal. Most often, you can even forget about the issue and pretend there's only a single version of Android. As game developers, we're less concerned with differences in APIs and more concerned with hardware capabilities. This is a different form of fragmentation, which is also a problem for platforms such as iOS, albeit not as pronounced. Throughout this book, we will cover the relevant fragmentation issues that might get in your way while you're developing your next game for Android.

The Role of Google

Although Android is officially the brainchild of the Open Handset Alliance, Google is the clear leader when it comes to implementing Android itself, as well as providing the necessary ecosystem for it to grow.

The Android Open Source Project

Google's efforts are summarized in the *Android Open Source Project*. Most of the code is licensed under Apache License 2, which is very open and nonrestrictive compared to other open source licenses, such as the GNU General Public License (GPL). Everyone is free to use this source code to build their own systems. However, systems that are proclaimed Android compatible first have to pass the Android Compatibility Program, a process ensuring baseline compatibility with third-party applications written by developers. Compatible systems are allowed to participate in the Android ecosystem, which also includes the Android Market.

The Android Market

The *Android Market* was opened to the public by Google in October 2008. It's an online software store that enables users to find and install third-party applications, or *apps*. The market is primarily available on Android devices, but also has a web front end where users can search, rate, download, and install apps. It isn't required, but the majority of Android devices have the Google Android Market app installed by default.

The market allows third-party developers to publish their programs either for free or as paid applications. Paid applications are available for purchase in many countries, and the integrated purchasing system handles exchange rates using Google Checkout. The Android Market also gives the option to price an app manually on a per-country basis.

A user gets access to the market after setting up a Google account. Applications can be purchased via credit card through Google Checkout or by using carrier billing. Buyers can decide to return an application within 15 minutes of the time of purchase for a full refund. Previously, the refund window was 24 hours, but it was shortened to curtail exploitation of the system.

Developers need to register an Android developer account with Google, for a one-time fee of $25, in order to be able to publish applications on the market. After successful registration, a developer can start publishing new applications in a matter of minutes.

The Android Market has no approval process, instead relying on a permission system. Before installing an application, the user is presented with a set of required permissions, which handle access to phone services, networking, Secure Digital (SD) cards, and so on. Only after the user has approved these permissions is the application installed. The system relies on user honesty. This approach isn't very successful on the PC, especially on Windows systems, but on Android, it seems to have worked so far; only a few applications have been pulled from the market due to malicious user behavior.

In order to sell applications, a developer additionally has to register a Google Checkout merchant account, which is free of charge. All financial transactions are handled through this account. Google also has an in-app purchase system, which is integrated with the Android Market and Google Checkout. A separate API is available for developers to process in-app purchase transactions.

Challenges, Device Seeding, and Google I/O

In an ongoing effort to draw more developers to the Android platform, Google introduced promotions in the form of challenges. The first of these, called the Android Developer Challenge (ADC), was launched in 2008 and offered relatively high cash prizes for the winning projects. The ADC was repeated the subsequent year, and was again a huge success in terms of developer participation. There was no ADC in either 2010 or 2011, probably because Android now has a considerable developer base and needs no further promotions aimed at getting new developers on board.

As an incentive for its developers, in early 2010 Google started a device-seeding program. Each developer with one or more applications on the market, that had more than 5,000 downloads and an average user rating of at least 3.5 stars, received a brand new Motorola Droid, Motorola Milestone, or Nexus One phone. This promotion was very well-received within the developer community. It was initially met with disbelief, though, as many considered the e-mail notifications that came out of the blue to be an elaborate hoax. Fortunately for the recipients, the promotion turned out to be real, and thousands of devices were sent to developers around the world—a great move by Google to keep its third-party developers happy, make them stick with the platform, and potentially attract new developers.

Google provides the special Android Dev Phone (ADP) for its developers. The first ADP was a version of the T-Mobile G1 (also known as the HTC Dream). The next iteration, called ADP2, was a variation of the HTC Magic. Google also released its own phone in the form of the Nexus One, originally available to end users. Although not initially released as an ADP, it was considered by many as the successor to the ADP2. Google eventually stopped selling the Nexus One to end users, and it is now available for shipment only to partners and developers. At the end of 2010, the latest ADP was released—a Samsung device running Android 2.3 (Gingerbread), called the Nexus S. ADPs can be bought on the Android Market, which requires you to have a developer account. The Nexus S can be bought via a separate Google site at www.google.com/phone.

The annual Google I/O conference is an event that every Android developer looks forward to each year. At Google I/O, the latest and greatest Google technologies and projects are revealed, among which Android has gained a special place in recent years. Google I/O usually features multiple sessions on Android-related topics, which are also available as videos on YouTube's Google Developers channel. At Google I/O 2011, Samsung and Google handed out Galaxy Tab 10.1 devices to all regular attendees. This really marked the start of the big push by Google to gain market share on the tablet side.

Android's Features and Architecture

Android is not just another Linux distribution for mobile devices. While developing for Android, you're not all that likely to meet the Linux kernel itself. The developer-facing side of Android is a platform that abstracts away the underlying Linux kernel and is programmed via Java. From a high-level view, Android possesses several nice features:

- An *application framework* that provides a rich set of APIs for creating various types of applications. It also allows the reuse and replacement of components provided by the platform and third-party applications.

- The *Dalvik virtual machine*, which is responsible for running applications on Android.

- A set of *graphics libraries* for 2D and 3D programming.

- *Media support* for common audio, video, and image formats, such as Ogg Vorbis, MP3, MPEG-4, H.264, and PNG. There's even a specialized API for playing back sound effects, which will come in handy in your game development adventures.

- *APIs for accessing peripherals* such as the camera, Global Positioning System (GPS), compass, accelerometer, touchscreen, trackball, keyboard, controller, and joystick. Note that not all Android devices have all these peripherals—hardware fragmentation in action.

Of course, there's a lot more to Android than the few features just mentioned. But, for your game development needs, these features are the most relevant.

Android's architecture is composed of stacked groups of components, and each layer builds on the components in the layer below it. Figure 1–1 gives an overview of Android's major components.

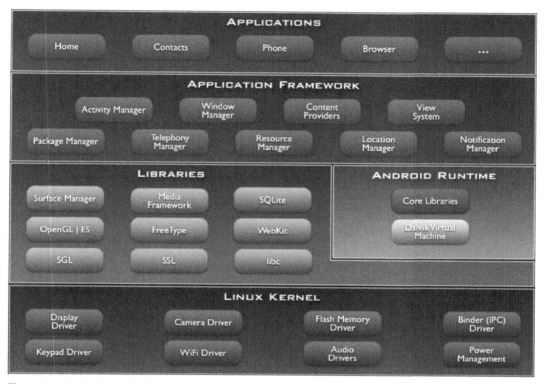

Figure 1–1. *Android architecture overview*

The Kernel

Starting at the bottom of the stack, you can see that the Linux kernel provides the basic drivers for the hardware components. Additionally, the kernel is responsible for such mundane things as memory and process management, networking, and so on.

The Runtime and Dalvik

The Android runtime is built on top of the kernel, and it is responsible for spawning and running Android applications. Each Android application is run in its own process with its own Dalvik VM.

Dalvik runs programs in the DEX bytecode format. Usually, you transform common Java .class files into DEX format using a special tool called *dx*, which is provided by the software development kit (SDK). The DEX format is designed to have a smaller memory footprint compared to classic Java .class files. This is achieved through heavy compression, tables, and merging of multiple .class files.

The Dalvik virtual machine interfaces with the core libraries, which provide the basic functionality that is exposed to Java programs. The core libraries provide some, but not all, of the classes available in Java Standard Edition (SE) through the use of a subset of the Apache Harmony Java implementation. This also means that there's no Swing or Abstract Window Toolkit (AWT) available, nor any classes that can be found in Java Micro Edition (ME). However, with some care, you can still use many of the third-party libraries available for Java SE on Dalvik.

Before Android 2.2 (Froyo), all bytecode was interpreted. Froyo introduced a tracing JIT compiler, which compiles parts of the bytecode to machine code on the fly. This considerably increases the performance of computationally intensive applications. The JIT compiler can use CPU features specifically tailored for special computations, such as a dedicated Floating Point Unit (FPU). Nearly every new version of Android improves upon the JIT compiler and enhances performance, usually at the cost of memory consumption. This is a scalable solution, though, as new devices contain more and more RAM as standard fare.

Dalvik also has an integrated garbage collector (GC). It's a mark-and-sweep, nongenerational GC that has the tendency to drive developers a little crazy at times. With some attention to detail, though, you can peacefully coexist with the GC in your day-to-day game development. The latest Android release (2.3) has an improved concurrent GC, which relieves some of the pain. You'll get to investigate GC issues in more detail later in the book.

Each application running in an instance of the Dalvik VM has a total of at least 16MB of heap memory available. Newer devices, specifically tablets, have much higher heap limits to facilitate higher-resolution graphics. Still, with games it is easy to use up all of that memory, so you have to keep that in mind as you juggle your image and audio resources.

System Libraries

Besides the core libraries, which provide some Java SE functionality, there's also a set of native C/C++ libraries (second layer in Figure 1–1), which build the basis for the application framework (third layer in Figure 1–1). These system libraries are mostly responsible for the computationally heavy tasks that would not be as well suited to the Dalvik VM, such as graphics rendering, audio playback, and database access. The APIs are *wrapped* by Java classes in the application framework, which you'll exploit when you start writing your games. You'll use the following libraries in one form or another:

> *Skia Graphics Library (Skia)*: This 2D graphics software is used for rendering the UI of Android applications. You'll use it to draw your first 2D game.

OpenGL for Embedded Systems (OpenGL ES): This is the industry standard for hardware-accelerated graphics rendering. OpenGL ES 1.0 and 1.1 are exposed to Java on all versions of Android. OpenGL ES 2.0, which brings shaders to the table, is only supported with Android 2.2 (Froyo) onward. It should be mentioned that the Java bindings for OpenGL ES 2.0 in Froyo are incomplete and lack a few vital methods. Fortunately, these methods were added in version 2.3. Also, the emulator and some of the older devices, which still make up a small share of the market, do not support OpenGL ES 2.0. For your purposes, stick with OpenGL ES 1.0 and 1.1, to maximize compatibility and allow you to ease into the world of Android 3D programming.

OpenCore: This is a media playback and recording library for audio and video. It supports a good mix of formats such as Ogg Vorbis, MP3, H.264, MPEG-4, and so on. You'll mostly deal with the audio portion, which is not directly exposed to the Java side, but rather wrapped in a couple of classes and services.

FreeType: This is a library used to load and render bitmap and vector fonts, most notably the TrueType format. FreeType supports the Unicode standard, including right-to-left glyph rendering for Arabic and similar special text. Sadly, this is not entirely true for the Java side, which still does not support Arabic typography. As with OpenCore, FreeType is not directly exposed to the Java side, but is wrapped in a couple of convenient classes.

These system libraries cover a lot of ground for game developers and perform most of the heavy lifting. They are the reason why you can write your games in plain old Java.

> **NOTE:** Although the capabilities of Dalvik are usually more than sufficient for your purposes, at times you might need more performance. This can be the case for very complex physics simulations or heavy 3D calculations, for which you would usually resort to writing native code. That aspect is not covered in this book. A couple of open source libraries for Android already exist that can help you stay on the Java side of things. See `http://code.google.com/p/libgdx/` for an example.

The Application Framework

The application framework ties together the system libraries and the runtime, creating the user side of Android. The framework manages applications and provides an elaborate structure within which applications operate. Developers create applications for this framework via a set of Java APIs that cover such areas as UI programming, background services, notifications, resource management, peripheral access, and so on. All out-of-the-box core applications provided by Android, such as the mail client, are written with these APIs.

Applications, whether they are UIs or background services, can communicate their capabilities to other applications. This communication enables an application to reuse components of other applications. A simple example is an application that needs to take a photo and then perform some operations on it. The application queries the system for a component of another application that provides this service. The first application can then reuse the component (for example, a built-in camera application or photo gallery). This significantly lowers the burden on programmers and also enables you to customize myriad aspects of Android's behavior.

As a game developer, you will create UI applications within this framework. As such, you will be interested in an application's architecture and life cycle, as well as its interactions with the user. Background services usually play a small role in game development, which is why they will not be discussed in detail.

The Software Development Kit

To develop applications for Android, you will use the Android software development kit (SDK). The SDK is composed of a comprehensive set of tools, documentation, tutorials, and samples that will help you get started in no time. Also included are the Java libraries needed to create applications for Android. These contain the APIs of the application framework. All major desktop operating systems are supported as development environments.

Prominent features of the SDK are as follows:

- The *debugger*, capable of debugging applications running on a device or in the emulator.
- A *memory and performance profile* to help you find memory leaks and identify slow code.
- The *device emulator*, accurate if a bit slow at times, is based on QEMU (an open source virtual machine for simulating different hardware platforms). *Command-line utilities* to communicate with devices.
- *Build scripts* and tools to package and deploy applications.

The SDK can be integrated with Eclipse, a popular and feature-rich open source Java integrated development environment (IDE). The integration is achieved through the Android Development Tools (ADT) plug-in, which adds a set of new capabilities to Eclipse for the following purposes: to create Android projects; to execute, profile, and debug applications in the emulator or on a device; and to package Android applications for their deployment to the Android Market. Note that the SDK can also be integrated into other IDEs, such as NetBeans. There is, however, no official support for this.

NOTE: Chapter 2 covers how to set up the development environment with the SDK and Eclipse.

The SDK and the ADT plug-in for Eclipse receive constant updates that add new features and capabilities. It's therefore a good idea to keep them updated.

Along with any good SDK comes extensive documentation. Android's SDK does not fall short in this area, and it includes a lot of sample applications. You can also find a developer guide and a full API reference for all the modules of the application framework at http://developer.android.com/guide/index.html.

The Developer Community

Part of the success of Android is its developer community, which gathers in various places around the Web. The most frequented site for developer exchange is the Android Developers group at http://groups.google.com/group/android-developers. This is the number one place to ask questions or seek help when you stumble across a seemingly unsolvable problem. The group is visited by all sorts of Android developers, from system programmers, to application developers, to game programmers. Occasionally, the Google engineers responsible for parts of Android also help out by offering valuable insights. Registration is free, and we highly recommend that you join this group now! Apart from providing a place for you to ask questions, it's also a great place to search for previously answered questions and solutions to problems. So, before asking a question, check whether it has been answered already.

Every developer community worth its salt has a mascot. Linux has Tux the penguin, GNU has its... well, gnu, and Mozilla Firefox has its trendy Web 2.0 fox. Android is no different, and has selected a little green robot as its mascot. Figure 1–2 shows you that little devil.

Figure 1–2. *Android's nameless mascot*

Although the choice of color may be debatable, this nameless little robot has already starred in a few popular Android games. Its most notable appearance was in Replica Island, a free open-source platform created by former Google developer advocate Chris Pruett as a 20 percent project. The term 20 percent project stands for the one day a week that Google employees get to spend on a project of their own choosing.

Devices, Devices, Devices!

Android is not locked into a single hardware ecosystem. Many prominent handset manufacturers, such as HTC, Motorola, Samsung, and LG, have jumped onto the Android bandwagon, and they offer a wide range of devices running Android. In addition to handsets, there are a slew of available tablet devices that build upon Android. Some key concepts are shared by all devices, though, which will make your life as game developer a little easier.

Hardware

Among the things that will be discussed later in the section on that moving target, Compatibility, Google originally issued the following minimum hardware specifications. Virtually all available Android devices fulfill, and often significantly surpass, these recommendations:

128MB RAM: This specification is a minimum. Current high-end devices already include 1GB RAM and, if Moore's law has its way, the upward trend won't end any time soon.

256MB flash memory: This is the minimum amount of memory required for storing the system image and applications. For a long time, lack of sufficient memory was the biggest gripe among Android users, as third-party applications could only be installed to flash memory. This changed with the release of Froyo.

Mini or Micro SD card storage: Most devices come with a few gigabytes of SD card storage, which can be replaced with higher-capacity SD cards by the user.

16-bit color Quarter Video Graphics Array (QVGA) Thin Film Transistor Liquid Crystal Display (TFT LCD): Before Android version 1.6, only Half-size VGA (HVGA) screens (480×320 pixels) were supported by the operating system. Since version 1.6, lower- and higher-resolution screens have been supported. The current high-end handsets have Wide VGA (WVGA) screens (800×480, 848×480, or 852×480 pixels), and some low-end devices support QVGA screens (320×280 pixels). Tablet screens come in various sizes, typically about 1280×800, and Google TV brings support for HDTV's 1920×1080 resolution! While many developers like to think that every device has a touchscreen, that is not the case. Android is pushing its way into set-top boxes and PC-like devices with traditional monitors. Neither of these have the same touchscreen input as a phone or tablet.

Dedicated hardware keys: These keys are used for navigation. Devices will always provide buttons specifically mapped to standard navigation commands, such as home and backs, usually set apart from on-screen touch commands. With Android the hardware range is huge, so make no assumptions!

Of course, most Android devices come with a lot more hardware than is required for the minimum specifications. Almost all handsets have *GPS*, an *accelerometer*, and a *compass*. Many also feature *proximity and light sensors*. These peripherals offer game developers new ways to let the user interact with games, and you can take a look at some of these later on. A few devices even have a full *QWERTY keyboard* and a *trackball*. The latter is most often found in HTC devices. *Cameras* are also available on almost all current portable devices. Some handsets and tablets have two cameras: one on the back and one on the front, for video chat.

Dedicated *graphics processing units (GPUs)* are especially crucial for game development. The earliest handset to run Android already had an OpenGL ES 1.0–compliant GPU. Newer portable devices have GPUs comparable in performance to the older Xbox or PlayStation 2, supporting OpenGL ES 2.0. If no graphics processor is available, the platform provides a fallback in the form of a software renderer called PixelFlinger. Many low-budget handsets rely on the software renderer, which is fast enough for most low-resolution screens.

Along with the graphics processor, any currently available Android device also has dedicated *audio hardware*. Many hardware platforms include special circuitry to decode different media formats, such as H.264. Connectivity is provided via hardware components for mobile telephony, Wi-Fi, and Bluetooth. All the hardware modules in an Android device are usually integrated in a single *system on chip (SoC)*, a system design also found in embedded hardware.

The Range of Devices

In the beginning, there was the G1. Developers eagerly awaited more devices, and several phones, with minute differences, soon followed, and these were considered "first generation." Over the years, hardware has become more and more powerful, and now there are phones, tablets, and set-top boxes ranging from devices with 2.5" QVGA screens, running only a software renderer on a 500MHz ARM CPU, all the way up to machines with dual 1GHz CPUs, with very powerful GPUs that can support HDTV.

We've already discussed fragmentation issues, but developers will also need to cope with this vast range of screen sizes, capabilities, and performance. The best way to do that is to understand the minimum hardware and make it the lowest common denominator for game design and performance testing.

The Minimum Practical Target

As of October 3, 2011, less than 3% of all Android devices are running a version of Android older than 2.1. This is important because it means that the game you start now will only have to support a minimum API level of 7 (2.1), and it will still reach 97% of all Android devices (by version) by the time it's completed. This isn't to say that you can't use the latest new features! You certainly can, and we'll show you how. You'll simply need to design your game with some fallback mechanisms to bring compatibility down to version 2.1. Current data is available via Google at `http://developer.android.com/resources/dashboard/platform-versions.html`, and a chart collected in mid-2011 is shown in Figure 1–3.

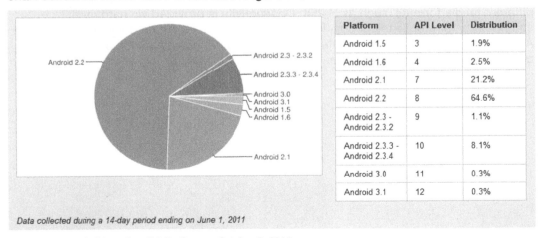

Platform	API Level	Distribution
Android 1.5	3	1.9%
Android 1.6	4	2.5%
Android 2.1	7	21.2%
Android 2.2	8	64.6%
Android 2.3 - Android 2.3.2	9	1.1%
Android 2.3.3 - Android 2.3.4	10	8.1%
Android 3.0	11	0.3%
Android 3.1	12	0.3%

Data collected during a 14-day period ending on June 1, 2011

Figure 1–3. *Android version distributions on October 3, 2011*

So, what's a good baseline device to use as a minimum target? Go back to the first Android 2.1 device released: the original *Motorola Droid*, shown in Figure 1–4. While it has since been updated to Android 2.2, the Droid is still a widely used device that is reasonably capable in terms of both CPU and GPU performance.

Figure 1–4. *The Motorola Droid*

The original Droid was coined the first "second generation" device, and it was released about a year after the first set of Qualcomm MSM7201A-based models, which included the G1, Hero, MyTouch, Eris, and many others. The Droid was the first phone to have a screen with a higher resolution than 480×320 and a discrete PowerVR GPU, and it was the first natively multi-touch Android device (though it had a few multi-touch issues, but more on that later).

Supporting the Droid means you're supporting devices that have the following set of specifications:

- A CPU speed between 550MHz and 1GHz with hardware floating-point support

- A programmable GPU supporting OpenGL ES 1.x and 2.0

- A WVGA screen

- Multi-touch support

- Android version 2.1 or 2.2+

The Droid is an excellent minimum target because it runs Android 2.2 and supports OpenGL ES 2.0. It also has a screen resolution similar to most phone-based handsets at 854×480. If a game works well on a Droid, it's likely to work well on 90% of all Android handsets. There are still going to be some old, and even some newer, devices that have a screen size of 480×320, so it's good to plan for it and at least test on them, but performance-wise, you're unlikely to need to support much less than the Droid to capture the vast majority of the Android market.

Cutting-Edge Devices

Honeycomb introduced very solid tablet support, and it's become apparent that tablets are a choice gaming platform. With the introduction of the NVIDIA Tegra 2 chip in early 2011 devices, both handsets and tablets started to receive fast, dual-core CPUs, and even more powerful GPUs have become the norm. It's difficult, when writing a book, to discuss what's modern because it changes so quickly, but at the time of this writing, it's becoming very common for devices to have ultra-fast processors all around, tons of storage, lots of RAM, high-resolution screens, two-handed multi-touch support, and even 3D stereoscopic display in a few of the new models.

The most common GPUs in Android devices are the PowerVR series, by Imagination Technologies, Snapdragon with integrated Adreno GPUs, by Qualcomm, and the Tegra series, by NVIDIA. The PowerVR currently comes in a few flavors: 530, 535, and 540. Don't be fooled by the small increments between model numbers; the 540 is an absolutely blazing-fast GPU compared to its predecessors, and it's shipped in the Samsung Galaxy S series, as well as the Google Nexus S. The 530 is in the Droid, and the 535 is scattered across a few models. Perhaps the most commonly used GPU is Qualcomm's, found in nearly every HTC device. The Tegra GPU is aimed at tablets, but it is also in several handsets. All three of these competing chip architectures are very comparable and very capable.

Samsung's Galaxy Tab 10.1 (see Figure 1–5) is currently the de facto standard Android tablet, and it sports the following features:

- NVIDIA Tegra 2 dual 1GHz CPU/GPU
- A programmable GPU supporting OpenGL ES 1.x and 2.0
- A 1280×800 screen
- Ten-point multi-touch support
- Android Honeycomb 3.1

Figure 1–5. *Samsung Galaxy Tab 10.1*

Supporting Galaxy Tab 10.1–class tablets is very important to sustain the growing number of users embracing this technology. Technically, supporting it is no different from supporting any other device. However, Google and Samsung have promised to maintain it with the most up-to-date version of Android for at least 18 months after release, so it's likely to receive the newest Android OS upgrades and features in the first wave of deployment. A tablet-sized screen is another aspect that may require a little extra consideration during the design phase, but you'll see more of that later.

The Future: Next Generation

Device manufacturers try to keep their latest handsets a secret for as long as possible, but some of the specifications always get leaked.

General trends for all future devices are toward more cores, more RAM, better GPUs, and higher screen resolutions. Competing chips are constantly coming out, boasting bigger numbers all the time, while Android itself grows and matures, both by improving performance and by gaining features in almost every subsequent release. The hardware market has been extremely competitive, and it doesn't show any signs of slowing down.

While Android started on a single phone, it has quickly evolved to work well on different types of devices, including e-book readers, set-top boxes, tablets, navigation systems, and hybrid handsets that plug into docks to become PCs. To create an Android game that works everywhere, developers need to take into account the very nature of Android; that is, a ubiquitous OS that can run embedded on almost anything. One shouldn't assume that Android will simply stay on the current types of devices. Its growth has been so great since 2008, and its reach so vast, that, for Android, it is clear that the sky's the limit.

Whatever the future brings, Android is here to stay!

Game Controllers

Given the different input methods available among the various Android handsets, a few manufacturers produce special game controllers. Because there's no API in Android for such controllers, game developers have to integrate support separately by using the SDK provided by the game controller manufacturer.

One such game controller is called the Zeemote JS1, shown in Figure 1–6. It features an analog stick along with a set of buttons.

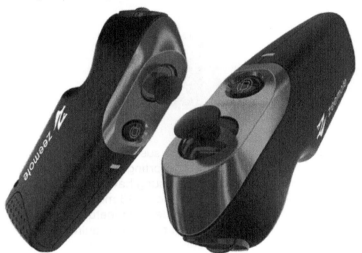

Figure 1–6. *The Zeemote JS1 game controller*

The controller is coupled with the Android device via Bluetooth. Game developers integrate support for the controller via a separate API provided by the Zeemote SDK. A couple of Android games already support the optional use of this controller.

In theory, a user could also couple the Nintendo Wii controller with an Android device via Bluetooth. A couple of prototypes exploiting the Wii controller exist, but there's no officially-supported SDK, which makes integration awkward.

The Game Gripper, shown in Figure 1–7, is an ingenious invention specifically designed for the Motorola Droid and Milestone. It is a simple rubber accessory that slides over the QWERTY keyboard of the phone, overlaying a more or less standard game controller layout on top of it. Game developers need only add keyboard controls to their game, and they don't have to integrate a special library to communicate with the Gripper. It's just a piece of rubber, after all.

Figure 1–7. *The Game Gripper in action*

Game controllers are still a bit esoteric in the realm of Android. However, some successful titles have integrated support for selected controllers, a move generally well received by Android gamers. Integrating support for such peripherals should therefore be considered.

Compatibility Across All Devices

After all of this discussion about phones, tablets, chipsets, peripherals, and so forth, it should be obvious that supporting the Android device market is not unlike supporting a PC market. Screen sizes range from a tiny 320×240 all the way up to 1920×1080 (and potentially higher on PC monitors!). On the lowest-end, first-gen device, you've got a paltry 500MHz ARM5 CPU and a very limited GPU without much memory. On the other end, you've got a high-bandwidth, multi-core 1-2GHz CPU with a massively parallelized GPU and tons of memory. First-gen handsets have an uncertain multi-touch system that can't detect discrete touch points. New tablets can support ten discrete touch points. Set-top boxes don't support any touching at all! What's a developer to do?

First of all, there is some sanity in all of this. Android itself has a compatibility program that dictates minimum specifications and ranges of values for various parts of an Android-compatible device. If a device fails to meet the standards, it is not allowed to bundle the Android Market app. Phew, that's a relief! The compatibility program is available at http://source.android.com/compatibility/overview.html.

The Android compatibility program is outlined in a document called the Compatibility Definition Document (CDD), which is available on the compatibility site. This document is updated for each release of the Android platform, and hardware manufacturers must update and retest their devices to stay compliant.

A few of the items that the CDD dictates as relevant to game developers are as follows:

- Minimum audio latency (varies)
- Minimum screen size (currently 2.5 inches)
- Minimum screen density (currently 100 dpi)
- Acceptable aspect ratios (currently 4:3 to 16:9)
- 3D Graphics Acceleration (OpenGL ES 1.0 is required)
- Input devices

Even if you can't make sense of some of the items listed above, fear not. You'll get to take a look at many of these topics in greater detail later in the book. The takeaway from this list is that there is a way to design a game that will work on the vast majority of Android devices. By planning things, such as the user interface and the general views in the game, so that they work on the different screen sizes and aspect ratios, as well as understanding that you want not only touch capability but also keyboard or additional input methods, you can successfully develop a very compatible game. Different games call for different techniques to achieve good user experiences on varying hardware, so unfortunately there is no silver bullet for solving these issues. But, rest assured: with time and a little proper planning, you'll be able to get good results.

Mobile Gaming Is Different

Gaming was a huge market segment long before the likes of iPhone and Android appeared on the scene. However, with these new forms of hybrid devices, the landscape has started to change. Gaming is no longer something just for nerdy kids. Serious business people have been seen playing the latest trendy game on their mobile phones in public, newspapers pick up stories of successful small game developers making a fortune on mobile phone application markets, and established game publishers have a hard time keeping up with the developments in the mobile space. Game developers must recognize this change and adjust accordingly. Let's see what this new ecosystem has to offer.

A Gaming Machine in Every Pocket

Mobile devices are everywhere. That's probably the key statement to take away from this section. From this, you can easily derive all the other facts about mobile gaming.

As hardware prices are constantly dropping and new devices have ever-increasing computational power, they also become ideal for gaming. Mobile phones are a must-have nowadays, so market penetration is huge. Many people are exchanging their old, classic mobile phones for newer-generation smartphones and discovering the new options available to them in the form of an incredibly wide range of applications.

Previously, if you wanted to play video games, you had to make the conscious decision to buy a video game system or a gaming PC. Now you get that functionality for free on mobile phones, tablets, and other devices. There's no additional cost involved (at least if you don't count the data plan you'll likely need), and your new gaming device is available to you at any time. Just grab it from your pocket or purse and you are ready to go—no need to carry a separate, dedicated system with you, because everything's integrated in one package.

Apart from the benefit of only having to carry a single device for your telephone, internet, and gaming needs, another factor makes gaming on mobile phones easily accessible to a much larger audience: you can fire up a dedicated market application on your device, pick a game that looks interesting, and immediately start to play. There's no need to go to a store or download something via your PC, only to find out, for example, that you don't have the USB cable you need to transfer that game to your phone.

The increased processing power of current-generation devices also has an impact on what's possible for you as a game developer. Even the middle class of devices is capable of generating gaming experiences similar to titles found on the older Xbox and PlayStation 2 systems. Given these capable hardware platforms, you can also start to explore elaborate games with physics simulations, an area offering great potential for innovation.

With new devices come new input methods, which have already been touched upon. A couple of games already take advantage of the GPS and/or compass available in most Android devices. The use of the accelerometer is already a mandatory feature of many games, and multi-touch screens offer new ways for the user to interact with the game world. Compared to classic gaming consoles (and ignoring the Wii, for the moment), this is quite a change for game developers. A lot of ground has been covered already, but there are still new ways to use all of this functionality in an innovative way.

Always Connected

Android devices are usually sold with data plans. This is driving an increasing amount of traffic on the Web. A smartphone user is very likely to be connected to the Web at any given time (disregarding poor reception caused by hardware design failures).

Permanent connectivity opens up a completely new world for mobile gaming. A user can challenge an opponent on the other side of the planet to a quick game of chess, explore virtual worlds populated with real people, or try fragging a best friend from another city in a gentlemen's death match. Moreover, all of this occurs on the go—on the bus, train, or in a most beloved corner of the local park.

Apart from multiplayer functionality, social networks have also started to influence mobile gaming. Games provide functionality to automatically tweet your latest high score directly to your Twitter account, or to inform a friend of the latest achievement you earned in that racing game you both love. Although growing social networks exist in the classical gaming world (for example, Xbox Live or PlayStation Network), the market penetration of services such as Facebook and Twitter is a lot higher, so the user is relieved of the burden of managing multiple networks at once.

Casual and Hardcore

The overwhelming user adoption of mobile devices also means that people who have never even touched a NES controller have suddenly discovered the world of gaming. Their idea of a good game often deviates quite a bit from that of the hardcore gamer.

According to the use cases for mobile phones, typical users tend to lean toward the more casual sort of game that they can fire up for a couple of minutes while on the bus or waiting in line at a fast food restaurant. These games are the equivalent those addictive little flash games on the PC that force many people in the workplace to Alt+Tab frantically every time they sense the presence of someone behind them. Ask yourself this: How much time each day would you be willing to spend playing games on your mobile phone? Can you imagine playing a "quick" game of Civilization on such a device?

Sure, there are probably serious gamers who would offer up their firstborn child if they could play their beloved Advanced Dungeons & Dragons variant on a mobile phone. But this group is a small minority, as evidenced by the top-selling games in the iPhone App Store and Android Market. The top-selling games are usually extremely casual in nature, but they have a neat trick up their sleeves: the average time it takes to play a round is in the range of minutes, but the games keep you coming back by employing various evil schemes. One game might provide an elaborate online achievement system that lets you virtually brag about your skills. Another could actually be a hardcore game in disguise. Offer users an easy way to save their progress and you are selling an epic RPG as a cute puzzle game!

Big Market, Small Developers

The low entry barrier is a main attractor for many hobbyists and independent developers. In the case of Android, this barrier is especially low: just get yourself the SDK and program away. You don't even need a device; just use the emulator (although having at least one development device is recommended). The open nature of Android also leads to a lot of activity on the Web. Information on all aspects of programming for the system can be found online for free. There's no need to sign a Non-Disclosure Agreement or wait for some authority to grant you access to their holy ecosystem.

At the time of this writing, the most successful games on the market were developed by one-person companies and small teams. Major publishers have not yet set foot in this market, at least not successfully. Gameloft serves as a prime example. Although big on the iPhone, Gameloft couldn't get a foothold in the Android market and decided instead to sell their games on their own website. Gameloft might not have been happy with the absence of a Digital Rights Management scheme (which is available on Android now), a move that considerably lowers the number of people who know about their games.

The Android environment also allows for a lot of experimentation and innovation, as bored people surfing the market are searching for little gems, including new ideas and game play mechanics. Experimentation on classic gaming platforms, such as the PC or consoles, often meets with failure. However, the Android Market enables you to reach a large audience that is willing to try experimental new ideas, and to reach them with a lot less effort.

This doesn't mean, of course, that you don't have to market your game. One way to do so is to inform various blogs and dedicated sites on the Web about your latest game. Many Android users are enthusiasts and regularly frequent such sites, checking in on the next big hit.

Another way to reach a large audience is to get featured in the Android Market. Once featured, your application will appear to users in a list that shows up when they start the market application. Many developers have reported a tremendous increase in downloads, which is directly correlated to getting featured in the market. How to get featured is a bit of a mystery, though. Having an awesome idea and executing it in the most polished way possible is your best bet, whether you are a big publisher or a small, one-person shop.

Summary

Android is an exciting little beast. You have seen what it's made of and gotten to know a little about its developer ecosystem. From a development standpoint, it offers you a very interesting system in terms of software and hardware, and the barrier of entry is extremely low, given the freely available SDK. The devices themselves are pretty powerful for handhelds, and they will enable us to present visually-rich gaming worlds to your users. The use of sensors, such as the accelerometer, lets you create innovative game ideas with new user interactions. And after you have finished developing your games, you can deploy them to millions of potential gamers in a matter of minutes. Sound exciting? Time to get your hands dirty with some code!

Chapter 2

First Steps with the Android SDK

The Android SDK provides a set of tools that allows you to create applications in no time. This chapter will guide you through the process of building a simple Android application with the SDK tools. This involves the following steps:

1. Setting up the development environment.

2. Creating a new project in Eclipse and writing your code.

3. Running the application on the emulator or on a device.

4. Debugging and profiling the application.

Let's start with setting up the development environment.

Setting Up the Development Environment

The Android SDK is flexible, and it integrates well with several development environments. Purists might choose to go hard core with command-line tools. We want things to be a little bit more comfortable, though, so we'll go for the simpler, more visual route using an IDE (integrated development environment).

Here's the list of software you'll need to download and install in the given order:

1. The Java Development Kit (JDK), version 5 or 6. We suggest using 6.

2. The Android Software Development Kit (Android SDK).

3. Eclipse for Java Developers, version 3.4 or newer.

4. The Android Development Tools (ADT) plug-in for Eclipse.

Let's go through the steps required to set up everything properly.

> **NOTE:** As the Web is a moving target, we don't provide URLs here. Fire up your favorite search engine and find the appropriate places to get the items listed above.

Setting Up the JDK

Download the JDK with one of the specified versions for your operating system. On most systems, the JDK comes in an installer or package, so there shouldn't be any hurdles. Once you have installed the JDK, you should add a new environment variable called JDK_HOME pointing to the root directory of the JDK installation. Additionally, you should add the $JDK_HOME/bin (%JDK_HOME%\bin on Windows) directory to your PATH environment variable.

Setting Up the Android SDK

The Android SDK is also available for the three mainstream desktop operating systems. Choose the one for your platform and download it. The SDK comes in the form of a ZIP or tar gzip file. Just uncompress it to a convenient folder (for example, c:\android-sdk on Windows or /opt/android-sdk on Linux). The SDK comes with several command-line utilities located in the tools/ folder. Create an environment variable called ANDROID_HOME pointing to the root directory of the SDK installation, and add $ANDROID_HOME/tools (%ANDROID_HOME%\tools on Windows) to your PATH environment variable. This way you can easily invoke the command-line tools from a shell later on if the need arises.

After performing the preceding steps, you'll have a bare-bones installation that consists of the basic command-line tools needed to create, compile, and deploy Android projects, as well as the SDK and AVD manager, a tool for installing SDK components and creating virtual devices used by the emulator. These tools alone are not sufficient to start developing, so you need to install additional components. That's where the SDK and AVD manager comes in. The manager is a package manager, much like the package management tools you find on Linux. The manager allows you to install the following types of components:

Android platforms: For every official Android release, there's a platform component for the SDK that includes the runtime libraries, a system image used by the emulator, and any version-specific tools.

SDK add-ons: Add-ons are usually external libraries and tools that are not specific to a platform. Some examples are the Google APIs that allow you to integrate Google maps in your application.

USB driver for Windows: This driver is necessary for running and debugging your application on a physical device on Windows. On Mac OS X and Linux, you don't need a special driver.

Samples: For each platform, there's also a set of platform-specific samples. These are great resources for seeing how to achieve specific goals with the Android runtime library.

Documentation: This is a local copy of the documentation for the latest Android framework API.

Being the greedy developers we are, we want to install all of these components to have the full set of this functionality at our disposal. Thus, first we have to start the SDK and AVD manager. On Windows, there's an executable called SDK manager.exe in the root directory of the SDK. On Linux and Mac OS X, you simply start the script android in the tools directory of the SDK.

Upon first startup, the SDK and AVD manager will connect to the package server and fetch a list of available packages. The manager will then present you with the dialog shown in Figure 2–1, which allows you to install individual packages. Simply check Accept All, click the Install button, and make yourself a nice cup of tea or coffee. The manager will take a while to install all the packages.

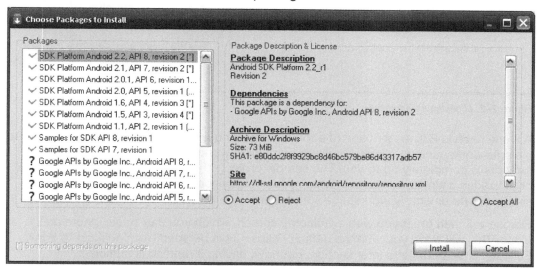

Figure 2–1. *First contact with the SDK and AVD manager*

You can use the SDK and AVD manager at anytime to update components or install new ones. The manager is also used to create new AVDs, which will be necessary later on when we start running and debugging our applications on the emulator.

Once the installation process is finished, you can move on to the next step in setting up your development environment.

Installing Eclipse

Eclipse comes in several different flavors. For Android developers, we suggest using Eclipse for Java Developers version 3.6. Similar to the Android SDK, Eclipse comes in the form of a ZIP or tar gzip package. Simply extract it to a folder of your choice. Once the package is uncompressed, you can create a shortcut on your desktop to the `eclipse` executable in the root directory of your Eclipse installation.

The first time you start Eclipse, you will be prompted to specify a workspace directory. Figure 2–2 shows you the dialog.

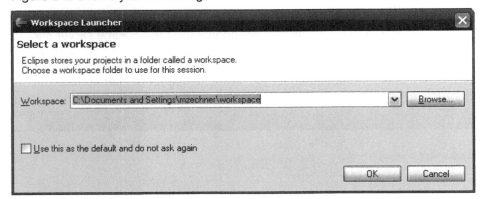

Figure 2–2. *Choosing a workspace*

A workspace is Eclipse's notion of a folder containing a set of projects. Whether you use a single workspace for all your projects or multiple workspaces that group just a few projects is completely up to you. The sample projects that accompany this book are all organized in a single workspace, which you could specify in this dialog. For now, we'll simply create an empty workspace somewhere.

Eclipse will then greet you with a welcome screen, which you can safely ignore and close. This will leave you with the default Eclipse Java perspective. You'll get to know Eclipse a little better in a later section. For now, having it running is sufficient.

Installing the ADT Eclipse Plug-In

The last piece in our setup puzzle is installing the ADT Eclipse plug-in. Eclipse is based on a plug-in architecture used to extend its capabilities by third-party plug-ins. The ADT plug-in marries the tools found in the Android SDK with the powers of Eclipse. With this combination, we can completely forget about invoking all the command-line Android SDK tools; the ADT plug-in integrates them transparently into our Eclipse workflow.

Installing plug-ins for Eclipse can be done either manually, by dropping the contents of a plug-in ZIP file into the plug-ins folder of Eclipse, or via the Eclipse plug-in manager integrated with Eclipse. Here we'll choose the second route.

1. To install a new plug-in, go to **Help ➤ Install New Software...**, which opens the installation dialog. In this dialog, you can then choose the source from which to install a plug-in. First, you have to add the plug-in repository from the ADT plug-in that is fetched. Click the Add button. You will be presented with the dialog depicted in Figure 2–3.

2. In the first text field, you can enter the name of the repository; something like "ADT repository" will do. The second text field specifies the URL of the repository. For the ADT plug-in, this field should be `https://dl-ssl.google.com/android/eclipse/`. Note that this URL might be different for newer versions, so check the ADT plug-in site for an up-to-date link.

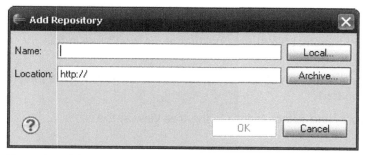

Figure 2–3. *Adding a repository*

3. After you've confirmed the dialog, you'll be brought back to the installation dialog, which should now be fetching the list of available plug-ins in the repository. Check the Developer Tools check box and click the Next button.

4. Eclipse will now calculate all the necessary dependencies, and then it will present you a new dialog that lists all the plug-ins and dependencies that are going to be installed. Confirm by clicking the Next button.

5. Another dialog will pop up prompting you to accept the license for each plug-in to be installed. You should, of course, accept those licenses and, finally, initiate the installation by clicking the Finish button.

NOTE: During the installation, you will be asked to confirm the installation of unsigned software. Don't worry, the plug-ins simply do not have a verified signature. Agree to the installation to continue the process.

6. Finally, Eclipse will ask you whether it should restart to apply the changes. You can opt for a full restart or for applying the changes without a restart. To play it safe, choose Restart Now, which will restart Eclipse as expected.

After Eclipse restarts, you'll be presented with the same Eclipse window as before. The toolbar features several new buttons specific to Android, which allow you to start the SDK and AVD manager directly from within Eclipse as well as create new Android projects. Figure 2–4 shows the new toolbar buttons.

Figure 2–4. *ADT toolbar buttons*

The first button on the left allows you to open the AVD and SDK manager. The next button is a shortcut to create a new Android project. The other two buttons will create a new unit test project or Android manifest file (functionality that we won't use in this book).

As one last step in finishing the installation of the ADT plug-in, you have to tell the plug-in where the Android SDK is located.

1. Open **Window ➤ Preferences**, and select **Android** in the tree view in the dialog that appears.

2. On the right side, click the Browse button to choose the root directory of your Android SDK installation.

3. Click the OK button to close the dialog. Now you'll be able to create your first Android application.

A Quick Tour of Eclipse

Eclipse is an open source IDE you can use to develop applications written in various languages. Usually, Eclipse is used in connection with Java development. Given Eclipse's plug-in architecture, many extensions have been created, so it is also possible to develop pure C/C++, Scala, or Python projects as well. The possibilities are endless; even plug-ins to write LaTeX projects exist, for example—something that only slightly resembles your usual code development tasks.

An instance of Eclipse works with a workspace that holds one or more projects. Previously, we defined a workspace at startup. All new projects you create will be stored in the workspace directory, along with a configuration that defines the look of Eclipse when using the workspace, among other things.

The user interface (UI) of Eclipse revolves around two concepts:

■ A *view*, a single UI component such as a source code editor, an output console, or a project explorer.

■ A *perspective*, a set of specific views that you'll most likely need for a specific development task, such as editing and browsing source code, debugging, profiling, synchronizing with a version control repository, and so on.

Eclipse for Java Developers comes with several predefined perspectives. The ones in which we are most interested are called Java and Debug. The Java perspective is the one shown in Figure 2–5. It features the Package Explorer view on the left side, a source-editing view in the middle (it's empty, as we didn't open a source file yet), a Task List view to the right, an Outline view, and a tabbed view that contains subviews called Problems view, Javadoc view, and Declaration view.

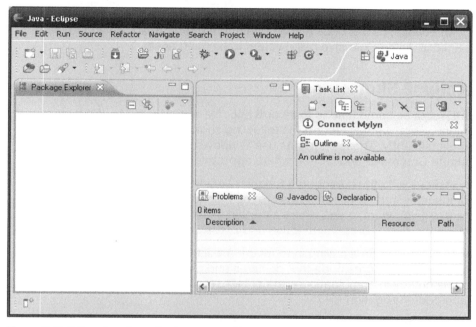

Figure 2–5. *Eclipse in action—the Java perspective*

You are free to rearrange the location of any view within a perspective via drag and drop. You can also resize views. Additionally, you can add and remove views to and from a perspective. To add a view, go to **Window ➤ Show View**, and either select one from the list presented or choose **Other...** to get a list of all available views.

To switch to another perspective, you can go to **Window ➤ Open Perspective** and choose the one you want. A faster way to switch between already open perspectives is given to you in the top-left corner of Eclipse. There you will see which perspectives are already open and which perspective is active. In Figure 2–5, notice that the Java perspective is open and active. It's the only currently open perspective. Once you open additional perspectives, they will also show up in that part of the UI.

The toolbars shown in Figure 2–5 are also just views. Depending on the perspective you are in at the time, the toolbars may change as well. Recall that several new buttons appeared in the toolbar after we installed the ADT plug-in. This is a common behavior of plug-ins: they will, in general, add new views and perspectives. In the case of the ADT plug-in, we can now also access a perspective called DDMS (Dalvik Debugging Monitor Server, which is specific to debugging and profiling Android applications) in addition to the standard Java Debug perspective. The ADT plug-in also adds several new views, including the LogCat view, which displays the live logging information about any attached device or emulator.

Once you get comfortable with the perspective and view concepts, Eclipse is a lot less intimidating. In the following subsections, we will explore some of the perspectives and views we'll use to write Android games. We can't possibly cover all the details of developing with Eclipse, as it is such a huge beast. We therefore advise you to learn more about Eclipse via its extensive help system if the need arises.

Helpful Eclipse Shortcuts

Every new IDE requires some time to learn and become accustomed to. After using Eclipse for many years, we have found the following shortcuts speed up software development significantly. These shortcuts use Windows terms, so Mac OS X users should substitute Command and Option where appropriate:

- Ctr+Shift+G with the cursor on a function or field will perform a workspace search for all references to the function or field. For instance, if you want to see where a certain function is called, just click to move the cursor onto the function and press Ctrl+Shift+G.

- F3 with the cursor on a calling in to function will follow that call and bring you to the source code that declares and defines the function. Use this hotkey in combination with Ctrl+Shift+G for easy Java source code navigation.

- Ctr+Space autocompletes the function or field name you are currently typing. Start typing and press the shortcut after you have entered a few characters. When there are multiple possibilities, a box will appear.

- Ctr+Z is undo.

- Ctr+X cuts.

- Ctr+C copies.

- Ctr+V pastes.

- Ctr+F11 runs the application.

- F11 debugs the application.

- Ctr+Shift+O organizes the Java imports of the current source file.

- ■ Ctr+Shift+F formats the current source file.

- ■ Ctr+Shift+T jumps to any Java class.

- ■ Ctr+Shift+R jumps to any resource file; that is, an image, a text file, and so on.

There are many more useful features in Eclipse, but mastering these basic keyboard shortcuts can significantly speed up your game development and make life in Eclipse just a little better. Eclipse is also very configurable. Any of these keyboard shortcuts can be reassigned to different keys in the Preferences.

Hello World, Android Style

With our development set up, we can now create our first Android project in Eclipse. The ADT plug-in installed several wizards that make creating new Android projects very easy.

Creating the Project

There are two ways to create a new Android project. The first one works by right-clicking in the Package Explorer view (see Figure 2–4) and then selecting **New ➤ Project...** from the pop-up menu. In the new dialog, select Android Project under the Android category. As you can see, there are many other options for project creation in that dialog. This is the standard way to create a new project of any type in Eclipse. After you confirm the dialog, the Android project wizard will open.

The second way is a lot easier: just click the button responsible for creating a new Android project (shown earlier in Figure 2–4).

Once you are in the Android project wizard dialog, you have to make a few decisions.

1. First, you must define the project name. The usual convention is to keep the name all lowercase. For this example, name the project "hello world."

2. Next, you have to specify the build target. For now, simply select the Android 1.5 build target, since this is the lowest common denominator and you don't need any fancy features like multitouch yet.

> **NOTE:** In Chapter 1, you saw that each new release of Android adds new classes to the Android framework API. The build target specifies which version of this API you want to use in your application. For example, if you choose the Android 3.1 build target, you get access to the latest and greatest API features. This comes at a risk, though: if your application is run on a device that uses a lower API version (say, a device running Android version 1.5), then your application will crash if you access API features that are available only in version 3.1. In this case, you'd need to detect the supported SDK version during runtime and access only the 3.1 features when you're sure that the Android version on the device supports this version. This may sound pretty nasty, but as you'll see in Chapter 5, given a good application architecture, you can easily enable and disable certain version-specific features without running the risk of crashing.

3. Next, you have to specify the name of your application (for example, `Hello World`), the name of the Java package in which all your source files will be located eventually (such as `com.helloworld`), and an activity name. An activity is similar to a window or dialog on a desktop operating system. Let's just name the activity `HelloWorldActivity`.

4. The Min SDK Version field allows you to specify the minimum Android version your application requires to run. This parameter is not required, but it's good practice to specify it. SDK versions are numbered starting from 1 (1.0) and increase with each release. Since 1.5 is the third release, specify 3 here. Remember that you had to specify a build target previously, which might be newer than the minimum SDK version. This allows you to work with a higher API level, but also deploy to older versions of Android (making sure that you call only the supported API methods for that version, of course).

5. Click Finish to create your first Android project.

> **NOTE:** Setting the minimum SDK version has some implications. The application can be run only on devices with an Android version equal to or greater than the minimum SDK version you specify. When a user browses the Android Market via the Market application, only applications with the appropriate minimum SDK version will be displayed.

Exploring the Project

In the Package Explorer, you should now see a project called "hello world." If you expand it and all its children, you'll see something like Figure 2–6. This is the general structure of most Android projects. Let's explore it a little bit.

- AndroidManifest.xml describes your application. It defines what activities and services comprise your application, what minimum and target Android version your application runs on (hypothetically), and what permissions it needs (for example, access to the SD card or networking).

- default.properties holds various settings for the build system. We won't touch upon this, as the ADT plug-in will take care of modifying it when necessary.

- src/ contains all your Java source files. Notice that the package has the same name as the one you specified in the Android project wizard.

- gen/ contains Java source files generated by the Android build system. You shouldn't modify them as, in some cases, they get regenerated automatically.

- assets/ is where you store file your application needs (such as configuration files, audio files, and the like). These files get packaged with your Android application.

- res/holds resources your application needs, such as icons, strings for internationalization, and UI layouts defined via XML. Like assets, the resources also get packaged with your application.

- Android 1.5 tells us that we are building against an Android version 1.5 target. This is actually a dependency in the form of a standard JAR file that holds the classes of the Android 1.5 API.

The Package Explorer view hides another directory, called bin/, which holds the compiled code ready for deployment to a device or emulator. As with the gen/ folder, we usually don't care what happens in this folder.

Figure 2–6. *Hello World project structure*

We can easily add new source files, folders, and other resources in the Package Explorer view by right-clicking the folder in which we want to put the new resources and selecting New plus the corresponding resource type we want to create. For now, though, we'll leave everything as is. Next, let's modify the source code a little.

Writing the Application Code

We still haven't written a single line of code, so let's change that. The Android project wizard created a template activity class for us called HelloWorldActivity, which will get displayed when we run the application on the emulator or a device. Open the source of the class by double-clicking the file in the Package Explorer view. We'll replace that template code with the code in Listing 2–1.

Listing 2–1. *HelloWorldActivity.java*

```
package com.helloworld;

import android.app.Activity;
import android.os.Bundle;
import android.view.View;
import android.widget.Button;

public class HelloWorldActivity extends Activity
                                implements View.OnClickListener {
```

```
    Button button;
    int touchCount;

    @Override
    public void onCreate(Bundle savedInstanceState) {
        super.onCreate(savedInstanceState);
        button = new Button(this);
        button.setText( "Touch me!" );
        button.setOnClickListener(this);
        setContentView(button);
    }

    public void onClick(View v) {
        touchCount++;
        button.setText("Touched me " + touchCount + " time(s)");
    }
}
```

Let's dissect Listing 2–1, so you can understand what it's doing. We'll leave the nitty-gritty details for later chapters. All we want is to get a sense of what's happening.

The source code file starts with the standard Java package declaration and several imports. Most Android framework classes are located in the android package.

```
package com.helloworld;

import android.app.Activity;
import android.os.Bundle;
import android.view.View;
import android.widget.Button;
```

Next, we define our HelloWorldActivity, and let it extend the base class Activity, which is provided by the Android framework API. An Activity is a lot like a window in classical desktop UIs, with the constraint that the Activity always fills the complete screen (except for the notification bar at the top of the Android UI). Additionally, we let the Activity implement the interface OnClickListener. If you have experience with other UI toolkits, you'll probably see what's coming next. More on that in a second.

```
public class HelloWorldActivity extends Activity
                        implements View.OnClickListener {
```

We let our Activity have two members: a Button and an integer that counts how often the Button is clicked.

```
    Button button;
    int touchCount;
```

Every Activity must implement the abstract method Activity.onCreate(), which gets called once by the Android system when the activity is first started. This replaces a constructor you'd normally expect to use to create an instance of a class. It is mandatory to call the base class onCreate() method as the first statement in the method body.

```
    @Override
public void onCreate(Bundle savedInstanceState) {
        super.onCreate(savedInstanceState);
```

Next, we create a Button and set its initial text. Button is one of the many widgets that the Android framework API provides. Widgets are synonymous with so-called Views on Android. Note that button is a member of our HelloWorldActivity class. We'll need a reference to it later on.

```
button = new Button(this);
button.setText( "Touch me!" );
```

The next line in onCreate() sets the OnClickListener of the Button. OnClickListener is a callback interface with a single method, OnClickListener.onClick(), which gets called when the Button is clicked. We want to be notified of clicks, so we let our HelloWorldActivity implement that interface and register it as the OnClickListener of the Button.

```
button.setOnClickListener(this);
```

The last line in the onCreate() method sets the Button as the so-called content View of our Activity. Views can be nested, and the content View of the Activity is the root of this hierarchy. In our case, we simply set the Button as the View to be displayed by the Activity. For simplicity's sake, we won't get into details of how the Activity will be laid out given this content View.

```
    setContentView(button);
}
```

The next step is simply the implementation of the OnClickListener.onClick() method, which the interface requires of our Activity. This method gets called each time the Button is clicked. In this method, we increase the touchCount counter and set the Button's text to a new string.

```
public void onClick(View v) {
    touchCount++;
    button.setText("Touched me" + touchCount + "times");
}
```

Thus, to summarize our Hello World application, we construct an Activity with a Button. Each time the Button is clicked, we reflect this by setting its text accordingly. (This may not be the most exciting application on the planet, but it will do for further demonstration purposes.)

Note that we never had to compile anything manually. The ADT plug-in, together with Eclipse, will recompile the project every time we add, modify, or delete a source file or resource. The result of this compilation process is an APK file ready to be deployed to the emulator or an Android device. The APK file is located in the bin/ folder of the project.

You'll use this application in the following sections to learn how to run and debug Android applications on emulator instances as well as devices.

Running and Debugging Android Applications

Once we've written the first iteration of our application code, we want to run and test it to identify potential problems or just be amazed at its glory. We have two ways we can achieve this:

- We can run our application on a real device connected to the development PC via USB.

- We can fire up the emulator included in the SDK and test our application there.

In both cases, we have to do a little bit of setup work before we can finally see our application in action.

Connecting a Device

Before we can connect our device for testing purposes, we have to make sure that it is recognized by the operating system. On Windows, this involves installing the appropriate driver, which is part of the SDK installation we installed earlier. Just connect your device and follow the standard driver installation project for Windows, pointing the process to the `driver/` folder in your SDK installation's root directory. For some devices, you might have to get the driver from the manufacturer's website. Many devices can use the Android ADB drivers that come with the SDK; however, a process is often required to add the specific device hardware ID to the INF file. A quick Google search for the device name and "Windows ADB" will often get you the information you need to get connected with that specific device.

On Linux and Mac OS X, you usually don't need to install any drivers, as they come with the operating system. Depending on your Linux flavor, you might have to fiddle with your USB device discovery a little bit, usually in the form of creating a new rules file for udev. This varies from device to device. A quick Web search should bring up a solution for your device.

Creating an Android Virtual Device

The SDK comes with an emulator that will run so-called Android virtual devices (AVDs). A *virtual device* consists of a system image of a specific Android version, a skin, and a set of attributes, which include the screen resolution, SD-card size, and so on.

To create an AVD, you have to fire up the SDK and AVD manager. You can do this either as described previously in the SDK installation step or directly from within Eclipse by clicking the SDK manager button in the toolbar.

1. Select Virtual Devices in the list on the left. You will be presented with a list of currently available AVDs. Unless you've already played around with the SDK manager, this list should be empty; let's change that.

2. To create a new AVD, click the **New...** button on the right, which will bring up the dialog shown in Figure 2–7.

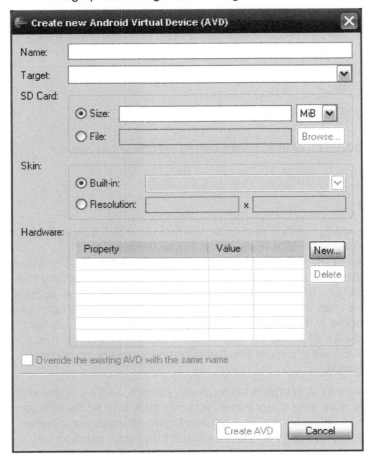

Figure 2–7. *The AVD creation dialog for the SDK manager*

3. Each AVD has a name by which you can refer to it later on. The target specifies the Android version that the AVD should use. Additionally, you can specify the size of the SD card of the AVD, as well as the screen size. For our simple "hello world" project, you can select an Android 1.5 target and leave everything else as it is. For real-life testing, you'd usually want to create multiple AVDs that cover all the Android versions and screen sizes you want your application to handle.

> **NOTE**: Unless you have dozens of different devices with different Android versions and screen sizes, you should use the emulator for additional testing of Android version/screen size combinations.

Running an Application

Now that you've set up your devices and AVDs, you can finally run the `Hello World` application. You can easily do this in Eclipse by right-clicking the "hello world" project in the Package Explorer view and then selecting **Run As ➤ Android Application** (or you can click the Run button on the toolbar). Eclipse will then perform the following steps in the background:

1. Compile the project to an APK file if any files have changed since the last compilation.

2. Create a new Run configuration for the Android project if one does not already exist. (We'll look at Run configurations in a minute.)

3. Install and run the application by starting or reusing an already running emulator instance with a fitting Android version or by deploying and running the application on a connected device (which must also run at least the minimum Android version you specified as the Min SDK Level parameter when you created the project).

If you created only an Android 1.5 AVD, as suggested in the previous section, then the ADT Eclipse plug-in will fire up a new emulator instance running that AVD, deploy the Hello World APK file, and start the application. The output should look like Figure 2–8.

Figure 2–8. *The Hello World application in action*

The emulator works almost exactly like a real device, and you can interact with it via your mouse just as you would with your finger on a device. Here are a few differences between a real device and the emulator:

- The emulator supports only single-touch input. Simply use your mouse cursor and pretend it is your finger.

- The emulator is missing some applications, such as the Android Market.

- To change the orientation of the device on the screen, don't tilt your monitor. Instead, use the 7 key on your numeric keypad to change the orientation. You have to press the Num Lock key above the numeric keypad first to disable its number functionality.

- The emulator is very slow. Do not assess the performance of your application by running it on the emulator.

> ▣ The emulator currently supports only OpenGL ES 1.0 with a few extensions. We'll talk about OpenGL ES in Chapter 7. This is fine for our purposes, except that the OpenGL ES implementation on the emulator is buggy, and it often gives you different results from those you would get on a real device. For now, just keep in mind that you should not test any OpenGL ES applications on the emulator.

Play around with it a little and get comfortable.

NOTE: Starting a fresh emulator instance takes considerable time (up to 10 minutes depending on your hardware). You can leave the emulator running for your whole development session so you don't have to restart it repeatedly, or you can check the "Snapshot" option when creating or editing the AVD, which will allow you to save and restore a snapshot of the VM, allowing for quick launch.

Sometimes when we run an Android application, the automatic emulator/device selection performed by the ADT plug-in is a hindrance. For example, we might have multiple devices/emulators connected, and we want to test our application on a specific device/emulator. To deal with this, we can turn off the automatic device/emulator selection in the Run configuration of the Android project. So, what is a Run configuration?

A Run configuration provides a way to tell Eclipse how it should start your application when you tell Eclipse to run the application. A Run configuration usually allows you to specify things such as command-line arguments passed to the application, VM arguments (in the case of Java SE desktop applications), and so on. Eclipse and third-party plug-ins offer different Run configurations for specific types of project s. The ADT plug-in adds an Android Application Run configuration to the set of available Run configurations. When we first ran our application earlier in the chapter, Eclipse and ADT created a new Android Application Run configuration for us in the background with default parameters.

To get to the Run configuration of your Android project, do the following:

1. Right-click the project in the Package Explorer view and select **Run As** ➤ **Run Configurations**.

2. From the list on the left side, select the "hello world" project.

3. On the right side of the dialog, you can now modify the name of the Run configuration, and change other settings on the Android, Target, and Commons tabs.

4. To change automatic deployment to manual deployment, click the Target tab and select Manual.

When you run your application again, you'll be prompted to select a compatible emulator or device on which to run the application. Figure 2–9 shows the dialog. In this figure, we added several AVDs with different targets and connected two devices.

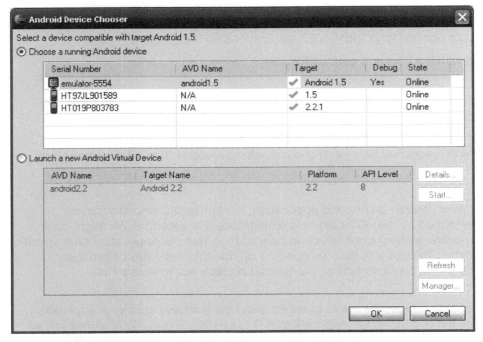

Figure 2–9. *Choosing an emulator/device on which to run the application*

The dialog shows all the running emulators and currently connected devices as well as all other AVDs not currently running. You can choose any emulator or device on which to run your application.

Debugging an Application

Sometimes your application will behave in unexpected ways or crash. To figure out what exactly is going wrong, you want to be able to debug your application.

Eclipse and ADT provide us with incredibly powerful debugging facilities for Android applications. We can set breakpoints in our source code, inspect variables and the current stack trace, and so forth.

Before we can debug our application, we have to modify its AndroidManifest.xml file to enable debugging. This presents a bit of a chicken-and-egg problem, as we haven't looked at manifest files in detail yet. For now, you should know simply that the manifest file specifies some attributes of your application. One of those attributes is whether the application is debuggable. This attribute is specified in the form of an xml attribute of the<application> tag in the manifest file. To enable debugging, we add the following attribute to the <application> in the manifest file:

```
android:debuggable="true"
```

While developing your application, you can safely leave that attribute in the manifest file. But don't forget to remove the attribute before you deploy your application in the market.

Now that you've set up your application to be debuggable, you can debug it on an emulator or device. Usually, you will set breakpoints before debugging to inspect the program state at certain points in the program.

To set a breakpoint, simply open the source file in Eclipse and double-click the gray area in front of the line at which you want to set the breakpoint. For demonstration purposes, do that for line 23 in the HelloWorldActivity class. This will make the debugger stop each time you click the button. The Source Code view should show you a small circle in front of that line after you double-click it, as shown in Figure 2–10. You can remove breakpoints by double-clicking them again in the Source Code view.

```
public void onClick(View v) {
    touchCount++;
    button.setText("Touched me "+touchCount+" time(s)");
}
}
```

Figure 2–10. *Setting a breakpoint*

Starting the debugging is much like running the application, as described in the previous section. Right-click the project in the Package Explorer view and select **Debug As ➤ Android Application**. This will create a new Debug configuration for your project, just as in the case of simply running the application. You can change the default settings of that Debug configuration by choosing **Debug As ➤ Debug Configurations** from the **Context** menu.

> **NOTE:** Instead of going through the **Context** menu of the project in the Package Explorer view, you can use the **Run** menu to run and debug applications as well as get access to the configurations.

If you start your first debugging session, Eclipse will ask whether you want to switch to the Debug perspective, which you can confirm. Let's have a look at that perspective first. Figure 2–11 shows how it would look after we start debugging our Hello World application.

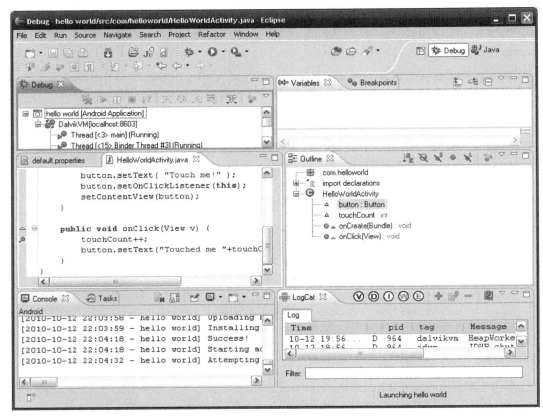

Figure 2–11. *The Debug perspective*

If you remember our quick tour of Eclipse, then you'll know there are several different perspectives, which consist of a set of views for a specific task. The Debug perspective looks quite different from the Java perspective.

- The first new view to notice is the Debug view at the top left. It shows all currently running applications and the stack traces of all their threads if the applications are run in debug mode.

- Below the Debug view is the source-editing view we also used in the Java perspective.

- The Console view prints out messages from the ADT plug-in, telling us what it is doing.

- The LogCat view will be one of your best friends on your journey. This view shows you logging output from the emulator/device on which your application is running. The logging output comes from system components, other applications, and your own application. The LogCat view will show you a stack trace when your application crashes and will also allow you to output your own logging messages at runtime. We'll take a closer look at LogCat in the next section.

- The Outline view is not very useful in the Debug perspective. You will usually be concerned with breakpoints and variables, and the current line on which the program is suspended while debugging. We often remove the Outline view from the Debug perspective to leave more space for the other views.

- The Variables view is especially useful for debugging purposes. When the debugger hits a breakpoint, you will be able to inspect and modify the variables in the current scope of the program.

- Finally, the Breakpoints view shows a list of breakpoints you've set so far.

If you are curious, you've probably already clicked the button in the running application to see how the debugger reacts. It will stop at line 23, as we instructed it by setting a breakpoint there. You will also have noticed that the Variables view now shows the variables in the current scope, which consist of the activity itself (`this`) and the parameter of the method (v). You can drill down further into the variables by expanding them.

The Debug view shows you the stack trace of the current stack down to the method you are in currently. Note that you might have multiple threads running and can pause them at any time in the Debug view.

Finally, notice that the line where we set the breakpoint is highlighted, indicating the position in the code where the program is currently paused.

You can instruct the debugger to execute the current statement (by pressing F6), step into any methods that get called in the current method (by pressing F5), or continue the program execution normally (by pressing F8). Alternatively, you can use the items on the Run menu to achieve the same. In addition, notice that there are more stepping options than the ones we've just mentioned. As with everything, we suggest you experiment to see what works for you and what doesn't.

> **NOTE:** Curiosity is a building block for successfully developing Android games. You have to get intimate with your development environment to get the most out of it. A book of this scope can't possible explain all the nitty-gritty details of Eclipse, so we urge you to experiment.

LogCat and DDMS

The ADT Eclipse plug-in installs many new views and perspectives to be used in Eclipse. One of the most useful views is the LogCat view, which we touched on briefly in the last section.

LogCat is the Android event-logging system that allows system components and applications to output logging information about various logging levels. Each log entry is composed of a time stamp, a logging level, the process ID from which the log came, a tag defined by the logging application itself, and the actual logging message.

The LogCat view gathers and displays this information from a connected emulator or device. Figure 2–12 shows some sample output from the LogCat view.

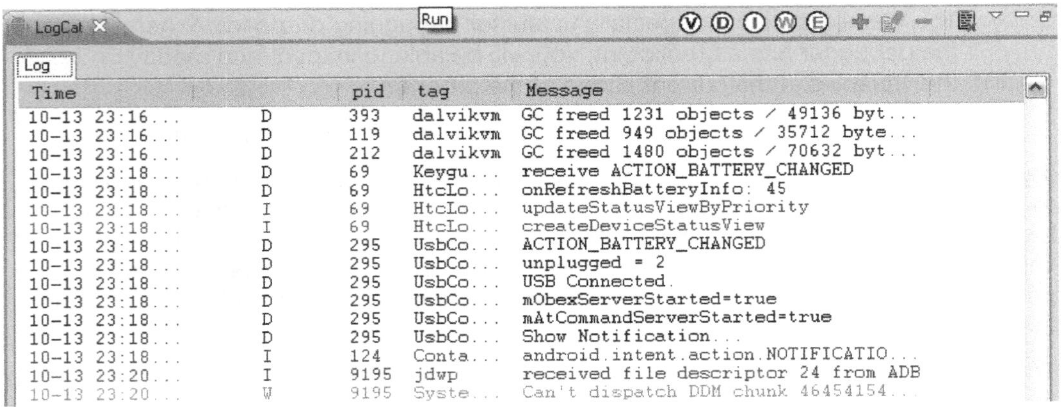

Figure 2–12. *The LogCat view*

Notice that there are a number of buttons at the top right of the LogCat view.

- The first five allow you to select the logging levels you want to see displayed.

- The green plus button lets you define a filter based on the tag, the process ID, and the log level, which comes in handy if you want to show only the log output of your own application (which will probably use a specific tag for logging).

- The other buttons allow you to edit a filter, delete a filter, or clear the current output.

If several devices and emulators are currently connected, then the LogCat view will output the logging data of only one. To get finer-grained control and even more inspection options, you can switch to the DDMS perspective.

DDMS (Dalvik Debugging Monitor Server) provides a lot of in-depth information about the processes and Dalvik VMs running on all connected devices. You can switch to the

DDMS perspective at any time via **Window ➤ Open Perspective ➤ Other ➤ DDMS**. Figure 2–13 shows what the DDMS perspective usually looks like.

As always, several specific views are suitable for our task at hand. In this case, we want to gather information about all the processes, their VMs and threads, the current state of the heap, LogCat information about a specific connected device, and so on.

- The Devices view displays all currently connected emulators and devices, as well as all the processes running on them. Via the toolbar buttons of this view, you can perform various actions, including debugging a selected process, recording heap and thread information, and taking a screenshot.

- The LogCat view is the same as in the previous perspective, with the difference being that it will display the output of the device currently selected in the Devices view.

- The Emulator Control view lets you alter the behavior of a running emulator instance. You can force the emulator to spoof GPS coordinates for testing, for example.

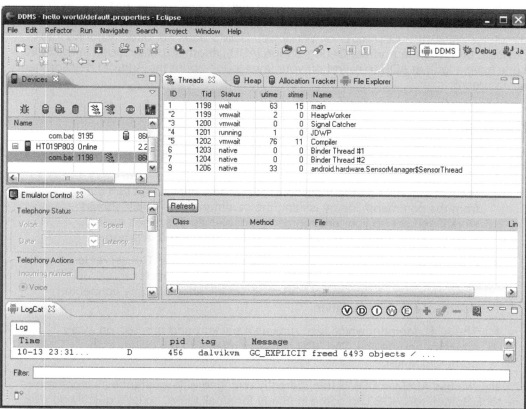

Figure 2–13. *DDMS in action*

- The Threads view displays information about the threads running on the process currently selected in the Devices view. The Threads view shows this information only if you also enable thread tracking, which can be achieved by clicking the fifth button from the left in the Devices view.

- The Heap view, which is not shown in Figure 2–13, gives information about the status of the heap on a device. As with the thread information, you have to enable heap tracking in the Devices view explicitly by clicking the second button from the left.

- The Allocation Tracker view shows which classes have been allocated the most within the last few moments. This view provides a great way to hunt down memory leaks.

- Finally, there's the File Explorer view, which allows you to modify files on the connected Android device or emulator instance. You can drag and drop files into this view as you would with your standard operating system file explorer.

DDMS is actually a standalone tool integrated with Eclipse via the ADT plug-in. You can also start DDMS as a standalone application from the $ANDROID_HOME/tools directory(%ANDROID_HOME%/tools on Windows). DDMS does not directly connect to devices, but uses the Android Debug Bridge (ADB), another tool included in the SDK. Let's have a look at ADB to round off your knowledge about the Android development environment.

Using ADB

ADB lets you manage connected devices and emulator instances. It is actually a composite of three components:

- A client that runs on the development machine, which you can start from the command line by issuing the command adb (which should work if you set up your environment variables as described earlier). When we talk about ADB, we refer to this command-line program.

- A server that also runs on your development machine. The server is installed as a background service, and it is responsible for communication between an ADB program instance and any connected device or emulator instance.

- The ADB daemon, which also runs as a background process on every emulator and device. The ADB server connects to this daemon for communication.

Usually, we use ADB via DDMS transparently and ignore its existence as a command-line tool. Sometimes ADB can come in handy for small tasks, so let's quickly go over some of its functionality.

> **NOTE:** Check out the ADB documentation on the Android Developers site at
> `http://developer.android.com` for a full reference list of the available commands.

A very useful task to perform with ADB is to query for all devices and emulators connected to the ADB server (and hence your development machine). To do this, execute the following command on the command line (note that > is not part of the command).

```
> adb devices
```

This will print a list of all connected devices and emulators with their respective serial numbers, and it will resemble the following output:

```
List of devices attached
HT97JL901589    device
HT019P803783    device
```

The serial number of a device or emulator is used to target specific subsequent commands at it. The following command will install an APK file called myapp.apk located on the development machine on the device with the serial number HT019P803783.

```
> adb –s HT019P803783 install myapp.apk
```

The –s argument can be used with any ADB command that performs an action that is targeted at a specific device.

Commands that will copy files to and from the device or emulator also exist. The following command copies a local file called myfile.txt to the SD card of a device with the serial number HT019P803783.

```
> adb –s HT019P803783 push myfile.txt  /sdcard/myfile.txt
```

To pull a file called myfile.txt from the SD card, you could issue the following command:

```
> abd pull /sdcard/myfile.txt myfile.txt
```

If there's only a single device or emulator currently connected to the ADB server, you can omit the serial number. The adb tool will automatically target the connected device or emulator for you.

Of course, the ADB tool offers many more possibilities. Most are exposed through DDMS, and we'll usually use that instead of going to the command line. For quick tasks, though, the command-line tool is ideal.

Summary

The Android development environment can be a bit intimidating at times. Luckily, you need only a subset of the available options to get started, and the last few pages of this chapter should have given you enough information to get started with some basic coding.

The big lesson to take away from this chapter is how the pieces fit together. The JDK and the Android SDK provide the basis for all Android development. They offer the tools to compile, deploy, and run applications on emulator instances and devices. To speed up development, we use Eclipse along with the ADT plug-in, which does all the hard work we'd otherwise have to do on the command line with the JDK and SDK tools. Eclipse itself is built on a few core concepts: workspaces, which manage projects; views, which provide specific functionality, such as source editing or LogCat output; perspectives, which tie together views for specific tasks such as debugging; and Run and Debug configurations, which allow you to specify the startup settings used when you run or debug applications.

The secret to mastering all this is practice, as dull as that may sound. Throughout the book, we'll implement several projects that should make you more comfortable with the Android development environment. At the end of the day, though, it is up to you to take it all one step further.

With all this information, you can move on to the reason you're reading this book in the first place: developing games.

Chapter 3

Game Development 101

Game development is hard—not so much because it's rocket science, but because there's a huge amount of information to digest before you can actually start writing the game of your dreams. On the programming side, you have to worry about such mundane things as file input/output (I/O), input handling, audio and graphics programming, and networking code. And those are only the basics! On top of that, you will want to build your actual game mechanics. The code for that needs structure as well, and it is not always obvious how to create the architecture of your game. You'll actually have to decide how to make your game world move. Can you get away with not using a physics engine and instead roll your own simple simulation code? What are the units and scale within which your game world is set? How does it translate to the screen?

There's actually another problem many beginners overlook, which is that, before you start hacking away, you'll actually have to design your game first. Countless projects never see the light of day and get stuck in the tech-demo phase because there was never any clear idea of how the game should actually behave. And I'm not talking about the basic game mechanics of your average first-person shooter. That's the easy part: WASD plus mouse, and you're done. You should ask yourself questions like: Is there a splash screen? What does it transition to? What's on the main menu screen? What head-up display elements are available on the actual game screen? What happens if I press the pause button? What options should be offered on the settings screen? How will my UI design work out on different screen sizes and aspect ratios?

The fun part is that there's no silver bullet; there's no standard way to approach all these questions. We will not pretend to give you the be-all and end-all solution to developing games. Instead, we'll try to illustrate how we usually approach the design of a game. You may decide to adapt it completely or modify it to better fit your needs. There are no rules—whatever works for you is OK. You should, however, always strive for an easy solution, both in code and on paper.

Genres: To Each One's Taste

At the start of your project, you usually decide on the genre to which your game will belong. Unless you come up with something completely new and previously unseen, chances are high that your game idea will fit into one of the broad genres currently popular. Most genres have established game mechanics standards (for example, control schemes, specific goals, and so forth.). Deviating from these standards can make a game a great hit, as gamers always long for something new. It can also be a great risk, though, so consider carefully if your new platformer/first-person shooter/real-time strategy game actually has an audience.

Let's check out some examples for the more popular genres on the Android Market.

Casual Games

Probably the biggest segment of games on the Android Market consists of so-called *casual games*. So what exactly is a casual game? That question has no concrete answer, but casual games share a few common traits. Usually, they feature great accessibility, so even non-gamers can pick them up easily, which immensely increases the pool of potential players. A game session is meant to take just a couple of minutes at most. However, the addictive nature of a casual game's simplicity often gets players hooked for hours. The actual game mechanics range from extremely simplistic puzzle games to one-button platformers to something as simple as tossing a paper ball into a basket. The possibilities are endless because of the blurry definition of the casual genre.

Abduction and *Abduction 2* (Figure 3–1), by the one-person shop Psym Mobile, is the perfect casual game example. It belongs to the subgenre of "jump-'em-up games" (at least that's what I call them). The goal of the game is it to direct the continually-jumping cow from platform to platform, and to reach the top of the level. On the way up, you'll battle breaking platforms, spikes, and flying enemies. You can pick up power-ups that help you reach the top and so on. You control the cow by tilting the phone, thereby influencing the direction it is jumping/falling. Easy-to-understand controls, a clear goal, and cute graphics made this game one of the first hits on the Android Market.

Figure 3–1. *Abduction (left) and Abduction 2 (right), by Psym Mobile*

Antigen (Figure 3–2), by Battery Powered Games LLC, is a completely different animal. This game was developed by one of the co-authors of this book, however, we aren't mentioning it to plug anything, but because it follows some of the input and compatibility methods we outline in this book. In Antigen, you play as an antibody that fights against different kinds of viruses. The game is actually a hybrid action puzzler. You control the antibody with the onscreen D-pad and rotation buttons at the top right. Your antibody has a set of connectors at each side that allow you to connect to viruses and thereby destroy them. While Abduction only features a single input mechanism via the accelerometer, the controls of Antigen are a little bit more involved. Not every device supports multitouch, so we came up with a couple of input schemes for all possible devices; Zeemote controls would be one of these. To reach the largest possible audience, special care was taken to make the game work even on low-end devices with 320×240 pixel screens, but it also scales up nicely to the modern tablets running at 1280×800.

Figure 3–2. *Antigen, by Battery Powered Games LLC*

A list of all of the possible subgenres of the casual game category would fill most of this book. Many more innovative game concepts can be found in this genre, and it is worth checking out the respective category in the market to get some inspiration.

Puzzle Games

Puzzle games need no introduction. We all know great games like *Tetris* and *Bejeweled*. They are a big part of the Android gaming market, and they are highly popular with all segments of the demographic. In contrast to PC-based puzzle games, , which usually just involves getting three objects of a color or shape together, many puzzle games on Android deviate from the classic match-3 formula and use more elaborate, physics-based puzzles.

Super Tumble (Figure 3–3) is a superb example of a physics puzzler. The goal of the game is to remove blocks by touching them, and to get the star sitting on top of the blocks safely to the bottom platform. While this may sound fairly simple, it can get rather involved in later levels. The game is powered by Box2D, a 2D physics engine.

Figure 3-3. *Super Tumble, by Camel Games*

U Connect (Figure 3–4), by BitLogik, is a minimalistic but entertaining little brain-teaser. The goal is to connect all the dots in the graph with a single line. Computer science students will probably recognize a familiar problem here.

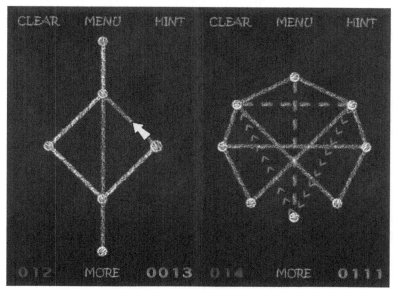

Figure 3-4. *U Connect, by BitLogik*

Of course, you can also find all kinds of Tetris clones, match-3 games, and other standard formulas on the market. The games listed here demonstrate that a puzzle game can be more than just another clone of a 20-year-old concept.

Action and Arcade Games

Action and arcade games usually unleash the full potential of the Android platform. Many of them feature stunning 3D visuals, demonstrating what is possible on the current generation of hardware. The genre has many sub-genres, including racing games, shoot-'em-ups, first- and third-person shooters, and platformers. This segment of the Android Market is still a little underdeveloped, as big companies that have the resources to produce these types of titles are hesitant to jump on the Android bandwagon. Some indie developers have taken it upon themselves to fill that niche, though.

Replica Island (Figure 3–5) is probably the most successful platformer on Android to date. It was developed by former Google engineer and game development advocate Chris Pruett in an attempt to show that one can write high-performance games in pure Java on Android. The game tries to accommodate all potential device configurations by offering a huge variety of input schemes. Special care was taken so that the game performs well even on low-end devices. The game itself involves a robot that is instructed to retrieve a mysterious artifact. The game mechanics resemble the old SNES 16-bit platformers. In the standard configuration, the robot is moved via an accelerometer and two buttons: one for enabling its thruster to jump over obstacles and the other to stomp enemies from above. The game is also open source, which is another plus.

Figure 3–5. *Replica Island, by Chris Pruett*

Exzeus (Figure 3–6), by HyperDevBox, is a classic rail shooter in the spirit of Starfox on the SNES, but with high-fidelity 3D graphics. The game features it all: different weapons, power-ups, big boss fights, and a ton of things to shoot. As with many other 3D titles, the game is meant to be played on high-end devices only. The main character is controlled via tilt and onscreen buttons—a rather intuitive control scheme for this type of game.

Figure 3–6. *Exzeus, by HyperDevBox*

Deadly Chambers (Figure 3–7), by Battery Powered Games LLC, is a third-person shooter in the style of such classics as Doom and Quake. Like *Antigen*, this game was developed by a co-author of this book. We mention it in order to contrast it with *Exzeus*. The game is a third-person/first-person shooter hybrid, with full OpenGL ES 3D animated graphics, guns, explosions, and everything else you'd expect from that sort of game. Unlike most games of this type, which only work on the latest hardware, we took great care to make it run even on low-end devices, such as the Hero and G1. The game also offers a variety of input schemes, so that you can play the game on single-touch screens, multitouch screens, keyboards, and the Zeemote JS1. Technically, the game is a major feat, especially considering that it was programmed by a single person over a period of roughly six months and is playable on a G1 phone.

Figure 3-7. *Deadly Chambers, by Battery Powered Games LLC*

Radiant (Figure 3–8), by Hexage, represents a brilliant evolutionary step from the old *Space Invaders* concept. Instead of offering a static playfield, the game presents side-scrolling levels, and it has quite a bit of variety in level and enemy design. You control the ship by tilting the phone, and you can upgrade the ship's weapon systems by buying new weapons with points you've earned by shooting enemies. The semi-pixelated style of the graphics gives this game a unique look and feel, while bringing back memories of the old days.

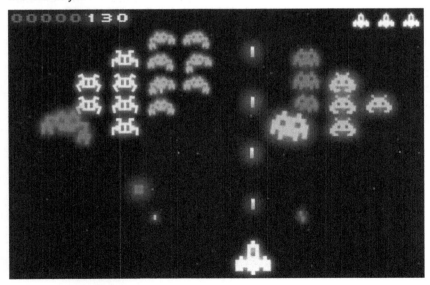

Figure 3-8. *Radiant, by Hexage*

The action and arcade genre is still a bit underrepresented on the market. Players are longing for good action titles, so maybe that is your niche!

Tower-Defense Games

Given their immense success on the Android platform, we felt the need to discuss tower-defense games as their own genre. Tower-defense games became popular as a variant of PC real-time strategy games developed by the modding community. The concept was soon translated to standalone games. Tower-defense games currently represent the best-selling genre on Android.

In a typical tower-defense game, some mostly evil force is sending out critters in so-called waves to attack your castle/base/crystals/you name it. Your task is to defend that special place on the game map by placing defense turrets that shoot the incoming enemies. For each enemy you kill, you usually get some amount of money or points that you can invest in new turrets or upgrades. The concept is extremely simple, but getting the balance of this type of game right is quite difficult.

Robo Defense (Figure 3–9), by Lupis Labs Software, is the mother of all tower-defense games on Android. It has occupied the number-one paid game spot in the market for most of Android's lifetime. The game follows the standard tower-defense formula, without any bells and whistles attached. It's a straightforward and dangerously addictive tower-defense implementation, with different pannable maps, achievements, and high scores. The presentation is sufficient to get the concept across, but not stellar, which offers more proof that a well-selling game doesn't necessarily need to feature cream-of-the-crop graphics and audio.

Figure 3–9. *Robo Defense, by Lupis Labs Software*

Innovation

Some games just can't be put into a category. They exploit the new capabilities and features of Android devices, such as the camera or the GPS, to create new sorts of experiences. This innovative crop of new games is social and location-aware, and it even introduces some elements from the field of augmented reality.

SpecTrek (Figure 3–10) is one of the winners of the second Android Developer Challenge. The goal of the game is to roam around, with GPS enabled, to find ghosts and catch them with your camera. The ghosts are simply laid over a camera view, and it is the player's task to keep them in focus and press the Catch button to score points.

Figure 3–10. *SpecTrek, by SpecTrekking.com*

Apparatus (Figure 3–11) is a game that was featured on Android tablets. It is an innovation on many previous physics-builder games, but is executed in such a way that players can't help but get hopelessly addicted to trying to solve the puzzles by creating the goal machine. It uses simple, but nice-to-look-at, 3D graphics, and it runs on nearly every device from Android 1.6 up.

Figure 3–11. *Apparatus, by BitHack*

Many new games, ideas, genres, and apps don't appear to be games at first, but they really are. Therefore, when entering the Android market, it's difficult to really pinpoint specifically what is now innovative. We've seen games where a tablet is used as the game host and then connected to a TV, which in turn is connected via Bluetooth to multiple Android handsets, each used as a controller. Casual, social games have been doing well for quite a while, and many popular titles that started on the Apple platform have now been ported to Android. Has everything possible already been done? No way! There will always be untapped markets and game ideas for those who are willing to take a few risks with some new game ideas. Hardware is becoming ever faster, and that opens up entire new realms of possibilities that were previously unfeasible due to lack of CPU horsepower.

So, now that you know what's already available on Android, we suggest that you fire up the Market application and checkout some of the games presented previously. Pay attention to their structure (for example, what screens lead to what other screens, what buttons do what, how game elements interact with each other, and so on). Getting a feeling for these things can actually be achieved by playing games with an analytical mindset. Push away the entertainment factor for a moment, and concentrate on deconstructing the game. Once you're done, come back and read on. We are going to design a very simple game on paper.

Game Design: The Pen Is Mightier Than the Code

As we said earlier, it is rather tempting to fire up the IDE and just hack together a nice tech demo. This is OK if you want to prototype experimental game mechanics and see if those actually work. However, once you do that, throw away the prototype. Pick up a pen and some paper, sit down in a comfortable chair, and think through all high-level aspects of your game. Don't concentrate on technical details yet—you'll do that later on. Right now, you want to concentrate on designing the user experience of your game. The best way to do this is by sketching up the following things:

- The core game mechanics, including a level concept if applicable.

- A rough backstory with the main characters.

- A list of items, powerups, or other things that modify the characters, mechanics, or environment if applicable.

- A rough sketch of the graphics style based on the backstory and characters.

- Sketches of all the screens involved as well as diagrams of transitions between screens, along with transition triggers (for example, for the game-over state).

If you've peeked at the Table of Contents, you know that we are going to implement *Snake* on Android. *Snake* is one of the most popular games ever to hit the mobile market. If you don't know about *Snake* already, look it up on the Web before reading on. I'll wait here in the meantime…

Welcome back. So, now that you know what *Snake* is all about, let us pretend we just came up with the idea ourselves and start laying out the design for it. Let's begin with the game mechanics.

Core Game Mechanics

Before we start, here's a list of what we need:

- A pair of scissors

- Something to write with

- Plenty of paper

In this phase of our game design, everything's a moving target. Instead of carefully crafting nice images in Paint, Gimp, or Photoshop, we suggest you create basic building blocks out of paper and rearrange them on a table until they fit. You can easily change things physically without having to cope with a silly mouse. Once you are OK with your paper design, you can take photos or scan the design in for future reference. Let's start by creating those basic blocks of our core game screen. Figure 3–12 shows you our version of what is needed for our core game mechanics.

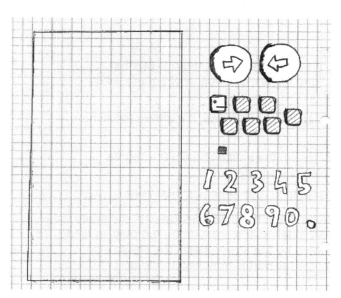

Figure 3–12. *Game design building blocks*

The leftmost rectangle is our screen, roughly the size of a Nexus One screen. That's where we'll place all the other elements. The next building blocks are two buttons that we'll use to control the snake. Finally, there's the snake's head, a couple of tail parts, and a piece it can eat. We also wrote out some numbers and cut them out. Those will be used to display the score. Figure 3–13 illustrates our vision of the initial playing field.

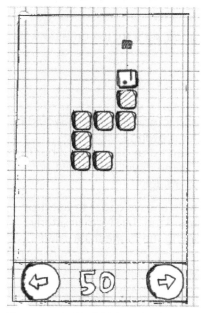

Figure 3–13. *The initial playing field*

Let's define the game mechanics:

- The snake advances in the direction in which its head is pointed, dragging along its tail. Head and tail are composed of equally-sized parts that do not differ much in their visuals.

- If the snake goes outside the screen boundaries, it reenters the screen on the opposite side.

- If the right or left button is pressed, the snake takes a 90-degree clockwise (right) or counterclockwise (left) turn.

- If the snake hits itself (for example, a part of its tail), the game is over.

- If the snake hits a piece with its head, the piece disappears, the score is increased by 10 points, and a new piece appears on the playing field in a location that is not occupied by the snake itself. The snake also grows by one tail part. That new tail part is attached to the end of the snake.

This is quite a complex description for such a simple game. Note that we ordered the items somewhat in ascending complexity. The behavior of the game when the snake eats a piece on the playing field is probably the most complex one. More elaborate games cannot, of course, be described in such a concise manner. Usually, you'd split these up into separate parts and design each part individually, connecting them in a final merge step at the end of the process.

The last game mechanics item has this implication: the game will end eventually, as all spaces on the screen will be used up by the snake.

Now that our totally original game mechanics idea looks good, let's try to come up with a backstory for it.

A Story and an Art Style

While an epic story with zombies, spaceships, dwarves, and lots of explosions would be fun, we have to realize that we are limited in resources. Our drawing skills, as exemplified in Figure 3–12, are somewhat lacking. We couldn't draw a zombie if our lives depended on it. So we did what any self-respecting indie game developer would do: resorted to the doodle style, and adjusted the settings accordingly.

Enter the world of Mr. Nom. Mr. Nom is a paper snake who's always eager to eat drops of ink that fall down from an unspecified source on his paper land. Mr. Nom is utterly selfish, and he has only a single, not-so-noble goal: becoming the biggest ink-filled paper snake in the world!

This little backstory allows us to define a few more things:

- The art style is doodly. We will actually scan in our building blocks later and use them in our game as graphical assets.

■ As Mr. Nom is an individualist, we will modify his blocky nature a little and give him a proper snake face. And a hat.

■ The digestible piece will be transformed into a set of ink stains.

■ We'll trick out the audio aspect of the game by letting Mr. Nom grunt each time he eats an ink stain.

■ Instead of going for a boring title like "Doodle Snake," let us call the game "Mr. Nom," a much more intriguing title.

Figure 3–14 shows Mr. Nom in his full glory, along with some ink stains that will replace the original block. We also sketched a doodly Mr. Nom logo that we can reuse throughout the game.

Figure 3–14. *Mr. Nom, his hat, ink stains, and the logo*

Screens and Transitions

With the game mechanics, backstory, characters, and art style fixed, we can now design our screens and the transitions between them. First, however, it's important to understand exactly what makes up a screen:

■ A screen is an atomic unit that fills the entire display, and it is responsible for exactly one part of the game (for example, the main menu, the settings menu, or the game screen where the action is happening).

■ A screen can be composed of multiple components (for example, buttons, controls, head-up displays, or the rendering of the game world).

■ A screen allows the user to interact with the screen's elements. These interactions can trigger screen transitions (for example, pressing a New Game button on the main menu could exchange the currently active main menu screen with the game screen or a level-selection screen).

With those definitions, we can put on our thinking caps and design all of the screens of our Mr. Nom game.

The first thing our game will present to the player is the main menu screen. What makes a good main menu screen?

■ Displaying the name of our game is a good idea in principle, so we'll put in the Mr. Nom logo.

■ To make things look more consistent, we also need a background. We'll reuse the playing field background for this.

■ Players will usually want to play the game, so let's throw in a Play button. This will be our first interactive component.

■ Players want to keep track of their progress and awesomeness, so we'll also add a high-score button, another interactive component.

■ There might be people out there that don't know *Snake*. Let's give them some help in the form of a Help button that will transition to a help screen.

■ While our sound design will be lovely, some players might still prefer to play in silence. Giving them a symbolic toggle button to enable and disable the sound will do the trick.

How we actually lay out those components on our screen is a matter of taste. You could start studying a subfield of computer science called human computer interfaces (HCI) to get the latest scientific opinion on how to present your application to the user. For Mr. Nom, that might be a little overkill, though. We settled with the simplistic design shown in Figure 3–15.

Figure 3–15. *The main menu screen*

Note that all of these elements (the logo, the menu buttons, and so forth) are all separate images.

We get an immediate advantage by starting with the main menu screen: we can directly derive more screens from the interactive components. In Mr. Nom's case, we will need a game screen, a high-scores screen, and a help screen. We get away with not including a settings screen since the only setting (sound) is already present on the main screen.

Let's ignore the game screen for a moment and concentrate first on the high-scores screen. We decided that high scores will be stored locally in Mr. Nom, so we'll only keep track of a single player's achievements. We also decided that only the five highest scores will be recorded. The high-scores screen will therefore look like Figure 3–16, showing the "HIGHSCORES" text at the top, followed by the five top scores and a single button with an arrow on it to indicate that you can transition back to something. We'll reuse the background of the playing field again because we like it cheap.

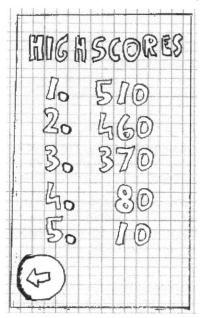

Figure 3–16. *The high-scores screen*

Next up is the help screen. It will inform the player of the backstory and the game mechanics. All of that information is a bit too much to be presented on a single screen. Therefore, we'll split up the help screen into multiple screens. Each of these screens will present one essential piece of information to the user: who Mr. Nom is and what he wants, how to control Mr. Nom to make him eat ink stains, and what Mr. Nom doesn't like (namely eating himself). That's a total of three help screens, as shown in Figure 3–17. Note that we added a button to each screen to indicate that there's more information to be read. We'll hook those screens up in a bit.

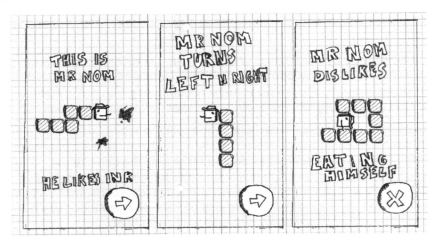

Figure 3–17. *The help screens*

Finally, there's our game screen, which we already saw in action. There are a few details we left out, though. First, the game shouldn't start immediately; we should give the player some time to get ready. The screen will therefore start off with a request to touch the screen to start the munching. This does not warrant a separate screen; we will directly implement that initial pause in the game screen.

Speaking of pauses, we'll also add a button that allows the user to pause the game. Once it's paused, we also need to give the user a way to resume the game. We'll just display a big Resume button in that case. In the pause state, we'll also display another button that will allow the user to return to the main menu screen.

In case Mr. Nom bites his own tail, we need to inform the player that the game is over. We could implement a separate game-over screen, or we could stay within the game screen and just overlay a big "Game Over" message. In this case, we'll opt for the latter. To round things out, we'll also display the score the player achieved, along with a button to get back to the main menu.

Think of those different states of the game screen as subscreens. We have four subscreens: the initial get-ready state, the normal game-playing state, the paused state, and the game-over state. Figure 3–18 shows these subscreens.

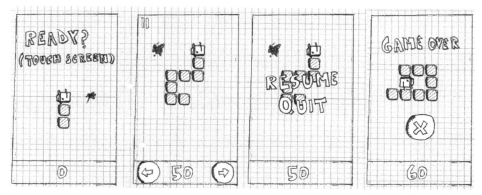

Figure 3–18. *The game screen and its four different states*

Now it's time to hook the screens together. Each screen has some interactive components that are made for transitioning to another screen.

- From the main menu screen, we can get to the game screen, the high-scores screen, and the help screen via their respective buttons.

- From the game screen, we can get back to the main screen either via the button in the paused state or the button in the game-over state.

- From the high-scores screen, we can get back to the main screen.

- From the first help screen, we can go to the second help screen; from the second to the third; and from the third to the fourth; from the fourth, we'll return back to the main screen.

That's all of our transitions! Doesn't look so bad, does it? Figure 3–19 visually summarizes all of the transitions, with arrows from each interactive component to the target screen. We also put in all of the elements that comprise our screens.

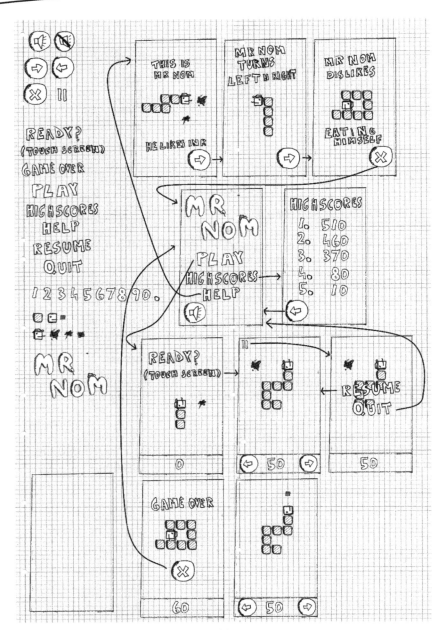

Figure 3–19. *All design elements and transitions*

We have now finished our first full game design. What's left is the implementation. How do we actually make this design into an executable game?

NOTE: The method we just used to create our game design is fine and dandy for smaller games. This book is called *Beginning Android Games*, so it's a fitting methodology. For larger projects, you will most likely work on a team, with each team member specializing in one aspect. While you can still apply the methodology described here in that context, you might need to tweak and tune it a little to accommodate the different environment. You will also work more iteratively, constantly refining your design.

Code: The Nitty-Gritty Details

Here's another chicken-and-egg situation: We only want to get to know the Android APIs that are relevant for game programming. However, we still don't know how to actually program a game. We have an idea of how to design one, but transforming it into an executable is still voodoo magic to us. In the following subsections, we want to give you an overview of what elements usually make up a game. We'll look at some pseudocode for interfaces that we'll later implement with what Android offers. Interfaces are awesome for two reasons: they allow us to concentrate on the semantics without needing to know the implementation details, and they allow us to exchange the implementation later (for example, instead of using 2D CPU rendering, we could exploit OpenGL ES to display Mr. Nom on the screen).

Every game needs a basic framework that abstracts away and eases the pain of communicating with the underlying operating system. Usually this is split up into modules, as follows:

Window management: This is responsible for creating a window and coping with things like closing the window or pausing/resuming the application in Android.

Input: This is related to the window management module, and it keeps track of user input (that is, touch events, keystrokes, periphery, and accelerometer readings).

File I/O: This allows us to get the bytes of our assets into our program from disk.

Graphics: This is probably the most complex module besides the actual game. It is responsible for loading graphics and drawing them on the screen.

Audio: This module is responsible for loading and playing everything that will hit our ears.

Game framework: This ties all the above together and provides an easy-to-use base for writing our games.

Each of these modules is composed of one or more interfaces. Each interface will have at least one concrete implementation that applies the semantics of the interface based on what the underlying platform (in our case Android) provides.

> **NOTE:** Yes, we deliberately left out networking from the preceding list. We will not implement multiplayer games in this book. That is a rather advanced topic, depending on the type of game. If you are interested in this topic, you can find a range of tutorials on the Web. (www.gamedev.net is a good place to start.)

In the following discussion, we will be as platform-agnostic as possible. The concepts are the same on all platforms.

Application and Window Management

A game is just like any other computer program that has a UI. It is contained in some sort of window (if the underlying operating system's UI paradigm is window based, which is the case for all mainstream operating systems). The window serves as a container, and we basically think of it as a canvas from which we draw our game content.

Most operating systems allow the user to interact with the window in a special way, besides touching the client area or pressing a key. On desktop systems, you can usually drag the window around, resize it, or minimize it to some sort of taskbar. In Android, resizing is replaced with accommodating an orientation change, and minimizing is similar to putting the application in the background, via a press of the home button or as a reaction to an incoming call.

The application and window management module is also responsible for actually setting up the window and making sure it is filled by a single UI component to which we can later render and that receives input from the user in the form of touching or pressing keys. That UI component might be rendered via the CPU or it can be hardware accelerated, as is the case with OpenGL ES.

The application and window management module does not have a concrete set of interfaces. We'll merge it with the game framework later on. The things we have to remember are the application states and window events that we have to manage:

Create: Called once when the window (and thus the application) is started up.

Pause: Called when the application is paused by some mechanism.

Resume: Called when the application is resumed and the window is again in the foreground.

NOTE: Some Android aficionados might roll their eyes at this point. Why use only a single window (activity in Android speak)? Why not use more than one UI widget for the game—say, for implementing complex UIs that our game might need? The main reason is that we want complete control over the look and feel of our game. It also allows us to focus on Android game programming instead of Android UI programming, a topic for which better books exist—for example, Mark Murphy's excellent *Beginning Android 2* (Apress, 2010).

Input

The user will surely want to interact with our game in some way. That's where the input module comes in. On most operating systems, input events such as touching the screen or pressing a key are dispatched to the currently-focused window. The window will then further dispatch the event to the UI component that has the focus. The dispatching process is usually transparent to us; our only concern is getting the events from the focused UI component. The UI APIs of the operating system provide a mechanism to hook into the event-dispatching system so that we can easily register and record the events. This hooking into and recording of events is the main task of the input module.

What can we do with the recorded information? There are two modi operandi:

Polling: With polling, we only check the current state of the input devices. Any states between the current check and the last check will be lost. This way of input handling is suitable for checking things like whether a user touches a specific button, for example. It is not suitable for tracking text input, as the order of key events is lost.

Event-based handling: This gives us a full chronological history of the events that have occurred since we last checked. It is a suitable mechanism to perform text input or any other task that relies on the order of events. It's also useful to detect when a finger first touched the screen or when the finger was lifted.

What input devices do we want to handle? On Android, we have three main input methods: touchscreen, keyboard/trackball, and accelerometer. The first two are suitable for both polling and event-based handling. The accelerometer is usually just polled. The touchscreen can generate three events:

Touch down: This happens when a finger is touched to the screen.

Touch drag: This occurs when a finger is dragged across the screen. Before a drag, there's always a down event.

Touch up: This happens when a finger is lifted from the screen.

Each touch event has additional information: the position relative to the UI component origin and a pointer index used in multitouch environments to identify and track separate fingers.

The keyboard can generate two types of events:

Key down: This happens when a key is pressed down.

Key up: This happens when a key is lifted. This event is always preceded by a key-down event.

Key events also carry additional information. Key-down events store the pressed key's code. Key-up events store the key's code and an actual Unicode character. There's a difference between a key's code and the Unicode character generated by a key-up event. In the latter case, the state of other keys is also taken into account, such as the Shift key. This way, we can get uppercase and lowercase letters in a key-up event, for example. With a key-down event, we only know that a certain key was pressed; we have no information on what character that keypress would actually generate.

Developers seeking to use custom USB hardware including joysticks, analog controllers, special keyboards, touchpads, or other Android supported peripherals can do this by utilizing the `android.hardware.usb` package APIs, which were introduced in API level 12 (Android 3.1) and also backported to Android 2.3.4 via the package `com.android.future.usb`. The USB APIs allow for an Android device to operate in either host mode, which allows for periphery to be attached to and used by the Android device, or accessory mode, which allows for the device to act as an accessory to another USB host. These APIs aren't quite beginner material, as the device access is very low level, offering data-streaming IO to the USB accessory, but it's important to note that the functionality is indeed there. If your game design revolves around a specific USB accessory, you will certainly want to develop a communication module for the accessory and prototype using it.

Finally, there's the accelerometer. It's important to understand that while nearly all handsets and tablets have accelerometers as standard hardware, many new devices, including set top boxes, may not have an accelerometer, so always plan on having multiple modes of input!

To use the accelerometer, we will always poll the accelerometer's state. The accelerometer reports the acceleration exerted by the gravity of our planet on one of three axes of the accelerometer. The axes are called x, y, and z. Figure 3–20 depicts each axis's orientation. The acceleration on each axis is expressed in meters per second squared (m/s²). From physics class, we know that an object will accelerate at roughly 9.8 m/s² when in free fall on planet Earth. Other planets have a different gravity, so the acceleration constant is also different. For the sake of simplicity, we'll only deal with planet Earth here. When an axis points away from the center of the Earth, the maximum acceleration is applied to it. If an axis points toward the center of the Earth, we get a negative maximum acceleration. If you hold your phone upright in portrait mode, then the y-axis will report an acceleration of 9.8 m/s², for example. In Figure 3–20, the z-axis would report an acceleration of 9.8 m/s², and the x- and y-axes would report and acceleration of zero.

Figure 3–20. *The accelerometer axes on an Android phone. The z-axis points out of the phone.*

Now, let's define an interface that gives us polling access to the touchscreen, the keyboard, and the accelerometer and that also gives us event-based access to the touchscreen and keyboard (see Listing 3–1).

Listing 3–1. *The Input Interface and the KeyEvent and TouchEvent Classes*

```java
package com.badlogic.androidgames.framework;

import java.util.List;

public interface Input {
    public static class KeyEvent {
        public static final int KEY_DOWN = 0;
        public static final int KEY_UP = 1;

        public int type;
        public int keyCode;
        public char keyChar;
    }

    public static class TouchEvent {
        public static final int TOUCH_DOWN = 0;
        public static final int TOUCH_UP = 1;
        public static final int TOUCH_DRAGGED = 2;

        public int type;
        public int x, y;
        public int pointer;
    }

    public boolean isKeyPressed(int keyCode);

    public boolean isTouchDown(int pointer);

    public int getTouchX(int pointer);

    public int getTouchY(int pointer);

    public float getAccelX();

    public float getAccelY();
```

```
    public float getAccelZ();

    public List<KeyEvent> getKeyEvents();

    public List<TouchEvent> getTouchEvents();
}
```

Our definition is started off by two classes, KeyEvent and TouchEvent. The KeyEvent class defines constants that encode a KeyEvent's type; the TouchEvent class does the same. A KeyEvent instance records its type, the key's code, and its Unicode character in case the event's type is KEY_UP.

The TouchEvent code is similar, and it holds the TouchEvent's type, the position of the finger relative to the UI component's origin, and the pointer ID that was given to the finger by the touchscreen driver. The pointer ID for a finger will stay the same for as long as that finger is on the screen. If two fingers are down and finger 0 is lifted, then finger 1 keeps its ID for as long as it is touching the screen. A new finger will get the first free ID, which would be 0 in this example. Pointer IDs are often assigned sequentially, but it is not guaranteed to happen that way. For example, a Sony Xperia Play uses 15 IDs and assigns them to touches in a round-robin manner. Do not ever make assumptions in your code about the ID of a new pointer—you can only read the ID of a pointer using the index and reference it until the pointer has been lifted.

Next are the polling methods of the Input interface, which should be pretty self-explanatory. Input.isKeyPressed() takes a keyCode and returns whether the corresponding key is currently pressed or not. Input.isTouchDown(), Input.getTouchX(), and Input.getTouchY() return whether a given pointer is down, as well as its current x- and y-coordinates. Note that the coordinates will be undefined if the corresponding pointer is not actually touching the screen.

Input.getAccelX(), Input.getAccelY(), and Input.getAccelZ() return the respective acceleration values of each accelerometer axis.

The last two methods are used for event-based handling. They return the KeyEvent and TouchEvent instances that got recorded since the last time we called these methods. The events are ordered according to when they occurred, with the newest event being at the end of the list.

With this simple interface and these helper classes, we have all our input needs covered. Let's move on to handling files.

NOTE: While mutable classes with public members are an abomination, we can get away with them in this case for two reasons: Dalvik is still slow when calling methods (getters in this case), and the mutability of the event classes does not have an impact on the inner workings of an Input implementation. Just take note that this is bad style in general, but that we will resort to this shortcut every once in a while for performance reasons.

File I/O

Reading and writing files is quite essential for our game development endeavor. Given that we are in Java land, we are mostly concerned with creating InputStream and OutputStream instances, the standard Java mechanisms for reading and writing data from and to a specific file. In our case, we are mostly concerned with reading files that we package with our game, such as level files, images, and audio files. Writing files is something we'll do a lot less often. Usually, we only write files if we want to maintain high-scores or game settings, or save a game state so that users can pick up from where they left off.

We want the easiest possible file-accessing mechanism. Listing 3–2 shows our proposal for a simple interface.

Listing 3–2. *The File I/O Interface*

```
package com.badlogic.androidgames.framework;

import java.io.IOException;
import java.io.InputStream;
import java.io.OutputStream;

public interface FileIO {
    public InputStream readAsset(String fileName) throws IOException;

    public InputStream readFile(String fileName) throws IOException;

    public OutputStream writeFile(String fileName) throws IOException;
}
```

That's rather lean and mean. We just specify a filename and get a stream in return. As we usually do in Java, we will throw an IOException in case something goes wrong. Where we read and write files from and to will depend on the implementation, of course. Assets will be read from our application's APK file, and files will be read from and written to on the SD card (also known as external storage).

The returned InputStreams and OutputStreams are plain-old Java streams. Of course, we have to close them once we are finished using them.

Audio

While audio programming is a rather complex topic, we can get away with a very simple abstraction. We will not do any advanced audio processing; we'll just play back sound effects and music that we load from files, much like we'll load bitmaps in the graphics module.

Before we dive into our module interfaces, though, let's stop for a moment and get some idea of what sound actually is and how it is represented digitally.

The Physics of Sound

Sound is usually modeled as a set of waves that travel in a medium such as air or water. The wave is not an actual physical object, but is the movement of the molecules within the medium. Think of a little pond into which you throw a stone. When the stone hits the pond's surface, it will push away a lot of water molecules within the pond, and those pushed-away molecules will transfer their energy to their neighbors, which will start to move and push as well. Eventually, you will see circular waves emerge from where the stone hit the pond.

Something similar happens when sound is created. Instead of a circular movement, you get spherical movement, though. As you may know from the highly scientific experiments you may have carried out in your childhood, water waves can interact with each other; they can cancel each other out or reinforce each other. The same is true for sound waves. All sound waves in an environment combine to form the tones and melodies you hear when you listen to music. The volume of a sound is dictated by how much energy the moving and pushing molecules exert on their neighbors and eventually on your ear.

Recording and Playback

The principle of recording and playing back audio is actually pretty simple in theory. For recording, we keep track of the point in time when certain amounts of pressure were exerted on an area in space by the molecules that form the sound waves. Playing back these data is a mere matter of getting the air molecules surrounding the speaker to swing and move like they did when we recorded them.

In practice, it is of course a little more complex. Audio is usually recorded in one of two ways: in analog or digitally. In both cases, the sound waves are recorded with some sort of microphone, which usually consists of a membrane that translates the pushing from the molecules to some sort of signal. How this signal is processed and stored is what makes the difference between analog and digital recording. We are working digitally, so let's just have a look at that case.

Recording audio digitally means that the state of the microphone membrane is measured and stored at discrete time steps. Depending on the pushing by the surrounding molecules, the membrane can be pushed inward or outward with regard to a neutral state. This process is called sampling, as we take membrane state samples at discrete points in time. The number of samples we take per time unit is called the *sampling rate*. Usually the time unit is given in seconds, and the unit is called Hertz (Hz). The more samples per second, the higher the quality of the audio. CDs play back at a sampling rate of 44,100 Hz, or 44.1 KHz. Lower sampling rates are found, for example, when transferring voice over the telephone line (8 KHz is common in this case).

The sampling rate is only one attribute responsible for a recording's quality. The way we store each membrane state sample also plays a role, and it is also subject to digitalization. Let's recall what the membrane state actually is: it's the distance of the membrane from its neutral state. Since it makes a difference whether the membrane is pushed inward or outward, we record the signed distance. Hence, the membrane state at a specific time step is a single negative or positive number. We can store this signed number in a variety of ways: as a signed 8-, 16-, or 32-bit integer, as a 32-bit float, or even as a 64-bit float. Every data type has limited precision. An 8-bit signed integer can store 127 positive and 128 negative distance values. A 32-bit integer provides a lot more resolution. When stored as a float, the membrane state is usually normalized to a range between −1 and 1. The maximum positive and minimum negative values represent the farthest distance the membrane can have from its neutral state. The membrane state is also called the amplitude. It represents the loudness of the sound that hits it.

With a single microphone, we can only record mono sound, which loses all spatial information. With two microphones, we can measure sound at different locations in space, and thus get so-called *stereo sound*. You might achieve stereo sound, for example, by placing one microphone to the left and another to the right of an object emitting sound. When the sound is played back simultaneously through two speakers, we can reasonably reproduce the spatial component of the audio. But this also means that we need to store twice the number of samples when storing stereo audio.

The playback is a simple matter in the end. Once we have our audio samples in digital form and with a specific sampling rate and data type, we can throw those data at our audio processing unit, which will transform the information into a signal for an attached speaker. The speaker interprets this signal and translates it into the vibration of a membrane, which in turn will cause the surrounding air molecules to move and produce sound waves. It's exactly what is done for recording, only reversed!

Audio Quality and Compression

Wow, lots of theory. Why do we care? If you paid attention, you can now tell whether an audio file is of high quality or not depending on the sampling rate and the data type used to store each sample. The higher the sampling rate and the higher the data type precision, the better the quality of the audio. However, that also means that we need more storage room for our audio signal.

Imagine that we record the same sound with a length of 60 seconds, but we record it twice: once at a sampling rate of 8 KHz at 8 bits per sample, and once at a sampling rate of 44 KHz at 16-bit precision. How much memory would we need to store each sound? In the first case, we need 1byte per sample. Multiply this by the sampling rate of 8,000 Hz, and we need 8,000 bytes per second. For our full 60 seconds of audio recording, that's 480,000 bytes, or roughly half a megabyte (MB). Our higher-quality recording needs quite a bit more memory: 2 bytes per sample, and 2 times 44,000 bytes per second. That's 88,000 bytes per second. Multiply this by 60 seconds, and we arrive at 5,280,000 bytes, or a little over 5 MB. Your usual 3–minute pop song would take up over 15 MB at that quality, and that's only a mono recording. For a stereo recording, you'd need twice that amount of memory. Quite a lot of bytes for a silly song!

Many smart people have come up with ways to reduce the number of bytes needed for an audio recording. They've invented rather complex psychoacoustic compression algorithms that analyze an uncompressed audio recording and output a smaller, compressed version. The compression is usually *lossy*, meaning that some minor parts of the original audio are omitted. When you playback MP3s or OGGs, you are actually listening to compressed lossy audio. So, using formats such as MP3 or OGG will help us reduce the amount of space needed to store our audio on disk.

What about playing back the audio from compressed files? While dedicated decoding hardware exists for various compressed audio formats, common audio hardware can often only cope with uncompressed samples. Before actually feeding the audio card with samples, we have to first read them in and decompress them. We can do this once and store all of the uncompressed audio samples in memory, or only stream in partitions from the audio file as needed.

In Practice

You have seen that even 3–minute songs can take up a lot of memory. When we play back our game's music, we will therefore stream the audio samples in on the fly instead of preloading all audio samples to memory. Usually, we only have a single music stream playing, so we only have to access the disk once.

For short sound effects, such as explosions or gunshots, the situation is a little different. We often want to play a sound effect multiple times simultaneously. Streaming the audio samples from disk for each instance of the sound effect is not a good idea. We are lucky, though, as short sounds do not take up a lot of memory. We will therefore read all samples of a sound effect into memory, from where we can directly and simultaneously play them back.

We have the following requirements:

- We need a way to load audio files for streaming playback and for playback from memory.

- We need a way to control the playback of streamed audio.

- We need a way to control the playback of fully loaded audio.

This directly translates into the Audio, Music, and Sound interfaces (shown in Listings 3–3 through 3–5, respectively).

Listing 3–3. *The Audio Interface*

```
package com.badlogic.androidgames.framework;

public interface Audio {
    public Music newMusic(String filename);

    public Sound newSound(String filename);
}
```

The Audio interface is our way to create new Music and Sound instances. A Music instance represents a streamed audio file. A Sound instance represents a short sound effect that we keep entirely in memory. The methods Audio.newMusic() and

Audio.newSound() both take a filename as an argument and throw an IOException in case the loading process fails (for example, when the specified file does not exist or is corrupt). The filenames refer to asset files in our application's APK file.

Listing 3–4. *The Music Interface*

```
package com.badlogic.androidgames.framework;

public interface Music {
    public void play();

    public void stop();

    public void pause();

    public void setLooping(boolean looping);

    public void setVolume(float volume);

    public boolean isPlaying();

    public boolean isStopped();

    public boolean isLooping();

    public void dispose();
}
```

The Music interface is a little bit more involved. It features methods to start playing the music stream, pausing and stopping it, and setting it to loop playback, which means it will automatically start from the beginning when it reaches the end of the audio file. Additionally, we can set the volume as a float in the range of 0 (silent) to 1 (maximum volume). A couple of getter methods are also available that allow us to poll the current state of the Music instance. Once we no longer need the Music instance, we have to dispose of it. This will close any system resources, such as the file from which the audio was streamed.

Listing 3–5. *The Sound Interface*

```
package com.badlogic.androidgames.framework;

public interface Sound {
    public void play(float volume);
,,,
    public void dispose();
}
```

The Sound interface is simpler. All we need to do is call its play() method, which again takes a float parameter to specify the volume. We can call the play() method anytime we want (for example, when Mr. Nom eats an ink stain). Once we no longer need the Sound instance, we have to dispose of it to free up the memory that the samples use, as well as other system resources that are potentially associated.

> **NOTE:** While we covered a lot of ground in this chapter, there's a lot more to learn about audio programming. We simplified some things to keep this section short and sweet. Usually you wouldn't specify the audio volume linearly, for example. In our context, it's OK to overlook this little detail. Just be aware that there's more to it!

Graphics

The last module at the core of our game framework is the graphics module. As you might have guessed, it will be responsible for drawing images (also known as bitmaps) to our screen. This may sound easy, but if you want high-performance graphics, you have to know at least the basics of graphics programming. Let's start with the basics of 2D graphics.

The first question we need to ask goes like this: how on Earth are the images output to my display? The answer is rather involved, and we do not necessarily need to know all the details. We'll just quickly review what's happening inside our computer and the display.

Of Rasters, Pixels, and Framebuffers

Today's displays are raster based. A *raster* is a two-dimensional grid of so-called picture elements. You might know them as *pixels*, and we'll refer to them as such in the subsequent text. The raster grid has a limited width and height, which we usually express as the number of pixels per row and per column. If you feel brave, you can turn on your computer and try to make out individual pixels on your display. Note that we're not responsible for any damage that does to your eyes, though.

A pixel has two attributes: a position within the grid and a color. A pixel's position is given as two-dimensional coordinates within a discrete coordinate system. *Discrete* means that a coordinate is always at an integer position. Coordinates are defined within a Euclidean coordinate system imposed on the grid. The origin of the coordinate system is the top-left corner of the grid. The positive x-axis points to the right and the y-axis points downward. The last item is what confuses people the most. We'll come back to it in a minute; there's a simple reason why this is the case.

Ignoring the silly y-axis, we can see that, due to the discrete nature of our coordinates, the origin is coincident with the top-left pixel in the grid, which is located at (0,0). The pixel to the right of the origin pixel is located at (1,0), the pixel beneath the origin pixel is at (0,1), and so on (see the left side of Figure 3–21). The display's raster grid is finite, so there's a limited number of meaningful coordinates. Negative coordinates are outside the screen. Coordinates greater than or equal to the width or height of the raster are also outside the screen. Note that the biggest x-coordinate is the raster's width minus 1, and the biggest y-coordinate is the raster's height minus 1. That's due to the origin being coincident with the top-left pixel. Off-by-one errors are a common source of frustration in graphics programming.

The display receives a constant stream of information from the graphics processor. It encodes the color of each pixel in the display's raster, as specified by the program or operating system in control of drawing to the screen. The display will refresh its state a few dozen times per second. The exact rate is called the refresh rate. It is expressed in Hertz. Liquid crystal displays (LCDs) usually have a refresh rate of 60 Hz per second; cathode ray tube (CRT) monitors and plasma monitors often have higher refresh rates.

The graphics processor has access to a special memory area known as video memory, or VRAM. Within VRAM there's a reserved area for storing each pixel to be displayed on the screen. This area is usually called the *framebuffer*. A complete screen image is therefore called a frame. For each pixel in the display's raster grid, there's a corresponding memory address in the framebuffer that holds the pixel's color. When we want to change what's displayed on the screen, we simply change the color values of the pixels in that memory area in VRAM.

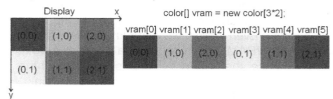

Figure 3–21. *Display raster grid and VRAM, oversimplified*

Now it's time to explain why the y-axis in the display's coordinate system is pointing downward. Memory, be it VRAM or normal RAM, is linear and one dimensional. Think of it as a one-dimensional array. So how do we map the two-dimensional pixel coordinates to one-dimensional memory addresses? Figure 3–21 shows a rather small display raster grid of three-by-two pixels, as well as its representation in VRAM. (We assume VRAM only consists of the framebuffer memory.)From this, we can easily derive the following formula to calculate the memory address of a pixel at (x,y):

```
int address = x + y * rasterWidth;
```

We can also go the other way around, from an address to the x- and y-coordinates of a pixel:

```
int x = address % rasterWidth;
int y = address / rasterWidth;
```

So, the y-axis is pointing downward because of the memory layout of the pixel colors in VRAM. This is actually a sort of legacy inherited from the early days of computer graphics. Monitors would update the color of each pixel on the screen, starting at the top-left corner, moving to the right, and tracing back to the left on the next line, until they reached the bottom of the screen. It was convenient to have the VRAM contents laid out in a manner that eased the transfer of the color information to the monitor.

> **NOTE:** If we had full access to the framebuffer, we could use the preceding equation to write a full-fledged graphics library to draw pixels, lines, rectangles, images loaded to memory, and so on. Modern operating systems do not grant us direct access to the framebuffer for various reasons. Instead, we usually draw to a memory area that is then copied to the actual framebuffer by the operating system. The general concepts hold true in this case as well, though! If you are interested in how to do these low-level things efficiently, search the Web for a guy called Bresenham and his line-and-circle-drawing algorithms.

Vsync and Double-Buffering

Now, if you remember the paragraph about refresh rates, you might have noticed that those rates seem rather low and that we might be able to write to the framebuffer faster than the display will refresh. That can happen. Even worse, we don't know when the display is grabbing its latest frame copy from VRAM, which could be a problem if we're in the middle of drawing something. In this case, the display will then show parts of the old framebuffer content and parts of the new state, which is an undesirable situation. You can see that effect in many PC games where it expresses itself as tearing (in which the screen simultaneously shows parts of the last frame and parts of the new frame).

The first part of the solution to this problem is called *double-buffering*. Instead of having a single framebuffer, the graphics processing unit (GPU) actually manages two of them: a front buffer and a back buffer. The front buffer, from which the pixel colors will be fetched, is available to the display, and the back buffer is available to draw our next frame while the display happily feeds off the front buffer. When we finish drawing our current frame, we tell the GPU to switch the two buffers with each other, which usually means just swapping the address of the front and back buffer. In graphics programming literature, and in API documentation, you may find the terms *page flip* and *buffer swap*, which refer to this process.

Double-buffering alone does not solve the problem entirely, though: the swap can still happen while the screen is in the middle of refreshing its content. That's where *vertical synchronization* (also known as *vsync*) comes into play. When we call the buffer swap method, the GPU will block until the display signals that it has finished its current refresh. If that happens, the GPU can safely swap the buffer addresses and all will be well.

Luckily, we barely need to care about these pesky details nowadays. VRAM and the details of double-buffering and vsyncing are securely hidden from us so that we cannot wreak havoc with them. Instead, we are provided with a set of APIs that usually limit us to manipulating the contents of our application window. Some of these APIs, such as OpenGL ES, expose hardware acceleration, which basically does nothing more than manipulate VRAM with specialized circuits on the graphics chip. See, it's not magic! The reason you should be aware of the inner workings, at least at a high level, is that it allows you to understand the performance characteristics of your application. When vsync is enabled, you can never go above the refresh rate of your screen, which might be puzzling if all you're doing is drawing a single pixel.

When we render with non-hardware-accelerated APIs, we don't directly deal with the display itself. Instead, we draw to one of the UI components in our window. In our case, we deal with a single UI component that is stretched over the whole window. Our coordinate system will therefore not stretch over the entire screen, but only our UI component. The UI component effectively becomes our display, with its own virtual framebuffer. The operating system will then manage compositing the contents of all the visible windows and ensuring that their contents are correctly transferred to the regions that they cover in the real framebuffer.

What Is Color?

You will notice that we have conveniently ignored colors so far. We made up a type called `color` in Figure 3–21 and pretended all is well. Let's see what color really is.

Physically, color is the reaction of your retina and visual cortex to electromagnetic waves. Such a wave is characterized by its wavelength and its intensity. We can see waves with a wavelength between roughly 400 and 700 nm. That sub-band of the electromagnetic spectrum is also known as the visible light spectrum. A rainbow shows all the colors of this visible light spectrum, going from violet to blue to green to yellow, followed by orange and ending at red. All a monitor does is emit specific electromagnetic waves for each pixel, which we experience as the color of each pixel. Different types of displays use different methods to achieve that goal. A simplified version of this process goes like this: every pixel on the screen is made up of three different fluorescent particles that will emit light with one of the colors red, green, or blue. When the display refreshes, each pixel's fluorescent particles will emit light by some means (for example, in the case of CRT displays, the pixel's particles get hit by a bunch of electrons). For each particle, the display can control how much light it emits. For example, if a pixel is entirely red, only the red particle will be hit with electrons at full intensity. If we want colors other than the three base colors, we can achieve that by mixing the base colors. Mixing is done by varying the intensity with which each particle emits its color. The electromagnetic waves will overlay each other on the way to our retina. Our brain interprets this mix as a specific color. A color can thus be specified by a mix of intensities of the base colors red, green, and blue.

Color Models

What we just discussed is called a color model, specifically the RGB color model. RGB stands for red, green, and blue, of course. There are many more color models we could use, such as YUV and CMYK. In most graphics programming APIs, the RGB color model is pretty much the standard, though, so we'll only discuss that here.

The RGB color model is called an additive color model, due to the fact that the final color is derived via mixing the additive primary colors red, green, and blue. You've probably experimented with mixing primary colors in school. Figure 3–22 shows you some examples for RGB color mixing to refresh your memory a little bit.

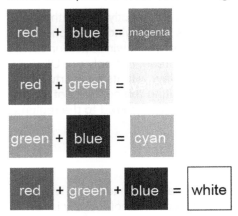

Figure 3–22. *Having fun with mixing the primary colors red, green, and blue*

We can, of course, generate a lot more colors than the ones shown in Figure 3–22 by varying the intensity of the red, green, and blue components. Each component can have an intensity value between 0 and some maximum value (say, 1). If we interpret each color component as a value on one of the three axes of a three-dimensional Euclidian space, we can plot a so-called *color cube*, as depicted in Figure 3–23. There are a lot more colors available to us if we vary the intensity of each component. A color is given as a triplet (red, green, blue) where each component is in the range between 0.0 and 1.0. 0.0 means no intensity for that color, and 1.0 means full intensity. The color black is at the origin (0,0,0), and the color white is at (1,1,1).

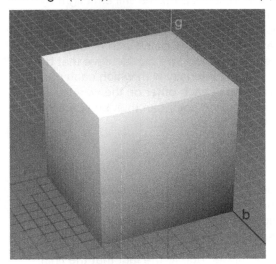

Figure 3–23. *The mighty RGB color cube*

Encoding Colors Digitally

How can we encode an RGB color triplet in computer memory? First, we have to define what data type we want to use for the color components. We could use floating-point numbers and specify the valid range as being between 0.0 and 1.0. This would give us quite some resolution for each component and would make a lot of different colors available to us. Sadly, this approach uses up a lot of space (3 times 4 or 8 bytes per pixel, depending on whether we use 32-bit or 64-bit floats).

We can do better—at the expense of losing a few colors—which is totally OK, since displays usually have a limited range of colors that they can emit. Instead of using a float for each component, we can use an unsigned integer. Now, if we use a 32-bit integer for each component, we haven't gained anything. Instead, we use an unsigned byte for each component. The intensity for each component then ranges from 0 to 255. For 1 pixel, we thus need 3 bytes, or 24 bits. That's 2 to the power of 24 (16,777,216) different colors. I'd say that's enough for our needs.

Can we get that down even more? Yes, we can. We can pack each component into a single 16-bit word, so each pixel needs 2 bytes of storage. Red uses 5 bits, green uses 6 bits, and blue uses the rest of 5 bits. The reason green gets 6 bits is that our eyes can see more shades of green than of red or blue. All bits together make 2 to the power of 16 (65,536) different colors that we can encode. Figure 3–24 shows how a color is encoded with the three encodings described previously.

float: (1.0, 0.5, 0.75)
24-bit: (255, 128, 196) = 0xFF80C4
16-bit: (31, 31, 45) = 0xFC0D

Figure 3–24. *Color encodings of a nice shade of pink (which will be gray in the print copy of this book, sorry)*

In the case of the float, we could use three 32-bit Java floats. In the 24-bit encoding case, we have a little problem: there's no 24-bit integer type in Java, so we could either store each component in a single byte or use a 32-bit integer, leaving the upper 8 bits unused. In case of the 16-bit encoding, we can again either use two separate bytes or store the components in a single short value. Note that Java does not have unsigned types. Due to the power of the two's complement, we can safely use signed integer types to store unsigned values.

For both 16- and 24-bit integer encodings, we also need to specify the order in which we store the three components in the short or integer value. Two methods are usually used: RGB and BGR. Figure 3–23 uses RGB encoding. The blue component is in the lowest 5 or 8 bits, the green component uses up the next 6 or 8 bits, and the red component uses the upper 5 or 8 bits. BGR encoding just reverses this order. The green bits stay where they are, and the red and blue bits swap places. We'll use the RGB order throughout this book, as Android's graphics APIs work with that order as well. Let's summarize the color encodings discussed so far:

- A 32-bit float RGB encoding has 12 bytes for each pixel, and intensities that vary between 0.0 and 1.0.

- A 24-bit integer RGB encoding has 3 or 4 bytes for each pixel, and intensities that vary between 0 and 255. The order of the components can be RGB or BGR. This is also known as RGB888 or BGR888 in some circles, where 8 specifies the number of bits per component.

- A 16-bit integer RGB encoding has 2 bytes for each pixel; red and blue have intensities between 0 and 31, and green has intensities between 0 and 63. The order of the components can be RGB or BGR. This is also known as RGB565 or BGR565 in some circles, where 5 and 6 specify the number of bits of the respective component.

The type of encoding we use is also called the color depth. Images we create and store on disk or in memory have a defined color depth, and so do the framebuffers of the actual graphics hardware and the display itself. Today's displays usually have a default color depth of 24bit, and they can be configured to use less in some cases. The framebuffer of the graphics hardware is also rather flexible, and it can use many different color depths. Our own images can, of course, also have any color depth we like.

> **NOTE:** There are a lot more ways to encode per-pixel color information. Apart from RGB colors, we could also have gray scale pixels, which only have a single component. As those are not used a lot, we'll ignore them at this point.

Image Formats and Compression

At some point in our game development process, our artist will provide us with images that were created with graphics software like Gimp, Paint.NET, or Photoshop. These images can be stored in a variety of formats on disk. Why is there a need for these formats in the first place? Can't we just store the raster as a blob of bytes on disk?

Well, we could, but let's check how much memory that would take up. Say that we want the best quality, so we choose to encode our pixels in RGB888at 24bits per pixel. The image would be 1,024 × 1,024 in size. That's 3 MB for a single puny image alone! Using RGB565, we can get that down to roughly 2 MB.

As in the case of audio, there's been a lot of research on how to reduce the memory needed to store an image. As usual, compression algorithms are employed, specifically tailored for the needs of storing images and keeping as much of the original color information as possible. The two most popular formats are JPEG and PNG. JPEG is a lossy format. This means that some of the original information is thrown away in the process of compression. PNG is a lossless format, and it will reproduce an image that's 100 percent true to the original. Lossy formats usually exhibit better compression characteristics and take up less space on disk. We can therefore choose what format to use depending on the disk memory constraints.

Similar to sound effects, we have to decompress an image fully when we load it into memory. So, even if your image is 20KB compressed on disk, you still need the full width times height times color depth storage space in RAM.

Once loaded and decompressed, the image will be available in the form of an array of pixel colors in exactly the same way the framebuffer is laid out in VRAM. The only difference is that the pixels are located in normal RAM, and that the color depth might differ from the framebuffer's color depth. A loaded image also has a coordinate system like the framebuffer, with the origin in its top-left corner, the x-axis pointing to the right, and the y-axis pointing downward.

Once an image is loaded, we can draw it in RAM to the framebuffer simply by transferring the pixel colors from the image to appropriate locations in the framebuffer. We don't do this by hand; instead, we use an API that provides that functionality.

Alpha Compositing and Blending

Before we can start designing our graphics module interfaces, we have to tackle one more thing: image compositing. For the sake of this discussion, assume that we have a framebuffer to which we can render, as well as a bunch of images loaded into RAM that we'll throw at the framebuffer. Figure 3–25 shows a simple background image, as well as Bob, a zombie-slaying ladies' man.

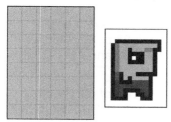

Figure 3–25. *A simple background and Bob, master of the universe*

To draw Bob's world, we'd first draw the background image to the framebuffer followed by Bob over the background image in the framebuffer. This process is called *compositing*, as we compose different images into a final image. The order in which we draw images is relevant, as any new draw call will overwrite the current contents in the framebuffer. So, what would be the final output of our compositing? Figure 3–26 shows it to you.

Figure 3–26. *Compositing the background and Bob into the framebuffer (not what we wanted)*

Ouch, that's not what we wanted. In Figure 3–26, notice that Bob is surrounded by white pixels. When we draw Bob on top of the background to the framebuffer, those white pixels also get drawn, effectively overwriting the background. How can we draw Bob's image so that only Bob's pixels are drawn and the white background pixels are ignored?

Enter alpha blending. Well, in Bob's case it's technically called alpha masking, but that's just a subset of alpha blending. Graphics software usually lets us not only specify the RGB values of a pixel, but also indicate its translucency. Think of it as yet another component of a pixel's color. We can encode it just like we encoded the red, green, and blue components.

We hinted earlier that we could store a 24-bit RGB triplet in a 32-bit integer. There are 8 unused bits in that 32-bit integer that we can grab and in which we can store our alpha value. We can then specify the translucency of a pixel from 0 to 255, where 0 is fully transparent and 255 is opaque. This encoding is known as ARGB8888 or BGRA8888, depending on the order of the components. There are also RGBA8888 and ABGR8888 formats, of course.

In the case of 16-bit encoding, we have a slight problem: all of the bits of our 16-bit short are taken up by the color components. Let's instead imitate the ARGB8888 format and define an ARGB4444 format analogously. That leaves 12 bits for our RGB values in total—4 bits per color component.

We can easily imagine how a rendering method for pixels that's fully translucent or opaque would work. In the first case, we'd just ignore pixels with an alpha component of zero. In the second case, we'd simply overwrite the destination pixel. When a pixel has neither a fully translucent nor fully opaque alpha component, however, things get a tiny bit more complicated.

When talking about blending in a formal way, we have to define a few things:

- Blending has two inputs and one output, each represented as an RGB triplet (C) plus an alpha value (α).

- The two inputs are called *source* and *destination*. The source is the pixel from the image we want to draw over the destination image (that is, the framebuffer). The destination is the pixel we are going to overdraw (partially) with our source pixel.

- The output is again a color expressed as an RGB triplet and an alpha value. Usually, we just ignore the alpha value, though. For simplicity we'll do that in this chapter.

- To simplify our math a little bit, we'll represent RGB and alpha values as floats in the range of 0.0 to 1.0.

Equipped with those definitions, we can create so-called blending equations. The simplest equation looks like this:

```
red = src.red * src.alpha + dst.red * (1 - src.alpha)
blue = src.green * src.alpha + dst.green * (1 - src.alpha)
green = src.blue * src.alpha + dst.blue * (1 - src.alpha)
```

`src` and `dst` are the pixels of the source and destination we want to blend with each other. We blend the two colors component-wise. Note the absence of the destination alpha value in these blending equations. Let's try an example and see what it does:

```
src = (1, 0.5, 0.5), src.alpha = 0.5, dst = (0, 1, 0)
red = 1 * 0.5 + 0 * (1 - 0.5) = 0.5
blue = 0.5 * 0.5 + 1 * (1 - 0.5) = 0.75
red = 0.5 * 0.5 + 0 * (1 - 0.5) = 0.25
```

Figure 3–27 illustrates the preceding equation. Our source color is a shade of pink, and the destination color is a shade of green. Both colors contribute equally to the final output color, resulting in a somewhat dirty shade of green or olive.

Figure 3–27. *Blending two pixels*

Two fine gentlemen named Porter and Duff came up with a slew of blending equations. We will stick with the preceding equation, though, as it covers most of our use cases. Try experimenting with it on paper or in the graphics software of your choice to get a feeling for what blending will do to your composition.

> **NOTE:** Blending is a wide field. If you want to exploit it to its fullest potential, we suggest that you search the Web for Porter and Duff's original work on the subject. For the games we will write, though, the preceding equation is sufficient.

Notice that there are a lot of multiplications involved in the preceding equations (six, to be precise). Multiplications are costly, and we should try to avoid them where possible. In the case of blending, we can get rid of three of those multiplications by pre-multiplying the RGB values of the source pixel color with the source alpha value. Most graphics software supports pre-multiplication of an image's RGB values with the respective alphas. If that is not supported, you can do it at load time in memory. However, when we use a graphics API to draw our image with blending, we have to make sure that we use the correct blending equation. Our image will still contain the alpha values, so the preceding equation would output incorrect results. The source alpha must not be multiplied with the source color. Luckily, all Android graphics APIs allow us to specify fully how we want to blend our images.

In Bob's case, we just set all the white pixels' alpha values to zero in our preferred graphics software program, load the image in ARGB8888 or ARGB4444 format, maybe pre-multiply the alpha, and use a drawing method that does the actual alpha blending with the correct blending equation. The result would look like Figure 3–28.

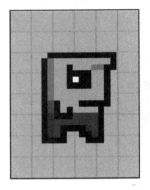 

Figure 3–28. *Bob blended is on the left, and Bob in Paint.NET.is on the right. The checkerboard illustrates that the alpha of the white background pixels is zero, so the background checkerboard shines through.*

> **NOTE:** The JPEG format does not support storage of alpha values per pixel. Use the PNG format in that case.

In Practice

With all of this information, we can finally start to design the interfaces for our graphics module. Let's define the functionality of those interfaces. Note that when we refer to the framebuffer, we actually mean the virtual framebuffer of the UI component to which we draw. We just pretend that we directly draw to the real framebuffer. We'll need to be able to perform the following operations:

- Load images from disk, and store them in memory for drawing them later on.
- Clear the framebuffer with a color so that we can erase what's still there from the last frame.
- Set a pixel in the framebuffer at a specific location to a specific color.
- Draw lines and rectangles to the framebuffer.
- Draw previously loaded images to the framebuffer. We'd like to be able to draw either the complete image or portions of it. We also need to be able to draw images with and without blending.
- Get the dimensions of the framebuffer.

We propose two simple interfaces: Graphics and Pixmap. Let's start with the Graphics interface, shown in Listing 3–6.

Listing 3–6. *The Graphics Interface*

```
package com.badlogic.androidgames.framework;

public interface Graphics {
    public static enum PixmapFormat {
        ARGB8888, ARGB4444, RGB565
    }

    public Pixmap newPixmap(String fileName, PixmapFormat format);

    public void clear(int color);

    public void drawPixel(int x, int y, int color);

    public void drawLine(int x, int y, int x2, int y2, int color);

    public void drawRect(int x, int y, int width, int height, int color);

    public void drawPixmap(Pixmap pixmap, int x, int y, int srcX, int srcY,
            int srcWidth, int srcHeight);

    public void drawPixmap(Pixmap pixmap, int x, int y);

    public int getWidth();

    public int getHeight();
}
```

We start with a public static enum called PixmapFormat. It encodes the different pixel formats we will support. Next, we have the different methods of our Graphics interface:

- The Graphics.newPixmap() method will load an image given in either JPEG or PNG format. We specify a desired format for the resulting Pixmap, which is a hint for the loading mechanism. The resulting Pixmap might have a different format. We do this so that we can somewhat control the memory footprint of our loaded images (for example, by loading RGB888 or ARGB8888 images as RGB565 or ARGB4444 images). The filename specifies an asset in our application's APK file.

- The Graphics.clear() method clears the complete framebuffer with the given color. All colors in our little framework will be specified as 32-bit ARGB8888 values (Pixmaps might of course have a different format).

- The Graphics.drawPixel() method will set the pixel at (x,y) in the framebuffer to the given color. Coordinates outside the screen will be ignored. This is called *clipping*.

- The Graphics.drawLine() method is analogous to the Graphics.drawPixel() method. We specify the start point and endpoint of the line, along with a color. Any portion of the line that is outside the framebuffer's raster will be ignored.

- The Graphics.drawRect() method draws a rectangle to the framebuffer. The (x,y) specifies the position of the rectangle's top-left corner in the framebuffer. The arguments width and height specify the number of pixels in x and y, and the rectangle will fill starting from (x,y). We fill downward in y. The color argument is the color that is used to fill the rectangle.

- The Graphics.drawPixmap() method draws rectangular portions of a Pixmap to the framebuffer. The (x,y) coordinates specify the top-left corner's position of the Pixmap's target location in the framebuffer. The arguments srcX and srcY specify the corresponding top-left corner of the rectangular region that is used from the Pixmap, given in the Pixmap's own coordinate system. Finally, srcWidth and srcHeight specify the size of the portion that we take from the Pixmap.

- Finally, the Graphics.getWidth() and Graphics.getHeight() methods return the width and height of the framebuffer in pixels.

All of the drawing methods except Graphics.clear() will automatically perform blending for each pixel they touch, as outlined in the previous section. We could disable blending on a case-by-case basis to speed up the drawing somewhat, but that would complicate our implementation. Usually, we can get away with having blending enabled all the time for simple games like Mr. Nom.

The Pixmap interface is given in Listing3–7.

Listing 3–7. *The Pixmap Interface*

```
package com.badlogic.androidgames.framework;

import com.badlogic.androidgames.framework.Graphics.PixmapFormat;

public interface Pixmap {
    public int getWidth();

    public int getHeight();

    public PixmapFormat getFormat();

    public void dispose();
}
```

We keep it very simple and immutable, as the compositing is done in the framebuffer.

- The Pixmap.getWidth() and Pixmap.getHeight() methods return the width and the height of the Pixmap in pixels.

- The Pixmap.getFormat() method returns the PixelFormat that the Pixmap is stored with in RAM.

- Finally, there's the `Pixmap.dispose()` method. `Pixmap` instances use up memory and potentially other system resources. If we no longer need them, we should dispose of them with this method.

With this simple graphics module, we can implement Mr. Nom easily later on. Let's finish this chapter with a discussion of the game framework itself.

The Game Framework

After all the groundwork we've done, we can finally talk about how to implement the game itself. For that, let's identify what tasks have to be performed by our game:

- The game is split up into different screens. Each screen performs the same tasks: evaluating user input, applying the input to the state of the screen, and rendering the scene. Some screens might not need any user input, but transition to another screen after some time has passed (for example, a splash screen).

- The screens need to be managed somehow (that is, we need to keep track of the current screen and have a way to transition to a new screen, which boils down to destroying the old screen and setting the new screen as the current screen).

- The game needs to grant the screens access to the different modules (for graphics, audio, input, and so forth) so that they can load resources, fetch user input, play sounds, render to the framebuffer, and so on.

- As our games will be in real-time (that means things will be moving and updating constantly), we have to make the current screen update its state and render itself as often as possible. We'd normally do that inside a loop called the *main loop*. The loop will terminate when the user quits the game. A single iteration of this loop is called a *frame*. The number of frames per second (FPS) that we can compute is called the *frame rate*.

- Speaking of time, we also need to keep track of the time span that has passed since our last frame. This is used for frame-independent movement, which we'll discuss in a minute.

- The game needs to keep track of the window state (that is, whether it was paused or resumed), and inform the current screen of these events.

- The game framework will deal with setting up the window and creating the UI component we render to and receive input from.

Let's boil this down to some pseudocode, ignoring the window management events like pause and resume for a moment:

```
createWindowAndUIComponent();

Input input = new Input();
Graphics graphics = new Graphics();
Audio audio = new Audio();
Screen currentScreen = new MainMenu();
Float lastFrameTime = currentTime();

while( !userQuit() ) {
    float deltaTime = currentTime() - lastFrameTime;
    lastFrameTime = currentTime();

    currentScreen.updateState(input, deltaTime);
    currentScreen.present(graphics, audio, deltaTime);
}

cleanupResources();
```

We start off by creating our game's window and the UI component to which we render and from which we receive input. Next, we instantiate all the modules necessary to do the low-level work. We instantiate our starting screen and make it the current screen, and we record the current time. Then we enter the main loop, which will terminate if the user indicates that he or she wants to quit the game.

Within the game loop, we calculate the so-called *delta time*. This is the time that has passed since the beginning of the last frame. We then record the time of the beginning of the current frame. The delta time and the current time are usually given in seconds. For the screen, the delta time indicates how much time has passed since it was last updated—information that is needed if we want to do frame-independent movement (which we'll come back to in a minute).

Finally, we simply update the current screen's state and present it to the user. The update depends on the delta time as well as the input state; hence, we provide those to the screen. The presentation consists of rendering the screen's state to the framebuffer, as well as playing back any audio the screen's state demands (that is, due to a shot that was fired in the last update). The presentation method might also need to know how much time has passed since it was last invoked.

When the main loop is terminated, we can clean up and release all resources and close the window.

And that is how virtually every game works at a high level. Process the user input, update the state, present the state to the user, and repeat ad infinitum (or until the user is fed up with our game).

UI applications on modern operating systems do not usually work in real-time. They work with an event-based paradigm, where the operating system informs the application of input events, as well as when to render itself. This is achieved by callbacks that the application registers with the operating system on startup; these are then responsible for processing received event notifications. All of this happens in the so-called *UI thread* — the main thread of a UI application. It is generally a good idea to return from the callbacks as fast as possible, so we would not want to implement our main loop in one of these.

Instead, we host our game's main loop in a separate thread that we'll spawn when our game is firing up. This means that we have to take some precautions when we want to receive UI thread events, such as input events or window events. But those are details that we'll handle later on, when we implement our game framework for Android. Just remember that we need to synchronize the UI thread and the game's main loop thread at certain points.

The Game and Screen Interfaces

With all of that said, let's try to design a game interface. Here's what an implementation of this interface has to do:

- Set up the window and UI component and hook into callbacks so that we can receive window and input events.

- Start the main loop thread.

- Keep track of the current screen, and tell it to update and present itself in every main loop iteration (aka frame).

- Transfer any window events (for example, pause and resume events) from the UI thread to the main loop thread and pass them on to the current screen so that it can change its state accordingly.

- Grant access to all the modules we developed earlier: Input, FileIO, Graphics, and Audio.

As game developers, we want to be agnostic about what thread our main loop is running on and whether we need to synchronize with a UI thread or not. We'd just like to implement the different game screens with a little help from the low-level modules and some notifications of window events. We will therefore create a very simple Game interface that hides all this complexity from us, as well as an abstract Screen class that we'll use to implement all of our screens. Listing 3–8 shows the Game interface.

Listing 3–8. *The Game Interface*

```
package com.badlogic.androidgames.framework;

public interface Game {
    public Input getInput();

    public FileIO getFileIO();

    public Graphics getGraphics();

    public Audio getAudio();

    public void setScreen(Screen screen);
```

```
    public Screen getCurrentScreen();

    public Screen getStartScreen();
}
```

As expected, a couple of getter methods are available that return the instances of our low-level modules, which the Game implementation will instantiate and track.

The Game.setScreen() method allows us to set the current Screen of the Game. These methods will be implemented once, along with all the internal thread creation, window management, and main loop logic that will constantly ask the current screen to present and update itself.

The Game.getCurrentScreen() method returns the currently active Screen.

We'll use an abstract class called AndroidGame later on to implement the Game interface, which will implement all methods except the Game.getStartScreen() method. This method will be an abstract method. If we create the AndroidGame instance for our actual game, we'll extend it and override the Game.getStartScreen() method, returning an instance to the first screen of our game.

To give you an impression of how easy it will be to set up our game, here's an example (assuming we have already implemented the AndroidGameclass):

```
public class MyAwesomeGame extends AndroidGame {
    public Screen getStartScreen () {
        return new MySuperAwesomeStartScreen(this);
    }
}
```

That is pretty awesome, isn't it? All we have to do is implement the screen that we want to use to start our game, and the AndroidGame class will do the rest for us. From that point onward, our MySuperAwesomeStartScreen will be asked to update and render itself by the AndroidGame instance in the main loop thread. Note that we pass the MyAwesomeGame instance itself to the constructor of our Screen implementation.

> **NOTE:** If you're wondering what actually instantiates our MyAwesomeGame class, we'll give you a hint: AndroidGame will be derived from `Activity`, which will be automatically instantiated by the Android operating system when a user starts our game.

The last piece in the puzzle is the abstract class Screen. We make it an abstract class instead of an interface so that we can implement some bookkeeping. This way, we have to write less boilerplate code in the actual implementations of the abstract Screen class. Listing 3–9 shows the abstract Screen class.

Listing 3–9. *The Screen Class*

```
package com.badlogic.androidgames.framework;

public abstract class Screen {
    protected final Game game;
```

```
    public Screen(Game game) {
        this.game = game;
    }

    public abstract void update(float deltaTime);

    public abstract void present(float deltaTime);

    public abstract void pause();

    public abstract void resume();

    public abstract void dispose();
}
```

It turns out that the bookkeeping isn't so bad after all. The constructor receives the Game instance and stores it in a final member that's accessible to all subclasses. Via this mechanism, we can achieve two things:

- We can get access to the low-level modules of the Game to play back audio, draw to the screen, get user input, and read and write files.

- We can set a new current Screen by invoking Game.setScreen() when appropriate (for example, when a button is pressed that triggers a transition to a new screen).

The first point is pretty much obvious: our Screen implementation needs access to these modules so that it can actually do something meaningful, like rendering huge numbers of unicorns with rabies.

The second point allows us to implement our screen transitions easily within the Screen instances themselves. Each Screen can decide when to transition to which other Screen based on its state (for example, when a menu button is pressed).

The methods Screen.update() and Screen.present()should be self-explanatory by now: they will update the screen state and present it accordingly. The Game instance will call them once in every iteration of the main loop.

The Screen.pause() and Screen.resume() methods will be called when the game is paused or resumed. This is again done by the Game instance and applied to the currently active Screen.

The Screen.dispose() method will be called by the Game instance in case Game.setScreen() is called. The Game instance will dispose of the current Screen via this method and thereby give the Screen an opportunity to release all its system resources (for example, graphical assets stored in Pixmaps) to make room for the new screen's resources in memory. The call to the Screen.dispose() method is also the last opportunity for a screen to make sure that any information that needs persistence is saved.

A Simple Example

Continuing with our MySuperAwesomeGame example, here is a very simple implementation of the MySuperAwesomeStartScreen class:

```java
public class MySuperAwesomeStartScreen extends Screen {
    Pixmap awesomePic;
    int x;

    public MySuperAwesomeStartScreen(Game game) {
        super(game);
        awesomePic = game.getGraphics().newPixmap("data/pic.png",
                PixmapFormat.RGB565);
    }

    @Override
    public void update(float deltaTime) {
        x += 1;
        if (x > 100)
            x = 0;
    }

    @Override
    public void present(float deltaTime) {
        game.getGraphics().clear(0);
        game.getGraphics().drawPixmap(awesomePic, x, 0, 0, 0,
                awesomePic.getWidth(), awesomePic.getHeight());
    }

    @Override
    public void pause() {
        // nothing to do here
    }

    @Override
    public void resume() {
        // nothing to do here
    }

    @Override
    public void dispose() {
        awesomePic.dispose();
    }
}
```

Let's see what this class, in combination with the MySuperAwesomeGame class, will do:

1. When the MySuperAwesomeGame class is created, it will set up the window, the UI component to which we render and from which we receive events, the callbacks to receive window and input events, and the main loop thread. Finally, it will call its own MySuperAwesomeGame.getStartScreen() method, which will return an instance of the MySuperAwesomeStartScreen() class.

2. In the MySuperAwesomeStartScreen constructor, we load a bitmap from disk and store it in a member variable. This completes our screen setup, and the control is handed back to the MySuperAwesomeGame class.

3. The main loop thread will now constantly call the MySuperAwesomeStartScreen.update() and MySuperAwesomeStartScreen.present() methods of the instance we just created.

4. In the MySuperAwesomeStartScreen.update() method, we increase a member called x by one each frame. This member holds the x-coordinate of the image we want to render. When the x-coordinate value is greater than 100, we reset it to 0.

5. In the MySuperAwesomeStartScreen.present() method, we clear the framebuffer with the color black (0x00000000 = 0) and render our Pixmap at position (x,0).

6. The main loop thread will repeat steps 3 to 5 until the user quits the game by pressing the back button on their device. The Game instance will call then call the MySuperAwesomeStartScreen.dispose() method, which will dispose of the Pixmap.

And that's our first (not so) exciting game! All a user will see is that an image is moving from left to right on the screen. Not exactly a pleasant user experience, but we'll work on that later. Note that, on Android, the game can be paused and resumed at any point in time. Our MyAwesomeGame implementation will then call the MySuperAwesomeStartScreen.pause() and MySuperAwesomeStartScreen.resume() methods. The main loop thread will be paused for as long as the application itself is paused.

There's one last problem we have to talk about: frame-rate independent movement.

Frame Rate–Independent Movement

Let's assume that the user's device can run our game from the last section at 60 FPS. Our Pixmap will advance 100 pixels in 100 frames as we increment the MySuperAwesomeStartScreen.x member by 1 pixel each frame. At a frame rate of 60 FPS, it will take roughly 1.66 seconds to reach position (100,0).

Now let's assume that a second user plays our game on a different device. That device is capable of running our game at 30 FPS. Each second, our Pixmap advances by 30 pixels, so it takes 3.33 seconds to reach position (100,0).

This is bad. It may not have an impact on the user experience that our simple game generates, but replace the Pixmap with Super Mario and think about what it would mean to move him in a frame-dependent manner. Say we hold down the right D-pad button so that Mario runs to the right. In each frame, we advance him by 1 pixel, as we do in case of our `Pixmap`. On a device that can run the game at 60 FPS, Mario would run twice as fast as on a device that runs the game at 30 FPS! This would totally change the user experience, depending on the performance of the device. We need to fix this.

The solution to this problem is called frame-independent movement. Instead of moving our `Pixmap` (or Mario) by a fixed amount each frame, we specify the movement speed in units per second. Say we want our `Pixmap` to advance 50 pixels per second. In addition to the 50-pixels-per-second value, we also need information on how much time has passed since we last moved the `Pixmap`. This is where this strange delta time comes into play. It tells us exactly how much time has passed since the last update. So our `MySuperAwesomeStartScreen.update()` method should look like this:

```
@Override
public void update(float deltaTime) {
    x += 50 * deltaTime;
    if(x > 100)
        x = 0;
}
```

If our game runs at a constant 60 FPS, the delta time passed to the method will always be 1 / 60 ~ 0.016 seconds. In each frame, we therefore advance by 50 × 0.016 ~ 0.83 pixels. At 60FPS, we advance 60 × 0.83 ~ 50 pixels! Let's test this with 30 FPS: 50 × 1 / 30 ~ 1.66. Multiplied by 30 FPS, we again move 50 pixels total each second. So, no matter how fast the device on which our game is running can execute our game, our animation and movement will always be consistent with actual wall clock time.

If we actually tried this with our preceding code, our `Pixmap` wouldn't move at all at 60 FPS. This is because of a bug in our code. We'll give you some time to spot it. It's rather subtle, but a common pitfall in game development. The x member that we use to increase each frame is actually an integer. Adding 0.83 to an integer will have no effect. To fix this, we simply have to store x as a float instead of an `int`. This also means that we have to add a cast to int when we call `Graphics.drawPixmap()`.

> **NOTE:** While floating-point calculations are usually slower on Android than integer operations are, the impact is mostly negligible, so we can get away with using more costly floating-point arithmetic.

And that is all there is to our game framework. We can directly translate the screens of our Mr. Nom design to our classes and the interface of the framework. Of course, still some implementation details still require attention, but we'll leave that for a later chapter. For now, you can be mighty proud of yourself. You kept on reading this chapter to the end and now you are ready to become a game developer for Android (and other platforms)!

Summary

Some fifty highly condensed and informative pages later, you should have a good idea of what is involved in creating a game. We checked out some of the most popular genres on the Android Market and drew some conclusions. We designed a complete game from the ground up using only scissors, a pen, and some paper. Finally, we explored the theoretical basis of game development, and we even created a set of interfaces and abstract classes that we'll use throughout this book to implement our game designs, based on those theoretical concepts. If you feel like you want to go beyond the basics covered here, then by all means consult the Web for more information. You are holding all the keywords in your hand. Understanding the principles is the key to developing stable and well-performing games. With that said, let's implement our game framework for Android!

Chapter 4

Android for Game Developers

Android's application framework is vast and confusing at times. For every possible task you can think of, there's an API you can use. Of course, you have to learn the APIs first. Luckily, we game developers only need an extremely limited set of these APIs. All we want is a window with a single UI component that we can draw to, and from which we can receive input, as well as the ability to play back audio. This covers all of our needs for implementing the game framework that we designed in the last chapter, and in a rather platform-agnostic way.

In this chapter, you'll learn the bare minimum number of Android APIs that you need to make Mr. Nom a reality. You'll be surprised at how little you actually need to know about these APIs to achieve that goal. Let's recall what ingredients we need:

- Window management
- Input
- File I/O
- Audio
- Graphics

For each of these modules, there's an equivalent in the application framework APIs. We'll pick and choose the APIs needed to handle those modules, discuss their internals, and finally implement the respective interfaces of the game framework that we designed in the last chapter.

Before we can dive into window management on Android, however, we have to revisit something we discussed only briefly in Chapter 2: defining our application via the manifest file.

Defining an Android Application: The Manifest File

An Android application can consist of a multitude of different components:

Activities: These are user-facing components that present a UI with which to interact.

Services: These are processes that work in the background and don't have a visible UI. For example, a service might be responsible for polling a mail server for new e-mails.

Content providers: These components make parts of your application data available to other applications.

Intents: These are messages created by the system or applications themselves. They are then passed on to any interested party. Intents might notify us of system events such as the SD card being removed or the USB cable being connected. Intents are also used by the system for starting components of our application, such as activities. We can also fire our own intents to ask other applications to perform an action, such as opening a photo gallery to display an image or starting the Camera application to take a photo.

Broadcast receivers: These react to specific intents, and they might execute an action, such as starting a specific activity or sending out another intent to the system.

An Android application has no single point of entry, as we are used to having on a desktop operating system (for example, in the form of Java's main() method). Instead, components of an Android application are started up or asked to perform a certain action by specific intents.

What components comprise our application and to which intents these components react are defined in the application's manifest file. The Android system uses this manifest file to get to know what makes up our application, such as the default activity to display when the application is started.

> **NOTE:** We are only concerned about activities in this book, so we'll only discuss the relevant portions of the manifest file for this type of component. If you want to make yourself dizzy, you can learn more about the manifest file on the Android Developers site.

The manifest file serves many more purposes than just defining an application's components. The following list summarizes the relevant parts of a manifest file in the context of game development:

- The version of our application as displayed and used on the Android Market
- The Android versions on which our application can run
- Hardware profiles our application requires (that is, multitouch, specific screen resolutions, or support for OpenGL ES 2.0)

■   Permissions for using specific components, such as for writing to the
     SD card or accessing the networking stack

We will create a template manifest in the following subsections that we can reuse, in a
slightly modified manner, in all the projects we'll develop throughout this book. For this,
we'll go through all the relevant XML tags we'll need to define our application.

The <manifest> Element

The <manifest>tag is the root element of an AndroidManifest.xml file. Here's a basic
example:

```
<manifest xmlns:android="http://schemas.android.com/apk/res/android"
      package="com.helloworld"
      android:versionCode="1"
      android:versionName="1.0"
      android:installLocation="preferExternal">
...
</manifest>
```

We are assuming that you have worked with XML before, so you should be familiar with
the first line. The <manifest> tag specifies a namespace called android, which is used
throughout the rest of the manifest file. The package attribute defines the root package
name of our application. Later on, we'll reference specific classes of our application
relative to this package name.

The versionCode and versionName attributes specify the version of our application in two
forms. The versionCode is an integer that we have to increment each time we publish a
new version of our application. It is used by the Android Market to track our
application's version. The versionName is displayed to users of the Android Market when
they browse our application. We can use any string we like here.

The installLocation attribute is only available to us if we set the build target of our
Android project in Eclipse to Android 2.2 or newer. It specifies where our application
should be installed. The string preferExternal tells the system that we'd like our
application to be installed to the SD card. This will only work on Android 2.2 or newer,
and this string is ignored by all earlier Android applications. On Android 2.2or newer, the
application will always get installed to internal storage where possible.

All attributes of the XML elements in a manifest file are generally prefixed with the
android namespace, as shown previously. For brevity, we will not specify the
namespace in the following sections when talking about a specific attribute.

Inside the <manifest> element, we then define the application's components,
permissions, hardware profiles, and supported Android versions.

The <application> Element

As in the case of the <manifest> element, let's discuss the <application> element in the form of an example:

```
<application android:icon="@drawable/icon" android:label="@string/app_name"
android:debuggable="true">
...
</application>
```

Now doesn't this look a bit strange? What's up with the @drawable/icon and @string/app_name strings? When developing a standard Android application, we usually write a lot of XML files, where each defines a specific portion of our application. Full definition of those portions requires that we are also able to reference resources that are not defined in the XML file, such as images or internationalized strings. These resources are located in subfolders of the res/ folder, as discussed in Chapter 2, when we dissected the Hello World project in Eclipse.

To reference resources, we use the preceding notation. The @ specifies that we want to reference a resource defined elsewhere. The following string identifies the type of the resource we want to reference, which directly maps to one of the folders or files in the res/directory. The final part specifies the name of the resource. In the preceding case, this is an image called icon and a string called app_name. In the case of the image, it's the actual filename we specify, as found in the res/drawable/folder. Note that the image name does not have a suffix like .png or .jpg. Android will infer the suffix automatically based on what's in the res/drawable/ folder. The app_name string is defined in the res/values/strings.xml file, a file where all the strings used by the application will be stored. The name of the string was defined in the strings.xml file.

> **NOTE:** Resource handling on Android is an extremely flexible, but also complex thing. For this book, we decided to skip most of resource handling for two reasons: it's utter overkill for game development, and we want to have full control over our resources. Android has the habit of modifying resources placed in the res/ folder, especially images (called drawables). That's something we, as game developers, do not want. The only use we'd suggest for the Android resource system in game development is internationalizing strings. We won't get into that in this book; instead, we'll use the more game development-friendly assets/ folder, which leaves our resources untouched and allows us to specify our own folder hierarchy.

The meaning of the attributes of the <application> element should become a bit clearer now. The icon attribute specifies the image from the res/drawable/ folder to be used as an icon for the application. This icon will be displayed in the Android Market as well as in the application launcher on the device. It is also the default icon for all the activities that we define within the <application> element.

The label attribute specifies the string being displayed for our application in the application launcher. In the preceding example, this references a string in the `res/values/string.xml` file, which is what we specified when we created the Android project in Eclipse. We could also set this to a raw string, such as `My Super Awesome Game`. The label is also the default label for all of the activities that we define in the `<application>` element. The label will be shown in the title bar of our application.

The `debuggable` attribute specifies whether or not our application can be debugged. For development, we should usually set this to `true`. When you deploy your application to the market, just switch it to `false`. If you don't set this to `true`, you won't be able to debug the application in Eclipse.

We have only discussed a very small subset of the attributes that you can specify for the `<application>` element. However, these are sufficient for our game development needs. If you want to know more, you can find the full documentation on the Android Developer's site.

The `<application>` element contains the definitions of all the application components, including activities and services, as well as any additional libraries used.

The <activity> Element

Now it's getting interesting. Here's a hypothetical example for our Mr. Nom game:

```
<activity android:name=".MrNomActivity"
          android:label="Mr. Nom"
          android:screenOrientation="portrait">
          android:configChanges="keyboard|keyboardHidden|orientation">
    <intent-filter>
        <action android:name="android.intent.action.MAIN" />
        <category android:name="android.intent.category.LAUNCHER" />
    </intent-filter>
</activity>
```

Let's have a look at the attributes of the `<activity>` tag first.

name: This specifies the name of the activity's class relative to the package attribute we specified in the `<manifest>`element. You can also specify a fully-qualified class name here.

label: We already specified the same attribute in the `<application>`. This label is displayed in the title bar of the activity (if it has one).The label will also be used as the text displayed in the application launcher if the activity we define is an entry point to our application. If we don't specify it, the label from the `<application>` element will be used instead. Note that we used a raw string here instead of a reference to a string in the `string.xml` file.

screenOrientation: This attribute specifies the orientation that the activity will use. Here we specified `portrait` for our Mr. Nom game, which will only work in portrait mode. Alternatively, we could specify `landscape` if we wanted to run in landscape mode. Both configurations will force the orientation of the activity to stay the same over the activity's life cycle, no matter how the device is actually oriented. If we leave out this attribute, then the activity will use the current orientation of the device, usually based on accelerometer data. This also means that whenever the device orientation changes, the activity will be destroyed and restarted—something that's undesirable in the case of a game. We usually fix the orientation of our game's activity either to landscape or portrait mode.

configChanges: Reorienting the device or sliding out the keyboard is considered a configuration change. In the case of such a change, Android will destroy and restart our application to accommodate the change. That's not desirable in the case of a game. The configChanges attribute of the <activity> element comes to the rescue. It allows us to specify which configuration changes we want to handle ourselves, without destroying and recreating our activity. Multiple configuration changes can be specified by using the | character to concatenate them. In the preceding case, we handle the changes keyboard, keyboardHidden, and orientation ourselves.

As with the <application> element, there are, of course, more attributes that you can specify for an<activity> element. For game development, we get away with the four attributes just discussed.

Now, you might have noticed that the <activity> element isn't empty, but it houses another element, which itself contains two more elements. What are those for?

As we pointed out earlier, there's no notion of a single main entry point to your application on Android. Instead, we can have multiple entry points in the form of activities and services that are started due to specific intents being sent out by the system or a third-party application. Somehow, we need to communicate to Android which activities and services of our application will react (and in what ways) to specific intents. That's where the <intent-filter> element comes into play.

In the preceding example, we specify two types of intent filters: an <action> and a <category>. The <action> element tells Android that our activity is a main entry point to our application. The <category> element specifies that we want that activity to be added to the application launcher. Both elements together allow Android to infer that, when the icon in the application launcher for the application is pressed, it should start that specific activity.

For both the <action> and <category> elements, the only thing that gets specified is the name attribute, which identifies the intent to which the activity will react. The intent android.intent.action.MAIN is a special intent that the Android system uses to start the main activity of an application. The intent android.intent.category.LAUNCHER is used to tell Android whether a specific activity of an application should have an entry in the application launcher.

Usually, we'll only have one activity that specifies these two intent filters. However, a standard Android application will almost always have multiple activities, and these need to be defined in the manifest.xml file as well. Here's an example definition of this type of a subactivity:

```
<activity android:name=".MySubActivity"
          android:label="Sub Activity Title"
          android:screenOrientation="portrait">
          android:configChanges="keyboard|keyboardHidden|orientation"/>
```

Here, no intent filters are specified—only the four attributes of the activity we discussed earlier. When we define an activity like this, it is only available to our own application. We start this type of activity programmatically with a special kind of intent; say, when a button is pressed in one activity to cause a new activity to open. We'll see in a later section how we can start an activity programmatically.

To summarize, we have one activity for which we specify two intent filters so that it becomes the main entry point of our application. For all other activities, we leave out the intent filter specification so that they are internal to our application. We'll start these programmatically.

> **NOTE:** As indicated earlier, we'll only ever have a single activity in our games. This activity will have exactly the same intent filter specification as shown previously. The reason we discussed how to specify multiple activities is that we are going to create a special sample application in a minute that will have multiple activities. Don't worry—it's going to be easy.

The <uses-permission> Element

We are leaving the `<application>` element now and coming back to elements that we normally define as children of the `<manifest>` element. One of these elements is the `<uses-permission>` element.

Android has an elaborate security model. Each application is run in its own process and VM, with its own Linux user and group, and it cannot influence other applications. Android also restricts the use of system resources, such as networking facilities, the SD card, and the audio-recording hardware. If our application wants to use any of these system resources, we have to ask for permission. This is done with the `<uses-permission>` element.

A permission always has the following form, where `string` specifies the name of the permission we want to be granted:

```
<uses-permission android:name="string"/>
```

Here are a few permission names that might come in handy:

`android.permission.RECORD_AUDIO`: This grants us access to the audio-recording hardware.

`android.permission.INTERNET`: This grants us access to all the networking APIs so we can, for example, fetch an image from the Net or upload high scores.

`android.permission.WRITE_EXTERNAL_STORAGE`: This allows us to read and write files on the external storage, usually the SD card of the device.

`android.permission.WAKE_LOCK`: This allows us to acquire a so-called *wake lock*. With this wake lock, we can keep the device from going to sleep if the screen hasn't been touched for some time. This could happen, for example, in a game that is controlled only by the accelerometer.

`android.permission.ACCESS_COARSE_LOCATION`: This is a very useful permission as it allows you to get non-gps-level access to things like the country in which the user is located, which can be useful for language defaults and analytics.

`android.permission.NFC`: This allows applications to perform I/O operations over NFC (near-field communication), which is useful for a variety of game features involving the quick exchange of small amounts of information.

To get access to the networking APIs, we'd thus specify the following element as a child of the `<manifest>` element:

```
<uses-permission android:name="android.permission.INTERNET"/>
```

For any additional permissions, we simply add more `<uses-permission>` elements. You can specify many more permissions; we again refer you to the official Android documentation. We'll only need the set just discussed.

Forgetting to add a permission for something like accessing the SD card is a common source of error. It manifests itself as a message in device log, which might survive undetected due to all the clutter in log. Think about the permissions your game will need, and specify them when you initially create the project.

Another thing to note is that, when a user installs your application, he or she will first be asked to review all of the permissions your application requires. Many users will just skip over these and happily install whatever they can get hold of. Some users are more conscious about their decisions and will review the permissions in detail. If you request suspicious permissions, like the ability to send out costly SMS messages or to get a user's location, you may receive some nasty feedback from users in the Comments section for your application when it's on the Market. If you must use one of those problematic permissions, you also should tell the user why you're using it in your application description. The best thing to do is to avoid those permissions in the first place or to provide functionality that legitimately uses them.

The `<uses-feature>` Element

If you are an Android user yourself and possess an older device with an old Android version like 1.5, you will have noticed that some awesome applications won't show up in the Android Market application on your device. One reason for this can be the use of the `<uses-feature>` element in the manifest file of the application.

The Android Market application will filter all available applications by your hardware profile. With the `<uses-feature>` element, an application can specify which hardware features it needs; for example, multitouch or support for OpenGL ES 2.0. Any device that does not have the specified features will trigger that filter so that the end user isn't shown the application in the first place.

A `<uses-feature>` element has the following attributes:

```
<uses-feature android:name="string" android:required=["true" | "false"]
android:glEsVersion="integer" />
```

The name attribute specifies the feature itself. The `required` attribute tells the filter whether we really need the feature under all circumstances or if it's just nice to have. The last attribute is optional and only used when a specific OpenGL ES version is required.

For game developers, the following features are most relevant:

`android.hardware.touchscreen.multitouch`: This requests that the device have a multitouch screen capable of basic multitouch interactions, such as pinch zooming and the like. These types of screens have problems with independent tracking of multiple fingers, so you have to evaluate if those capabilities are sufficient for your game.

`android.hardware.touchscreen.multitouch.distinct`: This is the big brother of the last feature. This requests full multitouch capabilities suitable for implementing things like onscreen virtual dual sticks for controls.

We'll look into multitouch in a later section of this chapter. For now, just remember that, when our game requires a multitouch screen, we can weed out all devices that don't support that feature by specifying a `<uses-feature>` element with one of the preceding feature names, like so:

```
<uses-feature android:name="android.hardware.touchscreen.multitouch"
android:required="true"/>
```

Another useful thing for game developers to do is to specify which OpenGL ES version is needed. In this book, we'll be concerned with OpenGL ES 1.0 and 1.1. For these, we usually don't specify a `<uses-feature>` element as they aren't all that different from each other. However, any device that implements OpenGL ES 2.0 can be assumed to be a graphics powerhouse. If our game is visually complex and needs a lot of processing power, we can require OpenGL ES 2.0 so that the game only shows up for devices that are able to render our awesome visuals at an acceptable frame rate. Note that we don't use OpenGL ES 2.0, but we just filter by hardware type so that our OpenGL ES 1.x code gets enough processing power. Here's how we can do this:

```
<uses-feature android:glEsVersion="0x00020000"android:required="true"/>
```

This will make our game only show up on devices that support OpenGL ES 2.0 and are thus assumed to have a fairly powerful graphics processor.

> **NOTE:** This feature is reported incorrectly by some devices out there, which will make your application invisible to otherwise perfectly fine devices. Use it with caution.

Let's say you want to have optional support of USB peripherals for your game so that the device can be a USB host and have controllers or other peripherals connected to it. The correct way of handling this is to add:

```
<uses-feature android:name="android.hardware.usb.host" android:required="false"/>
```

Setting "android:required" to false says to the market "We may use this feature, but it's not necessary to download and run the game." Setting usage of the optional hardware feature is a good way to future-proof your game for various pieces of hardware that you haven't yet encountered. It allows manufacturers to limit the apps only to ones that have declared support for their specific hardware and, if you declare optional support for it, you will be included in the apps that can be downloaded for that device.

Now, every specific requirement you have in terms of hardware potentially decreases the number of devices on which your game can be installed, which will direct affect your sales. Think twice before you specify any of the above. For example, if the standard mode of your game requires multitouch, but you can also think of a way to make it work on single-touch devices, you should strive to have two code paths—one for each hardware profile—so that your game can be deployed to a bigger market.

The <uses-sdk> Element

The last element we'll put in our manifest file is the <uses-sdk> element. It is a child of the <manifest> element. We implicitly defined this element when we created our Hello World project in Chapter 2 and we specified the minimum SDK version in the New Android Project dialog. So what does this element do? Here's an example:

```
<uses-sdk android:minSdkVersion="3" android:targetSdkVersion="13"/>
```

As we discussed in Chapter 2, each Android version has an integer assigned, also known as an *SDK version*. The <uses-sdk> element specifies the minimum version supported by our application and the target version of our application. In this example, we define our minimum version as Android 1.5 and our target version as This element allows us to deploy an application that uses APIs only available in newer versions to devices that have a lower version installed. One prominent example would be the multitouch APIs, which are supported from SDK version 5 (Android 2.0) onward. When we setup our Android project in Eclipse, we use a build target that supports that API; for example, SDK version 5 or higher (we usually set it to the latest SDK version, which is 13 at the time of writing). If we want our game to run on devices with SDK version 3 (Android 1.5) as well, we specify the minSdkVersion, as before, in the manifest file. Of course, we must be careful not to use any APIs that are not available in the lower version, at least on a 1.5 device. On a device with a higher version, we can use the newer APIs as well.

The preceding configuration is usually fine for most games (unless you can't provide a separate fallback code path for the higher-version APIs, in which case you will want to set the minSdkVersion attribute to the minimum SDK version you actually support).

Android Game Project Setup in Ten Easy Steps

Let's now combine all of the preceding information and develop a simple step-by-step method to create a new Android game project in Eclipse. Here's what we want from our project:

- It should be able to use the latest SDK version's features while maintaining compatibility with the lowest SDK version that some devices still run. That means that we want to support Android 1.5 and above.

- It should be installed to the SD card when possible so that we don't fill up the internal storage of the device.

- It should be debuggable.

- It should have a single main activity that will handle all configuration changes itself so that it doesn't get destroyed when the hardware keyboard is revealed or when the orientation of the device is changed.

- The activity should be fixed to either portrait or landscape mode.

- It should allow us to access the SD card.

- It should allow us to get a hold of a wake lock.

These are some easy goals to achieve with the information you just acquired. Here are the steps:

1. Create a new Android project in Eclipse by opening the New Android Project dialog, as described in Chapter 2.

2. In the New Android Project dialog, specify your project's name and set the build target to the latest available SDK version.

3. In the same dialog, specify the name of your game, the package in which all your classes will be stored, and the name of your main activity. Then set the minimum SDK version to 3. Press Finish to make the project a reality.

4. Open the `AndroidManifest.xml` file.

5. To make Android install the game on the SD card when available, add the `installLocation` attribute to the `<manifest>` element, and set it to `preferExternal`.

6. To make the game debuggable, add the `debuggable` attribute to the `<application>` element and set it to `true`.

7. To fix the orientation of the activity, add the `screenOrientation` attribute to the `<activity>` element, and specify the orientation you want (`portrait` or `landscape`).

8. To tell Android that we want to handle the `keyboard`, `keyboardHidden`, and `orientation` configuration changes, set the `configChanges` attribute of the `<activity>` element to `keyboard|keyboardHidden|orientation`.

9. Add two`<uses-permission>` elements to the `<manifest>` element, and specify the name attributes `android.permission.WRITE_EXTERNALSTORAGE` and `android.permission.WAKE_LOCK`.

10. Finally, add the `targetSdkVersion` attribute to the `<uses-sdk>` element and specify your target SDK. It should be the same as the one you specified for the build target in step 1.

There you have it. Ten easy steps that will generate a fully-defined application that will be installed to the SD card (on Android 2.2 and over), is debuggable, has a fixed orientation, will not explode on a configuration change, allows you to access the SD card and wake locks, and will work on all Android versions starting from 1.5 up to the latest version. Here's the final `AndroidManifest.xml` content after executing the preceding steps:

```xml
<?xml version="1.0" encoding="utf-8"?>
<manifest xmlns:android="http://schemas.android.com/apk/res/android"
    package="com.badlogic.awesomegame"
    android:versionCode="1"
    android:versionName="1.0"
    android:installLocation="preferExternal">
  <application android:icon="@drawable/icon"
              android:label="Awesomnium"
              android:debuggable="true">
     <activity android:name=".GameActivity"
              android:label="Awesomnium"
              android:screenOrientation="landscape"
              android:configChanges="keyboard|keyboardHidden|orientation">
        <intent-filter>
           <action android:name="android.intent.action.MAIN" />
           <category android:name="android.intent.category.LAUNCHER" />
        </intent-filter>
     </activity>
  </application>
  <uses-permission android:name="android.permission.WRITE_EXTERNAL_STORAGE"/>
  <uses-permission android:name="android.permission.WAKE_LOCK"/>
  <uses-sdk android:minSdkVersion="3" android:targetSdkVersion="9"/>
</manifest>
```

As you can see, we got rid of the `@string/app_name` in the label attributes of the `<application>` and `<activity>` element. This is not really necessary, but having the application definition in one place is preferred. From now on, it's all about the code! Or is it?

Market Filters

There are so many different Android devices, with so many different capabilities, that it's necessary for the hardware manufacturers to allow only compatible applications to be downloaded and run on their device, or the user will have the bad experience of trying to run something that's just not compatible. To deal with this, the Android Market filters out incompatible applications from the list of available applications for a specific device. For example, if you have a device without a camera, and you search for a game that requires a camera, it simply won't show up. For better or worse, it will appear to you, the user, like the app just doesn't exist.

Many of the previous manifest elements we've discussed are used as market filters. Besides <uses-feature>, <uses-sdk>and <uses-permission> that we went over, there are a few more elements that are specific to market filtering that you should keep in mind:

<supports-screens>: This allows you to declare the screen sizes and densities your game can run on. Ideally, your game will work on all screens, and we'll show you how to do that. However, in the manifest, you will want to declare support explicitly for every screen size you can.

<uses-configuration>: This lets you declare explicit support for an input configuration type on a device, such as a hard keyboard, qwerty-specific keyboard, touchscreen, or maybe trackball navigation input. Ideally, you'll support all of the above, but if your game requires very specific input, you will want to investigate and use this tag for market filtering.

<uses-library>: This allows for the declaration that a third-party library, on which your game is dependent, be present on the device. For example, you might require a text-to-speech library that is quite large, but very common, for your game. Declaring the library with this tag ensures that only devices with that library installed can see and download your game. A common use of this is to allow GPS/map-based games to work only on devices with the Google maps library installed.

As Android moves forward, more market filter tags are likely, so make sure to check the official market filters page on the developer's site to get up-to-date before you deploy.

Defining the Icon of Your Game

When you deploy your game to a device and open the application launcher, you will see that its entry has a nice, but not really unique, Android icon. The same icon would be shown for your game in the market. How can you change it to a custom icon?

Have a closer look at the <application> element again. There, we defined an attribute called icon. It references an image in the res/drawable directory called icon. So, it should be obvious what to do: replace the icon image in the drawable folder with your own icon image.

When you inspect the res/ folder, you'll see more than one drawable folder, as depicted in Figure 4–1.

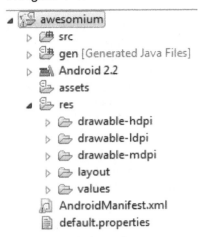

▲ 🖳 awesomium
   ▷ 🗂 src
   ▷ 🗂 gen [Generated Java Files]
   ▷ 🖳 Android 2.2
    🗂 assets
   ▲ 🗂 res
      ▷ 📁 drawable-hdpi
      ▷ 📁 drawable-ldpi
      ▷ 📁 drawable-mdpi
      ▷ 📁 layout
      ▷ 📁 values
    🗎 AndroidManifest.xml
    🗎 default.properties

Figure 4–1. *What happened to my res/ folder?*

Now, this is again a classic chicken-and-egg problem. In Chapter 2, only a single res/drawable folder was available in our Hello World project. This was due to the fact that we specified SDK version 3 as our build target. That version only supported a single screen size. That changed with Android 1.6 (SDK version 4). We saw in Chapter 1 that devices can have different sizes, but we didn't talk about how Android handles those. It turns out that there's an elaborate mechanism that allows you to define your graphical assets for a set of so-called screen densities. *Screen density* is a combination of physical screen size and the number of pixels of the screen. We'll look into that topic in a later section in more detail. For now, it suffices to know that Android defines three densities: ldpi for low-density screens, mdpi for standard-density screen, hdpi for high-density screens, and xhdpi for extra-high-density screens. For lower-density screens, we usually use smaller images; and for higher-density screens, we use high-resolution assets.

So, in the case of our icon, we need to provide four versions: one for each density. But how big should those versions each be? Luckily, we already have default icons in the res/drawable folders that we can use to reengineer the sizes of our own icons. The icon in res/drawable-ldpi has a resolution of 36×36 pixels, the icon in res/drawable-mdpi has a resolution of 48×48 pixels, the icon in res/drawable-hdpi has a resolution of 72×72 pixels, and the icon in res/drawable-xhdpi has a resolution of 96x96 pixels. All we need to do is create versions of our custom icon with the same resolutions and replace the icon.png file in each of the folders with our own icon.png file. We can leave the manifest file unaltered as long as we call our icon image file icon.png. Note that file references in the manifest file are case sensitive. Always use all lowercase letters in resource files, to play it safe.

For true Android 1.5 compatibility, we need to add a folder called res/drawable/and place the icon image from the res/drawable-mdpi/ folder there. Android 1.5 does not know about the other drawable folders, so it might not find our icon.

Finally, we are ready to get some Android coding done.

Android API Basics

In the rest of the chapter, we'll concentrate on playing around with those Android APIs that are relevant to our game development needs. For this, we'll do something rather convenient: we'll setup a test project that will contain all of our little test examples for the different APIs we are going to use. Let's get started.

Creating a Test Project

From the last section, we already know how to set up all our projects. So, the first thing we do is to execute the ten steps outlined earlier. We followed these steps, creating a project named ch04-android-basics with a single main activity called AndroidBasicsStarter. We are going to use some older and some newer APIs, so we set the minimum SDK version to 3 (Android 1.5) and the build target as well as the target SDK version to 9 (Android 2.3). From here on, all we'll do is create new activity implementations, each demonstrating parts of the Android APIs.

However, remember that we only have one main activity. So, what does our main activity look like? We want a convenient way to add new activities as well as the ability to start a specific activity easily. With one main activity, it should be clear that that activity will somehow provide us with a means to start a specific test activity. As discussed earlier, the main activity will be specified as the main entry point in the manifest file. Each additional activity that we add will be specified without the <intent-filter> child element. We'll start those programmatically from the main activity.

The AndroidBasicsStarter Activity

The Android API provides us with a special class called ListActivity, which derives from the Activity class that we used in the Hello World project. The ListActivity is a special type of activity whose single purpose is to display a list of things (for example, strings). We use it to display the names of our test activities. When we touch one of the list items, we'll start the corresponding activity programmatically. Listing 4–1 shows the code for our AndroidBasicsStarter main activity.

Listing 4–1. *AndroidBasicsStarter.java, Our Main Activity Responsible for Listing and Starting All Our Tests*

```
package com.badlogic.androidgames;

import android.app.ListActivity;
import android.content.Intent;
import android.os.Bundle;
import android.view.View;
```

```
import android.widget.ArrayAdapter;
import android.widget.ListView;

public class AndroidBasicsStarter extends ListActivity {
    String tests[] = { "LifeCycleTest", "SingleTouchTest", "MultiTouchTest",
            "KeyTest", "AccelerometerTest", "AssetsTest",
            "ExternalStorageTest", "SoundPoolTest", "MediaPlayerTest",
            "FullScreenTest", "RenderViewTest", "ShapeTest", "BitmapTest",
            "FontTest", "SurfaceViewTest" };

    public void onCreate(Bundle savedInstanceState) {
        super.onCreate(savedInstanceState);
        setListAdapter(new ArrayAdapter<String>(this,
                android.R.layout.simple_list_item_1, tests));
    }

    @Override
    protected void onListItemClick(ListView list, View view, int position,
            long id) {
        super.onListItemClick(list, view, position, id);
        String testName = tests[position];
        try {
            Class clazz = Class
                    .forName("com.badlogic.androidgames." + testName);
            Intent intent = new Intent(this, clazz);
            startActivity(intent);
        } catch (ClassNotFoundException e) {
            e.printStackTrace();
        }
    }
}
```

The package name we chose is com.badlogic.androidgames. The imports should also be pretty self-explanatory; these are simply all the classes we are going to use in our code. Our AndroidBasicsStarter class derives from the ListActivity class—still nothing special. The field tests is a string array that holds the names of all of the test activities that our starter application should display. Note that the names in that array are the exact Java class names of the activity classes we are going to implement later on.

The next piece of code should be familiar; it's the onCreate() method that we have to implement for each of our activities, and that will be called when the activity is created. Remember that we must call the onCreate() method of the base class of our activity. It's the first thing we must do in the onCreate() method of our own Activity implementation. If we don't, an exception will be thrown and the activity will not be displayed.

With that out of the way, the next thing we do is call a method called setListAdapter(). This method is provided to us by the ListActivity class we derived it from. It lets us specify the list items we want the ListActivity to display for us. These need to be passed to the method in the form of a class instance that implements the ListAdapter interface. We use the convenient ArrayAdapter to do this. The constructor of this class takes three arguments: the first is our activity, the second one we'll explain in a bit, and the third is the array of items that the ListActivity should display. We happily specify the tests array we defined earlier for the third argument, and that's all we need to do.

So what's this second argument to the ArrayAdapter constructor? To explain this, we'd have to go through all the Android UI API stuff, which we are not going to use in this book. So, instead of wasting pages on something we are not going to need, we'll give you the quick-and-dirty explanation: each item in the list is displayed via a View. The argument defines the layout of each View, along with the type of each View. The value android.R.layout.simple_list_item_1 is a predefined constant provided by the UI API for getting up and running quickly. It stands for a standard list item View that will display text. Just as a quick refresher, a View is a UI widget on Android, such as a button, a text field, or a slider. We talked about that while dissecting the HelloWorld activity in Chapter 2.

If we start our activity with just this onCreate() method, we'll see something that looks like the screen shown in Figure 4–2.

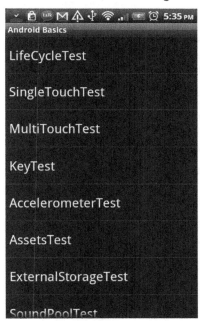

Figure 4–2. *Our test starter activity, which looks fancy but doesn't do a lot yet*

Now let's make something happen when a list item is touched. We want to start the respective activity that is represented by the list item we touched.

Starting Activities Programmatically

The ListActivity class has a protected method called onListItemClick() that will be called when an item is clicked. All we need to do is to override that method in our AndroidBasicsStarter class. And that's exactly what we did in Listing4–1.

The arguments to this method are the ListView that the ListActivity uses to display the items, the View that got touched and that's contained in that ListView, the position of the touched item in the list, and an ID, which doesn't interest us all that much. All we really care about is the position argument.

The onListItemClicked() method starts off by being a good citizen and calls the base class method first. This is always a good thing to do if we override methods of an activity. Next, we fetch the class name from the tests array, based on the position argument. That's the first piece of the puzzle.

Earlier, we discussed that we can start activities that we defined in the manifest file programmatically via an Intent. The Intent class has a nice and simple constructor to do this, which takes two arguments: a Context instance and a Class instance, which represent the Java class of the activity we want to start.

The Context is an interface that provides us with global information about our application. It is implemented by the Activity class, so we simply pass this reference to the Intent constructor.

To get the Class instance representing the activity we want to start, we use a little reflection, which will probably be familiar if you've worked with Java. The static method Class.forName() takes a string containing the fully-qualified name of a class for which we want to get a Class instance. All of the test activities we'll implement later will be contained in the com.badlogic.androidgames package. Concatenating the package name with the class name we fetched from the tests array will give us the fully-qualified name of the activity class we want to start. We pass that name to Class.forName() and get a nice Class instance that we can pass to the Intent constructor.

Once the Intent is constructed, we can start it with a call to the startActivity() method. This method is also defined in the Context interface. Since our activity implements that interface, we just call its implementation of that method. And that's it!

So how will our application behave? First, the starter activity will be displayed. Each time we touch an item on the list, the corresponding activity will be started. The starter activity will be paused and go into the background. The new activity will be created by the intent we send out and will replace the starter activity on the screen. When we press the back button on the phone, the activity is destroyed and the starter activity is resumed, taking back the screen.

Creating the Test Activities

When we create a new test activity, we have to perform the following steps:

1. Create the corresponding Java class in the com.badlogic.androidgames package and implement its logic.

2. Add an entry for it in the manifest file, using whatever attributes it needs (that is, android:configChanges or android:screenOrientation). Note that we won't specify an <intent-filter> element, as we'll start the activity programmatically.

3. Add the activity's class name to the `tests` array of the
    `AndroidBasicsStarter` class.

As long as we stick to this procedure, everything else will be taken care of by the logic
we implemented in the `AndroidBasicsStarter` class. The new activity will automatically
show up in the list, and it can be started by a simple touch.

One thing you might wonder is whether the test activity that gets started on a touch is
running in its own process and VM. It is not. An application composed of activities has
something called an *activity stack*. Every time we start a new activity, it gets pushed
onto that stack. When we close the new activity, the last activity that got pushed onto
the stack will get popped and resumed, becoming the new active activity on the screen.

This also has some other implications. First, all of the activities of the application (those
on the stack that are paused and the one that is active) share the same VM. They also
share the same memory heap. That can be a blessing and a curse. If you have static
fields in your activities, they will get memory on the heap as soon as they are started.
Being static fields, they will survive the destruction of the activity and the subsequent
garbage collection of the activity instance. This can lead to some bad memory leaks if
you carelessly use static fields. Think twice before using a static field.

As stated a couple of times already, we'll only ever have a single activity in our actual
games. The preceding activity starter is an exception to this rule to make our lives a little
easier. But don't worry; we'll have plenty of opportunities to get into trouble even with a
single activity.

> **NOTE:** This is as deep as we'll get into Android UI programming. From here on, we'll always use
> a single `View` in an activity to output things and to receive input. If you want to learn about things
> like layouts, view groups, and all the bells and whistles that the Android UI library offers, we
> suggest you check out Mark Murphy's book, *Beginning Android 2* (Apress, 2010), or the excellent
> developer guide on the Android Developer's site.

The Activity Life Cycle

The first thing we have to figure out when programming for Android is how an activity
behaves. On Android, this is called the *activity life cycle*. It describes the states and
transitions between those states through which an activity can live. Let's start by
discussing the theory behind this.

In Theory

An activity can be in one of three states:

> *Running*: In this state, it is the top-level activity that takes up the screen and directly
> interacts with the user.

Paused: This happens when the activity is still visible on the screen but partially obscured by either a transparent activity or a dialog, or if the phone screen is locked. A paused activity can be killed by the Android system at any point in time (for example, due to low memory). Note that the activity instance itself is still alive and kicking in the VM heap and waiting to be brought back to a running state.

Stopped: This happens when the activity is completely obscured by another activity and thus is no longer visible on the screen. Our AndroidBasicsStarter activity will be in this state if we start one of the test activities, for example. It also happens when a user presses the home button to go to the home screen temporarily. The system can again decide to kill the activity completely and remove it from memory if memory gets low.

In both the paused and stopped states, the Android system can decide to kill the activity at any point in time. It can do so politely, by first informing the activity of that by calling its finished() method, or by being bad and silently killing its process.

The activity can be brought back to a running state from a paused or stopped state. Note again that when an activity is resumed from a paused or stopped state, it is still the same Java instance in memory, so all the state and member variables are the same as before the activity was paused or stopped.

An activity has some protected methods that we can override to get information about state changes:

Activity.onCreate(): This is called when our activity is started up for the first time. Here, we setup all the UI components and hook into the input system. This will only get called once in the life cycle of our activity.

Activity.onRestart(): This is called when the activity is resumed from a stopped state. It is preceded by a call to onStop().

Activity.onStart(): This is called after onCreate() or when the activity is resumed from a stopped state. In the latter case, it is preceded by a call to onRestart().

Activity.onResume(): This is called after onStart() or when the activity is resumed from a paused state (for example when the screen is unlocked).

Activity.onPause(): This is called when the activity enters the paused state. It might be the last notification we receive, as the Android system might decide to kill our application silently. We should save all states we want to persist in this method!

Activity.onStop(): This is called when the activity enters the stopped state. It is preceded by a call to onPause(). This means that, before an activity is stopped, it is paused first. As with onPause(), it might be the last notification we get before the Android system silently kills the activity. We could also save persistent state here. However, the system might decide not to call this method and just kill the activity. As onPause() will always be called before onStop() and before the activity is silently killed, we'd rather save all our stuff in the onPause() method.

`Activity.onDestroy()`: This is called at the end of the activity life cycle when the activity is irrevocably destroyed. It's the last time we can persist any information we'd like to recover the next time our activity is created anew. Note that this method might actually never be called if the activity was destroyed silently after a call to `onPause()` or `onStop()` by the system.

Figure 4–3 illustrates the activity lifecycle and the method call order.

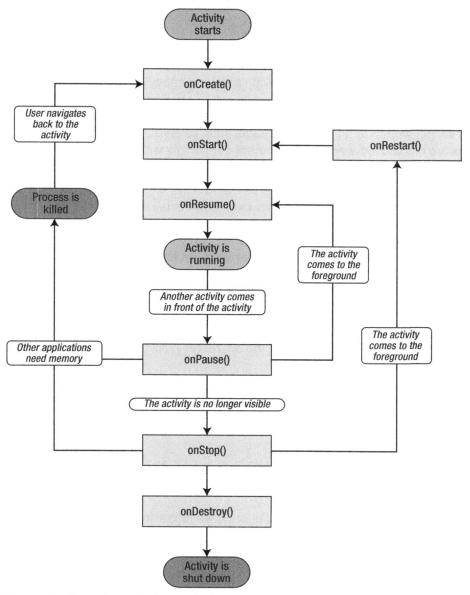

Figure 4–3. *The mighty, confusing activity lifecycle*

Here are the three big lessons we should take away from this:

1. Before our activity enters the running state, the onResume() method is always called, whether or not we resume from a stopped state or from a paused state. We can thus safely ignore the onRestart() and onStart() methods. We don't care whether we resumed from a stopped or a paused state. For our games, we only need to know that we are now actually running, and the onResume() method signals that to us.

2. The activity can be destroyed silently after onPause(). We should never assume that either onStop() or onDestroy() gets called. We also know that onPause() will always be called before onStop(). We can therefore safely ignore the onStop() and onDestroy() methods and just override onPause(). In this method, we have to make sure that all the states we want to persist, like high-scores and level progress, get written to an external storage, such as an SD card. After onPause(), all bets are off, and we won't know whether our activity will ever get the chance to run again.

3. We know that onDestroy() might never be called if the system decides to kill the activity after onPause() or onStop(). However, sometimes we'd like to know whether the activity is actually going to be killed. So how do we do that if onDestroy() is not going to get called? The Activity class has a method called Activity.isFinishing() that we can call at any time to check whether our activity is going to get killed. We are at least guaranteed that the onPause() method is called before the activity is killed. All we need to do is call this isFinishing() method inside the onPause() method to decide whether the activity is going to die after the onPause() call.

This makes life a lot easier. We only override the onCreate(), onResume(), and onPause() methods.

- In onCreate(), we setup our window and UI component to which we render and from which we receive input.

- In onResume(), we (re)start our main loop thread (discussed in the last chapter).

- In onPause(), we simply pause our main loop thread, and if Activity.isFinishing() returns true, we also save any state we want to persist to disk.

Many people struggle with the activity lifecycle, but if we follow these simple rules, our game will be capable of handling pausing and resuming as well as cleaning up.

In Practice

Let's write our first test example that demonstrates the activity life cycle. We'll want to have some sort of output that displays which state changes have happened so far. We'll do this in two ways:

1. The sole UI component that the activity will display is a so-called TextView. It displays text, and we've already used it implicitly for displaying each entry in our starter activity. Each time we enter a new state, we append a string to the TextView, which will display all the state changes that happened so far.

2. Since we won't be able to display the destruction event of our activity in the TextView as it will vanish from the screen too fast, we also output all state changes to LogCat. We do this with the Log class, which provides a couple of static methods to append messages to LogCat.

Remember what we need to do to add a test activity to our test application. First, we define it in the manifest file in the form of an<activity>element, which is a child of the<application>element:

```
<activity android:label="Life Cycle Test"
        android:name=".LifeCycleTest"
        android:configChanges="keyboard|keyboardHidden|orientation" />
```

Next we add a new Java class called LifeCycleTest to our com.badlogic.androidgames package. Finally, we add the class name to the tests member of the AndroidBasicsStarter class we defined earlier. (Of course, we already have that in there from when we wrote the class for demonstration purposes.)

We'll have to repeat all of these steps for any test activity that we create in the following sections. For brevity, we won't mention these steps again. Also note that we didn't specify an orientation for the LifeCycleTest activity. In this example, we can be either in landscape or portrait mode, depending on the device orientation. We did this so that you can see the effect on an orientation change on the life cycle (none, due to how we set the configChanges attribute). Listing 4–2 shows you the code of the entire activity.

Listing 4–2. *LifeCycleTest.java, Demonstrating the Activity Life Cycle*

```
package com.badlogic.androidgames;

import android.app.Activity;
import android.os.Bundle;
import android.util.Log;
import android.widget.TextView;

public class LifeCycleTest extends Activity {
    StringBuilder builder = new StringBuilder();
    TextView textView;

    private void log(String text) {
        Log.d("LifeCycleTest", text);
        builder.append(text);
```

```
        builder.append('\n');
        textView.setText(builder.toString());
    }

    @Override
    public void onCreate(Bundle savedInstanceState) {
        super.onCreate(savedInstanceState);
        textView = new TextView(this);
        textView.setText(builder.toString());
        setContentView(textView);
        log("created");
    }

    @Override
    protected void onResume() {
        super.onResume();
        log("resumed");
    }

    @Override
    protected void onPause() {
        super.onPause();
        log("paused");

        if (isFinishing()) {
            log("finishing");
        }
    }
}
```

Let's go through this code really quickly. The class derives from Activity—not a big surprise. We define two members: a StringBuilder, which will hold all the messages we have produced so far, and the TextView, which we use to display those messages directly in the Activity.

Next, we define a little private helper method that will log text to LogCat, append it to our StringBuilder, and update the TextView text. For the LogCat output, we use the static Log.d() method, which takes a tag as the first argument and the actual message as the second argument.

In the onCreate() method, we call the superclass method first, as always. We create the TextView and set it as the content view of our activity. It will fill the complete space of the activity. Finally, we log the message created to LogCat and update the TextView text with our previously defined helper method log().

Next, we override the onResume() method of the activity. As with any activity methods that we override, we first call the superclass method. All we do is call log() again with resumed as the argument.

The overridden onPause() method looks much like the onResume() method. We log the message as "paused" first. We also want to know whether the activity is going to be destroyed after the onPause() method call, so we check the Activity.isFinishing() method. If it returns true, we log the finishing event as well. Of course, we won't be able to see the updated TextView text as the activity will be destroyed before the change is displayed on the screen. Thus, we also output everything to LogCat, as discussed earlier.

Run the application, and play around with this test activity a little. Here's a sequence of actions you could execute:

1. Start up the test activity from the starter activity.

2. Lock the screen.

3. Unlock the screen.

4. Press the home button (which will get you back to the home screen).

5. On the home screen, hold the home button until you are presented with the currently running applications. Select the Android Basics Starter app to resume (which will bring the test activity back onscreen).

6. Press the back button (which will bring you back to the starter activity).

If your system didn't decide to kill the activity silently at any point when it was paused, you will see the output in Figure 4–4, (of course, only if you haven't pressed the back button yet).

Figure 4–4. *Running the LifeCycleTest activity*

On startup, onCreate() is called, followed by onResume(). When we lock the screen, onPause() is called. When we unlock the screen, onResume() is called. When we press the home button, onPause() is called. Going back to the activity will call onResume()again. The same messages are, of course, shown in LogCat, which you can observe in Eclipse in the LogCat view. Figure 4–5 shows what we wrote to LogCat while executing the preceding sequence of actions (plus pressing the back button).

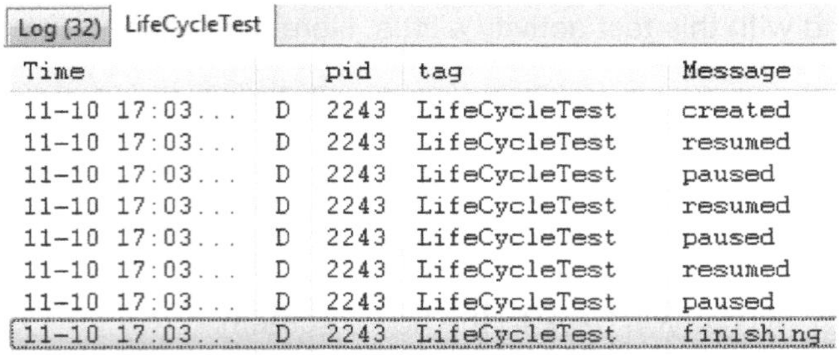

Log (32)	LifeCycleTest				
Time			pid	tag	Message
11-10 17:03...	D	2243		LifeCycleTest	created
11-10 17:03...	D	2243		LifeCycleTest	resumed
11-10 17:03...	D	2243		LifeCycleTest	paused
11-10 17:03...	D	2243		LifeCycleTest	resumed
11-10 17:03...	D	2243		LifeCycleTest	paused
11-10 17:03...	D	2243		LifeCycleTest	resumed
11-10 17:03...	D	2243		LifeCycleTest	paused
11-10 17:03...	D	2243		LifeCycleTest	finishing

Figure 4–5. *The LogCat output of LifeCycleTest*

Pressing the back button again invokes the onPause() method. As it also destroys the activity, the conditional in onPause() also gets triggered, informing us that this is the last we'll see of that activity.

That is the activity life cycle, demystified and simplified four our game programming needs. We now can easily handle any pause and resume events, and we are guaranteed to be notified when the activity is destroyed.

Input Device Handling

As discussed in previous chapters, we can get information from many different input devices on Android. In this section, we'll discuss three of the most relevant input devices on Android and how to work with them: the touchscreen, the keyboard, and the accelerometer.

Getting (Multi-)Touch Events

The touchscreen is probably the most important way to get input from the user. Until Android version 2.0, the API only supported processing single-finger touch events. Multitouch was introduced in Android 2.0 (SDK version 5). The multitouch event reporting was tagged onto the single-touch API, with some mixed results in usability. We'll first investigate handling single-touch events, which are available on all Android versions.

Processing Single-Touch Events

When we processed clicks on a button in Chapter 2, we saw that listener interfaces are the way Android reports events to us. Touch events are no different. Touch events are passed to an OnTouchListener interface implementation that we register with a View. The OnTouchListener interface has only a single method:

```
public abstract boolean onTouch (View v, MotionEvent event)
```

The first argument is the View to which the touch events get dispatched. The second argument is what we'll dissect to get the touch event.

An OnTouchListener can be registered with any View implementation via the View.setOnTouchListener() method. The OnTouchListener will be called before the MotionEvent is dispatched to the View itself. We can signal to the View in our implementation of the onTouch() method that we have already processed the event by returning true from the method. If we return false, the View itself will process the event.

The MotionEvent instance has three methods that are relevant to us:

MotionEvent.getX() and MotionEvent.getY(): These methods report the x- and y-coordinate of the touch event relative to the View. The coordinate system is defined with the origin in the top left of the view, the x-axis points to the right, and the y-axis points downward. The coordinates are given in pixels. Note that the methods return floats, and thus the coordinates have subpixel accuracy.

MotionEvent.getAction(): This returns the type of the touch event. It is an integer that takes on one of the values MotionEvent.ACTION_DOWN, MotionEvent.ACTION_MOVE, MotionEvent.ACTION_CANCEL, and MotionEvent.ACTION_UP.

Sounds simple, and it really is. The MotionEvent.ACTION_DOWN event happens when the finger touches the screen. When the finger moves, events with type MotionEvent.ACTION_MOVE are fired. Note that you will always get MotionEvent.ACTION_MOVE events, as you can't hold your finger still enough to avoid them. The touch sensor will recognize the slightest change. When the finger is lifted up again, the MotionEvent.ACTION_UP event is reported. MotionEvent.ACTION_CANCEL events are a bit of a mystery. The documentation says they will be fired when the current gesture is canceled. We have never seen that event in real life yet. However, we'll still process it and pretend it is a MotionEvent.ACTION_UP event when we start implementing our first game.

Let's write a simple test activity to see how this works in code. The activity should display the current position of the finger on the screen as well as the event type. Listing 4–3 shows you what we came up with.

Listing 4–3. *SingleTouchTest.java; Testing Single-Touch Handling*

```
package com.badlogic.androidgames;

import android.app.Activity;
import android.os.Bundle;
import android.util.Log;
import android.view.MotionEvent;
import android.view.View;
import android.view.View.OnTouchListener;
import android.widget.TextView;

public class SingleTouchTest extends Activity implements OnTouchListener {
    StringBuilder builder = new StringBuilder();
    TextView textView;
```

```
public void onCreate(Bundle savedInstanceState) {
    super.onCreate(savedInstanceState);
    textView = new TextView(this);
    textView.setText("Touch and drag (one finger only)!");
    textView.setOnTouchListener(this);
    setContentView(textView);
}

@Override
public boolean onTouch(View v, MotionEvent event) {
    builder.setLength(0);
    switch (event.getAction()) {
    case MotionEvent.ACTION_DOWN:
        builder.append("down, ");
        break;
    case MotionEvent.ACTION_MOVE:
        builder.append("move, ");
        break;
    case MotionEvent.ACTION_CANCEL:
        builder.append("cancle, ");
        break;
    case MotionEvent.ACTION_UP:
        builder.append("up, ");
        break;
    }
    builder.append(event.getX());
    builder.append(", ");
    builder.append(event.getY());
    String text = builder.toString();
    Log.d("TouchTest", text);
    textView.setText(text);
    return true;
}
}
```

We let our activity implement the OnTouchListener interface. We also have two members: one for the TextView and a StringBuilder we'll use to construct our event strings.

The onCreate() method is pretty self-explanatory. The only novelty is the call to TextView.setOnTouchListener(), where we register our activity with the TextView so that it receives MotionEvents.

What's left is the onTouch() method implementation itself. We ignore the view argument, as we know that it must be the TextView. All we are interested in is getting the touch event type, appending a string identifying it to our StringBuilder, appending the touch coordinates, and updating the TextView text. That's it. We also log the event to LogCat so that we can see the order in which the events happen, as the TextView will only show the last event that we processed (we clear the StringBuilder every time onTouch() is called).

One subtle detail in the onTouch() method is the return statement, where we return true. Usually, we'd stick to the listener concept and return false in order not to interfere with the event-dispatching process. If we do this in our example, we won't get any events other than the MotionEvent.ACTION_DOWN event. So, we tell the TextView that we just consumed the event. That behavior might differ between different View implementations. Luckily, we'll only need three other views in the rest of this book, and those will happily let us consume any event we want.

If we fire that application up on the emulator or a connected device, we can see how the TextView will always display the last event type and position reported to the onTouch() method. Additionally, you can see the same messages in LogCat.

We did not fix the orientation of the activity in the manifest file. If you rotate your device so that the activity is in landscape mode, the coordinate system changes, of course. Figure 4–6 shows you the activity in portrait and landscape mode. In both cases, we tried to touch the middle of the View. Note how the x- and y-coordinates seem to get swapped. The figure also shows you the x- and y-axes in both cases (the yellow lines), along with the point on the screen that we roughly touched (the green circle). In both cases, the origin is in the upper-left corner of the TextView, with the x-axis pointing to the right and the y-axis pointing downward.

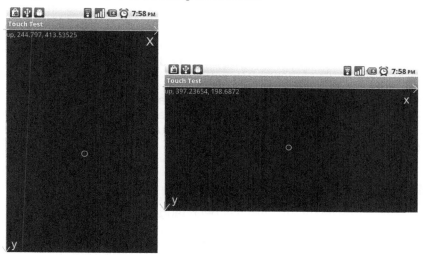

Figure 4–6. *Touching the screen in portrait and landscape modes*

Depending on the orientation, our maximum x and y values change, of course. The preceding images were taken on a Nexus One, which has a screen resolution of 480×800 pixels in portrait mode (800×480 in landscape mode). Since the touch coordinates are given relative to the View, and since the view doesn't fill the complete screen, our maximum y value will be smaller than the resolution height. We'll see later how we can enable full-screen mode so that the title bar and notification bar don't get in our way.

Sadly there are a few issues with touch events on older Android versions and first-generation devices:

Touch event flood: The driver will report as many touch events as possible when a finger is down on the touchscreen—on some devices hundreds per second. We can fix this issue by putting a Thread.sleep(16) call into our onTouch() method, which will put the UI thread on which those events are dispatched to sleep for 16 milliseconds. With this, we'll get 60 events per second at most, which is more than enough to have a responsive game. This is only a problem on devices with Android version 1.5.

Touching the screen eats the CPU: Even if we sleep in our onTouch() method, the system has to process the events in the kernel as reported by the driver. On old devices, such as the Hero or G1, this can use up to 50 percent of the CPU, which leaves a lot less processing power for our main loop thread. As a consequence, our perfectly fine frame rate will drop considerably, sometimes to the point where the game becomes unplayable. On second-generation devices, the problem is a lot less pronounced and can usually be ignored. Sadly, there's no solution for this on older devices.

In general, you will want to put Thread.sleep(16) in all your onTouch() methods just to make sure. On newer devices, it will have no effect; on older devices, it at least prevents the touch event flooding.

With first generation devices slowly dying out, this becomes less of a problem as more time passes. Nevertheless, it still causes major grief among game developers. Try to explain to your users that your game runs like molasses because something in the driver is using up all the CPU. Yeah, nobody will care.

Processing Multitouch Events

Warning: Major pain ahead! The multitouch API has been tagged onto the MotionEvent class, which originally handled only single touches. This makes for some major confusion when trying to decode multitouch events. Let's try to make some sense of it.

> **NOTE:** The multitouch API apparently is also confusing for the Android engineers that created it. It received a major overhaul in SDK version 8 (Android 2.2) with new methods, new constants, and even renamed constants. These changes should make working with multitouch a little bit easier. However, they are only available from SDK version 8 onward. To support all multitouch-capable Android versions (2.0 through 2.2.1), we have to use the API of SDK version 5.

Handling multitouch is very similar to handling single-touch events. We still implement the same OnTouchListener interface we implemented for single-touch events. We also get a MotionEvent instance from which to read the data. We also process the event types we processed before, like MotionEvent.ACTION_UP, plus a couple of new ones that aren't too big of a deal.

Pointer IDs and Indices

The differences start when we want to access the coordinates of a touch event. `MotionEvent.getX()` and `MotionEvent.getY()` return the coordinates of a single finger on the screen. When we process multitouch events, we use overloaded variants of these methods that take a so-called *pointer index*. This might look as follows:

```
event.getX(pointerIndex);
event.getY(pointerIndex);
```

Now, one would expect that `pointerIndex` directly corresponds to one of the fingers touching the screen (for example, the first finger that went down has `pointerIndex` 0, the next finger that went down has `pointerIndex` 1, and so forth). Sadly, this is not the case.

The `pointerIndex` is an index into internal arrays of the `MotionEvent` that holds the coordinates of the event for a specific finger that is touching the screen. The real identifier of a finger on the screen is called the *pointer identifier*. A pointer identifier is an arbitrary number that uniquely identifies one instance of a pointer touching down onto the screen. There's a separate method called `MotionEvent.getPointerIdentifier(int pointerIndex)` that returns the pointer identifier based on a pointer index. A pointer identifier will stay the same for a single finger as long as it touches the screen. This is not necessarily true for the pointer index. It's important to understand the distinction between the two and understand that you can't rely on the first touch to be index 0, id 0 because on some devices, notably the first version of the Xperia Play, the pointer id would always increment up to 15 and then start back over at 0, rather than reuse the lowest available number for an ID.

Let's start by examining how we can get to the pointer index of an event. We'll ignore the event type for now.

```
int pointerIndex = (event.getAction() & MotionEvent.ACTION_POINTER_ID_MASK) >>
MotionEvent.ACTION_POINTER_ID_SHIFT;
```

You probably have the same thoughts that we had when we first implemented this. Before we lose all faith in humanity, let's try to decipher what's happening here. We fetch the event type from the `MotionEvent` via `MotionEvent.getAction()`. Good, we've done that before. Next we perform a bitwise AND operation using the integer we get from the `MotionEvent.getAction()` method and a constant called `MotionEvent.ACTION_POINTER_ID_MASK`. Now the fun begins.

That constant has a value of 0xff00, so we essentially make all bits 0, other than bits 8 to 15, which hold the pointer index of the event. The lower eight bits of the integer returned by `event.getAction()` hold the value of the event type, such as `MotionEvent.ACTION_DOWN` and its siblings. We essentially throw away the event type by this bitwise operation. The shift should make a bit more sense now. We shift by `MotionEvent.ACTION_POINTER_ID_SHIFT`, which has a value of 8, so we basically move bits 8 through 15 to bits 0 through 7, arriving at the actual pointer index of the event. With this, we can then get the coordinates of the event, as well as the pointer identifier.

Notice that our magic constants are called XXX_POINTER_ID_XXX instead of XXX_POINTER_INDEX_XXX (which would make more sense, as we actually want to extract the pointer index, not the pointer identifier). Well, the Android engineers must have been confused as well. In SDK version 8, they deprecated those constants and introduced new constants called XXX_POINTER_INDEX_XXX, which have the exact same values as the deprecated ones. In order for legacy applications that are written against SDK version 5 to continue working on newer Android versions, the old constants are of course still made available.

So we now know how to get that mysterious pointer index that we can use to query for the coordinates and the pointer identifier of the event.

The Action Mask and More Event Types

Next, we have to get the pure event type minus the additional pointer index that is encoded in the integer returned by MotionEvent.getAction(). We just need to mask the pointer index out:

```
int action = event.getAction() & MotionEvent.ACTION_MASK;
```

OK, that was easy. Sadly, you'll only understand it if you know what that pointer index is, and that it is actually encoded in the action.

What's left is to decode the event type as we did before. We already said that there are a few new event types, so let's go through them:

MotionEvent.ACTION_POINTER_DOWN: This event happens for any additional finger that touches the screen after the first finger touches. The first finger will still produce a MotionEvent.ACTION_DOWN event.

MotionEvent.ACTION_POINTER_UP: This is analogous the previous action. This gets fired when a finger is lifted up from the screen and more than one finger is touching the screen. The last finger on the screen to go up will produce a MotionEvent.ACTION_UP event. This finger doesn't necessarily have to be the first finger that touched the screen.

Luckily, we can just pretend that those two new event types are the same as the old MotionEvent.ACTION_UP and MotionEvent.ACTION_DOWN events.

The last difference is the fact that a single MotionEvent can have data for multiple events. Yes, you read that right. For this to happen, the merged events have to have the same type. In reality, this will only happen for the MotionEvent.ACTION_MOVE event, so we only have to deal with this fact when processing said event type. To check how many events are contained in a single MotionEvent, we use the MotionEvent.getPointerCount() method, which tells us the number of fingers that have coordinates in the MotionEvent. We then can fetch the pointer identifier and coordinates for the pointer indices 0 to MotionEvent.getPointerCount() - 1 via the MotionEvent.getX(), MotionEvent.getY(), and MotionEvent.getPointerId() methods.

In Practice

Let's write an example for this fine API. We want to keep track of ten fingers at most (there's no device yet that can track more, so we are on the safe side here). The Android device will usually assign sequential pointer indices as we add more fingers to the screen, but it's not always guaranteed, so we rely on the pointer index for our arrays and will simply display which ID is assigned to the touch point. We keep track of each pointer's coordinates and touch state (touching or not), and output this information to the screen via a TextView. Let's call our test activity MultiTouchTest. Listing 4–4 shows the complete code.

Listing 4–4. *MultiTouchTest.java; Testing the Multitouch API*

```java
package com.badlogic.androidgames;

import android.app.Activity;
import android.os.Bundle;
import android.view.MotionEvent;
import android.view.View;
import android.view.View.OnTouchListener;
import android.widget.TextView;

public class MultiTouchTest extends Activity implements OnTouchListener {
    StringBuilder builder = new StringBuilder();
    TextView textView;
    float[] x = new float[10];
    float[] y = new float[10];
    boolean[] touched = new boolean[10];
    int[] id = new int[10];

    private void updateTextView() {
        builder.setLength(0);
        for (int i = 0; i < 10; i++) {
            builder.append(touched[i]);
            builder.append(", ");
            builder.append(id[i]);
            builder.append(", ");
            builder.append(x[i]);
            builder.append(", ");
            builder.append(y[i]);
            builder.append("\n");
        }
        textView.setText(builder.toString());
    }

    public void onCreate(Bundle savedInstanceState) {
        super.onCreate(savedInstanceState);
        textView = new TextView(this);
        textView.setText("Touch and drag (multiple fingers supported)!");
        textView.setOnTouchListener(this);
        setContentView(textView);
        for (int i = 0; i < 10; i++) {
            id[i] = -1;
        }
```

```java
            updateTextView();
    }

    @Override
    public boolean onTouch(View v, MotionEvent event) {
        int action = event.getAction() & MotionEvent.ACTION_MASK;
        int pointerIndex = (event.getAction() & MotionEvent.ACTION_POINTER_ID_MASK) >>
MotionEvent.ACTION_POINTER_ID_SHIFT;
        int pointerCount = event.getPointerCount();
        for (int i = 0; i < 10; i++) {
            if (i >= pointerCount) {
                touched[i] = false;
                id[i] = -1;
                continue;
            }
            if (event.getAction() != MotionEvent.ACTION_MOVE&& i != pointerIndex) {
                // if it's an up/down/cancel/out event, mask the id to see if we should
process it for this touch point
                continue;
            }
            int pointerId = event.getPointerId(i);
            switch (action) {
            case MotionEvent.ACTION_DOWN:
            case MotionEvent.ACTION_POINTER_DOWN:
                touched[i] = true;
                id[i] = pointerId;
                x[i] = (int) event.getX(i);
                y[i] = (int) event.getY(i);
                break;

            case MotionEvent.ACTION_UP:
            case MotionEvent.ACTION_POINTER_UP:
        case MotionEvent.ACTION_OUTSIDE:
            case MotionEvent.ACTION_CANCEL:
                touched[i] = false;
                id[i] = -1;
                x[i] = (int) event.getX(i);
                y[i] = (int) event.getY(i);
                break;

            case MotionEvent.ACTION_MOVE:
                touched[i] = true;
                id[i] = pointerId;
                x[i] = (int) event.getX(i);
                y[i] = (int) event.getY(i);
                break;
            }
        }

        updateTextView();
        return true;
    }
}
```

We implement the OnTouchListener interface as before. To keep track of the coordinates and touch state of the ten fingers, we add three new member arrays that will hold that information for us. The arrays x and y hold the coordinates for each pointer ID, and the array touched stores whether the finger with that pointer ID is down.

Next we took the freedom to create a little helper method that will output the current state of the fingers to the TextView. It simply iterates through all the ten finger states and concatenates them via a StringBuilder. The final text is set to the TextView.

The onCreate() method sets up our activity and registers it as an OnTouchListener with the TextView. We already know that part by heart.

Now for the scary part: the onTouch() method.

We start off by getting the event type by masking the integer returned by event.getAction(). Next, we extract the pointer index and fetch the corresponding pointer identifier from the MotionEvent, as discussed earlier.

The heart of the onTouch() method is that big nasty switch statement, which we already used in a reduced form to process single-touch events. We group all the events into three categories on a high level:

- A touch-down event happened: (MotionEvent.ACTION_DOWN orMotionEvent.ACTION_PONTER_DOWN). We set the touch state for the pointer identifier to true, and we also save the current coordinates of that pointer.

- A touch-up event happened: (MotionEvent.ACTION_UP,MotionEvent.ACTION_POINTER_UP, or MotionEvent.CANCEL). We set the touch state to false for that pointer identifier and save its last known coordinates.

- One or more fingers were dragged across the screen: (MotionEvent.ACTION_MOVE). We check how many events are contained in the MotionEvent and then update the coordinates for the pointer indices 0 to MotionEvent.getPointerCount()-1. For each event, we fetch the corresponding pointer identifier and update the coordinates.

Once the event is processed, we update the TextView via a call to the updateView() method we defined earlier. Finally we return true, indicating that we processed the touch event.

Figure 4–7 shows the output of the activity produced by touching 5 fingers on a Samsung Galaxy S and dragging them around a little.

Figure 4–7. *Fun with multitouch*

We can observe a few things when we run this example:

- If we start it on a device or emulator with an Android version lower than 2.0, we get a nasty exception, since we've used an API that is not available on those earlier versions. We can work around this by determining the Android version the application is running, using the single-touch code on devices with Android 1.5 and 1.6, and using the multitouch code on devices with Android 2.0 or newer. We'll get back to that in the next chapter.

- There's no multitouch on the emulator. The API is there if we create an emulator running Android version 2.0 or higher, but we only have a single mouse. Even if we had two mice, it wouldn't make a difference.

- Touch two fingers down, lift the first one, and touch it down again. The second finger will keep its pointer identifier after the first finger is lifted. When the first finger is touched down for the second time, it gets a new pointer identifier, which is usually 0 but can be any integer. Any new finger that touches the screen will get a new pointer identifier that could be anything that's not currently used by another active touch. That's a rule to remember.

■ If you try this on a Nexus One or a Droid, you will notice some strange behavior when your cross two fingers on one axis. This is due to the fact that the screens of those devices do not fully support the tracking of individual fingers. It's a big problem, but we can work around it somewhat by designing our UIs with some care. We'll have another look at the issue in a later chapter. The phrase to keep in mind is: *don't cross the streams!*

And that's how multitouch processing works on Android. It is a pain in the butt, but once you untangle all the terminology and come to peace with the bit twiddling, you will feel much more comfortable with the implementation and will be handling all those touch points like a pro.

> **NOTE:** We're sorry if this made your head explode. This section was rather heavy duty. Sadly, the official documentation for the API is extremely lacking, and most people "learn" the API by simply hacking away at it. We suggest you play around with the preceding code example until you fully grasp what's going on within it.

Processing Key Events

After the insanity of the last section, we deserve something dead simple. Welcome to processing key events.

To catch key events, we implement another listener interface, called `OnKeyListener`. It has a single method called onKey(), with the following signature:

```
public boolean onKey(View view, int keyCode, KeyEvent event)
```

The `View` specifies the view that received the key event, the `keyCode` argument is one of the constants defined in the `KeyEvent` class, and the final argument is the key event itself, which has some additional information.

What is a key code? Each key on the (onscreen) keyboard and each of the system keys has a unique number assigned to it. These key codes are defined in the `KeyEvent` class as static public final integers. One such key code is `KeyCode.KEYCODE_A`, which is the code for the A key. This has nothing to do with the character that is generated in a text field when a key is pressed. It really just identifies the key itself.

The `KeyEvent` class is similar to the `MotionEvent` class. It has two methods that are relevant for us:

> `KeyEvent.getAction()`:This method returns `KeyEvent.ACTION_DOWN`, `KeyEvent.ACTION_UP`, and `KeyEvent.ACTION_MULTIPLE`. For our purposes, we can ignore the last key event type. The other two will be sent when a key is either pressed or released.

> `KeyEvent.getUnicodeChar()`: This returns the Unicode character the key would produce in a text field. Say we hold down the Shift key and press the A key. This

would be reported as an event with a key code of KeyEvent.KEYCODE_A, but with a Unicode character A. We can use this method if we want to do text input ourselves.

To receive keyboard events, a View must have the focus. This can be forced with the following method calls:

```
View.setFocusableInTouchMode(true);
View.requestFocus();
```

The first method will guarantee that the View can be focused. The second method requests that the specific view gets the focus.

Let's implement a simple test activity to see how this works in combination. We want to get key events and display the last one we received in a TextView. The information we'll display is the key event type, along with the key code and the Unicode character, if one would be produced. Note that some keys do not produce a Unicode character on their own, but only in combination with other characters. Listing 4–5 demonstrates how we can achieve all of this in a couple of code lines.

Listing 4–5. *KeyTest.Java; Testing the Key Event API*

```
package com.badlogic.androidgames;

import android.app.Activity;
import android.os.Bundle;
import android.util.Log;
import android.view.KeyEvent;
import android.view.View;
import android.view.View.OnKeyListener;
import android.widget.TextView;

public class KeyTest extends Activity implements OnKeyListener {
    StringBuilder builder = new StringBuilder();
    TextView textView;

    public void onCreate(Bundle savedInstanceState) {
        super.onCreate(savedInstanceState);
        textView = new TextView(this);
        textView.setText("Press keys (if you have some)!");
        textView.setOnKeyListener(this);
        textView.setFocusableInTouchMode(true);
        textView.requestFocus();
        setContentView(textView);
    }

    @Override
    public boolean onKey(View view, int keyCode, KeyEvent event) {
        builder.setLength(0);
        switch (event.getAction()) {
        case KeyEvent.ACTION_DOWN:
            builder.append("down, ");
            break;
        case KeyEvent.ACTION_UP:
            builder.append("up, ");
            break;
```

```
        }
        builder.append(event.getKeyCode());
        builder.append(", ");
        builder.append((char) event.getUnicodeChar());
        String text = builder.toString();
        Log.d("KeyTest", text);
        textView.setText(text);

        if (event.getKeyCode() == KeyEvent.KEYCODE_BACK)
            return false;
        else
            return true;
    }
}
```

We start off by declaring that the activity implements the OnKeyListener interface. Next, we define two members with which we are already familiar: a StringBuilder to construct the text to be displayed and a TextView to display the text.

In the onCreate() method, we make sure the TextView has the focus so it can receive key events. We also register the activity as the OnKeyListener via the TextView.setOnKeyListener() method.

The onKey() method is also pretty straightforward. We process the two event types in the switch statement, appending a proper string to the StringBuilder. Next, we append the key code as well as the Unicode character from the KeyEvent itself and output it to LogCat as well as the TextView.

The last if statement is interesting: if the back key is pressed, we return false from the onKey() method, making the TextView process the event. Otherwise, we return true. Why differentiate here?

If we were to return true in the case of the back key, we'd mess with the activity life cycle a little. The activity would not be closed, as we decided to consume the back key ourselves. Of course, there are scenarios where we'd actually want to catch the back key so that our activity does not get closed. However, it is strongly advised not to do this unless absolutely necessary.

Figure 4–8 illustrates the output of the activity while holding down the Shift and A keys on the keyboard of a Droid.

Figure 4–8. *Pressing the Shift and A keys simultaneously*

There are a couple of things to note here:

- When you look at the LogCat output, notice that we can easily process simultaneous key events. Holding down multiple keys is not a problem.

- Pressing the D-pad and rolling the trackball are both reported as key events.

- As with touch events, key events can eat up considerable CPU resources on old Android versions and first-generation devices. However, they will not produce a flood of events.

That was pretty relaxing compared to the previous section, wasn't it?

> **NOTE:** The key processing API is a bit more complex than what we have shown here. However, for our game programming projects, the information contained here is more than sufficient. If you need something a bit more complex, refer to the official documentation on the Android Developer's site.

Reading the Accelerometer State

A very interesting input option for games is the accelerometer. All Android devices are required to contain a three-axis accelerometer. We talked about accelerometers a little bit in the last chapter. Generally, we'll only poll the state of the accelerometer.

So how do we get that accelerometer information? You guessed correctly—by registering a listener. The interface we need to implement is called SensorEventListener, which has two methods:

```
public void onSensorChanged(SensorEvent event);
public void onAccuracyChanged(Sensor sensor, int accuracy);
```

The first method is called when a new accelerometer event arrives. The second method is called when the accuracy of the accelerometer changes. We can safely ignore the second method for our purposes.

So where do we register our SensorEventListener? For this, we have to do a little bit of work. First, we need to check whether there actually is an accelerometer installed in the device. Now, we just told you that all Android devices must contain an accelerometer. This is still true, but it might change in the future. We therefore want to make 100 percent sure that that input method is available to us.

The first thing we need to do is get an instance of the so-called SensorManager. That guy will tell us whether an accelerometer is installed, and it is also where we register our listener. To get the SensorManager, we use a method of the Context interface:

```
SensorManager manager = (SensorManager)context.getSystemService(Context.SENSOR_SERVICE);
```

The SensorManager is a so-called *system service* that is provided by the Android system. Android is composed of multiple system services, each serving different pieces of system information to anyone who asks nicely.

Once we have the manager, we can check whether the accelerometer is available:

```
boolean hasAccel = manager.getSensorList(Sensor.TYPE_ACCELEROMETER).size() > 0;
```

With this bit of code, we poll the manager for all the installed sensors that have the type accelerometer. While this implies that a device can have multiple accelerometers, in reality this will only ever return one accelerometer sensor.

If an accelerometer is installed, we can fetch it from the SensorManager and register the SensorEventListener with it as follows:

```
Sensor sensor = manager.getSensorList(Sensor.TYPE_ACCELEROMETER).get(0);
boolean success = manager.registerListener(listener, sensor,
SensorManager.SENSOR_DELAY_GAME);
```

The argument SensorManager.SENSOR_DELAY_GAME specifies how often the listener should be updated with the latest state of the accelerometer. This is a special constant that is specifically designed for games, so we happily use that. Notice that the SensorManager.registerListener() method returns a Boolean, indicating whether the registration process worked or not. That means we have to check the Boolean afterwards to make sure we'll actually get any events from the sensor.

Once we have registered the listener, we'll receive SensorEvents in the SensorEventListener.onSensorChanged() method. The method name implies that it is only called when the sensor state has changed. This is a little bit confusing, since the accelerometer state is changed constantly. When we register the listener, we actually specify the desired frequency that we want for our sensor state updates.

So how do we process the SensorEvent? That's rather easy. The SensorEvent has a public float array member called SensorEvent.values that holds the current acceleration values of each of the three axes of the accelerometer. SensorEvent.values[0] holds the value of the x-axis, SensorEvent.values[1] holds the value of the y-axis, and SensorEvent.values[2] holds the value of the z-axis. We discussed what is meant by these values Chapter 3, so if you have forgotten that, go and check out the"Input"section again.

With this information, we can write a simple test activity. All we want to do is output the accelerometer values for each accelerometer axis in a TextView. Listing 4–6 shows you how to do this.

Listing 4–6.*AccelerometerTest.java; Testing the Accelerometer API*

```java
package com.badlogic.androidgames;

import android.app.Activity;
import android.content.Context;
import android.hardware.Sensor;
import android.hardware.SensorEvent;
import android.hardware.SensorEventListener;
import android.hardware.SensorManager;
import android.os.Bundle;
import android.widget.TextView;

package com.badlogic.androidgames;

import android.app.Activity;
import android.content.Context;
import android.hardware.Sensor;
import android.hardware.SensorEvent;
import android.hardware.SensorEventListener;
import android.hardware.SensorManager;
import android.os.Bundle;
import android.widget.TextView;

public class AccelerometerTest extends Activity implements SensorEventListener {
    TextView textView;
    StringBuilder builder = new StringBuilder();

    @Override
    public void onCreate(Bundle savedInstanceState) {
        super.onCreate(savedInstanceState);
        textView = new TextView(this);
        setContentView(textView);

        SensorManager manager = (SensorManager)
getSystemService(Context.SENSOR_SERVICE);
        if (manager.getSensorList(Sensor.TYPE_ACCELEROMETER).size() == 0) {
            textView.setText("No accelerometer installed");
        } else {
            Sensor accelerometer = manager.getSensorList(
                    Sensor.TYPE_ACCELEROMETER).get(0);
            if (!manager.registerListener(this, accelerometer,
```

```
                      SensorManager.SENSOR_DELAY_GAME)) {
                textView.setText("Couldn't register sensor listener");
            }
        }
    }

    @Override
    public void onSensorChanged(SensorEvent event) {
        builder.setLength(0);
        builder.append("x: ");
        builder.append(event.values[0]);
        builder.append(", y: ");
        builder.append(event.values[1]);
        builder.append(", z: ");
        builder.append(event.values[2]);
        textView.setText(builder.toString());
    }

    @Override
    public void onAccuracyChanged(Sensor sensor, int accuracy) {
        // nothing to do here
    }
}
```

We start by checking whether an accelerometer sensor is available. If it is, we fetch it from the SensorManager and try to register our activity, which implements the SensorEventListener interface. If any of this fails, we set the TextView to display a proper error message.

The onSensorChanged() method simply reads the axis values from the SensorEvent that are passed to it and updates the TextView text accordingly.

The onAccuracyChanged() method is there so that we fully implement the SensorEventListener interface. It serves no real other purpose.

Figure 4–9 shows you what values the axes take on in portrait and landscape modes when the device is held perpendicular to the ground.

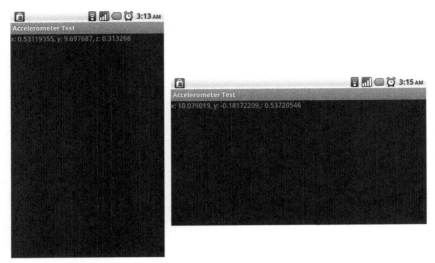

Figure 4–9. *Accelerometer axis values in portrait mode (left) and landscape mode (right) when the device is held perpendicular to the ground*

One thing that's a gotcha for Android accelerometer handling is the fact that the accelerometer values are relative to the default orientation of the device. This means that if your game is run only in landscape, you will have values 90-degrees different on a device where the default orientation is portrait versus one where the default orientation is landscape! So how does one cope with this? Use this handy-dandy code snippet and you should be good to go:

```
int screenRotation;
public void onResume() {
        WindowManager windowMgr =
(WindowManager)activity.getSystemService(Activity.WINDOW_SERVICE);
                // getOrientation() is deprecated in Android 8 but is the same as
getRotation() which is the rotation from the natural orientation of the device
        screenRotation = windowMgr.getDefaultDisplay().getOrientation();
}

static final int ACCELEROMETER_AXIS_SWAP[][] = {
    {1, -1, 0, 1}, // ROTATION_0
    {-1, -1, 1, 0}, // ROTATION_90
    {-1, 1, 0, 1}, // ROTATION_180
    {1, 1, 1, 0}}; // ROTATION_270
public void onSensorChanged(SensorEvent event) {
    final int[] as = ACCELEROMETER_AXIS_SWAP[screenRotation];
    float screenX = (float)as[0] * event.values[as[2]];
    float screenY = (float)as[1] * event.values[as[3]];
    float screenZ = event.values[2];
    // use screenX, screenY and screenZ as your accelerometer values now!
}
```

Here are a few closing comments on accelerometers:

- As you can see in the right screenshot in Figure 4–9, the accelerometer values might sometimes go over their specified range. This is due to small inaccuracies in the sensor, so you have to adjust for that if you need those values to be as exact as possible.

- The accelerometer axes always get reported in the same order, no matter the orientation of your activity.

- It is the responsibility of the application developer to rotate the accelerometer values based on the natural orientation of the device.

Reading the Compass State

Reading sensors other than the accelerometer, like the compass, is very similar. In fact, it is so similar that we can leave it to you simply to copy and paste the following in order to use our accelerometer test code as a compass test! Replace all instances of:

Sensor.`TYPE_ACCELEROMETER`

with

Sensor.`TYPE_ORIENTATION`

and re-run the test. You will now see that your x,y, and z values are doing something very different. If you hold the device flat with the screen up and parallel to the ground, x will read the number of degrees for a compass heading and y and z should be near 0. Now tilt the device around and see how those numbers change.The x should still be the primary heading (azimuth) but y and z are showing you the pitch and roll of the device. Since the constant for TYPE_ORIENTATION was deprecated, you can also receive the same compass data from a call to SensorManager.getOrientation(float[] R, float[] values) where R is a rotation matrix (see SensorManager.getRotationMatrix()) and values holds the three return values, this time in radians.

With this, we have discussed all of the input processing-related classes of the Android API that we'll need for game development.

> **NOTE:** As the name implies, the SensorManager class grants you access to other sensors as well. This includes the compass and light sensors. If you want to be creative, you could come up with a game idea that uses these sensors. Processing their events is done in a similar way to how we processed the data of the accelerometer. The documentation over at the Android Developer's site will give you more information.

File Handling

Android offers us a couple of ways to read and write files. In this section, we'll check out assets and how to access the external storage, mostly implemented as an SD card. Let's start with assets.

Reading Assets

In Chapter 2, we had a brief look at all the folders of an Android project. We identified the assets/ and res/ folders as the ones where we can put files that should get distributed with our application. When we discussed the manifest file, we told you that we're not going to make use of the res/ folder, as it implies restrictions on how we structure our file set. The assets/ directory is the place to put all our files, in whatever folder hierarchy we want.

The files in the assets/ folder are exposed via a class called AssetManager. We can obtain a reference to that manager for our application as follows:

```
AssetManager assetManager = context.getAssets();
```

We already saw the Context interface; it is implemented by the Activity class. In real life, we'd fetch the AssetManager from our activity.

Once we have the AssetManager, we can start opening files like crazy:

```
InputStream inputStream = assetManager.open("dir/dir2/filename.txt");
```

This method will return a plain-old Java InputStream, which we can use to read in any sort of file. The only argument to the AssetManager.open() method is the filename relative to the asset directory. In the preceding example, we have two directories in the assets/ folder, where the second one (dir2/) is a child of the first one (dir/). In our Eclipse project, the file would be located in assets/dir/dir2/.

Let's write a simple test activity that examines this functionality. We want to load a text file named myawesometext.txt from a subdirectory of the assets/ directory called texts. The content of the text file will be displayed in a TextView. Listing 4–7 shows the source for this awe-inspiring activity.

Listing 4–7. *AssetsTest.java, Demonstrating How to Read Asset Files*

```java
package com.badlogic.androidgames;

import java.io.ByteArrayOutputStream;
import java.io.IOException;
import java.io.InputStream;

import android.app.Activity;
import android.content.res.AssetManager;
import android.os.Bundle;
import android.widget.TextView;

public class AssetsTest extends Activity {
    @Override
```

```java
public void onCreate(Bundle savedInstanceState) {
    super.onCreate(savedInstanceState);
    TextView textView = new TextView(this);
    setContentView(textView);

    AssetManager assetManager = getAssets();
    InputStream inputStream = null;
    try {
        inputStream = assetManager.open("texts/myawesometext.txt");
        String text = loadTextFile(inputStream);
        textView.setText(text);
    } catch (IOException e) {
        textView.setText("Couldn't load file");
    } finally {
        if (inputStream != null)
            try {
                inputStream.close();
            } catch (IOException e) {
                textView.setText("Couldn't close file");
            }
    }
}

public String loadTextFile(InputStream inputStream) throws IOException {
    ByteArrayOutputStream byteStream = new ByteArrayOutputStream();
    byte[] bytes = new byte[4096];
    int len = 0;
    while ((len = inputStream.read(bytes)) > 0)
        byteStream.write(bytes, 0, len);
    return new String(byteStream.toByteArray(), "UTF8");
}
}
```

We see no big surprises here, other than finding that loading simple text from an InputStream is rather verbose in Java. We wrote a little method called loadTextFile() that will squeeze all the bytes out of the InputStream and return the bytes in the form of a string. We assume that the text file is encoded as UTF-8. The rest is just catching and handling various exceptions. Figure 4–10 shows you the output of this little activity.

Figure 4–10. *The text output of* AssetsTest

You should take away the following from this section:

■ Loading a text file from an InputStream in Java is a mess! Usually, we'd do that with something like Apache IOUtils. We'll leave that up for you as an exercise.

■ We can only read assets, not write them.

■ We could easily modify the loadTextFile() method to load binary data instead. We would just need to return the byte array instead of the string.

Accessing the External Storage

While assets are superb for shipping all our images and sounds with our application, there are times when we need to be able to persist some information and reload it later on. A common example would be with high-scores.

Android offers many different ways of doing this: you can use local shared preferences of an application, a small SQLite database, and so on. All of these options have one thing in common: they don't handle large binary files all that gracefully. Why would we need that anyway? While we can tell Android to install our application on the external storage device, and thus not waste memory in internal storage, this will only work on Android version 2.2 and above. For earlier versions, all our application data would get installed in internal storage. In theory, we could only include the code of our application in the APK file and download all the asset files from a server to the SD card the first time our application is started. Many of the high-profile games on Android do this.

There are also other scenarios where we'd want to have access to the SD card (which is pretty much synonymous with the term *external storage* on all currently available devices). We could allow our users to create their own levels with an in-game editor. We'd need to store these levels somewhere, and the SD card is perfect for just that purpose.

So, now that we've convinced you not to use the fancy mechanisms Android offers to store application preferences, let's have a look at how to read and write files on the SD card.

The first thing we have to do is request permission to access the external storage. This is done in the manifest file with the `<uses-permission>` element discussed earlier in this chapter.

The next thing we have to do is to check whether there is actually an external storage device available on the device we run. For example, if you create an AVD, you have the option of not having it simulate an SD card, so you couldn't write to it in your application. Another reason for failing to get access to the SD card could be that the external storage device is currently in use by something else (for example, the user may be exploring it via USB on a desktop PC). So, here's how we get the state of the external storage:

```
String state = Environment.getExternalStorageState();
```

Hmm, we get a string. The `Environment` class defines a couple of constants. One of these is called `Environment.MEDIA_MOUNTED`. It is also a string. If the string returned by the preceding method equals this constant, we have full read/write access to the external storage. Note that you really have to use the `equals()` method to compare the two strings; reference equality won't work in every case.

Once we have determined that we can actually access the external storage, we need to get its root directory name. If we then want to access a specific file, we need to specify it relative to this directory. To get that root directory, we use another `Environment` static method:

```
File externalDir = Environment.getExternalStorageDirectory();
```

From here on, we can use the standard Java I/O classes to read and write files.

Let's write a quick example that writes a file to the SD card, reads the file back in, displays its content in a `TextView`, and then deletes the file from the SD card again. Listing 4–8 shows the source code for this.

Listing 4–8. *The ExternalStorageTest Activity*

```
package com.badlogic.androidgames;

import java.io.BufferedReader;
import java.io.BufferedWriter;
import java.io.File;
import java.io.FileReader;
```

```java
import java.io.FileWriter;
import java.io.IOException;

import android.app.Activity;
import android.os.Bundle;
import android.os.Environment;
import android.widget.TextView;

public class ExternalStorageTest extends Activity {
    @Override
    public void onCreate(Bundle savedInstanceState) {
        super.onCreate(savedInstanceState);
        TextView textView = new TextView(this);
        setContentView(textView);

        String state = Environment.getExternalStorageState();
        if (!state.equals(Environment.MEDIA_MOUNTED)) {
            textView.setText("No external storage mounted");
        } else {
            File externalDir = Environment.getExternalStorageDirectory();
            File textFile = new File(externalDir.getAbsolutePath()
                    + File.separator + "text.txt");
            try {
                writeTextFile(textFile, "This is a test. Roger");
                String text = readTextFile(textFile);
                textView.setText(text);
                if (!textFile.delete()) {
                    textView.setText("Couldn't remove temporary file");
                }
            } catch (IOException e) {
                textView.setText("Something went wrong! " + e.getMessage());
            }
        }
    }

    private void writeTextFile(File file, String text) throws IOException {
        BufferedWriter writer = new BufferedWriter(new FileWriter(file));
        writer.write(text);
        writer.close();
    }

    private String readTextFile(File file) throws IOException {
        BufferedReader reader = new BufferedReader(new FileReader(file));
        StringBuilder text = new StringBuilder();
        String line;
        while ((line = reader.readLine()) != null) {
            text.append(line);
            text.append("\n");
        }
        reader.close();
        return text.toString();
    }
}
```

First, we check whether the SD card is actually mounted. If not, we bail out early. Next, we get the external storage directory and construct a new File instance that points to the file we are going to create in the next statement. The `writeTextFile()` method uses standard Java I/O classes to do its magic. If the file doesn't exist yet, this method will create it; otherwise, it will overwrite an already existing file. After we successfully dump our test text to the file on the external storage device, we read it in again and set it as the text of the `TextView`. As a final step, we delete the file from external storage again. All of this is done with standard safety measures in place that will report if something goes wrong by outputting an error message to the `TextView`. Figure 4–11 shows the output of the activity.

Figure 4–11. *Roger!*

Here are the lessons to take away from this section:

- Don't mess with any files that don't belong to you. Your users will be angry if you delete the photos of their last holiday.

- Always check whether the external storage device is mounted.

- Do not mess with any of the files on the external storage device! I mean it!

Because it is very easy to delete all the files on the external storage device, you might think twice before you install your next app from the Market that requests permissions to the SD card. The app has full control over your files once it's installed.

Shared Preferences

Android provides a simple API for storing key-value pairs for your application, called SharedPreferences. The SharedPreferences API is not unlike the standard Java Properties API. An activity can have a default SharedPreferences or it can use as many different SharedPreferences as required. Here are the typical ways to get an instance of SharedPreferences from an activity:

```
SharedPreferences prefs = PreferenceManager.getDefaultSharedPreferences(this);
```

or:

```
SharedPreferences prefs = getPreferences(MODE_PRIVATE);
```

The first method gives a common SharedPreferences that will be shared for that context (Activity, in our case). The second method does the same, but it lets you choose the privacy of the shared preferences. Options are: MODE_PRIVATE, which is default, MODE_WORLD_READABLE and MODE_WORLD_WRITEABLE. Using anything other than private is more advanced, and it isn't necessary for something like saving game settings.

To use the shared preferences, you first need to get the editor. This is done via:

```
Editor editor = prefs.edit()
```

Now we can insert some values:

```
editor.putString("key1", "banana");
editor.putInt("key2", 5);
```

And finally, when we want to save, we just add:

```
editor.commit();
```

Ready to read back? It's exactly as one would expect it:

```
String value1 = prefs.getString("key1", null);
int value2 = prefs.getInt("key2", 0);
```

In our example, value1 would be "banana" and value2 would be 5. The second parameter to the "get" calls of SharedPreferences are default values. These will be used if the key isn't found in the preferences. For example, if "key1" was never set, then value1 will be null after the getString call. SharedPreferences are so simple that we don't really need any test code to demonstrate. Just remember always to commit those edits!

Audio Programming

Android offers a couple of easy-to-use APIs for playing back sound effects and music files—just perfect for our game programming needs. Let's have a look at those APIs.

Setting the Volume Controls

If you have an Android device, you will have noticed that when you press the volume up and down buttons, you control different volume settings depending on the application you are currently using. In a call, you control the volume of the incoming voice stream. In a YouTube application, you control the volume of the video's audio. On the home screen, you control the volume of the ringer.

Android has different audio streams for different purposes. When we playback audio in our game, we use classes that output sound effects and music to a specific stream called the *music stream*. Before we think about playing back sound effects or music, we first have to make sure that the volume buttons will control the correct audio stream. For this, we use another method of the Context interface:

```
context.setVolumeControlStream(AudioManager.STREAM_MUSIC);
```

As always, the Context implementation of our choice will be our activity. After this call, the volume buttons will control the music stream to which we'll later output our sound effects and music. We need to call this method only once in our activity life cycle. The Activity.onCreate() method is the best place to do this.

Writing an example that only contains a single line of code is a bit of overkill. Thus, we'll refrain from doing that at this point. Just remember to use this method in all the activities that output sound.

Playing Sound Effects

In Chapter 3, we discussed the difference between streaming music and playing back sound effects. The latter are stored in memory and usually last no longer than a few seconds. Android provides us with a class called SoundPool that makes playing back sound effects really easy.

We can simply instantiate new SoundPool instances as follows:

```
SoundPool soundPool = new SoundPool(20, AudioManager.STREAM_MUSIC, 0);
```

The first parameter defines the maximum number of sound effects we can play simultaneously. This does not mean that we can't have more sound effects loaded; it only restricts how many sound effects can be played concurrently. The second parameter defines the audio stream where the SoundPool will output the audio. We choose the music stream where we have set the volume controls as well. The final parameter is currently unused and should default to 0.

To load a sound effect from an audio file into heap memory, we can use the SoundPool.load() method. We store all our files in the assets/directory, so we need to use the overloaded SoundPool.load() method, which takes an AssetFileDescriptor. How do we get that AssetFileDescriptor? Easy—via the AssetManager that we worked with before. Here's how we'd load an OGG file called explosion.ogg from the assets/ directory via the SoundPool:

```
AssetFileDescriptor descriptor = assetManager.openFd("explosion.ogg");
int explosionId = soundPool.load(descriptor, 1);
```

Getting the AssetFileDescriptor is straightforward via the AssetManager.openFd() method. Loading the sound effect via the SoundPool is just as easy. The first argument of the SoundPool.load() method is our AssetFileDescriptor, and the second argument specifies the priority of the sound effect. This is currently not used, and should be set to 1 for future compatibility.

The SoundPool.load() method returns an integer, which serves as a handle to the loaded sound effect. When we want to play the sound effect, we specify this handle so that the SoundPool knows what effect to play.

Playing the sound effect is again very easy:

```
soundPool.play(explosionId, 1.0f, 1.0f, 0, 0, 1);
```

The first argument is the handle we received from the SoundPool.load() method. The next two parameters specify the volume to be used for the left and right channels. These values should be in the range between 0 (silent) and 1 (ears explode).

Next comes two arguments that we'll rarely use. The first one is the priority, which is currently unused and should be set to 0. The other argument specifies how often the sound effect should be looped. Looping sound effects is not recommended, so you should generally use 0 here. The final argument is the playback rate. Setting it to something higher than 1 will allow the sound effect to be played back faster than it was recorded, while setting it to something lower than 1 will result in a slower playback.

When we no longer need a sound effect and want to free some memory, we can use the SoundPool.unload() method:

```
soundPool.unload(explosionId);
```

We simply pass in the handle we received from the SoundPool.load() method for that sound effect, and it will be unloaded from memory.

Generally, we'll have a single SoundPool instance in our game, which we'll use to load, play, and unload sound effects as needed. When we are done with all of our audio output and no longer need the SoundPool, we should always call the SoundPool.release() method, which will release all resources normally used up by the SoundPool. After the release, you can no longer use the SoundPool, of course. Also, all sound effects loaded by that SoundPool will be gone.

Let's write a simple test activity that will play back an explosion sound effect each time we tap the screen. We already know everything we need to know to implement this, so Listing 4–9 shouldn't hold any big surprises.

Listing 4–9. *SoundPoolTest.java; Playing Back Sound Effects*

```java
package com.badlogic.androidgames;

import java.io.IOException;

import android.app.Activity;
import android.content.res.AssetFileDescriptor;
import android.content.res.AssetManager;
import android.media.AudioManager;
import android.media.SoundPool;
import android.os.Bundle;
```

```java
import android.view.MotionEvent;
import android.view.View;
import android.view.View.OnTouchListener;
import android.widget.TextView;

public class SoundPoolTest extends Activity implements OnTouchListener {
    SoundPool soundPool;
    int explosionId = -1;

    @Override
    public void onCreate(Bundle savedInstanceState) {
        super.onCreate(savedInstanceState);
        TextView textView = new TextView(this);
        textView.setOnTouchListener(this);
        setContentView(textView);

        setVolumeControlStream(AudioManager.STREAM_MUSIC);
        soundPool = new SoundPool(20, AudioManager.STREAM_MUSIC, 0);

        try {
            AssetManager assetManager = getAssets();
            AssetFileDescriptor descriptor = assetManager
                    .openFd("explosion.ogg");
            explosionId = soundPool.load(descriptor, 1);
        } catch (IOException e) {
            textView.setText("Couldn't load sound effect from asset, "
                    + e.getMessage());
        }
    }

    @Override
    public boolean onTouch(View v, MotionEvent event) {
        if (event.getAction() == MotionEvent.ACTION_UP) {
            if (explosionId != -1) {
                soundPool.play(explosionId, 1, 1, 0, 0, 1);
            }
        }
        return true;
    }
}
```

We start off by deriving our class from `Activity` and letting it implement the `OnTouchListener` interface so that we can later process taps on the screen. Our class has two members: the `SoundPool`, and the handle to the sound effect we are going to load and play back. We set that to –1 initially, indicating that the sound effect has not yet been loaded.

In the `onCreate()` method, we do what we've done a couple of times before: create a `TextView`, register the activity as an `OnTouchListener`, and set the `TextView` as the content view.

The next line sets the volume controls to control the music stream, as discussed before. We then create the `SoundPool`, and configure it so it can play 20 concurrent effects at once. That should suffice for the majority of games.

Finally, we get an `AssetFileDescriptor` for the `explosion.ogg` file we put in the `assets/`directory from the `AssetManager`. To load the sound, we simply pass that descriptor to the `SoundPool.load()` method and store the returned handle. The `SoundPool.load()` method throws an exception in case something goes wrong while loading, in which case we catch that and display an error message.

In the `onTouch()` method, we simply check whether a finger went up, which indicates that the screen was tapped. If that's the case and the explosion sound effect was loaded successfully (indicated by the handle not being –1), we simply play back that sound effect.

When you execute this little activity, simply touch the screen to make the world explode. If you touch the screen in rapid succession, you'll notice that the sound effect is played multiple times in an overlapping manner. It would be pretty hard to exceed the 20 playbacks maximum that we configured into the `SoundPool`. However, if that happened, one of the currently playing sounds would just be stopped to make room for the newly-requested playback.

Notice that we didn't unload the sound or release the `SoundPool` in the preceding example. This is for brevity. Usually you'd release the `SoundPool` in the `onPause()` method when the activity is going to be destroyed. Just remember always to release or unload anything you no longer need.

While the `SoundPool` class is very easy to use, there are a couple of caveats you should remember:

- The `SoundPool.load()` method executes the actual loading asynchronously. This means that you have to wait briefly before you call the `SoundPool.play()` method with that sound effect, as the loading might not be finished yet. Sadly, there's no way to check when the sound effect is done loading. That's only possible with the SDK version 8 of `SoundPool`, and we want to support all Android versions. Usually it's not a big deal, since you will most likely load other assets as well before the sound effect is played for the first time.

- `SoundPool` is known to have problems with MP3 files and long sound files, where *long* is defined as "longer than 5 to 6 seconds." Both problems are undocumented, so there are no strict rules for deciding whether your sound effect will be troublesome or not. As a general rule, we'd suggest sticking to OGG audio files instead of MP3s, and trying for the lowest possible sampling rate and duration you can get away with before the audio quality becomes poor.

NOTE: As with any API we discuss, there's more functionality in SoundPool. We briefly told you that you can loop sound effects. For this, you get an ID from the `SoundPool.play()` method that you can use to pause or stop a looped sound effect. Check out the SoundPool documentation on the Android Developer's site if you need that functionality.

Streaming Music

Small sound effects fit into the limited heap memory an Android application gets from the operating system. Larger audio files containing longer music pieces don't fit. For this reason, we need to stream the music to the audio hardware, which means that we only read-in a small chunk at a time, enough to decode it to raw PCM data and throw that at the audio chip.

That sounds intimidating. Luckily, there's the MediaPlayer class, which handles all that business for us. All we need to do is point it at the audio file and tell it to play it back.

Instantiating the MediaPlayer class is dead simple:

```
MediaPlayer mediaPlayer = new MediaPlayer();
```

Next we need to tell the MediaPlayer what file to play back. That's again done via an AssetFileDescriptor:

```
AssetFileDescriptor descriptor = assetManager.openFd("music.ogg");
mediaPlayer.setDataSource(descriptor.getFileDescriptor(), descriptor.getStartOffset(),
descriptor.getLength());
```

There's a little bit more going on here than in the SoundPool case. The MediaPlayer.setDataSource() method does not directly take an AssetFileDescriptor. Instead, it wants a FileDescriptor, which we get via the AssetFileDescriptor.getFileDescriptor() method. Additionally, we have to specify the offset and the length of the audio file. Why the offset? Assets are all stored in a single file in reality. For the MediaPlayer to get to the start of the file, we have to provide it with the offset of the file within the containing asset file.

Before we can start playing back the music file, we have to call one more method that prepares the MediaPlayer for playback:

```
mediaPlayer.prepare();
```

This will actually open the file and check whether it can be read and played back by the MediaPlayer instance. From here on, we are free to play the audio file, pause it, stop it, set it to be looped, and change the volume.

To start the playback, we simply call the following method:

```
mediaPlayer.start();
```

Note that this can only be called after the MediaPlayer.prepare() method has been called successfully (you'll notice if it throws a runtime exception).

We can pause the playback after having started it with a call to the pause() method:

```
mediaPlayer.pause();
```

Calling this method is again only valid if we have successfully prepared the MediaPlayer and started playback already. To resume a paused MediaPlayer, we can call the MediaPlayer.start() method again without any preparation.

To stop the playback, we call the following method:

```
mediaPlayer.stop();
```

Note that when we want to start a stopped `MediaPlayer`, we first have to call the `MediaPlayer.prepare()` method again.

We can set the `MediaPlayer` to loop the playback with the following method:

```
mediaPlayer.setLooping(true);
```

To adjust the volume of the music playback, we can use this method:

```
mediaPlayer.setVolume(1, 1);
```

This will set the volume of the left and right channels. The documentation does not specify within what range these two arguments have to be. From experimentation, the valid range seems to be between 0 and 1.

Finally, we need a way to check whether the playback has finished. We can do this in two ways. For one, we can register an `OnCompletionListener` with the `MediaPlayer` that will be called when the playback has finished:

```
mediaPlayer.setOnCompletionListener(listener);
```

If we want to poll for the state of the `MediaPlayer`, we can use the following method instead:

```
boolean isPlaying = mediaPlayer.isPlaying();
```

Note that if the `MediaPlayer` is set to loop, none of the preceding methods will indicate that the `MediaPlayer` has stopped.

Finally, if we are done with that `MediaPlayer` instance, we make sure that all the resources it takes up are released by calling the following method:

```
mediaPlayer.release();
```

It's considered good practice always to do this before throwing away the instance.

In case we didn't set the `MediaPlayer` for looping and the playback has finished, we can restart the `MediaPlayer` by calling the `MediaPlayer.prepare()` and `MediaPlayer.start()` methods again.

Most of these methods work asynchronously, so even if you called `MediaPlayer.stop()`, the `MediaPlayer.isPlaying()` method might return for a short period after that. It's usually nothing we worry about. In most games, we set the `MediaPlayer` to be looped and then stop it when the need arises (for example, when we switch to a different screen where we want other music to be played).

Let's write a small test activity where we play back a sound file from the `assets/` directory in looping mode. This sound effect will be paused and resumed according to the activity life cycle—when our activity gets paused, so should the music, and when the activity is resumed, the music playback should pick up from where it left off. Listing 4–10 shows you how that's done.

Listing 4–10. *MediaPlayerTest.java; Playing Back Audio Streams*

```java
package com.badlogic.androidgames;

import java.io.IOException;

import android.app.Activity;
import android.content.res.AssetFileDescriptor;
import android.content.res.AssetManager;
import android.media.AudioManager;
import android.media.MediaPlayer;
import android.os.Bundle;
import android.widget.TextView;

public class MediaPlayerTest extends Activity {
    MediaPlayer mediaPlayer;

    @Override
    public void onCreate(Bundle savedInstanceState) {
        super.onCreate(savedInstanceState);
        TextView textView = new TextView(this);
        setContentView(textView);

        setVolumeControlStream(AudioManager.STREAM_MUSIC);
        mediaPlayer = new MediaPlayer();
        try {
            AssetManager assetManager = getAssets();
            AssetFileDescriptor descriptor = assetManager.openFd("music.ogg");
            mediaPlayer.setDataSource(descriptor.getFileDescriptor(),
                    descriptor.getStartOffset(), descriptor.getLength());
            mediaPlayer.prepare();
            mediaPlayer.setLooping(true);
        } catch (IOException e) {
            textView.setText("Couldn't load music file, " + e.getMessage());
            mediaPlayer = null;
        }
    }

    @Override
    protected void onResume() {
        super.onResume();
        if (mediaPlayer != null) {
            mediaPlayer.start();
        }
    }

    protected void onPause() {
        super.onPause();
        if (mediaPlayer != null) {
            mediaPlayer.pause();
            if (isFinishing()) {
                mediaPlayer.stop();
                mediaPlayer.release();
            }
        }
    }
}
```

We keep a reference to the MediaPlayer in the form of a member of our activity. In the onCreate() method, we simply create a TextView for outputting any error messages, as always.

Before we start playing around with the MediaPlayer, we make sure that the volume controls actually control the music stream. Having that set up, we instantiate the MediaPlayer. We fetch the AssetFileDescriptor from the AssetManager for a file called music.ogg located in the assets/ directory, and set it as the data source of the MediaPlayer. All that's left to do is to prepare the MediaPlayer instance and set it to loop the stream. In case anything goes wrong, we set the MediaPlayer member to null so we can later determine whether loading was successful. Additionally, we output some error text to the TextView.

In the onResume() method, we simply start the MediaPlayer (if creating it was successful). The onResume() method is the perfect place to do this as it is called after onCreate() and after onPause(). In the first case, it will start the playback for the first time; in the second case, it will simply resume the paused MediaPlayer.

The onResume() method pauses the MediaPlayer. If the activity is going to be killed, we stop the MediaPlayer and then release all of its resources.

If you play around with this, make sure you also test out how it reacts to pausing and resuming the activity, by either locking the screen or temporarily switching to the home screen. When resumed, the MediaPlayer will pick up from where it left when it was paused.

Here are a couple of things to remember:

- The methods MediaPlayer.start(), MediaPlayer.pause(), and MediaPlayer.resume() can only be called in certain states, as just discussed. Never try to call them when you haven't yet prepared the MediaPlayer. Call MediaPlayer.start() only after preparing the MediaPlayer or when you want to resume it after you've explicitly paused it via a call to MediaPlayer.pause().

- MediaPlayer instances are pretty heavyweight. Having many of them instanced will take up a considerable amount of resources. We should always try to have only one for music playback. Sound effects are better handled with the SoundPool class.

- Remember to set the volume controls to handle the music stream, or else your players won't be able to adjust the volume of your game.

We are almost done with this chapter, but one big topic still lies ahead of us: 2D graphics.

Basic Graphics Programming

Android offers us two big APIs for drawing to the screen. One is mainly used for simple 2D graphics programming, and the other is used for hardware-accelerated 3D graphics programming. This and the next chapter will focus on 2D graphics programming with the Canvas API, which is a nice wrapper around the Skia library and suitable for modestly complex 2D graphics. Before we get to that, we first need to talk about two things: going full-screen and wake locks.

Using Wake Locks

If you leave the tests we wrote so far alone for a few seconds, the screen of your phone will dim. Only if you touch the screen or hit a button will the screen go back to its full brightness. To keep our screen awake at all times, we can use a so-called *wake lock*.

The first thing we need to do is to add a proper <uses-permission> tag in the manifest file with the name android.permission.WAKE_LOCK. This will allow us to use the WakeLock class.

We can get a WakeLock instance from the PowerManager like this:

```
PowerManager powerManager =
(PowerManager)context.getSystemService(Context.POWER_SERVICE);
WakeLock wakeLock = powerManager.newWakeLock(PowerManager.FULL_WAKE_LOCK, "My Lock");
```

Like all other system services, we acquire the PowerManager from a Context instance. The PowerManager.newWakeLock() method takes two arguments: the type of the lock and a tag we can freely define. There are a couple of different wake lock types; for our purposes, the PowerManager.FULL_WAKE_LOCK type is the correct one. It will make sure that the screen will stay on, the CPU will work at full speed, and the keyboard will stay enabled.

To enable the wake lock, we have to call its acquire() method:

```
wakeLock.acquire();
```

The phone will be kept awake from this point on, no matter how much time passes without user interaction. When our application is paused or destroyed, we have to disable or release the wake lock again:

```
wakeLock.release();
```

Usually, we instantiate the WakeLock instance on the Activity.onCreate() method, call WakeLock.acquire() in the Activity.onResume() method, and call the WakeLock.release() method in the Activity.onPause() method. This way we guarantee that our application still performs well in the case of being paused or resumed. Since there are only four lines of code to add, we're not going to write a full-fledged example. Instead, we suggest you simply add the code to the full-screen example of the next section and observe the effects.

Going Full-Screen

Before we dive headfirst into drawing our first shapes with the Android APIs, let's fix something else. Up until this point, all of our activities have shown their title bars. The notification bar was visible as well. We'd like to immerse our players a little bit more by getting rid of those. We can do that with two simple calls:

```
requestWindowFeature(Window.FEATURE_NO_TITLE);
getWindow().setFlags(WindowManager.LayoutParams.FLAG_FULLSCREEN,
WindowManager.LayoutParams.FLAG_FULLSCREEN);
```

The first call gets rid of the activity's title bar. To make the activity go full-screen and thus eliminate the notification bar as well, we call the second method. Note that we have to call these methods before we set the content view of our activity.

Listing 4–11 shows you a very simple test activity that demonstrates how to go full-screen.

Listing 4–11. *FullScreenTest.java; Making Our Activity Go Full-Screen*

```
package com.badlogic.androidgames;

import android.os.Bundle;
import android.view.Window;
import android.view.WindowManager;

public class FullScreenTest extends SingleTouchTest {

    @Override
    public void onCreate(Bundle savedInstanceState) {
        requestWindowFeature(Window.FEATURE_NO_TITLE);
        getWindow().setFlags(WindowManager.LayoutParams.FLAG_FULLSCREEN,
                WindowManager.LayoutParams.FLAG_FULLSCREEN);
        super.onCreate(savedInstanceState);
    }
}
```

What's happening here? We simply derive from the TouchTest class we created earlier and override the onCreate() method. In the onCreate() method, we enable full-screen mode and then call the onCreate() method of the superclass (in this case, the TouchTest activity), which will set up all the rest of the activity. Note again that we have to call those two methods before we set the content view. Hence, the superclass onCreate() method is called after we execute these two methods.

We also fixed the orientation of the activity to portrait mode in the manifest file. You didn't forget to add <activity> elements in the manifest file for each test we wrote, right? From now on, we'll always fix it either to portrait or landscape mode, since we don't want a changing coordinate system all the time.

By deriving from TouchTest, we have a fully working example that we can now use to explore the coordinate system in which we are going to draw. The activity will show you the coordinates where you touch the screen, as in the old TouchTest example. The difference this time is that we are full-screen, which means that the maximum coordinates of our touch events are equal to the screen resolution (minus one in each dimension, as we start at [0,0]). For a Nexus One, the coordinate system would span the coordinates (0,0) to (479,799) in portrait mode (for a total of 480×800 pixels).

While it may seem that the screen is redrawn continuously, it actually is not. Remember from our TouchTest class that we update the TextView every time a touch event is processed. This, in turn, makes the TextView redraw itself. If we don't touch the screen, the TextView will not redraw itself. For a game, we need to be able to redraw the screen as often as possible, preferably within our main loop thread. We'll start off easy, and begin with continuous rendering in the UI thread.

Continuous Rendering in the UI Thread

All we've done up until now is to set the text of a TextView when needed. The actual rendering has been performed by the TextView itself. Let's create our own custom View whose sole purpose is to let us draw stuff to the screen. We also want it to redraw itself as often as possible, and we want a simple way to perform our own drawing in that mysterious redraw method.

Although this may sound complicated, in reality Android makes it really easy for us to create such a thing. All we have to do is to create a class that derives from the View class, and override a method called View.onDraw(). This method is called by the Android system every time it needs our View to redraw itself. Here's what that could look like:

```
class RenderView extends View {
    public RenderView(Context context) {
        super(context);
    }

    protected void onDraw(Canvas canvas) {
        // to be implemented
    }
}
```

Not exactly rocket science, is it? We get an instance of a class called Canvas passed to the onDraw() method. This will be our workhorse in the following sections. It lets us draw shapes and bitmaps to either another bitmap or a View (or a surface, which we'll talk about in a bit).

We can use this RenderView as we'd use a TextView. We just set it as the content view of our activity and hook up any input listeners we need. However, it's not all that useful yet, for two reasons: it doesn't actually draw anything and, even if it did, it would only do so when the activity needed to be redrawn (that is, when it is created or resumed, or when a dialog that overlaps it becomes invisible). How can we make it redraw itself?

Easy, like this:

```
protected void onDraw(Canvas canvas) {
    // all drawing goes here
    invalidate();
}
```

The call to the `View.invalidate()` method at the end of `onDraw()` will tell the Android system to redraw the `RenderView` as soon as it finds time to do that again. All of this still happens on the UI thread, which is a bit of a lazy horse. However, we actually have continuous rendering with the `onDraw()` method, albeit relatively slow continuous rendering. We'll fix that later; for now, it suffices for our needs.

So, let's get back to the mysterious `Canvas` class again. It is a pretty powerful class that wraps a custom low-level graphics library called Skia, specifically tailored to perform 2D rendering on the CPU. The `Canvas` class provides us with many drawing methods for various shapes, bitmaps, and even text.

Where do the draw methods draw to? That depends. A `Canvas` can render to a `Bitmap` instance; `Bitmap` is another class provided by the Android's 2D API, which we'll look into later on. In this case, it is drawing to the area on the screen that the `View` is taking up. Of course, this is an insane oversimplification. Under the hood, it will not directly draw to the screen, but to some sort of bitmap that the system will later use in combination with the bitmaps of all other `Views` of the activity to composite the final output image. That image will then be handed over to the GPU, which will display it on the screen through another set of mysterious paths.

We don't really need to care about the details. From our perspective, our `View` seems to stretch over the whole screen, so it may as well be drawing to the framebuffer of the system. For the rest of this discussion, we'll pretend that we directly draw to the framebuffer, with the system doing all the nifty things like vertical retrace and double-buffering for us.

The `onDraw()` method will be called as often as the system permits. For us, it is very similar to the body of our theoretical game main loop. If we were to implement a game with this method, we'd place all our game logic into this method. We won't do that for various reasons, performance being one of them.

So let's do something interesting. Every time you get access to a new drawing API, write a little test that checks if the screen is really redrawn frequently. It's a sort of a poor man's light show. All you need to do in each call to the redraw method is to fill the screen with a new random color. That way you only need to find the method of that API that allows you to fill the screen, without needing to know a lot about the nitty-gritty details. Let's write such a test with our own custom `RenderView` implementation.

The method of the `Canvas` to fill its rendering target with a specific color is called `Canvas.drawRGB()`:

```
Canvas.drawRGB(int r, int g, int b);
```

The r, g, and b arguments each stand for one component of the color that we will use to fill the "screen." Each of them has to be in the range 0 to 255, so we actually specify a color in the RGB888 format here. If you don't remember the details regarding colors, take a look at the "Encoding Colors Digitally" section of Chapter 3 again, as we'll be using that info throughout the rest of this chapter.

Listing 4–12 shows you the code for our little light show.

> **CAUTION:** Running this code will rapidly fill the screen with a random color. If you have epilepsy
> or are otherwise light-sensitive in any way, don't run it.

Listing 4–12. *The RenderViewTest Activity*

```java
package com.badlogic.androidgames;

import java.util.Random;

import android.app.Activity;
import android.content.Context;
import android.graphics.Canvas;
import android.os.Bundle;
import android.view.View;
import android.view.Window;
import android.view.WindowManager;

public class RenderViewTest extends Activity {
    class RenderView extends View {
        Random rand = new Random();

        public RenderView(Context context) {
            super(context);
        }

        protected void onDraw(Canvas canvas) {
            canvas.drawRGB(rand.nextInt(256), rand.nextInt(256),
                    rand.nextInt(256));
            invalidate();
        }
    }

    @Override
    public void onCreate(Bundle savedInstanceState) {
        super.onCreate(savedInstanceState);
        requestWindowFeature(Window.FEATURE_NO_TITLE);
        getWindow().setFlags(WindowManager.LayoutParams.FLAG_FULLSCREEN,
                WindowManager.LayoutParams.FLAG_FULLSCREEN);
        setContentView(new RenderView(this));
    }
}
```

For our first graphics demo, this is pretty concise. We define the RenderView class as an inner class of the RenderViewTest activity. The RenderView class derives from the View class, as discussed earlier, and has a mandatory constructor as well as the overridden onDraw() method. It also has an instance of the Random class as a member; we'll use that to generate our random colors.

The onDraw() method is dead simple. We first tell the Canvas to fill the whole view with a random color. For each color component, we simply specify a random number between 0 and 255 (Random.nextInt() is exclusive). After that, we tell the system that we want the onDraw() method to be called again as soon as possible.

The onCreate() method of the activity enables full-screen mode and sets an instance of our RenderView class as the content view. To keep the example short, we're leaving out the wake lock for now.

Taking a screenshot of this example is a little bit pointless. All it does is fill the screen with a random color as fast as the system allows on the UI thread. It's nothing to write home about. Let's do something more interesting instead: draw some shapes.

> **NOTE:** The preceding method of continuous rendering works, but we strongly recommend not using it! We should do as little work on the UI thread as possible. In a minute, we'll use a separate thread to discuss how to do it properly, where later on we can also implement our game logic.

Getting the Screen Resolution (and Coordinate Systems)

In Chapter 2, we talked a lot about the framebuffer and its properties. Remember that a framebuffer holds the colors of the pixels that get displayed on the screen. The number of pixels available to us is defined by the screen resolution, which is given by its width and height in pixels.

Now, with our custom View implementation, we don't actually render directly to the framebuffer. However, since our View spans the complete screen, we can pretend it does. In order to know where we can render our game elements, we need to know how many pixels there are on the x-axis and y-axis, or the width and height of the screen.

The Canvas class has two methods that provide us with that information:

```
int width = canvas.getWidth();
int height = canvas.getHeight();
```

This returns the width and height in pixels of the target to which the Canvas renders. Note that, depending on the orientation of our activity, the width might be smaller or larger than the height. A Nexus One, for example, has a resolution of 480×800 pixels in portrait mode, so the Canvas.getWidth() method would return 480 and the Canvas.getHeight() method would return 800. In landscape mode, the two values are simply swapped: Canvas.getWidth() would return 800 and Canvas.getHeight() would return 480.

The second piece of information we need to know is the organization of the coordinate system to which we render. First of all, only integer pixel coordinates make sense (there is a concept called subpixels, but we will ignore it). We also already know that the origin of that coordinate system at (0,0) is always at the top-left corner of the display, in both portrait or landscape mode. The positive x-axis is always pointing to the right, and the y-axis is always pointing downward. Figure 4–12 shows a hypothetical screen with a resolution of 48×32 pixels, in landscape mode.

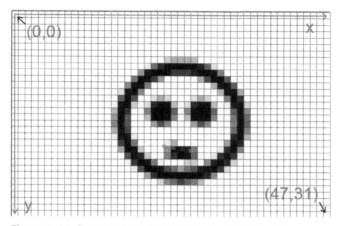

Figure 4–12. *The coordinate system of a 48×32-pixel-wide screen*

Note how the origin of the coordinate system in Figure 4–12 coincides with the top-left pixel of the screen. The bottom-left pixel of the screen is thus not at (48,32) as we'd expect, but at (47,31).In general, (width − 1, height − 1) is always the position of the bottom-right pixel of the screen.

Figure 4–12 shows you a hypothetical screen coordinate system in landscape mode. By now you should be able to imagine how the coordinate system would look in portrait mode.

All of the drawing methods of Canvas operate within this type of coordinate system. Usually, we can address many more pixels than we can in our 48×32-pixel example (e.g., 800×480). That said; let's finally draw some pixels, lines, circles, and rectangles.

> **NOTE:** You may have noticed that different devices can have difference screen resolutions. We'll look into that problem in the next chapter. For now, let's just concentrate on finally getting something on the screen ourselves.

Drawing Simple Shapes

One hundred fifty pages later, and we are finally on our way to drawing our first pixel. We'll quickly go over some of the drawing methods provided to us by the Canvas class.

Drawing Pixels

The first thing we want to know is how to draw a single pixel. That's done with the following method:

```
Canvas.drawPoint(float x, float y, Paint paint);
```

Two things to notice immediately are that the coordinates of the pixel are specified with floats, and that the Canvas doesn't let us specify the color directly, but instead it wants an instance of the Paint class from us.

Don't get confused by the fact that we specify coordinates as floats. Canvas has some very advanced functionality that allows us to render to noninteger coordinates, and that's where this is coming from. We won't need that functionality just yet, though; we'll come back to it in the next chapter.

The Paint class holds style and color information to be used for drawing shapes, text, and bitmaps. For drawing shapes, we are interested in only two things: the color the paint holds and the style. Since a pixel doesn't really have a style, let's concentrate on the color first. Here's how we instantiate the Paint class and set the color:

```
Paint paint = new Paint();
paint.setARGB(alpha, red, green, blue);
```

Instantiating the Paint class is pretty painless. The Paint.setARGB() method should also be easy to decipher. The arguments each represent one of the color components of the color, in the range from 0 to 255. We therefore specify an ARGB8888 color here.

Alternatively, we can use the following method to set the color of a Paint instance:

```
Paint.setColor(0xff00ff00);
```

We pass a 32-bit integer to this method. It again encodes an ARGB8888 color; in this case, it's the color green with alpha set to full opacity. The Color class defines some static constants that encode some standard colors like Color.RED, Color.YELLOW, and so on. You can use these if you don't want to specify a hexadecimal value yourself.

Drawing Lines

To draw a line, we can use the following Canvas method:

```
Canvas.drawLine(float startX, float startY, float stopX, float stopY, Paint paint);
```

The first two arguments specify the coordinates of the starting point of the line, the next two arguments specify the coordinates of the endpoint of the line, and the last argument specifies a Paint instance. The line that gets drawn will be one pixel thick. If we want the line to be thicker, we can specify its thickness in pixels by setting the stroke width of the Paint:

```
Paint.setStrokeWidth(float widthInPixels);
```

Drawing Rectangles

We can also draw rectangles with the Canvas:

```
Canvas.drawRect(float topleftX, float topleftY, float bottomRightX, float bottomRightY,
Paint paint);
```

The first two arguments specify the coordinates of the top-left corner of the rectangle, the next two arguments specify the coordinates of the bottom-left corner of the rectangle, and the Paint specifies the color and style of the rectangle. So what style can we have and how do we set it?

To set the style of a Paint instance, we call the following method:

```
Paint.setStyle(Style style);
```

Style is an enumeration that has the values Style.FILL, Style.STROKE, and Style.FILL_AND_STROKE. If we specify Style.FILL, the rectangle will be filled with the color of the Paint. If we specify Style.STROKE, only the outline of the rectangle will be drawn, again with the color and stroke width of the Paint. If Style.FILL_AND_STROKE is set, the rectangle will be filled, and the outline will be drawn with the given color and stroke width.

Drawing Circles

More fun can be had by drawing circles, either filled or stroked or both:

```
Canvas.drawCircle(float centerX, float centerY, float radius, Paint paint);
```

The first two arguments specify the coordinates of the center of the circle, the next argument specifies the radius in pixels, and the last argument is again a Paint instance. As with the Canvas.drawRectangle() method, the color and style of the Paint will be used to draw the circle.

One last thing of importance is that all of these drawing methods will perform alpha blending. Just specify the alpha of the color as something other than 255 (0xff), and your pixels, lines, rectangles, and circles will be translucent.

Putting It All Together

Let's write a quick test activity that demonstrates the preceding methods. This time, we want you to analyze the code in Listing 4–13 first. Figure out where on a 480×800 screen in portrait mode the different shapes will be drawn. When doing graphics programming, it is of utmost importance to imagine how the drawing commands you issue will behave. It takes some practice, but it really pays off.

Listing 4–13. *ShapeTest.java; Drawing Shapes Like Crazy*

```java
package com.badlogic.androidgames;

import android.app.Activity;
import android.content.Context;
import android.graphics.Canvas;
import android.graphics.Color;
import android.graphics.Paint;
import android.graphics.Paint.Style;
import android.os.Bundle;
import android.view.View;
import android.view.Window;
import android.view.WindowManager;

public class ShapeTest extends Activity {
```

```
class RenderView extends View {
    Paint paint;

    public RenderView(Context context) {
        super(context);
        paint = new Paint();
    }

    protected void onDraw(Canvas canvas) {
        canvas.drawRGB(255, 255, 255);
        paint.setColor(Color.RED);
        canvas.drawLine(0, 0, canvas.getWidth()-1, canvas.getHeight()-1, paint);

        paint.setStyle(Style.STROKE);
        paint.setColor(0xff00ff00);
        canvas.drawCircle(canvas.getWidth() / 2, canvas.getHeight() / 2, 40, paint);

        paint.setStyle(Style.FILL);
        paint.setColor(0x770000ff);
        canvas.drawRect(100, 100, 200, 200, paint);
        invalidate();
    }
}

@Override
public void onCreate(Bundle savedInstanceState) {
    super.onCreate(savedInstanceState);
    requestWindowFeature(Window.FEATURE_NO_TITLE);
    getWindow().setFlags(WindowManager.LayoutParams.FLAG_FULLSCREEN,
                         WindowManager.LayoutParams.FLAG_FULLSCREEN);
    setContentView(new RenderView(this));
}
}
```

Did you create that mental image already? Then let's analyze the RenderView.onDraw() method quickly. The rest is the same as in the last example.

We start off by filling the screen with the color white. Next we draw a line from the origin to the bottom-right pixel of the screen. We use a paint that has its color set to red, so the line will be red.

Next, we modify the paint slightly and set its style to Style.STROKE, its color to green, and its alpha to 255. The circle is drawn in the center of the screen with a radius of 40 pixels using the Paint we just modified. Only the outline of the circle will be drawn, due to the Paint's style.

Finally, we modify the Paint again. We set its style to Style.FILL and the color to full blue. Notice that we set the alpha to 0x77 this time, which equals 119 in decimal. This means that the shape we draw with the next call will be roughly 50 percent translucent.

Figure 4–13 shows you the output of the test activity on 480×800 and 320×480 screens in portrait mode.

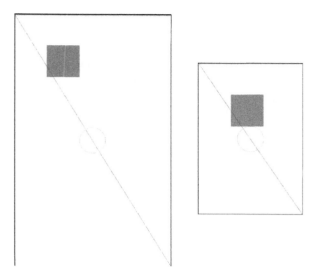

Figure 4–13. *The ShapeTest output on a 480×800 screen (left) and a 320×480 screen (right) (black border added afterward)*

Oh my, what happened here? That's what you get for rendering with absolute coordinates and sizes on different screen resolutions. The only thing that is constant in both images is the red line, which simply draws from the top-left corner to the bottom-right corner. This is done in a screen resolution-independent manner.

The rectangle is positioned at (100,100). Depending on the screen resolution, the distance to the screen center will differ. The size of the rectangle is 100×100 pixels. On the bigger screen, it takes up far less relative space than on the smaller screen.

The circle's position is again screen resolution-independent, but its radius is not. Therefore, it again takes up more relative space on the smaller screen than on the bigger one.

We already see that handling different screen resolutions might be a bit of a problem. It gets even worse when we factor in different physical screen sizes. However, we'll try to solve that issue in the next chapter. Just keep in mind that screen resolution and physical size matter.

> **NOTE:** The Canvas and Paint classes offer a lot more than what we just talked about. In fact, all of the standard Android Views draw themselves with this API, so you can image that there's more behind it. As always, check out the Android Developer's site for more information.

Using Bitmaps

While making a game with basic shapes such as lines or circles is a possibility, it's not exactly sexy. We want an awesome artist to create sprites and backgrounds and all that jazz for us, which we can then load from PNG or JPEG files. Doing this on Android is extremely easy.

Loading and Examining Bitmaps

The `Bitmap` class will become our best friend. We load a bitmap from a file by using the `BitmapFactory` singleton. As we store our images in the form of assets, let's see how we can load an image from the `assets/`directory:

```
InputStream inputStream = assetManager.open("bob.png");
Bitmap bitmap = BitmapFactory.decodeStream(inputStream);
```

The `Bitmap` class itself has a couple of methods that are of interest to us. First, we want to get to know its width and height in pixels:

```
int width = bitmap.getWidth();
int height = bitmap.getHeight();
```

The next thing we might want to know is the color format of the stored `Bitmap`:

```
Bitmap.Config config = bitmap.getConfig();
```

`Bitmap.Config` is an enumeration with the values:

- `Config.ALPHA_8`
- `Config.ARGB_4444`
- `Config.ARGB_8888`
- `Config.RGB_565`

From Chapter 3, you should know what these values mean. If not, we strongly suggest that you read the "Encoding Colors Digitally" section of Chapter 3 again.

Interestingly, there's no RGB888 color format. PNG only supports ARGB8888, RGB888, and palletized colors. What color format would be used to load an RGB888 PNG? `BitmapConfig.RGB_565` is the answer. This happens automatically for any RGB888 PNG we load via the `BitmapFactory`. The reason for this is that the actual framebuffer of most Android devices works with that color format. It would be a waste of memory to load an image with a higher bit depth per pixel, as the pixels would need to be converted to RGB565 anyway for final rendering.

So why is there the `Config.ARGB_8888` configuration then? The answer is because image composition can be done on the CPU prior to drawing the final image to the framebuffer. In the case of the alpha component, we also have a lot more bit depth than with `Config.ARGB_4444`, which might be necessary for some high-quality image processing.

An ARGB8888 PNG image would be loaded to a `Bitmap` with a `Config.ARGB_8888` configuration. The other two color formats are barely used. We can, however, tell the

BitmapFactory to try to load an image with a specific color format, even if its original format is different.

```
InputStream inputStream = assetManager.open("bob.png");
BitmapFactory.Options options = new BitmapFactory.Options();
options.inPreferredConfig = Bitmap.Config.ARGB_4444;
Bitmap bitmap = BitmapFactory.decodeStream(inputStream, null, options);
```

We use the overloaded BitmapFactory.decodeStream() method to pass a hint in the form of an instance of the BitmapFactory.Options class to the image decoder. We can specify the desired color format of the Bitmap instance via the BitmapFactory.Options.inPreferredConfig member, as shown previously. In this hypothetical example, the bob.png file would be an ARGB8888 PNG, and we want the BitmapFactory to load it and convert it to an ARGB4444 bitmap. The factory can ignore the hint, though.

This will free all the memory used by that Bitmap instance. Of course, you can no longer use the bitmap for rendering after a call to this method.

You can also create an empty Bitmap with the following static method:

```
Bitmap bitmap = Bitmap.createBitmap(int width, int height, Bitmap.Config config);
```

This might come in handy if you want to do custom image compositing yourself on the fly. The Canvas class also works on bitmaps:

```
Canvas canvas = new Canvas(bitmap);
```

You can then modify your bitmaps in the same way you modify the contents of a View.

Disposing of Bitmaps

The BitmapFactory can help us reduce our memory footprint when we load images. Bitmaps take up a lot of memory, as discussed in Chapter 3. Reducing the bits per pixel by using a smaller color format helps, but ultimately we will run out of memory if we keep on loading bitmap after bitmap. We should therefore always dispose of any Bitmap instance that we no longer need via the following method:

```
Bitmap.recycle();
```

Drawing Bitmaps

Once we have loaded our bitmaps, we can draw them via the Canvas. The easiest method to do this looks as follows:

```
Canvas.drawBitmap(Bitmap bitmap, float topLeftX, float topLeftY, Paint paint);
```

The first argument should be obvious. The arguments topLeftX and topLeftY specify the coordinates on the screen where the top-left corner of the bitmap will be placed. The last argument can be null. We could specify some very advanced drawing parameters with the Paint, but we don't really need those.

There's another method that will come in handy, as well:

```
Canvas.drawBitmap(Bitmap bitmap, Rect src, Rect dst, Paint paint);
```

This method is super-awesome. It allows us to specify a portion of the Bitmap to draw via the second parameter. The Rect class holds the top-left and bottom-right corner coordinates of a rectangle. When we specify a portion of the Bitmap via the src, we do it in the Bitmap's coordinate system. If we specify null, the complete Bitmap will be used.

The third parameter defines where to draw the portion of the Bitmap, again in the form of a Rect instance. This time, the corner coordinates are given in the coordinate system of the target of the Canvas, though (either a View or another Bitmap). The big surprise is that the two rectangles do not have to be the same size. If we specify the destination rectangle to be smaller in size than the source rectangle, then the Canvas will automatically scale for us. The same is true if we specify a larger destination rectangle, of course. We'll usually set the last parameter to null again. Note, however, that this scaling operation is very expensive. We should only use it when absolutely necessary.

So, you might wonder: If we have Bitmap instances with different color formats, do we need to convert them to some kind of standard format before we can draw them via a Canvas? The answer is no. The Canvas will do this for us automatically. Of course, it will be a bit faster if we use color formats that are equal to the native framebuffer format. Usually we just ignore this.

Blending is also enabled by default, so if our images contain an alpha component per pixel, it is actually interpreted.

Putting It All Together

With all of this information, we can finally load and render some Bobs. Listing 4–14 shows you the source of the BitmapTest activity that we wrote for demonstration purposes.

Listing 4–14. *The BitmapTest Activity*

```java
package com.badlogic.androidgames;

import java.io.IOException;
import java.io.InputStream;

import android.app.Activity;
import android.content.Context;
import android.content.res.AssetManager;
import android.graphics.Bitmap;
import android.graphics.BitmapFactory;
import android.graphics.Canvas;
import android.graphics.Rect;
import android.os.Bundle;
import android.util.Log;
import android.view.View;
import android.view.Window;
import android.view.WindowManager;
```

```java
public class BitmapTest extends Activity {
    class RenderView extends View {
        Bitmap bob565;
        Bitmap bob4444;
        Rect dst = new Rect();

        public RenderView(Context context) {
            super(context);

            try {
                AssetManager assetManager = context.getAssets();
                InputStream inputStream = assetManager.open("bobrgb888.png");
                bob565 = BitmapFactory.decodeStream(inputStream);
                inputStream.close();
                Log.d("BitmapText",
                        "bobrgb888.png format: " + bob565.getConfig());

                inputStream = assetManager.open("bobargb8888.png");
                BitmapFactory.Options options = new BitmapFactory.Options();
                options.inPreferredConfig = Bitmap.Config.ARGB_4444;
                bob4444 = BitmapFactory
                        .decodeStream(inputStream, null, options);
                inputStream.close();
                Log.d("BitmapText",
                        "bobargb8888.png format: " + bob4444.getConfig());

            } catch (IOException e) {
                // silently ignored, bad coder monkey, baaad!
            } finally {
                // we should really close our input streams here.
            }
        }

        protected void onDraw(Canvas canvas) {
            dst.set(50, 50, 350, 350);
            canvas.drawBitmap(bob565, null, dst, null);
            canvas.drawBitmap(bob4444, 100, 100, null);
            invalidate();
        }
    }

    @Override
    public void onCreate(Bundle savedInstanceState) {
        super.onCreate(savedInstanceState);
        requestWindowFeature(Window.FEATURE_NO_TITLE);
        getWindow().setFlags(WindowManager.LayoutParams.FLAG_FULLSCREEN,
                WindowManager.LayoutParams.FLAG_FULLSCREEN);
        setContentView(new RenderView(this));
    }
}
```

The onCreate() method of our activity is old hat, so let's move on to our custom View.

It has two Bitmap members, one storing an image of Bob (introduced in Chapter 3) in RGB565 format, and another storing Bob in ARGB4444 format. We also have a Rect member, where we store the destination rectangle for rendering.

In the constructor of the RenderView class, we first load Bob into the bob565 member of the View. Note that the image is loaded from an RGB888 PNG file, and that the BitmapFactory will automatically convert this to an RGB565 image. To prove this, we also output the Bitmap.Config of the Bitmap to LogCat. The RGB888 version of Bob has an opaque white background, so no blending needs to be performed.

Next we load Bob from an ARGB8888 PNG file stored in the assets/ directory. To save some memory, we also tell the BitmapFactory to convert this image of Bob to an ARGB4444 bitmap. The factory may not obey this request (for unknown reasons). To see whether it was nice to us, we output the Bitmap.Config file of this Bitmap to LogCat as well.

The onDraw() method is puny. All we do is draw bob565 scaled to 250×250 pixels (from his original size of 160×183 pixels) and draw bob4444 on top of him, unscaled but blended (which is done automagically by the Canvas). Figure 4–14 shows you the two Bobs in all their glory.

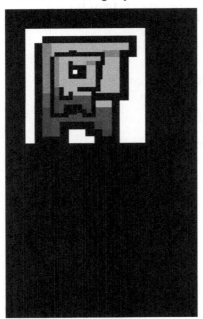

Figure 4–14. *Two Bobs on top of each other (at 480×800-pixel resolution)*

LogCat reports that bob565 indeed has the color format Config.RGB_565, and that bob4444 was converted to Config.ARGB_4444. The BitmapFactory did not fail us!

Here are some things you should take away from this section:

- Use the minimum color format that you can get away with to conserve memory. This might, however, come at the price of less visual quality and slightly reduced rendering speed.

■ Unless absolutely necessary, refrain from drawing bitmaps scaled. If you know their scaled size, prescale them offline or during loading time.

■ Always make sure you call the `Bitmap.recycle()` method if you no longer need a `Bitmap`. Otherwise you'll get some memory leaks or run low on memory.

Using LogCat all this time for text output is a bit tedious. Let's see how we can render text via the `Canvas`.

> **NOTE:** As with other classes, there's more to `Bitmap` than what we could describe in these couple of pages. We covered the bare minimum we need to write Mr. Nom. If you want more, check out the documentation on the Android Developer's site.

Rendering Text

While the text we'll output in the Mr. Nom game will be drawn by hand, it doesn't hurt to know how to draw text via TrueType fonts. Let's start by loading a custom TrueType font file from the `assets/` directory.

Loading Fonts

The Android API provides us with a class called `Typeface` that encapsulates a TrueType font. It provides a simple static method to load such a font file from the `assets/` directory:

```
Typeface font = Typeface.createFromAsset(context.getAssets(), "font.ttf");
```

Interestingly enough, this method does not throw any kind of `Exception` if the font file can't be loaded. Instead a `RuntimeException` is thrown. Why no explicit exception is thrown for this method is a bit of a mystery.

Drawing Text with a Font

Once we have our font, we set it as the `Typeface` of a `Paint` instance:

```
paint.setTypeFace(font);
```

Via the `Paint` instance, we also specify the size at which we want to render the font:

```
paint.setTextSize(30);
```

The documentation of this method is again a little sparse. It doesn't tell us whether the text size is given in points or pixels. We just assume the latter.

Finally, we can draw text with this font via the following `Canvas` method:

```
canvas.drawText("This is a test!", 100, 100, paint);
```

The first parameter is the text to draw. The next two parameters are the coordinates where the text should be drawn to. The last argument is familiar to us: it's the `Paint` instance that specifies the color, font, and size of the text to be drawn. By setting the color of the `Paint`, you also set the color of the text to be drawn.

Text Alignment and Boundaries

Now, you might wonder how the coordinates of the preceding method relate to the rectangle that the text string fills. Do they specify the top-left corner of the rectangle in which the text is contained? The answer is a bit more complicated. The `Paint` instance has an attribute called the *align setting*. It can be set via this method of the `Paint` class:

```
Paint.setTextAlign(Paint.Align align);
```

The `Paint.Align` enumeration has three values: `Paint.Align.LEFT`, `Paint.Align.CENTER`, and `Paint.Align.RIGHT`. Depending on what alignment is set, the coordinates passed to the `Canvas.drawText()` method are interpreted as either the top-left corner of the rectangle, the top-center pixel of the rectangle, or the top-right corner of the rectangle. The standard alignment is `Paint.Align.LEFT`.

Sometimes it's also useful to know the bounds of a specific string in pixels. For this, the `Paint` class offers the following method:

```
Paint.getTextBounds(String text, int start, int end, Rect bounds);
```

The first argument is the string for which we want to get the bounds. The second and third arguments specify the start character and the end character within the string that should be measured. The end argument is exclusive. The final argument, bounds, is a `Rect` instance we allocate ourselves and pass into the method. The method will write the width and height of the bounding rectangle into the `Rect.right` and `Rect.bottom` fields. For convenience, we can call `Rect.width()` and `Rect.height()` to get the same values.

Note that all of these methods work on a single line of text only. If we want to render multiple lines, we have to do the layout ourselves.

Putting It All Together

Enough talk: let's do some more coding. Listing 4–15 shows you text rendering in action.

Listing 4–15. *The FontTest Activity*

```
package com.badlogic.androidgames;

import android.app.Activity;
import android.content.Context;
import android.graphics.Canvas;
import android.graphics.Color;
import android.graphics.Paint;
import android.graphics.Rect;
import android.graphics.Typeface;
import android.os.Bundle;
```

```java
import android.view.View;
import android.view.Window;
import android.view.WindowManager;

public class FontTest extends Activity {
    class RenderView extends View {
        Paint paint;
        Typeface font;
        Rect bounds = new Rect();

        public RenderView(Context context) {
            super(context);
            paint = new Paint();
            font = Typeface.createFromAsset(context.getAssets(), "font.ttf");
        }

        protected void onDraw(Canvas canvas) {
            paint.setColor(Color.YELLOW);
            paint.setTypeface(font);
            paint.setTextSize(28);
            paint.setTextAlign(Paint.Align.CENTER);
            canvas.drawText("This is a test!", canvas.getWidth() / 2, 100,
                    paint);

            String text = "This is another test o_0";
            paint.setColor(Color.WHITE);
            paint.setTextSize(18);
            paint.setTextAlign(Paint.Align.LEFT);
            paint.getTextBounds(text, 0, text.length(), bounds);
            canvas.drawText(text, canvas.getWidth() - bounds.width(), 140,
                    paint);
            invalidate();
        }
    }

    @Override
    public void onCreate(Bundle savedInstanceState) {
        super.onCreate(savedInstanceState);
        requestWindowFeature(Window.FEATURE_NO_TITLE);
        getWindow().setFlags(WindowManager.LayoutParams.FLAG_FULLSCREEN,
                WindowManager.LayoutParams.FLAG_FULLSCREEN);
        setContentView(new RenderView(this));
    }
}
```

We won't discuss the onCreate() method of the activity, since we've seen it before.

Our RenderView implementation has three members: a Paint, a Typeface, and a Rect, where we'll store the bounds of a text string later on.

In the constructor, we create a new Paint instance and load a font from the file font.ttf in the assets/ directory.

In the onDraw() method, we set the Paint to the color yellow, set the font and its size, and specify the text alignment to be used when interpreting the coordinates in the call to

Canvas.drawText(). The actual drawing call renders the string This is a test!, centered horizontally at coordinate 100 on the y-axis.

For the second text-rendering call, we do something else: we want the text to be right-aligned with the right edge of the screen. We could do this by using Paint.Align.RIGHT and an x-coordinate of Canvas.getWidth() – 1. Instead, we do it the hard way by using the bounds of the string to practice very basic text layout a little. We also change the color and the size of the font for rendering. Figure 4–15 shows the output of this activity.

Figure 4–15. *Fun with text (480×800-pixel resolution)*

Another mystery of the Typeface class is that it does not explicitly allow us to release all its resources. We have to rely on the garbage collector to do the dirty work for us.

> **NOTE:** We only scratched the surface of text rendering here. If you want to know more . . . well, by now you know where to look.

Continuous Rendering with SurfaceView

This is the section where we become real men and women. It involves threading, and all the pain that is associated with it. We'll get through it alive. I promise!

Motivation

When we first tried to do continuous rendering, we did it the wrong way. Hogging the UI thread is unacceptable; we need a solution that does all the dirty work in a separate thread. Enter SurfaceView.

As the name gives away, the SurfaceView class is a View that handles a Surface, another class of the Android API. What is a Surface? It's an abstraction of a raw buffer that is used by the screen compositor for rendering that specific View. The screen compositor is the mastermind behind all rendering on Android, and it is ultimately responsible for pushing all pixels to the GPU. The Surface can be hardware accelerated in some cases. We don't care much about that fact, though. All we need to know is that it is a more direct way to render things to the screen.

Our goal is it to perform our rendering in a separate thread so that we do not hog the UI thread, which is busy with other things. The SurfaceView class provides us with a way to render to it from a thread other than the UI thread.

SurfaceHolder and Locking

In order to render to a SurfaceView from a different thread than the UI thread, we need to acquire an instance of the SurfaceHolder class, like this:

```
SurfaceHolder holder = surfaceView.getHolder();
```

The SurfaceHolder is a wrapper around the Surface, and does some bookkeeping for us. It provides us with two methods:

```
Canvas SurfaceHolder.lockCanvas();
SurfaceHolder.unlockAndPost(Canvas canvas);
```

The first method locks the Surface for rendering and returns a nice Canvas instance we can use. The second method unlocks the Surface again and makes sure that what we've drawn via the Canvas gets displayed on the screen. We will use these two methods in our rendering thread to acquire the Canvas, render with it, and finally make the image we just rendered visible on the screen. The Canvas we have to pass to the SurfaceHolder.unlockAndPost() method must be the one we received from the SurfaceHolder.lockCanvas() method.

The Surface is not immediately created when the SurfaceView is instantiated. Instead it is created asynchronously. The surface will be destroyed each time the activity is paused and recreated when the activity is resumed.

Surface Creation and Validity

We cannot acquire the Canvas from the SurfaceHolder as long as the Surface is not yet valid. However, we can check whether the Surface has been created or not via the following statement:

```
boolean isCreated = surfaceHolder.getSurface().isValid();
```

If this method returns true, we can safely lock the surface and draw to it via the Canvas we receive. We have to make absolutely sure that we unlock the Surface again after a call to SurfaceHolder.lockCanvas(), or else our activity might lock up the phone!

Putting It All Together

So how do we integrate all of this with a separate rendering thread as well as with the activity life cycle? The best way to figure this out is to look at some actual code. Listing 4–16 shows you a complete example that performs the rendering in a separate thread on a SurfaceView.

Listing 4–16. *The SurfaceViewTest Activity*

```
package com.badlogic.androidgames;

import android.app.Activity;
import android.content.Context;
import android.graphics.Canvas;
import android.os.Bundle;
import android.view.SurfaceHolder;
import android.view.SurfaceView;
import android.view.Window;
import android.view.WindowManager;

public class SurfaceViewTest extends Activity {
    FastRenderView renderView;

    public void onCreate(Bundle savedInstanceState) {
        super.onCreate(savedInstanceState);
        requestWindowFeature(Window.FEATURE_NO_TITLE);
        getWindow().setFlags(WindowManager.LayoutParams.FLAG_FULLSCREEN,
                        WindowManager.LayoutParams.FLAG_FULLSCREEN);
        renderView = new FastRenderView(this);
        setContentView(renderView);
    }

    protected void onResume() {
        super.onResume();
        renderView.resume();
    }

    protected void onPause() {
        super.onPause();
        renderView.pause();
    }

    class FastRenderView extends SurfaceView implements Runnable {
        Thread renderThread = null;
        SurfaceHolder holder;
        volatile boolean running = false;

        public FastRenderView(Context context) {
            super(context);
            holder = getHolder();
```

```
        }

        public void resume() {
            running = true;
            renderThread = new Thread(this);
            renderThread.start();
        }

        public void run() {
            while(running) {
                if(!holder.getSurface().isValid())
                    continue;

                Canvas canvas = holder.lockCanvas();
                canvas.drawRGB(255, 0, 0);
                holder.unlockCanvasAndPost(canvas);
            }
        }

        public void pause() {
            running = false;
            while(true) {
                try {
                    renderThread.join();
                } catch (InterruptedException e) {
                    // retry
                }
            }
        }
    }
}
```

This doesn't look all that intimidating, does it? Our activity holds a FastRenderView instance as a member. This is a custom SurfaceView subclass that will handle all the thread business and surface locking for us. To the activity, it looks like a plain-old View.

In the onCreate() method, we enable full-screen mode, create the FastRenderView instance, and set it as the content view of the activity.

We also override the onResume() method this time. In this method, we will start our rendering thread indirectly by calling the FastRenderView.resume() method, which does all the magic internally. This means that the thread will get started when the activity is initially created (because onCreate() is always followed by a call to onResume()). It will also get restarted when the activity is resumed from a paused state.

This, of course, implies that we have to stop the thread somewhere; otherwise, we'd create a new thread every time onResume() was called. That's where onPause() comes in. It calls the FastRenderView.pause() method, which will completely stop the thread. The method will not return before the thread is completely stopped.

So let's look at the core class of this example: FastRenderView. It's similar to the RenderView classes we implemented in the last couple of examples in that it derives from another View class. In this case, we directly derive it from the SurfaceView class. It also implements the Runnable interface so that we can pass it to the rendering thread in order for it to run the render thread logic.

The FastRenderView class has three members. The renderThread member is simply a reference to the Thread instance that will be responsible for executing our rendering thread logic. The holder member is a reference to the SurfaceHolder instance that we get from the SurfaceView superclass from which we derive. Finally, the running member is a simple Boolean flag we will use to signal the rendering thread that it should stop execution. The volatile modifier has a special meaning that we'll get to in a minute.

All we do in the constructor is call the superclass constructor and store the reference to the SurfaceHolder in the holder member.

Next comes the FastRenderView.resume() method. It is responsible for starting up the rendering thread. Notice that we create a new Thread each time this method is called. This is in line with what we discussed when we talked about the activity's onResume() and onPause() methods. We also set the running flag to true. You'll see how that's used in the rendering thread in a bit. The final piece to take away is that we set the FastRenderView instance itself as the Runnable of the thread. This will execute the next method of the FastRenderView in that new thread.

The FastRenderView.run() method is the workhorse of our custom View class. Its body is executed in the rendering thread. As you can see, it's merely composed of a loop that will stop executing as soon as the running flag is set to false. When that happens, the thread will also be stopped and die. Inside the while loop, we first check to ensure that the Surface is valid and, if it is, we lock it, render to it, and unlock it again, as discussed earlier. In this example, we simply fill the Surface with the color red.

The FastRenderView.pause() method looks a little strange. First we set the running flag to false. If you look up a little, you will see that the while loop in the FastRenderView.run() method will eventually terminate due to this, and hence stop the rendering thread. In the next couple of lines, we simply wait for the thread to die completely, by invoking Thread.join(). This method will wait for the thread to die, but might throw an InterruptedException before the thread actually dies. Since we have to make absolutely sure that the thread is dead before we return from that method, we perform the join in an endless loop until it is successful.

Let's come back to the volatile modifier of the running flag. Why do we need it? The reason is delicate: the compiler might decide to reorder the statements in the FastRenderView.pause() method if it recognizes that there are no dependencies between the first line in that method and the while block. It is allowed to do this if it thinks it will make the code execute faster. However, we depend on the order of execution that we specified in that method. Imagine if the running flag were set after we tried to join the thread. We'd go into an endless loop, as the thread would never terminate.

The volatile modifier prevents this from happening. Any statements where this member is referenced will be executed in order. This saves us from a nasty Heisenberg—a bug that comes and goes without the ability to be reproduced consistently.

There's one more thing that you might think will cause this code to explode. What if the surface is destroyed between the calls to SurfaceHolder.getSurface().isValid() and SurfaceHolder.lock()? Well, we are lucky—this can never happen. To understand why, we have to take a step back and see how the life cycle of the Surface works.

We know that the Surface is created asynchronously. It is likely that our rendering thread will execute before the Surface is valid. We safeguard against this by not locking the Surface unless it is valid. That covers the surface creation case.

The reason the rendering thread code does not explode from the Surface being destroyed, between the validity check and the locking, has to do with the point in time at which the Surface gets destroyed. The Surface is always destroyed after we return from the activity's onPause() method. Since we wait for the thread to die in that method via the call to FastRenderView.pause(), the rendering thread will no longer be alive when the Surface is actually destroyed. Sexy, isn't it? But it's also confusing.

We now perform our continuous rendering the correct way. We no longer hog the UI thread, but instead use a separate rendering thread. We made it respect the activity life cycle as well, so that it does not run in the background, eating the battery while the activity is paused. The whole world is a happy place again. Of course, we'll need to synchronize the processing of input events in the UI thread with our rendering thread. But that will turn out to be really easy, which you'll see in the next chapter, when we implement our game framework based on all the information you digested in this chapter.

Hardware Accelerated Rendering with Canvas

Android 3.0 Honeycomb added a remarkable feature in the form of the ability to enable GPU hardware acceleration for standard 2D canvas draw calls. The value of this feature varies by application and device, as some devices will actually perform better doing 2D draws on the CPU and others will benefit from the GPU. What the hardware acceleration does under the hood is that it analyzes the draw calls and converts them into OpenGL. For example, if we specify that a line should be drawn from 0,0 to 100,100, then the hardware acceleration will put together a special line-draw call using OpenGL and it will draw this to a hardware buffer that later gets composited to the screen.

Enabling this hardware acceleration is as simple as adding the following into your AndroidManifest.xml under the <application /> tag:

```
android:hardwareAccelerated="true"
```

Make sure to test your game with the acceleration turned on and off on a variety of devices, to determine if it's right for you. In the future, it may be fine to have it always on, but as with anything, we recommend that you take the approach of testing and determining this for yourself . Of course, there are more configuration options that let you set the hardware acceleration for a specific Application, Activity, Window or View, but since we're doing games, we only plan on having one of each, so setting it globally via Application would make the most sense.

The developer of this feature of Android, Romain Guy, has a very detailed blog article about the dos and don'ts of HW acceleration and some general guidelines to getting decent performance using it. The blog entry's URL is:http://android-developers.blogspot.com/2011/03/android-30-hardware-acceleration.html

Best Practices

Android (or rather Dalvik) has some strange performance characteristics at times. To round off this chapter, we'll present to you some of the most important best practices that you should follow to make your games as smooth as silk.

- The garbage collector is your biggest enemy. Once it obtains CPU time for doing its dirty work, it will stop the world for up to 600 ms. That's half a second that your game will not update or render. The user will complain. Avoid object creation as much as possible, especially in your inner loops.

- Objects can get created in some not-so-obvious places that you'll want to avoid. Don't use iterators, as they create new objects. Don't use any of the standard Set or Map collection classes, as they create new objects on each insertion; instead, use the SparseArray class provided by the Android API. Use StringBuffers instead of concatenating strings with the + operator. This will create a new StringBuffer each time. And for the love of all that's good in this world, don't use boxed primitives!

- Method calls have a larger associated cost in Dalvik than in other VMs. Use static methods if you can, as those perform best. Static methods are generally regarded as evil, much like static variables, as they promote bad design, so try to keep your design as clean as possible. Perhaps you should avoid getters and setters as well. Direct field access is about three times faster than method invocations without the JIT, and about seven times faster with the JIT. Nevertheless, think of your design before removing all your getters and setters.

- Floating-point operations are implemented in software on older devices and Dalvik versions without a JIT (anything before Android version 2.2). Old-school game developers would immediately fall back to fixed-point math. Don't do that either, since integer divisions are slow as well. Most of the time, you can get away with floats, and newer devices sport floating-point units (FPUs), which speed things up quite a bit once the JIT kicks in.

- Try to cram frequently-accessed values into local variables inside a method. Accessing local variables is faster than accessing members or calling getters.

Of course, you need to be careful about many other things. We'll sprinkle the rest of the book with some performance hints when the context allows it. If you follow the preceding recommendations, you should be on the safe side. Just don't let the garbage collector win!

Summary

This chapter covered everything we need to know in order to write a decent little 2D game for Android. We looked at how easy it is to set up a new game project with some defaults. We discussed the mysterious activity life cycle and how to live with it. We battled with touch (and more importantly, multitouch) events, processed key events, and checked the orientation of our device via the accelerometer. We explored how to read and write files. Outputting audio on Android turns out to be child's play, and apart from the threading issues with the SurfaceView, drawing stuff to the screen isn't that hard either. Mr. Nom can now become a reality—a terrible, hungry reality!

Chapter 5

An Android Game Development Framework

As you may have noticed, we've been through four chapters without writing a single line of game code. The reason we've put you through all of this boring theory and asked you to implement test programs is simple: if you want to write games, you have to know exactly what's going on. You can't just copy and paste code together from all over the Web and hope that it will form the next first-person shooter hit. By now, you should have a firm grasp on how to design a simple game from the ground up, how to structure a nice API for 2D game development, and which Android APIs will provide the functionality you need to implement your ideas.

To make Mr. Nom a reality, we have to do two things: implement the game framework interfaces and classes we designed in Chapter 3 and, based on that, code up Mr. Nom's game mechanics. Let's start with the game framework by merging what we designed in Chapter 3 with what we discussed in Chapter 4. Ninety percent of the code should be familiar to you already, since we covered most of it in the test programs in the previous chapter.

Plan of Attack

In Chapter 3, we laid out a minimal design for a game framework that abstracts away all the platform specifics so that we could concentrate on what we are here for: game development. Now, we'll implement all these interfaces and abstract classes in a bottom-up fashion, from easiest to hardest. The interfaces from Chapter 3 are located in the package, com.badlogic.androidgames.framework. We'll put the implementation from this chapter in the package, com.badlogic.androidgames.framework.impl, and indicate that it holds the actual implementation of the framework for Android. We'll prefix all our interface implementations with Android so that we can distinguish them from the interfaces. Let's start off with the easiest part, file I/O.

The code for this chapter and the next will be merged into a single Eclipse project. For now, you can just create a new Android project in Eclipse following the steps in the last chapter. At this point, it doesn't matter what you name your default activity.

The AndroidFileIO Class

The original FileIO interface was lean and mean. It contained four methods: one to get an InputStream for an asset, another to get an InputStream for a file in the external storage, a third that returned an OutputStream for a file on the external storage device, and a final one that got the SharedPreferences for the game. In Chapter 4, you learned how to open assets and files on the external storage using Android APIs. Listing 5–1 presents the implementation of the FileIO interface, based on knowledge from Chapter 4.

Listing 5–1. *AndroidFileIO.java; Implementing the FileIO Interface*

```java
package com.badlogic.androidgames.framework.impl;

import java.io.File;
import java.io.FileInputStream;
import java.io.FileOutputStream;
import java.io.IOException;
import java.io.InputStream;
import java.io.OutputStream;

import android.content.Context;
import android.content.SharedPreferences;
import android.content.res.AssetManager;
import android.os.Environment;
import android.preference.PreferenceManager;

import com.badlogic.androidgames.framework.FileIO;

public class AndroidFileIO implements FileIO {
    Context context;
    AssetManager assets;
    String externalStoragePath;

    public AndroidFileIO(Context context) {
        this.context = context;
        this.assets = context.getAssets();
        this.externalStoragePath = Environment.getExternalStorageDirectory()
                .getAbsolutePath() + File.separator;
    }

    @Override
    public InputStream readAsset(String fileName) throws IOException {
        return assets.open(fileName);
    }

    @Override
    public InputStream readFile(String fileName) throws IOException {
        return new FileInputStream(externalStoragePath + fileName);
    }
```

```
    @Override
    public OutputStream writeFile(String fileName) throws IOException {
        return new FileOutputStream(externalStoragePath + fileName);
    }

    public SharedPreferences getPreferences() {
        return PreferenceManager.getDefaultSharedPreferences(context);
    }
}
```

Everything is straightforward. We implement the FileIO interface, store the Context, which is the gateway to almost everything in Android, store an AssetManager, which we pull from the Context, store the external storage's path, and implement the four methods based on this path. Finally, we pass through any IOExceptions that get thrown so we'll know if anything is irregular on the calling side.

Our Game interface implementation will hold an instance of this class and return it via Game.getFileIO(). This also means that our Game implementation will need to pass through the Context in order for the AndroidFileIO instance to work.

Note that we do not check if the external storage is available. If it's not available, or if we forget to add the proper permission to the manifest file, we'll get an exception, so checking for errors is implicit. Now, we can move on to the next piece of our framework, which is audio.

AndroidAudio, AndroidSound, and AndroidMusic: Crash, Bang, Boom!

In Chapter 3, we designed three interfaces for all our audio needs: audio, sound, and music. Audio is responsible for creating sound and music instances from asset files. Sound lets us playback sound effects that are stored in RAM, and music streams bigger music files from the disk to the audio card. In Chapter 4, you learned which Android APIs are needed to implement this. We will start with the implementation of AndroidAudio, as shown in Listing 5-2.

Listing 5-2. *AndroidAudio.java; Implementing the Audio Interface*

```
package com.badlogic.androidgames.framework.impl;

import java.io.IOException;

import android.app.Activity;
import android.content.res.AssetFileDescriptor;
import android.content.res.AssetManager;
import android.media.AudioManager;
import android.media.SoundPool;

import com.badlogic.androidgames.framework.Audio;
import com.badlogic.androidgames.framework.Music;
import com.badlogic.androidgames.framework.Sound;
```

```java
public class AndroidAudio implements Audio {
    AssetManager assets;
    SoundPool soundPool;
```

The AndroidAudio implementation has an AssetManager and a SoundPool instance. The AssetManager is necessary for loading sound effects from asset files into the SoundPool on a call to AndroidAudio.newSound(). The AndroidAudio instance also manages the SoundPool.

```java
public AndroidAudio(Activity activity) {
        activity.setVolumeControlStream(AudioManager.STREAM_MUSIC);
    this.assets = activity.getAssets();
    this.soundPool = new SoundPool(20, AudioManager.STREAM_MUSIC, 0);
    }
```

There are two reasons why we pass our game's Activity in the constructor: it allows us to set the volume control of the media stream (we always want to do that), and it gives us an AssetManager instance, which we will happily store in the corresponding class member. The SoundPool is configured to play back 20 sound effects in parallel, which is adequate for our needs.

```java
@Override
public Music newMusic(String filename) {
    try {
        AssetFileDescriptor assetDescriptor = assets.openFd(filename);
        return new AndroidMusic(assetDescriptor);
    } catch (IOException e) {
        throw new RuntimeException("Couldn't load music '" + filename + "'");
    }
}
```

The newMusic() method creates a new AndroidMusic instance. The constructor of that class takes an AssetFileDescriptor, which it uses to create an internal MediaPlayer (more on that later). The AssetManager.openFd() method throws an IOException in case something goes wrong. We catch it and re-throw it as a RuntimeException. Why not hand the IOException to the caller? First, it would clutter the calling code considerably, so we would rather throw a RuntimeException that does not have to be caught explicitly. Second, we load the music from an asset file. It will only fail if we actually forget to add the music file to the assets/directory, or if our music file contains false bytes. False bytes constitute unrecoverable errors since we need that Music instance for our game to function properly. To avoid such an occurrence, we throw RuntimeExceptions instead of checked exceptions in a few more places in the framework of our game.

```java
@Override
public Sound newSound(String filename) {
    try {
        AssetFileDescriptor assetDescriptor = assets.openFd(filename);
        int soundId = soundPool.load(assetDescriptor, 0);
        return new AndroidSound(soundPool, soundId);
    } catch (IOException e) {
        throw new RuntimeException("Couldn't load sound '" + filename + "'");
    }
}
```

Finally, the newSound() method loads a sound effect from an asset into the SoundPool and returns an AndroidSound instance. The constructor of that instance takes a SoundPool and the ID of the sound effect assigned to it by the SoundPool. Again, we throw any checked exception and re-throw it as an unchecked RuntimeException.

> **NOTE:** We do not release the SoundPool in any of the methods. The reason for this is that there will always be a single Game instance holding a single Audio instance that holds a single SoundPool instance. The SoundPool instance will, thus, be alive as long as the activity (and with it our game) is alive. It will be destroyed automatically as soon as the activity ends.

Next, we will discuss the AndroidSound class, which implements the Sound interface. Listing 5–3 presents its implementation.

Listing 5–3. *Implementing the Sound Interface using AndroidSound.java.*

```
package com.badlogic.androidgames.framework.impl;

import android.media.SoundPool;

import com.badlogic.androidgames.framework.Sound;

public class AndroidSound implements Sound {
    int soundId;
    SoundPool soundPool;

    public AndroidSound(SoundPool soundPool, int soundId) {
        this.soundId = soundId;
        this.soundPool = soundPool;
    }

    @Override
    public void play(float volume) {
        soundPool.play(soundId, volume, volume, 0, 0, 1);
    }

    @Override
    public void dispose() {
        soundPool.unload(soundId);
    }
}
```

There are no surprises here. Via the play() and dispose() methods, we simply store the SoundPool and the ID of the loaded sound effect for later playback and disposal. It doesn't get any easier than this, thanks to the Android API.

Finally, we have to implement the AndroidMusic class returned by AndroidAudio.newMusic(). Listing 5–4 shows that class' code, which looks a little more complex than before. This is due to the state machine that the MediaPlayer uses, which will continuously throw exceptions if we call methods in certain states.

Listing 5–4. *AndroidMusic.java; Implementing the Music Interface*

```java
package com.badlogic.androidgames.framework.impl;

import android.content.res.AssetFileDescriptor;
import android.media.MediaPlayer;
import android.media.MediaPlayer.OnCompletionListener;

import com.badlogic.androidgames.framework.Music;

public class AndroidMusic implements Music, OnCompletionListener {
    MediaPlayer mediaPlayer;
    boolean isPrepared = false;
```

The AndroidMusic class stores a MediaPlayer instance along with a Boolean called isPrepared. Remember, we can only call MediaPlayer.start()/stop()/pause() when the MediaPlayer is prepared. This member helps us keep track of the MediaPlayer's state.

The AndroidMusic class implements the Music interface as well as the OnCompletionListener interface. In Chapter 3, we briefly defined this interface as a means of informing ourselves about when a MediaPlayer has stopped playing back a music file. If this happens, the MediaPlayer needs to be prepared again before we can invoke any of the other methods. The method OnCompletionListener.onCompletion() might be called in a separate thread, and since we set the isPrepared member in this method, we have to make sure that it is safe from concurrent modifications.

```java
public AndroidMusic(AssetFileDescriptor assetDescriptor) {
    mediaPlayer = new MediaPlayer();
    try {
        mediaPlayer.setDataSource(assetDescriptor.getFileDescriptor(),
                assetDescriptor.getStartOffset(),
                assetDescriptor.getLength());
        mediaPlayer.prepare();
        isPrepared = true;
        mediaPlayer.setOnCompletionListener(this);
    } catch (Exception e) {
        throw new RuntimeException("Couldn't load music");
    }
}
```

In the constructor, we create and prepare the MediaPlayer from the AssetFileDescriptor that is passed in, and we set the isPrepared flag, as well as register the AndroidMusic instance as an OnCompletionListener with the MediaPlayer. If anything goes wrong, we throw an unchecked RuntimeException once again.

```java
@Override
public void dispose() {
    if (mediaPlayer.isPlaying())
        mediaPlayer.stop();
    mediaPlayer.release();
}
```

The dispose() method checks if the MediaPlayer is still playing and, if so, stops it. Otherwise, the call to MediaPlayer.release() will throw a runtime exception.

```java
@Override
```

```
public boolean isLooping() {
    return mediaPlayer.isLooping();
}

@Override
public boolean isPlaying() {
    return mediaPlayer.isPlaying();
}

@Override
public boolean isStopped() {
    return !isPrepared;
}
```

The methods isLooping(), isPlaying(), and isStopped() are straightforward. The first two use methods provided by the MediaPlayer; the last one uses the isPrepared flag, which indicates if the MediaPlayer is stopped. This is something MediaPlayer.isPlaying() does not necessarily tell us since it returns false if the MediaPlayer is paused but not stopped.

```
@Override
public void pause() {
    if (mediaPlayer.isPlaying())
        mediaPlayer.pause();
}
```

The pause() method simply checks whether the MediaPlayer instance is playing and calls its pause() method if it is.

```
@Override
public void play() {
    if (mediaPlayer.isPlaying())
        return;
    try {
        synchronized (this) {
            if (!isPrepared)
                mediaPlayer.prepare();
            mediaPlayer.start();
        }
    } catch (IllegalStateException e) {
        e.printStackTrace();
    } catch (IOException e) {
        e.printStackTrace();
    }
}
```

The play() method is a little more involved. If we are already playing, we simply return from the function. Next we have a mighty try...catch block within which we check to see if the MediaPlayer is already prepared based on our flag; we prepare it if needed. If all goes well, we call the MediaPlayer.start() method, which will start the playback. This is conducted in a synchronized block, since we are using the isPrepared flag, which might get set on a separate thread because we are implementing the OnCompletionListener interface. In case something goes wrong, we throw an unchecked RuntimeException.

```
@Override
public void setLooping(boolean isLooping) {
```

```
            mediaPlayer.setLooping(isLooping);
    }

    @Override
    public void setVolume(float volume) {
        mediaPlayer.setVolume(volume, volume);
    }
```

The setLooping() and setVolume() methods can be called in any state of the MediaPlayer and delegated to the respective MediaPlayer methods.

```
    @Override
    public void stop() {
        mediaPlayer.stop();
        synchronized (this) {
            isPrepared = false;
        }
    }
```

The stop() method stops the MediaPlayer and sets the isPrepared flag in a synchronized block.

```
    @Override
    public void onCompletion(MediaPlayer player) {
        synchronized (this) {
            isPrepared = false;
        }
    }
}
```

Finally there's the OnCompletionListener.onCompletion() method that is implemented by AndroidMusic class. All it does is set the isPrepared flag in a synchronized block so that the other methods don't start throwing exceptions out of the blue. Next, we'll move on to our input-related classes.

AndroidInput and AccelerometerHandler

Using a couple of convenient methods, the Input interface we designed in Chapter 3 grants us access to the accelerometer, the touchscreen, and the keyboard in polling and event modes. The idea of putting all the code for an implementation of that interface into a single file is a bit nasty, so we outsource all the input event handling to handler classes. The Input implementation will use those handlers to pretend that it is actually performing all the work.

AccelerometerHandler: Which Side Is Up?

Let's start with the easiest of all handlers, the AccelerometerHandler. Listing 5–5 shows you its code.

Listing 5–5. *AccelerometerHandler.java; Performing All the Accelerometer Handling*

```
package com.badlogic.androidgames.framework.impl;
```

```java
import android.content.Context;
import android.hardware.Sensor;
import android.hardware.SensorEvent;
import android.hardware.SensorEventListener;
import android.hardware.SensorManager;

public class AccelerometerHandler implements SensorEventListener {
    float accelX;
    float accelY;
    float accelZ;

    public AccelerometerHandler(Context context) {
        SensorManager manager = (SensorManager) context
                .getSystemService(Context.SENSOR_SERVICE);
        if (manager.getSensorList(Sensor.TYPE_ACCELEROMETER).size() != 0) {
            Sensor accelerometer = manager.getSensorList(
                    Sensor.TYPE_ACCELEROMETER).get(0);
            manager.registerListener(this, accelerometer,
                    SensorManager.SENSOR_DELAY_GAME);
        }
    }

    @Override
    public void onAccuracyChanged(Sensor sensor, int accuracy) {
        // nothing to do here
    }

    @Override
    public void onSensorChanged(SensorEvent event) {
        accelX = event.values[0];
        accelY = event.values[1];
        accelZ = event.values[2];
    }

    public float getAccelX() {
        return accelX;
    }

    public float getAccelY() {
        return accelY;
    }

    public float getAccelZ() {
        return accelZ;
    }
}
```

Unsurprisingly, the class implements the SensorEventListener interface that we used in
Chapter 4. The class stores three members by holding the acceleration on each of the
three accelerometers' axes.

The constructor takes a Context, from which it gets a SensorManager instance to set up
the event listening. The rest of the code is equivalent to what we did in the last chapter.
Note that if no accelerometer is installed, the handler will happily return zero

acceleration on all axes throughout its life. Therefore, we don't need any extra error-checking or exception-throwing code.

The next two methods, onAccuracyChanged() and onSensorChanged(), should be familiar. In the first method, we don't do anything so there's nothing much to report. In the second one, we fetch the accelerometer values from the provided SensorEvent and store them in the handler's members. The final three methods simply return the current acceleration for each axis.

Note that we do not need to perform any synchronization here, even though the onSensorChanged() method might be called in a different thread. The Java memory model guarantees that writes and reads, to and from, primitive types such as Boolean, int, or byte are atomic. In this case, it's OK to rely on this fact since we aren't doing anything more complex than assigning a new value. We'd need to have proper synchronization if this were not the case (for example, if we did something with the member variables in the onSensorChanged() method).

CompassHandler

Just for fun, we're going to provide an example that is similar to the AccelerometerHandler, but this time we'll give you the compass values along with the pitch and roll of the phone. We'll call the compass value "yaw," since that's a standard orientation term that nicely defines the value we're seeing.

The only difference between the following code snippet and the previous accelerometer example is the change of the sensor type to TYPE_ORIENTATION and the renaming of the fields from "accel" to "yaw, pitch, and roll." Otherwise, it works in the same way, and you can easily swap this code into the game as the control handler! Listing 5–6 shows you its code.

Listing 5–6. *AccelerometerHandler.java; Performing All the Accelerometer Handling*

```java
package com.badlogic.androidgames.framework.impl;

import android.content.Context;
import android.hardware.Sensor;
import android.hardware.SensorEvent;
import android.hardware.SensorEventListener;
import android.hardware.SensorManager;

public class CompassHandler implements SensorEventListener {
    float yaw;
    float pitch;
    float roll;

    public CompassHandler(Context context) {
        SensorManager manager = (SensorManager) context
                .getSystemService(Context.SENSOR_SERVICE);
        if (manager.getSensorList(Sensor.TYPE_ORIENTATION).size() != 0) {
            Sensor compass = manager.getDefaultSensor(Sensor.TYPE_ORIENTATION);
            manager.registerListener(this, compass,
```

```
                    SensorManager.SENSOR_DELAY_GAME);
        }
    }

    @Override
    public void onAccuracyChanged(Sensor sensor, int accuracy) {
        // nothing to do here
    }

    @Override
    public void onSensorChanged(SensorEvent event) {
        yaw = event.values[0];
        pitch = event.values[1];
        roll = event.values[2];
    }

    public float getYaw() {
        return yaw;
    }

    public float getPitch() {
        return pitch;
    }

    public float getRoll() {
        return roll;
    }
}
```

The Pool Class: Because Reuse Is Good for You!

What's the worst thing that can happen to us as Android developers? World-stopping garbage collection! If you look at the Input interface definition in Chapter 3, you'll find the getTouchEvents() and getKeyEvents() methods. These methods return TouchEvents and KeyEvents lists. In our keyboard and touch event handlers, we constantly create instances of these two classes and store them in lists that are internal to the handlers. The Android input system fires many of these events when a key is pressed or a finger touches the screen, so we constantly create new instances that are collected by the garbage collector in short intervals. In order to avoid this, we implement a concept known as instance pooling. Instead of repeatedly creating new instances of a class, we simply reuse previously-created instances. The Pool class is a convenient way to implement that behavior. Let's have a look at its code in Listing 5–7.

Listing 5–7. *Pool.java; Playing Well with the Garbage Collector*

```
package com.badlogic.androidgames.framework;

import java.util.ArrayList;
import java.util.List;

public class Pool<T> {
```

Here are the generics: the first thing to recognize is that this is a generically typed class, much like collection classes such as ArrayList or HashMap. Generics allow us to store any type of object in our Pool without having to cast continuously. So what does the Pool class do?

```
    public interface PoolObjectFactory<T> {
        public T createObject();
    }
```

An interface called PoolObjectFactory is the first thing defined and is, once again, generic. It has a single method, createObject() that will return a new object with the generic type of the Pool/PoolObjectFactory instance.

```
    private final List<T> freeObjects;
    private final PoolObjectFactory<T> factory;
    private final int maxSize;
```

The Pool class has three members. These include an ArrayList to store pooled objects, a PoolObjectFactory that is used to generate new instances of the type held by the class, and a member that stores the maximum number of objects the Pool can hold. The last bit is needed so our Pool does not grow indefinitely; otherwise, we might run into an out-of-memory exception.

```
    public Pool(PoolObjectFactory<T> factory, int maxSize) {
        this.factory = factory;
        this.maxSize = maxSize;
        this.freeObjects = new ArrayList<T>(maxSize);
    }
```

The constructor of the Pool class takes a PoolObjectFactory and the maximum number of objects it should store. We store both parameters in the respective members and instantiate a new ArrayList with the capacity set to the maximum number of objects.

```
public T newObject() {
        T object = null;

if (freeObjects.size() == 0)
            object = factory.createObject();
else
            object = freeObjects.remove(freeObjects.size() - 1);

return object;
    }
```

The newObject() method is responsible for either handing us a brand-new instance of the type held by the Pool, via the PoolObjectFactory.newObject() method, or it returns a pooled instance in case there's one in the freeObjectsArrayList. If we use this method, we get recycled objects as long as the Pool has some stored in the freeObjects list. Otherwise, the method creates a new one via the factory.

```
public void free(T object) {
    if (freeObjects.size() < maxSize)
        freeObjects.add(object);
    }
}
```

The free() method lets us reinsert objects that we no longer use. It simply inserts the object into the freeObjects list if it is not yet filled to capacity. If the list is full, the object is not added, and it is likely to be consumed by the garbage collector the next time it executes.

So, how can we use that class? We'll look at some pseudocode usage of the Pool class in conjunction with touch events.

```
PoolObjectFactory<TouchEvent> factory = new PoolObjectFactory<TouchEvent>() {
    @Override
    public TouchEvent createObject() {
        return new TouchEvent();
    }
};
Pool<TouchEvent> touchEventPool = new Pool<TouchEvent>(factory, 50);
TouchEvent touchEvent = touchEventPool.newObject();
… do something here …
touchEventPool.free(touchEvent);
```

First, we define a PoolObjectFactory that creates TouchEvent instances. Next we instantiate the Pool by telling it to use our factory and that it should maximally store 50 TouchEvents. When we want a new TouchEvent from the Pool, we call the Pool's newObject() method. Initially, the Pool is empty, so it will ask the factory to create a brand new TouchEvent instance. When we no longer need the TouchEvent, we reinsert it into the Pool by calling the Pool's free() method. The next time we call the newObject() method, we get the same TouchEvent instance and recycle it to avoid problems with the garbage collector. This class is useful in a couple places. Please note that you must be careful to fully reinitialize reused when they're fetched from the Pool.

KeyboardHandler: Up, Up, Down, Down, Left, Right . . .

The KeyboardHandler must fulfill a couple tasks. First, it must connect with the View from which keyboard events are to be received. Next, it must store the current state of each key for polling. It must also keep a list of KeyEvent instances that we designed in Chapter 3 for event-based input handling. Finally, it must properly synchronize everything since it will receive events on the UI thread while being polled from our main game loop, which is executed on a different thread. This is a lot of work! As a refresher, we'll show you the KeyEvent class that we defined in Chapter 3 as part of the Input interface.

```
public static class KeyEvent {
    public static final int KEY_DOWN = 0;
    public static final int KEY_UP = 1;
```

```
    public int type;
    public int keyCode;
    public char keyChar;
}
```

This class simply defines two constants that encode the key event type along with three members while holding the type, key code, and Unicode character of the event. With this, we can implement our handler.

Listing 5–8 shows the implementation of the handler with the Android APIs discussed earlier and our new Pool class.

Listing 5–8. *KeyboardHandler.java: Handling Keys Since 2010*

```
package com.badlogic.androidgames.framework.impl;

import java.util.ArrayList;
import java.util.List;

import android.view.View;
import android.view.View.OnKeyListener;

import com.badlogic.androidgames.framework.Input.KeyEvent;
import com.badlogic.androidgames.framework.Pool;
import com.badlogic.androidgames.framework.Pool.PoolObjectFactory;

public class KeyboardHandler implements OnKeyListener {
    boolean[] pressedKeys = new boolean[128];
    Pool<KeyEvent> keyEventPool;
    List<KeyEvent> keyEventsBuffer = new ArrayList<KeyEvent>();
    List<KeyEvent> keyEvents = new ArrayList<KeyEvent>();
```

The KeyboardHandler class implements the OnKeyListener interface so that it can receive key events from a View. The members are next.

The first member is an array holding 128 Booleans. We store the current state (pressed or not) of each key in this array. It is indexed by the key's key code. Luckily for us, the android.view.KeyEvent.KEYCODE_XXX constants (which encode the key codes) are all between 0 and 127, so we can store them in a garbage collector–friendly form. Note that by an unlucky accident, our KeyEvent class shares its name with the Android KeyEvent class, of which instances get passed to our OnKeyEventListener.onKeyEvent() method. This slight confusion is only limited to this handler code. As there's no better name for a key event than "KeyEvent," we chose to live with this short-lived confusion.

The next member is a Pool that holds the instances of our KeyEvent class. We don't want to make the garbage collector angry, so we recycle all the KeyEvent objects we create.

The third member stores the KeyEvents that have not yet been consumed by our game. Each time we get a new key event on the UI thread, we add it to this list.

The last member stores the KeyEvents that we return by calling the
KeyboardHandler.getKeyEvents(). In the following sections, we'll see why we have to
double-buffer the key events.

```
public KeyboardHandler(View view) {
    PoolObjectFactory<KeyEvent> factory = new PoolObjectFactory<KeyEvent>() {
        @Override
        public KeyEvent createObject() {
            return new KeyEvent();
        }
    };
    keyEventPool = new Pool<KeyEvent>(factory, 100);
    view.setOnKeyListener(this);
    view.setFocusableInTouchMode(true);
    view.requestFocus();
}
```

The constructor has a single parameter consisting of the View from which we want to
receive key events. We create the Pool instance with a proper PoolObjectFactory,
register the handler as an OnKeyListener with the View, and finally, make sure that the
View will receive key events by making it the focused View.

```
@Override
public boolean onKey(View v, int keyCode, android.view.KeyEvent event) {
    if (event.getAction() == android.view.KeyEvent.ACTION_MULTIPLE)
        return false;

    synchronized (this) {
        KeyEvent keyEvent = keyEventPool.newObject();
        keyEvent.keyCode = keyCode;
        keyEvent.keyChar = (char) event.getUnicodeChar();
        if (event.getAction() == android.view.KeyEvent.ACTION_DOWN) {
            keyEvent.type = KeyEvent.KEY_DOWN;
            if(keyCode > 0 && keyCode < 127)
                pressedKeys[keyCode] = true;
        }
        if (event.getAction() == android.view.KeyEvent.ACTION_UP) {
            keyEvent.type = KeyEvent.KEY_UP;
            if(keyCode > 0 && keyCode < 127)
                pressedKeys[keyCode] = false;
        }
        keyEventsBuffer.add(keyEvent);
    }
    return false;
}
```

Next, we will discuss our implementation of the OnKeyListener.onKey() interface
method, which is called each time the View receives a new key event. We start by
ignoring any (Android) key events that encode a KeyEvent.ACTION_MULTIPLE event. These
are not relevant in our context. This is followed by a synchronized block. Remember, the
events are received on the UI thread and read on the main loop thread, so we have to
make sure that none of our members are accessed in parallel.

Within the synchronized block, we first fetch a KeyEvent instance (of our KeyEvent implementation) from the Pool. This will either get us a recycled instance or a brand new one, depending on the state of the Pool. Next, we set the KeyEvent's keyCode and keyChar members based on the contents of the Android KeyEvent that were passed to the method. Then, we decode the Android KeyEvent type and set the type of our KeyEvent, as well as the element in the pressedKey array, accordingly. Finally, we add our KeyEvent to the previously defined keyEventBuffer list.

```
public boolean isKeyPressed(int keyCode) {
    if (keyCode < 0 || keyCode > 127)
        return false;
    return pressedKeys[keyCode];
}
```

The next method of our handler the isKeyPressed() method, which implements the semantics of Input.isKeyPressed(). First, we pass in an integer that specifies the key code (one of the Android KeyEvent.KEYCODE_XXX constants) and returns whether that key is pressed or not. We do this by looking up the state of the key in the pressedKey array after some range checking. Remember, we set the elements of this array in the previous method, which gets called on the UI thread. Since we are working with primitive types again, there's no need for synchronization.

```
public List<KeyEvent> getKeyEvents() {
    synchronized (this) {
        int len = keyEvents.size();
        for (int i = 0; i < len; i++)
            keyEventPool.free(keyEvents.get(i));
        keyEvents.clear();
        keyEvents.addAll(keyEventsBuffer);
        keyEventsBuffer.clear();
        return keyEvents;
    }
}
```

The last method of our handler is called getKeyEvents(), and it implements the semantics of the Input.getKeyEvents() method. Once again, we start with a synchronized block and remember that this method will be called from a different thread.

Next, we loop through the keyEvents array, and insert all of its KeyEvents into our Pool. Remember, we fetch instances from the Pool in the onKey() method on the UI thread. Here, we reinsert them into the Pool. But isn't the keyEvents list empty? Yes, but only the first time we invoke that method. To understand why, you have to grasp the rest of the method.

After our mysterious Pool insertion loop, we clear the keyEvents list and fill it with the events in our keyEventsBuffer list. Finally, we clear the keyEventsBuffer list and return the newly–filled keyEvents list to the caller. What is happening here?

We'll use a simple example to illustrate this. First, we'll examine what happens to the keyEvents and the keyEventsBuffer lists, as well as to our Pool each time a new event arrives on the UI thread or the game fetches the events in the main thread:

```
UI thread: onKey() ->
        keyEvents = { }, keyEventsBuffer = {KeyEvent1}, pool = { }
Main thread: getKeyEvents() ->
        keyEvents = {KeyEvent1}, keyEventsBuffer = { }, pool { }
UI thread: onKey() ->
        keyEvents = {KeyEvent1}, keyEventsBuffer = {KeyEvent2}, pool { }
Main thread: getKeyEvents() ->
        keyEvents = {KeyEvent2}, keyEventsBuffer = { }, pool = {KeyEvent1}
UI thread: onKey() ->
        keyEvents = {KeyEvent2}, keyEventsBuffer = {KeyEvent1}, pool = { }
```

1. We get a new event in the UI thread. There's nothing in the Pool yet, so a new KeyEvent instance (KeyEvent1) is created and inserted into the keyEventsBuffer list.

2. We call getKeyEvents() on the main thread. getKeyEvents() takes KeyEvent1 from the keyEventsBuffer list and puts it into the keyEvents list that is returns to the caller.

3. We get another event on the UI thread. We still have nothing in the Pool, so a new KeyEvent instance (KeyEvent2) is created and inserted into the keyEventsBuffer list.

4. The main thread calls getKeyEvents() again. Now, something interesting happens. Upon entry into the method, the keyEvents list still holds KeyEvent1. The insertion loop will place that event into our Pool. It then clears the keyEvents list and inserts any KeyEvent into the keyEventsBuffer, in this case, KeyEvent2. We just recycled a key event.

5. Another key event arrives on the UI thread. This time, we have a free KeyEvent in our Pool, which we happily reuse. Incredibly, there's no garbage collection!

This mechanism comes with one caveat, which is that we have to call KeyboardHandler.getKeyEvents() frequently or the keyEvents list fills up quickly, and no objects are returned to the Pool. Problems can be avoided as long as we remember this.

Touch Handlers

Now it is time to consider fragmentation. In the last chapter, we revealed that multitouch is only supported on Android versions greater than 1.6. All the nice constants we used in our multitouch code (for example, MotionEvent.ACTION_POINTER_ID_MASK) are not available to us on Android 1.5 or 1.6. We can use them in our code if we set the build target of our project to an Android version that has this API; however, the application will crash on any device running Android 1.5 or 1.6. We want our games to run on all currently available Android versions, so how do we solve this problem?

We employ a simple trick. We write two handlers, one using the single-touch API in Android 1.5, and another using the multitouch API in Android 2.0 and above. This is safe as long as we don't execute the multitouch handler code on an Android device lower than version 2.0. The VM won't load the code, and it won't throw exceptions continuously. All we need to do is find out which Android version the device is running and instantiate the proper handler. You'll see how this works when we discuss the AndroidInput class. For now, let's concentrate on the two handlers.

The TouchHandler Interface

In order to use our two handler classes interchangeably, we need to define a common interface. Listing 5–9 presents the TouchHandler interface.

Listing 5–9. *TouchHandler.java, to Be Implemented for Android 1.5 and 1.6.*

```
package com.badlogic.androidgames.framework.impl;

import java.util.List;

import android.view.View.OnTouchListener;

import com.badlogic.androidgames.framework.Input.TouchEvent;

public interface TouchHandler extends OnTouchListener {
    public boolean isTouchDown(int pointer);

    public int getTouchX(int pointer);

    public int getTouchY(int pointer);

    public List<TouchEvent> getTouchEvents();
}
```

All TouchHandlers must implement the OnTouchListener interface, which is used to register the handler with a View. The methods of the interface correspond to the respective methods of the Input interface defined in Chapter 3. The first three are for polling the state of a specific pointer ID, and the last is for getting TouchEvents with which to perform event-based input handling. Note that the polling methods take pointer IDs that can be any number and are given by the touch event.

The SingleTouchHandler Class

In the case of our single-touch handler, we ignore any IDs other than zero. To recap, we'll recall the TouchEvent class defined in Chapter 3 as part of the Input interface.

```
public static class TouchEvent {
    public static final int TOUCH_DOWN = 0;
    public static final int TOUCH_UP = 1;
    public static final int TOUCH_DRAGGED = 2;

    public int type;
    public int x, y;
    public int pointer;
}
```

Like the KeyEvent class, it defines a couple of constants that echo the touch event's type, along with the x- and y-coordinates in the coordinate system of the View and the pointer ID. Listing 5–10 shows the implementation of the TouchHandler interface for Android 1.5 and 1.6.

Listing 5–10. *SingleTouchHandler.java; Good with Single Touch, Not So Good with Multitouch*

```
package com.badlogic.androidgames.framework.impl;

import java.util.ArrayList;
import java.util.List;

import android.view.MotionEvent;
import android.view.View;

import com.badlogic.androidgames.framework.Pool;
import com.badlogic.androidgames.framework.Input.TouchEvent;
import com.badlogic.androidgames.framework.Pool.PoolObjectFactory;

public class SingleTouchHandler implements TouchHandler {
    boolean isTouched;
    int touchX;
    int touchY;
    Pool<TouchEvent> touchEventPool;
    List<TouchEvent> touchEvents = new ArrayList<TouchEvent>();
    List<TouchEvent> touchEventsBuffer = new ArrayList<TouchEvent>();
    float scaleX;
    float scaleY;
```

We start by letting the class implement the TouchHandler interface, which also means that we must implement the OnTouchListener interface. Next, we have three members that store the current state of the touchscreen for one finger, followed by a Pool and two lists that hold the TouchEvents. This is the same as in the KeyboardHandler. We also have two members, scaleX and scaleY. We'll address these in the following sections and use them to cope with different screen resolutions.

> **NOTE:** Of course, we could make this more elegant by deriving the KeyboardHandler and SingleTouchHandler from a base class that handles all matters regarding pooling and synchronization. However, it would have complicated the explanation even more, so instead, we'll write a few more lines of code.

```
public SingleTouchHandler(View view, float scaleX, float scaleY) {
        PoolObjectFactory<TouchEvent> factory = new PoolObjectFactory<TouchEvent>() {
            @Override
            public TouchEvent createObject() {
                return new TouchEvent();
            }
        };
        touchEventPool = new Pool<TouchEvent>(factory, 100);
        view.setOnTouchListener(this);
```

```
            this.scaleX = scaleX;
            this.scaleY = scaleY;
    }
```

In the constructor, we register the handler as an OnTouchListener and set up the Pool that we use to recycle TouchEvents. We also store the scaleX and scaleY parameters that are passed to the constructor (ignore them for now).

```
@Override
    public boolean onTouch(View v, MotionEvent event) {
        synchronized(this) {
            TouchEvent touchEvent = touchEventPool.newObject();
            switch (event.getAction()) {
            case MotionEvent.ACTION_DOWN:
                touchEvent.type = TouchEvent.TOUCH_DOWN;
                isTouched = true;
                break;
            case MotionEvent.ACTION_MOVE:
                touchEvent.type = TouchEvent.TOUCH_DRAGGED;
                isTouched = true;
                break;
            case MotionEvent.ACTION_CANCEL:
            case MotionEvent.ACTION_UP:
                touchEvent.type = TouchEvent.TOUCH_UP;
                isTouched = false;
                break;
            }

            touchEvent.x = touchX = (int)(event.getX() * scaleX);
            touchEvent.y = touchY = (int)(event.getY() * scaleY);
            touchEventsBuffer.add(touchEvent);

            return true;
        }
    }
```

The onTouch() method achieves the same outcome as our KeyboardHandler's onKey() method; the only difference is that now we handle TouchEvents instead of KeyEvents. All the synchronization, pooling, and MotionEvent handling are already known to us. The only interesting thing is that we multiply the reported x- and y-coordinates of a touch event by scaleX and scaleY. This is important to remember as we'll return to it in the following sections.

```
@Override
    public boolean isTouchDown(int pointer) {
        synchronized(this) {
            if(pointer == 0)
                return isTouched;
            else
                return false;
        }
    }

    @Override
    public int getTouchX(int pointer) {
```

```
        synchronized(this) {
            return touchX;
        }
    }

    @Override
    public int getTouchY(int pointer) {
        synchronized(this) {
            return touchY;
        }
    }
```

The methods isTouchDown(), getTouchX(), and getTouchY() allow us to poll the state of the touchscreen based on the members that we set in the onTouch() method. The only noticeable thing about them is that they only return useful data for a pointer ID with a value of zero, since this class only supports single-touch screens.

```
@Override
    public List<TouchEvent> getTouchEvents() {
        synchronized(this) {
            int len = touchEvents.size();
            for( int i = 0; i < len; i++ )
                touchEventPool.free(touchEvents.get(i));
            touchEvents.clear();
            touchEvents.addAll(touchEventsBuffer);
            touchEventsBuffer.clear();
            return touchEvents;
        }
    }
}
```

The final method, SingleTouchHandler.getTouchEvents(), should be familiar to you, and is similar to the KeyboardHandler.getKeyEvents() methods. Remember that we call this method frequently the touchEvents list doesn't fill up.

The MultiTouchHandler

For multitouch handling, we use a class called MultiTouchHandler, as shown in Listing 5–11.

Listing 5–11. *MultiTouchHandler.java (More of the Same)*

```
package com.badlogic.androidgames.framework.impl;

import java.util.ArrayList;
import java.util.List;

import android.view.MotionEvent;
import android.view.View;

import com.badlogic.androidgames.framework.Input.TouchEvent;
import com.badlogic.androidgames.framework.Pool;
import com.badlogic.androidgames.framework.Pool.PoolObjectFactory;

public class MultiTouchHandler implements TouchHandler {
```

```java
        private static final int MAX_TOUCHPOINTS = 10;

    boolean[] isTouched = new boolean[MAX_TOUCHPOINTS];
    int[] touchX = new int[MAX_TOUCHPOINTS];
    int[] touchY = new int[MAX_TOUCHPOINTS];
    int[] id = new int[MAX_TOUCHPOINTS];
    Pool<TouchEvent> touchEventPool;
    List<TouchEvent> touchEvents = new ArrayList<TouchEvent>();
    List<TouchEvent> touchEventsBuffer = new ArrayList<TouchEvent>();
    float scaleX;
    float scaleY;

    public MultiTouchHandler(View view, float scaleX, float scaleY) {
        PoolObjectFactory<TouchEvent> factory = new PoolObjectFactory<TouchEvent>() {
            @Override
            public TouchEvent createObject() {
                return new TouchEvent();
            }
        };
        touchEventPool = new Pool<TouchEvent>(factory, 100);
        view.setOnTouchListener(this);

        this.scaleX = scaleX;
        this.scaleY = scaleY;
    }

    @Override
    public boolean onTouch(View v, MotionEvent event) {
        synchronized (this) {
            int action = event.getAction() & MotionEvent.ACTION_MASK;
            int pointerIndex = (event.getAction() & MotionEvent.ACTION_POINTER_ID_MASK)
>> MotionEvent.ACTION_POINTER_ID_SHIFT;
            int pointerCount = event.getPointerCount();
            TouchEvent touchEvent;
            for (int i = 0; i < MAX_TOUCHPOINTS; i++) {
                if (i >= pointerCount) {
                    isTouched[i] = false;
                    id[i] = -1;
                    continue;
                }
                int pointerId = event.getPointerId(i);
                if (event.getAction() != MotionEvent.ACTION_MOVE && i != pointerIndex) {
                    // if it's an up/down/cancel/out event, mask the id to see if we
should process it for this touch
                    // point
                    continue;
                }
                switch (action) {
                case MotionEvent.ACTION_DOWN:
                case MotionEvent.ACTION_POINTER_DOWN:
                    touchEvent = touchEventPool.newObject();
                    touchEvent.type = TouchEvent.TOUCH_DOWN;
                    touchEvent.pointer = pointerId;
                    touchEvent.x = touchX[i] = (int) (event.getX(i) * scaleX);
                    touchEvent.y = touchY[i] = (int) (event.getY(i) * scaleY);
```

```
                        isTouched[i] = true;
                        id[i] = pointerId;
                        touchEventsBuffer.add(touchEvent);
                        break;

                case MotionEvent.ACTION_UP:
                case MotionEvent.ACTION_POINTER_UP:
                case MotionEvent.ACTION_CANCEL:
                    touchEvent = touchEventPool.newObject();
                    touchEvent.type = TouchEvent.TOUCH_UP;
                    touchEvent.pointer = pointerId;
                    touchEvent.x = touchX[i] = (int) (event.getX(i) * scaleX);
                    touchEvent.y = touchY[i] = (int) (event.getY(i) * scaleY);
                    isTouched[i] = false;
                    id[i] = -1;
                    touchEventsBuffer.add(touchEvent);
                    break;

                case MotionEvent.ACTION_MOVE:
                    touchEvent = touchEventPool.newObject();
                    touchEvent.type = TouchEvent.TOUCH_DRAGGED;
                    touchEvent.pointer = pointerId;
                    touchEvent.x = touchX[i] = (int) (event.getX(i) * scaleX);
                    touchEvent.y = touchY[i] = (int) (event.getY(i) * scaleY);
                    isTouched[i] = true;
                    id[i] = pointerId;
                    touchEventsBuffer.add(touchEvent);
                    break;
                }
            }
        return true;
        }
    }

    @Override
    public boolean isTouchDown(int pointer) {
        synchronized (this) {
            int index = getIndex(pointer);
            if (index < 0 || index >= MAX_TOUCHPOINTS)
                return false;
            else
                return isTouched[index];
        }
    }

    @Override
    public int getTouchX(int pointer) {
        synchronized (this) {
            int index = getIndex(pointer);
            if (index < 0 || index >= MAX_TOUCHPOINTS)
                return 0;
            else
                return touchX[index];
        }
    }
```

```
        @Override
        public int getTouchY(int pointer) {
            synchronized (this) {
                int index = getIndex(pointer);
                if (index < 0 || index >= MAX_TOUCHPOINTS)
                    return 0;
                else
                    return touchY[index];
            }
        }

        @Override
        public List<TouchEvent> getTouchEvents() {
            synchronized (this) {
                int len = touchEvents.size();
                for (int i = 0; i < len; i++)
                    touchEventPool.free(touchEvents.get(i));
                touchEvents.clear();
                touchEvents.addAll(touchEventsBuffer);
                touchEventsBuffer.clear();
                return touchEvents;
            }
        }

        // returns the index for a given pointerId or -1 if no index.
        private int getIndex(int pointerId) {
            for (int i = 0; i < MAX_TOUCHPOINTS; i++) {
                if (id[i] == pointerId) {
                    return i;
                }
            }
            return -1;
        }
    }
```

The onTouch() method looks as intimidating as our test example in the last chapter. However, all we need to do is marry that test code with our event pooling and synchronization, which we've already talked about in detail. The only real difference from the SingleTouchHandler.onTouch() method is that we handle multiple pointers and set the TouchEvent.pointer member accordingly (instead of using a value of zero).

The polling methods, isTouchDown(), getTouchX(), and getTouchY( )should look familiar as well. We perform some error–checking and then fetch the corresponding pointer state for the corresponding pointer index from one of the member arrays that we fill in the onTouch() method.

```
@Override
    public List<TouchEvent> getTouchEvents() {
        synchronized (this) {
            int len = touchEvents.size();
            for (int i = 0; i < len; i++)
                touchEventPool.free(touchEvents.get(i));
            touchEvents.clear();
            touchEvents.addAll(touchEventsBuffer);
```

```
                touchEventsBuffer.clear();
                return touchEvents;
            }
        }
    }
```

The final method, getTouchEvents(), is exactly the same as the corresponding method
in SingleTouchHandler.getTouchEvents(). Now that we are equipped with all these
handlers, we can implement the Input interface.

AndroidInput: The Great Coordinator

The Input implementation of our game framework ties together all the handlers we have
developed. Any method calls are delegated to the corresponding handler. The only
interesting part of this implementation is choosing which TouchHandler implementation
to use, based on the Android version the device is running. Listing 5–12 shows you an
implementation called AndroidInput.

Listing 5–12. *AndroidInput.java; Handling the Handlers with Style*

```java
package com.badlogic.androidgames.framework.impl;

import java.util.List;

import android.content.Context;
import android.os.Build.VERSION;
import android.view.View;

import com.badlogic.androidgames.framework.Input;

public class AndroidInput implements Input {
    AccelerometerHandler accelHandler;
    KeyboardHandler keyHandler;
    TouchHandler touchHandler;
```

We start by letting the class implement the Input interface defined in Chapter 3. This
leads us to three members: an AccelerometerHandler, a KeyboardHandler, and a
TouchHandler.

```java
public AndroidInput(Context context, View view, float scaleX, float scaleY) {
    accelHandler = new AccelerometerHandler(context);
    keyHandler = new KeyboardHandler(view);
    if (Integer.parseInt(VERSION.SDK) < 5)
        touchHandler = new SingleTouchHandler(view, scaleX, scaleY);
    else
        touchHandler = new MultiTouchHandler(view, scaleX, scaleY);
}
```

These members are initialized in the constructor, which takes a Context, a View, and the
scaleX and scaleY parameters, which we can ignore again. The AccelerometerHandler
is instantiated via the Context parameter, as the KeyboardHandler needs the View that is
passed in.

To decide which TouchHandler to use, we simply check the Android version that the application uses to run. This can be done using the VERSION.SDK string, which is a constant provided by the Android API. It is unclear why this is a string since it directly encodes the SDK version numbers we use in our manifest file. Therefore, we need to make it into an integer in order to do some comparisons. The first Android version to support the multitouch API was version 2.0, which corresponds to SDK version 5. If the current device runs a lower Android version, we instantiate the SingleTouchHandler; otherwise, we use the MultiTouchHandler. At an API level, this is all the fragmentation we need to care about. When we start rendering OpenGL, we'll hit a few more fragmentation issues, but there is no need to worry—they are easily resolved, just like the touch API problems.

```java
@Override
public boolean isKeyPressed(int keyCode) {
    return keyHandler.isKeyPressed(keyCode);
}

@Override
public boolean isTouchDown(int pointer) {
    return touchHandler.isTouchDown(pointer);
}

@Override
public int getTouchX(int pointer) {
    return touchHandler.getTouchX(pointer);
}

@Override
public int getTouchY(int pointer) {
    return touchHandler.getTouchY(pointer);
}

@Override
public float getAccelX() {
    return accelHandler.getAccelX();
}

@Override
public float getAccelY() {
    return accelHandler.getAccelY();
}

@Override
public float getAccelZ() {
    return accelHandler.getAccelZ();
}

@Override
public List<TouchEvent> getTouchEvents() {
    return touchHandler.getTouchEvents();
}

@Override
public List<KeyEvent> getKeyEvents() {
```

```
        return keyHandler.getKeyEvents();
    }
}
```

The rest of this class is self-explanatory. Each method call is delegated to the appropriate handler, which does the actual work. With this, we have finished the input API of our game framework. Next, we'll discuss graphics.

AndroidGraphics and AndroidPixmap: Double Rainbow

It's time to get back to our most beloved topic, graphics programming. In Chapter 3, we defined two interfaces called Graphics and Pixmap. Now, we're going to implement them based on what you learned in Chapter 4. However, there's one thing we have yet to consider: how to handle different screen sizes and resolutions.

Handling Different Screen Sizes and Resolutions

Android has supported different screen resolutions since version 1.6. It can handle resolutions ranging from 240×320 pixels to a full HDTV resolution of 1920×1080. In the last chapter, we discussed the effect of different screen resolutions and physical screen sizes. For instance, drawing with absolute coordinates and sizes given in pixels will produce unexpected results. On again, Figure 5–1 shows you what happens when we render a 100×100-pixel rectangle with the upper-left corner at (219,379) on 480×800 and 320×480 screens.

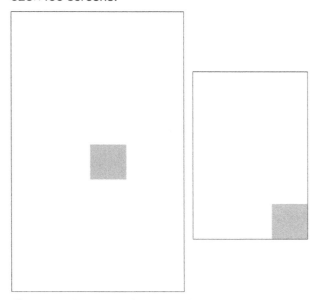

Figure 5–1. *A 100×100-pixel rectangle drawn at (219,379) on a 480×800 screen (left) and a 320×480 screen (right).*

This difference is problematic for two reasons. First, we can't draw our game and assume a fixed resolution. The second reason is more subtle: in Figure 5–1, we assumed that both screens have the same density (that is, each pixel has the same physical size on both devices), but this is rarely the case in reality.

Density

Density is usually specified in pixels per inch or pixels per centimeter (sometimes you'll hear about dots per inch, which is not technically correct). The Nexus One has a 480×800-pixel screen with a physical size of 8×4.8 centimeters. The older HTC Hero has a 320×480-pixel screen with a physical size of 6.5×4.5 centimeters. That's 100 pixels per centimeter on both axes on the Nexus One, and roughly 71 pixels per centimeter on both axes on the Hero. We can easily calculate the pixels per centimeter using the following equation.

pixels per centimeter (on x-axis) = width in pixels / width in centimeters

Or:

pixels per centimeter (on y-axis) = height in pixels / height in centimeters

Usually, we only need to calculate this on a single axis since the physical pixels are square (they're actually three pixels, but we'll ignore that here).

How big would a 100×100-pixel rectangle be in centimeters? On the Nexus One, we have a 1×1-centimeter rectangle; while the Hero has a 1.4×1.4-centimeter rectangle. This is something we need to account for if, for example, we are trying to provide buttons that are big enough for the average thumb on all screen sizes. This example implies that this is a major issue that could present huge problems; however, it usually doesn't. We need to make sure that our buttons are a decent size on high-density screens (for example, the Nexus One) since they will automatically be big enough on low-density screens.

Aspect Ratio

Aspect ratio is another problem to consider. The aspect ratio of a screen is the ratio between the width and height, either in pixels or centimeters. We can calculate aspect ratio using the following equation.

pixel aspect ratio = width in pixels / height in pixels

Or:

physical aspect ratio = width in centimeters / height in centimeters

Here *width* and *height* usually means the width and height in landscape mode. The Nexus One has a pixel and physical aspect ratio of ~1.66. The Hero has a pixel and physical aspect ratio of 1.5. What does this mean? On the Nexus One, we have more pixels available on the x-axis in landscape mode relative to height, than we have on the Hero. Figure 5–2 illustrates this with screenshots from Replica Island on both devices.

> **NOTE:** This book uses the metric system. We know this might be an inconvenience if you are familiar with inches and pounds. However, as we will be considering some physics problems in the following chapters, it's best get used to it now since physics problems are usually defined in the metric system. Remember that 1 inch is roughly 2.54 centimeters.

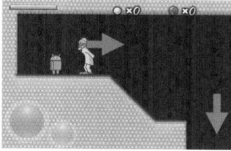

Figure 5–2. *Replica Island on the Nexus One (top) and the HTC Hero (bottom).*

The Nexus One displays a bit more on the x-axis. However, everything is identical on the y-axis. What did the creator of Replica Island do in this case?

Coping with Different Aspect Ratios

Replica Island serves as a very useful example of the aspect ratio problem. The game was originally designed to fit on a 480×320-pixel screen, including all "the sprites," such as the robot and the doctor, the tiles of "the world," and the UI elements (the buttons at the bottom left and the status info at the top of the screen). When the game is rendered on a Hero, each pixel in the sprite bitmaps, map to exactly one pixel on the screen. On a Nexus One, everything is scaled up while rendering, so one pixel of a sprite actually takes up 1.5 pixels on the screen. In other words, a 32×32-pixel sprite will be 48×48 pixels on the screen. This scaling factor is easily calculated using the following equation.

scaling factor (on x-axis) = screen width in pixels / target width in pixels

And:

scaling factor (on y-axis) = screen height in pixels / target height in pixels

The target width and height are equal to the screen resolution for which the graphical assets were designed; in Replica Island, the dimensions are 480×320 pixels. For the Nexus One, there is a scaling factor of 1.66 on the x-axis and a scaling factor of 1.5 on the y-axis. Why are the scaling factors on the two axes different?

This is due to the fact that two screen resolutions have different aspect ratios. If we simply stretch a 480×320-pixel image to an 800×480-pixel image, the original image is stretched on the x-axis. For most games, this will be insignificant so we can simply draw our graphical assets for a specific target resolution and stretch them to the actual screen resolution while rendering (remember the Bitmap.drawBitmap() method).

However, for some games, you might want to use a more complicated method. Figure 5–3 shows Replica Island scaled up from 480×320 to 800×480 pixels and overlaid with a faint image of how it actually looks.

Figure 5–3. *Replica Island stretched from 480×320 to 800×480 pixels, overlaid with a faint image of how it is rendered on an 800×480-pixel display.*

Replica Island performs normal stretching on the y-axis using the scaling factor we just calculated (1.5), but instead of using the x-axis scaling factor (1.66), which would squish the image, it uses the y-axis scaling factor. This trick allows all objects on the screen to keep their aspect ratio. A 32×32-pixel sprite becomes 48×48 pixels instead of 53×48 pixels. However, this also means that our coordinate system is no longer bounded between (0,0) and (479,319); instead, it ranges from (0,0) to (533,319). This is why we see more of Replica Island on a Nexus One than on an HTC Hero.

Note, however, that using this fancy method might be inappropriate for some games. For example, if the world size depends on the screen aspect ratio, players with wider screens could have an unfair advantage. This would be the case for a game like StarCraft 2.l Finally, if you want the entire game to fit onto a single screen, like in Mr. Nom, it is better to use the simpler stretching method; if we use the second version, there will be blank space left over on wider screens.

A Simpler Solution

One advantage of Replica Island is that it does all this stretching and scaling via OpenGL ES, which is hardware accelerated. So far, we've only discussed how to draw to a Bitmap and a View via the Canvas class, which involves slow number-crunching on the CPU and doesn't involve hardware acceleration on the GPU.

With this in mind, we perform a simple trick by creating a framebuffer in the form of a Bitmap instance with our target resolution. This way, we don't have to worry about the actual screen resolution when we design our graphical assets or render them via code. Instead, we pretend that the screen resolution is the same on all devices, and all our draw calls target this "virtual" framebuffer Bitmap via a Canvas instance. When we're done rendering a frame, we simply draw this framebuffer Bitmap to our SurfaceView via a call to the Canvas.drawBitmap() method, which allows us to draw a stretched Bitmap.

If we want to use the same technique as Replica Island, we need to adjust the size of our framebuffer on the bigger axis (that is, on the x-axis in landscape mode and on the y-axis in portrait mode). We also have to make sure to fill the extra pixels to avoid blank space.

The Implementation

Let's summarize everything in a work plan.

- We design all our graphic assets for a fixed target resolution (320×480 in the case of Mr. Nom).

- We create a Bitmap that is the same size as our target resolution and direct all our drawing calls to it, effectively working in a fixed-coordinate system.

- When we are done drawing a frame, we draw our framebuffer Bitmap that is stretched to the SurfaceView. On devices with a lower screen resolution, the image is scaled down; on devices with a higher resolution, it is scaled up.

- When we do our scaling trick, we make sure that all the UI elements with which the user interacts are big enough for all screen densities. We can do this in the graphic asset–design phase using the sizes of actual devices in combination with the previously mentioned formulas.

Now that we know how to handle different screen resolutions and densities, we can explain the scaleX and scaleY variables we encountered when we implemented the SingleTouchHandler and MultiTouchHandler in the previous sections.

All of our game code will work with our fixed target resolution (320×480 pixels). If we receive touch events on a device that has a higher or lower resolution, the x- and y-coordinates of those events will be defined in the View's coordinate system, but not in our target resolution coordinate system. Therefore, it is necessary to transform the coordinates from their original system to our system, which is based on the scaling factors. To do this, we use the following equations.

```
transformed touch x = real touch x * (target pixels on x axis / real pixels on x axis)
transformed touch y = real touch y * (target pixels on y axis / real pixels on y axis)
```

Let's calculate a simple example for a target resolution of 320×480 pixels and a device with a resolution of 480×800 pixels. If we touch the middle of the screen, we receive an event with the coordinates (240,400). Using the two preceding formulas, we arrive at the following equations, which are exactly in the middle of our target coordinate system.

```
transformed touch x = 240 * (320 / 480) = 160
transformed touch y = 400 * (480 / 800) = 240
```

Let's do another one, assuming a real resolution of 240×320, again touching the middle of the screen, at (120,160).

```
transformed touch x = 120 * (320 / 240) = 160
transformed touch y = 160 * (480 / 320) = 240
```

This works in both directions. If we multiply the real touch event coordinates by the target factor divided by the real factor, we don't have to worry about transforming our actual game code. All the touch coordinates will be expressed in our fixed–target coordinate system.

With that issue out of our way, we can implement the last few classes of our game framework.

AndroidPixmap: Pixels for the People

According to the design of our Pixmap interface from Chapter 3, there's not much to implement. Listing 5–13 presents the code.

Listing 5–13. *AndroidPixmap.java, a Pixmap Implementation Wrapping a Bitmap*

```java
package com.badlogic.androidgames.framework.impl;

import android.graphics.Bitmap;

import com.badlogic.androidgames.framework.Graphics.PixmapFormat;
import com.badlogic.androidgames.framework.Pixmap;

public class AndroidPixmap implements Pixmap {
    Bitmap bitmap;
    PixmapFormat format;
```

```java
    public AndroidPixmap(Bitmap bitmap, PixmapFormat format) {
        this.bitmap = bitmap;
        this.format = format;
    }

    @Override
    public int getWidth() {
        return bitmap.getWidth();
    }

    @Override
    public int getHeight() {
        return bitmap.getHeight();
    }

    @Override
    public PixmapFormat getFormat() {
        return format;
    }

    @Override
    public void dispose() {
        bitmap.recycle();
    }
}
```

All we need to do is store the `Bitmap` instance that we wrap, along with its format, which is stored as a `PixmapFormat` enumeration value, as defined in Chapter 3. Additionally, we implement the required methods of the `Pixmap` interface so that we can query the width and height of the `Pixmap`, as well as its format, and ensure that the pixels can be dumped from RAM. Note that the `bitmap` member is package private, so we can access it in `AndroidGraphics`, which we'll implement now.

AndroidGraphics: Serving Our Drawing Needs

The `Graphics` interface we designed in Chapter 3 is also lean and mean. It will draw pixels, lines, rectangles, and `Pixmaps` to the framebuffer. As discussed, we'll use a `Bitmap` as our framebuffer and direct all drawing calls to it via a `Canvas`. It is also responsible for creating `Pixmap` instances from asset files. Therefore, we'll also need another `AssetManager`. Listing 5–14 shows the code for our implementation of the interface, `AndroidGraphics`.

Listing 5–14. *AndroidGraphics.java; Implementing the Graphics Interface*

```java
package com.badlogic.androidgames.framework.impl;

import java.io.IOException;
import java.io.InputStream;

import android.content.res.AssetManager;
import android.graphics.Bitmap;
import android.graphics.Bitmap.Config;
import android.graphics.BitmapFactory;
```

```
import android.graphics.BitmapFactory.Options;
import android.graphics.Canvas;
import android.graphics.Paint;
import android.graphics.Paint.Style;
import android.graphics.Rect;

import com.badlogic.androidgames.framework.Graphics;
import com.badlogic.androidgames.framework.Pixmap;

public class AndroidGraphics implements Graphics {
    AssetManager assets;
    Bitmap frameBuffer;
    Canvas canvas;
    Paint paint;
    Rect srcRect = new Rect();
    Rect dstRect = new Rect();
```

The class implements the Graphics interface. It contains an AssetManager member that
we use to load Bitmap instances, a Bitmap member that represents our artificial
framebuffer, a Canvas member that we use to draw to the artificial framebuffer, a Paint
we need for drawing, and two Rect members we need for implementing the
AndroidGraphics.drawPixmap() methods. These last three members are there so we
don't have to create new instances of these classes on every draw call. That would
create a number of problems for the garbage collector.

```
public AndroidGraphics(AssetManager assets, Bitmap frameBuffer) {
    this.assets = assets;
    this.frameBuffer = frameBuffer;
    this.canvas = new Canvas(frameBuffer);
    this.paint = new Paint();
}
```

In the constructor, we get an AssetManager and Bitmap that represent our artificial
framebuffer from the outside. We store these in the respective members and create the
Canvas instance that will draw the artificial framebuffer, as well as the Paint, which we
use for some of the drawing methods.

```
@Override
public Pixmap newPixmap(String fileName, PixmapFormat format) {
    Config config = null;
    if (format == PixmapFormat.RGB565)
        config = Config.RGB_565;
    else if (format == PixmapFormat.ARGB4444)
        config = Config.ARGB_4444;
    else
        config = Config.ARGB_8888;

    Options options = new Options();
    options.inPreferredConfig = config;

    InputStream in = null;
    Bitmap bitmap = null;
    try {
        in = assets.open(fileName);
        bitmap = BitmapFactory.decodeStream(in);
```

```
            if (bitmap == null)
                throw new RuntimeException("Couldn't load bitmap from asset '"
                        + fileName + "'");
        } catch (IOException e) {
            throw new RuntimeException("Couldn't load bitmap from asset '"
                    + fileName + "'");
        } finally {
            if (in != null) {
                try {
                    in.close();
                } catch (IOException e) {
                }
            }
        }
    }

    if (bitmap.getConfig() == Config.RGB_565)
        format = PixmapFormat.RGB565;
    else if (bitmap.getConfig() == Config.ARGB_4444)
        format = PixmapFormat.ARGB4444;
    else
        format = PixmapFormat.ARGB8888;

    return new AndroidPixmap(bitmap, format);
}
```

The newPixmap() method tries to load a Bitmap from an asset file, using the specified
PixmapFormat. We start by translating the PixmapFormat into one of the constants of the
Android Config class used in Chapter 4. Next, we create a new Options instance and set
our preferred color format. Then, we try to load the Bitmap from the asset via the
BitmapFactory, and throw a RuntimeException if something goes wrong. Otherwise, we
check what format the BitmapFactory used to load the Bitmap and translate it into a
PixmapFormat enumeration value. Remember that the BitmapFactory might decide to
ignore our desired color format, so we have to check to determine what it used to
decode the image. Finally, we construct a new AndroidBitmap instance based on the
Bitmap we loaded, as well as its PixmapFormat, and return it to the caller.

```
@Override
public void clear(int color) {
    canvas.drawRGB((color & 0xff0000) >> 16, (color & 0xff00) >> 8,
            (color & 0xff));
}
```

The clear() method extracts the red, green, and blue components of the specified 32-
bit ARGB color parameter and calls the Canvas.drawRGB() method, which clears our
artificial framebuffer with that color. This method ignores any alpha value of the specified
color, so we don't have to extract it.

```
@Override
public void drawPixel(int x, int y, int color) {
    paint.setColor(color);
    canvas.drawPoint(x, y, paint);
}
```

The drawPixel() method draws a pixel of our artificial framebuffer via the Canvas.drawPoint() method. First, we set the color of our paint member variable and pass it to the drawing method in addition to the x- and y-coordinates of the pixel.

```
@Override
public void drawLine(int x, int y, int x2, int y2, int color) {
    paint.setColor(color);
    canvas.drawLine(x, y, x2, y2, paint);
}
```

The drawLine() method draws the given line of the artificial framebuffer, using the paint member to specify the color when calling the Canvas.drawLine() method.

```
@Override
public void drawRect(int x, int y, int width, int height, int color) {
    paint.setColor(color);
    paint.setStyle(Style.FILL);
    canvas.drawRect(x, y, x + width - 1, y + width - 1, paint);
}
```

The drawRect() method sets the Paint member's color and style attributes so that we can draw a filled, colored rectangle. In the actual Canvas.drawRect() call, we have to transform the x, y, width, and height parameters of the coordinates in the top-left and bottom-right corners of the rectangle. For the top-left corner, we simply use the x and y parameters. For the bottom-right corner, we add the width and height to x and y and subtract 1. For example, if we render a rectangle with an x and y of (10,10) and a width and height of 2 and 2 and we don't subtract 1, the resulting rectangle on the screen will be 3×3 pixels in size.

```
@Override
public void drawPixmap(Pixmap pixmap, int x, int y, int srcX, int srcY,
        int srcWidth, int srcHeight) {
    srcRect.left = srcX;
    srcRect.top = srcY;
    srcRect.right = srcX + srcWidth - 1;
    srcRect.bottom = srcY + srcHeight - 1;

    dstRect.left = x;
    dstRect.top = y;
    dstRect.right = x + srcWidth - 1;
    dstRect.bottom = y + srcHeight - 1;

    canvas.drawBitmap(((AndroidPixmap) pixmap).bitmap, srcRect, dstRect,
            null);
}
```

The drawPixmap() method, which allows us to draw a portion of a Pixmap, sets up the source and destination of the Rect members that are used in the actual drawing call. As with drawing a rectangle, we have to translate the x- and y-coordinates together with the width and height to the top-left and bottom-right corners. Again, we have to subtract 1, or else we will overshoot by 1 pixel. Next, we perform the actual drawing via the Canvas.drawBitmap() method, which will automatically do the blending if the Pixmap we draw has a PixmapFormat.ARGB4444 or a PixmapFormat.ARGB8888 color depth. Note that we have to cast the Pixmap parameter to an AndroidPixmap in order to fetch the bitmap member for drawing with the Canvas. That's a bit complicated, but we can be sure that the Pixmap instance that is passed in will be an AndroidPixmap.

```
@Override
public void drawPixmap(Pixmap pixmap, int x, int y) {
    canvas.drawBitmap(((AndroidPixmap)pixmap).bitmap, x, y, null);
}
```

The second drawPixmap() method draws the complete Pixmap to the artificial framebuffer at the given coordinates. Again, we must do some casting to get to the Bitmap member of the AndroidPixmap.

```
@Override
public int getWidth() {
    return frameBuffer.getWidth();
}

@Override
public int getHeight() {
    return frameBuffer.getHeight();
}
}
```

Finally, we have the methods getWidth() and getHeight(), which simply return the size of the artificial framebuffer stored by the AndroidGraphics to which it renders internally.

AndroidFastRenderView is the last class we need in order to implement.

AndroidFastRenderView: Loop, Stretch, Loop, Stretch

The name of this class should give away what lies ahead. In the last chapter, we discussed using a SurfaceView to perform continuous rendering in a separate thread that could also house our game's main loop. We developed a very simple class called FastRenderView, which was derived from the SurfaceView class, we made sure we play nice with the activity life cycle, and we set up a thread in order to constantly render the SurfaceView via a Canvas. Here, we'll reuse this FastRenderView class and augment it to do a few more things.

- It keeps a reference to a Game instance from which it can get the active Screen. We constantly call the Screen.update() and Screen.present() methods from within the FastRenderView thread.

- It keeps track of the delta time between frames that is passed to the active Screen.

It takes the artificial framebuffer to which the AndroidGraphics instance draws, and draws it to the SurfaceView, which is scaled if necessary.

Listing 5–15 shows the implementation of the AndroidFastRenderView class.

Listing 5–15. *AndroidFastRenderView.java, a Threaded SurfaceView Executing Our Game Code*

```java
package com.badlogic.androidgames.framework.impl;

import android.graphics.Bitmap;
import android.graphics.Canvas;
import android.graphics.Rect;
import android.view.SurfaceHolder;
import android.view.SurfaceView;

public class AndroidFastRenderView extends SurfaceView implements Runnable {
    AndroidGame game;
    Bitmap framebuffer;
    Thread renderThread = null;
    SurfaceHolder holder;
    volatile boolean running = false;
```

This should look familiar. We just need to add two more members—an AndroidGame instance and a Bitmap instance that represent our artificial framebuffer. The other members are the same as in our FastRenderView from Chapter 3.

```java
    public AndroidFastRenderView(AndroidGame game, Bitmap framebuffer) {
        super(game);
        this.game = game;
        this.framebuffer = framebuffer;
        this.holder = getHolder();
    }
```

In the constructor, we simply call the base class's constructor with the AndroidGame parameter (which is an Activity; this will be discussed in the following sections) and store the parameters in the respective members. Once again, we get a SurfaceHolder, as in previous sections.

```java
    public void resume() {
        running = true;
        renderThread = new Thread(this);
        renderThread.start();
    }
```

The resume() method is an exact copy of the FastRenderView.resume() method, so we won't discuss it again. In short, the method makes sure that our thread interacts nicely with the activity life cycle.

```java
    public void run() {
        Rect dstRect = new Rect();
        long startTime = System.nanoTime();
        while(running) {
            if(!holder.getSurface().isValid())
                continue;

            float deltaTime = (System.nanoTime()-startTime) / 1000000000.0f;
```

```
        startTime = System.nanoTime();

        game.getCurrentScreen().update(deltaTime);
        game.getCurrentScreen().present(deltaTime);

        Canvas canvas = holder.lockCanvas();
        canvas.getClipBounds(dstRect);
        canvas.drawBitmap(framebuffer, null, dstRect, null);
        holder.unlockCanvasAndPost(canvas);
    }
}
```

The run() method has a few more features. The first addition is its ability to track delta time between each frame. For this, we use System.nanoTime(), which returns the current time in nanoseconds as a long.

NOTE: A nanosecond is one-billionth of a second.

In each loop iteration, we start by taking the difference between the last loop iteration's start time and the current time. To make it easier to work with that delta, we convert it into seconds. Next, we save the current time stamp, which we'll use in the next loop iteration, to calculate the next delta time. With the delta time at hand, we call the current Screen's update() and present() methods, which will update the game logic and render things to the artificial framebuffer. Finally, we get a hold of the Canvas for the SurfaceView and draw the artificial framebuffer. The scaling is performed automatically in case the destination rectangle we pass to the Canvas.drawBitmap() method is smaller or bigger than the framebuffer.

Note that we've used a shortcut here to get a destination rectangle that stretches over the whole SurfaceView via the Canvas.getClipBounds() method. It will set the top and left members of dstRect to 0 and 0, respectively, and the bottom and right members to the actual screen dimensions (480×800 in portrait mode on a Nexus One). The rest of the method is exactly the same as what in our FastRenderView test. The method simply makes sure that the thread stops when the activity is paused or destroyed.

```
public void pause() {
        running = false;
        while(true) {
            try {
                renderThread.join();
                break;
            } catch (InterruptedException e) {
                // retry
            }
        }
    }
}
```

The last method of this class, pause(), is also the same as in the FastRenderView.pause() method – it simply terminates the rendering/main loop thread and waits for it to die completely before returning.

We are nearly done with our framework. The last piece of the puzzle is the implementation of the Game interface.

AndroidGame: Tying Everything Together

Our game development framework is nearly complete. All we need to do is tie the loose ends together by implementing the Game interface we designed in Chapter 3. To do this, we will use the classes we created in the previous sections of this chapter. The following is a list of responsibilities.

- Perform window management. In our context, this means setting up an activity and an AndroidFastRenderView, and handling the activity life cycle in a clean way.

- Use and manage a WakeLock so that the screen does not dim.

- Instantiate and hand out references to Graphics, Audio, FileIO, and Input to interested parties.

- Manage Screens and integrate them with the activity life cycle.

- Our general goal is it to have a single class called AndroidGame from which we can derive. We want to implement the Game.getStartScreen() method later on to start our game in the following way.

```
public class MrNom extends AndroidGame {
    @Override
    public Screen getStartScreen() {
        return new MainMenu(this);
    }
}
```

We hope you can see why it is beneficial to design a workable framework before diving headfirst into programming the actual game. We can reuse this framework for all future games that are not too graphically intensive. Now, let's discuss Listing 5–16, which shows the AndroidGame class.

Listing 5–16. *AndroidGame.java; Tying Everything Together*

```
package com.badlogic.androidgames.framework.impl;

import android.app.Activity;
import android.content.Context;
import android.content.res.Configuration;
import android.graphics.Bitmap;
import android.graphics.Bitmap.Config;
import android.os.Bundle;
import android.os.PowerManager;
import android.os.PowerManager.WakeLock;
import android.view.Window;
import android.view.WindowManager;
```

```
import com.badlogic.androidgames.framework.Audio;
import com.badlogic.androidgames.framework.FileIO;
import com.badlogic.androidgames.framework.Game;
import com.badlogic.androidgames.framework.Graphics;
import com.badlogic.androidgames.framework.Input;
import com.badlogic.androidgames.framework.Screen;

public abstract class AndroidGame extends Activity implements Game {
    AndroidFastRenderView renderView;
    Graphics graphics;
    Audio audio;
    Input input;
    FileIO fileIO;
    Screen screen;
    WakeLock wakeLock;
```

The class definition starts by letting AndroidGame extend the Activity class and
implement the Game interface. Next, we define a couple of members that should already
be familiar. The first member is the AndroidFastRenderView, to which we'll draw, and will
manage our main loop thread for us. Of course, we set the Graphics, Audio, Input, and
FileIO members to instances of AndroidGraphics, AndroidAudio, AndroidInput, and
AndroidFileIO. The next member holds the currently active Screen. Finally, there's a
member that holds a WakeLock that we use to keep the screen from dimming.

```
    @Override
    public void onCreate(Bundle savedInstanceState) {
        super.onCreate(savedInstanceState);

        requestWindowFeature(Window.FEATURE_NO_TITLE);
        getWindow().setFlags(WindowManager.LayoutParams.FLAG_FULLSCREEN,
                WindowManager.LayoutParams.FLAG_FULLSCREEN);

        boolean isLandscape = getResources().getConfiguration().orientation ==
Configuration.ORIENTATION_LANDSCAPE;
        int frameBufferWidth = isLandscape ? 480 : 320;
        int frameBufferHeight = isLandscape ? 320 : 480;
        Bitmap frameBuffer = Bitmap.createBitmap(frameBufferWidth,
                frameBufferHeight, Config.RGB_565);

        float scaleX = (float) frameBufferWidth
                / getWindowManager().getDefaultDisplay().getWidth();
        float scaleY = (float) frameBufferHeight
                / getWindowManager().getDefaultDisplay().getHeight();

        renderView = new AndroidFastRenderView(this, frameBuffer);
        graphics = new AndroidGraphics(getAssets(), frameBuffer);
        fileIO = new AndroidFileIO(getAssets());
        audio = new AndroidAudio(this);
        input = new AndroidInput(this, renderView, scaleX, scaleY);
        screen = getStartScreen();
        setContentView(renderView);

        PowerManager powerManager = (PowerManager)
getSystemService(Context.POWER_SERVICE);
        wakeLock = powerManager.newWakeLock(PowerManager.FULL_WAKE_LOCK, "GLGame");
    }
```

The onCreate() method, which is the familiar startup method of the Activity class, starts by calling the base class's onCreate() method, as required. Next, we make the Activity full-screen, as we did in a couple of other tests in the previous chapter. In the next few lines, we set up our artificial framebuffer. Depending on the orientation of the activity, we want to use a 320×480 framebuffer (portrait mode) or a 480×320 framebuffer (landscape mode). To determine the Activity's screen orientations, we fetch the orientation member from a class called Configuration, which we obtain via a call to getResources().getConfiguration(). Based on the value of that member, we then set the framebuffer size and instantiate a Bitmap, which we'll hand to the AndroidFastRenderView and the AndroidGraphics instances in the following chapters.

> **NOTE:** The Bitmap instance has an RGB565 color format. This way, we don't waste memory, and our drawing is completed a little faster.

We also calculate the scaleX and scaleY values that the SingleTouchHandler and the MultiTouchHandler classes will use to transform the touch event coordinates in our fixed-coordinate system.

Next, we instantiate the AndroidFastRenderView, AndroidGraphics, AndroidAudio, AndroidInput, and AndroidFileIO with the necessary constructor arguments. Finally, we call the getStartScreen() method, which our game will implement, and set the AndroidFastRenderView as the content view of the Activity. Of course, all the previously instantiated helper classes will do some more work in the background. For example, the AndroidInput class tells the selected touch handler to communicate with the AndroidFastRenderView.

```
@Override
public void onResume() {
    super.onResume();
    wakeLock.acquire();
    screen.resume();
    renderView.resume();
}
```

Next is the onResume() method of the Activity class, which we override. As usual, the first thing we do is call the superclass method. Next, we acquire the WakeLock and make sure the current Screen is informed that the game, and thereby, the activity, has been resumed. Finally, we tell the AndroidFastRenderView to resume the rendering thread, which will also kick off our game's main loop, where we tell the current Screen to update and present itself in each iteration.

```
@Override
public void onPause() {
    super.onPause();
    wakeLock.release();
    renderView.pause();
    screen.pause();

    if (isFinishing())
        screen.dispose();
```

}

First, the onPause() method calls the superclass method again. Next, it releases the WakeLock and makes sure that the rendering thread is terminated. If we don't terminate the thread before calling the current Screen's onPause(), we may run into concurrency issues since the UI thread and the main loop thread will both access the Screen at the same time. Once we are sure the main loop thread is no longer alive, we tell the current Screen that it should pause itself. In case the Activity is going to be destroyed, we also inform the Screen so that it can do any necessary cleanup work.

```
@Override
public Input getInput() {
    return input;
}

@Override
public FileIO getFileIO() {
    return fileIO;
}

@Override
public Graphics getGraphics() {
    return graphics;
}

@Override
public Audio getAudio() {
    return audio;
}
```

The getInput(), getFileIO(), getGraphics(), and getAudio() methods need no explanation. We simply return the respective instances to the caller. Later, the caller will always be one of our Screen implementations of our game.

```
@Override
public void setScreen(Screen screen) {
    if (screen == null)
        throw new IllegalArgumentException("Screen must not be null");

    this.screen.pause();
    this.screen.dispose();
    screen.resume();
    screen.update(0);
    this.screen = screen;
}
```

At first, the setScreen() method we inherit from the Game interface looks simple. We start with some traditional null-checking, since we can't allow a null Screen. Next, we tell the current Screen to pause and dispose of itself so that it can make room for the new Screen. The new Screen is asked to resume itself and update itself once with a delta time of zero. Finally, we set the Screen member to the new Screen.

Let's think about who will call this method and when. When we designed Mr. Nom, we identified all the transitions between various Screen instances. We'll usually call the

`AndroidGame.setScreen()` method in the `update()` method of one of these `Screen` instances.

For example, let's assume we have a main menu `Screen` where we check to see if the Play button is pressed in the `update()` method. If that is the case, we will transition to the next `Screen` by calling the `AndroidGame.setScreen()` method from within the `MainMenu.update()` method with a brand-new instance of that next `Screen`. The `MainMenu` screen will regain control after the call to `AndroidGame.setScreen()`, and should immediately return to the caller as it is no longer the active `Screen`. In this case, the caller is the `AndroidFastRenderView` in the main loop thread. If you check the portion of the main loop responsible for updating and rendering the active `Screen`, you'll see that the `update()` method will be called on the `MainMenu` class, but the `present()` method will be called on the new current `Screen`. This would be problematic, as we defined the `Screen` interface in a way that guarantees that the `resume()` and `update()` methods will be called at least once before the `Screen` is asked to present itself. That's why we call these two methods in the `AndroidGame.setScreen()` method on the new `Screen`. The `AndroidGame` class takes care of everything.

```
public Screen getCurrentScreen() {
        return screen;
    }
}
```

The last method is the `getCurrentScreen()` method, which simply returns the currently active `Screen`.

Finally, remember that `AndroidGame` derives from `Game`, which has another method called `getStartScreen()`. This is the method we have to implement to get things going for our game!

Now, we've created an easy-to-use Android game development framework. All we need to do is implement our game's `Screens`. We can also reuse the framework for any future games, as long as they do not need immense graphics power. If that is necessary, we have to use OpenGL ES. However, to do this, we only need to replace the graphics part of our framework. All the other classes for audio, input, and file I/O can be reused.

Summary

In this chapter, we implemented a full-fledged 2D Android game development framework from scratch that can be reused for all future games (as long as they are graphically modest). Great care was taken to achieve a good, extensible design. We could take the code and replace the rendering portions with OpenGL ES, thus making Mr. Nom 3D.

With all this boilerplate code in place, let's concentrate on what we are here for: writing games!

Chapter 6

Mr. Nom Invades Android

In Chapter 3, we churned out a full design for Mr. Nom, consisting of the game mechanics, a simple background story, handcrafted graphical assets, and definitions for all the screens based on some paper cutouts. In the last chapter, we developed a full-fledged game-development framework that allows us to transfer our design screens easily to code. But enough talking; let's start writing our first game!

Creating the Assets

We have two types of assets in Mr. Nom: audio assets and graphical assets. We recorded the audio assets via a nice open source application called Audacity and a bad netbook microphone. We created a sound effect to be played when a button is pressed or a menu item is chosen, one for when Mr. Nom eats a stain, and one for when he eats himself. We saved them as OGGs to the `assets/` folder, under the names `click.ogg`, `eat.ogg`, and `bitten.ogg`, respectively.

Earlier, we mentioned that we'll want to reuse those paper cutouts from the design phase as our real game graphics. For this, we first have to make them fit with our target resolution.

We chose a fixed target resolution of 320×480 (portrait mode) for which we'll design all our graphic assets. This might seem small, but it made it very quick and easy for us to develop the game and graphics and, after all, the point here is that you get to see the entire Android game development process.

For your production game, consider all of the resolutions and use higher-resolution graphics so that your game looks good on tablet-sized screens, perhaps targeting 800×1280 as a baseline. We scanned in all the paper cutouts and resized them a bit. We saved most of the assets in separate files and merged some of them into a single file. All images are saved in a PNG format. The background is the only image that is RGB888; all others are ARGB8888. Figure 6–1 shows you what we ended up with.

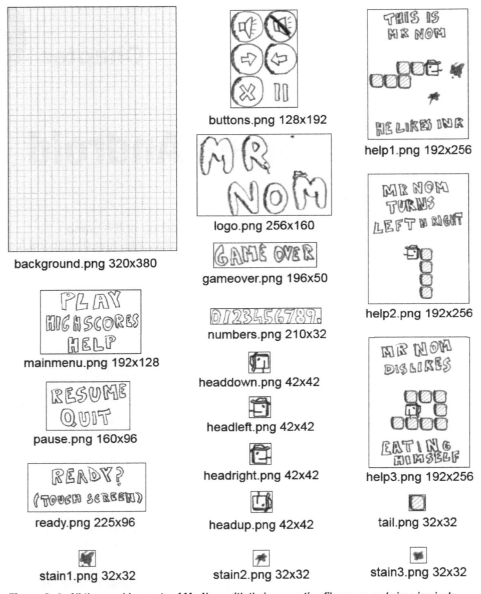

Figure 6–1. *All the graphic assets of Mr. Nom with their respective filenames and sizes in pixels.*

Let's break down those images a little:

background.png: This is our background image, which will be the first thing we'll draw to the framebuffer. It has the same size as our target resolution for obvious reasons.

`buttons.png`: This contains all the buttons we'll need in our game. We put them into a single file, as we can easily draw them via the `Graphics.drawPixmap()` method, which allows drawing portions of an image. We'll use that technique more often when we start drawing with OpenGL ES, so we better get used to it now. Merging several images into a single image is often called *atlasing*, and the image itself is called an *image atlas* (or texture atlas, or sprite sheet). Each button has a size of 64×64 pixels, which will come in handy when we have to decide whether a touch event has pressed a button on the screen.

`help1.png`, `help2.png`, *and* `help3.png`: These are the images we'll display on the three help screens of Mr. Nom. They are all the same size, which makes placing them on the screen easier.

`logo.png`: This is the logo we'll display on the main menu screen.

`mainmenu.png`: This contains the three options that we'll present to the player on the main menu. Selecting one of these will trigger a transition to the respective screen. Each option has a height of roughly 42 pixels, something we can use to easily detect which option was touched.

`ready.png`, `pause.png`, *and* `gameover.png`: We'll draw these when the game is about to be started, when it is paused, and when it is over.

`numbers.png`: This holds all the digits we'll need to render our high scores later on. What to remember about this image is that each digit has the same width and height, 20×32 pixels, except for the dot at the end, which is 10×32 pixels. We can use this to render any number that is thrown at us.

`tail.png`: This is the tail of Mr. Nom, or rather one part of his tail. It's 32×32 pixels in size, which has some implications that we'll discuss in a minute.

`headdown.png`, `headleft.png`, `headright.png`, *and* `headup.png`: These images are for the head of Mr. Nom; there's one for each direction in which he can move. Because of his hat, we have to make these images a little bigger than the tail image. Each head image is 42×42 pixels in size.

`stain1.png`, `stain2.png`, and `stain3.png`: These are the three types of stains that we can render. Having three types will make the game screen a little more diverse. They are 32×32 pixels in size, just like the tail image.

Great, now let's start implementing the screens!

Setting Up the Project

As mentioned in the last chapter, we will merge the code for Mr. Nom with our framework code. All the classes related to Mr. Nom will be placed in the package `com.badlogic.androidgames.mrnom`. Additionally, we have to modify the manifest file, as outlined in Chapter 4. Our default activity will be called `MrNomGame`. Just follow the ten steps outlined in the section "Android Game Project Setup in Ten Easy Steps" in Chapter 4 to set the `<activity>` attributes properly (that is, so that the game is fixed in portrait mode and configuration changes are handled by application) and to give our application the proper permissions (writing to external storage, using a wake lock, and so forth).

All the assets from the previous sections are located in the `assets/` folder of the project. Additionally, we have to put `icon.png` files into the `res/drawable`, `res/drawable-ldpi`, `res/drawable-mdpi`, and `res/drawable-hdpi` folders. We just took the `headright.png` of Mr. Nom, renamed it `icon.png`, and put a properly resized version of it in each of the folders.

All that's left is putting our game code into the `com.badlogic.androidgames.mrnom` package of the Eclipse project!

MrNomGame: The Main Activity

Our application needs a main entry point, also known as the default `Activity` on Android. We will call this default `ActivityMrNomGame` and let it derive from `AndroidGame`, the class we implemented in Chapter 5 to run our game. It will be responsible for creating and running our first screen later on. Listing 6–1 shows you our `MrNomGame` class.

Listing 6–1. *MrNomGame.java; Our Main Activity/Game Hybrid*

```
package com.badlogic.androidgames.mrnom;

import com.badlogic.androidgames.framework.Screen;
import com.badlogic.androidgames.framework.impl.AndroidGame;

public class MrNomGame extends AndroidGame {
    @Override
    public Screen getStartScreen() {
        return new LoadingScreen(this);
    }
}
```

All we need to do is derive from `AndroidGame` and implement the `getStartScreen()` method, which will return an instance of the `LoadingScreen` class (which we'll implement in a minute). Remember, this will get us started with all the things we need for our game, from setting up the different modules for audio, graphics, input, and file I/O to starting the main loop thread. Pretty easy, huh?

Assets: A Convenient Asset Store

The loading screen will load all the assets of our game. But where do we store them? To store them, we'll do something that is not seen very often in Java land: we'll create a class that has a ton of static public members that hold all the `Pixmaps` and `Sounds` that we've loaded from the assets. Listing 6–2 shows you that class.

Listing 6–2. *Assets.java; Holding All of Our Pixmaps and Sounds for Easy Access*

```java
package com.badlogic.androidgames.mrnom;

import com.badlogic.androidgames.framework.Pixmap;
import com.badlogic.androidgames.framework.Sound;

public class Assets {
    public static Pixmap background;
    public static Pixmap logo;
    public static Pixmap mainMenu;
    public static Pixmap buttons;
    public static Pixmap help1;
    public static Pixmap help2;
    public static Pixmap help3;
    public static Pixmap numbers;
    public static Pixmap ready;
    public static Pixmap pause;
    public static Pixmap gameOver;
    public static Pixmap headUp;
    public static Pixmap headLeft;
    public static Pixmap headDown;
    public static Pixmap headRight;
    public static Pixmap tail;
    public static Pixmap stain1;
    public static Pixmap stain2;
    public static Pixmap stain3;

    public static Sound click;
    public static Sound eat;
    public static Sound bitten;
}
```

We have a static member for every image and sound we load from the assets. If we want to use one of these assets, we can do something like this:

```java
game.getGraphics().drawPixmap(Assets.background, 0, 0)
```

or something like this:

```java
Assets.click.play(1);
```

Now that's convenient. However, note that nothing is keeping us from overwriting those static members, as they are not final. But as long as we don't overwrite them, we are safe. These public, non-final members actually make this "design pattern" an anti-pattern. For our game, it's OK to be a little lazy, though. A cleaner solution would hide the assets behind setters and getters in a so-called *singleton class*. We'll stick to our poor-man's asset manager.

Settings: Keeping Track of User Choices and High Scores

There are two other things that we need to load in the loading screen: the user settings and the high scores. If you look back at the main menu and high-scores screens in Chapter 3, you'll see that we allow the user to toggle the sounds and that we store the top five high scores. We'll save these settings to the external storage so that we can reload them the next time the game starts. For this, we'll implement another simple class called Settings, as shown in Listing 6–3.

Listing 6–3. *Settings.java; Which Stores Our Settings and Loads/Saves Them*

```java
package com.badlogic.androidgames.mrnom;

import java.io.BufferedReader;
import java.io.BufferedWriter;
import java.io.IOException;
import java.io.InputStreamReader;
import java.io.OutputStreamWriter;

import com.badlogic.androidgames.framework.FileIO;

public class Settings {
    public static boolean soundEnabled = true;
    public static int[] highscores = new int[] { 100, 80, 50, 30, 10 };
```

Whether sound effects are played back is determined by a public static Boolean called soundEnabled. The high scores are stored in a five-element integer array, sorted from highest to lowest. We define sensible defaults for both settings. We can access these two members the same way we accessed the members of the Assets class.

```java
    public static void load(FileIO files) {
        BufferedReader in = null;
        try {
            in = new BufferedReader(new InputStreamReader(
                    files.readFile(".mrnom")));
            soundEnabled = Boolean.parseBoolean(in.readLine());
            for (int i = 0; i < 5; i++) {
                highscores[i] = Integer.parseInt(in.readLine());
            }
        } catch (IOException e) {
            // :( It's ok we have defaults
        } catch (NumberFormatException e) {
            // :/ It's ok, defaults save our day
        } finally {
            try {
                if (in != null)
                    in.close();
            } catch (IOException e) {
            }
        }
    }
}
```

The static load() method tries to load the settings from a file called .mrnom from the external storage. It needs a FileIO instance for that, which we pass to the method. It assumes that the sound setting and each high-score entry is stored on a separate line and simply reads them in. If anything goes wrong (for example, if the external storage is not available or there is no settings file yet), we simply fall back to our defaults and ignore the failure.

```
public static void save(FileIO files) {
    BufferedWriter out = null;
    try {
        out = new BufferedWriter(new OutputStreamWriter(
            files.writeFile(".mrnom")));
        out.write(Boolean.toString(soundEnabled));
        for (int i = 0; i < 5; i++) {
            out.write(Integer.toString(highscores[i]));
        }

    } catch (IOException e) {
    } finally {
        try {
            if (out != null)
                out.close();
        } catch (IOException e) {
        }
    }
}
```

Next up is a method called save(). It takes the current settings and serializes them to the .mrnom file on the external storage (that is, /sdcard/.mrnom).The sound setting and each high-score entry is stored as a separate line in that file, as expected by the load() method. If something goes wrong, we just ignore the failure and use the default values defined earlier. In an AAA title, you might want to inform the user about this loading error.

It is worth noting that, in Android API 8, more specific methods were added for dealing with managed external storage. The method Context.getExternalFilesDir() was added, which provides a specific spot in the external storage that doesn't pollute the root directory of the SD Card or internal flash memory, and it also gets cleaned up when the application is uninstalled. Adding support for this, of course, means that you either have to load a class dynamically for API 8 and up, or set your minimum SDK to 8 and lose backward compatibility. Mr. Nom will use the old API 1 external storage spot for simplicity's sake, but should you need an example of how to load a class dynamically, look no further than our TouchHandler code.

```
public static void addScore(int score) {
    for (int i = 0; i < 5; i++) {
        if (highscores[i] < score) {
            for (int j = 4; j > i; j--)
                highscores[j] = highscores[j - 1];
            highscores[i] = score;
            break;
        }
    }
}
```

The final method, addScore(), is a convenience method. We will use it to add a new score to the high scores, automatically re-sorting them depending on the value we want to insert.

LoadingScreen: Fetching the Assets from Disk

With those classes at hand, we can now easily implement the loading screen. Listing 6–4 shows you the code.

Listing 6–4. *LoadingScreen.java; Which Loads All Assets and the Settings*

```java
package com.badlogic.androidgames.mrnom;

import com.badlogic.androidgames.framework.Game;
import com.badlogic.androidgames.framework.Graphics;
import com.badlogic.androidgames.framework.Screen;
import com.badlogic.androidgames.framework.Graphics.PixmapFormat;

public class LoadingScreen extends Screen {
    public LoadingScreen(Game game) {
        super(game);
    }
```

We let the LoadingScreen class derive from the Screen class we defined in Chapter 3. This requires that we implement a constructor that takes a Game instance, which we hand to the superclass constructor. Note that this constructor will be called in the MrNomGame.getStartScreen() method we defined earlier.

```java
    @Override
    public void update(float deltaTime) {
        Graphics g = game.getGraphics();
        Assets.background = g.newPixmap("background.png", PixmapFormat.RGB565);
        Assets.logo = g.newPixmap("logo.png", PixmapFormat.ARGB4444);
        Assets.mainMenu = g.newPixmap("mainmenu.png", PixmapFormat.ARGB4444);
        Assets.buttons = g.newPixmap("buttons.png", PixmapFormat.ARGB4444);
        Assets.help1 = g.newPixmap("help1.png", PixmapFormat.ARGB4444);
        Assets.help2 = g.newPixmap("help2.png", PixmapFormat.ARGB4444);
        Assets.help3 = g.newPixmap("help3.png", PixmapFormat.ARGB4444);
        Assets.numbers = g.newPixmap("numbers.png", PixmapFormat.ARGB4444);
        Assets.ready = g.newPixmap("ready.png", PixmapFormat.ARGB4444);
        Assets.pause = g.newPixmap("pausemenu.png", PixmapFormat.ARGB4444);
        Assets.gameOver = g.newPixmap("gameover.png", PixmapFormat.ARGB4444);
        Assets.headUp = g.newPixmap("headup.png", PixmapFormat.ARGB4444);
        Assets.headLeft = g.newPixmap("headleft.png", PixmapFormat.ARGB4444);
        Assets.headDown = g.newPixmap("headdown.png", PixmapFormat.ARGB4444);
        Assets.headRight = g.newPixmap("headright.png", PixmapFormat.ARGB4444);
        Assets.tail = g.newPixmap("tail.png", PixmapFormat.ARGB4444);
        Assets.stain1 = g.newPixmap("stain1.png", PixmapFormat.ARGB4444);
        Assets.stain2 = g.newPixmap("stain2.png", PixmapFormat.ARGB4444);
        Assets.stain3 = g.newPixmap("stain3.png", PixmapFormat.ARGB4444);
        Assets.click = game.getAudio().newSound("click.ogg");
        Assets.eat = game.getAudio().newSound("eat.ogg");
        Assets.bitten = game.getAudio().newSound("bitten.ogg");
        Settings.load(game.getFileIO());
        game.setScreen(new MainMenuScreen(game));
    }
```

Next up is our implementation of the update() method, where we load the assets and settings. For the image assets, we simply create new Pixmaps via the Graphics.newPixmap() method. Note that we specify which color format the Pixmaps should have. The background has an RGB565 format, and all other images have an ARGB4444 format (if the BitmapFactory respects our hint). We do this to conserve memory and increase our rendering speed a little later on. Our original images are stored in RGB888 and ARGB8888 formats, as PNGs. We also load in the three sound effects and store them in the respective members of the Assets class. Next, we load the settings from the external storage via the Settings.load() method. Finally, we initiate a screen transition to a Screen called MainMenuScreen, which will take over execution from that point on.

```java
    @Override
    public void present(float deltaTime) {

    }

    @Override
    public void pause() {

    }

    @Override
    public void resume() {

    }

    @Override
    public void dispose() {

    }
}
```

The other methods are just stubs and do not perform any actions. Since the update() method will immediately trigger a screen transition after all assets are loaded, there's nothing more to do on this screen.

The Main Menu Screen

The main menu screen is pretty dumb. It just renders the logo, the main menu options, and the sound setting in the form of a toggle button. All it does is react to touches on either the main menu options or the sound setting toggle button. To implement this behavior, we need to know two things: where on the screen we render the images, and what the touch areas are that will either trigger a screen transition or toggle the sound setting. Figure 6–2 shows where we'll render the different images on the screen. From that we can directly derive the touch areas.

Figure 6–2. *The main menu screen. The coordinates specify where we'll render the different images, and the outlines show the touch areas.*

The x-coordinates of the logo and main menu option images are calculated so that they are centered on the x-axis.

Next, let's implement the Screen. Listing 6–5 shows the code.

Listing 6–5. *MainMenuScreen.java; the Main Menu Screen*

```
package com.badlogic.androidgames.mrnom;

package com.badlogic.androidgames.mrnom;

import java.util.List;

import com.badlogic.androidgames.framework.Game;
import com.badlogic.androidgames.framework.Graphics;
import com.badlogic.androidgames.framework.Input.TouchEvent;
import com.badlogic.androidgames.framework.Screen;

public class MainMenuScreen extends Screen {
    public MainMenuScreen(Game game) {
        super(game);
    }
}
```

We let the class derive from Screen again and implement an adequate constructor for it.

```
    @Override
    public void update(float deltaTime) {
        Graphics g = game.getGraphics();
        List<TouchEvent> touchEvents = game.getInput().getTouchEvents();
        game.getInput().getKeyEvents();
```

```
        int len = touchEvents.size();
        for(int i = 0; i < len; i++) {
            TouchEvent event = touchEvents.get(i);
            if(event.type == TouchEvent.TOUCH_UP) {
                if(inBounds(event, 0, g.getHeight() - 64, 64, 64)) {
                    Settings.soundEnabled = !Settings.soundEnabled;
                    if(Settings.soundEnabled)
                        Assets.click.play(1);
                }
                if(inBounds(event, 64, 220, 192, 42) ) {
                    game.setScreen(new GameScreen(game));
                    if(Settings.soundEnabled)
                        Assets.click.play(1);
                    return;
                }
                if(inBounds(event, 64, 220 + 42, 192, 42) ) {
                    game.setScreen(new HighscoreScreen(game));
                    if(Settings.soundEnabled)
                        Assets.click.play(1);
                    return;
                }
                if(inBounds(event, 64, 220 + 84, 192, 42) ) {
                    game.setScreen(new HelpScreen(game));
                    if(Settings.soundEnabled)
                        Assets.click.play(1);
                    return;
                }
            }
        }
    }
```

Next, we have the update() method, in which we'll do all our touch event checking. We first fetch the TouchEvents and KeyEvents from the Input instance the Game provides us. Note that we do not use the KeyEvents, but we fetch them anyway in order to clear the internal buffer (yes, that's a tad bit nasty, but let's make it a habit). We then loop over all the TouchEvents until we find one with the type TouchEvent.TOUCH_UP. (We could alternatively look for TouchEvent.TOUCH_DOWN events, but in most UIs the up event is used to indicate that a UI component was pressed.)

Once we have a fitting event, we check whether it either pressed the sound toggle button or one of the menu entries. To make that code a little cleaner, we wrote a method called inBounds(), which takes a touch event, x- and y-coordinates, and a width and height. The method checks whether the touch event is inside the rectangle defined by those parameters, and it returns either true or false.

If the sound toggle button is pressed, we simply invert the Settings.soundEnabled Boolean value. In case any of the main menu entries are pressed, we transition to the appropriate screen by instancing it and setting it via Game.setScreen(). We can immediately return in that case, as the MainMenuScreen doesn't have anything to do anymore. We also play the click sounds if either the toggle button or a main menu entry is pressed and sound is enabled.

Remember that all the touch events will be reported relative to our target resolution of
320×480 pixels, thanks to the scaling magic we performed in the touch event handlers
discussed in Chapter 5.

```java
private boolean inBounds(TouchEvent event, int x, int y, int width, int height) {
    if(event.x > x && event.x < x + width - 1 &&
       event.y > y && event.y < y + height - 1)
        return true;
    else
        return false;
}
```

The inBounds() method works as previously discussed: put in a TouchEvent and a
rectangle, and it tells you whether the touch event's coordinates are inside that
rectangle.

```java
@Override
public void present(float deltaTime) {
    Graphics g = game.getGraphics();

    g.drawPixmap(Assets.background, 0, 0);
    g.drawPixmap(Assets.logo, 32, 20);
    g.drawPixmap(Assets.mainMenu, 64, 220);
    if(Settings.soundEnabled)
        g.drawPixmap(Assets.buttons, 0, 416, 0, 0, 64, 64);
    else
        g.drawPixmap(Assets.buttons, 0, 416, 64, 0, 64, 64);
}
```

The present() method is probably the one you've been waiting for most, but it isn't all that
exciting. Our little game framework makes it really simple to render our main menu screen.
All we do is render the background at (0, 0), which will basically erase our framebuffer, so no
call to Graphics.clear() is needed. Next, we draw the logo and main menu entries at the
coordinates shown in Figure 6–2. We end that method by drawing the sound toggle button
based on the current setting. As you can see, we use the same Pixmap, but only draw the
appropriate portion of it (the sound toggle button; see Figure 6–1). Now that was easy.

```java
@Override
public void pause() {
    Settings.save(game.getFileIO());
}
```

The final piece we need to discuss is the pause() method. Since we can change one of
the settings on that screen, we have to make sure that it gets persisted to the external
storage. With our Settings class, that's pretty easy!

```java
@Override
public void resume() {

}

@Override
public void dispose() {

}
}
```

The resume() and dispose() methods don't have anything to do in this Screen.

The HelpScreen Class(es)

Next, let's implement the HelpScreen, HighscoreScreen, and GameScreen classes we used previously in the update() method.

We defined three help screens in Chapter 3, each more or less explaining one aspect of the game play. We now directly translate those to Screen implementations called HelpScreen, HelpScreen2, and HelpScreen3. They all have a single button that will initiate a screen transition. The HelpScreen3 screen will transition back to the MainMenuScreen. Figure 6–3 shows the three help screens with the drawing coordinates and touch areas.

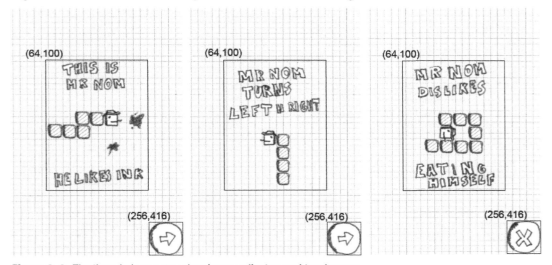

Figure 6–3. *The three help screens, drawing coordinates, and touch areas.*

Now that seems simple enough to implement. Let's start with the HelpScreen class shown in Listing 6–6.

Listing 6–6. *HelpScreen.java; the First Help Screen*

```java
package com.badlogic.androidgames.mrnom;

import java.util.List;

import com.badlogic.androidgames.framework.Game;
import com.badlogic.androidgames.framework.Graphics;
import com.badlogic.androidgames.framework.Input.TouchEvent;
import com.badlogic.androidgames.framework.Screen;

public class HelpScreen extends Screen {
    public HelpScreen(Game game) {
        super(game);
    }
```

```java
    @Override
    public void update(float deltaTime) {
        List<TouchEvent> touchEvents = game.getInput().getTouchEvents();
        game.getInput().getKeyEvents();

        int len = touchEvents.size();
        for(int i = 0; i < len; i++) {
            TouchEvent event = touchEvents.get(i);
            if(event.type == TouchEvent.TOUCH_UP) {
                if(event.x > 256 && event.y > 416 ) {
                    game.setScreen(new HelpScreen2(game));
                    if(Settings.soundEnabled)
                        Assets.click.play(1);
                    return;
                }
            }
        }
    }

    @Override
    public void present(float deltaTime) {
        Graphics g = game.getGraphics();
        g.drawPixmap(Assets.background, 0, 0);
        g.drawPixmap(Assets.help1, 64, 100);
        g.drawPixmap(Assets.buttons, 256, 416, 0, 64, 64, 64);
    }

    @Override
    public void pause() {

    }

    @Override
    public void resume() {

    }

    @Override
    public void dispose() {

    }
}
```

Again, very simple. We derive from Screen, and implement a proper constructor. Next, we have our familiar update() method, which simply checks if the button at the bottom was pressed. If that's the case, we play the click sound and transition to HelpScreen2.

The present() method just renders the background again, followed by the help image and the button.

The HelpScreen2 and HelpScreen3 classes look the same; the only difference is the help image they draw and the screen to which they transition. We can agree that we don't have to look at their code. On to the high-scores screen!

The High-Scores Screen

The high-scores screen simply draws the top five high scores we store in the Settings class, plus a fancy header telling the player that he or she is on the high-scores screen, and a button at the bottom left that will transition back to the main menu when pressed. The interesting part is how we render the high scores. Let's first have a look at where we render the images, which is shown in Figure 6–4.

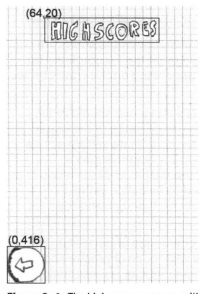

Figure 6–4. *The high-scores screen, without high scores.*

That looks as easy as the other screens we have implemented. But how can we draw the dynamic scores?

Rendering Numbers: An Excursion

We have an asset image called numbers.png that contains all digits from 0 to 9 plus a dot. Each digit is 20×32 pixels, and the dot is 10×32 pixels. The digits are arranged from left to right in ascending order. The high-scores screen should display five lines, each line showing one of the five high scores. One such line would start with the high score's position (for example, "1." or "5."), followed by a space, and then by the actual score. How can we do that?

We have two things at our disposal: the numbers.png image and Graphics.drawPixmap(), which allows us to draw portions of an image to the screen. Say we want the first line of the default high scores (with the string "1. 100") to be rendered at (20, 100), so that the top-left corner of the digit 1 coincides with those coordinates. We call Graphics.drawPixmap() like this:

```
game.getGraphics().drawPixmap(Assets.numbers, 20, 100, 20, 0, 20, 32);
```

We know that the digit 1 has a width of 20 pixels. The next character of our string would have to be rendered at (20+20,100). In the case of the string "1. 100," this character is the dot, which has a width of 10 pixels in the numbers.png image:

```
game.getGraphics().drawPixmap(Assets.numbers, 40, 100, 200, 0, 10, 32);
```

The next character in the string needs to be rendered at (20+20+10,100). That character is a space, which we don't need to draw. All we need to do is advance on the x-axis by 20 pixels again, as we assume that's the width of the space character. The next character, 1, would therefore be rendered at (20+20+10+20,100). See a pattern here?

Given the coordinates of the upper-left corner of our first character in the string, we can loop through each character of the string, draw it, and increment the x-coordinate for the next character to be drawn by either 20 or 10 pixels, depending on the character we just drew.

We also need to figure out which portion of the numbers.png image we should draw, given the current character. For that, we need the x- and y-coordinates of the upper-left corner of that portion, as well as its width and height. The y-coordinate will always be zero, which should be obvious when looking at Figure 6–1. The height is also a constant—32 in our case. The width is either 20 pixels (if the character of the string is a digit) or 10 pixels (if it is a dot). The only thing that we need to calculate is the x-coordinate of the portion in the numbers.png image. We can do that by using the following neat little trick.

The characters in a string can be interpreted as Unicode characters or as 16–bit integers. This means that we can actually do calculations with those character codes. By a lucky coincidence, the characters 0 to 9 have ascending integer representations. We can use this to calculate the x-coordinate of the portion of the number.png image for a digit like this:

```
char character = string.charAt(index);
int x = (character - '0') * 20;
```

That will give us 0 for the character 0, 3 × 20 = 60 for the character 3, and so on. That's exactly the x-coordinate of the portion of each digit. Of course, this won't work for the dot character, so we need to treat that specially. Let's summarize this in a method that can render one of our high-score lines, given the string of the line and the x- and y-coordinates where the rendering should start.

```
public void drawText(Graphics g, String line, int x, int y) {
    int len = line.length();
    for (int i = 0; i < len; i++) {
        char character = line.charAt(i);

        if (character == ' ') {
            x += 20;
            continue;
        }

        int srcX = 0;
```

```java
        int srcWidth = 0;
        if (character == '.') {
            srcX = 200;
            srcWidth = 10;
        } else {
            srcX = (character - '0') * 20;
            srcWidth = 20;
        }

        g.drawPixmap(Assets.numbers, x, y, srcX, 0, srcWidth, 32);
        x += srcWidth;
    }
}
```

We iterate over each character of the string. If the current character is a space, we just advance the x-coordinate by 20 pixels. Otherwise, we calculate the x-coordinate and width of the current character's region in the numbers.png image. The character is either a digit or a dot. We then render the current character and advance the rendering x-coordinate by the width of the character we've just drawn. This method will of course blow up if our string contains anything other than spaces, digits, and dots. Can you think of a way to make it work with any string?

Implementing the Screen

Equipped with this new knowledge, we can now easily implement the HighscoreScreen class, as shown in Listing 6–7.

Listing 6–7. *HighscoreScreen.java; Showing Us Our Best Achievements So Far*

```java
package com.badlogic.androidgames.mrnom;

import java.util.List;

import com.badlogic.androidgames.framework.Game;
import com.badlogic.androidgames.framework.Graphics;
import com.badlogic.androidgames.framework.Screen;
import com.badlogic.androidgames.framework.Input.TouchEvent;

public class HighscoreScreen extends Screen {
    String lines[] = new String[5];

    public HighscoreScreen(Game game) {
        super(game);

        for (int i = 0; i < 5; i++) {
            lines[i] = "" + (i + 1) + ". " + Settings.highscores[i];
        }
    }
```

As we want to stay friends with the garbage collector, we store the strings of the five high-score lines in a string array member. We construct the strings based on the Settings.highscores array in the constructor.

```
@Override
public void update(float deltaTime) {
    List<TouchEvent> touchEvents = game.getInput().getTouchEvents();
    game.getInput().getKeyEvents();

    int len = touchEvents.size();
    for (int i = 0; i < len; i++) {
        TouchEvent event = touchEvents.get(i);
        if (event.type == TouchEvent.TOUCH_UP) {
            if (event.x < 64 && event.y > 416) {
                if(Settings.soundEnabled)
                    Assets.click.play(1);
                game.setScreen(new MainMenuScreen(game));
                return;
            }
        }
    }
}
```

Next, we define the update() method, which is unsurprisingly boring. All we do is check for whether a touch-up event pressed the button in the bottom-left corner. If that's the case, we play the click sound and transition back to the MainMenuScreen.

```
@Override
public void present(float deltaTime) {
    Graphics g = game.getGraphics();

    g.drawPixmap(Assets.background, 0, 0);
    g.drawPixmap(Assets.mainMenu, 64, 20, 0, 42, 196, 42);

    int y = 100;
    for (int i = 0; i < 5; i++) {
        drawText(g, lines[i], 20, y);
        y += 50;
    }

    g.drawPixmap(Assets.buttons, 0, 416, 64, 64, 64, 64);
}
```

The present() method is pretty simple, with the help of the mighty drawText() method we previously defined. We render the background image first, as usual, followed by the "HIGHSCORES" portion of the Assets.mainmenu image. We could have stored this in a separate file, but we reuse it to free up more memory.

Next, we loop through the five strings for each high-score line we created in the constructor. We draw each line with the drawText() method. The first line starts at (20,100); the next line is rendered at (20,150), and so on. We just increase the y-coordinate for text rendering by 50 pixels for each line so that we have a nice vertical spacing between the lines. We finish the method off by drawing our button.

```java
public void drawText(Graphics g, String line, int x, int y) {
        int len = line.length();
        for (int i = 0; i < len; i++) {
            char character = line.charAt(i);

            if (character == ' ') {
                x += 20;
                continue;
            }

            int srcX = 0;
            int srcWidth = 0;
            if (character == '.') {
                srcX = 200;
                srcWidth = 10;
            } else {
                srcX = (character - '0') * 20;
                srcWidth = 20;
            }

            g.drawPixmap(Assets.numbers, x, y, srcX, 0, srcWidth, 32);
            x += srcWidth;
        }
    }

    @Override
    public void pause() {

    }

    @Override
    public void resume() {

    }

    @Override
    public void dispose() {

    }
}
```

The remaining methods should be self-explanatory. Let's get to the last missing piece of our Mr. Nom game: the game screen.

Abstracting…

So far, we've only implemented boring UI stuff and some housekeeping code for our assets and settings. We'll now abstract the world of Mr. Nom and all the objects in it. We'll also free Mr. Nom from the screen resolution and let him live in his own little world with his own little coordinate system.

Abstracting the World of Mr. Nom: Model, View, Controller

If you are a long-time coder, you've probably heard about design patterns. They are, more or less, strategies to design your code, given a scenario. Some of them are academic, and some have uses in the real world. For game development, we can borrow some ideas from the *Model-View-Controller (MVC)* design pattern. It's often used by the database and Web community to separate the data model from the presentation layer and the data manipulation layer. We won't strictly follow this design pattern, but rather adapt it in a simpler form.

So what does this mean for Mr. Nom? First of all, we need an abstract representation of our world that is independent of any bitmaps, sounds, framebuffers, or input events. Instead, we'll model Mr. Nom's world with a few simple classes in an object-oriented manner. We'll have a class for the stains in the world, and a class for Mr. Nom himself. Mr. Nom is composed of a head and tail parts, which we'll also represent by a separate class. To tie everything together, we'll have an all-knowing class representing the complete world of Mr. Nom, including the stains and Mr. Nom himself. All of this represents the *model* part of MVC.

The *view* in MVC will be the code that is responsible for rendering the world of Mr. Nom. We'll have a class or a method that takes the class for the world, reads its current state, and renders it to the screen. *How* it is rendered does not concern the model classes, which is the most important lesson to take away from MVC. The model classes are independent of everything, but the view classes and methods depend on the model classes.

Finally, we have the *controller* in MVC. It tells the model classes to change their state based on things like user input or the time ticking away. The model classes provide methods to the controller (for example, with instructions like "turn Mr. Nom to the left."), which the controller can then use to modify the state of the model. We don't have any code in the model classes that directly accesses things like the touchscreen or the accelerometer. This way, we can keep the model classes clear of any external dependencies.

This may sound complicated, and you may be wondering why we do things this way. However, there are a lot of benefits to this approach. We can implement all of our game logic without having to know about graphics, audio, or input devices. We can modify the rendering of the game world without having to change the model classes themselves. We could even go so far as to exchange a 2D world renderer with a 3D world renderer. We can easily add support for new input devices by using a controller. All it does is translate input events to method calls of the model classes. Want to turn Mr. Nom via the accelerometer? No problem—read the accelerometer values in the controller, and translate them to a "turn Mr. Nom left" or a "turn Mr. Nom right" method call on the model of Mr. Nom. Want to add support for the Zeemote? No problem, just do the same as in the case of the accelerometer! The best thing about using controllers is that we don't have to touch a single line of Mr. Nom's code to make all of this happen.

Let's start by defining Mr. Nom's world. To do this, we'll break away from the strict MVC pattern a little and use our graphic assets to illustrate the basic ideas. This will also help us to implement the view component later on (rendering Mr. Nom's abstract world in pixels).

Figure 6–5 shows the game screen upon which the world of Mr. Nom is superimposed, in the form of a grid.

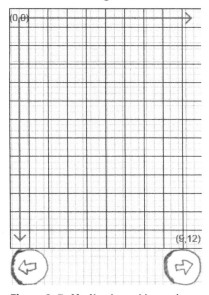

Figure 6–5. *Mr. Nom's world superimposed onto our game screen.*

Notice that Mr. Nom's world is confined to a grid of 10×13 cells. We address cells in a coordinate system with the origin in the upper-left corner at (0, 0), spanning to the bottom-right corner at (9, 12). Any part of Mr. Nom must be in one of these cells, and thus, must have integer x- and y-coordinates within this world. The same is true for the stains in this world. Each part of Mr. Nom fits into exactly one cell of 1×1 units. Note that the type of units doesn't matter—this is our own fantasy world free from the shackles of the SI system or pixels!

Mr. Nom can't travel outside this small world. If he passes an edge he'll just come out the other end, and all his parts will follow. (We have the same problem here on earth by the way—go in any direction for long enough and you'll come back to your starting point). Mr. Nom can also only advance cell by cell. All his parts will always be at integer coordinates. He'll never, for example, occupy two and a half cells.

> **NOTE:** As stated earlier, what we use here is not a strict MVC pattern. If you are interested in the real definition of an MVC pattern, we suggest you read *Design Patterns: Elements of Reusable Object-Oriented Software*, by Erich Gamm, Richard Helm, Ralph Johnson, and John M. Vlissides (a.k.a. the Gang of Four) (Addison-Wesley, 1994). In their book, the MVC pattern is known as the Observer pattern.

The Stain Class

The simplest object in Mr. Nom's world is a stain. It just sits in a cell of the world, waiting to be eaten. When we designed Mr. Nom, we created three different visual representations of a stain. The type of a stain does not make a difference in Mr. Nom's world, but we'll include it in our Stain class anyway. Listing 6–8 shows the Stain class.

Listing 6–8. *Stain.java*

```
package com.badlogic.androidgames.mrnom;

public class Stain {
    public static final int TYPE_1 = 0;
    public static final int TYPE_2 = 1;
    public static final int TYPE_3 = 2;
    public int x, y;
    public int type;

    public Stain(int x, int y, int type) {
        this.x = x;
        this.y = y;
        this.type = type;
    }
}
```

The Stain class defines three public static constants that encode the type of a stain. Each Stain has three members, x- and y-coordinates in Mr. Nom's world, and a type, which is one of the constants that were defined previously. To make our code simple, we don't include getters and setters, as is common practice. We finish the class off with a nice constructor that allows us to instantiate a Stain instance easily.

One thing to notice is the lack of any connection to graphics, sound, or other classes. The Stain class stands on its own, proudly encoding the attributes of a stain in Mr. Nom's world.

The Snake and SnakePart Classes

Mr. Nom is like a moving chain, composed of interconnected parts that will move along when we pick one part and drag it somewhere. Each part occupies a single cell in Mr. Nom's world, much like a stain. In our model, we do not distinguish between the head and tail parts, so we can have a single class that represents both types of parts of Mr.

Nom. Listing 6–9 shows the SnakePart class, which is used to define both parts of Mr. Nom.

Listing 6–9. *SnakePart.java*

```java
package com.badlogic.androidgames.mrnom;

public class SnakePart {
    public int x, y;

    public SnakePart(int x, int y) {
        this.x = x;
        this.y = y;
    }
}
```

This is essentially the same as the Stain class—we just removed the type member. The first really interesting class of our model of Mr. Nom's world is the Snake class. Let's think about what it has to be able to do:

- It must store the head and tail parts.

- It must know which way Mr. Nom is currently heading.

- It must be able to grow a new tail part when Mr. Nom eats a stain.

- It must be able to move by one cell in the current direction.

The first and second items are easy. We just need a list of SnakePart instances—the first part in that list being the head and the other parts making up the tail. Mr. Nom can move up, down, left, and right. We can encode that with some constants and store his current direction in a member of the Snake class.

The third item isn't all that complicated either. We just add another SnakePart to the list of parts we already have. The question is at what position should we add that part? It may sound surprising, but we give it the same position as the last part in the list. The reason for this becomes clearer when we look at how we can implement the last item on the preceding list: moving Mr. Nom.

Figure 6–6 shows Mr. Nom in his initial configuration. He is composed of three parts, the head, at (5, 6), and two tail parts, at (5, 7) and (5, 8).

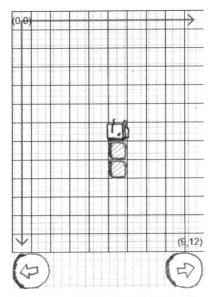

Figure 6–6. *Mr. Nom in his initial configuration.*

The parts in the list are ordered, beginning with the head and ending at the last tail part. When Mr. Nom advances by one cell, all the parts behind his head have to follow. However, Mr. Nom's parts might not be laid out in a straight line, as in Figure 6–6, so simply shifting all the parts in the direction Mr. Nom advances is not enough. We have to do something a little more sophisticated.

We need to start at the last part in the list, as counterintuitive as that may sound. We move it to the position of the part before it, and we repeat this for all other parts in the list, except for the head, as there's no part before it. In the case of the head, we check which direction Mr. Nom is currently heading and modify the head's position accordingly. Figure 6–7 illustrates this with a bit more complicated configuration of Mr. Nom.

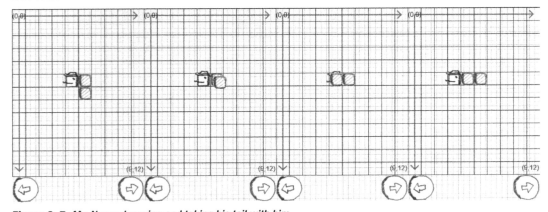

Figure 6–7. *Mr. Nom advancing and taking his tail with him.*

This movement strategy works well with our eating strategy. When we add a new part to Mr. Nom, it will stay at the same position as the part before it the next time Mr. Nom moves. Also, note that this will allow us to implement wrapping Mr. Nom easily to the other side of the world if he passes one of the edges. We just set the head's position accordingly, and the rest is done automatically.

With all this information, we can now implement the Snake class representing Mr. Nom. Listing 6–10 shows the code.

Listing 6–10. *Snake.java; Mr. Nom in Code*

```
package com.badlogic.androidgames.mrnom;

import java.util.ArrayList;
import java.util.List;

public class Snake {
    public static final int UP = 0;
    public static final int LEFT = 1;
    public static final int DOWN = 2;
    public static final int RIGHT = 3;

    public List<SnakePart> parts = new ArrayList<SnakePart>();
    public int direction;
```

We start off by defining a couple of constants that encode the direction of Mr. Nom. Remember that Mr. Nom can only turn left and right, so the way we define the constants' values is critical. It will later allow us to rotate the direction easily by plus and minus 90 degrees, just by incrementing and decrementing the current direction of the constant by one.

Next, we define a list called parts that holds all the parts of Mr. Nom. The first item in that list is the head, and the other items are the tail parts. The second member of the Snake class holds the direction in which Mr. Nom is currently heading.

```
public Snake() {
        direction = UP;
        parts.add(new SnakePart(5, 6));
        parts.add(new SnakePart(5, 7));
        parts.add(new SnakePart(5, 8));
    }
```

In the constructor, we set up Mr. Nom to be composed of his head and two additional tail parts, positioned more or less in the middle of the world, as shown previously in Figure 6–6. We also set the direction to Snake.UP, so that Mr. Nom will advance upward by one cell the next time he's asked to advance.

```
    public void turnLeft() {
        direction += 1;
        if(direction > RIGHT)
            direction = UP;
    }

    public void turnRight() {
        direction -= 1;
```

```
    if(direction < UP)
        direction = RIGHT;
}
```

The methods turnLeft() and turnRight() just modify the direction member of the Snake class. For a turn left, we increment it by one, and for a turn right, we decrement it by one. We also have to make sure that we wrap Mr. Nom around if the direction value gets outside the range of the constants we defined earlier.

```
public void eat() {
    SnakePart end = parts.get(parts.size()-1);
    parts.add(new SnakePart(end.x, end.y));
}
```

Next up is the eat() method. All it does is add a new SnakePart to the end of the list. This new part will have the same position as the current end part. The next time Mr. Nom advances, those two overlapping parts will move apart, as discussed earlier.

```
publicvoid advance() {
    SnakePart head = parts.get(0);

    int len = parts.size() - 1;
    for(int i = len; i > 0; i--) {
        SnakePart before = parts.get(i-1);
        SnakePart part = parts.get(i);
        part.x = before.x;
        part.y = before.y;
    }

    if(direction == UP)
        head.y -= 1;
    if(direction == LEFT)
        head.x -= 1;
    if(direction == DOWN)
        head.y += 1;
    if(direction == RIGHT)
        head.x += 1;

    if(head.x < 0)
        head.x = 9;
    if(head.x > 9)
        head.x = 0;
    if(head.y < 0)
        head.y = 12;
    if(head.y > 12)
        head.y = 0;
}
```

The next method, advance(), implements the logic illustrated in Figure 6–7. First, we move each part to the position of the part before it, starting with the last part. We exclude the head from this mechanism. Then, we move the head according to Mr. Nom's current direction. Finally, we perform some checks to make sure Mr. Nom doesn't go outside his world. If that's the case, we just wrap him around so that he comes out at the other side of the world.

```
public boolean checkBitten() {
        int len = parts.size();
        SnakePart head = parts.get(0);
        for(int i = 1; i < len; i++) {
            SnakePart part = parts.get(i);
            if(part.x == head.x && part.y == head.y)
                return true;
        }
        return false;
    }
}
```

The final method, checkBitten(), is a little helper method that checks if Mr. Nom has bitten his tail. All it does is check that no tail part is at the same position as the head. If that's the case, Mr. Nom will die and the game will end.

The World Class

The last of our model classes is called World. The World class has a couple of tasks to fulfill:

- Keeping track of Mr. Nom (in the form of a Snake instance), as well as the Stain that dropped on the World. There will only ever be a single stain in our world.

- Providing a method that will update Mr. Nom in a time-based manner (for example, he should advance by one cell every 0.5 seconds). This method will also check if Mr. Nom has eaten a stain or has bitten himself.

- Keeping track of the score; this is basically just the number of stains eaten so far times 10.

- Increasing the speed of Mr. Nom after every ten stains he's eaten. That will make the game a little more challenging.

- Keeping track of whether Mr. Nom is still alive. We'll use this to determine whether the game is over later on.

- Creating a new stain after Mr. Nom eats the current one (a subtle but important and surprisingly complex task).

There are only two items on this task list that we haven't discussed yet: updating the world in a time-based manner and placing a new stain.

Time-Based Movement of Mr. Nom

In Chapter 3, we talked about time-based movement. This basically means that we define velocities of all of our game objects, measure the time that has passed since the last update (a.k.a. the delta time), and advance the objects by multiplying their velocity by the delta time. In the example given in Chapter 3, we used floating-point values to achieve this. Mr. Nom's parts have integer positions, though, so we need to figure out how to advance the objects in this scenario.

Let's first define the velocity of Mr. Nom. The world of Mr. Nom has time, and we measure it in seconds. Initially, Mr. Nom should advance by one cell every 0.5 seconds. All we need to do is keep track of how much time has passed since we last advanced Mr. Nom. If that accumulated time goes over our 0.5-second threshold, we call the Snake.advance() method and reset our time accumulator. Where do we get those delta times from? Remember the Screen.update() method. It gets the frame delta time. We just pass that on to the update method of our World class, which will do the accumulation. To make the game more challenging, we will decrease that threshold by 0.05 seconds each time Mr. Nom eats another ten stains. We have to make sure, of course, that we don't reach a threshold of 0, or else Mr. Nom would travel at infinite speed—something Einstein wouldn't take kindly to.

Placing Stains

The second issue we have to solve is how to place a new stain when Mr. Nom has eaten the current one. It should appear in a random cell of the world. So we could just instantiate a new Stain with a random position, right? Sadly, it's not that easy.

Imagine Mr. Nom taking up a considerable number of cells. There is a reasonable probability that the stain would be placed in a cell that's already occupied by Mr. Nom, and it will increase the bigger Mr. Nom gets. Thus, we have to find a cell that is currently not occupied by Mr. Nom. Easy again, right? Just iterate over all cells, and use the first one that is not occupied by Mr. Nom.

Again, that's a little suboptimal. If we started our search at the same position, the stain wouldn't be placed randomly. Instead, we'll start at a random position in the world, scan all cells until we reach the end of the world, and then scan all cells above the start position, if we haven't found a free cell yet.

How do we check whether a cell is free? The naïve solution would be to go over all cells, take each cell's x- and y-coordinates, and check all the parts of Mr. Nom against those coordinates. We have $10 \times 13 = 130$ cells, and Mr. Nom can take up 55 cells. That would be $130 \times 55 = 7,150$ checks! Granted, most devices could handle that, but we can do better.

We'll create a two-dimensional array of Booleans, where each array element represents a cell in the world. When we have to place a new stain, we first go through all parts of Mr. Nom and set those elements that are occupied by a part in the array to true. We then simply choose a random position from which we start scanning until we find a free cell, in which we can place the new stain. With Mr. Nom being composed of 55 parts, it would take $130 + 55 = 185$ checks. That's a lot better!

Determining When the Game Is Over

There's one last thing we have to think about: what if all of the cells are taken up by Mr. Nom? In that case, the game would be over, as Mr. Nom would officially become the whole world. Given that we add 10 to the score each time Mr. Nom eats a stain, the maximally achievable score is $((10 \times 13) - 3) \times 10 = 1{,}270$ points (remember, Mr. Nom starts off with three parts already).

Implementing the World Class

Phew, we have a lot of stuff to implement, so let's get going. Listing 6–11 shows the code of the World class.

Listing 6–11. *World.java*

```java
package com.badlogic.androidgames.mrnom;

import java.util.Random;

public class World {
    static final int WORLD_WIDTH = 10;
    static final int WORLD_HEIGHT = 13;
    static final int SCORE_INCREMENT = 10;
    static final float TICK_INITIAL = 0.5f;
    static final float TICK_DECREMENT = 0.05f;

    public Snake snake;
    public Stain stain;
    public boolean gameOver = false;;
    public int score = 0;

    boolean fields[][] = new boolean[WORLD_WIDTH][WORLD_HEIGHT];
    Random random = new Random();
    float tickTime = 0;
    static float tick = TICK_INITIAL;
```

As always, we start off by defining a couple of constants—in this case, the world's width and height in cells, the value that we use to increment the score each time Mr. Nom eats a stain, the initial time interval used to advance Mr. Nom (called a *tick*), and the value we decrement the tick each time Mr. Nom has eaten ten stains in order to speed up things a little.

Next, we have some public members that hold a Snake instance, a Stain instance, a Boolean that stores whether the game is over, and the current score.

We define another four package private members: the 2D array we'll use to place a new stain; an instance of the Random class, through which we'll produce random numbers to place the stain and generate its type; the time accumulator variable, tickTime, to which we'll add the frame delta time; and the current duration of a tick, which defines how often we advance Mr. Nom.

```java
public World() {
    snake = new Snake();
    placeStain();
}
```

In the constructor, we create an instance of the Snake class, which will have the initial configuration shown in Figure 6–6. We also place the first random stain via the placeStain() method.

```java
private void placeStain() {
    for (int x = 0; x < WORLD_WIDTH; x++) {
        for (int y = 0; y < WORLD_HEIGHT; y++) {
            fields[x][y] = false;
        }
    }

    int len = snake.parts.size();
    for (int i = 0; i < len; i++) {
        SnakePart part = snake.parts.get(i);
        fields[part.x][part.y] = true;
    }

    int stainX = random.nextInt(WORLD_WIDTH);
    int stainY = random.nextInt(WORLD_HEIGHT);
    while (true) {
        if (fields[stainX][stainY] == false)
            break;
        stainX += 1;
        if (stainX >= WORLD_WIDTH) {
            stainX = 0;
            stainY += 1;
            if (stainY >= WORLD_HEIGHT) {
                stainY = 0;
            }
        }
    }
    stain = new Stain(stainX, stainY, random.nextInt(3));
}
```

The placeStain() method implements the placement strategy discussed previously. We start off by clearing the cell array. Next, we set all the cells occupied by parts of the snake to true. Finally, we scan the array for a free cell starting at a random position. Once we have found a free cell, we create a Stain with a random type. Note that if all cells are occupied by Mr. Nom, then the loop will never terminate. We'll make sure that will never happen in the next method.

```java
public void update(float deltaTime) {
    if (gameOver)
        return;

    tickTime += deltaTime;

    while (tickTime > tick) {
        tickTime -= tick;
        snake.advance();
```

```
            if (snake.checkBitten()) {
                gameOver = true;
                return;
            }

            SnakePart head = snake.parts.get(0);
            if (head.x == stain.x && head.y == stain.y) {
                score += SCORE_INCREMENT;
                snake.eat();
                if (snake.parts.size() == WORLD_WIDTH * WORLD_HEIGHT) {
                    gameOver = true;
                    return;
                } else {
                    placeStain();
                }

                if (score % 100 == 0 && tick - TICK_DECREMENT > 0) {
                    tick -= TICK_DECREMENT;
                }
            }
        }
    }
}
```

The update() method is responsible for updating the World and all the objects in it, based on the delta time we pass to it. This method will call each frame in the game screen so that the World is updated constantly. We start off by checking whether the game is over. If that's the case, then we don't need to update anything. Next, we add the delta time to our accumulator. The while loop will use up as many ticks that have been accumulated (for example, when tickTime is 1.2 and one tick should take 0.5 seconds, we can update the world twice, leaving 0.2 seconds in the accumulator). This is called a *fixed-time-step simulation*.

In each iteration, we first subtract the tick interval from the accumulator. Next, we tell Mr. Nom to advance. We check if he has bitten himself, and set the game-over flag if that's the case. Finally, we check whether Mr. Nom's head is in the same cell as the stain. If that's the case, we increment the score and tell Mr. Nom to grow. Next, we check if Mr. Nom is composed of as many parts as there are cells in the world. If that's the case, the game is over and we return from the function. Otherwise, we place a new stain with the placeStain() method. The last thing we do is check whether Mr. Nom has just eaten ten more stains. If that's the case, and our threshold is above zero, we decrease it by 0.05 seconds. The tick will be shorter, and thus, make Mr. Nom move faster.

This completes our set of model classes. The last thing we need to implement is the game screen!

The GameScreen Class

There's only one more screen to implement. Let's see what that screen does:

- As defined in Mr. Nom's design in Chapter 3, the game screen can be in one of four states: waiting for the user to confirm that he or she is ready, running the game, waiting in a paused state, and waiting for the user to click a button in the game-over state.

  - In the ready state, we simply ask the user to touch the screen to start the game.

  - In the running state, we update the world, render it, and also tell Mr. Nom to turn left and right when the player presses one of the buttons at the bottom of the screen.

  - In the paused state, we simply show two options: one to resume the game and one to quit it.

  - In the game-over state, we tell the user that the game is over and provide them with a button to touch so that he or she can get back to the main menu.

- For each state, we have different update and present methods to implement, as each state does different things and shows a different UI.

- Once the game is over, we have to make sure that we store the score, if it is a high score.

That's quite a bit of responsibility, which translates into more code than usual. Therefore, we'll split up the source listing of this class. Before we dive into the code, let's lay out how we arrange the different UI elements in each state. Figure 6–8 shows the four different states.

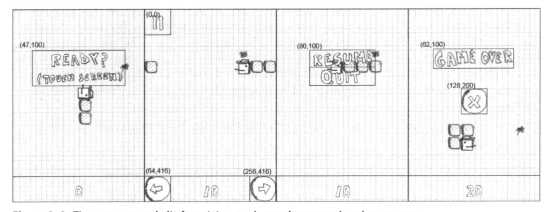

Figure 6–8. *The game screen in its four states: ready, running, paused, and game-over.*

Note that we also render the score at the bottom of the screen, along with a line that separates Mr. Nom's world from the buttons at the bottom. The score is rendered with the same routine that we used in the HighscoreScreen. Additionally, we center it horizontally, based on the score string width.

The last missing bit of information is how to render Mr. Nom's world based on its model. That's actually pretty easy. Take a look at Figure 6–1 and Figure 6–5 again. Each cell is exactly 32×32 pixels in size. The stain images are also 32×32 pixels in size, and so are the tail parts of Mr. Nom. The head images of Mr. Nom for all directions are 42×42 pixels, so they don't fit entirely into a single cell. That's not a problem, though. All we need to do to render Mr. Nom's world is take each stain and snake part, and multiply its world coordinates by 32 to arrive at the object's center in pixels on the screen—for example, a stain at (3,2) in world coordinates would have its center at 96×64 on the screen. Based on these centers, all that's left to do is to take the appropriate asset and render it centered around those coordinates. Let's get coding. Listing 6–12 shows the GameScreen class.

Listing 6–12. *GameScreen.java*

```java
package com.badlogic.androidgames.mrnom;

import java.util.List;

import android.graphics.Color;

import com.badlogic.androidgames.framework.Game;
import com.badlogic.androidgames.framework.Graphics;
import com.badlogic.androidgames.framework.Input.TouchEvent;
import com.badlogic.androidgames.framework.Pixmap;
import com.badlogic.androidgames.framework.Screen;

public class GameScreen extends Screen {
    enum GameState {
        Ready,
        Running,
        Paused,
        GameOver
    }

    GameState state = GameState.Ready;
    World world;
    int oldScore = 0;
    String score = "0";
```

We start off by defining an enumeration called GameState that encodes our four states (ready, running, paused, and game-over). Next, we define a member that holds the current state of the screen, another member that holds the World instance, and two more members that hold the currently-displayed score in the forms of an integer and a string. The reason we have the last two members is that we don't want to create new strings constantly from the World.score member each time we draw the score. Instead, we'll cache the string and only create a new one when the score changes. That way, we play nice with the garbage collector.

```
    public GameScreen(Game game) {
        super(game);
        world = new World();
    }
```

The constructor calls the superclass constructor and creates a new World instance. The game screen will be in the ready state after the constructor returns to the caller.

```
@Override
    public void update(float deltaTime) {
        List<TouchEvent> touchEvents = game.getInput().getTouchEvents();
        game.getInput().getKeyEvents();

        if(state == GameState.Ready)
            updateReady(touchEvents);
        if(state == GameState.Running)
            updateRunning(touchEvents, deltaTime);
        if(state == GameState.Paused)
            updatePaused(touchEvents);
        if(state == GameState.GameOver)
            updateGameOver(touchEvents);
    }
```

Next comes the screen's update() method. All it does is fetch the TouchEvents and KeyEvents from the input module and then delegate the update to one of the four update methods that we implement for each state based on the current state.

```
private void updateReady(List<TouchEvent> touchEvents) {
        if(touchEvents.size() > 0)
            state = GameState.Running;
    }
```

The next method is called updateReady(). It will be called when the screen is in the ready state. All it does is check if the screen was touched. If that's the case, it changes the state to running.

```
private void updateRunning(List<TouchEvent> touchEvents, float deltaTime) {
        int len = touchEvents.size();
        for(int i = 0; i < len; i++) {
            TouchEvent event = touchEvents.get(i);
            if(event.type == TouchEvent.TOUCH_UP) {
                if(event.x < 64 && event.y < 64) {
                    if(Settings.soundEnabled)
                        Assets.click.play(1);
                    state = GameState.Paused;
                    return;
                }
            }
            if(event.type == TouchEvent.TOUCH_DOWN) {
                if(event.x < 64 && event.y > 416) {
                    world.snake.turnLeft();
                }
                if(event.x > 256 && event.y > 416) {
                    world.snake.turnRight();
                }
            }
```

```
        }
        world.update(deltaTime);
        if(world.gameOver) {
            if(Settings.soundEnabled)
                Assets.bitten.play(1);
            state = GameState.GameOver;
        }
        if(oldScore != world.score) {
            oldScore = world.score;
            score = "" + oldScore;
            if(Settings.soundEnabled)
                Assets.eat.play(1);
        }
    }
```

The updateRunning() method first checks whether the pause button in the top-left corner of the screen was pressed. If that's the case, it sets the state to paused. It then checks whether one of the controller buttons at the bottom of the screen was pressed. Note that we don't check for touch-up events here, but for touch-down events. If either of the buttons were pressed, we tell the Snake instance of the World to turn left or right. That's right, the updateRunning() method contains the controller code of our MVC schema! After all the touch events have been checked, we tell the world to update itself with the given delta time. If the World signals that the game is over, we change the state accordingly and also play the bitten.ogg sound. Next, we check if the old score we have cached is different from the score that the World stores. If it is, then we know two things: Mr. Nom has eaten a stain, and the score string must be changed. In that case, we play the eat.ogg sound. And that's all there is to the running state update.

```java
private void updatePaused(List<TouchEvent> touchEvents) {
    int len = touchEvents.size();
    for(int i = 0; i < len; i++) {
        TouchEvent event = touchEvents.get(i);
        if(event.type == TouchEvent.TOUCH_UP) {
            if(event.x > 80 && event.x <= 240) {
                if(event.y > 100 && event.y <= 148) {
                    if(Settings.soundEnabled)
                        Assets.click.play(1);
                    state = GameState.Running;
                    return;
                }
                if(event.y > 148 && event.y < 196) {
                    if(Settings.soundEnabled)
                        Assets.click.play(1);
                    game.setScreen(new MainMenuScreen(game));
                    return;
                }
            }
        }
    }
}
```

The updatePaused() method just checks whether one of the menu options was touched and changes the state accordingly.

```
private void updateGameOver(List<TouchEvent> touchEvents) {
    int len = touchEvents.size();
    for(int i = 0; i < len; i++) {
        TouchEvent event = touchEvents.get(i);
        if(event.type == TouchEvent.TOUCH_UP) {
            if(event.x >= 128 && event.x <= 192 &&
               event.y >= 200 && event.y <= 264) {
                if(Settings.soundEnabled)
                    Assets.click.play(1);
                game.setScreen(new MainMenuScreen(game));
                return;
            }
        }
    }
}
```

The updateGameOver() method also checks if the button in the middle of the screen was pressed. If it has been pressed, then we initiate a screen transition back to the main menu screen.

```
@Override
public void present(float deltaTime) {
    Graphics g = game.getGraphics();

    g.drawPixmap(Assets.background, 0, 0);
    drawWorld(world);
    if(state == GameState.Ready)
        drawReadyUI();
    if(state == GameState.Running)
        drawRunningUI();
    if(state == GameState.Paused)
        drawPausedUI();
    if(state == GameState.GameOver)
        drawGameOverUI();

    drawText(g, score, g.getWidth() / 2 - score.length()*20 / 2, g.getHeight() - 42);
}
```

Next up are the rendering methods. The present() method first draws the background image, as that is needed in all states. Next, it calls the respective drawing method for the state we are in. Finally, it renders Mr. Nom's world and draws the score at the bottom-center of the screen.

```
private void drawWorld(World world) {
    Graphics g = game.getGraphics();
    Snake snake = world.snake;
    SnakePart head = snake.parts.get(0);
    Stain stain = world.stain;

    Pixmap stainPixmap = null;
    if(stain.type == Stain.TYPE_1)
        stainPixmap = Assets.stain1;
    if(stain.type == Stain.TYPE_2)
        stainPixmap = Assets.stain2;
    if(stain.type == Stain.TYPE_3)
```

```
            stainPixmap = Assets.stain3;
        int x = stain.x * 32;
        int y = stain.y * 32;
        g.drawPixmap(stainPixmap, x, y);

        int len = snake.parts.size();
        for(int i = 1; i < len; i++) {
            SnakePart part = snake.parts.get(i);
            x = part.x * 32;
            y = part.y * 32;
            g.drawPixmap(Assets.tail, x, y);
        }

        Pixmap headPixmap = null;
        if(snake.direction == Snake.UP)
            headPixmap = Assets.headUp;
        if(snake.direction == Snake.LEFT)
            headPixmap = Assets.headLeft;
        if(snake.direction == Snake.DOWN)
            headPixmap = Assets.headDown;
        if(snake.direction == Snake.RIGHT)
            headPixmap = Assets.headRight;
        x = head.x * 32 + 16;
        y = head.y * 32 + 16;
        g.drawPixmap(headPixmap, x - headPixmap.getWidth() / 2, y -
headPixmap.getHeight() / 2);
    }
```

The drawWorld() method draws the world, as we just discussed. It starts off by choosing the Pixmap to use for rendering the stain, and then it draws it and centers it horizontally at its screen position. Next, we render all the tail parts of Mr. Nom, which is pretty simple. Finally, we choose which Pixmap of the head to use, based on Mr. Nom's direction, and draw that Pixmap at the position of the head in the screen coordinates. As with the other objects, we also center the image around that position. And that's the code of the view in MVC.

```
private void drawReadyUI() {
        Graphics g = game.getGraphics();

        g.drawPixmap(Assets.ready, 47, 100);
        g.drawLine(0, 416, 480, 416, Color.BLACK);
    }

    private void drawRunningUI() {
        Graphics g = game.getGraphics();

        g.drawPixmap(Assets.buttons, 0, 0, 64, 128, 64, 64);
        g.drawLine(0, 416, 480, 416, Color.BLACK);
        g.drawPixmap(Assets.buttons, 0, 416, 64, 64, 64, 64);
        g.drawPixmap(Assets.buttons, 256, 416, 0, 64, 64, 64);
    }

    private void drawPausedUI() {
        Graphics g = game.getGraphics();

        g.drawPixmap(Assets.pause, 80, 100);
```

```
            g.drawLine(0, 416, 480, 416, Color.BLACK);
    }

    private void drawGameOverUI() {
        Graphics g = game.getGraphics();

        g.drawPixmap(Assets.gameOver, 62, 100);
        g.drawPixmap(Assets.buttons, 128, 200, 0, 128, 64, 64);
        g.drawLine(0, 416, 480, 416, Color.BLACK);
    }

    public void drawText(Graphics g, String line, int x, int y) {
        int len = line.length();
        for (int i = 0; i < len; i++) {
            char character = line.charAt(i);

            if (character == ' ') {
                x += 20;
                continue;
            }

            int srcX = 0;
            int srcWidth = 0;
            if (character == '.') {
                srcX = 200;
                srcWidth = 10;
            } else {
                srcX = (character - '0') * 20;
                srcWidth = 20;
            }

            g.drawPixmap(Assets.numbers, x, y, srcX, 0, srcWidth, 32);
            x += srcWidth;
        }
    }
```

The methods drawReadUI(), drawRunningUI(), drawPausedUI(), and drawGameOverUI()
are nothing new. They perform the same old UI rendering as always, based on the
coordinates shown Figure 6–8. The drawText() method is the same as the one in
HighscoreScreen, so we won't discuss that one either.

```
    @Override
    public void pause() {
        if(state == GameState.Running)
            state = GameState.Paused;

        if(world.gameOver) {
            Settings.addScore(world.score);
            Settings.save(game.getFileIO());
        }
    }

    @Override
    public void resume() {

    }
```

```
@Override
public void dispose() {

    }
}
```

Finally, there's one last vital method, pause(), which gets called when the activity is paused or the game screen is replaced by another screen. That's the perfect place to save our settings. First, we set the state of the game to paused. If the paused() method got called due to the activity being paused, this will guarantee that the user will be asked to resume the game when he or she returns to it. That's good behavior, as it would be stressful to pick up immediately from where one left the game. Next, we check whether the game screen is in a game-over state. If that's the case, we add the score the player achieved to the high scores (or not, depending on its value) and save all the settings to the external storage.

And that's it. We've written a full-fledged game for Android from scratch! We can be proud of ourselves, as we've conquered all the necessary topics to create almost any game we like. From here on, it's mostly just cosmetics.

Summary

In this chapter, we implemented a complete game on top of our framework with all the bells and whistles (minus music). You learned why it makes sense to separate the model from the view and the controller, and you learned that we don't need to define our game world in terms of pixels. We could take this code and replace the rendering portions with OpenGL ES, making Mr. Nom go 3D. We could also spice up the current renderer by adding animations to Mr. Nom, adding in some color, adding new game mechanics, and so on. We have just scratched the surface of the possibilities, however.

Before continuing with the book, we suggest taking the game code and playing around with it. Add some new game modes, power-ups, and enemies—anything you can think of.

Once you come back, in the next chapter, we'll beef up our knowledge of graphics programming to make our games look a bit fancier, and we'll also take your first steps into the third dimension!

Chapter 7

OpenGL ES: A Gentle Introduction

Mr. Nom was a great success. Due to its solid initial design and game framework, implementing Mr. Nom was a breeze for us. Best of all, the game runs smoothly even on low-end devices. Of course, Mr. Nom is not a very complex or graphically intense game, so using the Canvas API for rendering proved to be a good idea.

However, when you want to do something more complex—say, something like Replica Island—you will hit a wall: Canvas just can't keep up with the visual complexity of such a game. And if you want to go fancy-pants 3D, Canvas won't help you either. So . . . what can you do?

This is where OpenGL ES comes to the rescue. In this chapter, first we'll look briefly at what OpenGL ES actually is and does. We'll then focus on using OpenGL ES for 2D graphics without having to dive into the more mathematically complex realms of using the API for 3D graphics (we'll get to that in a later chapter). We'll take baby steps at first, as OpenGL ES can get quite complicated. Are you ready to get introduced to OpenGL ES?

What is OpenGL ES and Why Should I Care?

OpenGL ES is an industry standard for (3D) graphics programming. It is especially targeted at mobile and embedded devices. It is maintained by the Khronos Group, which is a conglomerate including ATI, NVIDIA, and Intel; together, these companies define and extend the standard.

Speaking of standards, there are currently three incremental versions of OpenGL ES: 1.0, 1.1, and 2.0. We are concerned with the first two in this book. All Android devices support OpenGL ES 1.0, and most also support version 1.1, which adds some new features to the 1.0 specification. OpenGL ES 2.0, however, breaks compatibility with the 1.x versions. You can use either 1.x or 2.0, but not both at the same time. The reason for this is that the 1.x versions use a programming model called *fixed-function pipeline*, while version 2.0 lets you programmatically define parts of the rendering pipeline via so-called *shaders*. Many of the second-generation devices already support OpenGL ES 2.0; however, the Java bindings are currently not in a usable state (unless you target the new Android 2.3). OpenGL ES 1.x is more than good enough for most games though, so we will stick to it here.

> **NOTE:** The emulator only supports OpenGL ES 1.0. While OpenGL ES is a standard, different manufacturers interpret it differently and performance across devices varies greatly, so make sure to test on a variety of devices to ensure compatibility.

OpenGL ES is an API that comes in the form of a set of C header files provided by the Khronos group, along with a very detailed specification of how the API defined in those headers should behave. This includes things such as how pixels and lines have to be rendered. Hardware manufacturers then take this specification and implement it for their GPUs on top of the GPU drivers. The quality of these implementations varies slightly: some companies strictly adhere to the standard (PowerVR), while others seem to have difficulty sticking to it. This can sometimes result in GPU-dependent bugs in the implementation that have nothing to do with Android itself, but with the hardware drivers provided by the manufacturers. We'll point out any device-specific issues for you along your journey into OpenGL ES land.

> **NOTE:** OpenGL ES is more or less a sibling of the more feature-rich desktop OpenGL standard. It deviates from the latter in that some of the functionality is reduced or completely removed. Nevertheless, it is possible to write an application that can run with both specifications, which is great if you want to port your game to your desktop as well.

So what does OpenGL ES actually do? The short answer is that it's a lean and mean triangle-rendering machine. The long answer is a little bit more involved.

The Programming Model: An Analogy

Generally speaking, OpenGL ES is a 3D graphics programming API. As such, it has a pretty nice and easy-to-understand programming model that we can illustrate with a simple analogy.

Think of OpenGL ES as working like a camera. To take a picture, you have to go to the scene you want to photograph. Your scene is composed of objects—say, a table with more objects on it. They all have a position and orientation relative to your camera as well as different materials and textures. Glass is translucent and reflective; a table is probably made out of wood; a magazine has the latest photo of a politician on it; and so on. Some of the objects might even move around (for example, a fruit fly you can't shoo). Your camera also has properties, such as focal length, field of view, image resolution, size of the photo that will be taken, and a unique position and orientation within the world (relative to some origin). Even if both objects and the camera are moving, when you press the shutter release, you catch a still image of the scene (for now, we'll neglect the shutter speed, which might cause a blurry image). For that infinitely small moment, everything stands still and is well defined, and the picture reflects exactly all those configurations of position, orientation, texture, materials, and lighting. Figure 7–1 shows an abstract scene with a camera, light, and three objects with different materials.

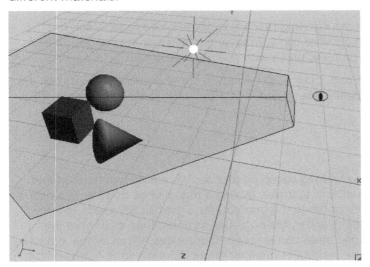

Figure 7–1. *An abstract scene*

Each object has a position and orientation relative to the scene's origin. The camera, indicated by the eye, also has a position in relation to the scene's origin. The pyramid in Figure 7–1 is the so-called *view volume* or *view frustum*, which shows how much of the scene the camera captures and how the camera is oriented. The little white ball with the rays is the light source in the scene, which also has a position relative to the origin.

We can directly map this scene to OpenGL ES, but to do so we need to define a couple of things:

- *Objects (a.k.a. models)*: These are generally composed of four sets of attributes: geometry, color, texture, and material. The geometry is specified as a set of triangles. Each triangle is composed of three points in 3D space, so we have x-, y-, and z-coordinates defined relative to the coordinate system origin, as shown in Figure 7–1. Note that the z-axis points toward us. The color is usually specified as an RGB triple, which we are used to already. Textures and materials are a little bit more involved. We'll get to those later on.

- *Lights*: OpenGL ES offers a couple different light types with various attributes. They are just mathematical objects with positions and/or directions in 3D space, plus attributes such as color.

- *Camera*: This is also a mathematical object that has a position and orientation in 3D space. Additionally, it has parameters that govern how much of the image we see, similar to a real camera. All these things together define a view volume or view frustum (indicated by the pyramid with the top cut off in Figure 7–1). Anything inside this pyramid can be seen by the camera; anything outside will not make it into the final picture.

- *Viewport*: This defines the size and resolution of the final image. Think of it as the type of film you put into your analog camera or the image resolution you get for pictures taken with your digital camera.

Given all this, OpenGL ES can construct a 2D bitmap of our scene from the camera's point of view. Notice that we define everything in 3D space. So, how can OpenGL ES map that to two dimensions?

Projections

This 2D mapping is done via something called *projection*. We already mentioned that OpenGL ES is mainly concerned with triangles. A single triangle has three points defined in 3D space. To render such a triangle to the framebuffer, OpenGL ES needs to know the coordinates of these 3D points within the pixel-based coordinate system of the framebuffer. Once it knows those three corner-point coordinates, it can simply draw the pixels in the framebuffer that are inside the triangle. We could even write our own little OpenGL ES implementation by projecting 3D points to 2D, and simply draw lines between them via the Canvas.

There are two kinds of projections that are commonly used in 3D graphics.

- *Parallel (or orthographic) projection*: If you've ever played with a CAD application, you might already know about this. A parallel projection doesn't care how far an object is away from the camera; the object will always have the same size in the final image. This type of projection is typically used for rendering 2D graphics in OpenGL ES.

- *Perspective projection*: Your eyes use this type of projection every day. Objects further away from you appear smaller on your retina. Perspective projection is typically used when we do 3D graphics with OpenGL ES.

In both cases, you need something called a *projection plane*, which is nearly exactly the same as your retina—it's where the light is actually registered to form the final image. While a mathematical plane is infinite in terms of area, our retina is limited. Our OpenGL ES "retina" is equal to the rectangle at the top of the view frustum seen in Figure 7–1. This part of the view frustum is where OpenGL ES will project the points. This area is called the *near clipping plane*, and it has its own little 2D coordinate system. Figure 7–2 shows that near clipping plane again, from the camera's point of view, with the coordinate system superimposed.

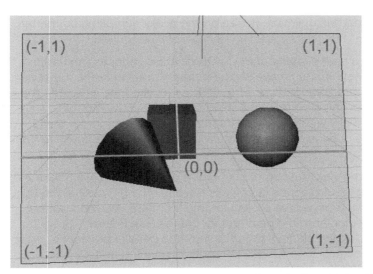

Figure 7–2. *The near clipping plane (also known as the projection plane) and its coordinate system*

Note that the coordinate system is by no means fixed. We can manipulate it so that we can work in any projected coordinate system we like; for example, we could instruct OpenGL ES to let the origin be in the bottom-left corner, and let the visible area of the "retina" be 480 units on the x-axis, and 320 units on the y-axis. Sounds familiar? Yes, OpenGL ES allows you to specify any coordinate system you want for the projected points.

Once we specify our view frustum, OpenGL ES then takes each point of a triangle and shoots a ray from it through the projection plane. The difference between a parallel and a perspective projection is how the directions of those rays are constructed. Figure 7–3 shows the difference between the two, viewed from above.

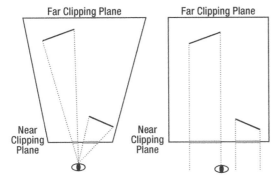

Figure 7–3. *A perspective projection (left) and a parallel projection (right)*

A perspective projection shoots the rays from the triangle points through the camera (or eye, in this case). Objects further away will thus appear smaller on the projection plane. When we use a parallel projection, the rays are shot perpendicular to the projection plane. In this scenario, an object will maintain its size on the projection plane no matter how far away it is.

Our projection plane is called a *near clipping plane* in OpenGL ES lingo, as pointed out earlier. All of the sides of the view frustum have similar names. The one furthest away from the camera is called the *far clipping plane*. The others are called the *left*, *right*, *top*, and *bottom* clipping planes. Anything outside or behind those planes will not be rendered. Objects that are partially within the view frustum will be clipped from these planes, meaning that the parts outside the view frustum get cut away. That's where the name *clipping plane* comes from.

You might be wondering why the view frustum of the parallel projection case in Figure 7–3 is rectangular. It turns out that the projection is actually governed by how we define our clipping planes. In the case of a perspective projection, the left, right, top, and bottom clipping planes are not perpendicular to the near and far planes (see Figure 7–3, which shows only the left and right clipping planes). In the case of the parallel projection, these planes are perpendicular, which tells OpenGL ES to render everything at the same size no matter how far away it is from the camera.

Normalized Device Space and the Viewport

Once OpenGL ES has figured out the projected points of a triangle on the near clipping plane, it can finally translate them to pixel coordinates in the framebuffer. For this, it must first transform the points to so-called *normalized device space*. This equals the coordinate system depicted in Figure 7–2. Based on these normalized device space coordinates, OpenGL ES calculates the final framebuffer pixel coordinates via the following simple formulas:

```
pixelX = (norX + 1) / (viewportWidth + 1) + norX
pixelY = (norY + 1) / (viewportHeight +1) + norY
```

Where norX and norY are the normalized device coordinates of a 3D point, and viewportWidth and viewportHeight are the size of the viewport in pixels on the x- and y-axes. We don't have to worry about the normalized device coordinates all that much, as OpenGL will do the transformation for us automatically. What we do care about, though, are the viewport and the view frustum.

Matrices

Later, you will see how to specify a view frustum, and thus a projection. OpenGL ES expresses projections in the form of *matrices*. We don't need to know the internals of matrices. We only need to know what they do to the points we define in our scene. Here's the executive summary of matrices:

- A matrix encodes transformations to be applied to a point. A transformation can be a projection, a translation (in which the point is moved around), a rotation around another point and axis, or a scale, among other things.

- By multiplying such a matrix with a point, we apply the transformation to the point. For example, multiplying a point with a matrix that encodes a translation by 10 units on the x-axis will move the point 10 units on the x-axis and thereby modify its coordinates.

- We can concatenate transformations stored in separate matrices into a single matrix by multiplying the matrices. When we multiply this single concatenated matrix with a point, all the transformations stored in that matrix will be applied to that point. The order in which the transformations are applied is dependent on the order in which we multiplied the matrices.

- There's a special matrix called an *identity matrix*. If we multiply a matrix or a point with it, nothing will happen. Think of multiplying a point or matrix by an identity matrix as multiplying a number by 1. It simply has no effect. The relevance of the identity matrix will become clear once you learn how OpenGL ES handles matrices (see the section "Matrix Modes and Active Matrices")—a classic chicken and egg problem.

> **NOTE:** When we talk about points in this context, we actually mean 3D vectors.

OpenGL ES has three different matrices that it applies to the points of our models:

- *Model-view matrix*: We can use this matrix to move, rotate, or scale the points of our triangles (this is the *model* part of the model-view matrix). This matrix is also used to specify the position and orientation of our camera (this is the *view* part).

- *Projection matrix*: The name says it all—this matrix encodes a projection, and thus the view frustum of our camera.

- *Texture matrix*: This matrix allows us to manipulate texture coordinates (which we'll discuss later). However, we'll avoid using this matrix in this book since this part of OpenGL ES is broken on a couple of devices thanks to buggy drivers.

The Rendering Pipeline

OpenGL ES keeps track of these three matrices. Each time we set one of the matrices, it will remember it until we change the matrix again. In OpenGL ES speak, this is called a *state*. OpenGL keeps track of more than just the matrix states though; it also keeps track of whether we want to alpha-blend triangles, whether we want lighting to be taken into account, which texture should be applied to our geometry, and so on; in fact, OpenGL ES is one huge state machine. We set its current state, feed it the geometries of our objects, and tell it to render an image for us. Let's see how a triangle passes through this mighty triangle-rendering machine. Figure 7–4 shows a very high-level, simplified view of the OpenGL ES pipeline.

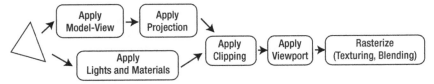

Figure 7–4. *The way of the triangle*

The way of a triangle through this pipeline looks as follows:

1. Our brave triangle is first transformed by the model-view matrix. This means that all its points are multiplied with this matrix. This multiplication will effectively move the triangle's points around in the world.

2. The resulting output is then multiplied by the projection matrix, effectively transforming the 3D points onto the 2D projection plane.

3. In between these two steps (or parallel to them), the currently set lights and materials are also applied to our triangle, giving it its color.

4. Once all that is done, the projected triangle is clipped to our "retina" and transformed to framebuffer coordinates.

5. As a final step, OpenGL fills in the pixels of the triangle based on the colors from the lighting stage, textures to be applied to the triangle, and the blending state in which each pixel of the triangle might or might not be combined with the pixel in the framebuffer.

All you need to learn is how to throw geometry and textures at OpenGL ES, and to set the states used by each of the preceding steps. Before you can do that, you need to see how Android grants you access to OpenGL ES.

> **NOTE:** While the high-level description of the OpenGL ES pipeline is mostly correct, it is heavily simplified and leaves out some details that will become important in a later chapter. Another thing to note is that when OpenGL ES performs projections, it doesn't actually project onto a 2D coordinate system; instead, it projects into something called a *homogenous coordinate system*, which is actually four dimensional. This is a very involved mathematical topic, so for the sake of simplicity, we'll just stick to the simplified premise that OpenGL ES projects to 2D coordinates.

Before We Begin

Throughout the rest of this chapter, we'll provide many brief examples, as we did in Chapter 4 when we discussed Android API basics. We'll use the same starter class that we did in Chapter 4, which shows you a list of test Activities you can start. The only things that will change are the names of the Activities you instantiate via reflection, and the package in which they are located. All the examples in the rest of this chapter will be in the package com.badlogic.androidgames.glbasics. The rest of the code will stay the same. Your new starter Activity will be called GLBasicsStarter. You will also copy over all the source code from Chapter 5, which contains your framework classes, as you of course want to reuse those. Finally, you will write some new framework and helper classes, which will go in the com.badlogic.androidgames.framework package and subpackages.

We also have a manifest file again. As each of the following examples will be an Activity, we also have to make sure each activity has an entry in the manifest. All the examples will use a fixed orientation (either portrait or landscape, depending on the example), and will tell Android that they can handle keyboard, keyboardHidden, and orientationChange events.

With that out of our way, let the fun begin!

GLSurfaceView: Making Things Easy Since 2008

The first thing we need is some type of View that will allow us to draw via OpenGL ES. Luckily, there's such a View in the Android API—it's called GLSurfaceView, and it's a descendent of the SurfaceView class, which we already used for drawing the world of Mr. Nom.

We also need a separate main loop thread again so that we don't bog down the UI thread. Surprise: GLSurfaceView already sets up such a thread for us! All we need to do is implement a listener interface called GLSurfaceView.Renderer and register it with the GLSurfaceView. The interface has three methods.

```
interface Renderer {
    public void onSurfaceCreated(GL10 gl, EGLConfig config);

    public void onSurfaceChanged(GL10 gl, int width, int height);

    public void onDrawFrame(GL10 gl);
}
```

The onSurfaceCreated() method is called each time the GLSurfaceView surface is created. This happens the first time we fire up the Activity and each time we come back to the Activity from a paused state. The method takes two parameters: a GL10 instance and an EGLConfig. The GL10 instance allows us to issue commands to OpenGL ES. The EGLConfig just tells us about the attributes of the surface, such as the color, depth, and so on. We usually ignore it. We will set up our geometries and textures in the onSurfaceCreated() method.

The onSurfaceChanged() method is called each time the surface is resized. We get the new width and height of the surface in pixels as parameters, along with a GL10 instance if we want to issue OpenGL ES commands.

The onDrawFrame() method is where the fun happens. It is similar in spirit to our Screen.render() method, which gets called as often as possible by the rendering thread that the GLSurfaceView sets up for us. In this method, we perform all our rendering.

Besides registering a Renderer listener, we also have to call GLSurfaceView.onPause()/onResume() in our Activity's onPause()/onResume() methods. The reason for this is simple. The GLSurfaceView will start up the rendering thread in its onResume() method and tear it down in its onPause()method. This means that our listener will not be called while our Activity is paused, since the rendering thread which calls our listener will also be paused.

Here comes the only bummer: each time our Activity is paused, the surface of the GLSurfaceView will be destroyed. When the Activity is resumed again—and GLSurfaceView.onResume() is called—the GLSurfaceView instantiates a new OpenGL ES rendering surface, and informs us of this by calling our listener's onSurfaceCreated() method. This would all be well and good if not for a single problem: all the OpenGL ES states that we've set so far will be lost. This also includes things such as textures, which we'll have to reload. This problem is known as a *context loss*. The word *context* stems from the fact that OpenGL ES associates a context with each surface we create, which holds the current states. When we destroy that surface, the context is lost as well. It's not all that bad though, given that we design our games properly to handle this context loss.

> **NOTE:** Actually, EGL is responsible for context and surface creation and destruction. EGL is another Khronos Group standard; it defines how an operating system's UI works together with OpenGL ES, and how the operating system grants OpenGL ES access to the underlying graphics hardware. This includes surface creation as well as context management. Since GLSurfaceView handles all the EGL stuff for us, we can safely ignore it in almost all cases.

Following tradition, let's write a small example that will clear the screen with a random color each frame. Listing 7–1 shows the code.

Listing 7–1. *GLSurfaceViewTest.java; Screen-Clearing Madness*

```java
package com.badlogic.androidgames.glbasics;

import java.util.Random;

import javax.microedition.khronos.egl.EGLConfig;
import javax.microedition.khronos.opengles.GL10;

import android.app.Activity;
import android.opengl.GLSurfaceView;
import android.opengl.GLSurfaceView.Renderer;
import android.os.Bundle;
import android.util.Log;
import android.view.Window;
import android.view.WindowManager;

public class GLSurfaceViewTest extends Activity {
    GLSurfaceView glView;
```

```
public void onCreate(Bundle savedInstanceState) {
    super.onCreate(savedInstanceState);
    requestWindowFeature(Window.FEATURE_NO_TITLE);
    getWindow().setFlags(WindowManager.LayoutParams.FLAG_FULLSCREEN,
            WindowManager.LayoutParams.FLAG_FULLSCREEN);
    glView = new GLSurfaceView(this);
    glView.setRenderer(new SimpleRenderer());
    setContentView(glView);
}
```

We keep a reference to a GLSurfaceView instance as a member of the class. In the onCreate() method, we make our application go full-screen, create the GLSurfaceView, set our Renderer implementation, and make the GLSurfaceView the content view of our Activity.

```
@Override
public void onResume() {
    super.onPause();
    glView.onResume();
}

@Override
public void onPause() {
    super.onPause();
    glView.onPause();
}
```

In the onResume() and onPause() methods, we call the supermethods as well as the respective GLSurfaceView methods. These will start up and tear down the rendering thread of the GLSurfaceView, which in turn will trigger the callback methods of our Renderer implementation at appropriate times.

```
static class SimpleRenderer implements Renderer {
    Random rand = new Random();

    @Override
    public void onSurfaceCreated(GL10 gl, EGLConfig config) {
        Log.d("GLSurfaceViewTest", "surface created");
    }

    @Override
    public void onSurfaceChanged(GL10 gl, int width, int height) {
        Log.d("GLSurfaceViewTest", "surface changed: " + width + "x"
                + height);
    }

    @Override
    public void onDrawFrame(GL10 gl) {
        gl.glClearColor(rand.nextFloat(), rand.nextFloat(),
                rand.nextFloat(), 1);
        gl.glClear(GL10.GL_COLOR_BUFFER_BIT);
    }
}
```

The final piece of the code is our Renderer implementation. It just logs some information in the onSurfaceCreated() and onSurfaceChanged() methods. The really interesting part is the onDrawFrame() method.

As stated earlier, the GL10 instance gives us access to the OpenGL ES API. The 10 in GL10 indicates that it offers us all the functions defined in the OpenGL ES 1.0 standard. For now, we can be happy with that. All the methods of that class map to a corresponding C function, as defined in the standard. Each method begins with the prefix gl, an old tradition of OpenGL ES.

The first OpenGL ES method we call is glClearColor(). You probably already know what that will do. It sets the color to be used when we issue a command to clear the screen. Colors in OpenGL ES are almost always RGBA, where each component has a range between 0 and 1. There are ways to define a color in, say, RGB565, but for now, let's stick to the floating-point representation. We could set the color used for clearing only once and OpenGL ES would remember it. The color we set with glClearColor() is one of OpenGL ES's states.

The next call actually clears the screen with the clear color we just specified. The method glClear() takes a single argument that specifies which buffer to clear. OpenGL ES does not only have the notation of a framebuffer that holds pixels, but also other types of buffers. You'll get to know them in Chapter 10, but for now, all we care about is the framebuffer that holds our pixels, which OpenGL ES calls the *color buffer*. To tell OpenGL ES that we want to clear that exact buffer, we specify the constant GL10.GL_COLOR_BUFFER_BIT.

OpenGL ES has a lot of constants, which are all defined as static public members of the GL10 interface. Like the methods, each constant has the prefix GL_.

So, that was our first OpenGL ES application. We'll spare you the impressive screenshot, since you probably know what it looks like.

> **NOTE:** Thou shalt never call OpenGL ES from another thread! First and last commandment! The reason is that OpenGL ES is designed to be used in single threaded environments only, and it is not thread-safe. It can be made to work somewhat on multiple threads, but many drivers have problems with this and there's no real benefit to doing so.

GLGame: Implementing the Game Interface

In the previous chapter, we implemented the AndroidGame class, which ties together all the submodules for audio, file I/O, graphics, and user input handling. We want to reuse most of this for our upcoming 2D OpenGL ES game, so let's implement a new class called GLGame that implements the Game interface we defined earlier.

The first thing you will notice is that you can't possibly implement the Graphics interface with your current knowledge of OpenGL ES. Here's a surprise: you won't implement it. OpenGL does not lend itself well to the programming model of your Graphics interface;

instead, we'll implement a new class, GLGraphics, which will keep track of the GL10 instance we get from the GLSurfaceView. Listing 7–2 shows the code.

Listing 7–2. *GLGraphics.java; Keeping Track of the GLSurfaceView and the GL10 Instance*

```java
package com.badlogic.androidgames.framework.impl;

import javax.microedition.khronos.opengles.GL10;

import android.opengl.GLSurfaceView;

public class GLGraphics {
    GLSurfaceView glView;
    GL10 gl;

    GLGraphics(GLSurfaceView glView) {
        this.glView = glView;
    }

    public GL10 getGL() {
        return gl;
    }

    void setGL(GL10 gl) {
        this.gl = gl;
    }

    public int getWidth() {
        return glView.getWidth();
    }

    public int getHeight() {
        return glView.getHeight();
    }
}
```

This class has just a few getters and setters. Note that we will use this class in the rendering thread set up by the GLSurfaceView. As such, it might be problematic to call methods of a View, which lives mostly on the UI thread. In this case, it's OK, as we only query for the GLSurfaceView's width and height, so we get away with it.

The GLGame class is a bit more involved. It borrows most of its code from the AndroidGame class. The synchronization between the rendering and UI threads is a little bit more complex. Let's have a look at it in Listing 7–3.

Listing 7–3. *GLGame.java, the Mighty OpenGL ES Game Implementation*

```java
package com.badlogic.androidgames.framework.impl;

import javax.microedition.khronos.egl.EGLConfig;
import javax.microedition.khronos.opengles.GL10;

import android.app.Activity;
import android.content.Context;
import android.opengl.GLSurfaceView;
import android.opengl.GLSurfaceView.Renderer;
```

```java
import android.os.Bundle;
import android.os.PowerManager;
import android.os.PowerManager.WakeLock;
import android.view.Window;
import android.view.WindowManager;

import com.badlogic.androidgames.framework.Audio;
import com.badlogic.androidgames.framework.FileIO;
import com.badlogic.androidgames.framework.Game;
import com.badlogic.androidgames.framework.Graphics;
import com.badlogic.androidgames.framework.Input;
import com.badlogic.androidgames.framework.Screen;

public abstract class GLGame extends Activity implements Game, Renderer {
    enum GLGameState {
        Initialized,
        Running,
        Paused,
        Finished,
        Idle
    }

    GLSurfaceView glView;
    GLGraphics glGraphics;
    Audio audio;
    Input input;
    FileIO fileIO;
    Screen screen;
    GLGameState state = GLGameState.Initialized;
    Object stateChanged = new Object();
    long startTime = System.nanoTime();
    WakeLock wakeLock;
```

The class extends the Activity class and implements the Game and
GLSurfaceView.Renderer interface. It has an enum called GLGameState that keeps track
of the state that the GLGame instance is in. You'll see how those are used in a bit.

The members of the class consist of a GLSurfaceView and GLGraphics instance. The
class also has Audio, Input, FileIO, and Screen instances, which we need for writing our
game, just as we did for the AndroidGame class. The state member keeps track of the
state via one of the GLGameState enums. The stateChanged member is an object we'll
use to synchronize the UI and rendering threads. Finally, we have a member to keep
track of the delta time and a WakeLock that we'll use to keep the screen from dimming.

```java
@Override
public void onCreate(Bundle savedInstanceState) {
    super.onCreate(savedInstanceState);
    requestWindowFeature(Window.FEATURE_NO_TITLE);
    getWindow().setFlags(WindowManager.LayoutParams.FLAG_FULLSCREEN,
                         WindowManager.LayoutParams.FLAG_FULLSCREEN);
    glView = new GLSurfaceView(this);
    glView.setRenderer(this);
    setContentView(glView);

    glGraphics = new GLGraphics(glView);
```

```
        fileIO = new AndroidFileIO(getAssets());
        audio = new AndroidAudio(this);
        input = new AndroidInput(this, glView, 1, 1);
        PowerManager powerManager = (PowerManager)
getSystemService(Context.POWER_SERVICE);
        wakeLock = powerManager.newWakeLock(PowerManager.FULL_WAKE_LOCK, "GLGame");
    }
```

In the onCreate() method, we perform the usual setup routine. We make the Activity go full-screen and instantiate the GLSurfaceView, setting it as the content View. We also instantiate all the other classes that implement framework interfaces, such as the AndroidFileIO or AndroidInput classes. Note that we reuse the classes we used in the AndroidGame class, except for AndroidGraphics. Another important point is that we no longer let the AndroidInput class scale the touch coordinates to a target resolution, as in AndroidGame. The scale values are both 1, so we will get the real touch coordinates. It will become clear later on why we do that. The last thing we do is create the WakeLock instance.

```
    public void onResume() {
        super.onResume();
        glView.onResume();
        wakeLock.acquire();
    }
```

In the onResume() method, we let the GLSurfaceView start the rendering thread with a call to its onResume() method. We also acquire the WakeLock.

```
    @Override
    public void onSurfaceCreated(GL10 gl, EGLConfig config) {
        glGraphics.setGL(gl);

        synchronized(stateChanged) {
            if(state == GLGameState.Initialized)
                screen = getStartScreen();
            state = GLGameState.Running;
            screen.resume();
            startTime = System.nanoTime();
        }
    }
```

The onSurfaceCreate() method will be called next, which is, of course, invoked on the rendering thread. Here, you can see how the state enums are used. If the application is started for the first time, the state will be GLGameState.Initialized. In this case, we call the getStartScreen() method to return the starting screen of the game. If the game is not in an initialized state but was already been running, we know that we have just resumed from a paused state. In any case, we set the state to GLGameState.Running and call the current Screen's resume() method. We also keep track of the current time, so we can calculate the delta time later on.

The synchronization is necessary, since the members we manipulate within the synchronized block could be manipulated in the onPause() method on the UI thread. That's something we have to prevent, so we use an object as a lock. We could have also used the GLGame instance itself, or a proper lock.

```
    @Override
    public void onSurfaceChanged(GL10 gl, int width, int height) {
    }
```

The onSurfaceChanged() method is basically just a stub. There's nothing for us to do here.

```
    @Override
    public void onDrawFrame(GL10 gl) {
        GLGameState state = null;

        synchronized(stateChanged) {
            state = this.state;
        }

        if(state == GLGameState.Running) {
            float deltaTime = (System.nanoTime()-startTime) / 1000000000.0f;
            startTime = System.nanoTime();

            screen.update(deltaTime);
            screen.present(deltaTime);
        }

        if(state == GLGameState.Paused) {
            screen.pause();
            synchronized(stateChanged) {
                this.state = GLGameState.Idle;
                stateChanged.notifyAll();
            }
        }

        if(state == GLGameState.Finished) {
            screen.pause();
            screen.dispose();
            synchronized(stateChanged) {
                this.state = GLGameState.Idle;
                stateChanged.notifyAll();
            }
        }
    }
```

The onDrawFrame() method is where the bulk of all the work is performed. It is called by the rendering thread as often as possible. Here, we check the state our game is in and react accordingly. As the state can be set on the onPause() method on the UI thread, we have to synchronize the access to it.

If the game is running, we calculate the delta time and tell the current Screen to update and present itself.

If the game is paused, we tell the current Screen to pause itself as well. We then change the state to GLGameState.Idle, indicating that we have received the pause request from the UI thread. Since we wait for this to happen in the onPause() method in the UI thread, we notify the UI thread that it can now truly pause the application. This notification is necessary, as we have to make sure that the rendering thread is paused/shut down properly in case our Activity is paused or closed on the UI thread.

If the Activity is being closed (and not paused), we react to GLGameState.Finished. In this case, we tell the current Screen to pause and dispose of itself, and then send another notification to the UI thread, which waits for the rendering thread to shut things down properly.

```
@Override
public void onPause() {
    synchronized(stateChanged) {
        if(isFinishing())
            state = GLGameState.Finished;
        else
            state = GLGameState.Paused;
        while(true) {
            try {
                stateChanged.wait();
                break;
            } catch(InterruptedException e) {
            }
        }
    }
    wakeLock.release();
    glView.onPause();
    super.onPause();
}
```

The onPause() method is our usual Activity notification method that's called on the UI thread when the Activity is paused. Depending on whether the application is closed or paused, we set the state accordingly and wait for the rendering thread to process the new state. This is achieved with the standard Java wait/notify mechanism.

Finally, we release the WakeLock and tell the GLSurfaceView and the Activity to pause themselves, effectively shutting down the rendering thread and destroying the OpenGL ES surface, which triggers the dreaded OpenGL ES context loss mentioned earlier.

```
public GLGraphics getGLGraphics() {
    return glGraphics;
}
```

The getGLGraphics() method is a new method that is only accessible via the GLGame class. It returns the instance of GLGraphics we store so that we can get access to the GL10 interface in our Screen implementations later on.

```
@Override
public Input getInput() {
    return input;
}

@Override
public FileIO getFileIO() {
    return fileIO;
}

@Override
public Graphics getGraphics() {
    throw new IllegalStateException("We are using OpenGL!");
```

```
        }

        @Override
        public Audio getAudio() {
            return audio;
        }

        @Override
        public void setScreen(Screen screen) {
            if (screen == null)
                throw new IllegalArgumentException("Screen must not be null");

            this.screen.pause();
            this.screen.dispose();
            screen.resume();
            screen.update(0);
            this.screen = screen;
        }

        @Override
        public Screen getCurrentScreen() {
            return screen;
        }
}
```

The rest of the class works as before. In case we accidentally try to access the standard Graphics instance, we throw an exception, as it is not supported by GLGame. Instead we'll work with the GLGraphics method we get via the GLGame.getGLGraphics() method.

Why did we go through all the pain of synchronizing with the rendering thread? Well, it will make our Screen implementations live entirely on the rendering thread. All the methods of Screen will be executed there, which is necessary if we want to access OpenGL ES functionality. Remember, we can only access OpenGL ES on the rendering thread.

Let's round this out with an example. Listing 7–4 shows how our first example in this chapter looks when using GLGame and Screen.

Listing 7–4. *GLGameTest.java; More Screen Clearing, Now with 100 Percent More GLGame*

```
package com.badlogic.androidgames.glbasics;

import java.util.Random;

import javax.microedition.khronos.opengles.GL10;

import com.badlogic.androidgames.framework.Game;
import com.badlogic.androidgames.framework.Screen;
import com.badlogic.androidgames.framework.impl.GLGame;
import com.badlogic.androidgames.framework.impl.GLGraphics;

public class GLGameTest extends GLGame {
    @Override
    public Screen getStartScreen() {
        return new TestScreen(this);
    }
```

```
class TestScreen extends Screen {
    GLGraphics glGraphics;
    Random rand = new Random();

    public TestScreen(Game game) {
        super(game);
        glGraphics = ((GLGame) game).getGLGraphics();
    }

    @Override
    public void present(float deltaTime) {
        GL10 gl = glGraphics.getGL();
        gl.glClearColor(rand.nextFloat(), rand.nextFloat(),
                rand.nextFloat(), 1);
        gl.glClear(GL10.GL_COLOR_BUFFER_BIT);
    }

    @Override
    public void update(float deltaTime) {
    }

    @Override
    public void pause() {
    }

    @Override
    public void resume() {
    }

    @Override
    public void dispose() {
    }
}
}
```

This is the same program as our last example, except that we now derive from GLGame instead of Activity, and we provide a Screen implementation instead of a GLSurfaceView.Renderer implementation.

In the following examples, we'll only have a look at the relevant parts of each example's Screen implementation. The overall structure of our examples will stay the same. Of course, we have to add the example GLGame implementations to our starter Activity, as well as to the manifest file.

With that out of our way, let's render our first triangle.

Look Mom, I Got a Red Triangle!

You already learned that OpenGL ES needs a couple of things set before we can tell it to draw some geometry. The two things about which we are most concerned are the projection matrix (and with it our view frustum) and the viewport, which governs the size of our output image and the position of our rendering output in the framebuffer.

Defining the Viewport

OpenGL ES uses the viewport as a way to translate the coordinates of points projected to the near clipping plane to framebuffer pixel coordinates. We can tell OpenGL ES to use only a portion of our framebuffer—or all of it—with the following method:

```
GL10.glViewport(int x, int y, int width, int height)
```

The x- and y-coordinates specify the top-left corner of the viewport in the framebuffer, and width and height specify the viewport's size in pixels. Note that OpenGL ES assumes the framebuffer coordinate system to have its origin in the lower left of the screen. Usually we set x and y to zero and width and height to our screen resolution, as we are using full-screen mode. We could instruct OpenGL ES to use only a portion of the framebuffer with this method. It would then take the rendering output and automatically stretch it to that portion.

> **NOTE:** While this method looks like it sets up a 2D coordinate system for us to render to, it actually does not. It only defines the portion of the framebuffer OpenGL ES uses to output the final image. Our coordinate system is defined via the projection and model-view matrices.

Defining the Projection Matrix

The next thing we need to define is the projection matrix. As we are only concerned with 2D graphics in this chapter, we want to use a parallel projection. How do we do that?

Matrix Modes and Active Matrices

We already discussed that OpenGL ES keeps track of three matrices: the projection matrix, the model-view matrix, and the texture matrix (which we'll continue to ignore). OpenGL ES offers a couple specific methods to modify these matrices. Before we can use these methods, however, we have to tell OpenGL ES which matrix we want to manipulate. This is done with the following method:

```
GL10.glMatrixMode(int mode)
```

The mode parameter can be GL10.GL_PROJECTION, GL10.GL_MODELVIEW, or GL10.GL_TEXTURE. It should be clear which of these constants will make which matrix active. Any subsequent calls to the matrix manipulation methods will target the matrix we set with this method until we change the active matrix again via another call to this method. This matrix mode is one of OpenGL ES's states (which will get lost when we lose the context if our application is paused and resumed). To manipulate the projection matrix with any subsequent calls, we can call the method like this:

```
gl.glMatrixMode(GL10.GL_PROJECTION);
```

Orthographic Projection with glOrthof

OpenGL ES offers the following method for setting the active matrix to an orthographic (parallel) projection matrix:

```
GL10.glOrthof(int left, int right, int bottom, int top, int near, int far)
```

Hey, that looks like it has something to do with our view frustum's clipping planes . . . and indeed it does! So what values do we specify here?

OpenGL ES has a standard coordinate system, as depicted in Figure 7–4. The positive x-axis points to the right, the positive y-axis points upward, and the positive z-axis points toward us. With glOrthof(), we define the view frustum of our parallel projection in this coordinate system. If you look back at Figure 7–3, you can see that the view frustum of a parallel projection is a box. We can interpret the parameters for glOrthof() as specifying two of these corners of our view frustum box. Figure 7–5 illustrates this.

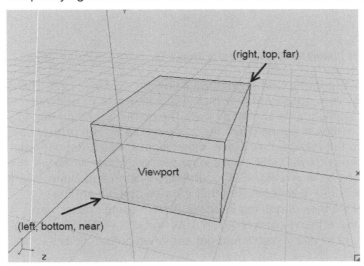

Figure 7–5. *An orthographic view frustum*

The front side of our view frustum will be directly mapped to our viewport. In the case of a full-screen viewport from, say, (0,0) to (480,320) (for example, landscape mode on a Hero), the bottom-left corner of the front side would map to the bottom-left corner of our screen, and the top-right corner of the front side would map to the top-left corner of our screen. OpenGL will perform the stretching automatically for us.

Since we want to do 2D graphics, we will specify the corner points—left, bottom, near, and right, top, far (see figure 7–5)—in a way that allows us to work in a sort of pixel coordinate system, as we did with the Canvas and Mr. Nom. Here's how we could set up such a coordinate system:

```
gl.glOrthof(0, 480, 0, 320, 1, -1);
```

Figure 7-6 shows the view frustum.

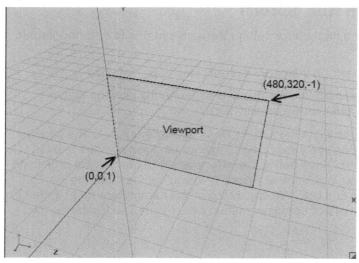

Figure 7-6. *Our parallel projection view frustum for 2D rendering with OpenGL ES*

Our view frustum is pretty thin, but that's OK because we'll only be working in 2D. The visible part of our coordinate system goes from (0,0,1) to (480,320,–1). Any points we specify within this box will be visible on the screen as well. The points will be projected onto the front side of this box, which is our beloved near clipping plane. The projection will then get stretched out onto the viewport, whatever dimensions it has. Suppose we have a Nexus One with a resolution of 800×480 pixels in landscape mode. When we specify our view frustum, we can work in a 480×320 coordinate system and OpenGL will stretch it to the 800×480 framebuffer (if we specified that the viewport covers the complete framebuffer). Best of all, there's nothing keeping us from using crazier view frustums. We could also use one with the corners (–1,–1,100) and (2,2,–100). Everything we specify that falls inside this box will be visible and get stretched automatically— pretty nifty!

Note that we also set the near and far clipping planes. Since we are going to neglect the z-coordinate completely in this chapter, you might be tempted to use zero for both near and far; however, that's a bad idea for various reasons. To play it safe, we grant the view frustum a little buffer in the z-axis. All our geometries' points will be defined in the x-y plane with z set to zero—2D all the way.

NOTE: You might have noticed that the y-axis is pointing upward now, and the origin is in the lower-left corner of our screen. While the Canvas, UI framework, and many other 2D-rendering APIs use the y-down, origin-top-left convention, it is actually more convenient to use this "new" coordinate system for game programming. For example, if Super Mario is jumping, wouldn't you expect his y-coordinate to increase instead of decrease while he's on his way up? Want to work in the other coordinate system? Fine, just swap the bottom and top parameters of glOrthof(). Also, while the illustration of the view frustum is mostly correct from a geometric point of view, the near and far clipping planes are actually interpreted a little differently by glOrthof(). Since that is a little involved, we'll just pretend the preceding illustrations are correct.

A Helpful Snippet

Here's a small snippet that will be used in all of our examples in this chapter. It clears the screen with black, sets the viewport to span the whole framebuffer, and sets up the projection matrix (and thereby the view frustum) so that we can work in a comfortable coordinate system with the origin in the lower-left corner of the screen and the y-axis pointing upward.

```
gl.glClearColor(0,0,0,1);
gl.glClear(GL10.GL_COLOR_BUFFER_BIT);
gl.glViewport(0, 0, glGraphics.getWidth(), glGraphics.getHeight());
gl.glMatrixMode(GL10.GL_PROJECTION);
gl.glLoadIdentity();
gl.glOrthof(0, 320, 0, 480, 1, -1);
```

Wait, what does glLoadIdentity() do in there? Well, most of the methods OpenGL ES offers us to manipulate the active matrix don't actually set the matrix; instead, they construct a temporary matrix from whatever parameters they take and multiply it with the current matrix. The glOrthof() method is no exception. For example, if we calledglOrthof() each frame, we'd multiply the projection matrix to death with itself. Instead of doing that, we make sure that we have a clean identity matrix in place before we multiply the projection matrix. Remember, multiplying a matrix by the identity matrix will output the matrix itself again, and that's what glLoadIdentity() is for. Think of it as first loading the value 1 and then multiplying it with whatever we have; in our case, the projection matrix produced by glOrthof().

Note that our coordinate system now goes from (0,0,1) to (320,480,–1)—that's for portrait mode rendering.

Specifying Triangles

Next, we have to figure out how we can tell OpenGL ES about the triangles we want it to render. First, let's define what comprises a triangle:

- A triangle is comprised of three points.

- Each point is called a vertex.

- A vertex has a position in 3D space.

- A position in 3D space is given as three floats, specifying the x-, y-, and z-coordinates.

- A vertex can have additional attributes, such as a color or texture coordinates (which we'll talk about later). These can be represented as floats as well.

OpenGL ES expects to send our triangle definitions in the form of arrays; however, given that OpenGL ES is actually a C API, we can't just use standard Java arrays. Instead, we have to use Java NIO buffers, which are just memory blocks of consecutive bytes.

A Small NIO Buffer Digression

To be totally exact, we need to use *direct* NIO buffers. This means that the memory is not allocated in the virtual machine's heap memory, but in native heap memory. To construct such a direct NIO buffer, we can use the following code snippet:

```
ByteBuffer buffer = ByteBuffer.allocateDirect(NUMBER_OF_BYTES);
buffer.order(ByteOrder.nativeOrder());
```

This will allocate a ByteBuffer that can hold NUMBER_OF_BYTES bytes in total, and make sure that the byte order is equal to the byte order used by the underlying CPU. An NIO buffer has three attributes.

- Capacity: The number of elements the buffer can hold in total.

- Position: The current position to which the next element would be written or read from.

- Limit: The index of the last element that has been defined, plus one.

The capacity of a buffer is its actual size. In the case of a ByteBuffer, it is given in bytes. The position and limit attributes can be thought of as defining a segment within the buffer starting at position and ending at limit (exclusive).

Since we want to specify our vertices as floats, it would be nice not to have to cope with bytes. Luckily, we can convert the ByteBuffer instance to a FloatBuffer instance, which allows us to do just that: work with floats.

```
FloatBuffer floatBuffer = buffer.asFloatBuffer();
```

Capacity, position, and limit are given in floats in the case of a `FloatBuffer`. Our usage pattern of these buffers will be pretty limited—it goes like this:

```
float[] vertices = { ... definitions of vertex positions etc  ...;
floatBuffer.clear();
floatBuffer.put(vertices);
floatBuffer.flip();
```

We first define our data in a standard Java float array. Before we put that float array into the buffer, we tell the buffer to clear itself via the `clear()` method. This doesn't actually erase any data, but it sets the position to zero and the limit to the capacity. Next, we use the `FloatBuffer.put(float[] array)` method to copy the content of the complete array to the buffer, beginning at the buffer's current position. After the copying, the position of the buffer will be increased by the length of the array. Next, the call to the `put()` method appends the additional data to the data of the last array we copied to the buffer. The final call to `FloatBuffer.flip()` just swaps the position and limit.

For this example, let's assume that our vertices array is five floats in size and that our `FloatBuffer` has enough capacity to store those five floats. After the call to `FloatBuffer.put()`, the position of the buffer will be 5 (indices 0 to 4 are taken up by the five floats from our array). The limit will still be equal to the capacity of the buffer. After the call to `FloatBuffer.flip()`, the position will be set to 0 and the limit will be set to 5. Any party interested in reading the data from the buffer will then know that it should read the floats from index 0 to 4 (remember that the limit is exclusive); and that's exactly what OpenGL ES needs to know as well. Note, however, that it will happily ignore the limit. Usually, we have to tell it the number of elements to read in addition to passing the buffer to it. There's no error checking done, so watch out.

Sometimes, it's useful to set the position of the buffer manually after we've filled it. This can be done via a call to the following method:

```
FloatBuffer.position(int position)
```

This will come in handy later on, when we temporarily set the position of a filled buffer to something other than zero for OpenGL ES to start reading at a specific position.

Sending Vertices to OpenGL ES

So how do we define the positions of the three vertices of our first triangle? Easy—assuming our coordinate system is (0,0,1) to (320,480,–1), as we defined it in the preceding code snippet—we can do the following:

```
ByteBuffer byteBuffer = ByteBuffer.allocateDirect(3 * 2 * 4);
byteBuffer.order(ByteOrder.nativeOrder());
FloatBuffer vertices = byteBuffer.asFloatBuffer();
vertices.put(new float[] {    0.0f,    0.0f,
                            319.0f,    0.0f,
                            160.0f, 479.0f  });
vertices.flip();
```

The first three lines should be familiar already. The only interesting part is how many bytes we allocate. We have three vertices, each composed of a position given as x- and y-coordinates. Each coordinate is a float, and thus takes up 4 bytes. That's three vertices times two coordinates times four bytes, for a total of 24 bytes for our triangle.

> **NOTE:** We can specify vertices with x- and y-coordinates only, and OpenGL ES will automatically set the z-coordinate to zero for us.

Next, we put a float array holding our vertex positions into the buffer. Our triangle starts at the bottom-left corner (0,0), goes to the right edge of the view frustum/screen (319,0), and then goes to the middle of the top edge of the view frustum/screen. Being the good NIO buffer users we are, we also call the flip() method on our buffer. Thus, the position will be 0 and the limit will be 6 (remember, FloatBuffer limits and positions are given in floats, not bytes).

Once we have our NIO buffer ready, we can tell OpenGL ES to draw it with its current state (that is, viewport and projection matrix). This can be done with the following snippet:

```
gl.glEnableClientState(GL10.GL_VERTEX_ARRAY);
gl.glVertexPointer( 2, GL10.GL_FLOAT, 0, vertices);
gl.glDrawArrays(GL10.GL_TRIANGLES, 0, 3);
```

The call to glEnableClientState() is a bit of a relic. It tells OpenGL ES that the vertices we are going to draw have a position. This is a bit silly for two reasons:

- The constant is called GL10.GL_VERTEX_ARRAY, which is a bit confusing. It would make more sense if it were called GL10.GL_POSITION_ARRAY.

- There's no way to draw anything that has no position, so the call to this method is a little bit superfluous. We do it anyway, however, to make OpenGL ES happy.

In the call to glVertexPointer(), we tell OpenGL ES where it can find the vertex positions and give it some additional information. The first parameter tells OpenGL ES that each vertex position is composed of two coordinates, x and y. If we would have specified x, y, and z, we would have passed three to the method. The second parameter tells OpenGL ES the data type we used to store each coordinate. In this case, it's GL10.GL_FLOAT, indicating that we used floats encoded as 4 bytes each. The third parameter, stride, tells OpenGL how far apart each of our vertex positions are from each other in bytes. In the preceding case, stride is zero, as the positions are tightly packed [vertex 1 (x,y), vertex 2(x,y), and so on]. The final parameter is our FloatBuffer, for which there are two things to remember:

- The FloatBuffer represents a memory block in the native heap, and thus has a starting address.

- The position of the FloatBuffer is an offset from that starting address.

OpenGL ES will take the buffer's starting address and add the buffer's positions to arrive at the float in the buffer from which it will start reading the vertices when we tell it to draw the contents of the buffer. The vertex pointer (which again should be called the *position pointer*) is a state of OpenGL ES. As long as we don't change it (and the context isn't lost), OpenGL ES will remember it and use it for all subsequent calls that need vertex positions.

Finally, there's the call to `glDrawArrays()`. It will draw our triangle. The first parameter specifies what type of primitive we are going to draw. In this case, we say that we want to render a list of triangles, which is specified via `GL10.GL_TRIANGLES`. The next parameter is an offset relative to the first vertex to which the vertex pointer points. The offset is measured in vertices, not bytes or floats. If we would have specified more than one triangle, we could use this offset to render only a subset of our triangle list. The final argument tells OpenGL ES how many vertices it should use for rendering. In our case, that's three vertices. Note that we always have to specify a multiple of 3 if we draw `GL10.GL_TRIANGLES`. Each triangle is composed of three vertices, so that makes sense. For other primitive types, the rules are a little different.

Once we issue the `glVertexPointer()` command, OpenGL ES will transfer the vertex positions to the GPU and store them there for all subsequent rendering commands. Each time we tell OpenGL ES to render vertices, it takes their positions from the data we last specified via `glVertexPointer()`.

Each of our vertices might have more attributes than just a position. One other attribute might be a vertex's color. We usually refer to those attributes as *vertex attributes*.

You might be wondering how OpenGL ES knows what color our triangle should have, as we have only specified positions. It turns out that OpenGL ES has sensible defaults for any vertex attribute that we don't specify. Most of these defaults can be set directly. For example, if we want to set a default color for all vertices that we draw, we can use the following method:

`GL10.glColor4f(`**float** `r,` **float** `g,` **float** `b,` **float** `a)`

This method will set the default color to be used for all vertices for which one wasn't specified. The color is given as RGBA values in the range of 0.0 to 1.0, as was the case for the clear color earlier. The default color OpenGL ES starts with is (1,1,1,1)—that is, fully opaque white.

That's all the code we need to render a triangle with a custom parallel projection—a mere 16 lines of code for clearing the screen, setting the viewport and projection matrix, creating an NIO buffer in which we store our vertex positions, and drawing the triangle! Now compare that to the six pages it took us to explain this to you. We could have, of course, left out the details and used coarser language. The problem is that OpenGL ES is a pretty complex beast at times and, to avoid getting an empty screen, it's best to learn what it's all about rather than just copying and pasting code.

Putting It Together

To round this section out, let's put all this together via a nice GLGame and Screen implementation. Listing 7–5 shows the complete example.

Listing 7–5. *FirstTriangleTest.java*

```java
package com.badlogic.androidgames.glbasics;

import java.nio.ByteBuffer;
import java.nio.ByteOrder;
import java.nio.FloatBuffer;

import javax.microedition.khronos.opengles.GL10;

import com.badlogic.androidgames.framework.Game;
import com.badlogic.androidgames.framework.Screen;
import com.badlogic.androidgames.framework.impl.GLGame;
import com.badlogic.androidgames.framework.impl.GLGraphics;

public class FirstTriangleTest extends GLGame {
    @Override
    public Screen getStartScreen() {
        return new FirstTriangleScreen(this);
    }
}
```

The FirstTriangleTest class derives from GLGame, and thus has to implement the Game.getStartScreen() method. In that method, we create a new FirstTriangleScreen, which will then be called frequently to update and present itself by the GLGame. Note that when this method is called, we are already in the main loop—or rather, the GLSurfaceView rendering thread—so we can use OpenGL ES methods in the constructor of the FirstTriangleScreen class. Let's have a closer look at that Screen implementation.

```java
class FirstTriangleScreen extends Screen {
    GLGraphics glGraphics;
    FloatBuffer vertices;

    public FirstTriangleScreen(Game game) {
        super(game);
        glGraphics = ((GLGame)game).getGLGraphics();

        ByteBuffer byteBuffer = ByteBuffer.allocateDirect(3 * 2 * 4);
        byteBuffer.order(ByteOrder.nativeOrder());
        vertices = byteBuffer.asFloatBuffer();
        vertices.put( new float[] {   0.0f,   0.0f,
                                    319.0f,   0.0f,
                                    160.0f, 479.0f});
        vertices.flip();
    }
```

The FirstTriangleScreen class holds two members: a GLGraphics instance and our trusty FloatBuffer, which stores the 2D positions of the three vertices of our triangle. In the constructor, we fetch the GLGraphics instance from the GLGame and create and fill the

FloatBuffer according to our previous code snippet. Since the Screen constructor gets a Game instance, we have to cast it to a GLGame instance so that we can use the GLGame.getGLGraphics() method.

```
@Override
public void present(float deltaTime) {
    GL10 gl = glGraphics.getGL();
    gl.glViewport(0, 0, glGraphics.getWidth(), glGraphics.getHeight());
    gl.glClear(GL10.GL_COLOR_BUFFER_BIT);
    gl.glMatrixMode(GL10.GL_PROJECTION);
    gl.glLoadIdentity();
    gl.glOrthof(0, 320, 0, 480, 1, -1);

    gl.glColor4f(1, 0, 0, 1);
    gl.glEnableClientState(GL10.GL_VERTEX_ARRAY);
    gl.glVertexPointer( 2, GL10.GL_FLOAT, 0, vertices);
    gl.glDrawArrays(GL10.GL_TRIANGLES, 0, 3);
}
```

The present() method reflects what we just discussed: we set the viewport, clear the screen, set the projection matrix so that we can work in our custom coordinate system, set the default vertex color (red in this case), specify that our vertices will have positions, tell OpenGL ES where it can find those vertex positions, and finally, render our awesome little red triangle.

```
@Override
public void update(float deltaTime) {
    game.getInput().getTouchEvents();
    game.getInput().getKeyEvents();
}

@Override
public void pause() {

}

@Override
public void resume() {

}

@Override
public void dispose() {

}
    }
}
```

The rest of the class is just boilerplate code. In the update() method, we make sure that our event buffers don't get filled up. The rest of the code does nothing.

> **NOTE:** From here on, we'll only focus on the Screen classes themselves, as the enclosing GLGame derivatives, such as FirstTriangleTest, will always be the same. We'll also reduce the code size a little by leaving out any empty or boilerplate methods of the Screen class. The following examples will all just differ in terms of members, constructors, and present methods.

Figure 7–7 shows the output of the preceding example.

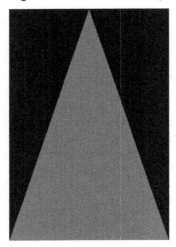

Figure 7–7. *Our first attractive triangle*

Here's what we did wrong in this example in terms of OpenGL ES best practices:

- We set the same states to the same values over and over again without any need. State changes in OpenGL ES are expensive—some a little bit more— others a little bit less. We should always try to reduce the number of state changes we make in a single frame.

- The viewport and projection matrix will never change once we set them. We could move that code to the resume() method, which is only called once each time the OpenGL ES surface gets (re-)created; this also handles OpenGL ES context loss.

- We could also move setting the color used for clearing and setting the default vertex color to the resume() method. These two colors won't change either.

- We could move the glEnableClientState() and glVertexPointer() methods to the resume() method.

- The only things that we need to call each frame are glClear() and glDrawArrays(). Both use the current OpenGL ES states, which will stay the same as long as we don't change them and as long as we don't lose the context due to the Activity being paused and resumed.

If we had put these optimizations into practice, we would have only two OpenGL ES calls in our main loop. For the sake of clarity, we'll refrain from using these kinds of minimal state change optimizations for now. When we start writing our first OpenGL ES game, though, we'll have to follow those practices as best as we can to guarantee good performance.

Let's add some more attributes to our triangle's vertices, starting with color.

> **NOTE:** Very, very alert readers might have noticed that the triangle in Figure 7–7 is actually missing a pixel in the bottom-right corner. This may look like a typical off-by-one error, but it's actually due to the way OpenGL ES rasterizes (draws the pixels of) the triangle. There's a specific triangle rasterization rule that is responsible for that artifact. Worry not—we are mostly concerned with rendering 2D rectangles (composed of two triangles), where this effect will vanish.

Specifying Per Vertex Color

In the last example, we set a global default color for all vertices we drew via glColor4f(). Sometimes we want to have more granular control (for example, we want to set a color per vertex). OpenGL ES offers us this functionality, and it's really easy to use. All we have to do is add RGBA float components to each vertex and tell OpenGL ES where it can find the color for each vertex, similar to how we told it where it can find the position for each vertex. Let's start by adding the colors to each vertex.

```
int VERTEX_SIZE = (2 + 4) * 4;
ByteBuffer byteBuffer = ByteBuffer.allocateDirect(3 * VERTEX_SIZE);
byteBuffer.order(ByteOrder.nativeOrder());
FloatBuffer vertices = byteBuffer.asFloatBuffer();
vertices.put( new float[] {   0.0f,   0.0f, 1, 0, 0, 1,
                            319.0f,   0.0f, 0, 1, 0, 1,
                            160.0f, 479.0f, 0, 0, 1, 1});
vertices.flip();
```

We first have to allocate a ByteBuffer for our three vertices. How big should that ByteBuffer be? We have two coordinates and four (RGBA) color components per vertex, so that's six floats in total. Each float value takes up 4 bytes, so a single vertex uses 24 bytes. We store this information in VERTEX_SIZE. When we call ByteBuffer.allocateDirect(), we just multiply VERTEX_SIZE by the number of vertices we want to store in the ByteBuffer. The rest is fairly self-explanatory. We get a FloatBuffer view to our ByteBuffer and put() the vertices into the ByteBuffer. Each row of the float array holds the x- and y-coordinates and the R, G, B, and A components of a vertex, in that order.

If we want to render this, we have to tell OpenGL ES that our vertices not only have a position, but they also have a color attribute. We start off, as before, by calling glEnableClientState().

```
gl.glEnableClientState(GL10.GL_VERTEX_ARRAY);
gl.glEnableClientState(GL10.GL_COLOR_ARRAY);
```

Now that OpenGL ES knows that it can expect position and color information for each vertex, we have to tell it where it can find that information:

```
vertices.position(0);
gl.glVertexPointer(2, GL10.GL_FLOAT, VERTEX_SIZE, vertices);
vertices.position(2);
gl.glColorPointer(4, GL10.GL_FLOAT, VERTEX_SIZE, vertices);
```

We start of by setting the position of our FloatBuffer, which holds our vertices to 0. The position thus points to the x-coordinate of our first vertex in the buffer. Next, we call glVertexPointer(). The only difference from the previous example is that we now also specify the vertex size (remember, it's given in bytes). OpenGL ES will then start reading in vertex positions from the position in the buffer from which we told it to start. For the second vertex position, it will add VERTEX_SIZE bytes to the first position's address, and so on.

Next, we set the position of the buffer to the R component of the first vertex and call glColorPointer(), which tells OpenGL ES where it can find the colors of our vertices. The first argument is the number of components per color. This is always four, as OpenGL ES demands an R, G, B, and A component per vertex from us. The second parameter specifies the type of each component. As with the vertex coordinates, we use GL10.GL_FLOAT again to indicate that each color component is a float in the range between 0 and 1. The third parameter is the stride between vertex colors. It's of course the same as the stride between vertex positions. The final parameter is our vertices buffer again.

Since we called vertices.position(2) before the glColorPointer() call, OpenGL ES knows that the first vertex color can be found starting from the third float in the buffer. If we wouldn't have set the position of the buffer to 2, OpenGL ES would have started reading in the colors from position 0. That would have been bad, as that's where the x-coordinate of our first vertex is. Figure 7–8 shows from where OpenGL ES will read our vertex attributes, and how it jumps from one vertex to the next for each attribute.

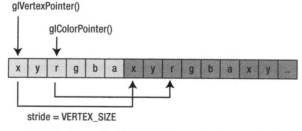

Figure 7–8. *Our vertices FloatBuffer, start addresses for OpenGL ES from which to read position/color, and stride used to jump to the next position/color*

To draw our triangle, we again call glDrawElements(), which tells OpenGL ES to draw a triangle using the first three vertices of our FloatBuffer.

```
gl.glDrawElements(GL10.GL_TRIANGLES, 0, 3);
```

Since we enabled the GL10.GL_VERTEX_ARRAY and GL10.GL_COLOR_ARRAY, OpenGL ES knows that it should use the attributes specified by glVertexPointer() and glColorPointer(). It will ignore the default color, as we provide our own per-vertex colors.

> **NOTE:** The way we just specified our vertices' positions and colors is called *interleaving*. This means that we pack the attributes of a vertex in one continuous memory block. There's another way we could have achieved this: *non-interleaved vertex arrays*. We could have used two FloatBuffers, one for the positions and one for the colors. However, interleaving performs much better due to memory locality, so we won't discuss non-interleaved vertex arrays here.

Putting it all together into a new GLGame and Screen implementation should be a breeze. Listing 7–6 shows an excerpt from the file ColoredTriangleTest.java. We left out the boilerplate code.

Listing 7–6. *Excerpt from ColoredTriangleTest.java; Interleaving Position and Color Attributes*

```java
class ColoredTriangleScreen extends Screen {
    final int VERTEX_SIZE = (2 + 4) * 4;
    GLGraphics glGraphics;
    FloatBuffer vertices;

    public ColoredTriangleScreen(Game game) {
        super(game);
        glGraphics = ((GLGame) game).getGLGraphics();

        ByteBuffer byteBuffer = ByteBuffer.allocateDirect(3 * VERTEX_SIZE);
        byteBuffer.order(ByteOrder.nativeOrder());
        vertices = byteBuffer.asFloatBuffer();
        vertices.put( new float[] {   0.0f,   0.0f, 1, 0, 0, 1,
                                    319.0f,   0.0f, 0, 1, 0, 1,
                                    160.0f, 479.0f, 0, 0, 1, 1});
        vertices.flip();
    }

    @Override
    public void present(float deltaTime) {
        GL10 gl = glGraphics.getGL();
        gl.glViewport(0, 0, glGraphics.getWidth(), glGraphics.getHeight());
        gl.glClear(GL10.GL_COLOR_BUFFER_BIT);
        gl.glMatrixMode(GL10.GL_PROJECTION);
        gl.glLoadIdentity();
        gl.glOrthof(0, 320, 0, 480, 1, -1);

        gl.glEnableClientState(GL10.GL_VERTEX_ARRAY);
        gl.glEnableClientState(GL10.GL_COLOR_ARRAY);

        vertices.position(0);
        gl.glVertexPointer(2, GL10.GL_FLOAT, VERTEX_SIZE, vertices);
        vertices.position(2);
        gl.glColorPointer(4, GL10.GL_FLOAT, VERTEX_SIZE, vertices);
```

```
        gl.glDrawArrays(GL10.GL_TRIANGLES, 0, 3);
    }
```

Cool—that still looks pretty straightforward. Compared to the previous example, we simply added the four color components to each vertex in our FloatBuffer and enabled the GL10.GL_COLOR_ARRAY. The best thing about it is that any additional vertex attributes we add in the following examples will work the same way. We just tell OpenGL ES not to use the default value for that specific attribute; instead, we tell it to look up the attributes in our FloatBuffer, starting at a specific position and moving from vertex to vertex by VERTEX_SIZE bytes.

Now, we could also turn off the GL10.GL_COLOR_ARRAY so that OpenGL ES uses the default vertex color again, which we can specify via glColor4f() as we did previously. For this we can call

```
gl.glDisableClientState(GL10.GL_COLOR_ARRAY);
```

OpenGL ES will just turn off the feature to read the colors from our FloatBuffer. If we already set a color pointer via glColorPointer(), OpenGL ES will remember the pointer even though we just told OpenGL ES to not use it.

To round this example out, let's have a look at the output of the preceding program. Figure 7–9 shows a screenshot.

Figure 7–9. *Per-vertex colored triangle*

Whoa, this is pretty neat! We didn't make any assumptions about how OpenGL ES will use the three colors we specified (red for the bottom-left vertex, green for the bottom-right vertex, and blue for the top vertex). It turns out that it will interpolate the colors between the vertices for us. With this, we can easily create nice gradients.; however, colors alone will not make us happy for very long. We want to draw images with OpenGL ES. And that's where so-called texture mapping comes into play.

Texture Mapping: Wallpapering Made Easy

When we wrote Mr. Nom, we loaded some bitmaps and directly drew them to the framebuffer—no rotation involved, just a little bit of scaling, which is pretty easy to achieve. In OpenGL ES, we are mostly concerned with triangles, which can have any orientation or scale we want them to have. So, how can we render bitmaps with OpenGL ES?

Easy, just load up the bitmap to OpenGL ES (and for that matter to the GPU, which has its own dedicated RAM), add a new attribute to each of our triangle's vertices, and tell OpenGL ES to render our triangle and apply the bitmap (also known as *texture* in OpenGL ES speak) to the triangle. Let's first look at what these new vertex attributes actually specify.

Texture Coordinates

To map a bitmap to a triangle, we need to add *texture coordinates* to each vertex of the triangle. What is a texture coordinate? It specifies a point within the texture (our uploaded bitmap) to be mapped to one of the triangle's vertices. Texture coordinates are usually 2D.

While we call our positional coordinates x, y, and z, texture coordinates are usually called u and v or s and t, depending on the circle of graphics programmers of which you're a member. OpenGL ES calls them s and t, so that's what we'll stick to. If you read resources on the Web that use the u/v nomenclature, don't get confused: it's the same as s and t. What does the coordinate system look like? Figure 7–10 shows Bob in the texture coordinate system after we uploaded him to OpenGL ES.

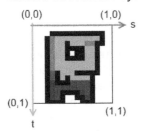

Figure 7–10. *Bob, uploaded to OpenGL ES, shown in the texture coordinate system*

There are a couple of interesting things going on here. First of all, s equals the x-coordinate in a standard coordinate system, and t is equal to the y-coordinate. The s-axis points to the right, and the t-axis points downward. The origin of the coordinate system coincides with the top-left corner of Bob's image. The bottom-right corner of the image maps to (1,1).

So, what happened to pixel coordinates? It turns out that OpenGL ES doesn't like them a lot. Instead, any image we upload, no matter its width and height in pixels, will be embedded into this coordinate system. The top-left corner of the image will always be at

(0,0), and the bottom-right corner will always be at (1,1)—even if, say, the width is twice as large as the height. We call these *normalized coordinates*, and they actually make our lives easier at times. Now, how can we map Bob to our triangle? Easy, we just give each vertex of the triangle a texture coordinate pair in Bob's coordinate system. Figure 7–11 shows a few configurations.

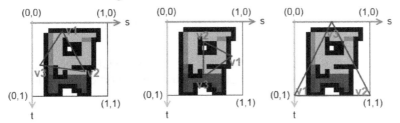

Figure 7–11. *Three different triangles mapped to Bob; the names v1, v2, and v3 each specify a vertex of the triangle.*

We can map our triangle's vertices to the texture coordinate system however we want. Note that the orientation of the triangle in the positional coordinate system does not have to be the same as it is in the texture coordinate system. The coordinate systems are completely decoupled. So, let's see how we can add those texture coordinates to our vertices.

```
int VERTEX_SIZE = (2 + 2) * 4;
ByteBuffer byteBuffer = ByteBuffer.allocateDirect(3 * VERTEX_SIZE);
byteBuffer.order(ByteOrder.nativeOrder());
vertices = byteBuffer.asFloatBuffer();
vertices.put( new float[] {   0.0f,   0.0f, 0.0f, 1.0f,
                            319.0f,   0.0f, 1.0f, 1.0f,
                            160.0f, 479.0f, 0.5f, 0.0f});
vertices.flip();
```

That was easy. All we have to do is to make sure that we have enough room in our buffer and then append the texture coordinates to each vertex. The preceding code corresponds to the rightmost mapping in Figure 7–10. Note that our vertex positions are still given in the usual coordinate system we defined via our projection. If we wanted to, we could also add the color attributes to each vertex, as in the previous example. OpenGL ES would then mix the interpolated vertex colors with the colors from the pixels of the texture to which the triangle maps on the fly. Of course, we'd need to adjust the size of our buffer as well as the VERTEX_SIZE constant accordingly; for example, (2 + 4 + 2) × 4. To tell OpenGL ES that our vertices have texture coordinates, we again use glEnableClientState() together with the glTexCoordPointer() method, which behaves exactly the same as glVertexPointer() and glColorPointer() (can you see a pattern here?).

```
gl.glEnableClientState(GL10.GL_VERTEX_ARRAY);
gl.glEnableClientState(GL10.GL_TEXTURE_COORD_ARRAY);

vertices.position(0);
gl.glVertexPointer(2, GL10.GL_FLOAT, VERTEX_SIZE, vertices);
vertices.position(2);
gl.glTexCoordPointer(2, GL10.GL_FLOAT, VERTEX_SIZE, vertices);
```

Nice—that looks very familiar. So, the remaining question is how can we upload the texture to OpenGL ES and tell it to map it to our triangle? Naturally, that's a little bit more involved. But fear not, it's still pretty easy.

Uploading Bitmaps

First, we have to load our bitmap. We already know how to do that on Android.

```
Bitmap bitmap = BitmapFactory.decodeStream(game.getFileIO().readAsset("bobrgb888.png"));
```

Here we load Bob in an RGB888 configuration. The next thing we need to do is tell OpenGL ES that we want to create a new texture. OpenGL ES has the notion of objects for a couple of things, such as textures. To create a texture object, we can call the following method:

```
GL10.glGenTextures(int numTextures, int[] ids, int offset)
```

The first parameter specifies how many texture objects we want to create. Usually, we only want to create one. The next parameter is an int array to which OpenGL ES will write the IDs of the generated texture objects. The final parameter just tells OpenGL ES to where it should start writing the IDs to in the array.

You've already learned that OpenGL ES is a C API. Naturally, it can't return a Java object for a new texture; instead, it gives us an ID (or handle) to that texture. Each time we want OpenGL ES to do something with that specific texture, we specify its ID. So here's a more complete code snippet showing how to generate a single new texture object and get its ID:

```
int textureIds[] = new int[1];
gl.glGenTextures(1, textureIds, 0);
int textureId = textureIds[0];
```

The texture object is still empty, which means it doesn't have any image data yet. Let's upload our bitmap. For this, we first have to bind the texture. To bind something in OpenGL ES means that we want OpenGL ES to use that specific object for all subsequent calls until we change the binding again. Here, we want to bind a texture object for which the method glBindTexture() is available. Once we have bound a texture, we can manipulate its attributes, such as image data. Here's how we can upload Bob to our new texture object:

```
gl.glBindTexture(GL10.GL_TEXTURE_2D, textureId);
GLUtils.texImage2D(GL10.GL_TEXTURE_2D, 0, bitmap, 0);
```

First, we bind the texture object with glBindTexture(). The first parameter specifies the type of texture we want to bind. Our image of Bob is 2D, so we use GL10.GL_TEXTURE_2D. There are other texture types, but we don't have a need for them in this book. We'll always specifyGL10.GL_TEXTURE_2D for the methods that need to know the texture type with which we want to work. The second parameter of that method is our texture ID. Once the method returns, all subsequent methods that work with a 2D texture will work with our texture object.

The next method call invokes a method of the GLUtils class, which is provided by the Android framework. Usually, the task of uploading a texture image is pretty involved; this little helper class eases our pain quite a bit. All we need to do is specify the texture type (GL10.GL_TEXTURE_2D), the mipmapping level (we'll look at that in Chapter 11; it defaults to zero), the bitmap we want to upload, and another argument, which has to be set to zero in all cases. After this call, our texture object has image data attached to it.

> **NOTE:** The texture object and its image data are actually held in video RAM, not in our usual RAM. The texture object (and the image data) will get lost when the OpenGL ES context is destroyed (for example, when our activity is paused and resumed). This means that we have to re-create the texture object and re-upload our image data every time the OpenGL ES context is (re-)created. If we don't do this, all we'll see is a white triangle.

Texture Filtering

There's one last thing we need to define before we can use the texture object. It has to do with the fact that our triangle might take up more or less pixels on the screen than there are pixels in the mapped region of the texture. For example, the image of Bob in Figure 7–10 has a size of 128×128 pixels. Our triangle maps to half that image, so it uses (128×128) /2 pixels from the texture (which are also called *texels*). When we draw the triangle to the screen with the coordinates we defined in the preceding snippet, it will take up (320×480) / 2 pixels. That's a lot more pixels that we use on the screen than we fetch from the texture map. It can, of course, also be the other way around: we use fewer pixels on the screen than from the mapped region of the texture. The first case is called *magnification*, and the second is called *minification*. For each case, we need to tell OpenGL ES how it should upscale or downscale the texture. The up- and downscaling are also referred to as *minification* and *magnification filters* in OpenGL ES lingo. These filters are attributes of our texture object, much like the image data itself. To set them, we first have to make sure that the texture object is bound via a call to glBindTexture(). If that's the case, we can set them like this:

```
gl.glTexParameterf(GL10.GL_TEXTURE_2D, GL10.GL_TEXTURE_MIN_FILTER, GL10.GL_NEAREST);
gl.glTexParameterf(GL10.GL_TEXTURE_2D, GL10.GL_TEXTURE_MAG_FILTER, GL10.GL_NEAREST);
```

Both times we use the method GL10.glTexParameterf(), which sets an attribute of the texture. In the first call, we specify the minification filter; in the second, we call the magnification filter. The first parameter to that method is the texture type, which defaults to GL10.GL_TEXTURE_2D. The second argument tells the method which attributes we want to set; in our case, the GL10.GL_TEXTURE_MIN_FILTER and the GL10.GL_TEXTURE_MAG_FILTER. The last parameter specifies the type of filter that should be used. We have two options here: GL10.GL_NEARESTandGL10.GL_LINEAR.

The first filter type will always choose the nearest texel in the texture map to be mapped to a pixel. The second filter type will sample the four nearest texels for a pixel of the triangle and average them to arrive at the final color. We use the first type of filter if we want to have a pixelated look and the second if we want a smooth look. Figure 7–12 shows the difference between the two types of filters.

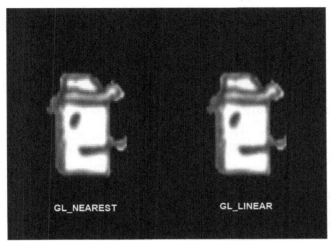

Figure 7–12. *GL10.GL_NEAREST vs. GL10.GL_LINEAR; the first filter type makes for a pixelated look; the second one smoothes things out a little.*

Our texture object is now fully defined: we created an ID, set the image data, and specified the filters to be used in case our rendering is not pixel perfect. It is a common practice to unbind the texture once we are done defining it. We should also recycle the `Bitmap` we loaded, as we no longer need it. Why waste memory? That can be achieved with the following snippet:

```
gl.glBindTexture(GL10.GL_TEXTURE_2D, 0);
bitmap.recycle();
```

Here, 0 is a special ID that tells OpenGL ES that it should unbind the currently bound object. If we want to use the texture for drawing our triangles, we need to bind it again, of course.

Disposing of Textures

It is also useful to know how to delete a texture object from video RAM if we no longer need it (like we use `Bitmap.recycle()` to release the memory of a bitmap). This can be achieved with the following snippet:

```
gl.glBindTexture(GL10.GL_TEXTURE_2D, 0);
int textureIds = { textureid };
gl.glDeleteTextures(1, textureIds, 0);
```

Note that we first have to make sure that the texture object is not currently bound before we can delete it. The rest is similar to how we used `glGenTextures()` to create a texture object.

A Helpful Snippet

For your reference, here's the complete snippet to create a texture object, load image data, and set the filters on Android:

```
Bitmap bitmap = BitmapFactory.decodeStream(game.getFileIO().readAsset("bobrgb888.png"));
int textureIds[] = new int[1];
gl.glGenTextures(1, textureIds, 0);
int textureId = textureIds[0];
gl.glBindTexture(GL10.GL_TEXTURE_2D, textureId);
GLUtils.texImage2D(GL10.GL_TEXTURE_2D, 0, bitmap, 0);
gl.glTexParameterf(GL10.GL_TEXTURE_2D, GL10.GL_TEXTURE_MIN_FILTER, GL10.GL_NEAREST);
gl.glTexParameterf(GL10.GL_TEXTURE_2D, GL10.GL_TEXTURE_MAG_FILTER, GL10.GL_NEAREST);
gl.glBindTexture(GL10.GL_TEXTURE_2D, 0);
bitmap.recycle();
```

Not so bad after all. The most important part of all this is to recycle the Bitmap once we're done; otherwise, we'd waste memory. Our image data is safely stored in video RAM in the texture object (until the context is lost and we need to reload it again).

Enabling Texturing

There's one more thing before we can draw our triangle with the texture. We need to bind the texture, and we need to tell OpenGL ES that it should actually apply the texture to all triangles we render. Whether or not texture mapping is performed is another state of OpenGL ES, which we can enable and disable with the following methods:

```
GL10.glEnable(GL10.GL_TEXTURE_2D);
GL10.glDisable(GL10.GL_TEXTURE_2D);
```

These look vaguely familiar. When we enabled/disabled vertex attributes in the previous sections, we used glEnableClientState()/glDisableClientState(). As we noted earlier, those are relics from the infancy of OpenGL itself. There's a reason why those are not merged with glEnable()/glDisable(), but we won't go into that here. Just remember to use glEnableClientState()/glDisableClientState() to enable and disable vertex attributes, and use glEnable()/glDisable() for any other states of OpenGL, such as texturing.

Putting It Together

With that out of our way, we can now write a small example that puts all of this together. Listing 7–7 shows an excerpt of theTexturedTriangleTest.java source file, listing only the relevant parts of the TexturedTriangleScreen class contained in it.

Listing 7–7.*Excerpt from TexturedTriangleTest.java; Texturing a Triangle*

```
class TexturedTriangleScreen extends Screen {
    final int VERTEX_SIZE = (2 + 2) * 4;
    GLGraphics glGraphics;
    FloatBuffer vertices;
    int textureId;
```

```java
    public TexturedTriangleScreen(Game game) {
        super(game);
        glGraphics = ((GLGame) game).getGLGraphics();

        ByteBuffer byteBuffer = ByteBuffer.allocateDirect(3 * VERTEX_SIZE);
        byteBuffer.order(ByteOrder.nativeOrder());
        vertices = byteBuffer.asFloatBuffer();
        vertices.put( new float[] {    0.0f,   0.0f, 0.0f, 1.0f,
                                     319.0f,   0.0f, 1.0f, 1.0f,
                                     160.0f, 479.0f, 0.5f, 0.0f});
        vertices.flip();
        textureId = loadTexture("bobrgb888.png");
    }

    public int loadTexture(String fileName) {
        try {
            Bitmap bitmap =
BitmapFactory.decodeStream(game.getFileIO().readAsset(fileName));
            GL10 gl = glGraphics.getGL();
            int textureIds[] = new int[1];
            gl.glGenTextures(1, textureIds, 0);
            int textureId = textureIds[0];
            gl.glBindTexture(GL10.GL_TEXTURE_2D, textureId);
            GLUtils.texImage2D(GL10.GL_TEXTURE_2D, 0, bitmap, 0);
            gl.glTexParameterf(GL10.GL_TEXTURE_2D, GL10.GL_TEXTURE_MIN_FILTER,
GL10.GL_NEAREST);
            gl.glTexParameterf(GL10.GL_TEXTURE_2D, GL10.GL_TEXTURE_MAG_FILTER,
GL10.GL_NEAREST);
            gl.glBindTexture(GL10.GL_TEXTURE_2D, 0);
            bitmap.recycle();
            return textureId;
        } catch(IOException e) {
            Log.d("TexturedTriangleTest", "couldn't load asset 'bobrgb888.png'!");
            throw new RuntimeException("couldn't load asset '" + fileName + "'");
        }
    }

    @Override
    public void present(float deltaTime) {
        GL10 gl = glGraphics.getGL();
        gl.glViewport(0, 0, glGraphics.getWidth(), glGraphics.getHeight());
        gl.glClear(GL10.GL_COLOR_BUFFER_BIT);
        gl.glMatrixMode(GL10.GL_PROJECTION);
        gl.glLoadIdentity();
        gl.glOrthof(0, 320, 0, 480, 1, -1);

        gl.glEnable(GL10.GL_TEXTURE_2D);
        gl.glBindTexture(GL10.GL_TEXTURE_2D, textureId);

        gl.glEnableClientState(GL10.GL_VERTEX_ARRAY);
        gl.glEnableClientState(GL10.GL_TEXTURE_COORD_ARRAY);

        vertices.position(0);
        gl.glVertexPointer(2, GL10.GL_FLOAT, VERTEX_SIZE, vertices);
        vertices.position(2);
        gl.glTexCoordPointer(2, GL10.GL_FLOAT, VERTEX_SIZE, vertices);
```

```
        gl.glDrawArrays(GL10.GL_TRIANGLES, 0, 3);
    }
```

We took the freedom to put the texture loading into a method called loadTexture(), which simply takes the filename of a bitmap to be loaded. The method returns the texture object ID generated by OpenGL ES, which we'll use in the present() method to bind the texture.

The definition of our triangle shouldn't be a big surprise; we just added texture coordinates to each vertex.

The present() method does what it always does: it clears the screen and sets the projection matrix. Next, we enable texture mapping via a call to glEnable() and bind our texture object. The rest is just what we did before: enable the vertex attributes we want to use; tell OpenGL ES where it can find them and what strides to use; and finally, draw the triangle with a call to glDrawArrays(). Figure 7–13 shows the output of the preceding code.

Figure 7–13. *Texture mapping Bob onto our triangle*

There's one last thing we haven't mentioned yet, and it's of great importance:

All bitmaps we load must have a width and height of a power of two.

Stick to it or else things will explode.

So what does this actually mean? The image of Bob that we used in our example has a size of 128×128 pixels. The value 128 is 2 to the power of 7 (2×2×2×2×2×2×2). Other valid image sizes would be 2×8, 32×16, 128×256, and so on. There's also a limit to how big our images can be. Sadly, it varies depending on the hardware on which our application is running. The OpenGL ES 1.x standard doesn't specify a minimally supported texture size; however, from experience, it seems that 512×512-pixel textures work on all current Android devices (and most likely will work on all future devices as well). We'd even go so far to say that 1024×1024 is OK as well.

Another issue that we have pretty much ignored so far is the color depth of our textures. Luckily, the method GLUtils.texImage2D(), which we used to upload our image data to the GPU, handles this for us fairly well. OpenGL ES can cope with color depths like RGBA8888, RGB565, and so on. We should always strive to use the lowest possible color depth to decrease bandwidth. For this, we can employ the BitmapFactory.Options class, as in previous chapters, to load an RGB888 Bitmap to a RGB565 Bitmap in memory, for example. Once we have loaded our Bitmap instance with the color depth we want it to have, GLUtils.texImage2D() takes over and makes sure that OpenGL ES gets the image data in the correct format. Of course, you should always check whether the reduction in color depth has a negative impact on the visual fidelity of your game.

A Texture Class

To reduce the code needed for subsequent examples, we wrote a little helper class called Texture. It will load a bitmap from an asset and create a texture object from it. It also has a few convenience methods to bind the texture and dispose of it. Listing 7–8 shows the code.

Listing 7–8. *Texture.java, a Little OpenGL ES Texture Class*

```
package com.badlogic.androidgames.framework.gl;

import java.io.IOException;
import java.io.InputStream;

import javax.microedition.khronos.opengles.GL10;

import android.graphics.Bitmap;
import android.graphics.BitmapFactory;
import android.opengl.GLUtils;

import com.badlogic.androidgames.framework.FileIO;
import com.badlogic.androidgames.framework.impl.GLGame;
import com.badlogic.androidgames.framework.impl.GLGraphics;

public class Texture {
    GLGraphics glGraphics;
    FileIO fileIO;
    String fileName;
    int textureId;
    int minFilter;
    int magFilter;

    public Texture(GLGame glGame, String fileName) {
        this.glGraphics = glGame.getGLGraphics();
        this.fileIO = glGame.getFileIO();
        this.fileName = fileName;
        load();
    }

    private void load() {
        GL10 gl = glGraphics.getGL();
        int[] textureIds = new int[1];
```

```java
        gl.glGenTextures(1, textureIds, 0);
        textureId = textureIds[0];

        InputStream in = null;
        try {
            in = fileIO.readAsset(fileName);
            Bitmap bitmap = BitmapFactory.decodeStream(in);
            gl.glBindTexture(GL10.GL_TEXTURE_2D, textureId);
            GLUtils.texImage2D(GL10.GL_TEXTURE_2D, 0, bitmap, 0);
            setFilters(GL10.GL_NEAREST, GL10.GL_NEAREST);
            gl.glBindTexture(GL10.GL_TEXTURE_2D, 0);
        } catch(IOException e) {
            throw new RuntimeException("Couldn't load texture '" + fileName +"'", e);
        } finally {
            if(in != null)
                try { in.close(); } catch (IOException e) { }
        }
    }

    public void reload() {
        load();
        bind();
        setFilters(minFilter, magFilter);
        glGraphics.getGL().glBindTexture(GL10.GL_TEXTURE_2D, 0);
    }

    public void setFilters(int minFilter, int magFilter) {
        this.minFilter = minFilter;
        this.magFilter = magFilter;
        GL10 gl = glGraphics.getGL();
        gl.glTexParameterf(GL10.GL_TEXTURE_2D, GL10.GL_TEXTURE_MIN_FILTER, minFilter);
        gl.glTexParameterf(GL10.GL_TEXTURE_2D, GL10.GL_TEXTURE_MAG_FILTER, magFilter);
    }

    public void bind() {
        GL10 gl = glGraphics.getGL();
        gl.glBindTexture(GL10.GL_TEXTURE_2D, textureId);
    }

    public void dispose() {
        GL10 gl = glGraphics.getGL();
        gl.glBindTexture(GL10.GL_TEXTURE_2D, textureId);
        int[] textureIds = { textureId };
        gl.glDeleteTextures(1, textureIds, 0);
    }
}
```

The only interesting thing about this class is the reload() method, which we can use when the OpenGL ES context is lost. Also note that the setFilters() method will only work if the Texture is actually bound. Otherwise, it will set the filters of the currently bound texture.

We could also write a little helper method for our vertices buffer. But before we can do this, we have to discuss one more thing: indexed vertices.

Indexed Vertices: Because Re-use is Good for You

Up until this point, we have always defined lists of triangles, where each triangle has its own set of vertices. We have actually only ever drawn a single triangle, but adding more would not have been a big deal.

There are cases, however, where two or more triangles can share some vertices. Let's think about how we'd render a rectangle with our current knowledge. We'd simply define two triangles that would have two vertices with the same positions, colors, and texture coordinates. We can do better. Figure 7–14 shows the old way and the new way of rendering a rectangle.

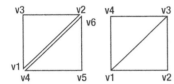

Figure 7–14. *Rendering a rectangle as two triangles with six vertices (left), and rendering it with four vertices (right)*

Instead of duplicating vertex v1 and v2 with vertex v4 and v6, we only define these vertices once. We still render two triangles in this case, but we tell OpenGL ES explicitly which vertices to use for each triangle (that is, use v1, v2, and v3 for the first triangle and v3, v4, and v1 for the second one)—which vertices to use for each triangle are defined via indices in our vertices array. The first vertex in our array has index 0, the second vertex has index 1, and so on. For the preceding rectangle, we'd have a list of indices like this:

```
short[] indices = { 0, 1, 2,
                    2, 3, 0 };
```

Incidentally, OpenGL ES wants us to specify the indices as shorts (which is not entirely correct; we could also use bytes). However, as with the vertex data, we can't just pass a short array to OpenGL ES. It wants a direct ShortBuffer. We already know how to handle that.

```
ByteBuffer byteBuffer = ByteBuffer.allocate(indices.length * 2);
byteBuffer.order(ByteOrder.nativeOrder());
ShortBuffer shortBuffer = byteBuffer.asShortBuffer();
shortBuffer.put(indices);
shortBuffer.flip();
```

A short needs 2 bytes of memory, so we allocate indices.length × 2 bytes for our ShortBuffer. We set the order to native again and get a ShortBuffer view so that we can handle the underlying ByteBuffer more easily. All that's left is putting our indices into the ShortBuffer and flipping it so the limit and position are set correctly.

If we wanted to draw Bob as a rectangle with two indexed triangles, we could define our vertices like this:

```
ByteBuffer byteBuffer = ByteBuffer.allocateDirect(4 * VERTEX_SIZE);
byteBuffer.order(ByteOrder.nativeOrder());
vertices = byteBuffer.asFloatBuffer();
vertices.put(new float[] {  100.0f, 100.0f, 0.0f, 1.0f,
                            228.0f, 100.0f, 1.0f, 1.0f,
                            228.0f, 229.0f, 1.0f, 0.0f,
                            100.0f, 228.0f, 0.0f, 0.0f });
vertices.flip();
```

The order of the vertices is exactly the same as in the right part of Figure 7–13. We tell OpenGL ES that we have positions and texture coordinates for our vertices and where it can find these vertex attributes via the usual calls to glEnableClientState() and glVertexPointer()/glTexCoordPointer(). The only difference is the method we call to draw the two triangles.

```
gl.glDrawElements(GL10.GL_TRIANGLES, 6, GL10.GL_UNSIGNED_SHORT, indices);
```

This method is actually very similar to glDrawArrays(). The first parameter specifies the type of primitive we want to render—in this case, a list of triangles. The next parameter specifies how many vertices we want to use, which equals six in our case. The third parameter specifies what type the indices have—we specify unsigned short. Note that Java has no unsigned types; however, given the one-complement encoding of signed numbers, it's OK to use a ShortBuffer that actually holds signed shorts. The last parameter is our ShortBuffer holding the six indices.

So, what will OpenGL ES do? It knows that we want to render triangles; it knows that we want to render two triangles, as we specified six vertices; but instead of fetching six vertices sequentially from the vertices array, OpenGL ES goes sequentially through the index buffer and uses the vertices it has indexed.

Putting It Together

When we put it all together, we arrive at the code in Listing 7–9.

Listing 7–9. *Excerpt from IndexedTest.java; Drawing Two Indexed Triangles*

```
class IndexedScreen extends Screen {
    final int VERTEX_SIZE = (2 + 2) * 4;
    GLGraphics glGraphics;
    FloatBuffer vertices;
    ShortBuffer indices;
    Texture texture;

    public IndexedScreen(Game game) {
        super(game);
        glGraphics = ((GLGame) game).getGLGraphics();

        ByteBuffer byteBuffer = ByteBuffer.allocateDirect(4 * VERTEX_SIZE);
        byteBuffer.order(ByteOrder.nativeOrder());
        vertices = byteBuffer.asFloatBuffer();
        vertices.put(new float[] {  100.0f, 100.0f, 0.0f, 1.0f,
                                    228.0f, 100.0f, 1.0f, 1.0f,
                                    228.0f, 228.0f, 1.0f, 0.0f,
                                    100.0f, 228.0f, 0.0f, 0.0f });
```

```
        vertices.flip();

        byteBuffer = ByteBuffer.allocateDirect(6 * 2);
        byteBuffer.order(ByteOrder.nativeOrder());
        indices = byteBuffer.asShortBuffer();
        indices.put(new short[] { 0, 1, 2,
                                  2, 3, 0 });
        indices.flip();

        texture = new Texture((GLGame)game, "bobrgb888.png");
    }

    @Override
    public void present(float deltaTime) {
        GL10 gl = glGraphics.getGL();
        gl.glViewport(0, 0, glGraphics.getWidth(), glGraphics.getHeight());
        gl.glClear(GL10.GL_COLOR_BUFFER_BIT);
        gl.glMatrixMode(GL10.GL_PROJECTION);
        gl.glLoadIdentity();
        gl.glOrthof(0, 320, 0, 480, 1, -1);

        gl.glEnable(GL10.GL_TEXTURE_2D);
        texture.bind();

        gl.glEnableClientState(GL10.GL_TEXTURE_COORD_ARRAY);
        gl.glEnableClientState(GL10.GL_VERTEX_ARRAY);

        vertices.position(0);
        gl.glVertexPointer(2, GL10.GL_FLOAT, VERTEX_SIZE, vertices);
        vertices.position(2);
        gl.glTexCoordPointer(2, GL10.GL_FLOAT, VERTEX_SIZE, vertices);

        gl.glDrawElements(GL10.GL_TRIANGLES, 6, GL10.GL_UNSIGNED_SHORT, indices);
    }
```

Note the use of our awesome Texture class, which brings down the code size considerably. Figure 7–15 shows the output, and Bob in all his glory.

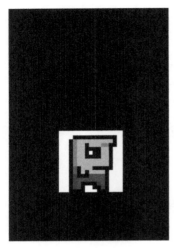

Figure 7–15. *Bob, indexed*

Now, this is pretty close to how we worked with Canvas. We have a lot more flexibility as well, since we are not limited to axis-aligned rectangles anymore.

This example has covered all we need to know about vertices for now. We saw that every vertex must have at least a position, and can have additional attributes, such as a color, given as four RGBA float values and texture coordinates. We also saw that we can reuse vertices via indexing in case we want to avoid duplication. This gives us a little performance boost, since OpenGL ES does not have to multiply more vertices by the projection and model-view matrices than absolutely necessary (which, again, is not entirely correct, but let's stick to this interpretation).

A Vertices Class

Let's make our code easier to write by creating a Vertices class that can hold a maximum number of vertices and, optionally, indices to be used for rendering. It should also take care of enabling all the states needed for rendering, as well as cleaning up the states after rendering has finished, so that other code can rely on a clean set of OpenGL ES states. Listing 7–10 shows our easy–to–use Vertices class.

Listing 7–10. *Vertices.java; Encapsulating (Indexed) Vertices*

```
package com.badlogic.androidgames.framework.gl;

import java.nio.ByteBuffer;
import java.nio.ByteOrder;
import java.nio.FloatBuffer;
import java.nio.ShortBuffer;

import javax.microedition.khronos.opengles.GL10;

import com.badlogic.androidgames.framework.impl.GLGraphics;
```

```java
public class Vertices {
    final GLGraphics glGraphics;
    final boolean hasColor;
    final boolean hasTexCoords;
    final int vertexSize;
    final FloatBuffer vertices;
    final ShortBuffer indices;
```

The Vertices class has a reference to the GLGraphics instance, so we can get ahold of the GL10 instance when we need it. We also store whether the vertices have colors and texture coordinates. This gives us great flexibility as we can choose the minimal set of attributes we need for rendering. Additionally, we store a FloatBuffer that holds our vertices and a ShortBuffer that holds the optional indices.

```java
    public Vertices(GLGraphics glGraphics, int maxVertices, int maxIndices, boolean hasColor, boolean hasTexCoords) {
        this.glGraphics = glGraphics;
        this.hasColor = hasColor;
        this.hasTexCoords = hasTexCoords;
        this.vertexSize = (2 + (hasColor?4:0) + (hasTexCoords?2:0)) * 4;

        ByteBuffer buffer = ByteBuffer.allocateDirect(maxVertices * vertexSize);
        buffer.order(ByteOrder.nativeOrder());
        vertices = buffer.asFloatBuffer();

        if(maxIndices > 0) {
            buffer = ByteBuffer.allocateDirect(maxIndices * Short.SIZE / 8);
            buffer.order(ByteOrder.nativeOrder());
            indices = buffer.asShortBuffer();
        } else {
            indices = null;
        }
    }
```

In the constructor, we specify how many vertices and indices our Vertices instance can hold maximally, as well as whether the vertices have colors or texture coordinates. Inside the constructor, we then set the members accordingly and instantiate the buffers. Note that the ShortBuffer will be set to null if maxIndices is zero. Our rendering will be performed non-indexed in that case.

```java
    public void setVertices(float[] vertices, int offset, int length) {
        this.vertices.clear();
        this.vertices.put(vertices, offset, length);
        this.vertices.flip();
    }

    public void setIndices(short[] indices, int offset, int length) {
        this.indices.clear();
        this.indices.put(indices, offset, length);
        this.indices.flip();
    }
```

Next up are the setVertices() and setIndices() methods. The latter will throw a NullPointerException in case the Vertices instance does not store indices. All we do is clear the buffers and copy the contents of the arrays.

```java
        public void draw(int primitiveType, int offset, int numVertices) {
            GL10 gl = glGraphics.getGL();

            gl.glEnableClientState(GL10.GL_VERTEX_ARRAY);
            vertices.position(0);
            gl.glVertexPointer(2, GL10.GL_FLOAT, vertexSize, vertices);

            if(hasColor) {
                gl.glEnableClientState(GL10.GL_COLOR_ARRAY);
                vertices.position(2);
                gl.glColorPointer(4, GL10.GL_FLOAT, vertexSize, vertices);
            }

            if(hasTexCoords) {
                gl.glEnableClientState(GL10.GL_TEXTURE_COORD_ARRAY);
                vertices.position(hasColor?6:2);
                gl.glTexCoordPointer(2, GL10.GL_FLOAT, vertexSize, vertices);
            }

            if(indices!=null) {
                indices.position(offset);
                gl.glDrawElements(primitiveType, numVertices, GL10.GL_UNSIGNED_SHORT,
    indices);
            } else {
                gl.glDrawArrays(primitiveType, offset, numVertices);
            }

            if(hasTexCoords)
                gl.glDisableClientState(GL10.GL_TEXTURE_COORD_ARRAY);

            if(hasColor)
                gl.glDisableClientState(GL10.GL_COLOR_ARRAY);
        }
    }
```

The final method of the Vertices class is draw(). It takes the type of the primitive (for example, GL10.GL_TRIANGLES), the offset into the vertices buffer (or the indices buffer if we use indices), and the number of vertices to use for rendering. Depending on whether the vertices have colors and texture coordinates, we enable the relevant OpenGL ES states and tell OpenGL ES where to find the data. We do the same for the vertex positions, of course, which are always needed. Depending on whether indices are used, we either call glDrawElements() or glDrawArrays() with the parameters passed to the method. Note that the offset parameter can also be used in case of indexed rendering: we simply set the position of the indices buffer accordingly so that OpenGL ES starts reading the indices from that offset instead of the first index of the indices buffer. The last thing we do in the draw() method is clean up the OpenGL ES state a little. We call glDisableClientState() with either GL10.GL_COLOR_ARRAY or GL10.GL_TEXTURE_COORD_ARRAY in case our vertices have these attributes. We need to do this, as another instance of Vertices might not use those attributes. If we rendered that other Vertices instance, OpenGL ES would still look for colors and/or texture coordinates.

We could replace all the tedious code in the constructor of our preceding example with the following snippet:

```
Vertices vertices = new Vertices(glGraphics, 4, 6, false, true);
vertices.setVertices(new float[] { 100.0f, 100.0f, 0.0f, 1.0f,
                                   228.0f, 100.0f, 1.0f, 1.0f,
                                   228.0f, 228.0f, 1.0f, 0.0f,
                                   100.0f, 228.0f, 0.0f, 0.0f }, 0, 16);
vertices.setIndices(new short[] { 0, 1, 2, 2, 3, 0 }, 0, 6);
```

Likewise, we could replace all the calls for setting up our vertex attribute arrays and rendering with a single call to the following:

```
vertices.draw(GL10.GL_TRIANGLES, 0, 6);
```

Together with our Texture class, we now have a pretty nice basis for all of our 2D OpenGL ES rendering. In order to reproduce all our Canvas rendering abilities completely, however, we are still missing blending. Let's have a look at that.

Alpha Blending: I Can See Through You

Alpha blending in OpenGL ES is pretty easy to enable. We only need two method calls:

```
gl.glEnable(GL10.GL_BLEND);
gl.glBlendFunc(GL10.GL_SRC_ALPHA, GL10.GL_ONE_MINUS_SRC_ALPHA);
```

The first method call should be familiar: it just tells OpenGL ES that it should apply alpha blending to all triangles we render from this point on. The second method is a little bit more involved. It specifies how the source and destination color should be combined. If you remember what we discussed in Chapter 3, the way a source color and a destination color are combined is governed by a simple blending equation. The method glBlendFunc() just tells OpenGL ES which kind of equation to use. The preceding parameters specify that we want the source color to be mixed with the destination color exactly as specified in the blending equation in Chapter 3. This is equal to how the Canvas blended Bitmaps for us.

Blending in OpenGL ES is pretty powerful and complex, and there's a lot more to it. For our purposes, we can ignore all those details, though, and just use the preceding blending function whenever we want to blend our triangles with the framebuffer—the same way we blended Bitmaps with the Canvas.

The second question is where the source and destination colors come from. The latter is easy to explain: it's the color of the pixel in the framebuffer we are going to overwrite with the triangle we draw. The source color is actually a combination of two colors.

The vertex color: This is the color we either specify via glColor4f() for all vertices or on a per-vertex basis by adding a color attribute to each vertex.

The texel color: As mentioned before, a texel is a pixel from a texture. When our triangle is rendered with a texture mapped to it, OpenGL ES will mix the texel colors with the vertex colors for each pixel of a triangle.

So, if our triangle is not texture mapped, the source color for blending is equal to the vertex color. If the triangle is texture mapped, the source color for each of the triangle's pixels is a mixture of the vertex color and the texel color. We could specify how the vertex and texel colors are combined by using the glTexEnv() method. The default is to *modulate* the vertex color by the texel color, which basically means that the two colors are multiplied with each other component-wise (vertex r × texel r, and so on). For all our use cases in this book, this is exactly what we want, so we won't go into glTexEnv(). There are also some very specialized cases where you might want to change how the vertex and texel colors are combined. As with glBlendFunc(), we'll ignore the details and just use the default.

When we load a texture image that doesn't have an alpha channel, OpenGL ES will automatically assume an alpha value of 1 for each pixel. If we load an image in RGBA8888 format, OpenGL ES will happily use the supplied alpha values for blending.

For vertex colors, we always have to specify an alpha component, either by using glColor4f(), where the last argument is the alpha value, or by specifying the four components per vertex, where again, the last component is the alpha value.

Let's put this into practice with a brief example. We want to draw Bob twice: once by using the image bobrgb888.png, which does not have an alpha channel per pixel, and a second time by using the image bobargb8888.png, which has alpha information. Note that the PNG image actually stores the pixels in ARGB8888 format instead of RGBA8888. Luckily, the GLUtils.texImage2D() method we use to upload the image data for a texture will do the conversion for us automatically. Listing 7–11 shows the code of our little experiment using the Texture and Vertices classes.

Listing 7–11. *Excerpt from BlendingTest.java; Blending in Action*

```
class BlendingScreen extends Screen {
    GLGraphics glGraphics;
    Vertices vertices;
    Texture textureRgb;
    Texture textureRgba;

    public BlendingScreen(Game game) {
        super(game);
        glGraphics = ((GLGame)game).getGLGraphics();

        textureRgb = new Texture((GLGame)game, "bobrgb888.png");
        textureRgba = new Texture((GLGame)game, "bobargb8888.png");

        vertices = new Vertices(glGraphics, 8, 12, true, true);
        float[] rects = new float[] {
                100, 100, 1, 1, 1, 0.5f, 0, 1,
                228, 100, 1, 1, 1, 0.5f, 1, 1,
                228, 228, 1, 1, 1, 0.5f, 1, 0,
                100, 228, 1, 1, 1, 0.5f, 0, 0,

                100, 300, 1, 1, 1, 1, 0, 1,
                228, 300, 1, 1, 1, 1, 1, 1,
                228, 428, 1, 1, 1, 1, 1, 0,
                100, 428, 1, 1, 1, 1, 0, 0
```

```
        };
        vertices.setVertices(rects, 0, rects.length);
        vertices.setIndices(new short[] {0, 1, 2, 2, 3, 0,
                                         4, 5, 6, 6, 7, 4 }, 0, 12);
    }
```

Our little `BlendingScreen` implementation holds a single `Vertices` instance where we'll store the two rectangles, as well as two `Texture` instances—one holding the RGBA8888 image of Bob and the other one storing the RGB888 version of Bob. In the constructor, we load both textures from the files bobrgb888.png and bobargb8888.png and rely on the `Texture` class and `GLUtils.texImag2D()` to convert the ARGB8888 PNG to RGBA8888, as needed by OpenGL ES. Next up, we define our vertices and indices. The first rectangle, consisting of four vertices, maps to the RGB888 texture of Bob. The second rectangle maps to the RGBA8888 version of Bob and is rendered 200 units above the RGB888 Bob rectangle. Note that the vertices of the first rectangle all have the color (1,1,1,0.5f), while the vertices of the second rectangle have the color (1,1,1,1).

```
    @Override
    public void present(float deltaTime) {
        GL10 gl = glGraphics.getGL();
        gl.glViewport(0, 0, glGraphics.getWidth(), glGraphics.getHeight());
        gl.glClearColor(1,0,0,1);
        gl.glClear(GL10.GL_COLOR_BUFFER_BIT);
        gl.glMatrixMode(GL10.GL_PROJECTION);
        gl.glLoadIdentity();
        gl.glOrthof(0, 320, 0, 480, 1, -1);

        gl.glEnable(GL10.GL_BLEND);
        gl.glBlendFunc(GL10.GL_SRC_ALPHA, GL10.GL_ONE_MINUS_SRC_ALPHA);

        gl.glEnable(GL10.GL_TEXTURE_2D);
        textureRgb.bind();
        vertices.draw(GL10.GL_TRIANGLES, 0, 6 );

        textureRgba.bind();
        vertices.draw(GL10.GL_TRIANGLES, 6, 6 );
    }
```

In our `present()` method, we clear the screen with red and set the projection matrix as we are used to doing. Next, we enable alpha blending and set the correct blend equation. Finally, we enable texture mapping and render the two rectangles. The first rectangle is rendered with the RGB888 texture bound, and the second rectangle is rendered with the RGBA8888 texture bound. We store both rectangles in the same `Vertices` instance and thus use offsets with the `vertices.draw()` methods. Figure 7–16 shows the output of this little gem.

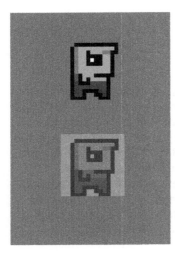

Figure 7–16. *Bob, vertex color blended (bottom) and texture blended (top)*

In the case of RGB888 Bob, the blending is performed via the alpha values in the per-vertex colors. Since we set those to 0.5f, Bob is 50 percent translucent.

In the case of RGBA8888 Bob, the per-vertex colors all have an alpha value of 1. However, since the background pixels of that texture have alpha values of 0, and since the vertex and texel colors are modulated, the background of this version of Bob disappears. If we'd have set the per-vertex colors' alpha values to 0.5f as well, then Bob himself would also have been 50 percent as translucent as his clone in the bottom of the screen. Figure 7–17 shows what that would have looked like.

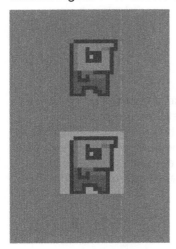

Figure 7–17. *An alternative version of RGBA8888 Bob using per-vertex alpha of 0.5f (top of the screen)*

That's basically all we need to know about blending with OpenGL ES in 2D.

However, there is one more very important thing we'd like to point out: *Blending is expensive!* Seriously, don't overuse it. Current mobile GPUs are not all that good at blending massive amounts of pixels. You should only use blending if absolutely necessary.

More Primitives: Points, Lines, Strips, and Fans

When we told you that OpenGL ES was a big, nasty triangle-rendering machine, we were not being 100 percent honest; in fact, OpenGL ES can also render points and lines. Best of all, these are also defined via vertices, and thus, all of the above also applies to them (texturing, per-vertex colors, and so forth). All we need to do to render these primitives is use something other than GL10.GL_TRIANGLES when we call glDrawArrays()/glDrawElements(). We can also perform indexed rendering with these primitives, although that's a bit redundant (in the case of points at least). Figure 7–18 shows a list of all the primitive types OpenGL ES offers.

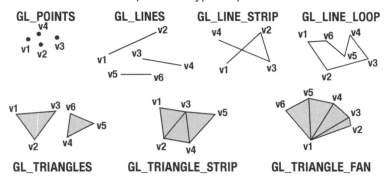

Figure 7–18. *All the primitives OpenGL ES can render*

Let's go through all of these primitives really quickly:

Point: With a point, each vertex is its own primitive.

Line: A line is made up of two vertices. As with triangles, we can just have $2 \times n$ vertices to define *n* lines.

Line strip: All the vertices are interpreted as belonging to one long line.

Line loop: This is similar to a line strip, with the difference being that OpenGL ES will automatically draw an additional line from the last vertex to the first vertex.

Triangle: This we already know. Each triangle is made up of three vertices.

Triangle strip: Instead of specifying three vertices, we just specify *number of triangles* + 1 vertices. OpenGL ES will then construct the first triangle from vertices (v1,v2,v3), the next triangle from vertices (v2,v3,v4), and so on.

Triangle fan: This has one base vertex (v1) that is shared by all triangles. The first triangle will be (v1,v2,v3), the next triangle (v1,v3,v4), and so on.

Triangle strips and fans are a little bit less flexible than pure triangle lists. But they can give a little performance boost, as fewer vertices have to be multiplied by the projection and model-view matrices. We'll stick to triangle lists in all our code, though, as they are easier to use and can be made to achieve similar performance by using indices.

Points and lines are a little bit strange in OpenGL ES. When we use a pixel-perfect orthographic projection—for example, our screen resolution is 320×480 pixels and our glOrthof() call uses those exact values—we still don't get pixel-perfect rendering in all cases. The positions of the point and line vertices have to be offset by 0.375f due to something called the *diamond exit rule*. Keep that in mind if you want to render pixel-perfect points and lines. We already saw that something similar applies to triangles. However, given that we usually draw rectangles in 2D, we don't run into that problem.

Given that all you have to do to render primitives other than GL10.GL_TRIANGLES is use one of the other constants in Figure 7–17, we'll spare you an example program. We'll stick to triangle lists for the most part, especially when doing 2D graphics programming.

Let's now dive into one more thing OpenGL ES offers us: the almighty model-view matrix!

2D Transformations: Fun with the Model-View Matrix

All we've done so far is define static geometries in the form of triangle lists. There was nothing moving, rotating, or scaling. Also, even when the vertex data itself stayed the same (that is, the width and height of a rectangle composed of two triangles along with texture coordinates and color), we still had to duplicate the vertices if we wanted to draw the same rectangle at different places. Look back at Listing 7–11 and ignore the color attributes of the vertices for now. The two rectangles only differ in their y-coordinates by 200 units. If we had a way to move those vertices without actually changing their values, we could get away with defining the rectangle of Bob only once and simply draw him at different locations— and that's exactly how we can use the model-view matrix.

World and Model Space

To understand how this works, we literally have to think outside of our little orthographic view frustum box. Our view frustum is in a special coordinate system called the *world space*. This is the space where all our vertices are going to end up eventually.

Up until now, we have specified all vertex positions in absolute coordinates relative to the origin of this world space (compare with Figure 7–5). What we really want is to make the definition of the positions of our vertices independent from this world space coordinate system. We can achieve this by giving each of our models (for example, Bob's rectangle, a spaceship, and so forth.) its own coordinate system.

This is what we usually call *model space*, the coordinate system within which we define the positions of our model's vertices. Figure 7–19 illustrates this concept in 2D, and the same rules apply to 3D as well (just add a z-axis).

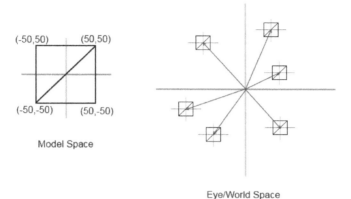

Figure 7–19. *Defining our model in model space, re-using it, and rendering it at different locations in the world space*

In Figure 7–19, we have a single model defined via a Vertices instance—for example, like this:

```
Vertices vertices = new Vertices(glGraphics, 4, 12, false, false);
vertices.setVertices(new float[] { -50, -50,
                                    50, -50,
                                    50,  50,
                                   -50,  50 }, 0, 8);
vertices.setIndices(new short[] {0, 1, 2, 2, 3, 0}, 0, 6);
```

For our discussion, we just leave out any vertex colors or texture coordinates. Now, when we render this model without any further modifications, it will be placed around the origin in the world space in our final image. If we want to render it at a different position—say, its center being at (200,300) in world space—we could redefine the vertex positions like this:

```
vertices.setVertices(new float[] { -50 + 200, -50 + 300,
                                    50 + 200, -50 + 300,
                                    50 + 200,  50 + 300,
                                   -50 + 200,  50 + 300 }, 0, 8);
```

On the next call to vertices.draw(), the model would be rendered with its center at (200,300), but this is a tad bit tedious isn't it?

Matrices Again

Remember when we briefly talked about matrices? We discussed how matrices can encode transformations, such as translations (moving stuff around), rotations, and scaling. The projection matrix we use to project our vertices onto the projection plane encodes a special type of transformation: a projection.

Matrices are the key to solving our previous problem more elegantly. Instead of manually moving our vertex positions around by redefining them, we simply set a matrix that encodes a translation. Since the projection matrix of OpenGL ES is already occupied by the orthogonal graphics projection matrix we specified via glOrthof(), we use a different OpenGL ES matrix: the model-view matrix. Here's how we could render our model with its origin moved to a specific location in eye/world space:

```
gl.glMatrixMode(GL10.GL_MODELVIEW);
gl.glLoadIdentity();
gl.glTranslatef(200, 300, 0);
vertices.draw(GL10.GL_TRIANGLES, 0, 6);
```

We first have to tell OpenGL ES which matrix we want to manipulate. In our case, that's the model-view matrix, which is specified by the constant GL10.GL_MODELVIEW. Next, we make sure that the model-view matrix is set to an identity matrix. Basically, we just overwrite anything that was in there already—we sort of clear the matrix. The next call is where the magic happens.

The method glTranslatef() takes three arguments: the translation on the x-, y-, and z-axes. Since we want the origin of our model to be placed at (200,300) in eye/world space, we specify a translation by 200 units on the x-axis and a translation by 300 units on the y-axis. As we are working in 2D, we simply ignore the z-axis and set the translation component to zero. We didn't specify a z-coordinate for our vertices, so these will default to zero. Adding zero to zero equals zero, so our vertices will stay in the x-y plane.

From this point on, the model-view matrix of OpenGL ES encodes a translation by (200,300,0), which will be applied to all vertices that pass through the OpenGL ES pipeline. If you refer back to Figure 7–4, you'll see that OpenGL ES will multiply each vertex with the model-view matrix first and then apply the projection matrix. Until now, the model-view matrix was set to an identity matrix (the default of OpenGL ES); therefore, it did not have an effect on our vertices. Our little glTranslatef() call changes this, and it will move all vertices first before they are projected.

This is, of course, done on the fly; the values in our Vertices instance do not change at all. We would have noticed any permanent change to our Vertices instance, because, by that logic, the projection matrix would have changed it already.

An Initial Example Using Translation

What can we use translation for? Say we want to render 100 Bobs at different positions in our world. Additionally, we want them to move around on the screen and change direction each time they hit an edge of the screen (or rather, a plane of our parallel projection view frustum, which coincides with the extents of our screen). We could do this by having one large Vertices instance that holds the vertices of the 100 rectangles—one for each Bob—and re-calculate the vertex positions of each frame. The easier method is to have one small Vertices instance that only holds a single rectangle (the model of Bob) and reuse it by translating it with the model-view matrix on the fly. Let's define our Bob model.

```
Vertices bobModel = new Vertices(glGraphics, 4, 12, false, true);
bobModel.setVertices(new float[] { -16, -16, 0, 1,
                                    16, -16, 1, 1,
                                    16,  16, 1, 0,
                                   -16,  16, 0, 0, }, 0, 8);
bobModel.setIndices(new short[] {0, 1, 2, 2, 3, 0}, 0, 6);
```

So, each Bob is 32×32 units in size. We also texture map him—we'll use bobrgb888.png to see the extents of each Bob.

Bob Becomes a Class

Let's define a simple Bob class. It will be responsible for holding a Bob's position and advancing his position in his current direction based on the delta time, just like we advanced Mr. Nom (with the difference being that we don't move in a grid anymore). The update() method will also make sure that Bob doesn't escape our view volume bounds. Listing 7–12 shows the Bob class.

Listing 7–12. *Bob.java*

```java
package com.badlogic.androidgames.glbasics;

import java.util.Random;

class Bob {
    static final Random rand = new Random();
    public float x, y;
    float dirX, dirY;

    public Bob() {
        x = rand.nextFloat() * 320;
        y = rand.nextFloat() * 480;
        dirX = 50;
        dirY = 50;
    }

    public void update(float deltaTime) {
        x = x + dirX * deltaTime;
        y = y + dirY * deltaTime;

        if (x < 0) {
            dirX = -dirX;
            x = 0;
        }

        if (x > 320) {
            dirX = -dirX;
            x = 320;
        }

        if (y < 0) {
            dirY = -dirY;
            y = 0;
        }
```

```
            if (y > 480) {
                dirY = -dirY;
                y = 480;
            }
        }
    }
}
```

Each Bob will place himself at a random location in the world when we construct him. All the Bobs will initially move in the same direction: 50 units to the right and 50 units upward per second (as we multiply by the deltaTime). In the update() method, we simply advance Bob in his current direction in a time-based manner and then check if he left the view frustum bounds. If that's the case, we invert his direction and make sure he's still in the view frustum.

Now let's assume we are instantiating 100 Bobs, like this:

```
Bob[] bobs = new Bob[100];
for(int i = 0; i < 100; i++) {
    bobs[i] = new Bob();
}
```

To render each of these Bobs, we'd do something like this (assuming we've already cleared the screen, set the projection matrix, and bound the texture):

```
gl.glMatrixMode(GL10.GL_MODELVIEW);
for(int i = 0; i < 100; i++) {
    bob.update(deltaTime);
    gl.glLoadIdentity();
    gl.glTranslatef(bobs[i].x, bobs[i].y, 0);
    bobModel.render(GL10.GL_TRIANGLES, 0, 6);
}
```

That is pretty sweet, isn't it? For each Bob, we call his update() method, which will advance his position and make sure he stays within the bounds of our little world. Next, we load an identity matrix into the model-view matrix of OpenGL ES so we have a clean slate. We then use the current Bob's x- and y-coordinates in a call to glTranslatef(). When we render the Bob model in the next call, all the vertices will be offset by the current Bob's position—exactly what we wanted.

Putting It Together

Let's make this a full-blown example. Listing 7–13 shows the code.

Listing 7–13. *BobTest.java; 100 Moving Bobs!*

```
package com.badlogic.androidgames.glbasics;

import javax.microedition.khronos.opengles.GL10;

import com.badlogic.androidgames.framework.Game;
import com.badlogic.androidgames.framework.Screen;
import com.badlogic.androidgames.framework.gl.FPSCounter;
import com.badlogic.androidgames.framework.gl.Texture;
import com.badlogic.androidgames.framework.gl.Vertices;
import com.badlogic.androidgames.framework.impl.GLGame;
```

```
import com.badlogic.androidgames.framework.impl.GLGraphics;

public class BobTest extends GLGame {

    @Override
    public Screen getStartScreen() {
        return new BobScreen(this);
    }

    class BobScreen extends Screen {
        static final int NUM_BOBS = 100;
        GLGraphics glGraphics;
        Texture bobTexture;
        Vertices bobModel;
        Bob[] bobs;
```

Our BobScreen class holds a Texture (loaded from bobrbg888.png), a Vertices instance holding the model of Bob (a simple textured rectangle), and an array of Bob instances. We also define a little constant named NUM_BOBS so that we can modify the number of Bobs we want to have on the screen.

```
        public BobScreen(Game game) {
            super(game);
            glGraphics = ((GLGame)game).getGLGraphics();

            bobTexture = new Texture((GLGame)game, "bobrgb888.png");

            bobModel = new Vertices(glGraphics, 4, 12, false, true);
            bobModel.setVertices(new float[] { -16, -16, 0, 1,
                                                16, -16, 1, 1,
                                                16,  16, 1, 0,
                                               -16,  16, 0, 0, }, 0, 16);
            bobModel.setIndices(new short[] {0, 1, 2, 2, 3, 0}, 0, 6);


            bobs = new Bob[100];
            for(int i = 0; i < 100; i++) {
                bobs[i] = new Bob();
            }
        }
```

The constructor just loads the texture, creates the model, and instantiates NUM_BOBS Bob instances.

```
    @Override
        public void update(float deltaTime) {
            game.getInput().getTouchEvents();
            game.getInput().getKeyEvents();

            for(int i = 0; i < NUM_BOBS; i++) {
                bobs[i].update(deltaTime);
            }
        }
```

The update() method is where we let our Bobs update themselves. We also make sure our input event buffers are emptied.

```
@Override
      public void present(float deltaTime) {
          GL10 gl = glGraphics.getGL();
          gl.glClearColor(1,0,0,1);
          gl.glClear(GL10.GL_COLOR_BUFFER_BIT);
          gl.glMatrixMode(GL10.GL_PROJECTION);
          gl.glLoadIdentity();
          gl.glOrthof(0, 320, 0, 480, 1, -1);

          gl.glEnable(GL10.GL_TEXTURE_2D);
          bobTexture.bind();

          gl.glMatrixMode(GL10.GL_MODELVIEW);
          for(int i = 0; i < NUM_BOBS; i++) {
              gl.glLoadIdentity();
              gl.glTranslatef(bobs[i].x, bobs[i].y, 0);
              gl.glRotatef(45, 0, 0, 1);
              gl.glScalef(2, 0.5f, 0);
              bobModel.draw(GL10.GL_TRIANGLES, 0, 6);
          }
      }
```

In the render() method, we clear the screen, set the projection matrix, enable texturing, and bind the texture of Bob. The last couple of lines are responsible for actually rendering each Bob instance. Since OpenGL ES remembers its states, we have to set the active matrix only once; in this case, we are going to modify the model-view matrix in the rest of the code. We then loop through all the Bobs, set the model-view matrix to a translation matrix based on the position of the current Bob, and render the model, which will be translated by the model view-matrix automatically.

```
      @Override
      public void pause() {
      }

      @Override
      public void resume() {
      }

      @Override
      public void dispose() {
      }
   }
}
```

That's it. Best of all, we employed the MVC pattern we used in Mr. Nom again. It really lends itself well to game programming. The logical side of Bob is completely decoupled from his appearance, which is nice, as we can easily replace his appearance with something more complex. Figure 7–20 shows the output of our little program after running it for a few seconds.

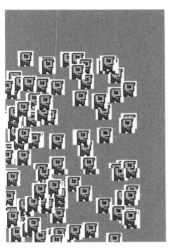

Figure 7-20. *That's a lot of Bobs!*

That's not the end of all of our fun with transformations yet. If you remember what we said a couple of pages ago, you'll know what's coming: rotations and scaling.

More Transformations

Besides the glTranslatef() method, OpenGL ES also offers us two methods for transformations: glRotatef() and glScalef().

Rotation

Here's the signature of glRotatef():

GL10.glRotatef(**float** angle, **float** axisX, **float** axisY, **float** axisZ);

The first parameter is the angle in degrees by which we want to rotate our vertices. What do the rest of the parameters mean?

When we rotate something, we rotate it around an axis. What is an axis? Well, we already know three axes: the x-axis, the y-axis, and the z-axis. We can express these three axes as so-called *vectors*. The positive x-axis would be described as (1,0,0), the positive y-axis would be (0,1,0), and the positive z-axis would be (0,0,1). As you can see, a vector actually encodes a direction; in our case, in 3D space. Bob's direction is also a vector, but in 2D space. Vectors can also encode positions, like Bob's position in 2D space.

To define the axis around which we want to rotate the model of Bob, we need to go back to 3D space. Figure 7-21 shows the model of Bob (with a texture applied for orientation), as defined in the previous code in 3D space.

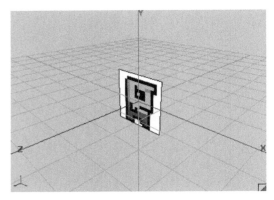

Figure 7–21. *Bob in 3D*

Since we haven't defined z-coordinates for Bob's vertices, he is embedded in the x-y plane of our 3D space (which is actually the model space, remember?). If we want to rotate Bob, we can do so around any axis we can think of: the x-, y-, or z-axis, or even a totally crazy axis like (0.75,0.75,0.75). However, for our 2D graphics programming needs, it makes sense to rotate Bob in the x-y plane; hence, we'll use the positive z-axis as our rotation axis, which can be defined as (0,0,1). The rotation will be counterclockwise around the z-axis. A call to glRotatef(), like this would cause the vertices of Bob's model to be rotated as shown in Figure 7–22.

```
gl.glRotatef(45, 0, 0, 1);
```

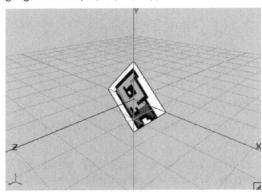

Figure 7–22.*Bob, rotated around the z-axis by 45 degrees*

Scaling

We can also scale Bob's model with glScalef(), like this:

```
glScalef(2, 0.5f, 1);
```

Given Bob's original model pose, this would result in the new orientation depicted in Figure 7–23.

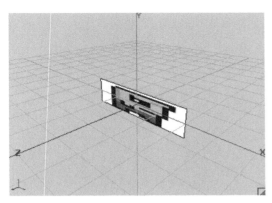

Figure 7–23. *Bob, scaled by a factor of 2 on the x-axis and a factor of 0.5 on the y-axis . . . ouch.*

Combining Transformations

Now, we also discussed that we can combine the effect of multiple matrices by multiplying them together to form a new matrix. All the methods—glTranslatef(), glScalef(), glRotatef(), and glOrthof()—do just that. They multiply the current active matrix by the temporary matrix they create internally based on the parameters we pass to them. So, let's combine the rotation and scaling of Bob.

```
gl.glRotatef(45, 0, 0, 1);
gl.glScalef(2, 0.5f, 1);
```

This would make Bob's model look like Figure 7–24 (remember, we are still in model space).

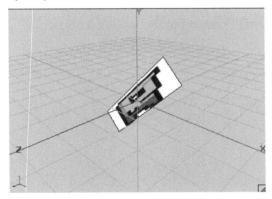

Figure 7–24. *Bob, first scaled and then rotated (still not looking happy)*

What would happen if we applied the transformations the other way around?

```
gl.glScalef(2, 0.5, 0);
gl.glRotatef(45, 0, 0, 1)
```

Figure 7–25 gives you the answer.

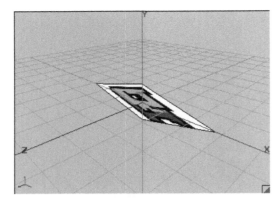

Figure 7–25. *Bob, first rotated and then scaled*

Wow, this is not the Bob we used to know. What happened here? If you look at the code snippets, you'd actually expect Figure 7–24 to look like Figure 7–25, and Figure 7–25 to look like Figure 7–24. In the first snippet, we apply the rotation first and then scale Bob, right?

Wrong. The way OpenGL ES multiplies matrices with each other dictates the order in which the transformations the matrices encode are applied to a model. The last matrix with which we multiply the currently active matrix will be the first that gets applied to the vertices. So if we want to scale, rotate, and translate Bob in that exact order, we have to call the methods like this:

```
glTranslatef(bobs[i].x, bobs[i].y, 0);
glRotatef(45, 0, 0, 1);
glScalef(2, 0.5f, 1);
```

If we changed the loop in our BobScreen.present() method to the following code:

```
gl.glMatrixMode(GL10.GL_MODELVIEW);
for(int i = 0; i <NUM_BOBS; i++) {
    gl.glLoadIdentity();
    gl.glTranslatef(bobs[i].x, bobs[i].y, 0);
    gl.glRotatef(45, 0, 0, 1);
    gl.glScalef(2, 0.5f, 0);
    bobModel.draw(GL10.GL_TRIANGLES, 0, 6);
}
```

The output would look like Figure 7–25.

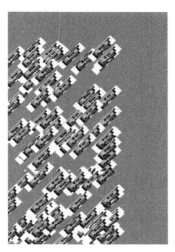

Figure 7–26. *A hundred Bobs scaled, rotated, and translated (in that order) to their positions in world space*

It's easy to mix up the order of these matrix operations when you first start out with OpenGL on the desktop. To remember how to do it correctly, use the mnemonic device called the LASFIA principle: last specified, first applied (Yeah, this mnemonic isn't all that great huh?).

The easiest way to get comfortable with model-view transformations is to use them heavily. We suggest you take the BobTest.java source file, modify the inner loop for some time, and observe the effects. Note that you can specify as many transformations as you want for rendering each model. Add more rotations, translations, and scaling. Go crazy.

With this last example, we basically know everything we need to know about OpenGL ES to write 2D games . . . or do we?

Optimizing for Performance

When we run this example on a beefy second-generation device like a Droid or a Nexus One, everything will run smooth as silk. If we run it on a Hero, everything will start to stutter and look pretty unpleasant. But hey, didn't we say that OpenGL ES was the silver bullet for fast graphics rendering? Well, it is, but only if we do things the way OpenGL ES wants us to do them.

Measuring Frame Rate

BobTest provides a perfect example to start with some optimizations. Before we can do that though, we need a way to assess performance. Manual visual inspection ("doh, it looks like it stutters a little") is not precise enough. A better way to measure how fast our program performs is to count the number of frames we render per second. If you remember Chapter 3, we talked about something called the vertical synchronization, or vsync for short. This is enabled on all Android devices that are on the market so far, and it limits the maximum frames per second (FPS) we can achieve to 60. We know our code is good enough when we run at that frame rate.

> **NOTE:** While 60 FPS would be nice to have, in reality it is pretty hard to achieve such performance on many Android devices. High-resolution tablets have a lot of pixels to fill, even if we're just clearing the screen. We'll be happy if our game renders the world at more than 30 FPS in general. More frames don't hurt, though.

Let's write a little helper class that counts the FPS and outputs that value periodically. Listing 7–14 shows the code of a class called FPSCounter.

Listing 7–14. *FPSCounter.java; Counting Frames and Logging Them to LogCat Each Second*

```
package com.badlogic.androidgames.framework.gl;

import android.util.Log;

public class FPSCounter {
    long startTime = System.nanoTime();
    int frames = 0;

    public void logFrame() {
        frames++;
        if(System.nanoTime() - startTime >= 1000000000) {
            Log.d("FPSCounter", "fps: " + frames);
            frames = 0;
            startTime = System.nanoTime();
        }
    }
}
```

We can put an instance of this class in our BobScreen class and call the logFrame() method once in the BobScreen.present() method. We just did this, and here is the output for a Hero (running Android 1.5), a Droid (running Android 2.2), and a Nexus One (running Android 2.2.1).

```
Hero:
12-10 03:27:05.230: DEBUG/FPSCounter(17883): fps: 22
12-10 03:27:06.250: DEBUG/FPSCounter(17883): fps: 22
12-10 03:27:06.820: DEBUG/dalvikvm(17883): GC freed 21818 objects / 524280 bytes in
132ms
12-10 03:27:07.270: DEBUG/FPSCounter(17883): fps: 20
12-10 03:27:08.290: DEBUG/FPSCounter(17883): fps: 23

Droid:
12-10 03:29:44.825: DEBUG/FPSCounter(8725): fps: 39
12-10 03:29:45.864: DEBUG/FPSCounter(8725): fps: 38
12-10 03:29:46.879: DEBUG/FPSCounter(8725): fps: 38
12-10 03:29:47.879: DEBUG/FPSCounter(8725): fps: 39
12-10 03:29:48.887: DEBUG/FPSCounter(8725): fps: 40
```

```
Nexus One:
12-10 03:28:05.923: DEBUG/FPSCounter(930): fps: 43
12-10 03:28:06.933: DEBUG/FPSCounter(930): fps: 43
12-10 03:28:07.943: DEBUG/FPSCounter(930): fps: 44
12-10 03:28:08.963: DEBUG/FPSCounter(930): fps: 44
12-10 03:28:09.973: DEBUG/FPSCounter(930): fps: 44
12-10 03:28:11.003: DEBUG/FPSCounter(930): fps: 43
12-10 03:28:12.013: DEBUG/FPSCounter(930): fps: 44
```

Upon first inspection, we can see the following:

- The Hero is twice as slow as the Droid and the Nexus One.

- The Nexus One is slightly faster than the Droid.

- We generate garbage on the Hero in our process (17883).

Now, the last item on that list is somewhat puzzling. We run the same code on all three devices. Upon further inspection, we do not allocate any temporary objects in either the present() or update() method. So what's happening on the Hero?

The Curious Case of the Hero on Android 1.5

It turns out that there is a bug in Android 1.5. Well, it's not *really* a bug, it's just some extremely sloppy programming. Remember that we use direct NIO buffers for our vertices and indices? These are actually memory blocks in native heap memory. Each time we call glVertexPointer(), glColorPointer(), or any other of the glXXXPointer() methods, OpenGL ES will try to fetch the native heap memory address of that buffer to look up the vertices to transfer the data to video RAM. The problem on Android 1.5 is that each time we request the memory address from a direct NIO buffer, it will generate a temporary object called PlatformAddress. Since we have a lot of calls to the glXXXPointer() and glDrawElements() methods (remember, the latter fetches the address from a direct ShortBuffer), Android allocates a metric ton of temporary PlatformAddress instances, and there's nothing we can do about it (a workaround is out there, but for now we won't discuss it). Let's just accept the fact that using NIO buffers on Android 1.5 is horribly broken and move on.

What's Making My OpenGL ES Rendering So Slow?

That the Hero is slower than the second-generation devices is no big surprise. However, the PowerVR chip in the Droid is slightly faster than the Adreno chip in the Nexus One, so the preceding results are a little bit strange at first sight. Upon further inspection, we can probably attribute the difference, not to the GPU power, but to the fact that we call many OpenGL ES methods each frame, which are costly Java Native Interface methods. This means that they actually call into C code, which costs more than calling a Java method on Dalvik. The Nexus One has a JIT compiler and can optimize a little bit there. So, let's just assume that the difference stems from the JIT compiler (which is probably not entirely correct).

Now, let's examine what's bad for OpenGL ES:

- Changing states a lot per frame (that is, blending, enabling/disabling texture mapping, and so on)

- Changing matrices a lot per frame

- Binding textures a lot per frame

- Changing the vertex, color, and texture coordinate pointers a lot per frame

It all boils down to changing states really. Why is this costly? GPUs work like an assembly line in a factory. While the front of the line processes new incoming pieces, the end of the line finishes off pieces already processed by previous stages of the line. Let's try it with a little car factory analogy.

The production line has a few states, such as the tools that are available to factory workers, the type of bolts that are used to assemble parts of the cars, the color with which the cars get painted, and so on. Yes, real car factories have multiple assembly lines, but let's just pretend there's only one. Now, each stage of the line will be busy as long as we don't change any of the states. As soon as we change a single state, however, the line will stall until all the cars currently being assembled are finished off. Only then can we actually change the state and assemble cars with the new paint, bolts, or whatever.

The key insight is that a call to glDrawElements() or glDrawArrays() is not immediately executed; instead, the command is put into a buffer that is processed asynchronously by the GPU. This means that the calls to the drawing methods will not block. It's therefore a bad idea to measure the time a call to glDrawElements() takes, as the actual work might be performed in the future. That's why we measure FPS instead. When the framebuffer is swapped (yes, we use double-buffering with OpenGL ES as well), OpenGL ES will make sure that all pending operations will be executed.

So, translating the car factory analogy to OpenGL ES means the following: While new triangles enter the command buffer via a call to glDrawElements() or glDrawArrays(), the GPU pipeline might finish off the rendering of currently processed triangles from earlier calls to the render methods (for example, a triangle can be currently processed in the rasterization state of the pipeline). This has the following implications:

- Changing the currently bound texture is expensive. Any triangles in the command buffer that have not been processed yet and that use the texture must be rendered first. The pipeline will stall.

- Changing the vertex, color, and texture coordinate pointers is expensive. Any triangles in the command buffer that haven't been rendered yet and use the old pointers must be rendered first. The pipeline will stall.

- Changing blending state is expensive. Any triangles in the command buffer that need/don't need blending and haven't been rendered yet must be rendered first. The pipeline will stall.

- Changing the model-view or projection matrix is expensive. Any triangles in the command buffer that haven't been processed yet and to which the old matrices should be applied must be rendered first. The pipeline will stall.

The quintessence of all this is *reduce your state changes*—all of them.

Removing Unnecessary State Changes

Let's look at the present() method of BobTest and see what we can change. Here's the snippet for reference—we add the FPSCounter and we also use glRotatef() and glScalef()):

```
@Override
public void present(float deltaTime) {
    GL10 gl = glGraphics.getGL();
    gl.glViewport(0, 0, glGraphics.getWidth(), glGraphics.getHeight());
    gl.glClearColor(1,0,0,1);
    gl.glClear(GL10.GL_COLOR_BUFFER_BIT);
    gl.glMatrixMode(GL10.GL_PROJECTION);
    gl.glLoadIdentity();
    gl.glOrthof(0, 320, 0, 480, 1, -1);

    gl.glEnable(GL10.GL_TEXTURE_2D);
    bobTexture.bind();

    gl.glMatrixMode(GL10.GL_MODELVIEW);
    for(int i = 0; i < NUM_BOBS; i++) {
        gl.glLoadIdentity();
        gl.glTranslatef(bobs[i].x, bobs[i].y, 0);
        gl.glRotatef(45, 0, 0, 1);
        gl.glScalef(2, 0.5f, 1);
        bobModel.draw(GL10.GL_TRIANGLES, 0, 6);
    }
    fpsCounter.logFrame();
}
```

The first thing we could do is to move the calls to glViewport() and glClearColor(), as well as the method calls that set the projection matrix to the BobScreen.resume() method. The clear color will never change; the viewport and the projection matrix won't change either. Why not put the code to set up all persistent OpenGL states like the viewport or projection matrix in the constructor of BobScreen? Well, we need to battle context loss. All OpenGL ES state modifications we perform will get lost, and when our screen's resume() method is called, we know that the context has been re-created, and it is thus missing all the states that we might have set before. We can also put the glEnable() and the texture-binding call into the resume() method. After all, we want texturing to be enabled all the time, and we also only want to use that single Bob texture. For good measure, we also call texture.reload() in the resume() method, so that our texture image data is also reloaded in the case of a context loss. Here are our modified present() and resume() methods:

```java
@Override
public void resume() {
    GL10 gl = glGraphics.getGL();
    gl.glViewport(0, 0, glGraphics.getWidth(), glGraphics.getHeight());
    gl.glClearColor(1, 0, 0, 1);
    gl.glMatrixMode(GL10.GL_PROJECTION);
    gl.glLoadIdentity();
    gl.glOrthof(0, 320, 0, 480, 1, -1);

    bobTexture.reload();
    gl.glEnable(GL10.GL_TEXTURE_2D);
    bobTexture.bind();
}

@Override
public void present(float deltaTime) {
    GL10 gl = glGraphics.getGL();
    gl.glClear(GL10.GL_COLOR_BUFFER_BIT);

    gl.glMatrixMode(GL10.GL_MODELVIEW);
    for(int i = 0; i < NUM_BOBS; i++) {
        gl.glLoadIdentity();
        gl.glTranslatef(bobs[i].x, bobs[i].y, 0);
        gl.glRotatef(45, 0, 0, 1);
        gl.glScalef(2, 0.5f, 0);
        bobModel.draw(GL10.GL_TRIANGLES, 0, 6);
    }

    fpsCounter.logFrame();
}
```

Running this "improved" version gives the following performance on the three devices:

```
Hero:
12-10 04:41:56.750: DEBUG/FPSCounter(467): fps: 23
12-10 04:41:57.770: DEBUG/FPSCounter(467): fps: 23
12-10 04:41:58.500: DEBUG/dalvikvm(467): GC freed 21821 objects / 524288 bytes in 133ms
12-10 04:41:58.790: DEBUG/FPSCounter(467): fps: 19
12-10 04:41:59.830: DEBUG/FPSCounter(467): fps: 23

Droid:
12-10 04:45:26.906: DEBUG/FPSCounter(9116): fps: 39
12-10 04:45:27.914: DEBUG/FPSCounter(9116): fps: 41
12-10 04:45:28.922: DEBUG/FPSCounter(9116): fps: 41
12-10 04:45:29.937: DEBUG/FPSCounter(9116): fps: 40

Nexus One:
12-10 04:37:46.097: DEBUG/FPSCounter(2168): fps: 43
12-10 04:37:47.127: DEBUG/FPSCounter(2168): fps: 45
12-10 04:37:48.147: DEBUG/FPSCounter(2168): fps: 44
12-10 04:37:49.157: DEBUG/FPSCounter(2168): fps: 44
12-10 04:37:50.167: DEBUG/FPSCounter(2168): fps: 44
```

As you can see, all of the devices have already benefited a tiny bit from our optimizations. Of course, the effects are not exactly huge. This can be attributed to the fact that when we originally called all those methods at the beginning of the frame, there were no triangles in the pipeline.

Reducing Texture Size Means Fewer Pixels to be Fetched

So what else could be changed? Something that is not all that obvious. Our Bob instances are 32×32 units in size. We use a projection plane that is 320×480 units in size. On a Hero, that will give us pixel-perfect rendering. On a Nexus One or a Droid, a single unit in our coordinate system would take up a little under a pixel. In any event, our texture is actually 128×128 pixels in size. We don't need that much resolution, so let's resize the texture image bobrgb888.png to 32×32 pixels. We'll call the new image bobrgb888-32x32.png. Using this smaller texture, we get the following FPS for each device:

```
Hero:
12-10 04:48:03.940: DEBUG/FPSCounter(629): fps: 23
12-10 04:48:04.950: DEBUG/FPSCounter(629): fps: 23
12-10 04:48:05.860: DEBUG/dalvikvm(629): GC freed 21812 objects / 524256 bytes in 134ms
12-10 04:48:05.990: DEBUG/FPSCounter(629): fps: 21
12-10 04:48:07.030: DEBUG/FPSCounter(629): fps: 24

Droid:
12-10 04:51:11.601: DEBUG/FPSCounter(9191): fps: 56
12-10 04:51:12.609: DEBUG/FPSCounter(9191): fps: 56
12-10 04:51:13.625: DEBUG/FPSCounter(9191): fps: 55
12-10 04:51:14.641: DEBUG/FPSCounter(9191): fps: 55

Nexus One:
12-10 04:48:18.067: DEBUG/FPSCounter(2238): fps: 53
12-10 04:48:19.077: DEBUG/FPSCounter(2238): fps: 56
12-10 04:48:20.077: DEBUG/FPSCounter(2238): fps: 53
12-10 04:48:21.097: DEBUG/FPSCounter(2238): fps: 54
```

Wow, that makes a huge difference on the second-generation devices! It turns out that the GPUs of those devices hate nothing more than having to scan over a large amount of pixels. This is true for fetching texels from a texture, as well as actually rendering triangles to the screen. The rate at which those GPUs can fetch texels and render pixels to the framebuffer is called the *fill rate*. All second-generation GPUs are heavily fill-rate limited, so we should try to use textures that are as small as possible (or map our triangles only to a small portion of them), and not render extremely huge triangles to the screen. We should also look out for overlap: the fewer overlapping triangles, the better.

> **NOTE:** Actually, overlap is not an extremely big problem with GPUs such as the PowerVR SGX 530 on the Droid. These GPUs have a special mechanism called *tile-based deferred rendering* that can eliminate a lot of that overlap under certain conditions. We should still care about pixels that will never be seen on the screen, though.

The Hero only slightly benefitted from the decrease in texture image size. So what could be the culprit here?

Reducing Calls to OpenGL ES/JNI Methods

The first suspects are the many OpenGL ES calls we issue per frame when we render the model for each Bob. First of all, we have four matrix operations per Bob. If we don't need rotation or scaling, we can bring that down to two calls. Here are the FPS numbers for each device when we only use glLoadIdentity() and glTranslatef() in the inner loop:

```
Hero:
12-10 04:57:49.610: DEBUG/FPSCounter(766): fps: 27
12-10 04:57:49.610: DEBUG/FPSCounter(766): fps: 27
12-10 04:57:50.650: DEBUG/FPSCounter(766): fps: 28
12-10 04:57:50.650: DEBUG/FPSCounter(766): fps: 28
12-10 04:57:51.530: DEBUG/dalvikvm(766): GC freed 22910 objects / 568904 bytes in 128ms

Droid:
12-10 05:08:38.604: DEBUG/FPSCounter(1702): fps: 56
12-10 05:08:39.620: DEBUG/FPSCounter(1702): fps: 57
12-10 05:08:40.628: DEBUG/FPSCounter(1702): fps: 58
12-10 05:08:41.644: DEBUG/FPSCounter(1702): fps: 57

Nexus One:
12-10 04:58:01.277: DEBUG/FPSCounter(2509): fps: 54
12-10 04:58:02.287: DEBUG/FPSCounter(2509): fps: 54
12-10 04:58:03.307: DEBUG/FPSCounter(2509): fps: 55
12-10 04:58:04.317: DEBUG/FPSCounter(2509): fps: 55
```

Well, it improved the performance on the Hero quite a bit, and the Droid and Nexus One also benefitted a little from removing the two matrix operations. Of course, there's a little bit of cheating involved: if we need to rotate and scale our Bobs, there's no way around issuing those two additional calls. However, when all we do is 2D rendering, there's a neat little trick we can use that will get rid of all matrix operations (we'll look into this in the next chapter).

OpenGL ES is a C API provided to Java via a JNI wrapper. This means that any OpenGL ES method we call has to cross that JNI wrapper to call the actual C native function. This was somewhat costly on earlier Android versions, but has gotten better with more recent versions. As shown, the impact is not all that huge, especially if the actual operations take up more time than issuing the call itself.

The Concept of Binding Vertices

So, is there anything else we can improve? Let's look at our current present() method one more time [with removed glRotatef() and glScalef()]:

```
public void present(float deltaTime) {
    GL10 gl = glGraphics.getGL();
    gl.glClear(GL10.GL_COLOR_BUFFER_BIT);
```

```
    gl.glMatrixMode(GL10.GL_MODELVIEW);
    for(int i = 0; i < NUM_BOBS; i++) {
        gl.glLoadIdentity();
        gl.glTranslatef(bobs[i].x, bobs[i].y, 0);
        bobModel.draw(GL10.GL_TRIANGLES, 0, 6);
    }

    fpsCounter.logFrame();
}
```

That looks pretty much optimal, doesn't it? Well, in fact it is not optimal. First, we can also move the gl.glMatrixMode() call to the resume() method, but that won't have a huge impact on performance, as we've already seen. The second thing that can be optimized is a little more subtle.

We use the Vertices class to store and render the model of our Bobs. Remember the Vertices.draw() method? Here it is one more time:

```
public void draw(int primitiveType, int offset, int numVertices) {
    GL10 gl = glGraphics.getGL();

    gl.glEnableClientState(GL10.GL_VERTEX_ARRAY);
    vertices.position(0);
    gl.glVertexPointer(2, GL10.GL_FLOAT, vertexSize, vertices);

    if(hasColor) {
        gl.glEnableClientState(GL10.GL_COLOR_ARRAY);
        vertices.position(2);
        gl.glColorPointer(4, GL10.GL_FLOAT, vertexSize, vertices);
    }

    if(hasTexCoords) {
        gl.glEnableClientState(GL10.GL_TEXTURE_COORD_ARRAY);
        vertices.position(hasColor?6:2);
        gl.glTexCoordPointer(2, GL10.GL_FLOAT, vertexSize, vertices);
    }

    if(indices!=null) {
        indices.position(offset);
        gl.glDrawElements(primitiveType, numVertices, GL10.GL_UNSIGNED_SHORT, indices);
    } else {
        gl.glDrawArrays(primitiveType, offset, numVertices);
    }

    if(hasTexCoords)
        gl.glDisableClientState(GL10.GL_TEXTURE_COORD_ARRAY);

    if(hasColor)
        gl.glDisableClientState(GL10.GL_COLOR_ARRAY);
}
```

Now look at preceding the loop again. Notice something? For each Bob, we enable the same vertex attributes over and over again via glEnableClientState(). We actually only need to set those once, as each Bob uses the same model that always uses the same vertex attributes. The next big problem are the calls to glXXXPointer() for each Bob. Since those pointers are also OpenGL ES states, we only need to set them once as well, as they will never change once they're set. So how can we fix that? Let's rewrite the Vertices.draw() method a little:

```
public void bind() {
    GL10 gl = glGraphics.getGL();

    gl.glEnableClientState(GL10.GL_VERTEX_ARRAY);
    vertices.position(0);
    gl.glVertexPointer(2, GL10.GL_FLOAT, vertexSize, vertices);

    if(hasColor) {
        gl.glEnableClientState(GL10.GL_COLOR_ARRAY);
        vertices.position(2);
        gl.glColorPointer(4, GL10.GL_FLOAT, vertexSize, vertices);
    }

    if(hasTexCoords) {
        gl.glEnableClientState(GL10.GL_TEXTURE_COORD_ARRAY);
        vertices.position(hasColor?6:2);
        gl.glTexCoordPointer(2, GL10.GL_FLOAT, vertexSize, vertices);
    }
}

public void draw(int primitiveType, int offset, int numVertices) {
    GL10 gl = glGraphics.getGL();

    if(indices!=null) {
        indices.position(offset);
        gl.glDrawElements(primitiveType, numVertices, GL10.GL_UNSIGNED_SHORT, indices);
    } else {
        gl.glDrawArrays(primitiveType, offset, numVertices);
    }
}

public void unbind() {
    GL10 gl = glGraphics.getGL();
    if(hasTexCoords)
        gl.glDisableClientState(GL10.GL_TEXTURE_COORD_ARRAY);

    if(hasColor)
        gl.glDisableClientState(GL10.GL_COLOR_ARRAY);
}
```

Can you see what we've done here? We can treat our vertices and all those pointers just like we treat a texture. We "bind" the vertex pointers via a single call to Vertices.bind(). From this point on, every Vertices.draw() call will work with those "bound" vertices, just like the draw call will also use the currently bound texture. Once we are done rendering stuff with that Vertices instance, we call Vertices.unbind() to disable any vertex attributes that another Vertices instance might not need. Keeping our OpenGL ES state clean is a good thing. Here's how our present() method looks now [We moved the glMatrixMode(GL10.GL_MODELVIEW) call to resume() as well]:

```
@Override
public void present(float deltaTime) {
    GL10 gl = glGraphics.getGL();
```

```
gl.glClear(GL10.GL_COLOR_BUFFER_BIT);

bobModel.bind();
for(int i = 0; i < NUM_BOBS; i++) {
    gl.glLoadIdentity();
    gl.glTranslatef(bobs[i].x, bobs[i].y, 0);
    bobModel.draw(GL10.GL_TRIANGLES, 0, 6);
}
bobModel.unbind();

fpsCounter.logFrame();
}
```

This effectively calls the glXXXPointer() and glEnableClientState() methods only once per frame. We thus save nearly 100 × 6 calls to OpenGL ES. That should have a huge impact on performance, right?

```
Hero:
12-10 05:16:59.710: DEBUG/FPSCounter(865): fps: 51
12-10 05:17:00.720: DEBUG/FPSCounter(865): fps: 46
12-10 05:17:01.720: DEBUG/FPSCounter(865): fps: 47
12-10 05:17:02.610: DEBUG/dalvikvm(865): GC freed 21815 objects / 524272 bytes in 131ms
12-10 05:17:02.740: DEBUG/FPSCounter(865): fps: 44
12-10 05:17:03.750: DEBUG/FPSCounter(865): fps: 50

Droid:
12-10 05:22:27.519: DEBUG/FPSCounter(2040): fps: 57
12-10 05:22:28.519: DEBUG/FPSCounter(2040): fps: 57
12-10 05:22:29.526: DEBUG/FPSCounter(2040): fps: 57
12-10 05:22:30.526: DEBUG/FPSCounter(2040): fps: 55

Nexus One:
12-10 05:18:31.915: DEBUG/FPSCounter(2509): fps: 56
12-10 05:18:32.935: DEBUG/FPSCounter(2509): fps: 56
12-10 05:18:33.935: DEBUG/FPSCounter(2509): fps: 55
12-10 05:18:34.965: DEBUG/FPSCounter(2509): fps: 54
```

All three devices are nearly on par now. The Droid performs the best, followed by the Nexus One. Our little Hero performs great as well. We are up to 50 FPS from 22 FPS in the non-optimized case. That's an increase in performance of over 100 percent. We can be proud of ourselves. Our optimized Bob test is pretty much optimal.

Of course, our new bindable Vertices class has a few restrictions now:

- We can only set the vertex and index data when the Vertices instance is not bound, as the upload of that information is performed in Vertices.bind().

- We can't bind two Vertices instances at once. This means that we can only render with a single Vertices instance at any point in time. That's usually not a big problem though, and given the impressive increase in performance, we will live with it.

In Closing

There's one more optimization we can apply that is suited for 2D graphics programming with flat geometry, such as with rectangles. We'll look into that in the next chapter. The keyword to search for is *batching*, which means reducing the number of glDrawElements()/glDrawArrays() calls. An equivalent for 3D graphics exists as well, called *instancing*, but that's not possible with OpenGL ES 1.x.

We want to mention two more things before we close this chapter. First of all, when you run either BobText or OptimizedBobTest (which contains the super-optimized code we just developed), notice that the Bobs wobble around the screen somewhat. This is due to the fact that their positions are passed to glTranslatef() as floats. The problem with pixel-perfect rendering is that OpenGL ES is really sensitive to vertex positions with fractional parts in their coordinates. We can't really work around this problem; the effect will be less pronounced or even non-existent in a real game, as we'll see when we implement our next game. We can hide the effect to some extent by using a more diverse background, among other things.

The second thing we want to point out is how we interpret the FPS measurements. As you can see from the preceding output, the FPS fluctuates a little. This can be attributed to background processes that run alongside our application. We will never have all of the system resources for our game, so we have to learn to live with this issue. When you are optimizing your program, don't fake the environment by killing all background processes. Run the application on a phone that is in a normal state, as you'd use it yourself during the day. This will reflect the same experience that a user will have.

Our nice achievement concludes this chapter. As a word of warning, only start optimizing your rendering code after you have it working, and only then after you actually have a performance problem. Premature optimization is often a cause for having to rewrite your entire rendering code, as it may become unmaintainable.

Summary

OpenGL ES is a huge beast. We managed to boil all that down to a size that makes it easily usable for our game programming needs. We discussed what OpenGL ES is (a lean, mean triangle-rendering machine) and how it works. We then explored how to make use of OpenGL ES functionality by specifying vertices, how to create textures, and how to use states (such as blending) for some nice effects. We also looked a little bit into projections and how they are connected to matrices. While we didn't discuss what a matrix does internally, we explored how to use them to rotate, scale, and translate reusable models from model space to world space. When we use OpenGL ES for 3D programming later, you'll notice that you've already learned 90 percent of what you need to know. All we'll do is change the projection and add a z-coordinate to our vertices (well, there are a few more things, but on a high level that's actually it). Before that, however, we'll write a nice 2D game with OpenGL ES. In the next chapter, you'll get to know some of the 2D programming techniques we might need for that.

Chapter 8

2D Game Programming Tricks

Chapter 7 demonstrated that OpenGL ES offers quite a lot of features to exploit for 2D graphics programming, such as easy rotation and scaling and the automatic stretching of your view frustum to the viewport. It also offers performance benefits over using the Canvas.

Now it's time to look at some of the more advanced topics of 2D game programming. You used some of these concepts intuitively when you wrote Mr. Nom, including time-based state updates and image atlases. A lot of what's to come is also indeed very intuitive, and chances are high that you'd have come up with the same solution sooner or later. But it doesn't hurt to learn about these things explicitly.

There are a handful of crucial concepts for 2D game programming. Some of them will be graphics related, and others will deal with how you represent and simulate your game world. All of these have one thing in common: they rely on a little linear algebra and trigonometry. Fear not, the level of math needed to write games like Super Mario Brothers is not exactly mind blowing. You can begin by reviewing some concepts of 2D linear algebra and trigonometry.

Before We Begin

As with the previous "theoretical" chapters, you are going to create a couple of examples to get a feel for what's happening. For this chapter, you can reuse what you developed in the last chapter, mainly the GLGame, GLGraphics, Texture, and Vertices classes, along with the rest of the framework classes.

Your demo project consists of a starter called GameDev2DStarter, which presents a list of tests to run. Reuse the code of the GLBasicsStarter and simply replace the class names of the tests. Add each of the tests to the manifest in the form of <activity> elements.

Each of the tests is again an instance of the Game interface, and the actual test logic is implemented in the form of a Screen contained in the Game implementation of the test, as in the previous chapter. Only the relevant portions of the Screen will be presented to conserve some pages. The naming conventions are again XXXTest and XXXScreen for the GLGame and Screen implementation of each test.

With that out of your way, it's time to talk about vectors.

In the Beginning . . . There Was the Vector

In the last chapter, you learned that vectors shouldn't be mixed up with positions. This is not entirely true, as you can (and will) represent a position in some spaces via a vector. A vector can actually have many interpretations:

- *Position*: You already used this in the previous chapters to encode the coordinates of our entities relative to the origin of the coordinate system.

- *Velocity and acceleration*: These are physical quantities you'll hear about in the next section. While you are likely used to thinking about velocity and acceleration as being a single value, they should actually be represented as 2D or 3D vectors. They encode not only the speed of an entity (for example, a car driving at 100 km/h), but also the direction in which the entity is traveling. Note that this kind of vector interpretation does not state that the vector is given relative to the origin. This makes sense, since the velocity and direction of a car is independent of its position. Think of a car traveling northwest on a straight highway at 100 km/h. As long as its speed and direction don't change, the velocity vector won't change either.

- *Directions and distances*: Directions are similar to velocities, but generally lack physical quantities. You can use such a vector interpretation to encode states, such as *this entity is pointing southeast*. Distances just tell us how far away, and in what direction, a position is from another position.

Figure 8–1 shows these interpretations in action.

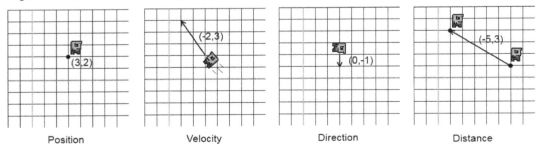

Figure 8–1. *Bob, with position, velocity, direction, and distance expressed as vectors*

Figure 8–1 is, of course, not exhaustive. Vectors can have a lot more interpretations. For yourgame development needs, however, these four basic interpretations suffice.

One thing that's left out from Figure 8–1 is the units the vector components have. Make sure that these are sensible (for example, Bob's velocity could be in meters per second, so that he travels 2 m to the left and 3 m up in 1 s). The same is true for positions and distances, which could also be expressed in meters. The direction of Bob is a special case, though—it is unitless. This will come in handy if you want to specify the general direction of an object while keeping the direction's physical features separate. You can do this for the velocity of Bob, storing the direction of his velocity as a direction vector and his speed as a single value. Single values are also known as *scalars*. The direction vector must be of length 1, as will be discussed later on.

Working with Vectors

The power of vectors stems from the fact that you can easily manipulate and combine them. Before you can do that, though, you need to define how you represent vectors:

$v = (x,y)$

Now, this isn't a big surprise; you've done this a gazillion times already. Every vector has an x and a y component in your 2D space. (Yes, you'll be staying in two dimensions in this chapter.) You can also add two vectors:

$c = a + b = (a.x, a.y) + (b.x, b.y) = (a.x + b.x, a.y + b.y)$

All you need to do is add the components together to arrive at the final vector. Try it out with the vectors given in Figure 8–1. Say you take Bob's position, $p = (3,2)$, and add his velocity, $v = (-2,3)$. You arrive at a new position, $p' = (3 + -2, 2 + 3) = (1,5)$. Don't get confused by the apostrophe behind the p here; it's just there to denote that you have a new vector p. Of course, this little operation only makes sense when the units of the position and the velocity fit together. In this case, you assume the position is given in meters (m) and the velocity is given in meters per second (m/s), which fits perfectly.

Of course, you can also subtract vectors:

$c = a - b = (a.x, a.y) - (b.x, b.y) = (a.x - b.x, a.y - b.y)$

Again, all you do is combine the components of the two vectors. Note, however, that the order in which you subtract one vector from the other is important. Take the rightmost image in Figure 8–1, for example. You have a green Bob at pg = (1,4) and a red Bob at pr = (6,1), where pg and pr stand for position green and position red, respectively. When you take the distance vector from green Bob to red Bob, you calculate the following:

$d = pg - pr = (1, 4) - (6, 1) = (-5, 3)$

Now this is strange. This vector is actually pointing from red Bob to green Bob! To get the direction vector from green Bob to red Bob, you have to reverse the order of subtraction:

$d = pr - pg = (6, 1) - (1, 4) = (5, -3)$

If you want to find the distance vector from position *a* to position *b*, use the following general formula:

$d = b - a$

In other words, always subtract the start position from the end position. That's a little confusing at first, but if you think about it, it makes absolute sense. Try it out on some graph paper!

You can also multiply a vector by a scalar (remember, a scalar is just a single value):

$a' = a * scalar = (a.x * scalar, a.y * scalar)$

You multiply each of the components of the vector by the scalar. This allows you to scale the length of a vector. Take the direction vector in Figure 8–1 as an example. It's specified as $d=(0,-1)$. If you multiply it with the scalar $s=2$, you effectively double its length: $d \times s = (0,-1 \times 2) = (0,-2)$. You can, of course, make it smaller, by using a scalar less than 1—for example, d multiplied by $s=0.5$ creates a new vector $d'=(0,-0.5)$.

Speaking of length, you can also calculate the length of a vector (in the units it's given in):

$|a| = sqrt(a.x*a.x + a.y*a.y)$

The $|a|$ notation simply explains that this represents the length of the vector. If you didn't sleep through your linear algebra class at school, you might recognize the formula for the vector length. It's simply the Pythagorean Theorem applied to your fancy 2D vector. The x and y components of the vector form two sides of a right triangle, and the third side is the length of the vector. Figure 8–2 illustrates this.

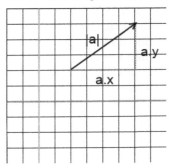

Figure 8–2. *Pythagoras would love vectors too*

The vector length is always positive or zero, given the properties of the square root. If you apply this to the distance vector between the red and green Bob, you can figure out that how far apart they are from each other (if their positions are given in meters):

$|pr - pg| = sqrt(5*5 + -3*-3) = sqrt(25 + 9) = sqrt(34) \sim= 5.83m$

Note that if you calculated $|pg - pr|$, you'd arrive at the same value, as the length is independent of the direction of the vector. This new knowledge also has another implication: when you multiply a vector with a scalar, its length changes accordingly.

Given a vector $d=(0,-1)$, with an original length of 1 unit, you can multiply it by 2.5 and arrive at a new vector, with a length of 2.5 units.

Direction vectors usually don't have any units associated with them. You can give them a unit by multiplying them with a scalar—for example, you can multiply a direction vector $d = (0,1)$ with a speed constant $s = 100$ m/s to get a velocity vector $v = (0 \times 100, 1 \times 100)$ $= (0,100)$. It's always a good idea to let your direction vectors have a length of 1. Vectors with a length of 1 are called *unit vectors*. You can make any vector a unit vector by dividing each of its components by its length:

$$d' = (d.x/|d|, d.y/|d|)$$

Remember that $|d|$ just means the length of the vector d. Try it out. Say you want a direction vector that points exactly northeast: $d = (1,1)$. It might seem that this vector is already a unit length, as both components are 1, right? Wrong:

$$|d| = sqrt(1*1 + 1*1) = sqrt(2) \sim= 1.44$$

You can easily fix that by making the vector a unit vector:

$$d' = (d.x/|d|, d.y/|d|) = (1/|d|, 1/|d|) \sim= (1/1.44, 1/1.44) = (0.69, 0.69)$$

This is also called *normalizing* a vector, which just means that you ensure it has a length of 1. With this little trick, you can, for example, create a unit-length direction vector out of a distance vector. Of course, you have to watch out for zero-length vectors, as you'd have to divide by zero in that case!

A Little Trigonometry

It's time to turn to trigonometry for a minute. There are two essential functions in trigonometry: *cosine* and *sine*. Each takes a single argument: an *angle*. You are probably used to specifying angles in degrees (for example, 45° or 360°). In most math libraries, however, trigonometry functions expect the angle in radians. You can easily do conversions between degrees and radians using the following equations:

```
degreesToRadians(angleInDegrees) = angleInDegrees / 180 * pi
radiansToDegrees(angle) = angleInRadians / pi * 180
```

Here, `pi` is the beloved superconstant, with an approximate value of 3.14159265. `pi` radians equal 180°, so that's how the preceding functions came to be.

So what do cosine and sine actually calculate, given an angle? They calculate the x and y components of a unit-length vector relative to the origin. Figure 8–3 illustrates this.

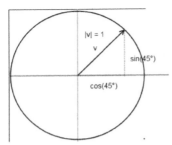

Figure 8–3. *Cosine and sine produce a unit vector, with its endpoint lying on the unit circle*

Given an angle, you can therefore create a unit-length direction vector like this:

v = (cos(angle), sin(angle))

You can go the other way around, as well, and calculate the angle of a vector with respect to the x-axis:

angle = atan2(v.y, v.x)

The atan2 function is actually an artificial construct. It uses the arcus tangent function (which is the inverse of the tangent function, another fundamental function in trigonometry) to construct an angle in the range of –180° to 180° (or –pi to pi, if the angle is returned in radians). The internals are a somewhat involved, and do not matter all that much in this discussion. The arguments are the y and x components of your vector. Note that the vector does not have to be a unit vector for the atan2 function to work. Also, note that the y component is usually given first, and then the x component—but this depends on the selected math library. This is a common source of errors.

Try a few examples. Given a vector *v*=(cos(97°), sin(97°)), the result of atan2(sin(97°),cos(97°)) is 97°. Great, that was easy. Using a vector *v*=(1,–1), you get atan2(–1,1)= –45°. So if your vector's y component is negative, you' ll get a negative angle in the range 0° to –180°. You can fix this by adding 360° (or 2 pi) if the output of atan2 is negative. In the preceding example, you would then get 315°.

The final operation you want to be able to apply to your vectors is rotating them by some angle. The derivations of the equations that follow are again rather involved. Luckily, you can just use these equations as is, without knowing about orthogonal base vectors. (*Hint:* that's the key phrase to search for on the Web if you want to know what's going on under the hood.) Here's the magical pseudocode:

v.x' = cos(angle) * v.x - sin(angle) * v.y
v.y' = sin(angle) * v.x + cos(angle) * v.y

Whoa, that was less complicated than expected. This will rotate any vector counter-clockwise around the origin, no matter what interpretation you have of the vector.

Together with vector addition, subtraction, and multiplication by a scalar, you can actually implement all the OpenGL matrix operations yourself. This is one part of the solution for further increasing the performance of your BobTest from the last chapter. This will be discussed in one of the following sections. For now, concentrate on what was discussed and transfer it to code.

Implementing a Vector Class

Now you can create an easy-to-use vector class for 2D vectors. Call it Vector2. It should have two members for holding the x and y components of the vector. Additionally, it should have a couple of nice methods that allow us to the following:

- Add and subtract vectors

- Multiply the vector components with a scalar

- Measure the length of a vector

- Normalize a vector

- Calculate the angle between a vector and the x-axis

- Rotate the vector

Java lacks operator overloading, so you have to come up with a mechanism that makes working with the Vector2 class less cumbersome. Ideally, you should have something like the following:

```
Vector2 v = new Vector2();
v.add(10,5).mul(10).rotate(54);
```

You can easily achieve this by letting each of the Vector2 methods return a reference to the vector itself. Of course, you also want to overload methods like Vector2.add() so that you can either pass in two floats or an instance of another Vector2. Listing 8–1 shows your Vector2 class in its full glory.

Listing 8–1. *Vector2.java: Implementing Some Nice 2D Vector Functionality*

```java
package com.badlogic.androidgames.framework.math;

import android.util.FloatMath;

public class Vector2 {
    public static float TO_RADIANS = (1 / 180.0f) * (float) Math.PI;
    public static float TO_DEGREES = (1 / (float) Math.PI) * 180;
    public float x, y;

    public Vector2() {
    }

    public Vector2(float x, float y) {
        this.x = x;
        this.y = y;
    }

    public Vector2(Vector2 other) {
        this.x = other.x;
        this.y = other.y;
    }
```

Put that class in the package com.badlogic.androidgames.framework.math, where you'll also house any other math-related classes.

Start off by defining two static constants, TO_RADIANS and TO_DEGREES. To convert an angle given in radians, simply multiply it by TO_DEGREES; to convert an angle given in degrees to radians, multiply it by TO_RADIANS. You can double-check this by looking at the two previously defined equations that govern degree-to-radian conversion. With this little trick, you can shave off some division and speed things up.

Next, define the members x and y, which store the components of the vector, and a couple of constructors—nothing too complex:

```
public Vector2 cpy() {
    return new Vector2(x, y);
}
```

The cpy() method will create a duplicate instance of the current vector and return it. This might come in handy if you want to manipulate a copy of a vector, preserving the value of the original vector.

```
public Vector2 set(float x, float y) {
    this.x = x;
    this.y = y;
    return this;
}

public Vector2 set(Vector2 other) {
    this.x = other.x;
    this.y = other.y;
    return this;
}
```

The set() methods allow you to set the x and y components of a vector, based on either two float arguments or another vector. The methods return a reference to this vector, so you can chain operations, as discussed previously.

```
public Vector2 add(float x, float y) {
    this.x += x;
    this.y += y;
    return this;
}

public Vector2 add(Vector2 other) {
    this.x += other.x;
    this.y += other.y;
    return this;
}

public Vector2 sub(float x, float y) {
    this.x -= x;
    this.y -= y;
    return this;
}

public Vector2 sub(Vector2 other) {
```

```
        this.x -= other.x;
        this.y -= other.y;
        return this;
    }
```

The add() and sub() methods come in two flavors: in one case, they work with two float arguments, while in the other case, they take another Vector2 instance. All four methods return a reference to this vector so that you can chain operations.

```
    public Vector2 mul(float scalar) {
        this.x *= scalar;
        this.y *= scalar;
        return this;
    }
```

The mul() method simply multiplies the x and y components of the vector with the given scalar value, and it returns a reference to the vector itself, for chaining.

```
    public float len() {
        return FloatMath.sqrt(x * x + y * y);
    }
```

The len() method calculates the length of the vector exactly, as defined previously. Note that you use the FastMath class instead of the usual Math class that Java SE provides. This is a special Android API class that works with floats instead of doubles, and it is a little bit faster than the Math equivalent.

```
    public Vector2 nor() {
        float len = len();
        if (len != 0) {
            this.x /= len;
            this.y /= len;
        }
        return this;
    }
```

The nor() method normalizes the vector to unit length. You use the len() method internally to first calculate the length. If it is zero, you can bail out early and avoid a division by zero. Otherwise, divide each component of the vector by its length to arrive at a unit-length vector. For chaining, you return the reference to this vector again.

```
    public float angle() {
        float angle = (float) Math.atan2(y, x) * TO_DEGREES;
        if (angle < 0)
            angle += 360;
        return angle;
    }
```

The angle() method calculates the angle between the vector and the x-axis using the atan2() method, as discussed previously. You have to use the Math.atan2() method, as the FastMath class doesn't have this method. The returned angle is given in radians, so you convert it to degrees by multiplying it by TO_DEGREES. If the angle is less than zero, you add 360° to it so that you can return a value in the range 0 to 360°.

```
    public Vector2 rotate(float angle) {
```

```
        float rad = angle * TO_RADIANS;
        float cos = FloatMath.cos(rad);
        float sin = FloatMath.sin(rad);

        float newX = this.x * cos - this.y * sin;
        float newY = this.x * sin + this.y * cos;

        this.x = newX;
        this.y = newY;

        return this;
    }
```

The rotate() method simply rotates the vector around the origin by the given angle. Since the FastMath.cos() and FastMath.sin() methods expect the angle to be given in radians, you first convert them from degrees to radians. Next, use the previously defined equations to calculate the new x and y components of the vector, and then return the vector itself, again for chaining.

```
    public float dist(Vector2 other) {
        float distX = this.x - other.x;
        float distY = this.y - other.y;
        return FloatMath.sqrt(distX * distX + distY * distY);
    }

    public float dist(float x, float y) {
        float distX = this.x - x;
        float distY = this.y - y;
        return FloatMath.sqrt(distX * distX + distY * distY);
    }
}
```

Finally, you have two methods that calculate the distance between this vector and another vector.

And that's your shiny Vector2 class, which you can use to represent positions, velocities, distances, and directions in the code that follows. To get a feeling for your new class, use it in a simple example.

A Simple Usage Example

Here's a proposal for a simple test:

- Create a sort of cannon represented by a triangle that has a fixed position in your world. The center of the triangle will be at (2.4,0.5).

- Each time you touch the screen, you want to rotate the triangle to face the touch point.

- Your view frustum will show us the region of the world between (0,0) and (4.8,3.2). You do not operate in pixel coordinates, but instead define your own coordinate system, where one unit equals one meter. Also, you'll be working in landscape mode.

There are a couple of things you need to think about. You already know how to define a triangle in model space—you can use a Vertices instance for this. Your cannon should point to the right at an angle of 0 degrees in its default orientation. Figure 8–4 shows the cannon triangle in model space.

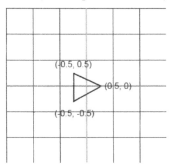

Figure 8–4. *The cannon triangle in model space*

When you render that triangle, simply use glTranslatef() to move it to its place in the world at (2.4,0.5).

You also want to rotate the cannon so that its tip points in the direction of the point on the screen that you last touched. For this, you need to figure out the location of the last touch event in your world. The GLGame.getInput().getTouchX() and getTouchY() methods will return the touch point in screen coordinates, with the origin in the top-left corner. The Input instance will not scale the events to a fixed coordinate system, as it did in Mr. Nom. Instead, you will receive the coordinates by touching the bottom-right corner of the (landscape-oriented) screen on a Hero or a Nexus One (479,319 and 799,479, respectively). You need to convert these touch coordinates to world coordinates. You already did this in the touch handlers in Mr. Nom and the Canvas-based game framework; the only difference this time is that the coordinate system extents are a little smaller, and your world's y-axis is pointing upward. Here's the pseudocode showing how you can achieve the conversion in a general case, which is nearly the same as in the touch handlers of Chapter 5:

```
worldX = (touchX / Graphics.getWidth()) * viewFrustmWidth
worldY = (1 - touchY / Graphics.getHeight()) * viewFrustumHeight
```

You normalize the touch coordinates to the range (0,1) by dividing them by the screen resolution. In the case of the y-coordinate, you subtract the normalized y-coordinate of the touch event from 1 to flip the y-axis. All that's left is scaling the x- and y-coordinates by the view frustum's width and height—in your case, that's 4.8 and 3.2. From worldX and worldY, you can then construct a Vector2 that stores the position of the touch point in your world's coordinates.

The last thing you need to do is calculate the angle with which to rotate the canon. Let's look at Figure 8–5, which shows your cannon and a touch point in world coordinates.

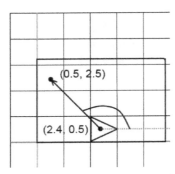

Figure 8–5. *Your cannon in its default state, pointing to the right (angle = 0°), a touch point, and the angle by which you need to rotate the cannon. The rectangle is the area of the world that your view frustum will show on the screen: (0,0) to (4.8,3.2).*

All you need to do is create a distance vector from the cannon's center at (2.4,0.5) to the touch point (and remember, you have to subtract the cannon's center from the touch point, not the other way around). Once you have that distance vector, you can calculate the angle with the Vector2.angle() method. This angle can then be used to rotate your model via glRotatef().

Let's code that. Listing 8–2 shows the relevant portion of your CannonScreen, part of the CannonTest class.

Listing 8–2. *Excerpt from CannonTest.java; Touching the Screen Will Rotate the Cannon*

```
class CannonScreen extends Screen {
    float FRUSTUM_WIDTH = 4.8f;
    float FRUSTUM_HEIGHT = 3.2f;
    GLGraphics glGraphics;
    Vertices vertices;
    Vector2 cannonPos = new Vector2(2.4f, 0.5f);
    float cannonAngle = 0;
    Vector2 touchPos = new Vector2();
```

Start off with two constants that define your frustum's width and height, as discussed earlier. Next, have a GLGraphics instance, as well as a Vertices instance. Store the cannon's position in a Vector2 and its angle in a float. Finally, we have another Vector2, which you can use to calculate the angle between a vector from the origin to the touch point and the x-axis.

Why do you store the Vector2 instances as class members? You can instantiate them every time you need them, but that would make the garbage collector angry. In general, try to instantiate all the Vector2 instances once and then reuse them as often as possible.

```
    public CannonScreen(Game game) {
        super(game);
        glGraphics = ((GLGame) game).getGLGraphics();
        vertices = new Vertices(glGraphics, 3, 0, false, false);
        vertices.setVertices(new float[] { -0.5f, -0.5f,
                                            0.5f, 0.0f,
                                           -0.5f, 0.5f }, 0, 6);
    }
```

In the constructor, fetch the GLGraphics instance and create the triangle according to Figure 8–4.

```
@Override
public void update(float deltaTime) {
    List<TouchEvent> touchEvents = game.getInput().getTouchEvents();
    game.getInput().getKeyEvents();

    int len = touchEvents.size();
    for (int i = 0; i < len; i++) {
        TouchEvent event = touchEvents.get(i);

        touchPos.x = (event.x / (float) glGraphics.getWidth())
                * FRUSTUM_WIDTH;
        touchPos.y = (1 - event.y / (float) glGraphics.getHeight())
                * FRUSTUM_HEIGHT;
        cannonAngle = touchPos.sub(cannonPos).angle();
    }
}
```

Next up is the update() method. Simply loop over all TouchEvents and calculate the angle for the cannon. This can be done in a couple steps. First, transform the screen coordinates of the touch event to the world coordinate system, as discussed earlier. Store the world coordinates of the touch event in the touchPoint member. You then subtract the position of the cannon from the touchPoint vector, which will result in the vector depicted in Figure 8–5. You then calculate the angle between this vector and the x-axis. And that's all there is to it!

```
@Override
public void present(float deltaTime) {

    GL10 gl = glGraphics.getGL();
    gl.glViewport(0, 0, glGraphics.getWidth(), glGraphics.getHeight());
    gl.glClear(GL10.GL_COLOR_BUFFER_BIT);
    gl.glMatrixMode(GL10.GL_PROJECTION);
    gl.glLoadIdentity();
    gl.glOrthof(0, FRUSTUM_WIDTH, 0, FRUSTUM_HEIGHT, 1, -1);
    gl.glMatrixMode(GL10.GL_MODELVIEW);
    gl.glLoadIdentity();

    gl.glTranslatef(cannonPos.x, cannonPos.y, 0);
    gl.glRotatef(cannonAngle, 0, 0, 1);
    vertices.bind();
    vertices.draw(GL10.GL_TRIANGLES, 0, 3);
    vertices.unbind();
}
```

The present() method does the same boring things as it did before. Set the viewport, clear the screen, set up the orthographic projection matrix using your frustum's width and height, and tell OpenGL ES that all subsequent matrix operations will work on the model-view matrix. Load an identity matrix to the model-view matrix to "clear" it. Next, multiply the (identity) model-view matrix with a translation matrix, which will move the vertices of your triangle from model space to world space. Call glRotatef() with the angle you calculated in the update() method, so that your triangle gets rotated in model

space before it is translated. Remember, transformations are applied in reverse order—
the last specified transform is applied first. Finally, bind the vertices of the triangle,
render it, and unbind it.

```
@Override
public void pause() {

}

@Override
public void resume() {

}

@Override
public void dispose() {

}
}
```

Now you have a triangle that will follow your every touch. Figure 8–6 shows the output
after touching the upper-left corner of the screen.

Figure 8–6. *Your triangle cannon reacting to a touch event in the upper-left corner*

Note that it doesn't really matter whether you render a triangle at the cannon position or
a rectangle texture mapped to an image of a cannon—OpenGL ES doesn't really care.
You also have all the matrix operations in the present() method. The truth of the matter
is that it is easier to keep track of OpenGL ES states this way, and you can use multiple
view frustums in one present() call (for example, one view frustum setting up a world in
meters, for rendering your world, and another setting up a world in pixels, for rendering
UI elements). The impact on performance is not all that big, as described in the last
chapter, so it's acceptable to do it this way most of the time. Just remember that you
can optimize this if the need arises.

Vectors will be your best friends from now on. You can use them to specify virtually everything in your world. You will also be able to do some very basic physics with vectors. What's a cannon good for if it can't shoot, right?

A Little Physics in 2D

In this section, you'll use a very simple and limited version of physics. Games are all about being good fakes. They cheat wherever possible in order to avoid potentially heavy calculations. The behavior of objects in a game does not need to be 100 percent physically accurate; it just needs to be good enough to look believable. Sometimes you won't even want physically accurate behavior (that is, you might want one set of objects to fall downward, and another, crazier, set of objects to fall upward).

Even the original Super Mario Brothers used at least some basic principles of Newtonian physics. These principles are really simple and easy to implement. Only the absolute minimum required for implementing a simple physics model for your game objects will be discussed.

Newton and Euler, Best Friends Forever

Your main concern is with the motion physics of so-called *point masses*, which refers to the change in position, velocity, and acceleration of an object over time. Point mass means that you approximate all objects with an infinitesimally small point that has an associated mass. You do not have to deal with things like torque—the rotational velocity of an object around its center of mass—because that is a complex problem domain about which more than one complete book has been written. Just look at these three properties for an object:

- The position of an object is simply a vector in some space—in your case, a 2D space. You represent it as a vector. Usually the position is given in meters.

- The velocity of an object is its change in position per second. Velocity is given as a 2D velocity vector, which is a combination of the unit-length direction vector in which the object is heading and the speed at which the object will move, given in meters per second. Note that the speed just governs the length of the velocity vector; if you normalize the velocity vector by the speed, you get a nice unit-length direction vector.

- The acceleration of an object is its change in velocity per second. You can either represent this as a scalar that only affects the speed of the velocity (the length of the velocity vector), or as a 2D vector, so that you can have different acceleration in the x- and y-axes. Here you'll choose the latter, as it allows you to use things such as ballistics more easily. Acceleration is usually given in meters per second per second (m/s²). No, that's not a typo—you change the velocity by some amount given in meters per second, each second.

When you know the properties of an object for a given point in time, you can integrate them in order to simulate the object's path through the world over time. This may sound scary, but you already did this with Mr. Nom and your Bob test. In those cases, you didn't use acceleration; you simply set the velocity to a fixed vector. Here's how you can integrate the acceleration, velocity, and position of an object in general:

```
Vector2 position = new Vector2();
Vector2 velocity = new Vector2();
Vector2 acceleration = new Vector2(0, -10);
while(simulationRuns) {
    float deltaTime = getDeltaTime();
    velocity.add(acceleration.x * deltaTime, acceleration.y * deltaTime);
    position.add(velocity.x * deltaTime, velocity.y * deltaTime);
}
```

This is called *numerical Euler integration*, and it is the most intuitive of the integration methods used in games. You start off with a position at (0,0), a velocity given as (0,0), and an acceleration of (0,−10), which means that the velocity will increase by 1 m/s on the y-axis. There will be no movement on the x-axis. Before you enter the integration loop, your object is standing still. Within the loop, you first update the velocity, based on the acceleration multiplied by the delta time, and then update the position, based on the velocity multiplied by the delta time. That's all there is to the big, scary word *integration*.

> **NOTE:** As usual, that's not even half of the story. Euler integration is an "unstable" integration method and should be avoided when possible. Usually, one would employ a variant of the so-called *verlet integration*, which is just a bit more complex. For your purposes, however, the easier Euler integration is sufficient.

Force and Mass

You might wonder where the acceleration comes from. That's a good question, with many answers. The acceleration of a car comes from its engine. The engine applies a force to the car that causes it to accelerate. But that's not all. A car will also accelerate toward the center of the earth, due to gravity. The only thing that keeps it from falling through to the center of the earth is the ground, which it can't pass through. The ground cancels out this gravitational force. The general idea is this:

force = mass × acceleration

You can rearrange this to the following equation:

acceleration = force / mass

Force is given in the SI unit *Newton*. (Guess who came up with this.) If you specify acceleration as a vector, then you also have to specify the force as a vector. A force can thus have a direction. For example, the gravitational force pulls downward in the direction (0,–1). The acceleration is also dependent on the mass of an object. The greater the mass of an object, the more force you need to apply in order to make it accelerate as fast as an object of less weight. This is a direct consequence of the preceding equations.

For simple games you can, however, ignore the mass and force, and just work with the velocity and acceleration directly. In the preceding pseudocode, you set the acceleration to (0,–10) m/s per second (again, not a typo), which is roughly the acceleration of an object when it is falling toward the earth, no matter its mass (ignoring things like air resistance). It's true, ask Galileo!

Playing Around, Theoretically

Use the preceding example to play with an object falling toward earth. Let's assume that you let the loop iterate ten times, and that getDeltaTime() will always return 0.1 s. You'll get the following positions and velocities for each iteration:

```
time=0.1, position=(0.0,-0.1), velocity=(0.0,-1.0)
time=0.2, position=(0.0,-0.3), velocity=(0.0,-2.0)
time=0.3, position=(0.0,-0.6), velocity=(0.0,-3.0)
time=0.4, position=(0.0,-1.0), velocity=(0.0,-4.0)
time=0.5, position=(0.0,-1.5), velocity=(0.0,-5.0)
time=0.6, position=(0.0,-2.1), velocity=(0.0,-6.0)
time=0.7, position=(0.0,-2.8), velocity=(0.0,-7.0)
time=0.8, position=(0.0,-3.6), velocity=(0.0,-8.0)
time=0.9, position=(0.0,-4.5), velocity=(0.0,-9.0)
time=1.0, position=(0.0,-5.5), velocity=(0.0,-10.0)
```

After 1 s, your object will fall 5.5 m and have a velocity of (0,–10) m/s, moving straight down to the core of the earth (until it hits the ground, of course).

Your object will increase its downward speed without end, as you haven't factored in air resistance. (As mentioned before, you can easily cheat your own system.) You can simply enforce a maximum velocity by checking the current velocity length, which equals the speed of the object.

All-knowing Wikipedia indicates that a human in free fall can have a maximum, or terminal, velocity of roughly 125 mph. Converting that to meters per second (125 × 1.6 × 1000 / 3600), you get 55.5 m/s. To make your simulation more realistic, you can modify the loop, as follows:

```
while(simulationRuns) {
    float deltaTime = getDeltaTime();
    if(velocity.len() < 55.5)
        velocity.add(acceleration.x * deltaTime, acceleration.y * deltaTime);
    position.add(velocity.x * deltaTime, velocity.y * deltaTime);
}
```

As long as the speed of the object (the length of the velocity vector) is smaller than 55.5 m/s, you can increase the velocity by the acceleration. When you've reached the terminal velocity, you simply stop increasing it by the acceleration. This simple capping of velocities is a trick that is used heavily in many games.

You can add wind to the equation by adding another acceleration in the x direction, say (-1,0) m/s². For this, add the gravitational acceleration to the wind acceleration before you add it to the velocity:

```
Vector2 gravity = new Vector2(0,-10);
Vector2 wind = new Vector2(-1,0);
while(simulationRuns) {
    float deltaTime = getDeltaTime();
    acceleration.set(gravity).add(wind);
    if(velocity.len() < 55.5)
        velocity.add(acceleration.x * deltaTime, acceleration.y * deltaTime);
    position.add(velocity.x * deltaTime, velocity.y * deltaTime);
}
```

You can also ignore acceleration altogether and let your objects have a fixed velocity. You did exactly this in the BobTest. You changed the velocity of each Bob only if he hit an edge, and you did so instantly.

Playing Around, Practically

The possibilities, even with this simple model, are endless. Let's extend your little CannonTest so that you can actually shoot a cannonball. Here's what you want to do:

- As long as the user drags his or her finger over the screen, the canon will follow it. That's how you can specify the angle at which you'll shoot the ball.

- As soon as you receive a touch-up event, you can fire a cannonball in the direction the cannon is pointing. The initial velocity of the cannonball will be a combination of the cannon's direction and the speed the cannonball has from the start. The speed is equal to the distance between the cannon and the touch point. The further away you touch, the faster the cannonball will fly.

- The cannonball will fly as long as there's no new touch-up event.

- You can double the size of your view frustum to (0,0) to (9.6, 6.4) so that you can see more of your world. Additionally, you can place the cannon at (0,0). Note that all units of the world are now given in meters.

- You can render the cannonball as a red rectangle of the size 0.2×0.2 m, or 20×20 cm—close enough to a real cannonball. The pirates among you may choose a more realistic size, of course.

Initially, the position of the cannonball will be (0,0)—the same as the cannon's position. The velocity will also be (0,0). Since you apply gravity in each update, the cannonball will simply fall straight down.

Once a touch-up event is received, set the ball's position back to (0,0) and its initial velocity to (Math.cos(cannonAngle),Math.sin(cannonAngle)). This will ensure that the cannonball flies in the direction the cannon is pointing. Also, set the speed simply by multiplying the velocity by the distance between the touch point and the cannon. The closer the touch point to the cannon, the more slowly the cannonball will fly.

Sounds easy enough, so now you can try implementing it. Copy over the code from the CannonTest to a new file, called CannonGravityTest.java. Rename the classes contained in that file to CannonGravityTest and CannonGravityScreen. Listing 8–3 shows the CannonGravityScreen.

Listing 8–3. *Excerpt from CannonGravityTest*

```
class CannonGravityScreen extends Screen {
    float FRUSTUM_WIDTH = 9.6f;
    float FRUSTUM_HEIGHT = 6.4f;
    GLGraphics glGraphics;
    Vertices cannonVertices;
    Vertices ballVertices;
    Vector2 cannonPos = new Vector2();
    float cannonAngle = 0;
    Vector2 touchPos = new Vector2();
    Vector2 ballPos = new Vector2(0,0);
    Vector2 ballVelocity = new Vector2(0,0);
    Vector2 gravity = new Vector2(0,-10);
```

Not a lot has changed. You simply doubled the size of the view frustum, and reflected that by setting FRUSTUM_WIDTH and FRUSTUM_HEIGHT to 9.6 and 6.2, respectively. This means that you can see a rectangle of 9.2x6.2 m of the world. Since you also want to draw the cannonball, add another Vertices instance, called ballVertices, which will hold the four vertices and six indices of the rectangle of the cannonball. The new members ballPos and ballVelocity store the position and velocity of the cannonball, and the member gravity is the gravitational acceleration, which will stay at a constant (0,–10) m/s² over the lifetime of your program.

```
    public CannonGravityScreen(Game game) {
        super(game);
        glGraphics = ((GLGame) game).getGLGraphics();
        cannonVertices = new Vertices(glGraphics, 3, 0, false, false);
        cannonVertices.setVertices(new float[] { -0.5f, -0.5f,
                                                  0.5f, 0.0f,
                                                 -0.5f, 0.5f }, 0, 6);
        ballVertices = new Vertices(glGraphics, 4, 6, false, false);
        ballVertices.setVertices(new float[] { -0.1f, -0.1f,
                                                0.1f, -0.1f,
                                                0.1f,  0.1f,
                                               -0.1f,  0.1f }, 0, 8);
        ballVertices.setIndices(new short[] {0, 1, 2, 2, 3, 0}, 0, 6);
    }
```

In the constructor, simply create the additional Vertices instance for the rectangle of the cannonball. Define it in model space with the vertices (–0.1,–0.1), (0.1,–0.1), (0.1,0.1), and (–0.1,0.1). Use indexed drawing, and thus specify six vertices in this case.

```
    @Override
    public void update(float deltaTime) {
        List<TouchEvent> touchEvents = game.getInput().getTouchEvents();
        game.getInput().getKeyEvents();
```

```
            int len = touchEvents.size();
            for (int i = 0; i < len; i++) {
                TouchEvent event = touchEvents.get(i);

                touchPos.x = (event.x / (float) glGraphics.getWidth())
                        * FRUSTUM_WIDTH;
                touchPos.y = (1 - event.y / (float) glGraphics.getHeight())
                        * FRUSTUM_HEIGHT;
                cannonAngle = touchPos.sub(cannonPos).angle();

                if(event.type == TouchEvent.TOUCH_UP) {
                    float radians = cannonAngle * Vector2.TO_RADIANS;
                    float ballSpeed = touchPos.len();
                    ballPos.set(cannonPos);
                    ballVelocity.x = FloatMath.cos(radians) * ballSpeed;
                    ballVelocity.y = FloatMath.sin(radians) * ballSpeed;
                }
            }

            ballVelocity.add(gravity.x * deltaTime, gravity.y * deltaTime);
            ballPos.add(ballVelocity.x * deltaTime, ballVelocity.y * deltaTime);
        }
```

The update() method has changed only slightly. The calculation of the touch point in
world coordinates and the angle of the cannon are still the same. The first addition is the
if statement inside the event-processing loop. In case you get a touch-up event, you
prepare the cannonball to be shot. Transfomr the cannon's aiming angle to radians, as
you'll use FastMath.cos() and FastMath.sin() later on. Next, calculate the distance
between the cannon and the touch point. This will be the speed of the cannonball. Set
the ball's position to the cannon's position. Finally, calculate the initial velocity of the
cannonball. Use sine and cosine, as discussed in the previous section, to construct a
direction vector from the cannon's angle. Multiply this direction vector by the
cannonball's speed to arrive at the final cannonball velocity. This is interesting, as the
cannonball will have this velocity from the start. In the real world, the cannonball would,
of course, accelerate from 0 m/s to whatever it could reach given air resistance, gravity,
and the force applied to it by the cannon. You can cheat here, though, as that
acceleration would happen in a very tiny time window (a couple hundred milliseconds).
The last thing you do in the update() method is update the velocity of the cannonball
and, based on that, adjust its position.

```
@Override
    public void present(float deltaTime) {

        GL10 gl = glGraphics.getGL();
        gl.glViewport(0, 0, glGraphics.getWidth(), glGraphics.getHeight());
        gl.glClear(GL10.GL_COLOR_BUFFER_BIT);
        gl.glMatrixMode(GL10.GL_PROJECTION);
        gl.glLoadIdentity();
        gl.glOrthof(0, FRUSTUM_WIDTH, 0, FRUSTUM_HEIGHT, 1, -1);
        gl.glMatrixMode(GL10.GL_MODELVIEW);

        gl.glLoadIdentity();
        gl.glTranslatef(cannonPos.x, cannonPos.y, 0);
```

```
        gl.glRotatef(cannonAngle, 0, 0, 1);
        gl.glColor4f(1,1,1,1);
        cannonVertices.bind();
        cannonVertices.draw(GL10.GL_TRIANGLES, 0, 3);
        cannonVertices.unbind();

        gl.glLoadIdentity();
        gl.glTranslatef(ballPos.x, ballPos.y, 0);
        gl.glColor4f(1,0,0,1);
        ballVertices.bind();
        ballVertices.draw(GL10.GL_TRIANGLES, 0, 6);
        ballVertices.unbind();
    }
```

In the present() method, simply add the rendering of the cannonball rectangle. You do this after rendering the cannon's triangle, which means that you have to "clean" the model-view matrix before you can render the rectangle. Do this with glLoadIdentity(), and then use glTranslatef() to convert the cannonball's rectangle from model space to world space at the ball's current position.

```
    @Override
    public void pause() {

    }

    @Override
    public void resume() {

    }

    @Override
    public void dispose() {

    }
}
```

If you run the example and touch the screen a couple of times, you'll get a pretty good feel for how the cannonball will fly. Figure 8–7 shows the output (which is not all that impressive, since it is a still image).

Figure 8–7. *A triangle cannon that shoots red rectangles. Impressive!*

That's enough physics for your purposes. With this simple model, you can simulate much more than cannonballs. Super Mario, for example, could be simulated in much the same way. If you have ever played Super Mario Brothers, then you will notice that Mario takes a bit of time before he reaches his maximum velocity when running. This can be implemented with a very fast acceleration and velocity capping, as in the preceding pseudocode. Jumping can be implemented in much the same way as shooting the cannonball. Mario's current velocity would be adjusted by an initial jump velocity on the y-axis (remember that you can add velocities like any other vectors). You would always apply a negative y acceleration (gravity), which makes him come back to the ground, or fall into a pit, after jumping. The velocity in the x direction is not influenced by what's happening on the y-axis. You can still press left and right to change the velocity of the x-axis. The beauty of this simple model is that it allows you to implement very complex behavior with very little code. You can use this type of physics when you write your next game.

Simply shooting a cannonball is not a lot of fun. You want to be able to hit objects with the cannonball. For this, you need something called collision detection, which you can investigate in the next section.

Collision Detection and Object Representation in 2D

Once you have moving objects in your world, you want them to interact. One such mode of interaction is simple *collision detection*. Two objects are said to be colliding when they overlap in some way. You already did a little collision detection in Mr. Nom when you checked whether Mr. Nom bit himself or ate an ink stain.

Collision detection is accompanied by *collision response*: once you determine that two objects have collided, you need to respond to that collision by adjusting the position and/or movement of your objects in a sensible manner. For example, when Super Mario jumps on a Goomba, the Goomba goes to Goomba heaven and Mario performs another little jump. A more elaborate example is the collision and response of two or more billiard balls. You won't need to get into this kind of collision response now, as it is overkill for your purposes. Your collision responses will usually consist of changing the state of an object (for example, letting an object explode or die, collecting a coin, setting the score, and so forth). This type of response is game dependent, so it won't be discussed in this section.

So how do you figure out whether two objects have collided? First you need to think about when to check for collisions. If your objects follow a simple physics model, as discussed in the last section, you could check for collisions after you move all your objects for the current frame and time step.

Bounding Shapes

Once you have the final positions of your objects, you can perform collision tests, which boils down to testing for overlap. But what is it that overlaps? Each of your objects needs to have some mathematically defined form or shape that provides bounds for it. The correct term in this case is *bounding shape*. Figure 8–8 shows a few choices for bounding shapes.

Triangle Mesh   Axis Aligned Bounding Box   Bounding Circle

Figure 8–8. *Various bounding shapes around Bob*

The properties of the three types of bounding shapes in Figure 8–8 are as follows:

- *Triangle mesh*: This bounds the object as tightly as possible by approximating its silhouette with a few triangles. It requires the most storage space, and it's hard to construct and expensive to test against. It gives the most precise results, however. You won't necessarily use the same triangles for rendering, but simply store them for collision detection. The mesh can be stored as a list of vertices, with each subsequent three vertices forming a triangle. To conserve memory, you could also use indexed vertex lists.

- *Axis-aligned bounding box*: This bounds the object via a rectangle that is axis aligned, which means that the bottom and top edges are always aligned with the x-axis, and the left and right edges are aligned with the y-axis. This is also fast to test against, but less precise than a triangle mesh. A bounding box is usually stored in the form of the position of its lower-left corner, plus its width and height. (In the case of 2D, these are also referred to as *bounding rectangles*).

■ *Bounding circle*: This bounds the object with the smallest circle that can contain the object. It's very fast to test against, but it is the least precise bounding shape. The circle is usually stored in the form of its center position and its radius.

Every object in your game gets a bounding shape that encloses it, in addition to its position, scale, and orientation. Of course, you need to adjust the bounding shape's position, scale, and orientation according to the object's position, scale, and orientation when you move the object, say, in a physics integration step.

Adjusting for position changes is easy: you simply move the bounding shape accordingly. In the case of the triangle mesh, simply move each vertex; in the case of the bounding rectangle, move the lower-left corner; and in the case of the bounding circle, simply move the center.

Scaling a bound shape is a little harder. You need to define the point around which you scale. This is usually the object's position, which is often given as the center of the object. If you use this convention, then scaling is easy. For the triangle mesh, you scale the coordinates of each vertex; for the bounding rectangle, you scale its width, height, and lower-left corner position; and for the bounding circle, you scale its radius (the circle center is equal to the object's center).

Rotating a bounding shape is also dependent on the definition of a point around which to rotate. Using the convention just mentioned (where the object center is the rotation point), rotation also becomes easy. In the case of the triangle mesh, simply rotate all vertices around the object's center. In the case of the bounding circle, you do not have to do anything, as the radius will stay the same no matter how you rotate your object. The bounding rectangle is a little more involved. You need to construct all four corner points, rotate them, and then find the axis-aligned bounding rectangle that encloses those four points. Figure 8–9 shows the three bounding shapes after rotation.

Figure 8–9. *Rotated bounding shapes, with the center of the object as the rotation point*

While rotating a triangle mesh or a bounding circle is rather easy, the results for the axis-aligned bounding box are not all that satisfying. Notice that the bounding box of the original object fits tighter than its rotated version. This leads to the question of how you got your bounding shapes for Bob in the first place.

Constructing Bounding Shapes

In this example, simply construct the bounding shapes by hand, based on Bob's image. But what if Bob's image is given in pixels, and your world operates in, say, meters? The solutions to this problem involves normalization and model space. Imagine the two triangles you use for Bob in model space when you render him with OpenGL. The rectangle is centered at the origin in model space and has the same aspect ratio (width/height) as Bob's texture image (that is, 32×32 pixels in the texture map, as compared to 2×2 m in model space). Now you can apply Bob's texture and figure out the locations of the points of the bounding shape in model space. Figure 8–10 shows how you can construct the bounding shapes around Bob in model space.

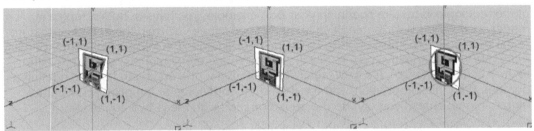

Figure 8–10. *Bounding shapes around Bob in model space*

This process may seem a little cumbersome, but the steps involved are not all that hard. The first thing you have to remember is how texture mapping works. You specify the texture coordinates for each vertex of Bob's rectangle (which is composed of two triangles) in texture space. The upper-left corner of the texture image in texture space is at (0,0), and the lower-left corner is at (1,1), no matter the actual width and height of the image in pixels. To convert from the pixel space of your image to texture space, you can use this simple transformation:

```
u = x / imageWidth
v = y / imageHeight
```

where u and v are the texture coordinates of the pixel given by x and y in image space. The imageWidth and imageHeight are set to the image's dimensions in pixels (32×32 in Bob's case). Figure 8–11 shows how the center of Bob's image maps to texture space.

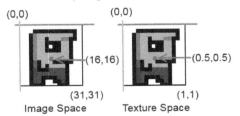

Figure 8–11. *Mapping a pixel from image space to texture space*

The texture is applied to a rectangle that you define in model space. In Figure 8–10, you have an example with the upper-left corner at (–1,1) and the lower-right corner at (1,–1). You can use meters as the units in your world, so the rectangle has a width and height of 2 m. Additionally, you know that the upper-left corner has the texture coordinates (0,0) and the lower-right corner has the texture coordinates (1,1), so you map the complete texture to Bob. This won't always be the case, as you'll see in one of the following sections.

Now you need a generic way to map from texture to model space. You can make your life a little easier by constraining your mapping to only axis-aligned rectangles in texture and model space. Assume that an axis-aligned rectangular region in texture space is mapped to an axis-aligned rectangle in model space. For the transformation, you need to know the width and height of the rectangle in model space and the width and height of the rectangle in texture space. In your Bob example, you have a 2×2 rectangle in model space and a 1×1 rectangle in texture space (since you map the complete texture to the rectangle). You also need to know the coordinates of the upper-left corner of each rectangle in its respective space. For the model space rectangle, that's (–1,1); for the texture space rectangle, it's (0,0) (again, since you map the complete texture, not just a portion). With this information, and the u- and v-coordinates of the pixel you want to map to model space, you can do the transformation with these two equations:

```
mx = (u - minU) / (tWidth) x mWidth + minX
my = (1 - ((v - minV) / (tHeight))x mHeight - minY
```

The variables u and v are the coordinates calculated in the last transformation from pixel to texture space. The variables minU and minV are the coordinates of the top-left corner of the region you map from texture space. The variables tWidth and tHeight are the width and height of your texture space region. The variables mWidth and mHeight are the width and height of your model space rectangle. The variables minX and minY are—you guessed it—the coordinates of the top-left corner of the rectangle in model space. Finally, you have mx and my, which are the transformed coordinates in model space.

These equations take the u- and v-coordinates, map them to the range 0 to 1, and then scale and position them in model space. Figure 8–12 shows a texel in texture space and how it is mapped to a rectangle in model space. On the sides, you see tWidth and tHeight, and mWidth and mHeight. The top-left corner of each rectangle corresponds to (minU, minV) in texture space and (minX, minY) in model space.

Figure 8–12. *Mapping from texture space to model space*

Substituting the first two equations, you can go directly from pixel space to model space:

```
mx = ((x/imageWidth) - minU) / (tWidth) * mWidth + minX
my = (1 - (((y/imageHeight) - minV) / (tHeight)) * mHeight - minY
```

You can use these two equations to calculate the bounding shapes of your objects based on the image you map to their rectangles via texture mapping. In the case of the triangle mesh, this can get a little tedious; the bounding rectangle and bounding circle cases are a lot easier. Usually, you won't need to take this hard route, but rather create your textures so that the bounding rectangles at least have the same aspect ratio as the rectangle you render for the object via OpenGL ES. This way, you can construct the bounding rectangle from the object's image dimension directly. The same is true for the bounding circle. Hopefully this has showed you how you can construct an arbitrary bounding shape given an image that gets mapped to a rectangle in model space.

You should now know how to construct a nicely-fitted bounding shape for your 2D objects. But remember, define those bounding shape sizes manually when you create your graphical assets, and define the units and sizes of your objects in the game world. You can then use these sizes in your code to collide objects.

Game Object Attributes

Bob just got fatter. In addition to the mesh you use for rendering (the rectangle mapping to Bob's image texture), you now have a second data structure holding his bounds in some form. It is crucial to realize that, while you model the bounds after the mapped version of Bob in model space, the actual bounds are independent of the texture region to which you map Bob's rectangle. Of course, try to have a close match to the outline of Bob's image in the texture when you create the bounding shape. It does not matter, however, whether the texture image is 32×32 or 128×128 pixels. An object in your world thus has three attribute groups:

- Its position, orientation, scale, velocity, and acceleration. With these you can apply your physics model from the previous section. Of course, some objects might be static, and thus will only have position, orientation, and scale. Often you can even leave out orientation and scale. The position of the object usually coincides with the origin in model space, as seen in Figure 8–10. This makes some calculations easier.

- Its bounding shape (usually constructed in model space around the object's center), which coincides with its position and is aligned with the object's orientation and scale, as shown in Figure 8–10. This gives your object a boundary and defines its size in the world. You can make this shape as complex as you want. You could, for example, make it a composite of several bounding shapes.

■ Its graphical representation. As shown in Figure 8–12, you still use two triangles to form a rectangle for Bob and texture-map his image onto the rectangle. The rectangle is defined in model space, but does not necessarily equal the bounding shape, as shown in Figure 8–10. The graphical rectangle of Bob that you send to OpenGL ES is slightly larger than Bob's bounding rectangle.

This separation of attributes allows you to apply your Model-View-Controller (MVC) pattern.

■ On the model side, you have Bob's physical attributes, composed of his position, scale, rotation, velocity, acceleration, and bounding shape. Bob's position, scale, and orientation govern where his bounding shape is located in world space.

■ The view simply takes Bob's graphical representation (that is, the two texture-mapped triangles defined in model space) and renders them at their world space position according to Bob's position, rotation, and scale. Here you can use the OpenGL ES matrix operations as you did previously.

■ The controller is responsible for updating Bob's physical attributes according to user input (for example, a left button press could move him to the left), and according to physical forces, such as gravitational acceleration (like you applied to the cannonball in the previous section).

Of course, there's some correspondence between Bob's bounding shape and his graphical representation in the texture, as you base the bounding shape on that graphical representation. Your MVC pattern is thus not entirely clean, but you can live with that.

Broad-Phase and Narrow-Phase Collision Detection

You still don't know how to check for collisions between your objects and their bounding shapes, however. There are two phases in collision detection:

Broad phase: In this phase, you try to figure out which objects might potentially collide. Imagine having 100 objects that could collide with each other. You'd need to perform 100 × 100 / 2 overlap tests if you chose, naively, to test each object against the other objects. This naïve overlap testing approach is of $O(n^2)$ asymptotic complexity, meaning it would take n^2 steps to complete (it actually could be finished in half that many steps, but the asymptotic complexity leaves out any constants). In a good, non-brute-force broad phase, you can try to figure out which pairs of objects are actually in danger of colliding. Other pairs (for example, two objects that are too far apart for a collision to happen) will not be checked. You can reduce the computational load this way, as narrow-phase testing is usually pretty expensive.

Narrow phase: Once you know which pairs of objects can potentially collide, you test whether they really collide or not by doing an overlap test on their bounding shapes.

You can focus on the narrow phase first and leave the broad phase for later.

Narrow Phase

Once done with the broad phase, you have to check whether the bounding shapes of the potentially colliding objects overlap. It was mentioned earlier that you have a couple of options for bounding shapes. Triangle meshes are the most computationally expensive and cumbersome to create. It turns out that you can get away with bounding rectangles and bounding circles in most 2D games, so that's what you can concentrate on here.

Circle Collision

Bounding circles are the cheapest way to check whether two objects collide. Let's define a simple Circle class. Listing 8–4 shows the code.

Listing 8–4. *Circle.java, a Simple Circle Class*

```
package com.badlogic.androidgames.framework.math;

public class Circle {
    public final Vector2 center = new Vector2();
    public float radius;

    public Circle(float x, float y, float radius) {
        this.center.set(x,y);
        this.radius = radius;
    }
}
```

You store the center as a Vector2 and the radius as a simple float. How can you check whether two circles overlap? Look at Figure 8–13.

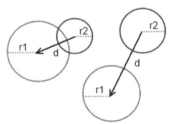

Figure 8–13. *Two circles overlapping (left), and two circles not overlapping (right)*

It's very simple and computationally efficient. All you need to do is figure out the distance between the two centers. If the distance is greater than the sum of the two radii, then you know the two circles do not overlap. In code, this will appear as follows:

```
public boolean overlapCircles(Circle c1, Circle c2) {
```

```
    float distance = c1.center.dist(c2.center);
    return distance <= c1.radius + c2.radius;
}
```

First, measure the distance between the two centers, and then check to see if the distance is smaller or equal to the sum of the radii.

You have to take a square root in the Vector2.dist() method. This is unfortunate, as taking the square root is a costly operation. Can you make this faster? Yes, you can—all you need to do is reformulate your condition:

sqrt(dist.x × dist.x + dist.y × dist.y) <= radius1 + radius2

You can get rid of the square root by exponentiating both sides of the inequality, as follows:

dist.x × dist.x + dist.y × dist.y <= (radius 1 + radius2) × (radius1 + radius2)

You trade the square root for another addition and multiplication on the right side. This is a lot better. Now you can create aVector2.distSquared() function that will return the squared distance between two vectors:

```
public float distSquared(Vector2 other) {
    float distX = this.x - other.x;
    float distY = this.y - other.y;
    return distX*distX + distY*distY;
}
```

The overlapCircles() method then becomes the following:

```
public boolean overlapCircles(Circle c1, Circle c2) {
    float distance = c1.center.distSquared(c2.center);
    float radiusSum = c1.radius + c2.radius;
    return distance <= radiusSum * radiusSum;
}
```

Rectangle Collision

Now you can move on to rectangles. First, you need a class that can represent a rectangle. As previously mentioned, you want a rectangle to be defined by its lower-left corner position, plus its width and height. You do just that in Listing 8–5.

Listing 8–5. *Rectangle.java, a Rectangle Class*

```
package com.badlogic.androidgames.framework.math;

public class Rectangle {
    public final Vector2 lowerLeft;
    public float width, height;

    public Rectangle(float x, float y, float width, float height) {
        this.lowerLeft = new Vector2(x,y);
        this.width = width;
        this.height = height;
    }
}
```

Store the lower-left corner's position in a `Vector2` and the width and height in two floats. How can you check whether two rectangles overlap? Figure 8–14 should give you a hint.

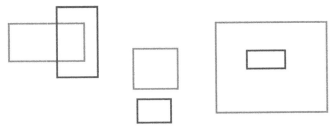

Figure 8–14. *Lots of overlapping and non-overlapping rectangles*

The first two cases of partial overlap and non-overlap are easy. The last one is a surprise. A rectangle can, of course, be completely contained in another rectangle. This can happen in the case of circles, as well. However, your circle overlap test will return the correct result if one circle is contained in the other circle.

Checking for overlap in the rectangle case looks complex at first. However, you can create a very simple test if you use a little logic. Here's the simplest method to check for overlap between two rectangles:

```
public boolean overlapRectangles(Rectangle r1, Rectangle r2) {
    if(r1.lowerLeft.x < r2.lowerLeft.x + r2.width &&
        r1.lowerLeft.x + r1.width > r2.lowerLeft.x &&
        r1.lowerLeft.y < r2.lowerLeft.y + r2.height &&
        r1.lowerLeft.y + r1.height > r2.lowerLeft.y)
        return true;
    else
        return false;
}
```

This looks a little confusing at first sight, so let's go over each condition. The first condition states that the left edge of the first rectangle must be to the left of the right edge of the second rectangle. The next condition states that the right edge of the first rectangle must be to the right of the left edge of the second rectangle. The other two conditions state the same for the top and bottom edges of the rectangles. If all these conditions are met, then the two rectangles overlap. Double-check this with Figure 8–14. It also covers the containment case.

Circle/Rectangle Collision

Can you check for overlap between a circle and a rectangle? Yes, you can. However, this is a little more involved. Take a look at Figure 8–15.

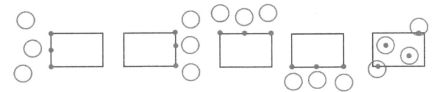

Figure 8–15. *Overlap-testing a circle and a rectangle by finding the point on/in the rectangle that is closest to the circle*

The overall strategy to test for overlap between a circle and a rectangle goes like this:

- Find the x-coordinate on or in the rectangle that is closest to the circle's center. This coordinate can either be a point on the left or right edge of the rectangle, unless the circle center is contained in the rectangle, in which case the closest x-coordinate is the circle center's x-coordinate.

- Find the y-coordinate on or in the rectangle that is closest to the circle's center. This coordinate can either be a point on the top or bottom edge of the rectangle, unless the circle center is contained in the rectangle, in which case the closest y-coordinate is the circle center's y-coordinate.

- If the point composed of the closest x- and y-coordinates is within the circle, the circle and rectangle overlap.

While not depicted in Figure 8–15, this method also works for circles that completely contain the rectangle. Code it up:

```
public boolean overlapCircleRectangle(Circle c, Rectangle r) {
    float closestX = c.center.x;
    float closestY = c.center.y;

    if(c.center.x < r.lowerLeft.x) {
        closestX = r.lowerLeft.x;
    }
    else if(c.center.x > r.lowerLeft.x + r.width) {
        closestX = r.lowerLeft.x + r.width;
    }

    if(c.center.y < r.lowerLeft.y) {
        closestY = r.lowerLeft.y;
    }
    else if(c.center.y > r.lowerLeft.y + r.height) {
        closestY = r.lowerLeft.y + r.height;
    }

    return c.center.distSquared(closestX, closestY) < c.radius * c.radius;
}
```

The description looked a lot scarier than the implementation. You determine the closest point on the rectangle to the circle and then simply check whether the point lies inside the circle. If that's the case, there is an overlap between the circle and the rectangle.

Note that you add an overloaded distSquared() method to Vector2 that takes two float arguments instead of another Vector2. You do the same for the dist()function.

Putting It All Together

Checking whether a point lies inside a circle or rectangle can also be useful. You can code up two more methods and put them in a class called OverlapTester, together with the other three methods you just defined. Listing 8–6 shows the code.

Listing 8–6. *OverlapTester.java; Testing Overlap Between Circles, Rectangles, and Points*

```
package com.badlogic.androidgames.framework.math;

public class OverlapTester {
    public static boolean overlapCircles(Circle c1, Circle c2) {
        float distance = c1.center.distSquared(c2.center);
        float radiusSum = c1.radius + c2.radius;
        return distance <= radiusSum * radiusSum;
    }

    public static boolean overlapRectangles(Rectangle r1, Rectangle r2) {
        if(r1.lowerLeft.x < r2.lowerLeft.x + r2.width &&
           r1.lowerLeft.x + r1.width > r2.lowerLeft.x &&
           r1.lowerLeft.y < r2.lowerLeft.y + r2.height &&
           r1.lowerLeft.y + r1.height > r2.lowerLeft.y)
            return true;
        else
            return false;
    }

    public static boolean overlapCircleRectangle(Circle c, Rectangle r) {
        float closestX = c.center.x;
        float closestY = c.center.y;

        if(c.center.x < r.lowerLeft.x) {
            closestX = r.lowerLeft.x;
        }
        else if(c.center.x > r.lowerLeft.x + r.width) {
            closestX = r.lowerLeft.x + r.width;
        }

        if(c.center.y < r.lowerLeft.y) {
            closestY = r.lowerLeft.y;
        }
        else if(c.center.y > r.lowerLeft.y + r.height) {
            closestY = r.lowerLeft.y + r.height;
        }

        return c.center.distSquared(closestX, closestY) < c.radius * c.radius;
    }
}
```

```
    public static boolean pointInCircle(Circle c, Vector2 p) {
        return c.center.distSquared(p) < c.radius * c.radius;
    }

    public static boolean pointInCircle(Circle c, float x, float y) {
        return c.center.distSquared(x, y) < c.radius * c.radius;
    }

    public static boolean pointInRectangle(Rectangle r, Vector2 p) {
        return r.lowerLeft.x <= p.x && r.lowerLeft.x + r.width >= p.x &&
               r.lowerLeft.y <= p.y && r.lowerLeft.y + r.height >= p.y;
    }

    public static boolean pointInRectangle(Rectangle r, float x, float y) {
        return r.lowerLeft.x <= x && r.lowerLeft.x + r.width >= x &&
               r.lowerLeft.y <= y && r.lowerLeft.y + r.height >= y;
    }
}
```

Sweet, now you have a fully-functional 2D math library you can use for all your little physics models and for collision detection. Now you can look at the broad phase in a little more detail.

Broad Phase

So how can you achieve the magic that the broad phase promises? Look at Figure 8–16, which shows a typical Super Mario Brothers scene.

Figure 8–16. *Super Mario and his enemies. Boxes around objects are their bounding rectangles; the big boxes make up a grid imposed on the world.*

Can you guess what you can do to eliminate some checks? The blue grid in Figure 8–16 represents cells with which you can partition your world. Each cell has the exact same size, and the whole world is covered in cells. Mario is currently in two of those cells, and the other objects with which Mario could potentially collide are in different cells. Thus, you don't need to check for any collisions, as Mario is not in the same cells as any of the other objects in the scene. All you need to do is the following:

- Update all objects in the world based on your physics and controller step.

- Update the position of the bounding shape of each object according to the object's position. You can, of course, also include the orientation and scale.

- Figure out in which cell or cells each object is contained, based on the bounding shape, and add these to the list of objects contained in those cells.

- Check for collisions, but only between object pairs that can collide (for example, Goombas don't collide with other Goombas) and are in the same cell.

This is called a *spatial hash grid* broad phase, and it is very easy to implement. The first thing you have to define is the size of each cell. This is highly dependent on the scale and units you use for your game's world.

An Elaborate Example

Develop a spatial hash grid broad phase based on your last cannonball example. You will completely rework it to incorporate everything covered in this section so far. In addition to the cannon and the ball, you also want to have targets. Make your life easy and just use 0.5×0.5 m squares as targets. These squares don't move; they're static. Your cannon is also static. The only thing that moves is the cannonball itself. You can generally categorize objects in your game world as static objects or dynamic objects. Now you can devise a class that represents such objects.

GameObject, DynamicGameObject, and Cannon

Let's start with the static case, or base case, in Listing 8–7.

Listing 8–7. *GameObject.java, a Static Game Object with a Position and Bounds*

```
package com.badlogic.androidgames.gamedev2d;

import com.badlogic.androidgames.framework.math.Rectangle;
import com.badlogic.androidgames.framework.math.Vector2;

public class GameObject {
    public final Vector2 position;
    public final Rectangle bounds;
```

```
    public GameObject(float x, float y, float width, float height) {
        this.position = new Vector2(x,y);
        this.bounds = new Rectangle(x-width/2, y-height/2, width, height);
    }
}
```

Every object in your game has a position that coincides with its center. Additionally, let each object have a single bounding shape—a rectangle, in this case. In your constructor, set the position and bounding rectangle (which is centered around the center of the object) according to the parameters.

For dynamic objects (that is, objects which move), you also need to keep track of velocity and acceleration (if they're actually accelerated by themselves—for example, via an engine or thruster). Listing 8–8 shows the code for the DynamicGameObject class.

Listing 8–8. *DynamicGameObject.java: Extending the GameObject with a Velocity and Acceleration Vector*

```
package com.badlogic.androidgames.gamedev2d;

import com.badlogic.androidgames.framework.math.Vector2;

public class DynamicGameObject extends GameObject {
    public final Vector2 velocity;
    public final Vector2 accel;

    public DynamicGameObject(float x, float y, float width, float height) {
        super(x, y, width, height);
        velocity = new Vector2();
        accel = new Vector2();
    }
}
```

You extend the GameObject class to inherit the position and bounds members. Additionally, create vectors for the velocity and acceleration. A new dynamic game object will have zero velocity and acceleration after it has been initialized.

In your cannonball example, you have the cannon, the cannonball, and the targets. The cannonball is a DynamicGameObject, as it moves according to your simple physics model. The targets are static and can be implemented using the standard GameObject. The cannon can also be implemented via the GameObject class. You will derive a Cannon class from the GameObject class and add a field storing the cannon's current angle. Listing 8–9 shows the code.

Listing 8–9. *Cannon.java: Extending the GameObject with an Angle*

```
package com.badlogic.androidgames.gamedev2d;

public class Cannon extends GameObject {
    public float angle;

    public Cannon(float x, float y, float width, float height) {
        super(x, y, width, height);
        angle = 0;
    }
}
```

This nicely encapsulates all the data needed to represent an object in your cannon world. Every time you need a special kind of object, like the cannon, you can simply derive one from GameObject, if it is a static object, or from DynamicGameObject, if it has a velocity and acceleration.

> **NOTE:** The overuse of inheritance can lead to severe headaches and very ugly code architecture. Do not use it just for the sake of using it. The simple class hierarchy just used is OK, but you shouldn't let it go a lot deeper (for example, by extending Cannon). There are alternative representations of game objects that do away with all inheritance by composition. For your purposes, simple inheritance is more than enough, though. If you are interested in other representations, search for "composites" or "mixins" on the Web.

The Spatial Hash Grid

Your cannon will be bounded by a rectangle of 1×1 m, the cannonball will have a bounding rectangle of 0.2×0.2 m, and the targets will each have a bounding rectangle of 0.5×0.5 m. The bounding rectangles are centered on each object's position to make your life a little easier.

When your cannon example starts up, you can simply place a number of targets at random positions. Here's how you can set up the objects in your world:

```
Cannon cannon = new Cannon(0, 0, 1, 1);
DynamicGameObject ball = new DynamicGameObject(0, 0, 0.2f, 0.2f);
GameObject[] targets = new GameObject[NUM_TARGETS];
for(int i = 0; i < NUM_TARGETS; i++) {
    targets[i] = new GameObject((float)Math.random() * WORLD_WIDTH,
                                (float)Math.random() * WORLD_HEIGHT,
                                0.5f, 0.5f);
}
```

The constants WORLD_WIDTH and WORLD_HEIGHT define the size of your game world. Everything should happen inside the rectangle bounded by (0,0) and (WORLD_WIDTH,WORLD_HEIGHT). Figure 8–17 shows a little mock-up of the game world so far.

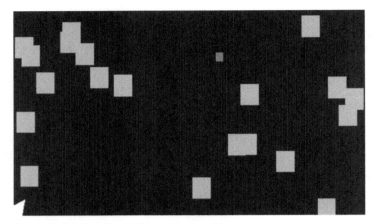

Figure 8–17. *A mock-up of your game world*

Your world will look like this later on, but for now you can overlay a spatial hash grid. How big should the cells of the hash grid be? There's no silver bullet, but it helps to have them five times bigger than the biggest object in the scene. In your example, the biggest object is the cannon, but you don't collide anything with the cannon, so you can base the grid size on the next biggest objects in your scene, the targets. These are 0.5×0.5 m in size. A grid cell should thus have a size of 2.5×2.5 m. Figure 8–18 shows the grid overlaid onto your world.

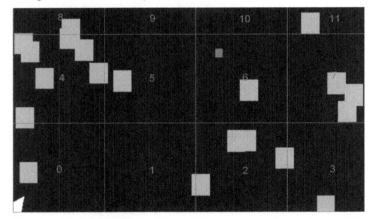

Figure 8–18. *Your cannon world, overlaid with a spatial hash grid consisting of 12 cells*

You have a fixed number of cells—in the case of the cannon world, 12. Give each cell a unique number, starting at the bottom-left cell, which gets the ID 0. Note that the top cells actually extend outside the world. This is not a problem; you simply need to make sure all your objects stay inside the boundaries of the world.

What you want to do is figure out to which cell(s) an object belongs. Ideally, you want to calculate the IDs of the cells in which the object is contained. This allows you to use the following simple data structure to store your cells:

```
List<GameObject>[] cells;
```

That's right; you represent each cell as a list of GameObjects. The spatial hash grid itself is just composed of an array of lists of GameObjects.

Now you can figure out the IDs of the cells in which an object is contained. Figure 8–18 shows a couple of targets that span two cells. In fact, a small object can span up to four cells, and an object bigger than a grid cell can span more than four cells. You can make sure this never happens by choosing the grid cell size to be a multiple of the size of the biggest object in your game. This leaves us with the possibility of one object being contained in, at most, four cells.

To calculate the cell IDs for an object, simply take the four corner points of the bounding rectangle and check which cell each corner point is in. Determining the cell that a point is in is easy—you just need to divide its coordinates by the cell width. Say you have a point at (3,4) and a cell size of 2.5×2.5 m: the point would be in the cell with ID 5, as in Figure 8–18.

You can divide each the point's coordinates by the cell size to get 2D integer coordinates, as follows:

```
cellX = floor(point.x / cellSize) = floor(3 / 2.5) = 1
cellY = floor(point.y / cellSize) = floor(4 / 2.5) = 1
```

And from these cell coordinates, you can easily get the cell ID:

```
cellId = cellX + cellY × cellsPerRow = 1 + 1 × 4 = 5
```

The constant cellsPerRow is simply the number of cells you need to cover your world with cells on the x-axis:

```
cellsPerRow = ceil(worldWidth / cellSize) = ceil(9.6 / 2.5) = 4
```

You can calculate the number of cells needed per column like this:

```
cellsPerColumn = ceil(worldHeight / cellSize) = ceil(6.4 / 2.5) = 3
```

Based on this, you can implement the spatial hash grid rather easily. You set it up by giving it the world's size and the desired cell size. Assume that all the action is happening in the positive quadrant of the world. This means that all the x- and y-coordinates of the points in the world will be positive. This is a constraint you can accept.

From the parameters, the spatial hash grid can figure out how many cells it needs (cellsPerRow × cellsPerColumn). You can also add a simple method to insert an object into the grid that will use the object's boundaries to determine the cells in which it is contained. The object will then be added to each cell's list of the objects that it contains. If one of the corner points of the bounding shape of the object is outside the grid, you can just ignore that corner point.

Reinsert every object into the spatial hash grid of each frame after you update its position. However, there are objects in your cannon world that don't move, so inserting them anew for each frame is very wasteful. Make a distinction between dynamic objects and static objects by storing two lists per cell. One will be updated each frame, and only hold moving objects, and the other will be static, and it will only be modified when a new static object is inserted.

Finally, you need a method that returns a list of objects in the cells of the object you'd like to collide with other objects. All this method does is check which cells the object in question is in, retrieve the list of dynamic and static objects in those cells, and return them to the caller. Of course, you have to make sure that you don't return any duplicates, which can happen if an object is in multiple cells.

Listing 8–10 shows the code (well, most of it). The SpatialHashGrid.getCellIds() method will be discussed in a minute, as it is a little involved.

Listing 8–10. *Excerpt from SpatialHashGrid.java: A Spatial Hash Grid Implementation*

```java
package com.badlogic.androidgames.framework.gl;

import java.util.ArrayList;
import java.util.List;

import com.badlogic.androidgames.gamedev2d.GameObject;

import android.util.FloatMath;

public class SpatialHashGrid {
    List<GameObject>[] dynamicCells;
    List<GameObject>[] staticCells;
    int cellsPerRow;
    int cellsPerCol;
    float cellSize;
    int[] cellIds = new int[4];
    List<GameObject> foundObjects;
```

As discussed, you store two cell lists, one for dynamic and one for static objects. You also store the cells per row and column, so that you can later decide whether a point you check is inside or outside the world. The cell size also needs to be stored. The cellIds array is a working array that you can use to store the four cell IDs a GameObject is contained in temporarily. If it is only contained in one cell, then only the first element of the array will be set to the cell ID of the cell that contains the object entirely. If the object is contained in two cells, then the first two elements of that array will hold the cell ID, and so on. To indicate the number of cell IDs, you set all "empty" elements of the array to –1. The foundObjects list is also a working list, which you can return upon a call to getPotentialColliders(). Why do you keep those two members rather instantiating a new array and list each time one is needed? Remember the garbage collector monster.

```java
    @SuppressWarnings("unchecked")
    public SpatialHashGrid(float worldWidth, float worldHeight, float cellSize) {
        this.cellSize = cellSize;
        this.cellsPerRow = (int)FloatMath.ceil(worldWidth/cellSize);
        this.cellsPerCol = (int)FloatMath.ceil(worldHeight/cellSize);
        int numCells = cellsPerRow * cellsPerCol;
        dynamicCells = new List[numCells];
        staticCells = new List[numCells];
        for(int i = 0; i < numCells; i++) {
            dynamicCells[i] = new ArrayList<GameObject>(10);
```

```
        staticCells[i] = new ArrayList<GameObject>(10);
    }
    foundObjects = new ArrayList<GameObject>(10);
}
```

The constructor of that class takes the world's size and the desired cell size. From those
arguments, calculate how many cells are needed, and instantiate the cell arrays and the
lists holding the objects contained in each cell. Initialize the foundObjects list. All the
ArrayLists you instantiate will have an initial capacity of ten GameObjects. You do this to
avoid memory allocations. The assumption is that it is unlikely that one single cell will
contain more than ten GameObjects. As long as that is true, the arrays don't need to be
resized.

```
    public void insertStaticObject(GameObject obj) {
        int[] cellIds = getCellIds(obj);
        int i = 0;
        int cellId = -1;
        while(i <= 3 && (cellId = cellIds[i++]) != -1) {
            staticCells[cellId].add(obj);
        }
    }

    public void insertDynamicObject(GameObject obj) {
        int[] cellIds = getCellIds(obj);
        int i = 0;
        int cellId = -1;
        while(i <= 3 && (cellId = cellIds[i++]) != -1) {
            dynamicCells[cellId].add(obj);
        }
    }
```

Next up are the methods insertStaticObject() and insertDynamicObject(). They
calculate the IDs of the cells in which the object is contained, via a call to getCellIds(),
and insert the object into the appropriate lists accordingly. The getCellIds() method
will actually fill the cellIds member array.

```
    public void removeObject(GameObject obj) {
        int[] cellIds = getCellIds(obj);
        int i = 0;
        int cellId = -1;
        while(i <= 3 && (cellId = cellIds[i++]) != -1) {
            dynamicCells[cellId].remove(obj);
            staticCells[cellId].remove(obj);
        }
    }
```

You also have a removeObject() method, which you can use to figure out what cells the
object is in, and then delete it from the dynamic and static lists accordingly. This will be
needed when a game object dies, for example.

```
    public void clearDynamicCells(GameObject obj) {
        int len = dynamicCells.length;
        for(int i = 0; i < len; i++) {
            dynamicCells[i].clear();
        }
```

```
        }
```

The clearDynamicCells() method will be used to clear all dynamic cell lists. You need to call this each frame before you reinsert the dynamic objects, as discussed earlier.

```java
    public List<GameObject> getPotentialColliders(GameObject obj) {
        foundObjects.clear();
        int[] cellIds = getCellIds(obj);
        int i = 0;
        int cellId = -1;
        while(i <= 3 && (cellId = cellIds[i++]) != -1) {
            int len = dynamicCells[cellId].size();
            for(int j = 0; j < len; j++) {
                GameObject collider = dynamicCells[cellId].get(j);
                if(!foundObjects.contains(collider))
                    foundObjects.add(collider);
            }

            len = staticCells[cellId].size();
            for(int j = 0; j < len; j++) {
                GameObject collider = staticCells[cellId].get(j);
                if(!foundObjects.contains(collider))
                    foundObjects.add(collider);
            }
        }
        return foundObjects;
    }
```

Finally, there's the getPotentialColliders() method. It takes an object and returns a list of neighboring objects that are contained in the same cells as that object. Use the working list foundObjects to store the list of found objects. Again, you do not want to instantiate a new list each time this method is called. All you need to do is figure out which cells the object passed to the method is in. You then simply add all the dynamic and static objects found in those cells to the foundObjects list and make sure that there are no duplicates. Using foundObjects.contains() to check for duplicates is, of course, suboptimal, but given that the number of found objects will never be large, it is acceapatble to use it in this case. If you run into performance problems, then this is your number one candidate for optimization. Sadly, this isn't trivial. You can use a Set, of course, but that allocates new objects internally each time you add an object to it. For now, just leave it as it is, knowing that you can come back to it if anything goes wrong performance-wise.

The method left out is SpatialHashGrid.getCellIds(). Listing 8–11 shows its code. Don't be afraid, it just looks menacing.

Listing 8–11. *The Rest of SpatialHashGrid.java: Implementing getCellIds()*

```java
    public int[] getCellIds(GameObject obj) {
        int x1 = (int)FloatMath.floor(obj.bounds.lowerLeft.x / cellSize);
        int y1 = (int)FloatMath.floor(obj.bounds.lowerLeft.y / cellSize);
        int x2 = (int)FloatMath.floor((obj.bounds.lowerLeft.x + obj.bounds.width) /
cellSize);
        int y2 = (int)FloatMath.floor((obj.bounds.lowerLeft.y + obj.bounds.height) /
cellSize);
```

```
        if(x1 == x2 && y1 == y2) {
            if(x1 >= 0 && x1 < cellsPerRow && y1 >= 0 && y1 < cellsPerCol)
                cellIds[0] = x1 + y1 * cellsPerRow;
            else
                cellIds[0] = -1;
            cellIds[1] = -1;
            cellIds[2] = -1;
            cellIds[3] = -1;
        }
        else if(x1 == x2) {
            int i = 0;
            if(x1 >= 0 && x1 < cellsPerRow) {
                if(y1 >= 0 && y1 < cellsPerCol)
                    cellIds[i++] = x1 + y1 * cellsPerRow;
                if(y2 >= 0 && y2 < cellsPerCol)
                    cellIds[i++] = x1 + y2 * cellsPerRow;
            }
            while(i <= 3) cellIds[i++] = -1;
        }
        else if(y1 == y2) {
            int i = 0;
            if(y1 >= 0 && y1 < cellsPerCol) {
                if(x1 >= 0 && x1 < cellsPerRow)
                    cellIds[i++] = x1 + y1 * cellsPerRow;
                if(x2 >= 0 && x2 < cellsPerRow)
                    cellIds[i++] = x2 + y1 * cellsPerRow;
            }
            while(i <= 3) cellIds[i++] = -1;
        }
        else {
            int i = 0;
            int y1CellsPerRow = y1 * cellsPerRow;
            int y2CellsPerRow = y2 * cellsPerRow;
            if(x1 >= 0 && x1 < cellsPerRow && y1 >= 0 && y1 < cellsPerCol)
                cellIds[i++] = x1 + y1CellsPerRow;
            if(x2 >= 0 && x2 < cellsPerRow && y1 >= 0 && y1 < cellsPerCol)
                cellIds[i++] = x2 + y1CellsPerRow;
            if(x2 >= 0 && x2 < cellsPerRow && y2 >= 0 && y2 < cellsPerCol)
                cellIds[i++] = x2 + y2CellsPerRow;
            if(x1 >= 0 && x1 < cellsPerRow && y2 >= 0 && y2 < cellsPerCol)
                cellIds[i++] = x1 + y2CellsPerRow;
            while(i <= 3) cellIds[i++] = -1;
        }
        return cellIds;
    }

}
```

The first four lines of this method calculate the cell coordinates of the bottom-left and top-right corners of the object's bounding rectangle. This calculation was discussed earlier. To understand the rest of this method, think about how an object can overlap grid cells. There are four possibilities:

- The object is contained in a single cell. The bottom-left and top-right corners of the bounding rectangle thus have the same cell coordinates.

- The object overlaps two cells horizontally. The bottom-left corner is in one cell, and the top-right corner is in the cell to the right.

- The object overlaps two cells vertically. The bottom-left corner is in one cell, and the top-right corner is in the cell above.

- The object overlaps four cells. The bottom-left corner is in one cell, the bottom-right corner is in the cell to the right, the top-right corner is in the cell above that, and the top-left corner is in the cell above the first cell.

All this method does is make a special case for each of these possibilities. The first `if` statement checks for the single-cell case, the second `if` statement checks for the horizontal double-cell case, the third `if` statement checks for the vertical double-cell case, and the `else` block handles the case of an object overlapping four grid cells. In each of the four blocks, make sure that you only set the cell ID if the corresponding cell coordinates are within the world. And that's all there is to this method.

Now, the method looks like it should take a lot of computational power. And indeed it does, but less than its size would suggest. The most common case will be the first one, and processing that is pretty cheap. Can you see opportunities to optimize this method further?

Putting It All Together

Let's put all the knowledge you gathered in this section together to form a nice little example. You can extend the cannon example of the last section, as discussed a few pages back. Use a `Cannon` object for the cannon, a `DynamicGameObject` for the cannonball, and a number of `GameObjects` for the targets. Each target will have a size of 0.5×0.5 m and be placed randomly in the world.

You want to be able to shoot these targets. For this, you need collision detection. You could just loop over all targets and check them against the cannonball, but that would be boring. Use your fancy new `SpatialHashGrid` class to speed up the process of finding potential-collision targets for the current ball position. Don't insert the ball or the cannon into the grid, though, as that wouldn't really help you.

Since this example is already pretty big, split it into multiple listings. Call the test `CollisionTest` and the corresponding screen `CollisionScreen`. As always, you only look at the screen. Let's start with the members and the constructor in Listing 8–12.

Listing 8–12. *Excerpt from CollisionTest.java: Members and Constructor*

```
class CollisionScreen extends Screen {
    final int NUM_TARGETS = 20;
    final float WORLD_WIDTH = 9.6f;
```

```java
    final float WORLD_HEIGHT = 4.8f;
    GLGraphics glGraphics;
    Cannon cannon;
    DynamicGameObject ball;
    List<GameObject> targets;
    SpatialHashGrid grid;

    Vertices cannonVertices;
    Vertices ballVertices;
    Vertices targetVertices;

    Vector2 touchPos = new Vector2();
    Vector2 gravity = new Vector2(0,-10);

    public CollisionScreen(Game game) {
        super(game);
        glGraphics = ((GLGame)game).getGLGraphics();

        cannon = new Cannon(0, 0, 1, 1);
        ball = new DynamicGameObject(0, 0, 0.2f, 0.2f);
        targets = new ArrayList<GameObject>(NUM_TARGETS);
        grid = new SpatialHashGrid(WORLD_WIDTH, WORLD_HEIGHT, 2.5f);
        for(int i = 0; i < NUM_TARGETS; i++) {
            GameObject target = new GameObject((float)Math.random() * WORLD_WIDTH,
                                               (float)Math.random() * WORLD_HEIGHT,
                                               0.5f, 0.5f);
            grid.insertStaticObject(target);
            targets.add(target);
        }

        cannonVertices = new Vertices(glGraphics, 3, 0, false, false);
        cannonVertices.setVertices(new float[] { -0.5f, -0.5f,
                                                  0.5f, 0.0f,
                                                 -0.5f, 0.5f }, 0, 6);

        ballVertices = new Vertices(glGraphics, 4, 6, false, false);
        ballVertices.setVertices(new float[] { -0.1f, -0.1f,
                                                0.1f, -0.1f,
                                                0.1f,  0.1f,
                                               -0.1f,  0.1f }, 0, 8);
        ballVertices.setIndices(new short[] {0, 1, 2, 2, 3, 0}, 0, 6);

        targetVertices = new Vertices(glGraphics, 4, 6, false, false);
        targetVertices.setVertices(new float[] { -0.25f, -0.25f,
                                                  0.25f, -0.25f,
                                                  0.25f,  0.25f,
                                                 -0.25f,  0.25f }, 0, 8);
        targetVertices.setIndices(new short[] {0, 1, 2, 2, 3, 0}, 0, 6);
    }
```

You can bring over a lot from the CannonGravityScreen. Start off with a couple of constant definitions, governing the number of targets and your world's size. Next, you have the GLGraphics instance, as well as the objects for the cannon, the ball, and the targets, which you store in a list. You also have a SpatialHashGrid, of course. For rendering your world, you need a few meshes: one for the cannon, one for the ball, and one to render each target. Remember that you only needed a single rectangle in BobTest to render the 100 Bobs to the screen. Reuse that principle here, rather than having a single Vertices instance holding the triangles (rectangles) of your targets. The last two members are the same as those in the CannonGravityTest. You use them to shoot the ball and apply gravity when the user touches the screen.

The constructor does all the things discussed previously. Instantiate your world objects and meshes. The only interesting thing is that you also add the targets as static objects to the spatial hash grid.

Now you check out the next method of the CollisionTest class in Listing 8–13.

Listing 8–13. *Excerpt from CollisionTest.java: The update() Method*

```
@Override
public void update(float deltaTime) {
    List<TouchEvent> touchEvents = game.getInput().getTouchEvents();
    game.getInput().getKeyEvents();

    int len = touchEvents.size();
    for (int i = 0; i < len; i++) {
        TouchEvent event = touchEvents.get(i);

        touchPos.x = (event.x / (float) glGraphics.getWidth())* WORLD_WIDTH;
        touchPos.y = (1 - event.y / (float) glGraphics.getHeight()) * WORLD_HEIGHT;

        cannon.angle = touchPos.sub(cannon.position).angle();

        if(event.type == TouchEvent.TOUCH_UP) {
            float radians = cannon.angle * Vector2.TO_RADIANS;
            float ballSpeed = touchPos.len() * 2;
            ball.position.set(cannon.position);
            ball.velocity.x = FloatMath.cos(radians) * ballSpeed;
            ball.velocity.y = FloatMath.sin(radians) * ballSpeed;
            ball.bounds.lowerLeft.set(ball.position.x - 0.1f, ball.position.y - 0.1f);
        }
    }

    ball.velocity.add(gravity.x * deltaTime, gravity.y * deltaTime);
    ball.position.add(ball.velocity.x * deltaTime, ball.velocity.y * deltaTime);
    ball.bounds.lowerLeft.add(ball.velocity.x * deltaTime, ball.velocity.y * deltaTime);

    List<GameObject> colliders = grid.getPotentialColliders(ball);
    len = colliders.size();
    for(int i = 0; i < len; i++) {
        GameObject collider = colliders.get(i);
        if(OverlapTester.overlapRectangles(ball.bounds, collider.bounds)) {
            grid.removeObject(collider);
            targets.remove(collider);
        }
    }
}
```

As always, first fetch the touch and key events, and only iterate over the touch events. The handling of touch events is nearly the same as in the CannonGravityTest. The only difference is that you use the Cannon object instead of the vectors you had in the old example, and you reset the ball's bounding rectangle when the cannon is ready to shoot after a touch-up event.

The next change is in how you update the ball. Instead of straight vectors, use the members of the DynamicGameObject that you instantiated for the ball. Neglect the DynamicGameObject.acceleration member, and instead add your gravity to the ball's velocity. Multiply the ball's speed by 2, so that the cannonball flies a little faster. The interesting thing is that you update not only the ball's position, but also the position of the lower-left corner of the bounding rectangle. This is crucial, as otherwise your ball will move, while its bounding rectangle won't. Is there a reason why you don't simply use the ball's bounding rectangle to store the ball's position? You might want to have multiple bounding shapes attached to an object. Which bounding shape would then hold the actual position of the object? Separating these two things is thus beneficial, and it introduces only a slight computational overhead. You could, of course, optimize this by multiplying the velocity with the delta time only once. The overhead would then boil down to two further additions—a small price to pay for the flexibility you gain.

The final portion of this method is your collision detection code. Find the targets in the spatial hash grid that are in the same cells as your cannonball. Use the SpatialHashGrid.getPotentialColliders() method for this. Since the cells in which the ball is contained are evaluated in that method directly, you do not need to insert the ball into the grid. Next, loop through all the potential colliders and check to see if there really is an overlap between the ball's bounding rectangle and a potential collider's bounding rectangle. If there is, simply remove the target from the target list. Remember, you only add targets as static objects to the grid.

And those are your complete game mechanics. The last piece of the puzzle is the actual rendering, which shouldn't really surprise you. See the code in Listing 8–14.

Listing 8–14. *Excerpt from CollisionTest.java: The present() Method*

```java
@Override
public void present(float deltaTime) {
    GL10 gl = glGraphics.getGL();
    gl.glViewport(0, 0, glGraphics.getWidth(), glGraphics.getHeight());
    gl.glClear(GL10.GL_COLOR_BUFFER_BIT);
    gl.glMatrixMode(GL10.GL_PROJECTION);
    gl.glLoadIdentity();
    gl.glOrthof(0, WORLD_WIDTH, 0, WORLD_HEIGHT, 1, -1);
    gl.glMatrixMode(GL10.GL_MODELVIEW);

    gl.glColor4f(0, 1, 0, 1);
    targetVertices.bind();
    int len = targets.size();
    for(int i = 0; i < len; i++) {
        GameObject target = targets.get(i);
        gl.glLoadIdentity();
        gl.glTranslatef(target.position.x, target.position.y, 0);
        targetVertices.draw(GL10.GL_TRIANGLES, 0, 6);
    }
    targetVertices.unbind();

    gl.glLoadIdentity();
```

```
        gl.glTranslatef(ball.position.x, ball.position.y, 0);
        gl.glColor4f(1,0,0,1);
        ballVertices.bind();
        ballVertices.draw(GL10.GL_TRIANGLES, 0, 6);
        ballVertices.unbind();

        gl.glLoadIdentity();
        gl.glTranslatef(cannon.position.x, cannon.position.y, 0);
        gl.glRotatef(cannon.angle, 0, 0, 1);
        gl.glColor4f(1,1,1,1);
        cannonVertices.bind();
        cannonVertices.draw(GL10.GL_TRIANGLES, 0, 3);
        cannonVertices.unbind();
}
```

Nothing new here. As always, set the projection matrix and viewport, and clear the screen first. Next, render all targets, reusing the rectangular model stored in targetVertices. This is essentially the same thing you did in BobTest, but this time you render targets instead. Next, render the ball and the cannon, as you did in the CollisionGravityTest.

The only thing to note here is that you change the drawing order so that the ball will always be above the targets and the cannon will always be above the ball. You also color the targets green with a call to glColor4f().

The output of this little test is exactly the same as in Figure 8–17, so you can spare yourself the repetition. When you fire the cannonball, it will plow through the field of targets. Any target that gets hit by the ball will be removed from the world.

This example could actually be a nice game if you polish it up a little and add some motivating game mechanics. Can you think of additions? Play around with the example a little to get a feeling for the new tools you have developed over the course of the last couple of pages.

There are a few more things to discuss in this chapter: cameras, texture atlases, and sprites. These use graphics-related tricks that are independent of your model of the game world. Time to get going!

A Camera in 2D

Up until now, you haven't had the concept of a camera in your code; you've only had the definition of your view frustum via glOrthof(), like this:

```
gl.glMatrixMode(GL10.GL_PROJECTION);
gl.glLoadIdentity();
gl.glOrthof(0, FRUSTUM_WIDTH, 0, FRUSTUM_HEIGHT, 1, -1);
```

From Chapter 6, you know that the first two parameters define the x-coordinates of the left and right edges of your frustum in the world, the next two parameters define the y-coordinates of the bottom and top edges of the frustum, and the last two parameters define the near and far clipping planes. Figure 8–19 shows that frustum again.

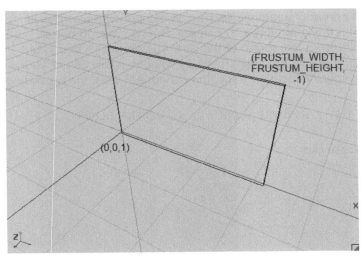

Figure 8–19. *The view frustum for your 2D world, again*

So you only see the region (0,0,1) to (FRUSTUM_WIDTH, FRUSTUM_HEIGHT,–1) of your world. Wouldn't it be nice if you could move the frustum, say, to the left? Of course that would be nice, and it is also dead simple:

```
gl.glOrthof(x, x + FRUSTUM_WIDTH, 0, FRUSTUM_HEIGHT, 1, -1);
```

In this case, x is just some offset that you define. You can, of course, also move on the x- and y-axes:

```
gl.glOrthof(x, x + FRUSTUM_WIDTH, y, y +FRUSTUM_HEIGHT, 1, -1);
```

Figure 8–20 shows what that means.

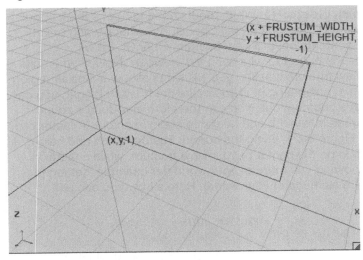

Figure 8–20. *Moving the frustum around*

Simply specify the bottom-left corner of your view frustum in the world space. This is already sufficient to implement a freely-movable 2D camera. But you can do better. What about not specifying the bottom-left corner of the view frustum with x and y, but instead specifying the center of the view frustum? This way you can easily center your view frustum on an object at a specific location—say, the cannonball from the preceding example:

```
gl.glOrthof(x - FRUSTUM_WIDTH / 2, x + FRUSTUM_WIDTH / 2, y - FRUSTUM_HEIGHT / 2, y
+FRUSTUM_HEIGHT / 2, 1, -1);
```

Figure 8–21 shows what this looks like.

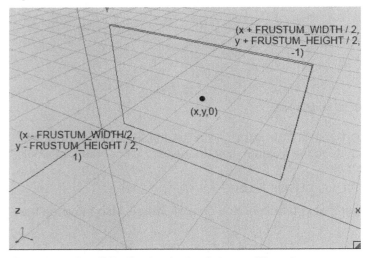

Figure 8–21. *Specifying the view frustum in terms of its center*

That's still not all you can do with glOrthof(). What about zooming? Let's think about this. You know that, via glViewportf(), you can tell OpenGL ES what portion of your screen you wish to render the contents of your view frustum. OpenGL ES will automatically stretch and scale the output to align with the viewport. Now, if you make the width and height of your view frustum smaller, you will simply show a smaller region of your world on the screen—that's zooming in. If you make the frustum bigger, you can show more of your world—that's zooming out. You can therefore introduce a zoom factor and multiply it by your frustum's width and height to zoom in an out. A factor of 1 will show you the world, as in Figure 8–21, using the normal frustum width and height. A factor smaller than 1 will zoom in on the center of your view frustum, while a factor bigger than 1 will zoom out, showing you more of your world (for example, setting the zoom factor to 2 will show twice as much of your world). Here's how you can use glOrthof() to do that:

```
gl.glOrthof(x - FRUSTUM_WIDTH / 2 * zoom, x + FRUSTUM_WIDTH / 2 * zoom, y -
FRUSTUM_HEIGHT / 2 * zoom, y +FRUSTUM_HEIGHT / 2 * zoom, 1, -1);
```

Dead simple! You can now create a camera class that has a position at which it is looking (the center of the view frustum), a standard frustum width and height, and a zoom factor that makes the frustum smaller or bigger, thereby showing either less of your world (zooming in) or more of your world (zooming out). Figure 8–22 shows a view frustum with a zoom factor of 0.5 (the inner gray box), and one with a zoom factor of 1 (the outer, transparent box).

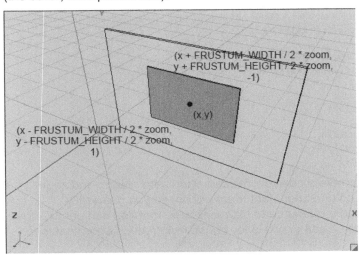

Figure 8–22. *Zooming, by manipulating the frustum size*

To make your life complete, you should add one more thing. Imagine that you touch the screen and want to figure out which point in your 2D world you touched. You already did this a couple of times in your iteratively improving cannon examples. With a view frustum configuration that does not factor in the camera's position and zoom, as seen in Figure 8–19, you had the following equations (see the update() method of your cannon examples):

```
worldX = (touchX / Graphics.getWidth()) x FRUSTUM_WIDTH;
worldY = (1 - touchY / Graphics.getHeight()) x FRUSTUM_HEIGHT;
```

First, normalize the touch x- and y-coordinates to the range 0 to 1 by dividing by the screen's width and height, and then scale them so that they are expressed in terms of your world space by multiplying them with the frustum's width and height. All you need to do is factor in the position of the view frustum, as well as the zoom factor. Here's how you do that:

```
worldX = (touchX / Graphics.getWidth()) x FRUSTUM_WIDTH + x - FRUSTUM_WIDTH / 2;
worldY = (1 - touchY / Graphics.getHeight()) x FRUSTUM_HEIGHT + y - FRUSTUM_HEIGHT / 2;
```

Here, x and y are your camera's position in world space.

The Camera2D Class

Let's put all this together into a single class. You want it to store the camera's position, the standard frustum width and height, and the zoom factor. You also want a convenient method that sets the viewport (always use the whole screen) and projection matrix correctly. Additionally, you want a method that can translate touch coordinates to world coordinates. Listing 8–15 shows your new Camera2D class.

Listing 8–15. *Camera2D.java, Your Shiny New Camera Class for 2D Rendering*

```
package com.badlogic.androidgames.framework.gl;

import javax.microedition.khronos.opengles.GL10;

import com.badlogic.androidgames.framework.impl.GLGraphics;
import com.badlogic.androidgames.framework.math.Vector2;

public class Camera2D {
    public final Vector2 position;
    public float zoom;
    public final float frustumWidth;
    public final float frustumHeight;
    final GLGraphics glGraphics;
```

As discussed, you store the camera's position, frustum width and height, and zoom factor as members. The position and zoom factor are public, so you can easily manipulate them. You also need a reference to GLGraphics so that you can get the up-to-date width and height of the screen in pixels for transforming touch coordinates to world coordinates.

```
    public Camera2D(GLGraphics glGraphics, float frustumWidth, float frustumHeight) {
        this.glGraphics = glGraphics;
        this.frustumWidth = frustumWidth;
        this.frustumHeight = frustumHeight;
        this.position = new Vector2(frustumWidth / 2, frustumHeight / 2);
        this.zoom = 1.0f;
    }
```

In the constructor, take a GLGraphics instance, and the frustum's width and height at the zoom factor 1, as parameters. You store them and initialize the position of the camera to look at the center of the box bounded by (0,0,1) and (frustumWidth, frustumHeight,-1), as shown in Figure 8–19. The initial zoom factor is set to 1.

```
    public void setViewportAndMatrices() {
        GL10 gl = glGraphics.getGL();
        gl.glViewport(0, 0, glGraphics.getWidth(), glGraphics.getHeight());
        gl.glMatrixMode(GL10.GL_PROJECTION);
        gl.glLoadIdentity();
        gl.glOrthof(position.x - frustumWidth * zoom / 2,
                    position.x + frustumWidth * zoom/ 2,
                    position.y - frustumHeight * zoom / 2,
                    position.y + frustumHeight * zoom/ 2,
                    1, -1);
        gl.glMatrixMode(GL10.GL_MODELVIEW);
        gl.glLoadIdentity();
    }
```

The setViewportAndMatrices() method sets the viewport to span the whole screen, and sets the projection matrix in accordance with your camera's parameters, as discussed previously. At the end of the method, tell OpenGL ES that all further matrix operations are targeting the model view matrix and load an identity matrix. Call this method each frame so that you can start from a clean slate. No more direct OpenGL ES calls to set up your viewport and projection matrix.

```
public void touchToWorld(Vector2 touch) {
    touch.x = (touch.x / (float) glGraphics.getWidth()) * frustumWidth * zoom;
    touch.y = (1 - touch.y / (float) glGraphics.getHeight()) * frustumHeight * zoom;
    touch.add(position).sub(frustumWidth * zoom / 2, frustumHeight * zoom / 2);
}
}
```

The touchToWorld() method takes a Vector2 instance containing touch coordinates and transforms the vector to world space. This is the same as was just discussed; the only difference is that you can use your fancy Vector2 class.

An Example

Use the Camera2D class in your cannon example. Copy the CollisionTest file and rename it Camera2DTest. Rename the GLGame class inside the file Camera2DTest, and rename the CollisionScreen classCamera2DScreen. There are a few little changes you have to make to use your new Camera2D class.

The first thing you do is add a new member to the Camera2DScreen class:

```
Camera2D camera;
```

You initialize this member in the constructor, as follows:

```
camera = new Camera2D(glGraphics, WORLD_WIDTH, WORLD_HEIGHT);
```

Pass in your GLGraphics instance and the world's width and height, which you previously used as the frustum's width and height in your call to glOrthof(). All you need to do now is replace your direct OpenGL ES calls in the present() method, which looked like this:

```
gl.glViewport(0, 0, glGraphics.getWidth(), glGraphics.getHeight());
gl.glClear(GL10.GL_COLOR_BUFFER_BIT);
gl.glMatrixMode(GL10.GL_PROJECTION);
gl.glLoadIdentity();
gl.glOrthof(0, WORLD_WIDTH, 0, WORLD_HEIGHT, 1, -1);
gl.glMatrixMode(GL10.GL_MODELVIEW);
```

You replace them with this:

```
gl.glClear(GL10.GL_COLOR_BUFFER_BIT);
camera.setViewportAndMatrices();
```

You still have to clear the framebuffer, of course, but all the other direct OpenGL ES calls are nicely hidden inside the Camera2D.setViewportAndMatrices() method. If you run that code, you'll see that nothing has changed. Everything works like before—all you did was make things a little nicer and more flexible.

You can also simplify the update() method of the test. Since you added the Camera2D.touchToWorld() method to the camera class, you might as well use it. You can replace this snippet from the update method:

```
touchPos.x = (event.x / (float) glGraphics.getWidth())* WORLD_WIDTH;
touchPos.y = (1 - event.y / (float) glGraphics.getHeight()) * WORLD_HEIGHT;
```

with this:

```
camera.touchToWorld(touchPos.set(event.x, event.y));
```

Neat—now everything is nicely encapsulated. But it would be very boring if you didn't use the features of your camera class to their full extent. Here's the plan: you want to have the camera look at the world in the "normal" way as long as the cannonball does not fly. That's easy; you're already doing that. You can determine whether the cannonball flies or not by checking whether the y-coordinate of its position is less than or equal to zero. Since you always apply gravity to the cannonball, it will fall even if you don't shoot it, so that's a cheap way to check matters.

Your new addition will come into effect when the cannonball is flying (when the y-coordinate is greater than zero). You want the camera to follow the cannonball. You can achieve this by simply setting the camera's position to the cannonball's position. That will always keep the cannonball in the center of the screen. You also want to try out your zooming functionality. Therefore, you can increase the zoom factor depending on the y-coordinate of the cannonball: the further away from zero, the higher the zoom factor. If the cannonball has a higher y-coordinate, this will make the camera zoom out. Here's what you need to add at the end of the update() method in your test's screen:

```
if(ball.position.y > 0) {
    camera.position.set(ball.position);
    camera.zoom = 1 + ball.position.y / WORLD_HEIGHT;
} else {
    camera.position.set(WORLD_WIDTH / 2, WORLD_HEIGHT / 2);
    camera.zoom = 1;
}
```

As long as the y-coordinate of your ball is greater than zero, the camera will follow it and zoom out. Just add a value to the standard zoom factor of 1. That value is just the relation between the ball's y-position and the world's height. If the ball's y-coordinate is at WORLD_HEIGHT, the zoom factor will be 2, so you'll see more of your world. The way this is done can be really arbitrary; you can come up with any formula that you want here—there's nothing magical about it. In case the ball's position is less than or equal to zero, you show the world normally, as you did in the previous examples.

Texture Atlas: Because Sharing Is Caring

Up until this point, you have only used a single texture in your programs. What if you not only want to render Bob, but other superheroes, enemies, explosions, or coins as well? You could have multiple textures, each holding the image of one object type. But OpenGL ES wouldn't like that too much, since you' d need to switch textures for every object type you render (that is, bind Bob's texture, render Bobs, bind the coin texture, render coins, and so on). You can do it more effectively by putting multiple images into a single texture. And that's a texture atlas: a single texture containing multiple images. You only need to bind that texture once, and you can then render any entity types for which there is an image in the atlas. That saves some state change overhead and increases your performance. Figure 8–23 shows such a texture atlas.

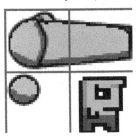

Figure 8–23. *A texture atlas*

There are three objects in Figure 8–23: a cannon, a cannonball, and Bob. The grid is not part of the texture; it's only there to illustrate how you usually create texture atlases.

The texture atlas is 64×64 pixels in size, and each grid is 32×32 pixels. The cannon takes up two cells, the cannonball a little less than one-quarter of a cell, and Bob a single cell. Now, if you look back at how you defined the bounds (and graphical rectangles) of the cannon, cannonball, and targets, you will notice that the relation of their sizes to each other is very similar to what you have in the grid. The target is 0.5×0.5 m in your world and the cannon is 0.2×0.2 m. In your texture atlas, Bob takes up 32×32 pixels and the cannonball a little less than 16×16 pixels. The relationship between the texture atlas and the object sizes in your world should be clear: 32 pixels in the atlas equals 0.5 m in your world. Now the cannon was 1×1 m in your original example, but you can, of course, change this. According to your texture atlas, in which the cannon takes up 64×32 pixels, you should let your cannon have a size of 1×0.5 m in your world. Wow, that is exceptionally easy, isn't it?

So why choose 32 pixels to match 1 meter in your world? Remember that textures must have power-of-two widths and heights. Using a power-of-two pixel unit like 32 to map to 0.5 m in your world is a convenient way for the artist to cope with the restriction on texture sizes. It also makes it easier to get the size relations of different objects in your world right in the pixel art.

Note that there's nothing keeping you from using more pixels per world unit. You could choose 64 pixels or 50 pixels to match 0.5 m in your world. So what's a good pixel-to-meters size, then? That again depends on the screen resolution at which the game will run. Let's do some calculations.

Your cannon world is bounded by (0,0) in the bottom-left corner and (9.6,4.8) in the top-left corner. This is mapped to your screen. Let's figure out how many pixels per world unit you have on the screen of a Hero (480×320 pixels in landscape mode):

```
pixelsPerUnitX = screenWidth / worldWidth = 480 / 9.6 = 50 pixels / meter
pixelsPerUnitY = screenHeight / worldHeight = 320 / 6.4 = 50 pixels / meter
```

Your cannon, which will now take up 1×0.5 m in the world, will thus use 50×25 pixels on the screen. You can use a 64×32-pixel region from your texture, so you can actually downscale the texture image a little when rendering the cannon. That's totally fine—

OpenGL ES will do this automatically for you. Depending on the minification filter you set for the texture, the result will either be crisp and pixelated (GL_NEAREST) or a little smoothed out (GL_LINEAR). If you wanted a pixel-perfect rendering on the Hero, you need to scale your texture images a little. You could use a grid size of 25×25 pixels instead of 32×32. However, if you just resized the atlas image (or rather redrew everything by hand), you'd have a 50×50-pixel image—a no-go with OpenGL ES. You'd have to add padding to the left and bottom to obtain a 64×64 image (since OpenGL ES requires power-of-two widths and heights). Thus OpenGL ES is fine for scaling your texture image down on the Hero.

How's the situation on higher-resolution devices like the Nexus One (800×480 in landscape mode)? Let's perform the calculations for this screen configuration via the following equations:

```
pixelsPerUnitX = screenWidth / worldWidth = 800 / 9.6 =  83 pixels / meter
pixelsPerUnitY = screenHeight / worldHeight = 480 / 6.4 = 75 pixels / meter
```

You have different pixels per unit on the x- and y-axes because the aspect ratio of your view frustum (9.6 / 6.4 = 1.5) is different from the screen's aspect ratio (800 / 480 = 1.66). This was discussed in Chapter 4 and a couple solutions were outlined. Back then, you targeted a fixed pixel size and aspect ratio; now you can adopt that scheme and target a fixed frustum width and height. In the case of the Nexus One, the cannon, the cannonball, and Bob would get scaled up and stretched, due to the higher resolution and different aspect ratio. Accept this fact, since you want all players to see the same region of your world. Otherwise, players with higher aspect ratios would have the advantage of being able to see more of the world.

So, how do you use such a texture atlas? You just remap your rectangles. Instead of using all of the texture, you just use portions of it. To figure out the texture coordinates of the corners of the images contained in the texture atlas, you can reuse the equations from one of the last examples. Here's a quick refresher:

```
u = x / imageWidth
v = y / imageHeight
```

Here, u and v are the texture coordinates and x and y are the pixel coordinates. Bob's top-left corner in pixel coordinates is at (32,32). If you plug that into the preceding equation, you get (0.5,0.5) as texture coordinates. You can do the same for any other corners you need, and based on this set the correct texture coordinates for the vertices of your rectangles.

An Example

Add this texture atlas to your previous example to make it look more beautiful. Bob will be your target.

Copy the Camera2DTest and modify it a little. Place the copy in a file called TextureAtlasTest.java and rename the two classes contained in it (TextureAtlasTest and TextureAtlasScreen) accordingly.

The first thing you do is add a new member to the TextureAtlasScreen:

```
Texture texture;
```

Instead of creating a Texture in the constructor, create it in the resume() method. Remember that textures will get lost when your application comes back from a paused state, so you have to re-create them in the resume() method:

```
@Override
public void resume() {
    texture = new Texture(((GLGame)game), "atlas.png");
}
```

Put the image in Figure 8–23 in the assets/ folder of your project and name it atlas.png. (Of course, it doesn't contain the gridlines shown in the figure.)

Next, you need to change the definitions of the vertices. You have one Vertices instance for each entity type (cannon, cannonball, and Bob) holding a single rectangle of four vertices and six indices, making up three triangles. All you need to do is add texture coordinates to each of the vertices in accordance with the texture atlas. You also change the cannon from being represented as a triangle to being represented by a 1×0.5 m rectangle. Here's what you use to replace the old vertex creation code in the constructor:

```
cannonVertices = new Vertices(glGraphics, 4, 6, false, true);
cannonVertices.setVertices(new float[] { -0.5f, -0.25f, 0.0f, 0.5f,
                                          0.5f, -0.25f, 1.0f, 0.5f,
                                          0.5f,  0.25f, 1.0f, 0.0f,
                                         -0.5f,  0.25f, 0.0f, 0.0f },
                                          0, 16);
cannonVertices.setIndices(new short[] {0, 1, 2, 2, 3, 0}, 0, 6);

ballVertices = new Vertices(glGraphics, 4, 6, false, true);
ballVertices.setVertices(new float[] { -0.1f, -0.1f, 0.0f, 0.75f,
                                        0.1f, -0.1f, 0.25f, 0.75f,
                                        0.1f,  0.1f, 0.25f, 0.5f,
                                       -0.1f,  0.1f, 0.0f, 0.5f },
                                        0, 16);
ballVertices.setIndices(new short[] {0, 1, 2, 2, 3, 0}, 0, 6);

targetVertices = new Vertices(glGraphics, 4, 6, false, true);
targetVertices.setVertices(new float[] { -0.25f, -0.25f, 0.5f, 1.0f,
                                          0.25f, -0.25f, 1.0f, 1.0f,
                                          0.25f,  0.25f, 1.0f, 0.5f,
                                         -0.25f,  0.25f, 0.5f, 0.5f },
                                          0, 16);
targetVertices.setIndices(new short[] {0, 1, 2, 2, 3, 0}, 0, 6);
```

Each of your meshes is now comprised of four vertices, each having a 2D position and texture coordinates. Add six indices to the mesh, specifying the two triangles you want to render. The cannon is a little smaller on the y-axis. It now has a size of 1×0.5 m instead of 1×1 m. This is also reflected in the construction of the Cannon object earlier in the constructor:

```
cannon = new Cannon(0, 0, 1, 0.5f);
```

Since you don't do any collision detection with the cannon itself, it doesn't really matter what size you set in that constructor; just do it for consistency.

The last thing you need to change is your render method. Here it is in its full glory:

```java
@Override
public void present(float deltaTime) {
    GL10 gl = glGraphics.getGL();
    gl.glClear(GL10.GL_COLOR_BUFFER_BIT);
    camera.setViewportAndMatrices();

    gl.glEnable(GL10.GL_BLEND);
    gl.glBlendFunc(GL10.GL_SRC_ALPHA, GL10.GL_ONE_MINUS_SRC_ALPHA);
    gl.glEnable(GL10.GL_TEXTURE_2D);
    texture.bind();

    targetVertices.bind();
    int len = targets.size();
    for(int i = 0; i < len; i++) {
        GameObject target = targets.get(i);
        gl.glLoadIdentity();
        gl.glTranslatef(target.position.x, target.position.y, 0);
        targetVertices.draw(GL10.GL_TRIANGLES, 0, 6);
    }
    targetVertices.unbind();

    gl.glLoadIdentity();
    gl.glTranslatef(ball.position.x, ball.position.y, 0);
    ballVertices.bind();
    ballVertices.draw(GL10.GL_TRIANGLES, 0, 6);
    ballVertices.unbind();

    gl.glLoadIdentity();
    gl.glTranslatef(cannon.position.x, cannon.position.y, 0);
    gl.glRotatef(cannon.angle, 0, 0, 1);
    cannonVertices.bind();
    cannonVertices.draw(GL10.GL_TRIANGLES, 0, 6);
    cannonVertices.unbind();
}
```

Here, you enable blending, set a proper blending function, enable texturing, and bind your atlas texture. You also slightly adapt the cannonVertices.draw() call, which now renders two triangles instead of one. That's all there is to it. Figure 8–24 shows the results of your face-lifting operation.

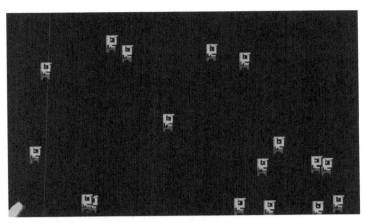

Figure 8–24. *Beautifying the cannon example with a texture atlas*

There are a few more things you need to know about texture atlases:

- When you use GL_LINEAR as the minification and/or magnification filter, there might be artifacts when two images within the atlas are touching each other. This is due to the texture mapper actually fetching the four nearest texels from a texture for a pixel on the screen. When it does that for the border of an image, it will also fetch texels from the neighboring image in the atlas. You can eliminate this problem by introducing an empty border of 2 pixels between your images. Even better, you can duplicate the border pixel of each image. The first solution is easier—just make sure your texture stays a power of two.

- There's no need to lay out all the images in the atlas in a fixed grid. You could put arbitrarily-sized images in the atlas as tightly as possible. All you need to know is where an image starts and ends in the atlas, so that you can calculate proper texture coordinates for it. Packing arbitrarily-sized images is a nontrivial problem, however. There are a couple of tools on the Web that can help you with creating a texture atlas; just do a search and you'll be hit with a plethora of options.

- Often you cannot group all the images of your game into a single texture. Remember that there's a maximum texture size that varies from device to device. You can safely assume that all devices support a texture size of 512×512 pixels (or even 1024×1024). So, you can just have multiple texture atlases. You should try to group objects that will be seen on the screen together in one atlas, though—say, all the objects of level 1 in one atlas, all the objects of level 2 in another, all the UI elements in another, and so on. Think about the logical grouping before finalizing your art assets.

- Remember how you drew numbers dynamically in Mr. Nom? You used a texture atlas for that. In fact, you can perform all dynamic text rendering via a texture atlas. Just put all the characters you need for your game into an atlas and render them on demand, via multiple rectangle mapping to the appropriate characters in the atlas. There are tools you can find on the Web that will generate a so-called *bitmap font* for you. For your purposes in the coming chapters, stick to the approach used in Mr. Nom: static text will be prerendered as a whole, and only dynamic text (for example, numbers in high scores) will be rendered via an atlas.

You might have noticed that Bobs disappear before they are graphically hit by the cannonball. This is because your bounding shapes are a little too big. You have some white space around Bob and the cannonball. What's the solution? Just make the bounding shapes a little smaller. You should get a feel for this, so manipulate the source until the collision feels right. You will often find such fine-tuning "opportunities" while developing a game. Fine tuning is probably one of the most crucial parts, aside from good level design. Getting things to feel right can be hard, but it is highly satisfactory once you have achieved the level of perfection in Super Mario Brothers. Sadly, this is nothing that can be taught, as it is dependent on the look and feel of your game. Consider it the magic sauce that sets good and bad games apart.

> **NOTE:** To handle the disappearance issue just mentioned, make the bounding rectangles a little smaller than their graphical representations to allow for some overlap before a collision is triggered.

Texture Regions, Sprites, and Batches: Hiding OpenGL ES

Your code so far, for the cannon example, is made up of a lot of boilerplate, some of which can be reduced. One such area is the definition of the Vertices instances. It's tedious to have seven lines of code just to define a single textured rectangle. Another area you could improve is the manual calculation of texture coordinates for images in a texture atlas. Finally, there's a lot of highly-repetitive code involved when you want to render your 2D rectangles. There is also a better way of rendering many objects than having one draw call per object. You can solve all these issues by introducing a few new concepts:

- *Texture regions*: You worked with texture regions in the last example. A texture region is a rectangular area within a single texture (for example, the area that contains the cannon in your atlas). You want a nice class that can encapsulate all the nasty calculations for translating pixel coordinates to texture coordinates.

- *Sprites*: A sprite is a lot like a game object. It has a position (and possibly orientation and scale), as well as a graphical extent. You render a sprite via a rectangle, just as you render Bob or the cannon. In fact, the graphical representations of Bob and the other objects can and should be considered sprites. A sprite also maps to a region in a texture. That's where texture regions come in. While it is tempting to combine sprites in the game directly, you keep them separated, following the Model-View-Controller pattern. This clean separation between graphics and mode code makes for a better design.

- *Sprite batchers*: A sprite batcher is responsible for rendering multiple sprites in one go. To do this, the sprite batcher needs to know each sprite's position, size, and texture region. The sprite batcher will be your magic ingredient to get rid of multiple draw calls and matrix operations per object.

These concepts are highly interconnected and will be discussed next.

The TextureRegion Class

Since you've worked with texture regions already, it should be straightforward to figure out what you need. You know how to convert from pixel coordinates to texture coordinates. You want to have a class where you can specify pixel coordinates of an image in a texture atlas, which then stores the corresponding texture coordinates of the atlas region for further processing (for example, when you want to render a sprite). Without further ado, Listing 8–16 shows your TextureRegion class.

Listing 8–16. TextureRegion.java: Converting Pixel Coordinates to Texture Coordinates

```
package com.badlogic.androidgames.framework.gl;

public class TextureRegion {
    public final float u1, v1;
    public final float u2, v2;
    public final Texture texture;

    public TextureRegion(Texture texture, float x, float y, float width, float height) {
        this.u1 = x / texture.width;
        this.v1 = y / texture.height;
        this.u2 = this.u1 + width / texture.width;
        this.v2 = this.v1 + height / texture.height;
        this.texture = texture;
    }
}
```

The TextureRegion stores the texture coordinates of the top-left corner (u1,v1) and bottom-right corner (u2,v2) of the region in texture coordinates. The constructor takes a Texture and the top-left corner, as well as the width and height of the region, in pixel coordinates. To construct a texture region for the Cannon, you could do this:

```
TextureRegion cannonRegion = new TextureRegion(texture, 0, 0, 64, 32);
```

Similarly, you could construct a region for Bob:

```
TextureRegion bobRegion = new TextureRegion(texture, 32, 32, 32, 32);
```

And so on and so forth. You can use this in the example code that you've already created, and use the TextureRegion.u1, v1, u2, and v2 members for specifying the texture coordinates of the vertices of your rectangles. But you won't need do that, since you want to get rid of these tedious definitions altogether. That's what you can use the sprite batcher to do.

The SpriteBatcher Class

As already discussed, a sprite can be easily defined by its position, size, and texture region (and, optionally, its rotation and scale). It is simply a graphical rectangle in your world space. To make things easier, stick to the conventions, with the position being in the center of the sprite and the rectangle constructed around that center. Now you can have a Sprite class and use it like this:

```
Sprite bobSprite = new Sprite(20, 20, 0.5f, 0.5f, bobRegion);
```

That would construct a new sprite, with its center at (20,20) in the world, extending 0.25 m to each side, and using the bobRegion TextureRegion. But you could do this instead:

```
spriteBatcher.drawSprite(bob.x, bob.y, BOB_WIDTH, BOB_HEIGHT, bobRegion);
```

Now that looks a lot better. You don't need to construct yet another object to represent the graphical side of your object. Instead, draw an instance of Bob on demand. You could also have an overloaded method:

```
spriteBatcher.drawSprite(cannon.x, cannon.y, CANNON_WIDTH, CANNON_HEIGHT, cannon.angle,
cannonRegion);
```

That would draw the cannon, rotated by its angle. So how can you implement the sprite batcher? Where are the Vertices instances? Let's think about how the batcher could work.

What is batching anyway? In the graphics community, batching is defined as collapsing multiple draw calls into a single draw call. This makes the GPU happy, as discussed in the previous chapter. A sprite batcher offers one way to make this happen. Here's how:

- The batcher has a buffer that is empty initially (or becomes empty after you signal it to be cleared). That buffer will hold vertices. It will be a simple float array, in your case.

- Each time you call the SpriteBatcher.drawSprite() method, you add four vertices to the buffer based on the position, size, orientation, and texture region that were specified as arguments. This also means that you have to rotate and translate the vertex positions manually, without the help of OpenGL ES. Fear not, though, the code of your Vector2 class will come in handy here. This is the key to eliminating all the draw calls.

- Once you have specified all the sprites you want to render, you tell the sprite batcher to submit the vertices for all the rectangles of the sprites to the GPU in one go and then call the actual OpenGL ES drawing method to render all the rectangles. For this, you can transfer the contents of the float array to a `Vertices` instance and use it to render the rectangles.

> **NOTE:** You can only batch sprites that use the same texture. However, it's not a huge problem, since you'll use texture atlases, anyway.

The usual usage pattern of a sprite batcher looks like this:

```
batcher.beginBatch(texture);
// call batcher.drawSprite() as often as needed, referencing regions in the texture
batcher.endBatch();
```

The call to `SpriteBatcher.beginBatch()` will tell the batcher two things: it should clear its buffer, and use the texture you pass in. You will bind the texture within this method for convenience.

Next, render as many sprites that reference regions within this texture as you need. This will fill the buffer, adding four vertices per sprite.

The call to `SpriteBatcher.endBatch()` signals to the sprite batcher that you are done rendering the batch of sprites and that it should now upload the vertices to the GPU for actual rendering. You are going to use indexed rendering with a `Vertices` instance, so you also need to specify the indices, in addition to the vertices in the float array buffer. However, since you are always rendering rectangles, you can generate the indices beforehand once in the constructor of the `SpriteBatcher`. For this, you need to know how many sprites the batcher can draw per batch. By putting a hard limit on the number of sprites that can be rendered per batch, you don't need to grow any arrays of other buffers; you can just allocate these arrays and buffers once in the constructor.

The general mechanics are rather simple. The `SpriteBatcher.drawSprite()` method may seem like a mystery, but it's not a big problem (if you leave out rotation and scaling for a moment). All you need to do is calculate the vertex positions and texture coordinates, as defined by the parameters. You have done this manually already in previous examples—for instance, when you defined the rectangles for the cannon, the cannonball, and Bob. You can do more or less the same in the `SpriteBatcher.drawSprite()` method, only automatically, based on the parameters of the method. So let's check out the `SpriteBatcher`. Listing 8–17 shows the code.

Listing 8–17. *Excerpt from SpriteBatcher.java, Without Rotation and Scaling*

```
package com.badlogic.androidgames.framework.gl;

import javax.microedition.khronos.opengles.GL10;

import android.util.FloatMath;
```

```
import com.badlogic.androidgames.framework.impl.GLGraphics;
import com.badlogic.androidgames.framework.math.Vector2;

public class SpriteBatcher {
    final float[] verticesBuffer;
    int bufferIndex;
    final Vertices vertices;
    int numSprites;
```

Look at the members first. The member verticesBuffer is the temporary float array in which you store the vertices of the sprites of the current batch. The member bufferIndex indicates where in the float array you should start to write the next vertices. The member vertices is the Vertices instance used to render the batch. It also stores the indices that you'll define in a minute. The member numSprites holds the number drawn so far in the current batch.

```
    public SpriteBatcher(GLGraphics glGraphics, int maxSprites) {
        this.verticesBuffer = new float[maxSprites*4*4];
        this.vertices = new Vertices(glGraphics, maxSprites*4, maxSprites*6, false,
true);
        this.bufferIndex = 0;
        this.numSprites = 0;

        short[] indices = new short[maxSprites*6];
        int len = indices.length;
        short j = 0;
        for (int i = 0; i < len; i += 6, j += 4) {
                indices[i + 0] = (short)(j + 0);
                indices[i + 1] = (short)(j + 1);
                indices[i + 2] = (short)(j + 2);
                indices[i + 3] = (short)(j + 2);
                indices[i + 4] = (short)(j + 3);
                indices[i + 5] = (short)(j + 0);
        }
        vertices.setIndices(indices, 0, indices.length);
    }
```

Moving to the constructor, you have two arguments: the GLGraphics instance you need for creating the Vertices instance, and the maximum number of sprites the batcher should be able to render in one batch. The first thing you do in the constructor is create the float array. You have four vertices per sprite, and each vertex takes up four floats (two for the x- and y-coordinates and another two for the texture coordinates). You can have maxSprites sprites maximally, so that's 4 × 4 × maxSprites floats that you need for the buffer.

Next, create the Vertices instance. You need it to store maxSprites × 4 vertices and maxSprites × 6 indices. Tell the Vertices instance that you have not only positional attributes, but also texture coordinates for each vertex. You then initialize the bufferIndex and numSprites members to zero. Create the indices for your Vertices instance. You need to do this only once, as the indices will never change. The first sprite in a batch will always have the indices 0, 1, 2, 2, 3, 0; the next sprite will have 4, 5, 6, 6,

7, 4; and so on. You can precompute these and store them in the Vertices instance. This way, you only need to set them once, instead of once for each sprite.

```java
public void beginBatch(Texture texture) {
    texture.bind();
    numSprites = 0;
    bufferIndex = 0;
}
```

Next up is the beginBatch() method. It binds the texture and resets the numSprites and bufferIndex members so that the first sprite's vertices will get inserted at the front of the verticesBuffer float array.

```java
public void endBatch() {
    vertices.setVertices(verticesBuffer, 0, bufferIndex);
    vertices.bind();
    vertices.draw(GL10.GL_TRIANGLES, 0, numSprites * 6);
    vertices.unbind();
}
```

The next method is endBatch(); you'll call it to finalize and draw the current batch. It first transfers the vertices defined for this batch from the float array to the Vertices instance. All that's left is binding the Vertices instance, drawing numSprites × 2 triangles, and unbinding the Vertices instance again. Since you use indexed rendering, specify the number of indices to use—which is six indices per sprite, times numSprites. That's all there is to rendering.

```java
    public void drawSprite(float x, float y, float width, float height, TextureRegion
region) {
        float halfWidth = width / 2;
        float halfHeight = height / 2;
        float x1 = x - halfWidth;
        float y1 = y - halfHeight;
        float x2 = x + halfWidth;
        float y2 = y + halfHeight;

        verticesBuffer[bufferIndex++] = x1;
        verticesBuffer[bufferIndex++] = y1;
        verticesBuffer[bufferIndex++] = region.u1;
        verticesBuffer[bufferIndex++] = region.v2;

        verticesBuffer[bufferIndex++] = x2;
        verticesBuffer[bufferIndex++] = y1;
        verticesBuffer[bufferIndex++] = region.u2;
        verticesBuffer[bufferIndex++] = region.v2;

        verticesBuffer[bufferIndex++] = x2;
        verticesBuffer[bufferIndex++] = y2;
        verticesBuffer[bufferIndex++] = region.u2;
        verticesBuffer[bufferIndex++] = region.v1;

        verticesBuffer[bufferIndex++] = x1;
        verticesBuffer[bufferIndex++] = y2;
        verticesBuffer[bufferIndex++] = region.u1;
        verticesBuffer[bufferIndex++] = region.v1;
```

```
            numSprites++;
      }
```

The next method is the workhorse of the SpriteBatcher. It takes the x- and y-
coordinates of the center of the sprite, its width and height, and the TextureRegion to
which it maps. The method's responsibility is to add four vertices to the float array
starting at the current bufferIndex. These four vertices form a texture-mapped
rectangle. You calculate the position of the bottom-left corner (x1,y1) and the top-right
corner (x2,y2), and use these four variables to construct the vertices together with the
texture coordinates from the TextureRegion. The vertices are added in counterclockwise order, starting at the bottom-left vertex. Once they are added to the float
array, you increment the numSprites counter and wait for another sprite to be added or
for the batch to be finalized.

And that is all there is to do. You just eliminated a lot of drawing methods simply by
buffering pre-transformed vertices in a float array and rendering them in one go. That will
increase your 2D sprite-rendering performance considerably, compared to the method
you were using before. Fewer OpenGL ES state changes and fewer drawing calls make
the GPU happy.

There's one more thing you need to implement: a SpriteBatcher.drawSprite() method
that can draw a rotated sprite. All you need to do is construct the four corner vertices
without adding the position, rotate them around the origin, add the position of the sprite
so that the vertices are placed in the world space, and then proceed as in the previous
drawing method. You could use Vector2.rotate() for this, but that would mean some
functional overhead. You therefore reproduce the code in Vector2.rotate(), and
optimize where possible. The final method of the SpriteBatcher looks like Listing 8–18.

Listing 8–18. *The Rest of SpriteBatcher.java: A Method to Draw Rotated Sprites*

```java
    public void drawSprite(float x, float y, float width, float height, float angle,
TextureRegion region) {
          float halfWidth = width / 2;
          float halfHeight = height / 2;

          float rad = angle * Vector2.TO_RADIANS;
          float cos = FloatMath.cos(rad);
          float sin = FloatMath.sin(rad);

          float x1 = -halfWidth * cos - (-halfHeight) * sin;
          float y1 = -halfWidth * sin + (-halfHeight) * cos;
          float x2 = halfWidth * cos - (-halfHeight) * sin;
          float y2 = halfWidth * sin + (-halfHeight) * cos;
          float x3 = halfWidth * cos - halfHeight * sin;
          float y3 = halfWidth * sin + halfHeight * cos;
          float x4 = -halfWidth * cos - halfHeight * sin;
          float y4 = -halfWidth * sin + halfHeight * cos;

          x1 += x;
          y1 += y;
          x2 += x;
          y2 += y;
          x3 += x;
```

```
        y3 += y;
        x4 += x;
        y4 += y;

        verticesBuffer[bufferIndex++] = x1;
        verticesBuffer[bufferIndex++] = y1;
        verticesBuffer[bufferIndex++] = region.u1;
        verticesBuffer[bufferIndex++] = region.v2;

        verticesBuffer[bufferIndex++] = x2;
        verticesBuffer[bufferIndex++] = y2;
        verticesBuffer[bufferIndex++] = region.u2;
        verticesBuffer[bufferIndex++] = region.v2;

        verticesBuffer[bufferIndex++] = x3;
        verticesBuffer[bufferIndex++] = y3;
        verticesBuffer[bufferIndex++] = region.u2;
        verticesBuffer[bufferIndex++] = region.v1;

        verticesBuffer[bufferIndex++] = x4;
        verticesBuffer[bufferIndex++] = y4;
        verticesBuffer[bufferIndex++] = region.u1;
        verticesBuffer[bufferIndex++] = region.v1;

        numSprites++;
    }
}
```

You do the same as in the simpler drawing method, except that you construct all four corner points instead of just the two opposite ones. This is needed for the rotation. The rest is the same as before.

What about scaling? You do not explicitly need another method, since scaling a sprite only requires scaling its width and height. You can do that outside the two drawing methods, so there's no need to have another bunch of methods for the scaled drawing of sprites.

And that's the big secret behind lightning-fast sprite rendering with OpenGL ES.

Using the SpriteBatcher Class

Now you can incorporate the TextureRegion and SpriteBatcher classes in your cannon example. Copy the TextureAtlas example and rename it SpriteBatcherTest. The classes contained in it can be called SpriteBatcherTest and SpriteBatcherScreen.

Get rid of the Vertices members in the screen class. You don't need them anymore, since the SpriteBatcher will do all the dirty work for you. Instead, add the following members:

```
TextureRegion cannonRegion;
TextureRegion ballRegion;
TextureRegion bobRegion;
SpriteBatcher batcher;
```

You now have a TextureRegion for each of the three objects in your atlas, as well as a SpriteBatcher.

Next, modify the constructor of the screen. Get rid of all the Vertices instantiation and initialization code, and replace it with a single line of code:

```
batcher = new SpriteBatcher(glGraphics, 100);
```

That will set out batcher member to a fresh SpriteBatcher instance that can render 100 sprites in one batch.

The TextureRegions get initialized in the resume() method, as they depend on the Texture:

```
@Override
public void resume() {
    texture = new Texture(((GLGame)game), "atlas.png");
    cannonRegion = new TextureRegion(texture, 0, 0, 64, 32);
    ballRegion = new TextureRegion(texture, 0, 32, 16, 16);
    bobRegion = new TextureRegion(texture, 32, 32, 32, 32);
}
```

No surprises here. The last thing you need to change is the present() method. You'll be surprised how clean it's looking now. Here it is:

```
@Override
public void present(float deltaTime) {
    GL10 gl = glGraphics.getGL();
    gl.glClear(GL10.GL_COLOR_BUFFER_BIT);
    camera.setViewportAndMatrices();

    gl.glEnable(GL10.GL_BLEND);
    gl.glBlendFunc(GL10.GL_SRC_ALPHA, GL10.GL_ONE_MINUS_SRC_ALPHA);
    gl.glEnable(GL10.GL_TEXTURE_2D);

    batcher.beginBatch(texture);

    int len = targets.size();
    for(int i = 0; i < len; i++) {
        GameObject target = targets.get(i);
        batcher.drawSprite(target.position.x, target.position.y, 0.5f, 0.5f, bobRegion);
    }

    batcher.drawSprite(ball.position.x, ball.position.y, 0.2f, 0.2f, ballRegion);
    batcher.drawSprite(cannon.position.x, cannon.position.y, 1, 0.5f, cannon.angle, cannonRegion);
    batcher.endBatch();
}
```

That is super sweet. The only OpenGL ES calls you issue now are for clearing the screen, enabling blending and texturing, and setting the blend function. The rest is pure SpriteBatcher and Camera2D goodness. Since all your objects share the same texture atlas, you can render them in a single batch. You call batcher.beginBatch() with the atlas texture, render all the Bob targets using the simple drawing method, render the ball (again with the simple drawing method), and finally render the cannon using the drawing method that can rotate a sprite. You end the method by calling batcher.endBatch(), which will actually transfer the geometry of your sprites to the GPU and render everything.

Measuring Performance

So how much faster is the SpriteBatcher method than the method you used in BobTest? Add an FPSCounter to the code and timing it on a Hero, a Droid, and a Nexus One, as you did in the case of BobTest. Incerse the number of targets to 100 and set the maximum number of sprites the SpriteBatcher can render to 102, since you render 100 targets, 1 ball, and 1 cannon. Here are the results:

```
Hero (1.5):
12-27 23:51:09.400: DEBUG/FPSCounter(2169): fps: 31
12-27 23:51:10.440: DEBUG/FPSCounter(2169): fps: 31
12-27 23:51:11.470: DEBUG/FPSCounter(2169): fps: 32
12-27 23:51:12.500: DEBUG/FPSCounter(2169): fps: 32

Droid (2.1.1):
12-27 23:50:23.416: DEBUG/FPSCounter(8145): fps: 56
12-27 23:50:24.448: DEBUG/FPSCounter(8145): fps: 56
12-27 23:50:25.456: DEBUG/FPSCounter(8145): fps: 56
12-27 23:50:26.456: DEBUG/FPSCounter(8145): fps: 55

Nexus One (2.2.1):
12-27 23:46:57.162: DEBUG/FPSCounter(754): fps: 61
12-27 23:46:58.171: DEBUG/FPSCounter(754): fps: 61
12-27 23:46:59.181: DEBUG/FPSCounter(754): fps: 61
12-27 23:47:00.181: DEBUG/FPSCounter(754): fps: 60
```

Before you come to any conclusions, let's test the old method, as well. Since the example is not equivalent to the old BobTest, modify TextureAtlasTest, which is the same as the current example—the only difference being that it uses the old BobTest method for rendering. Here are the results:

```
Hero (1.5):
12-27 23:53:45.950: DEBUG/FPSCounter(2303): fps: 46
12-27 23:53:46.720: DEBUG/dalvikvm(2303): GC freed 21811 objects / 524280 bytes in 135ms
12-27 23:53:46.970: DEBUG/FPSCounter(2303): fps: 40
12-27 23:53:47.980: DEBUG/FPSCounter(2303): fps: 46
12-27 23:53:48.990: DEBUG/FPSCounter(2303): fps: 46

Droid (2.1.1):
12-28 00:03:13.004: DEBUG/FPSCounter(8277): fps: 52
12-28 00:03:14.004: DEBUG/FPSCounter(8277): fps: 52
12-28 00:03:15.027: DEBUG/FPSCounter(8277): fps: 53
12-28 00:03:16.027: DEBUG/FPSCounter(8277): fps: 53

Nexus One (2.2.1):
12-27 23:56:09.591: DEBUG/FPSCounter(873): fps: 61
12-27 23:56:10.591: DEBUG/FPSCounter(873): fps: 60
12-27 23:56:11.601: DEBUG/FPSCounter(873): fps: 61
12-27 23:56:12.601: DEBUG/FPSCounter(873): fps: 60
```

The Hero performs a lot worse with your new SpriteBatcher method, as compared to the old way of using glTranslate() and similar methods. The Droid actually benefits from the new SpriteBatcher method, and the Nexus One doesn't really care what you use. If you increased the number of targets by another 100, you'd see that the SpriteBatcher method would also be faster on the Nexus One.

So what's up with the Hero? The problem in BobTest was that you called too many OpenGL ES methods, so why is it performing worse now that you're using fewer OpenGL ES method calls?

Working Around a Bug in FloatBuffer

The reason for this isn't obvious. Your SpriteBatcher puts a float array into a direct ByteBuffer each frame when you call Vertices.setVertices(). The method boils down to calling FloatBuffer.put(float[]), and that's the culprit for your performance hit. While desktop Java implements that FloatBuffer method via a real bulk memory move, the Harmony version calls FloatBuffer.put(float) for each element in the array. And that's extremely unfortunate, as that method is a JNI method, which has a lot of overhead (much like the OpenGL ES methods, which are also JNI methods).

There are a couple solutions. IntBuffer.put(int[]) does not suffer from this problem, for example. You could replace the FloatBuffer in your Vertices class with an IntBuffer, and modify Vertices.setVertices() so that it first transfers the floats from the float array to a temporary int array and then copies the contents of that int array to the IntBuffer. This solution was proposed by Ryan McNally, a fellow game developer, who also reported the bug on the Android bug tracker. It produces a five-times performance increase on the Hero, and a little less on other Android devices.

Modify the Vertices class to include this fix. Change the vertices member to an IntBuffer. Add a new member called tmpBuffer, which is an int[] array. The tmpBuffer array is initialized in the constructor of Vertices, as follows:

```
this.tmpBuffer = new int[maxVertices * vertexSize / 4];
```

You also get an IntBuffer view from the ByteBuffer in the constructor, instead of a FloatBuffer:

```
vertices = buffer.asIntBuffer();
```

And the Vertices.setVertices() method looks like this now:

```
public void setVertices(float[] vertices, int offset, int length) {
    this.vertices.clear();
    int len = offset + length;
    for(int i=offset, j=0; i < len; i++, j++)
        tmpBuffer[j] = Float.floatToRawIntBits(vertices[i]);
    this.vertices.put(tmpBuffer, 0, length);
    this.vertices.flip();
}
```

First, transfer the contents of the vertices parameter to the tmpBuffer. The static methodFloat.floatToRawIntBits() reinterprets the bit pattern of a float as an int. You then need to copy the contents of the int array to the `IntBuffer`, formerly known as a `FloatBuffer`. Does it improve performance? Running the `SpriteBatcherTest` produces the following output now on the Hero, Droid, and Nexus One:

```
Hero (1.5):
12-28 00:24:54.770: DEBUG/FPSCounter(2538): fps: 61
12-28 00:24:54.770: DEBUG/FPSCounter(2538): fps: 61
12-28 00:24:55.790: DEBUG/FPSCounter(2538): fps: 62
12-28 00:24:55.790: DEBUG/FPSCounter(2538): fps: 62

Droid (2.1.1):
12-28 00:35:48.242: DEBUG/FPSCounter(1681): fps: 61
12-28 00:35:49.258: DEBUG/FPSCounter(1681): fps: 62
12-28 00:35:50.258: DEBUG/FPSCounter(1681): fps: 60
12-28 00:35:51.266: DEBUG/FPSCounter(1681): fps: 59

Nexus One (2.2.1):
12-28 00:27:39.642: DEBUG/FPSCounter(1006): fps: 61
12-28 00:27:40.652: DEBUG/FPSCounter(1006): fps: 61
12-28 00:27:41.662: DEBUG/FPSCounter(1006): fps: 61
12-28 00:27:42.662: DEBUG/FPSCounter(1006): fps: 61
```

Yes—I know you double-checked—this is not a typo. The Hero really achieves 60 FPS now. A workaround consisting of five lines of code increases your performance by 50 percent. The Droid also benefited a little from this fix.

The problem is fixed in the latest release of Android. However, not all devices will receive the latest version, so you should keep this workaround to maintain backwards compatibility.

> **NOTE:** There's another, even faster workaround. It involves a custom JNI method that does the memory move in native code. You can find it if you search for the "Android Game Development Wiki" on the Net. You can use this most of the time, rather than the pure Java workaround. However, including JNI methods is a bit more complex, which is why the pure-Java workaround is described here.

Sprite Animation

If you've ever played a 2D video game, you know that you are still missing a vital component: sprite animation. The animation consists of so-called *keyframes*, which produce the illusion of movement. Figure 8–25 shows a nice animated sprite by Ari Feldmann (part of his royalty-free SpriteLib).

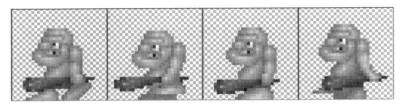

Figure 8–25. *A walking caveman, by Ari Feldmann (grid not in original)*

The image is 256×64 pixels in size, and each keyframe is 64×64 pixels. To produce animation, you just draw a sprite using the first keyframe for an amount of time—say, 0.25 s—and then you switch to the next keyframe, and so on. When you reach the last frame you have two options: you can stay at the last keyframe or start at the beginning again (and perform what is called a *looping animation*).

You can easily do this with your TextureRegion and SpriteBatcher classes. Usually, you'd not only have a single animation, like the one in Figure 8–25, but many more in a single atlas. Besides the walk animation, you could have a jump animation, an attack animation, and so on. For each animation, you need to know the frame duration, which tells you how long to keep using a single keyframe of the animation before switching to the next frame.

The Animation Class

From this, you can define the requirements for an Animation class, which stores the data for a single animation, such as the walk animation in Figure 8–25:

- An Animation holds a number of TextureRegions, which store where each keyframe is located in the texture atlas. The order of the TextureRegions is the same as that used for playing back the animation.

- The Animation also stores the frame duration, which has to pass before you switch to the next frame.

- The Animation should provide you with a method to which you pass the time you've been in the state that the Animation represents (for example, walking left), and that will return the appropriate TextureRegion. The method should take into consideration whether you want the Animation to loop or to stay at the last frame when the end is reached.

This last bullet point is important because it allows you to store a single Animation instance to be used by multiple objects in your world. An object just keeps track of its current state (that is, whether it is walking, shooting, or jumping, and how long it has been in that state). When you render this object, use the state to select the animation you want to play back and the state time to get the correct TextureRegion from the Animation. Listing 8–19 shows the code of your new Animation class.

Listing 8–19. *Animation.java, a Simple Animation Class*

```java
package com.badlogic.androidgames.framework.gl;

public class Animation {
    public static final int ANIMATION_LOOPING = 0;
    public static final int ANIMATION_NONLOOPING = 1;

    final TextureRegion[] keyFrames;
    final float frameDuration;

    public Animation(float frameDuration, TextureRegion ... keyFrames) {
        this.frameDuration = frameDuration;
        this.keyFrames = keyFrames;
    }

    public TextureRegion getKeyFrame(float stateTime, int mode) {
        int frameNumber = (int)(stateTime / frameDuration);

        if(mode == ANIMATION_NONLOOPING) {
            frameNumber = Math.min(keyFrames.length-1, frameNumber);
        } else {
            frameNumber = frameNumber % keyFrames.length;
        }
        return keyFrames[frameNumber];
    }
}
```

First, define two constants to be used with the getKeyFrame() method. The first one says the animation should be looping, and the second one says that it should stop at the last frame.

Next, define two members: an array holding the TextureRegions and a float storing the frame duration.

You pass the frame duration and the TextureRegions that hold the keyframes to the constructor, which simply stores them. You can make a defensive copy of the keyFrames array, but that would allocate a new object, which would make the garbage collector a little mad.

The interesting piece is the getKeyFrame() method. You pass in the time that the object has been in the state that the animation represents, as well as the mode, either Animation.ANIMATION_LOOPING or Animation.NON_LOOPING. Calculate how many frames have already been played for the given state, based on the stateTime. If the animation shouldn't be looping, simply clamp the frameNumber to the last element in the TextureRegion array. Otherwise, take the modulus, which will automatically create the looping effect you desire (for example, 4 % 3 = 1). All that's left is returning the proper TextureRegion.

An Example

Let's create an example called AnimationTest, with a corresponding screen called AnimationScreen. As always, only the screen itself will be discussed.

You want to render a number of cavemen, all walking to the left. Your world will be the same size as your view frustum, which has the size 4.8×3.2 m. (This is arbitrary; you could use any size.) A caveman is a DynamicGameObject with a size of 1×1 m. You will derive from DynamicGameObject and create a new class called Caveman, which will store an additional member that keeps track of how long the caveman has been walking. Each caveman will move 0.5 m/s, either to the left or to the right. Add an update() method to the Caveman class to update the caveman's position, based on the delta time and his velocity. If a caveman reaches the left or right edge of the world, set him to the other side of the world. Use the image in Figure 8–25 and create TextureRegions and an Animation instance, accordingly. For rendering, use a Camera2D instance and a SpriteBatcher because they are fancy. Listing 8–20 shows the code of the Caveman class.

Listing 8–20. *Excerpt from AnimationTest, Showing the Inner Caveman Class.*

```
static final float WORLD_WIDTH = 4.8f;
static final float WORLD_HEIGHT = 3.2f;

static class Caveman extends DynamicGameObject {
    public float walkingTime = 0;

    public Caveman(float x, float y, float width, float height) {
        super(x, y, width, height);
        this.position.set((float)Math.random() * WORLD_WIDTH,
                          (float)Math.random() * WORLD_HEIGHT);
        this.velocity.set(Math.random() > 0.5f?-0.5f:0.5f, 0);
        this.walkingTime = (float)Math.random() * 10;
    }

    public void update(float deltaTime) {
        position.add(velocity.x * deltaTime, velocity.y * deltaTime);
        if(position.x < 0) position.x = WORLD_WIDTH;
        if(position.x > WORLD_WIDTH) position.x = 0;
        walkingTime += deltaTime;
    }
}
```

The two constants WORLD_WIDTH and WORLD_HEIGHT are part of the enclosing AnimationTest class, and are used by the inner classes. Your world is 4.8×3.2 m in size.

Next up is the inner Caveman class, which extends DynamicGameObject, since you will move cavemen based on velocity. You define an additional member that keeps track of how long the caveman has been walking. In the constructor, place the caveman at a random position and let him walk to the left or the right. Initialize the walkingTime member to a number between 0 and 10; this way your cavemen won't walk in sync.

The update() method advances the caveman based on his velocity and the delta time. If he leaves the world, reset him to either the left or right edge. Add the delta time to the walkingTime to keep track of how long he's been walking.

Listing 8–21 shows the AnimationScreen class.

Listing 8–21. *Excerpt from AnimationTest.java: The AnimationScreen Class*

```java
class AnimationScreen extends Screen {
    static final int NUM_CAVEMEN = 10;
    GLGraphics glGraphics;
    Caveman[] cavemen;
    SpriteBatcher batcher;
    Camera2D camera;
    Texture texture;
    Animation walkAnim;
```

Your screen class has the usual suspects as members. You have a GLGraphics instance, a Caveman array, a SpriteBatcher, a Camera2D, the Texture containing the walking keyframes, and an Animation instance.

```java
    public AnimationScreen(Game game) {
        super(game);
        glGraphics = ((GLGame)game).getGLGraphics();
        cavemen = new Caveman[NUM_CAVEMEN];
        for(int i = 0; i < NUM_CAVEMEN; i++) {
            cavemen[i] = new Caveman((float)Math.random(), (float)Math.random(), 1, 1);
        }
        batcher = new SpriteBatcher(glGraphics, NUM_CAVEMEN);
        camera = new Camera2D(glGraphics, WORLD_WIDTH, WORLD_HEIGHT);
    }
```

In the constructor, you create the Caveman instances, as well as the SpriteBatcher and Camera2D.

```java
    @Override
    public void resume() {
        texture = new Texture(((GLGame)game), "walkanim.png");
        walkAnim = new Animation( 0.2f,
                            new TextureRegion(texture, 0, 0, 64, 64),
                            new TextureRegion(texture, 64, 0, 64, 64),
                            new TextureRegion(texture, 128, 0, 64, 64),
                            new TextureRegion(texture, 192, 0, 64, 64));
    }
```

In the resume() method, you load the texture atlas containing the animation keyframes from the asset file walkanim.png, which is the same as seen in Figure 8–25. Afterward, you create the Animation instance, setting the frame duration to 0.2 s and passing in a TextureRegion for each of the keyframes in the texture atlas.

```java
    @Override
    public void update(float deltaTime) {
        int len = cavemen.length;
        for(int i = 0; i < len; i++) {
            cavemen[i].update(deltaTime);
        }
    }
```

The update() method just loops over all Caveman instances and calls their Caveman.update() method with the current delta time. This will make the cavemen move and update their walking times.

```java
    @Override
```

```
    public void present(float deltaTime) {
        GL10 gl = glGraphics.getGL();
        gl.glClear(GL10.GL_COLOR_BUFFER_BIT);
        camera.setViewportAndMatrices();

        gl.glEnable(GL10.GL_BLEND);
        gl.glBlendFunc(GL10.GL_SRC_ALPHA, GL10.GL_ONE_MINUS_SRC_ALPHA);
        gl.glEnable(GL10.GL_TEXTURE_2D);

        batcher.beginBatch(texture);
        int len = cavemen.length;
        for(int i = 0; i < len; i++) {
            Caveman caveman = cavemen[i];
            TextureRegion keyFrame = walkAnim.getKeyFrame(caveman.walkingTime,
Animation.ANIMATION_LOOPING);
            batcher.drawSprite(caveman.position.x, caveman.position.y,
caveman.velocity.x < 0?1:-1, 1, keyFrame);
        }
        batcher.endBatch();
    }

    @Override
    public void pause() {
    }

    @Override
    public void dispose() {
    }
}
```

Finally, you have the present() method. Start off by clearing the screen and setting the viewport and projection matrix via your camera. Next, enable blending and texture mapping, and set the blend function. Start rendering by telling the sprite batcher that you want to start a new batch using the animation texture atlas. Next, loop through all the cavemen and render them. For each caveman, you first fetch the correct keyframe from the Animation instance based on the caveman's walking time. You specify that the animation should be looping. Then you draw the caveman with the correct texture region at his position.

But what do you do with the width parameter here? Remember that your animation texture only contains keyframes for the "walk left" animation. You want to flip the texture horizontally in case the caveman is walking to the right, which you can do by specifying a negative width. If you don't trust us, go back to the SpriteBatcher code and check whether this works. You essentially flip the rectangle of the sprite by specifying a negative width. You could do the same vertically, as well, by specifying a negative height.

Figure 8–26 shows your walking cavemen.

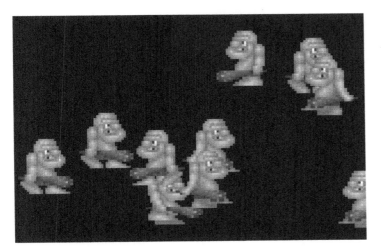

Figure 8–26. *Cavemen walking*

And that is all you need to know to produce a nice 2D game with OpenGL ES. Note how you still separate the game logic and the presentation from each other. A caveman does not need to know that he is being rendered. He therefore doesn't keep any rendering-related members, such as an Animation instance or a Texture. All you need to do is keep track of the state of the caveman, and how long he's been in that state. Together with his position and size, you can then easily render him by using your little helper classes.

Summary

You should now be well equipped to create almost any 2D game you want. You've learned about vectors and how to work with them, resulting in a nice, reusable Vector2 class. You also looked into basic physics for creating things like ballistic cannonballs. Collision detection is also a vital part of most games, and you should now know how to do it correctly and efficiently via a SpatialHashGrid. You explored a way to keep your game logic and objects separated from the rendering by creating GameObject and DynamicGameObject classes that keep track of the state and shape of objects. You covered how easy it is to implement the concept of a 2D camera via OpenGL ES, all based on a single method called glOrthof(). You learned about texture atlases, why you need them, and how you can use them. This was expanded by introducing texture regions, sprites, and how you can render them efficiently via a SpriteBatcher. Finally, you looked into sprite animations, which turn out to be extremely simple to implement.

It should be worth noting that all of the topics covered in this chapter, including broad and narrow-phase collision detection, physics simulation, movement integration, and differently-shaped bounds are implemented robustly in many open-source libraries, such as Box2D, Chipmunk Physics, Bullet Physics, and more. All of these libraries were originally developed in C or C++, but there are Android wrappers or Java implementations for a few that make them options worth checking out as you plan your game.

In the next chapter, you'll create a new game with your new tools . You'll be surprised how easy it is.

Chapter 9

Super Jumper: A 2D OpenGL ES Game

Time to put all we've learned together into a game. As discussed in Chapter 3, there are a couple of very popular genres in the mobile space that we can choose. For our next game, we decided to go the more casual route. We'll implement a jump-'em-up game similar to Abduction or Doodle Jump. As with Mr. Nom, we'll start by defining our game mechanics.

Core Game Mechanics

We'd suggest you quickly install Abduction on your Android device or look up videos of this game on the Web. From this example, we can condense the core game mechanics of our game, which will be called Super Jumper. Here are some details:

- The protagonist is constantly jumping upward, moving from platform to platform. The game world spans multiple screens vertically.

- Horizontal movement can be controlled by tilting the phone to the left or the right.

- When the protagonist leaves one of the horizontal screen boundaries, he reenters the screen on the opposite side.

- Platforms can be static or moving horizontally.

- Some platforms will be pulverized randomly when the protagonist hits them.

- Along the way up, the protagonist can collect items to score points.

- Besides coins, there are also springs on some platforms that will make the protagonist jump higher.

- Evil forces populate the game world, moving horizontally. When our protagonist hits one of them, he dies and the game is over.

- When our protagonist falls below the bottom edge of the screen, the game is over.

- At the top of the level is some sort of goal. When the protagonist hits that goal, a new level begins.

While the list is longer than the one we created for Mr. Nom, it doesn't seem a lot more complex. Figure 9–1 shows an initial mock-up of the core principles. This time we went straight to Paint.NET for creating the mock-up. Let's come up with a backstory.

Figure 9–1. *Our initial game mechanics mock-up, showing the protagonist, platforms, coins, evil forces, and goal at the top of the level.*

A Backstory and Art Style

We are going to be totally creative here and come up with the following unique story for our game.

Bob, our protagonist, suffers from chronic jumperitis. He is doomed to jump every time he touches the ground. Even worse, his beloved princess, who shall remain nameless, was kidnapped by an evil army of killer flying squirrels and placed in a castle in the sky. Bob's condition proves beneficial after all, and he begins the hunt for his loved one, battling the evil squirrel forces.

This classic video game story lends itself well to the 8-bit graphics style, which can be found in games such as the original Super Mario Brothers on the NES. The mock-up in Figure 9–1 shows the final game graphics for all the elements of our game. Bob, coins, squirrels, and pulverized platforms are of course animated. We'll also use music and sound effects that fit our visual style.

Screens and Transitions

We are now able to define our screens and transitions. We'll follow the same formula we used in Mr. Nom:

- We'll have a main screen with a logo; PLAY, HIGHSCORES, and HELP menu items; and a button to disable and enable sound.

- We'll have a game screen that will ask the player to get ready and handle running, paused, game-over, and next-level states gracefully. The only new addition to what we used in Mr. Nom will be the next-level state of the screen, which will be triggered once Bob hits the castle. In that case, a new level will be generated, and Bob will start at the bottom of the world again, keeping his score.

- We'll have a high-scores screen that will show the top five scores the player has achieved so far.

- We'll have help screens that present the game mechanics and goals to the player. We'll be sneaky and leave out a description of how to control the player. Kids these days should be able to handle the complexity we faced back in the '80s and early '90s, when games didn't provide you with any instructions.

That is more or less the same as what we had in Mr. Nom. Figure 9–2 shows all screens and transitions. Note that we don't have any buttons on the game screen or its subscreens, except for the pause button. Users will intuitively touch the screen when asked to be ready.

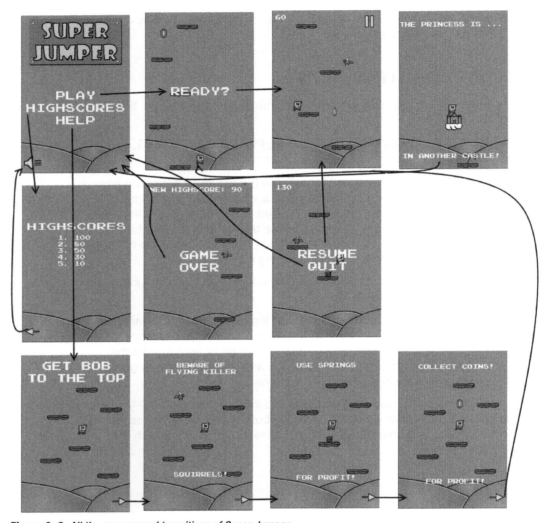

Figure 9–2. *All the screens and transitions of Super Jumper.*

With that out of our way, we can now think about our world's size and units, as well as how that maps to the graphical assets.

Defining the Game World

The classic chicken-and-egg problem haunts us again. You learned in the last chapter that we have a correspondence between world units (for example, meters) and pixels. Our objects are defined physically in world space. Bounding shapes and positions are given in meters; velocities are given in meters per second. The graphical representations of our objects are defined in pixels though, so we have to have some sort of mapping. We overcome this problem by first defining a target resolution for our graphical assets.

As with Mr. Nom, we will use a target resolution of 320×480 pixels (aspect ratio of 1.5). We're using this target because it's the lowest practical resolution but, if you're targeting tablets specifically, you may want to use a resolution like 800×1280 or perhaps something in between, such as 480×800 (a typical Android handset). Despite your target resolution, the principals remain the same.

The next thing we have to do is establish a correspondence between pixels and meters in our world. The mock-up in Figure 9–1 gives us a sense of how much screen space different objects use, as well as their proportions relative to each other. We recommend choosing a mapping of 32 pixels to 1 meter for 2D games. So let's overlay our mock-up, which is 320×380 pixels in size, with a grid where each cell is 32×32 pixels. In our world space, this would map to 1×1 meter cells. Figure 9–3 shows our mock-up and the grid.

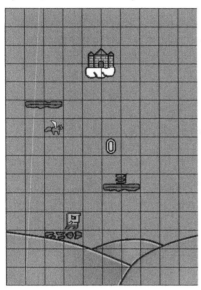

Figure 9–3. *The mock-up overlaid with a grid. Each cell is 32×32 pixels and corresponds to a 1×1-meter area in the game world.*

Figure 9–3 is of course a little bit cheated. We arranged the graphics in a way so that they line up nicely with the grid cells. In the real game, we'll place the objects at noninteger positions.

So, what can we make of Figure 9–3? First of all, we can directly estimate the width and height of each object in our world in meters. Here are the values we'll use for the bounding rectangles of our objects:

- Bob is 0.8×0.8 meters; he does not entirely span a complete cell.

- A platform is 2×0.5 meters, taking up two cells horizontally and half a cell vertically.

- A coin is 0.8×0.5 meters. It nearly spans a cell vertically and takes up roughly half a cell horizontally.

- A spring is 0.5×0.5 meters, talking up half a cell in each direction. The spring is actually a little bit taller than it is wide. We make its bounding shape square so that the collision testing is a little bit more forgiving.

- A squirrel is 1×0.8 meters.

- A castle is 0.8×0.8 meters.

With those sizes, we also have the sizes of the bounding rectangles of our objects for collision detection. We can adjust them if they turn out to be a little too big or small, depending on how the game plays out with those values.

Another thing we can derive from Figure 9–3 is the size of our view frustum. It will show us 10×15 meters of our world.

The only thing left to define are the velocities and accelerations we have in the game. This is highly dependent on how we want our game to feel. Usually, you'd have to do some experimentation to get those values right. Here's what we came up with after a few iterations of tuning:

- The gravity acceleration vector is $(0,-13)$ m/s^2, slightly more than what we have here on earth and what we used in our cannon example.

- Bob's initial jump velocity vector is $(0,11)$ m/s. Note that the jump velocity only affects the movement on the y-axis. The horizontal movement will be defined by the current accelerometer readings.

- Bob's jump velocity vector will be 1.5 times his normal jump velocity when he hits a spring. That's equivalent to $(0,16.5)$ m/s. Again, this value is purely derived from experimentation.

- Bob's horizontal movement speed is 20 m/s. Note that that's a directionless speed, not a vector. We'll explain in a minute how that works together with the accelerometer.

- The squirrels will patrol from the left to the right and back continuously. They'll have a constant movement speed of 3 m/s. Expressed as a vector, that's either $(-3,0)$ m/s if the squirrel moves to the left or $(3,0)$ m/s if the squirrel moves to the right.

So how will Bob's horizontal movement work? The movement speed we defined before is actually Bob's maximum horizontal speed. Depending on how much the player tilts his or her phone, Bob's horizontal movement speed will be between 0 (no tilt) and 20 m/s (fully tilted to one side).

We'll use the value of the accelerometer's x-axis since our game will run in portrait mode. When the phone is not tilted, the axis will report an acceleration of 0 m/s^2. When fully tilted to the left so that the phone is in landscape orientation, the axis will report roughly -10 m/s^2. When fully tilted to the right, the axis will report an acceleration of roughly 10 m/s^2. All we need to do is normalize the accelerometer reading by dividing it by the maximum absolute value (10) and then multiplying Bob's maximum horizontal speed by that. Bob will thus travel 20 m/s to the left or right when the phone is fully tilted to one side and less if the phone is tilted less. Bob can move around the screen twice per second when the phone is fully tilted.

We'll update this horizontal movement velocity each frame based on the current accelerometer value on the x-axis and combine it with Bob's vertical velocity, which is derived from the gravity acceleration and his current vertical velocity, as we did for the cannonball in the earlier examples.

One essential aspect of the world is the portion we see of it. Since Bob will die when he leaves the screen on the bottom edge, our camera also plays a role in the game mechanics. While we'll use a camera for rendering and move it upward when Bob jumps, we won't use it in our world simulation classes. Instead we record Bob's highest y-coordinate so far. If he's below that value minus half the view frustum height, we know he has left the screen. Thus, we don't have a completely clean separation between the model (our world simulation classes) and the view, since we need to know the view frustum's height to determine whether Bob is dead. We can live with this.

Let's have a look at the assets we need.

Creating the Assets

Our new game has two types of graphical assets: UI elements and actual game, or world, elements. Let's start with the UI elements.

The UI Elements

The first thing to notice is that the UI elements (buttons, logos, and so forth) do not depend on our pixel-to-world unit mapping. As in Mr. Nom, we design them to fit a target resolution—in our case 320×480 pixels. Looking at Figure 9–2, we can determine which UI elements we have.

The first UI elements we create are the buttons we need for the different screens. Figure 9–4 shows all the buttons of our game.

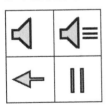

Figure 9–4. *Various buttons, each 64×64 pixels in size.*

We prefer to create all graphical assets in a grid with cells having sizes of 32×32 or 64×64 pixels. The buttons in Figure 9–4 are laid out in a grid with each cell having 64×64 pixels. The buttons in the top row are used on the main menu screen to signal whether sound is enabled or not. The arrow at the bottom left is used in a couple of screens to navigate to the next screen. The button in the bottom right is used in the game screen when the game is running to allow the user to pause the game.

You might wonder why there's no arrow pointing to the right. Remember that, with our fancy sprite batcher, we can easily flip things we draw by specifying negative width and/or height values. We'll use that trick for a couple of graphical assets to save some memory.

Next up are the elements we need on the main menu screen. There we have a logo, the menu entries, and the background. Figure 9–5 shows all those elements.

Figure 9–5. *The background image, the main menu entries, and the logo.*

The background image is used not only on the main menu screen, but on all screens. It is the same size as our target resolution, 320×480 pixels. The main menu entries make up 300×110 pixels. The black background you see in Figure 9–5 is there since white on white wouldn't look all that good. In the actual image, the background is made up of transparent pixels, of course. The logo is 274×142 pixels with some transparent pixels at the corners.

Next up are the help screen images. Instead of compositing each of them with a couple of elements, we lazily made them all full-screen images of size 320×480 instead. That will reduce the size of our drawing code a little while not adding a lot to our program's size. You can see all of the help screens in Figure 9–2. The only thing we'll composite these images with is the arrow button.

For the high-scores screen, we'll reuse the portion of the main menu entries image that says HIGHSCORES. The actual scores are rendered with a special technique we'll look into later on in this chapter. The rest of that screen is again composed of the background image and a button.

The game screen has a few more textual UI elements, namely the READY? label, the menu entries for the paused state (RESUME and QUIT), and the GAME OVER label. Figure 9–6 shows them in all their glory.

Figure 9–6.The READY?, RESUME, QUIT, and GAME OVER labels

Handling Text with Bitmap Fonts

So, how do we render the other textual elements in the game screen? With the same technique we used in Mr. Nom to render the scores. Instead of just having numbers, we also have characters now. We use an image atlas where each subimage represents one character (for example, *0* or *a*). This image atlas is called a bitmap font. Figure 9–7 shows the bitmap font we'll use.

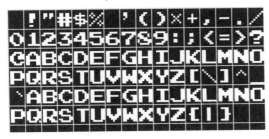

Figure 9–7. A bitmap font.

The black background and the grid in Figure 9–7 are, of course, not part of the actual image. Bitmap fonts are a very old technique to render text on the screen in a game. They usually contain images for a range of ASCII characters. One such character image is referred to as a *glyph*. ASCII is one of the predecessors of Unicode. There are 128 characters in the ASCII character set, as shown in Figure 9–8.

ASCII Table

Dec	Hex	Oct	Char	Dec	Hex	Oct	Char	Dec	Hex	Oct	Char	Dec	Hex	Oct	Char
0	0	0		32	20	40	[space]	64	40	100	@	96	60	140	'
1	1	1		33	21	41	!	65	41	101	A	97	61	141	a
2	2	2		34	22	42	"	66	42	102	B	98	62	142	b
3	3	3		35	23	43	#	67	43	103	C	99	63	143	c
4	4	4		36	24	44	$	68	44	104	D	100	64	144	d
5	5	5		37	25	45	%	69	45	105	E	101	65	145	e
6	6	6		38	26	46	&	70	46	106	F	102	66	146	f
7	7	7		39	27	47	'	71	47	107	G	103	67	147	g
8	8	10		40	28	50	(	72	48	110	H	104	68	150	h
9	9	11		41	29	51	)	73	49	111	I	105	69	151	i
10	A	12		42	2A	52	*	74	4A	112	J	106	6A	152	j
11	B	13		43	2B	53	+	75	4B	113	K	107	6B	153	k
12	C	14		44	2C	54	,	76	4C	114	L	108	6C	154	l
13	D	15		45	2D	55	-	77	4D	115	M	109	6D	155	m
14	E	16		46	2E	56	.	78	4E	116	N	110	6E	156	n
15	F	17		47	2F	57	/	79	4F	117	O	111	6F	157	o
16	10	20		48	30	60	0	80	50	120	P	112	70	160	p
17	11	21		49	31	61	1	81	51	121	Q	113	71	161	q
18	12	22		50	32	62	2	82	52	122	R	114	72	162	r
19	13	23		51	33	63	3	83	53	123	S	115	73	163	s
20	14	24		52	34	64	4	84	54	124	T	116	74	164	t
21	15	25		53	35	65	5	85	55	125	U	117	75	165	u
22	16	26		54	36	66	6	86	56	126	V	118	76	166	v
23	17	27		55	37	67	7	87	57	127	W	119	77	167	w
24	18	30		56	38	70	8	88	58	130	X	120	78	170	x
25	19	31		57	39	71	9	89	59	131	Y	121	79	171	y
26	1A	32		58	3A	72	:	90	5A	132	Z	122	7A	172	z
27	1B	33		59	3B	73	;	91	5B	133	[	123	7B	173	{
28	1C	34		60	3C	74	<	92	5C	134	\	124	7C	174		
29	1D	35		61	3D	75	=	93	5D	135	]	125	7D	175	}
30	1E	36		62	3E	76	>	94	5E	136	^	126	7E	176	~
31	1F	37		63	3F	77	?	95	5F	137	_	127	7F	177	

Figure 9–8. *ASCII characters and their decimal, hexadecimal, and octal values.*

Out of those 128 characters, 96 are printable (characters 32 to 127). Our bitmap font only contains printable characters. The first row in the bitmap font contains the characters 32 to 47; the next row contains the characters 48 to 63, and so on. ASCII is only useful if you want to store and display text that uses the standard Latin alphabet. There's an extended ASCII format that uses the values 128 to 255 to encode other common characters of Western languages, such as ö or é. More expressive character sets (for example, for Chinese or Arabic) are represented via Unicode and can't be encoded via ASCII. For our game, the standard ASCII character set suffices.

So, how do we render text with a bitmap font? That turns out to be really easy. First, we create 96 texture regions, each mapping to a glyph in the bitmap font. We can store those texture regions in an array as follows:

```
TextureRegion[] glyphs = new TextureRegion[96];
```

Java strings are encoded in 16-bit Unicode. Luckily for us, the ASCII characters we have in our bitmap font have the same values in ASCII and Unicode. To fetch the region for a character in a Java string, we just need to do this:

```
int index = string.charAt(i) - 32;
```

This gives us a direct index into the texture region array. We just subtract the value for the space character (32) from the current character in the string. If the index is smaller than zero or bigger than 95, we have a Unicode character that is not in our bitmap font. Usually, we just ignore such a character.

To render multiple characters in a line, we need to know how much space there should be between characters. The bitmap font in Figure 9–7 is a so-called fixed-width font.

That means that each glyph has the same width. Our bitmap font glyphs have a size of 16×20 pixels each. When we advance our rendering position from character to character in a string, we just need to add 20 pixels. The number of pixels we move the drawing position from character to character is called *advance*. For our bitmap font, it is fixed; however, it is generally variable depending on the character we draw. A more complex form of *advance* takes both the current character we are about to draw and the next character into consideration for calculating the advance. This technique is called *kerning*, if you want to look it up on the Web. We'll only use fixed-width bitmap fonts, as they make our lives considerably easier.

So, how did we generate that ASCII bitmap font? We used one of the many tools available on the Web for generating bitmap fonts. The one we used is called Codehead's Bitmap Font Generator, and it is freely available. You can select a font file on your hard drive and specify the height of the font, and the generator will produce an image from it for the ASCII character set. The tool has a lot more options that we can't discuss here. We recommend that you check it out and play around with it a little.

We'll draw all the remaining strings in our game with this technique. Later, you'll see a concrete implementation of a bitmap font class. Let's get on with our assets.

With the bitmap font, we now have assets for all our graphical UI elements. We will render them via a `SpriteBatcher` using a camera that sets up a view frustum that directly maps to our target resolution. This way we can specify all the coordinates in pixel coordinates.

The Game Elements

What are left are the actual game objects. Those are dependent on our pixel-to-world unit mappings, as discussed earlier. To make the creation of those as easy as possible, we used a little trick: we started each drawing with a grid of 32×32 pixels per cell. All the objects are centered in one or more such cells, so that they correspond easily with the physical sizes they have in our world. Let's start with Bob, depicted in Figure 9–9.

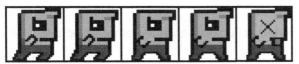

Figure 9–9. Bob and his five animation frames.

Figure 9-9 shows two frames for jumping, two frames for falling, and one frame for being dead. Each image is 160×32 pixels in size, and each animation frame is 32×32 pixels in size. The background pixels are transparent.

Bob can be in three states: jumping, falling, and dead. We have animation frames for each of these states. Granted, the difference between the two jumping frames is minor—only his forelock is wiggling. We'll create an `Animation` instance for each of the three animations of Bob, and we'll use them for rendering according to his current state. We also don't have duplicate frames for Bob heading left. As with the arrow button, we'll just specify a negative width with the SpriteBatcher.drawSprite() call to flip Bob's image horizontally.

Figure 9–10 depicts the evil squirrel. We have two animation frames again, so the squirrel appears to be flapping its evil wings.

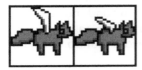

Figure 9–10. *An evil flying squirrel and its two animation frames.*

The image in Figure 9–10 is 64×32 pixels, and each frame is 32×32 pixels.

The coin animation in Figure 9–11 is special. Our keyframe sequence will not be 1, 2, 3, 1, but 1, 2, 3, 2, 1. Otherwise, the coin would go from its collapsed state in frame 3 to its fully-extended state in frame 1. We can conserve a little space by reusing the second frame.

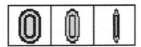

Figure 9–11.*The coin and its animation frames.*

The image in Figure 9–11 is 96×32 pixels, and each frame is 32×32 pixels.

Not a lot has to be said about the spring image in Figure 9–12. The spring just sits there happily in the center of the image.

Figure 9–12. *The spring. The image is 32×32 pixels.*

The castle in Figure 9–13 is also not animated. It is bigger than the other objects (64×64 pixels).

Figure 9–13. *The castle.*

The platform in Figure 9–14 (64x64 pixels) has four animation frames. According to our game mechanics, some platforms will be pulverized when Bob hits them. We'll play back the full animation of the platform in that case once. For static platforms, we'll just use the first frame.

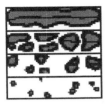

Figure 9–14. *The platform and its animation frames.*

Texture Atlas to the Rescue

That's all the graphical assets we have in our game. We already talked about how textures need to have power-of-two widths and heights. Our background image and all the help screens have a size of 320×480 pixels. We'll store those in 512×512-pixel images so that we can load them as textures. That's already six textures.

Do we create separate textures for all the other images as well? No. We create a single texture atlas. It turns out that everything else fits nicely in a single 512×512 pixel atlas, which we can load as a single texture—something that will make the GPU really happy, since we only need to bind one texture for all game elements, except the background and help screen images. Figure 9–15 shows the atlas.

The image in Figure 9–15 is 512×512 pixels in size. The grids and red outlines are not part of the image, and the background pixels are transparent. This is also true for the black background pixels of the UI labels and the bitmap font. The grid cells are 32×32 pixels in size. The cool thing about using a texture atlas like this is that, if you want to support higher resolution screens, you don't need to change anything but the size of this texture atlas! Scale it up to 1024×1024 with higher-fidelity graphics and, even though our target was 320×480, OpenGL gives you the better graphics with no game changes!

We placed all the images in the atlas at corners with coordinates that are multiples of 32. This makes creating TextureRegions easier.

Figure 9–15.*The mighty texture atlas.*

Music and Sound

We also need sound effects and music. Since our game is an 8-bit retro-style game, it's fitting to use so-called *chip tunes*. Chip tunes are sound effects and music generated by a synthesizer. The most famous chip tunes were generated by Nintendo's NES, SNES, and GameBoy. For the sound effects, we used a tool called *sfxr*, by Tomas Pettersson (or rather the Flash version, called *as3sfxr*). It can be found at www.superflashbros.net/as3sfxr. Figure 9–16 shows its user interface.

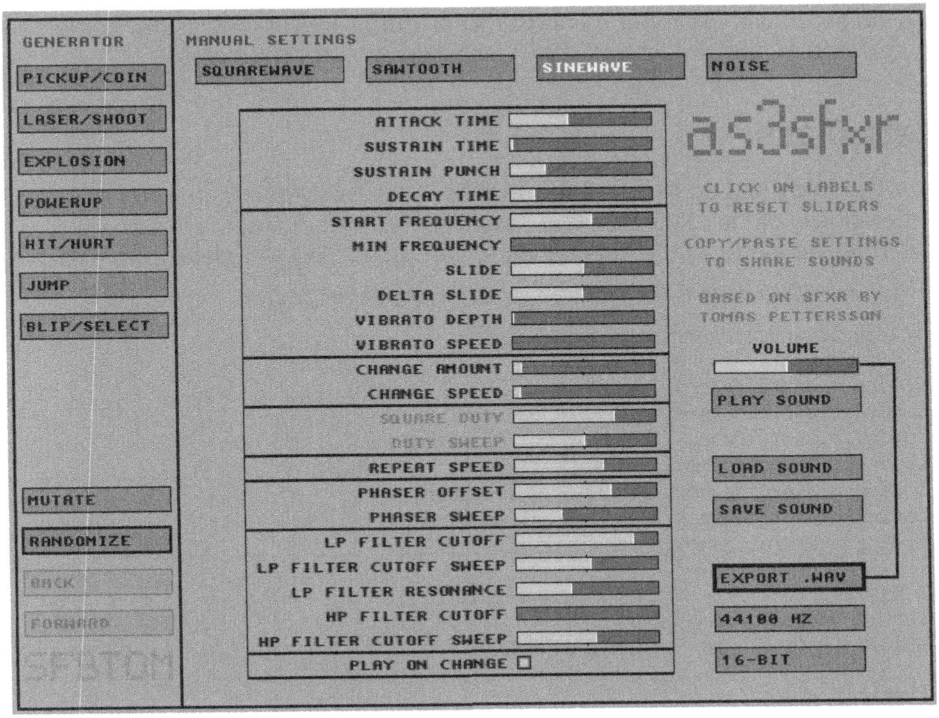

Figure 9–16. as3sfxr, a Flash port of sfxr, by Tomas Pettersson.

We created sound effects for jumping, hitting a spring, hitting a coin, and hitting a squirrel. We also created a sound effect for clicking UI elements. All we did was mash the buttons to the left of as3sfxr for each category until we found a fitting sound effect.

Music for games is usually a little bit harder to come by. There are a few sites on the Web that feature 8-bit chip tunes fitting for a game like Super Jumper. We'll use a single song called "New Song," by Geir Tjelta. The song can be found at www.freemusicarchive.org. It's licensed under the Creative Commons Attribution-NonCommercial-NoDerivatives (a.k.a. Music Sharing) license. This means we can use it in noncommercial projects, such as our open source Super Jumper game, as long as we give attribution to Geir and don't modify the original piece. When you scout the Web for music to be used in your games, always make sure that you adhere to the license. People put a lot of work into those songs. If the license doesn't fit your project (that is, if it is a commercial one), then you can't use it.

Implementing Super Jumper

Implementing Super Jumper will be pretty easy. We can reuse our complete framework from the previous chapter and follow the architecture we had in Mr. Nom on a high level. This means we'll have a class for each screen, and each of these classes will implement the logic and presentation expected from that screen. Besides that, we'll also have our standard project setup with a proper manifest file, all our assets in the assets/ folder, an icon for our application, and so on. Let's start with our main Assets class.

The Assets Class

In Mr. Nom, we already had an Assets class that consisted only of a metric ton of Pixmap and Sound references held in static member variables. We'll do the same in Super Jumper. This time, we'll add a little loading logic, though. Listing 9–1 shows the code.

Listing 9–1. *Assets.java, Which Holds All Our Assets Except for the Help Screen Textures*

```java
package com.badlogic.androidgames.jumper;

import com.badlogic.androidgames.framework.Music;
import com.badlogic.androidgames.framework.Sound;
import com.badlogic.androidgames.framework.gl.Animation;
import com.badlogic.androidgames.framework.gl.Font;
import com.badlogic.androidgames.framework.gl.Texture;
import com.badlogic.androidgames.framework.gl.TextureRegion;
import com.badlogic.androidgames.framework.impl.GLGame;

public class Assets {
    public static Texture background;
    public static TextureRegion backgroundRegion;

    public static Texture items;
    public static TextureRegion mainMenu;
    public static TextureRegion pauseMenu;
    public static TextureRegion ready;
    public static TextureRegion gameOver;
    public static TextureRegion highScoresRegion;
    public static TextureRegion logo;
    public static TextureRegion soundOn;
    public static TextureRegion soundOff;
    public static TextureRegion arrow;
    public static TextureRegion pause;
    public static TextureRegion spring;
    public static TextureRegion castle;
    public static Animation coinAnim;
    public static Animation bobJump;
    public static Animation bobFall;
    public static TextureRegion bobHit;
    public static Animation squirrelFly;
    public static TextureRegion platform;
    public static Animation brakingPlatform;
    public static Font font;

    public static Music music;
    public static Sound jumpSound;
    public static Sound highJumpSound;
    public static Sound hitSound;
    public static Sound coinSound;
    public static Sound clickSound;
```

The class holds references to all the Texture, TextureRegion, Animation, Music, and Sound instances we need throughout our game. The only thing we don't load here are the images for the help screens.

```java
public static void load(GLGame game) {
    background = new Texture(game, "background.png");
    backgroundRegion = new TextureRegion(background, 0, 0, 320, 480);

    items = new Texture(game, "items.png");
    mainMenu = new TextureRegion(items, 0, 224, 300, 110);
    pauseMenu = new TextureRegion(items, 224, 128, 192, 96);
    ready = new TextureRegion(items, 320, 224, 192, 32);
    gameOver = new TextureRegion(items, 352, 256, 160, 96);
    highScoresRegion = new TextureRegion(Assets.items, 0, 257, 300, 110 / 3);
    logo = new TextureRegion(items, 0, 352, 274, 142);
    soundOff = new TextureRegion(items, 0, 0, 64, 64);
    soundOn = new TextureRegion(items, 64, 0, 64, 64);
    arrow = new TextureRegion(items, 0, 64, 64, 64);
    pause = new TextureRegion(items, 64, 64, 64, 64);

    spring = new TextureRegion(items, 128, 0, 32, 32);
    castle = new TextureRegion(items, 128, 64, 64, 64);
    coinAnim = new Animation(0.2f,
                        new TextureRegion(items, 128, 32, 32, 32),
                        new TextureRegion(items, 160, 32, 32, 32),
                        new TextureRegion(items, 192, 32, 32, 32),
                        new TextureRegion(items, 160, 32, 32, 32));
    bobJump = new Animation(0.2f,
                        new TextureRegion(items, 0, 128, 32, 32),
                        new TextureRegion(items, 32, 128, 32, 32));
    bobFall = new Animation(0.2f,
                        new TextureRegion(items, 64, 128, 32, 32),
                        new TextureRegion(items, 96, 128, 32, 32));
    bobHit = new TextureRegion(items, 128, 128, 32, 32);
    squirrelFly = new Animation(0.2f,
                        new TextureRegion(items, 0, 160, 32, 32),
                        new TextureRegion(items, 32, 160, 32, 32));
    platform = new TextureRegion(items, 64, 160, 64, 16);
    brakingPlatform = new Animation(0.2f,
                        new TextureRegion(items, 64, 160, 64, 16),
                        new TextureRegion(items, 64, 176, 64, 16),
                        new TextureRegion(items, 64, 192, 64, 16),
                        new TextureRegion(items, 64, 208, 64, 16));

    font = new Font(items, 224, 0, 16, 16, 20);

    music = game.getAudio().newMusic("music.mp3");
    music.setLooping(true);
    music.setVolume(0.5f);
    if(Settings.soundEnabled)
        music.play();
    jumpSound = game.getAudio().newSound("jump.ogg");
    highJumpSound = game.getAudio().newSound("highjump.ogg");
    hitSound = game.getAudio().newSound("hit.ogg");
```

```
        coinSound = game.getAudio().newSound("coin.ogg");
        clickSound = game.getAudio().newSound("click.ogg");
    }
```

The load() method, which will be called once at the start of our game, is responsible for populating all the static members of the class. It loads the background image and creates a corresponding TextureRegion for it. Next, it loads the texture atlas and creates all the necessary TextureRegions and Animations. Compare the code to Figure 9–15 and the other figures in the last section. The only noteworthy thing about the code for loading graphical assets is the creation of the coin Animation instance. As discussed, we reuse the second frame at the end of the animation frame sequence. All the animations use a frame time of 0.2 seconds.

We also create an instance of the Font class, which we have not yet discussed. It will implement the logic to render text with the bitmap font embedded in the atlas. The constructor takes the Texture, which contains the bitmap font glyphs, the pixel coordinates of the top-left corner of the area that contains the glyphs, the number of glyphs per row, and the size of each glyph in pixels.

We also load all the Music and Sound instances in that method. As you can see, we work with our old friend the Settings class again. We can reuse it from the Mr. Nom project pretty much as is, with one slight modification as you'll see in a minute. Note that we set the Music instance to be looping and its volume to 0.5, so it is a little quieter than the sound effects. The music will only start playing if the user hasn't previously disabled the sound, which is stored in the Settings class, as in Mr. Nom.

```
    public static void reload() {
        background.reload();
        items.reload();
        if(Settings.soundEnabled)
            music.play();
    }
```

Next, we have a mysterious method called reload(). Remember that the OpenGL ES context will get lost when our application is paused. We have to reload the textures when the application is resumed, and that's exactly what this method does. We also resume the music playback in case sound is enabled.

```
    public static void playSound(Sound sound) {
        if(Settings.soundEnabled)
            sound.play(1);
    }
}
```

The final method of this class is a helper method we'll use in the rest of the code to play back audio. Instead of having to check whether sound is enabled everywhere, we encapsulate that check in this method.

Let's have a look at the modified Settings class.

The Settings Class

Not a lot has changed. Listing 9–2 shows the code of our slightly modified Settings class.

Listing 9–2. *Settings.java, Our Slightly Modified Settings Class, Stolen from Mr. Nom.*

```java
package com.badlogic.androidgames.jumper;

import java.io.BufferedReader;
import java.io.BufferedWriter;
import java.io.IOException;
import java.io.InputStreamReader;
import java.io.OutputStreamWriter;

import com.badlogic.androidgames.framework.FileIO;

public class Settings {
    public static boolean soundEnabled = true;
    public final static int[] highscores = new int[] { 100, 80, 50, 30, 10 };
    public final static String file = ".superjumper";

    public static void load(FileIO files) {
        BufferedReader in = null;
        try {
            in = new BufferedReader(new InputStreamReader(files.readFile(file)));
            soundEnabled = Boolean.parseBoolean(in.readLine());
            for(int i = 0; i < 5; i++) {
                highscores[i] = Integer.parseInt(in.readLine());
            }
        } catch (IOException e) {
            // :( It's ok we have defaults
        } catch (NumberFormatException e) {
            // :/ It's ok, defaults save our day
        } finally {
            try {
                if (in != null)
                    in.close();
            } catch (IOException e) {
            }
        }
    }

    public static void save(FileIO files) {
        BufferedWriter out = null;
        try {
            out = new BufferedWriter(new OutputStreamWriter(
                    files.writeFile(file)));
            out.write(Boolean.toString(soundEnabled));
            out.write("\n");
            for(int i = 0; i < 5; i++) {
                out.write(Integer.toString(highscores[i]));
                out.write("\n");
            }
```

```
            } catch (IOException e) {
            } finally {
                try {
                    if (out != null)
                        out.close();
                } catch (IOException e) {
                }
            }
        }

    public static void addScore(int score) {
        for(int i=0; i < 5; i++) {
            if(highscores[i] < score) {
                for(int j= 4; j > i; j--)
                    highscores[j] = highscores[j-1];
                highscores[i] = score;
                break;
            }
        }
    }
}
```

The only difference from the Mr. Nom version of this class is the file from and to which we read and write the settings. Instead of .mrnom, we now use the file .superjumper.

The Main Activity

We need an Activity as the main entry point of our game. We'll call it SuperJumper. Listing 9–3 shows its code.

Listing 9–3. *SuperJumper.java, the Main Entry Point Class*

```
package com.badlogic.androidgames.jumper;

import javax.microedition.khronos.egl.EGLConfig;
import javax.microedition.khronos.opengles.GL10;

import com.badlogic.androidgames.framework.Screen;
import com.badlogic.androidgames.framework.impl.GLGame;

public class Settings {
    public static boolean soundEnabled = true;
    public final static int[] highscores = new int[] { 100, 80, 50, 30, 10 };
    public final static String file = ".superjumper";

    public static void load(FileIO files) {
        BufferedReader in = null;
        try {
            in = new BufferedReader(new InputStreamReader(files.readFile(file)));
            soundEnabled = Boolean.parseBoolean(in.readLine());
            for(int i = 0; i < 5; i++) {
                highscores[i] = Integer.parseInt(in.readLine());
            }
        } catch (IOException e) {
```

```
            // :( It's ok we have defaults
        } catch (NumberFormatException e) {
            // :/ It's ok, defaults save our day
        } finally {
            try {
                if (in != null)
                    in.close();
            } catch (IOException e) {
            }
        }
    }

    public static void save(FileIO files) {
        BufferedWriter out = null;
        try {
            out = new BufferedWriter(new OutputStreamWriter(
                    files.writeFile(file)));
            out.write(Boolean.toString(soundEnabled));
            out.write("\n");
            for(int i = 0; i < 5; i++) {
                out.write(Integer.toString(highscores[i]));
                out.write("\n");
            }

        } catch (IOException e) {
        } finally {
            try {
                if (out != null)
                    out.close();
            } catch (IOException e) {
            }
        }
    }

    public static void addScore(int score) {
        for(int i=0; i < 5; i++) {
            if(highscores[i] < score) {
                for(int j= 4; j > i; j--)
                    highscores[j] = highscores[j-1];
                highscores[i] = score;
                break;
            }
        }
    }
}
```

We derive from GLGame and implement the getStartScreen() method, which returns a MainMenuScreen instance. The other two methods are a little less obvious.

We override onSurfaceCreate(), which is called each time the OpenGL ES context is re-created (compare with the code of GLGame in Chapter 6). If the method is called for the first time, we use the Assets.load() method to load all assets and also load the settings from the settings file on the SD card, if available. Otherwise, all we need to do is reload the textures and start playback of the music via the Assets.reload() method. We also override the onPause() method to pause the music in the case it is playing.

We do both of these things so that we don't have to repeat them in the resume() and pause() methods of our screens.

Before we dive into the screen implementations, let's have a look at our new Font class.

The Font Class

We are going to use bitmap fonts to render arbitrary (ASCII) text. We already discussed how this works on a high level, so let's look at the code in Listing 9–4.

Listing 9–4. *Font.java, a Bitmap Font–Rendering Class*

```
package com.badlogic.androidgames.framework.gl;

public class Font {
    public final Texture texture;
    public final int glyphWidth;
    public final int glyphHeight;
    public final TextureRegion[] glyphs = new TextureRegion[96];
```

The class stores the texture containing the font's glyph, the width and height of a single glyph, and an array of TextureRegions—one for each glyph. The first element in the array holds the region for the space glyph, the next one holds the region for the exclamation mark glyph, and so on. In other words, the first element corresponds to the ASCII character with the code 32, and the last element corresponds to the ASCII character with the code 127.

```
    public Font(Texture texture,
                int offsetX, int offsetY,
                int glyphsPerRow, int glyphWidth, int glyphHeight) {
        this.texture = texture;
        this.glyphWidth = glyphWidth;
        this.glyphHeight = glyphHeight;
        int x = offsetX;
        int y = offsetY;
        for(int i = 0; i < 96; i++) {
            glyphs[i] = new TextureRegion(texture, x, y, glyphWidth, glyphHeight);
            x += glyphWidth;
            if(x == offsetX + glyphsPerRow * glyphWidth) {
                x = offsetX;
                y += glyphHeight;
            }
        }
    }
}
```

In the constructor, we store the configuration of the bitmap font and generate the glyph regions. The offsetX and offsetY parameters specify the top-left corner of the bitmap font area in the texture. In our texture atlas, that's the pixel at (224,0). The parameter glyphsPerRow tells us how many glyphs there are per row, and the parameters glyphWidth and glyphHeight specify the size of a single glyph. Since we use a fixed-width bitmap font, that size is the same for all glyphs. The glyphWidth is also the value by which we will advance when rendering multiple glyphs.

```java
    public void drawText(SpriteBatcher batcher, String text, float x, float y) {
        int len = text.length();
        for(int i = 0; i < len; i++) {
            int c = text.charAt(i) - ' ';
            if(c < 0 || c > glyphs.length - 1)
                continue;

            TextureRegion glyph = glyphs[c];
            batcher.drawSprite(x, y, glyphWidth, glyphHeight, glyph);
            x += glyphWidth;
        }
    }
}
```

The drawText() method takes a SpriteBatcher instance, a line of text, and the x and y positions at which to start drawing the text. The x- and y-coordinates specify the center of the first glyph. All we do is get the index for each character in the string, check whether we have a glyph for it, and, if so, render it via the SpriteBatcher. We then increment the x-coordinate by the glyphWidth so that we can start rendering the next character in the string.

You might wonder why we don't need to bind the texture containing the glyphs. We assume that this is done before a call to drawText(). The reason is that the text rendering might be part of a batch, in which case the texture must already be bound. Why unnecessarily bind it again in the drawText() method? Remember, OpenGL ES loves nothing more than minimal state changes.

Of course, we can only handle fixed-width fonts with this class. If we want to support more general fonts, we also need to have information about the advance of each character. One solution would be to use kerning as described in the section "Handling Text with Bitmap Fonts." We are happy with our simple solution though.

GLScreen

In the examples in the last two chapters, we always got the reference to GLGraphics by casting. Let's fix this with a little helper class called GLScreen, which will do the dirty work for us and store the reference to GLGraphics in a member. Listing 9–5 shows the code.

Listing 9–5. *GLScreen.java, a Little Helper Class.*

```java
package com.badlogic.androidgames.framework.impl;

import com.badlogic.androidgames.framework.Game;
import com.badlogic.androidgames.framework.Screen;

public abstract class GLScreen extends Screen {
    protected final GLGraphics glGraphics;
    protected final GLGame glGame;

    public GLScreen(Game game) {
        super(game);
        glGame = (GLGame)game;
```

```
            glGraphics = ((GLGame)game).getGLGraphics();
    }

}
```

We store the `GLGraphics` and `GLGame` instances. Of course, this will crash if the `Game` instance passed as a parameter to the constructor is not a `GLGame`. But we'll make sure it is. All the screens of Super Jumper will derive from this class.

The Main Menu Screen

This is the screen that is returned by `SuperJumper.getStartScreen()`, so it's the first screen the player will see. It renders the background and UI elements and simply waits there for us to touch any of the UI elements. Based on the element that was hit, we either change the configuration (sound enabled/disabled) or transition to a new screen. Listing 9–6 shows the code.

Listing 9–6. *MainMenuScreen.java: The Main Menu Screen.*

```java
package com.badlogic.androidgames.jumper;

import java.util.List;

import javax.microedition.khronos.opengles.GL10;

import com.badlogic.androidgames.framework.Game;
import com.badlogic.androidgames.framework.Input.TouchEvent;
import com.badlogic.androidgames.framework.gl.Camera2D;
import com.badlogic.androidgames.framework.gl.SpriteBatcher;
import com.badlogic.androidgames.framework.impl.GLScreen;
import com.badlogic.androidgames.framework.math.OverlapTester;
import com.badlogic.androidgames.framework.math.Rectangle;
import com.badlogic.androidgames.framework.math.Vector2;

public class MainMenuScreen extends GLScreen {
    Camera2D guiCam;
    SpriteBatcher batcher;
    Rectangle soundBounds;
    Rectangle playBounds;
    Rectangle highscoresBounds;
    Rectangle helpBounds;
    Vector2 touchPoint;
```

The class derives from `GLScreen`, so we can access the `GLGraphics` instance more easily.

There are a couple of members in this class. The first one is a `Camera2D` instance called `guiCam`. We also need a `SpriteBatcher` to render our background and UI elements. We'll use `Rectangle`s to determine if the user touched a UI element. Since we use a `Camera2D`, we also need a `Vector2` instance to transform the touch coordinates to world coordinates.

```java
    public MainMenuScreen(Game game) {
        super(game);
        guiCam = new Camera2D(glGraphics, 320, 480);
        batcher = new SpriteBatcher(glGraphics, 100);
```

```
        soundBounds = new Rectangle(0, 0, 64, 64);
        playBounds = new Rectangle(160 - 150, 200 + 18, 300, 36);
        highscoresBounds = new Rectangle(160 - 150, 200 - 18, 300, 36);
        helpBounds = new Rectangle(160 - 150, 200 - 18 - 36, 300, 36);
        touchPoint = new Vector2();
    }
```

In the constructor, we simply set up all the members. And there's a surprise. The
Camera2D instance will allow us to work in our target resolution of 320×480 pixels. All we
need to do is set the view frustum width and height to the proper values. The rest is
done by OpenGL ES on the fly. Note, however, that the origin is still in the bottom-left
corner and the y-axis is pointing upward. We'll use such a GUI camera in all screens that
have UI elements so that we can lay them out in pixels instead of world coordinates. Of
course, we cheat a little on screens that are not 320×480 pixels wide, but we already did
that in Mr. Nom, so we don't need to feel bad about it. The Rectangles we set up for
each UI element are thus given in pixel coordinates.

```
    @Override
    public void update(float deltaTime) {
        List<TouchEvent> touchEvents = game.getInput().getTouchEvents();
        game.getInput().getKeyEvents();

        int len = touchEvents.size();
        for(int i = 0; i < len; i++) {
            TouchEvent event = touchEvents.get(i);
            if(event.type == TouchEvent.TOUCH_UP) {
                touchPoint.set(event.x, event.y);
                guiCam.touchToWorld(touchPoint);

                if(OverlapTester.pointInRectangle(playBounds, touchPoint)) {
                    Assets.playSound(Assets.clickSound);
                    game.setScreen(new GameScreen(game));
                    return;
                }
                if(OverlapTester.pointInRectangle(highscoresBounds, touchPoint)) {
                    Assets.playSound(Assets.clickSound);
                    game.setScreen(new HighscoresScreen(game));
                    return;
                }
                if(OverlapTester.pointInRectangle(helpBounds, touchPoint)) {
                    Assets.playSound(Assets.clickSound);
                    game.setScreen(new HelpScreen(game));
                    return;
                }
                if(OverlapTester.pointInRectangle(soundBounds, touchPoint)) {
                    Assets.playSound(Assets.clickSound);
                    Settings.soundEnabled = !Settings.soundEnabled;
                    if(Settings.soundEnabled)
                        Assets.music.play();
                    else
                        Assets.music.pause();
                }
            }
        }
    }
```

Next is the update() method. We loop through the TouchEvents returned by our Input instance and check for touch-up events. In case we have such an event, we first translate the touch coordinates to world coordinates. Since the camera is set up in a way so that we work in our target resolution, this transformation boils down simply to flipping the y-coordinate on a 320×480 pixel screen. On larger or smaller screens, we just transform the touch coordinates to the target resolution. Once we have our world touch point, we can check it against the rectangles of the UI elements. If PLAY, HIGHSCORES, or HELP was hit, we transition to the respective screen. In case the sound button was pressed, we change the setting and either resume or pause the music. Also note that we play the click sound in case a UI element was pressed via the Assets.playSound() method.

```
@Override
public void present(float deltaTime) {
    GL10 gl = glGraphics.getGL();
    gl.glClear(GL10.GL_COLOR_BUFFER_BIT);
    guiCam.setViewportAndMatrices();

    gl.glEnable(GL10.GL_TEXTURE_2D);

    batcher.beginBatch(Assets.background);
    batcher.drawSprite(160, 240, 320, 480, Assets.backgroundRegion);
    batcher.endBatch();

    gl.glEnable(GL10.GL_BLEND);
    gl.glBlendFunc(GL10.GL_SRC_ALPHA, GL10.GL_ONE_MINUS_SRC_ALPHA);

    batcher.beginBatch(Assets.items);

    batcher.drawSprite(160, 480 - 10 - 71, 274, 142, Assets.logo);
    batcher.drawSprite(160, 200, 300, 110, Assets.mainMenu);
    batcher.drawSprite(32, 32, 64, 64,
Settings.soundEnabled?Assets.soundOn:Assets.soundOff);

    batcher.endBatch();

    gl.glDisable(GL10.GL_BLEND);
}
```

The present() method shouldn't really need any explanation at this point. We clear the screen, set up the projection matrices via the camera, and render the background and UI elements. Since the UI elements have transparent backgrounds, we enable blending temporarily to render them. The background does not need blending, so we don't use it to conserve some GPU cycles. Again, note that the UI elements are rendered in a coordinate system with the origin in the lower left of the screen and the y-axis pointing upward.

```
@Override
public void pause() {
    Settings.save(game.getFileIO());
}

@Override
public void resume() {
```

```
    }

    @Override
    public void dispose() {
    }
}
```

The last method that actually does something is the pause() method. Here, we make sure that the settings are saved to the SD card since the user can change the sound settings on this screen.

The Help Screens

We have a total of five help screens that all work the same: load the help screen image, render it along with the arrow button, and wait for a touch of the arrow button to move to the next screen. The only thing in which the screens differ is the image that they each load and the screen to which they transition. For this reason, we'll only present you with the code of the first help screen, which transitions to the second one. The image files for the help screens are named help1.png, help1.png, and so on, up to help5.png. The respective screen classes are called HelpScreen, Help2Screen, and so on. The last screen, Help5Screen, transitions to the MainMenuScreen again.

```java
package com.badlogic.androidgames.jumper;

import java.util.List;

import javax.microedition.khronos.opengles.GL10;

import com.badlogic.androidgames.framework.Game;
import com.badlogic.androidgames.framework.Input.TouchEvent;
import com.badlogic.androidgames.framework.gl.Camera2D;
import com.badlogic.androidgames.framework.gl.SpriteBatcher;
import com.badlogic.androidgames.framework.gl.Texture;
import com.badlogic.androidgames.framework.gl.TextureRegion;
import com.badlogic.androidgames.framework.impl.GLScreen;
import com.badlogic.androidgames.framework.math.OverlapTester;
import com.badlogic.androidgames.framework.math.Rectangle;
import com.badlogic.androidgames.framework.math.Vector2;

public class HelpScreen extends GLScreen {
    Camera2D guiCam;
    SpriteBatcher batcher;
    Rectangle nextBounds;
    Vector2 touchPoint;
    Texture helpImage;
    TextureRegion helpRegion;
```

We have a couple of members again holding a camera, a SpriteBatcher, the rectangle for the arrow button, a vector for the touch point, and a Texture and TextureRegion for the help image.

```java
    public HelpScreen(Game game) {
        super(game);
```

```
        guiCam = new Camera2D(glGraphics, 320, 480);
        nextBounds = new Rectangle(320 - 64, 0, 64, 64);
        touchPoint = new Vector2();
        batcher = new SpriteBatcher(glGraphics, 1);
    }
```

In the constructor, we set up all members pretty much the same way we did in the
MainMenuScreen.

```
    @Override
    public void resume() {
        helpImage = new Texture(glGame, "help1.png" );
        helpRegion = new TextureRegion(helpImage, 0, 0, 320, 480);
    }

    @Override
    public void pause() {
        helpImage.dispose();
    }
```

In the resume() method, we load the actual help screen texture and create a
corresponding TextureRegion for rendering with the SpriteBatcher. We do the loading
in this method, as the OpenGL ES context might be lost. The textures for the
background and the UI elements are handled by the Assets and SuperJumper classes, as
discussed before. We don't need to deal with them in any of our screens. Additionally,
we dispose of the help image texture in the pause() method again to clean up memory.

```
    @Override
    public void update(float deltaTime) {
        List<TouchEvent> touchEvents = game.getInput().getTouchEvents();
        game.getInput().getKeyEvents();
        int len = touchEvents.size();
        for(int i = 0; i < len; i++) {
            TouchEvent event = touchEvents.get(i);
            touchPoint.set(event.x, event.y);
            guiCam.touchToWorld(touchPoint);

            if(event.type == TouchEvent.TOUCH_UP) {
                if(OverlapTester.pointInRectangle(nextBounds, touchPoint)) {
                    Assets.playSound(Assets.clickSound);
                    game.setScreen(new HelpScreen2(game));
                    return;
                }
            }
        }
    }
```

Next up is the update() method, which simply checks whether the arrow button was
pressed. In which case, we transition to the next help screen. We also play the click
sound.

```
    @Override
    public void present(float deltaTime) {
        GL10 gl = glGraphics.getGL();
        gl.glClear(GL10.GL_COLOR_BUFFER_BIT);
```

```
        guiCam.setViewportAndMatrices();

        gl.glEnable(GL10.GL_TEXTURE_2D);

        batcher.beginBatch(helpImage);
        batcher.drawSprite(160, 240, 320, 480, helpRegion);
        batcher.endBatch();

        gl.glEnable(GL10.GL_BLEND);
        gl.glBlendFunc(GL10.GL_SRC_ALPHA, GL10.GL_ONE_MINUS_SRC_ALPHA);

        batcher.beginBatch(Assets.items);
        batcher.drawSprite(320 - 32, 32, -64, 64, Assets.arrow);
        batcher.endBatch();

        gl.glDisable(GL10.GL_BLEND);
    }

    @Override
    public void dispose() {
    }
}
```

In the present() method, we clear the screen, set up the matrices, render the help image in one batch, and then render the arrow button. Of course, we don't need to render the background image here as the help image already contains that.

The other help screens are analogous as outlined before.

The High-Scores Screen

Next on our list is the high-scores screen. Here, we'll use part of the main menu UI labels (the HIGHSCORES portion) and render the high scores stored in Settings via the Font instance we store in the Assets class. Of course, we have an arrow button so that the player can get back to the main menu. Listing 9–7 shows the code.

Listing 9–7. *HighscoresScreen.java: The High-Scores Screen.*

```java
package com.badlogic.androidgames.jumper;

import java.util.List;

import javax.microedition.khronos.opengles.GL10;

import com.badlogic.androidgames.framework.Game;
import com.badlogic.androidgames.framework.Input.TouchEvent;
import com.badlogic.androidgames.framework.gl.Camera2D;
import com.badlogic.androidgames.framework.gl.SpriteBatcher;
import com.badlogic.androidgames.framework.impl.GLScreen;
import com.badlogic.androidgames.framework.math.OverlapTester;
import com.badlogic.androidgames.framework.math.Rectangle;
import com.badlogic.androidgames.framework.math.Vector2;

public class HighscoreScreen extends GLScreen {
    Camera2D guiCam;
```

```
SpriteBatcher batcher;
Rectangle backBounds;
Vector2 touchPoint;
String[] highScores;
float xOffset = 0;
```

As always, we have a couple of members for the camera, the SpriteBatcher, bounds for the arrow button, and so on. In the highscores array, we store the formatted strings for each high score we present to the player. The xOffset member is a value we compute to offset the rendering of each line so that the lines are centered horizontally.

```
public HighscoreScreen(Game game) {
    super(game);

    guiCam = new Camera2D(glGraphics, 320, 480);
    backBounds = new Rectangle(0, 0, 64, 64);
    touchPoint = new Vector2();
    batcher = new SpriteBatcher(glGraphics, 100);
    highScores = new String[5];
    for(int i = 0; i < 5; i++) {
        highScores[i] = (i + 1) + ". " + Settings.highscores[i];
        xOffset = Math.max(highScores[i].length() * Assets.font.glyphWidth,
xOffset);
    }
    xOffset = 160 - xOffset / 2;
}
```

In the constructor, we set up all members as usual and compute that xOffset value. We do so by evaluating the size of the longest string out of the five strings we create for the five high scores. Since our bitmap font is fixed-width, we can easily calculate the number of pixels needed for a single line of text by multiplying the number of characters with the glyph width. This will, of course, not account for nonprintable characters or characters outside of the ASCII character set. Since we know that we won't be using those, we can get away with this simple calculation. The last line in the constructor then subtracts half of the longest line width from 160 (the horizontal center of our target screen of 320×480 pixels) and adjusts it further by subtracting half of the glyph width. This is needed since the Font.drawText() method uses the glyph centers instead of one of the corner points.

```
@Override
public void update(float deltaTime) {
    List<TouchEvent> touchEvents = game.getInput().getTouchEvents();
    game.getInput().getKeyEvents();
    int len = touchEvents.size();
    for(int i = 0; i < len; i++) {
        TouchEvent event = touchEvents.get(i);
        touchPoint.set(event.x, event.y);
        guiCam.touchToWorld(touchPoint);

        if(event.type == TouchEvent.TOUCH_UP) {
            if(OverlapTester.pointInRectangle(backBounds, touchPoint)) {
                game.setScreen(new MainMenu(game));
                return;
            }
        }
```

```
            }
        }
    }
```

The update() method just checks whether the arrow button was pressed, in which case, it plays the click sound and transitions back to the main menu screen.

```java
@Override
public void present(float deltaTime) {
    GL10 gl = glGraphics.getGL();
    gl.glClear(GL10.GL_COLOR_BUFFER_BIT);
    guiCam.setViewportAndMatrices();

    gl.glEnable(GL10.GL_TEXTURE_2D);

    batcher.beginBatch(Assets.background);
    batcher.drawSprite(160, 240, 320, 480, Assets.backgroundRegion);
    batcher.endBatch();

    gl.glEnable(GL10.GL_BLEND);
    gl.glBlendFunc(GL10.GL_SRC_ALPHA, GL10.GL_ONE_MINUS_SRC_ALPHA);

    batcher.beginBatch(Assets.items);
    batcher.drawSprite(160, 360, 300, 33, Assets.highScoresRegion);

    float y = 240;
    for(int i = 4; i >= 0; i--) {
        Assets.font.drawText(batcher, highScores[i], xOffset, y);
        y += Assets.font.glyphHeight;
    }

    batcher.drawSprite(32, 32, 64, 64, Assets.arrow);
    batcher.endBatch();

    gl.glDisable(GL10.GL_BLEND);
}

@Override
public void resume() {
}

@Override
public void pause() {
}

@Override
public void dispose() {
}
}
```

The present() method is again very straightforward. We clear the screen, set the matrices, render the background, render the highscores portion of the main menu labels, and then render the five highscore lines using the xOffset we calculated in the constructor. Now we can see why the Font does not do any texture binding: we can batch the five calls to Font.drawText(). Of course, we have to make sure that the SpriteBatcher instance can batch as many sprites (or glyphs in this case) as are needed for rendering our texts. We made sure it can when creating it in the constructor with a maximum batch size of 100 sprites (glyphs).

Now it's time to look at the classes of our simulation.

The Simulation Classes

Before we can dive into the game screen, we need to create our simulation classes. We'll follow the same pattern as in Mr. Nom, with a class for each game object and an all-knowing superclass called World that ties together the loose ends and makes our game world tick. We'll need classes for the following:

- Bob
- Squirrels
- Springs
- Coins
- Platforms

Bob, squirrels, and platforms can move, so we'll base their classes on the DynamicGameObject we created in the last chapter. Springs and coins are static, so those will derive from the GameObject class. The tasks of each of our simulation classes are as follows:

- Store the position, velocity, and bounding shape of the object.
- Store the state and length of time that the object has been in that state (state time) if needed.
- Provide an update() method that will advance the object if needed according to its behavior.
- Provide methods to change an object's state (for example, tell Bob he's dead or hit a spring).

The World class will then keep track of multiple instances of these objects, update them each frame, check collisions between objects and Bob, and carry out the collision responses (that is, let Bob die, collect a coin, and so forth). We will go through each class, from simplest to most complex.

The Spring Class

Let's start with the Spring class in Listing 9–8.

Listing 9–8. *Spring.java, the Spring Class.*

```
package com.badlogic.androidgames.jumper;

import com.badlogic.androidgames.framework.GameObject;

public class Spring extends GameObject {
    public static float SPRING_WIDTH = 0.3f;
```

```
    public static float SPRING_HEIGHT = 0.3f;

    public Spring(float x, float y) {
        super(x, y, SPRING_WIDTH, SPRING_HEIGHT);
    }
}
```

The Spring class derives from the GameObject class: we only need a position and bounding shape since a spring does not move.

Next, we define two constants that are publicly accessible: the spring width and height in meters. We estimated those values previously, and we just reuse them here.

The final piece is the constructor, which takes the x- and y-coordinates of the spring's center. With this, we call the constructor of the superclass GameObject, which takes the position as well as the width and height of the object from which to construct a bounding shape (a Rectangle centered around the given position). With this information, our Spring is fully defined, having a position and bounding shape against which to collide.

The Coin Class

Next up is the class for coins in Listing 9–9.

Listing 9–9. *Coin.java, the Coin Class.*

```
package com.badlogic.androidgames.jumper;

import com.badlogic.androidgames.framework.GameObject;

public class Coin extends GameObject {
    public static final float COIN_WIDTH = 0.5f;
    public static final float COIN_HEIGHT = 0.8f;
    public static final int COIN_SCORE = 10;

    float stateTime;
    public Coin(float x, float y) {
        super(x, y, COIN_WIDTH, COIN_HEIGHT);
        stateTime = 0;
    }

    public void update(float deltaTime) {
        stateTime += deltaTime;
    }
}
```

The Coin class is pretty much the same as the Spring class, with only one difference: we keep track of the duration the coin has been alive already. This information is needed when we want to render the coin later on using an Animation. We did the same thing for our cavemen in the last example of the last chapter. It is a technique we'll use for all our simulation classes. Given a state and a state time, we can select an Animation, as well as the keyframe of that Animation to use for rendering. The coin only has a single state, so we only need to keep track of the state time. For that we have the update() method, which will increase the state time by the delta time passed to it.

The constants defined at the top of the class specify a coin's width and height as we defined it before, as well as the number of points Bob earns if he hits a coin.

The Castle Class

Next up, we have a class for the castle at the top of our world. Listing 9–10 shows the code.

Listing 9–10. *Castle.java, the Castle Class.*

```
package com.badlogic.androidgames.jumper;

import com.badlogic.androidgames.framework.GameObject;

public class Castle extends GameObject {
    public static float CASTLE_WIDTH = 1.7f;
    public static float CASTLE_HEIGHT = 1.7f;

    public Castle(float x, float y) {
        super(x, y, CASTLE_WIDTH, CASTLE_HEIGHT);
    }

}
```

Not too complex. All we need to store is the position and bounds of the castle. The size of a castle is defined by the constants CASTLE_WIDTH and CASTLE_HEIGHT, using the values we discussed earlier.

The Squirrel Class

Next is the Squirrel class in Listing 9–11.

Listing 9–11. *Squirrel.java, the Squirrel Class.*

```
package com.badlogic.androidgames.jumper;

import com.badlogic.androidgames.framework.DynamicGameObject;

public class Squirrel extends DynamicGameObject {
    public static final float SQUIRREL_WIDTH = 1;
    public static final float SQUIRREL_HEIGHT = 0.6f;
    public static final float SQUIRREL_VELOCITY = 3f;

    float stateTime = 0;

    public Squirrel(float x, float y) {
        super(x, y, SQUIRREL_WIDTH, SQUIRREL_HEIGHT);
        velocity.set(SQUIRREL_VELOCITY, 0);
    }

    public void update(float deltaTime) {
```

```
        position.add(velocity.x * deltaTime, velocity.y * deltaTime);
        bounds.lowerLeft.set(position).sub(SQUIRREL_WIDTH / 2, SQUIRREL_HEIGHT / 2);

        if(position.x < SQUIRREL_WIDTH / 2 ) {
            position.x = SQUIRREL_WIDTH / 2;
            velocity.x = SQUIRREL_VELOCITY;
        }
        if(position.x > World.WORLD_WIDTH - SQUIRREL_WIDTH / 2) {
            position.x = World.WORLD_WIDTH - SQUIRREL_WIDTH / 2;
            velocity.x = -SQUIRREL_VELOCITY;
        }
        stateTime += deltaTime;
    }
}
```

Squirrels are moving objects, so we let the class derive from DynamicGameObject, which gives us a velocity and acceleration vector as well. The first thing we do is define a squirrel's size, as well as its velocity. Since a squirrel is animated, we also keep track of its state time. A squirrel has a single state, like a coin: moving horizontally. Whether it moves to the left or right can be decided based on the velocity vector's x-component, so we don't need to store a separate state member for that.

In the constructor, we of course call the superclass's constructor with the initial position and size of the squirrel. We also set the velocity vector to (SQUIRREL_VELOCITY,0). All squirrels will thus move to the right in the beginning.

The update() method updates the position and bounding shape of the squirrel based on the velocity and delta time. It's our standard Euler integration step, which we talked about and used a lot in the last chapter. We also check whether the squirrel hit the left or right edge of the world. If that's the case, we simply invert its velocity vector so that it starts moving in the opposite direction. Our world's width is fixed at a value of 10 meters, as discussed earlier. The last thing we do is update the state time based on the delta time so that we can decide which of the two animation frames we need to use for rendering that squirrel later on.

The Platform Class

The Platform class is shown in Listing 9–12.

Listing 9–12. *Platform.java, the Platform Class.*

```
package com.badlogic.androidgames.jumper;

import com.badlogic.androidgames.framework.DynamicGameObject;

public class Platform extends DynamicGameObject {
    public static final float PLATFORM_WIDTH = 2;
    public static final float PLATFORM_HEIGHT = 0.5f;
    public static final int PLATFORM_TYPE_STATIC = 0;
    public static final int PLATFORM_TYPE_MOVING = 1;
    public static final int PLATFORM_STATE_NORMAL = 0;
    public static final int PLATFORM_STATE_PULVERIZING = 1;
    public static final float PLATFORM_PULVERIZE_TIME = 0.2f * 4;
```

```java
public static final float PLATFORM_VELOCITY = 2;
```

Platforms are a little bit more complex, of course. Let's go over the constants defined in the class. The first two constants define the width and height of a platform, as discussed earlier. A platform has a type; it can be either a static platform or a moving platform. We denote this via the constants PLATFORM_TYPE_STATIC and PLATFORM_TYPE_MOVING. A platform can also be in one of two states: it can be in a normal state—that is, either sitting there statically or moving—or it can be pulverized. The state is encoded via one of the constants PLATFORM_STATE_NORMAL or PLATFORM_STATE_PULVERIZING. Pulverization is, of course, a process limited in time. We therefore define the time it takes for a platform to be completely pulverized, which is 0.8 seconds. This value is simply derived from the number of frames in the Animation of the platform and the duration of each frame—one of the little quirks we have to accept while trying to follow the MVC pattern. Finally, we define the speed of moving platforms to be 2 m/s, as discussed earlier. A moving platform will behave exactly like a squirrel in that it just travels in one direction until it hits the world's horizontal boundaries, in which case it just inverts its direction.

```java
int type;
int state;
float stateTime;

public Platform(int type, float x, float y) {
    super(x, y, PLATFORM_WIDTH, PLATFORM_HEIGHT);
    this.type = type;
    this.state = PLATFORM_STATE_NORMAL;
    this.stateTime = 0;
    if(type == PLATFORM_TYPE_MOVING) {
        velocity.x = PLATFORM_VELOCITY;
    }
}
```

To store the type, the state, and the state time of the Platform instance, we need three members. These get initialized in the constructor based on the type of the Platform, which is a parameter of the constructor, along with the platform center's position.

```java
public void update(float deltaTime) {
    if(type == PLATFORM_TYPE_MOVING) {
        position.add(velocity.x * deltaTime, 0);
        bounds.lowerLeft.set(position).sub(PLATFORM_WIDTH / 2, PLATFORM_HEIGHT / 2);

        if(position.x < PLATFORM_WIDTH / 2) {
            velocity.x = -velocity.x;
            position.x = PLATFORM_WIDTH / 2;
        }
        if(position.x > World.WORLD_WIDTH - PLATFORM_WIDTH / 2) {
            velocity.x = -velocity.x;
            position.x = World.WORLD_WIDTH - PLATFORM_WIDTH / 2;
        }
    }

    stateTime += deltaTime;
}
```

The update() method will move the platform and check for the out-of-world condition, acting accordingly by inverting the velocity vector. This is exactly the same thing we did in the Squirrel.update() method. We also update the state time at the end of the method.

```
public void pulverize() {
    state = PLATFORM_STATE_PULVERIZING;
    stateTime = 0;
    velocity.x = 0;
}
}
```

The final method of this class is called pulverize(). It switches the state from PLATFORM_STATE_NORMAL to PLATFORM_STATE_PULVERIZING and resets the state time and velocity. This means that moving platforms will stop moving. The method will be called if the World class detects a collision between Bob and the Platform, and it decides to pulverize the Platform based on a random number. We'll talk about that in a bit.

The Bob Class

First we need to talk about Bob. The Bob class is shown in Listing 9–13.

Listing 9–13. *Bob.java.*

```
package com.badlogic.androidgames.jumper;

import com.badlogic.androidgames.framework.DynamicGameObject;

public class Bob extends DynamicGameObject{
    public static final int BOB_STATE_JUMP = 0;
    public static final int BOB_STATE_FALL = 1;
    public static final int BOB_STATE_HIT = 2;
    public static final float BOB_JUMP_VELOCITY = 11;
    public static final float BOB_MOVE_VELOCITY = 20;
    public static final float BOB_WIDTH = 0.8f;
    public static final float BOB_HEIGHT = 0.8f;
```

We start with a couple of constants again. Bob can be in one of three states: jumping upward, falling downward, or being hit. He also has a vertical jump velocity, which is only applied on the y-axis, and a horizontal move velocity, which is only applied on the x-axis. The final two constants define Bob's width and height in the world. Of course, we also have to store Bob's state and state time.

```
    int state;
    float stateTime;

    public Bob(float x, float y) {
        super(x, y, BOB_WIDTH, BOB_HEIGHT);
        state = BOB_STATE_FALL;
        stateTime = 0;
    }
```

The constructor just calls the superclass's constructor so that Bob's center position and bounding shape are initialized correctly, and then initializes the state and stateTime member variables.

```java
public void update(float deltaTime) {
        velocity.add(World.gravity.x * deltaTime, World.gravity.y * deltaTime);
        position.add(velocity.x * deltaTime, velocity.y * deltaTime);
        bounds.lowerLeft.set(position).sub(bounds.width / 2, bounds.height / 2);

        if(velocity.y > 0 && state != BOB_STATE_HIT) {
            if(state != BOB_STATE_JUMP) {
                state = BOB_STATE_JUMP;
                stateTime = 0;
            }
        }

        if(velocity.y < 0 && state != BOB_STATE_HIT) {
            if(state != BOB_STATE_FALL) {
                state = BOB_STATE_FALL;
                stateTime = 0;
            }
        }

        if(position.x < 0)
            position.x = World.WORLD_WIDTH;
        if(position.x > World.WORLD_WIDTH)
            position.x = 0;

        stateTime += deltaTime;
    }
```

The update() method starts off by updating Bob's position and bounding shape based on gravity and his current velocity. Note that the velocity is a composite of the gravity and Bob's own movement due to jumping and moving horizontally. The next two big conditional blocks set Bob's state to either BOB_STATE_JUMPING or BOB_STATE_FALLING, and reinitialize his state time depending on the y component of his velocity. If it is greater than zero, Bob is jumping; if it is smaller than zero, Bob is falling. We only do this if Bob hasn't been hit and if he isn't already in the correct state. Otherwise, we'd always reset the state time to zero, which wouldn't play nice with Bob's animation later on. We also wrap Bob from one edge of the world to the other if he leaves the world to the left or right. Finally, we update the stateTime member again.

From where does Bob get his velocity apart from gravity? That's where the other methods come in.

```java
    public void hitSquirrel() {
        velocity.set(0,0);
        state = BOB_STATE_HIT;
        stateTime = 0;
    }

    public void hitPlatform() {
        velocity.y = BOB_JUMP_VELOCITY;
        state = BOB_STATE_JUMP;
        stateTime = 0;
```

```
    }

    public void hitSpring() {
        velocity.y = BOB_JUMP_VELOCITY * 1.5f;
        state = BOB_STATE_JUMP;
        stateTime = 0;
    }
}
```

The method `hitSquirrel()` is called by the `World` class in case Bob hits a squirrel. If that's the case, Bob stops moving by himself and enters the `BOB_STATE_HIT` state. Only gravity will apply to Bob from this point on; the player can't control him anymore, and he doesn't interact with platforms any longer. That's similar to the behavior Super Mario exhibits when he gets hit by an enemy. He just falls down.

The `hitPlatform()` method is also called by the `World` class. It will be invoked when Bob hits a platform while falling downward. If that's the case, then we set his y velocity to `BOB_JUMP_VELOCITY`, and we also set his state and state time accordingly. From this point on, Bob will move upward until gravity wins again, making Bob fall down.

The last method, `hitSpring()`, is invoked by the `World` class if Bob hits a spring. It does the same thing as the `hitPlatform()` method, with one exception; that is, the initial upward velocity is set to 1.5 times `BOB_JUMP_VELOCITY`. This means that Bob will jump a little higher when hitting a spring compared with when he hits a platform.

The World Class

The last class we have to discuss is the `World` class. It's a little longer, so we'll split it up. Listing 9–14 shows the first part of the code.

Listing 9–14. *Excerpt from World.java: Constants, Members, and Initialization.*

```
package com.badlogic.androidgames.jumper;

import java.util.ArrayList;
import java.util.List;
import java.util.Random;

import com.badlogic.androidgames.framework.math.OverlapTester;
import com.badlogic.androidgames.framework.math.Vector2;

public class World {
    public interface WorldListener {
        public void jump();
        public void highJump();
        public void hit();
        public void coin();
    }
```

The first thing we define is an interface called `WorldListener`. What does it do? We need it to solve a little MVC problem: when do we play sound effects? We could just add invocations of `Assets.playSound()` to the respective simulation classes, but that's not very clean. Instead, we'll let a user of the `World` class register a `WorldListener`, which will be called when Bob jumps from a platform, jumps from a spring, gets hit by a squirrel, or collects a coin. We will later register a listener that plays back the proper sound effects for each of those events, keeping the simulation classes clean from any direct dependencies on rendering and audio playback.

```java
public static final float WORLD_WIDTH = 10;
public static final float WORLD_HEIGHT = 15 * 20;
public static final int WORLD_STATE_RUNNING = 0;
public static final int WORLD_STATE_NEXT_LEVEL = 1;
public static final int WORLD_STATE_GAME_OVER = 2;
public static final Vector2 gravity = new Vector2(0, -12);
```

Next, we define a couple of constants. The WORLD_WIDTH and WORLD_HEIGHT specify the extents of our world horizontally and vertically. Remember that our view frustum will show a region of 10×15 meters of our world. Given the constants defined here, our world will span 20 view frustums or screens vertically. Again, that's a value we came up with by tuning. We'll get back to it when we discuss how we generate a level. The world can also be in one of three states: running, waiting for the next level to start, or the game-over state—when Bob falls too far (outside of the view frustum). We also define our gravity acceleration vector as a constant here.

```java
public final Bob bob;
public final List<Platform> platforms;
public final List<Spring> springs;
public final List<Squirrel> squirrels;
public final List<Coin> coins;
public Castle castle;
public final WorldListener listener;
public final Random rand;

public float heightSoFar;
public int score;
public int state;
```

Next up are all the members of the World class. It keeps track of Bob; all the Platforms, Springs, Squirrels, and Coins; and the Castle. Additionally, it has a reference to a WorldListener and an instance of Random, which we'll use to generate random numbers for various purposes. The last three members keep track of the highest height Bob has reached so far, as well as the World's state and the score achieved.

```java
public World(WorldListener listener) {
    this.bob = new Bob(5, 1);
    this.platforms = new ArrayList<Platform>();
    this.springs = new ArrayList<Spring>();
    this.squirrels = new ArrayList<Squirrel>();
    this.coins = new ArrayList<Coin>();
    this.listener = listener;
    rand = new Random();
    generateLevel();

    this.heightSoFar = 0;
    this.score = 0;
    this.state = WORLD_STATE_RUNNING;
```

```
    }
```

The constructor initializes all members and also stores the `WorldListener` passed as a parameter. Bob is placed in the middle of the world horizontally and a little bit above the ground at (5,1). The rest is pretty much self-explanatory, with one exception: the `generateLevel()` method.

Generating the World

You might have wondered already how we actually create and place the objects in our world. We use a method called procedural generation. We come up with a simple algorithm that will generate a random level for us. Listing 9–15 shows the code.

Listing 9–15. *Excerpt from World.java: The generateLevel() Method.*

```java
private void generateLevel() {
    float y = Platform.PLATFORM_HEIGHT / 2;
    float maxJumpHeight = Bob.BOB_JUMP_VELOCITY * Bob.BOB_JUMP_VELOCITY
            / (2 * -gravity.y);
    while (y < WORLD_HEIGHT - WORLD_WIDTH / 2) {
        int type = rand.nextFloat() > 0.8f ? Platform.PLATFORM_TYPE_MOVING
                : Platform.PLATFORM_TYPE_STATIC;
        float x = rand.nextFloat()
                * (WORLD_WIDTH - Platform.PLATFORM_WIDTH)
                + Platform.PLATFORM_WIDTH / 2;

        Platform platform = new Platform(type, x, y);
        platforms.add(platform);

        if (rand.nextFloat() > 0.9f
                && type != Platform.PLATFORM_TYPE_MOVING) {
            Spring spring = new Spring(platform.position.x,
                    platform.position.y + Platform.PLATFORM_HEIGHT / 2
                            + Spring.SPRING_HEIGHT / 2);
            springs.add(spring);
        }

        if (y > WORLD_HEIGHT / 3 && rand.nextFloat() > 0.8f) {
            Squirrel squirrel = new Squirrel(platform.position.x
                    + rand.nextFloat(), platform.position.y
                    + Squirrel.SQUIRREL_HEIGHT + rand.nextFloat() * 2);
            squirrels.add(squirrel);
        }

        if (rand.nextFloat() > 0.6f) {
            Coin coin = new Coin(platform.position.x + rand.nextFloat(),
                    platform.position.y + Coin.COIN_HEIGHT
                            + rand.nextFloat() * 3);
            coins.add(coin);
        }

        y += (maxJumpHeight - 0.5f);
        y -= rand.nextFloat() * (maxJumpHeight / 3);
    }
```

```
    castle = new Castle(WORLD_WIDTH / 2, y);
}
```

Let's outline the general idea of the algorithm in plain words:

1. Start at the bottom of the world at y = 0.

2. While we haven't reached the top of the world yet, do the following:

   a. Create a platform, either moving or stationary at the current y position with a random x position.

   b. Fetch a random number between 0 and 1 and, if it is greater than 0.9 and if the platform is not moving, create a spring on top of the platform.

   c. If we are above the first third of the level, fetch a random number and, if it is above 0.8, create a squirrel offset randomly from the platform's position.

   d. Fetch a random number and, if it is greater than 0.6, create a coin offset randomly from the platform's position.

   e. Increase y by the maximum normal jump height of Bob, decrease it a tiny bit randomly—but only so far that it doesn't fall below the last y value—and go to 2.

3. Place the castle at the last y position, centered horizontally.

The big secret of this procedure is how we increase the y position for the next platform in step 2e. We have to make sure that each subsequent platform is reachable by Bob by jumping from the current platform. Bob can only jump as high as gravity allows, given his initial jump velocity of 11 m/s vertically. How can we calculate how high Bob will jump? We can do this with the following formula:

```
height = velocity x velocity / (2 x  gravity) = 11 x 11 / (2 x 13) ~= 4.6m
```

This means that we should have a distance of 4.6 meters vertically between each platform so that Bob can still reach it. To make sure that all platforms are reachable, we use a value that's a little bit less than the maximum jump height. This guarantees that Bob will always be able to jump from one platform to the next. The horizontal placement of platforms is again random. Given Bob's horizontal movement speed of 20 m/s, we can be more than sure that he will not only be able to reach a platform vertically but also horizontally.

The other objects are created based on chance. The method `Random.nextFloat()` returns a random number between 0 and 1 on each invocation, where each number has the same probability of occurring. Squirrels are only generated when the random number we fetch from `Random` is greater than 0.8. This means that we'll generate a squirrel with a probability of 20 percent (1 – 0.8). The same is true for all other randomly-created objects. By tuning these values, we can have more or fewer objects in our world.

Updating the World

Once we have generated our world, we can update all objects in it and check for collisions. Listing 9–16 shows the update methods of the World class.

Listing 9–16. *Excerpt from World.java: The Update Methods*

```java
public void update(float deltaTime, float accelX) {
    updateBob(deltaTime, accelX);
    updatePlatforms(deltaTime);
    updateSquirrels(deltaTime);
    updateCoins(deltaTime);
    if (bob.state != Bob.BOB_STATE_HIT)
        checkCollisions();
    checkGameOver();
}
```

The method update() is the one called by our game screen later on. It receives the delta time and acceleration on the x-axis of the accelerometer as an argument. It is responsible for calling the other update methods, as well as performing the collision checks and game-over check. We have an update method for each object type in our world.

```java
private void updateBob(float deltaTime, float accelX) {
    if (bob.state != Bob.BOB_STATE_HIT && bob.position.y <= 0.5f)
        bob.hitPlatform();
    if (bob.state != Bob.BOB_STATE_HIT)
        bob.velocity.x = -accelX / 10 * Bob.BOB_MOVE_VELOCITY;
    bob.update(deltaTime);
    heightSoFar = Math.max(bob.position.y, heightSoFar);
}
```

The updateBob() method is responsible for updating Bob's state. The first thing it does is check whether Bob is hitting the bottom of the world, in which case Bob is instructed to jump. This means that, at the start of each level, Bob is allowed to jump off the ground of our world. As soon as the ground is out of sight, this won't work anymore, of course. Next, we update Bob's horizontal velocity that is based on the value of the x-axis of the accelerometer we get as an argument. As discussed, we normalize this value from a range of –10 to 10 to a range of –1 to 1 (full left tilt to full right tilt), and then multiply it by Bob's standard movement velocity. Next, we tell Bob to update himself by calling the Bob.update() method. The last thing we do is keep track of the highest y position Bob has reached so far. We need this to determine whether Bob has fallen too far later on.

```java
private void updatePlatforms(float deltaTime) {
    int len = platforms.size();
    for (int i = 0; i < len; i++) {
        Platform platform = platforms.get(i);
        platform.update(deltaTime);
        if (platform.state == Platform.PLATFORM_STATE_PULVERIZING
                && platform.stateTime > Platform.PLATFORM_PULVERIZE_TIME) {
            platforms.remove(platform);
            len = platforms.size();
        }
```

```
    }
}
```

Next, we update all the platforms in updatePlatforms(). We loop through the list of platforms and call each platform's update() method with the current delta time. In case the platform is in the process of pulverization, we check for how long that has been going on. If the platform is in the PLATFORM_STATE_PULVERIZING state for more than PLATFORM_PULVERIZE_TIME, we simply remove the platform from our list of platforms.

```java
private void updateSquirrels(float deltaTime) {
    int len = squirrels.size();
    for (int i = 0; i < len; i++) {
        Squirrel squirrel = squirrels.get(i);
        squirrel.update(deltaTime);
    }
}

private void updateCoins(float deltaTime) {
    int len = coins.size();
    for (int i = 0; i < len; i++) {
        Coin coin = coins.get(i);
        coin.update(deltaTime);
    }
}
```

In the updateSquirrels() method, we update each Squirrel instance via its update() method, passing in the current delta time. We do the same for coins in the updateCoins() method.

Collision Detection and Response

Looking back at our original World.update() method, we can see that the next thing we do is check for collisions between Bob and all the other objects with which he can collide in the world. We only do this if Bob is in a state not equal to BOB_STATE_HIT, in which case he just continues to fall down due to gravity. Let's have a look at those collision-checking methods in Listing 9–17.

Listing 9–17. *Excerpt from World.java: The Collision-Checking Methods.*

```java
private void checkCollisions() {
    checkPlatformCollisions();
    checkSquirrelCollisions();
    checkItemCollisions();
    checkCastleCollisions();
}
```

The checkCollisions() method is more or less another master method, which simply invokes all the other collision-checking methods. Bob can collide with a couple of things in the world: platforms, squirrels, coins, springs, and the castle. For each of those object types, we have a separate collision-checking method. Remember that we invoke this method and the slave methods after we have updated the positions and bounding shapes of all objects in our world. Think of it as a snapshot of the state of our world at the given point in time. All we do is observe this still image and see whether anything overlaps. We can then take action and make sure that the objects that collide react to those overlaps or collisions in the next frame by manipulating their states, positions, velocities, and so on.

```java
private void checkPlatformCollisions() {
    if (bob.velocity.y > 0)
        return;

    int len = platforms.size();
    for (int i = 0; i < len; i++) {
        Platform platform = platforms.get(i);
        if (bob.position.y > platform.position.y) {
            if (OverlapTester
                    .overlapRectangles(bob.bounds, platform.bounds)) {
                bob.hitPlatform();
                listener.jump();
                if (rand.nextFloat() > 0.5f) {
                    platform.pulverize();
                }
                break;
            }
        }
    }
}
```

In the checkPlatformCollisions() method, we test for overlap between Bob and any of the platforms in our world. We break out of that method early in case Bob is currently on his way up. This way Bob can pass through platforms from below. For Super Jumper, that's good behavior; in a game like Super Mario Brothers, we'd probably want Bob to fall down if he hits a block from below.

Next, we loop through all platforms and check whether Bob is above the current platform. If he is, we test whether his bounding rectangle overlaps the bounding rectangle of the platform, in which case, we tell Bob that he hit a platform via a call to Bob.hitPlatform(). Looking back at that method, we see that it will trigger a jump and set Bob's states accordingly. Next, we call the WorldListener.jump() method to inform the listener that Bob has just started to jump again. We'll use this later on to play back a corresponding sound effect in the listener. The last thing we do is fetch a random number and, if it is above 0.5, we tell the platform to pulverize itself. It will be alive for another PLATFORM_PULVERIZE_TIME seconds (0.8) and will then be removed in the updatePlatforms() method shown earlier. When we render that platform, we'll use its state time to determine which of the platform animation keyframes to play back.

```java
private void checkSquirrelCollisions() {
    int len = squirrels.size();
    for (int i = 0; i < len; i++) {
        Squirrel squirrel = squirrels.get(i);
        if (OverlapTester.overlapRectangles(squirrel.bounds, bob.bounds)) {
            bob.hitSquirrel();
            listener.hit();
        }
    }
}
```

The method checkSquirrelCollisions() tests Bob's bounding rectangle against the bounding rectangle of each squirrel. If Bob hits a squirrel, we tell him to enter the BOB_STATE_HIT state, which will make him fall down without the player being able to control him any further. We also tell the WorldListener about it so that he can play back a sound effect, for example.

```java
private void checkItemCollisions() {
    int len = coins.size();
    for (int i = 0; i < len; i++) {
        Coin coin = coins.get(i);
        if (OverlapTester.overlapRectangles(bob.bounds, coin.bounds)) {
            coins.remove(coin);
            len = coins.size();
            listener.coin();
            score += Coin.COIN_SCORE;
        }

    }

    if (bob.velocity.y > 0)
        return;

    len = springs.size();
    for (int i = 0; i < len; i++) {
        Spring spring = springs.get(i);
        if (bob.position.y > spring.position.y) {
            if (OverlapTester.overlapRectangles(bob.bounds, spring.bounds)) {
                bob.hitSpring();
                listener.highJump();
            }
        }
    }
}
```

The checkItemCollisions() method checks Bob against all coins in the world and against all springs. In case Bob hits a coin, we remove the coin from our world, tell the listener that a coin was collected, and increase the current score by COIN_SCORE. In case Bob is falling downward, we also check Bob against all springs in the world. In case he hits one, we tell him about it so that he'll perform a higher jump than usual. We also inform the listener of this event.

```java
private void checkCastleCollisions() {
    if (OverlapTester.overlapRectangles(castle.bounds, bob.bounds)) {
        state = WORLD_STATE_NEXT_LEVEL;
    }
}
```

The final method checks Bob against the castle. If Bob hits it, we set the world's state to WORLD_STATE_NEXT_LEVEL, signaling any outside entity (such as our game screen) that we should transition to the next level, which will again be a randomly generated instance of World.

Game Over, Buddy!

The last method in the `World` class, which is invoked in the last line of the
`World.update()` method, is shown in Listing 9–18.

Listing 9–18. *The Rest of World.java: The Game Over–Checking Method.*

```
    private void checkGameOver() {
        if (heightSoFar - 7.5f > bob.position.y) {
            state = WORLD_STATE_GAME_OVER;
        }
    }
}
```

Remember how we defined the game-over state: Bob must leave the bottom of the view
frustum. The view frustum is, of course, governed by a `Camera2D` instance, which has a
position. The y-coordinate of that position is always equal to the biggest y-coordinate
Bob has had so far, so the camera will somewhat follow Bob on his way upward. Since
we want to keep the rendering and simulation code separate, we don't have a reference
to the camera in our world though. We thus keep track of Bob's highest y-coordinate in
`updateBob()` and store that value in `heightSoFar`. We know that our view frustum will
have a height of 15 meters. Thus, we also know that if Bob's y-coordinate is below
`heightSoFar` – 7.5, then he has left the view frustum on the bottom edge. That's when
Bob is declared to be dead. Of course, this is a tiny bit hackish, as it is based on the
assumption that the view frustum's height will always be 15 meters and that the camera
will always be at the highest y-coordinate Bob has been able to reach so far. If we had
allowed zooming or used a different camera-following method, this would no longer hold
true. Instead of overcomplicating things, we'll just leave it as is though. You will often
face such decisions in game development, as it is hard at times to keep everything clean
from a software engineering point of view (as evidenced by our overuse of public or
package private members).

You may be wondering why we don't use the `SpatialHashGrid` class we developed in
the last chapter. We'll show you the reason in a minute. Let's get our game done by
implementing the `GameScreen` class first.

The Game Screen

We are nearing the completion of Super Jumper. The last thing we need to implement is
the game screen, which will present the actual game world to the player and allow it to
interact with it. The game screen consists of five subscreens as shown in Figure 9–2. We
have the ready screen, the normal running screen, the next-level screen, the game-over
screen, and the pause screen. The game screen in Mr. Nom was similar to this; it only
lacked a next-level screen as there was only one level. We will use the same approach
as in Mr. Nom: we'll have separate update and present methods for all subscreens that
update and render the game world, as well as the UI elements that are part of the
subscreens. Since the game screen code is a little longer, we'll split it up into multiple
listings here. Listing 9–19 shows the first part of the game screen.

Listing 9–19. *Excerpt from GameScreen.java: Members and Constructor.*

```java
package com.badlogic.androidgames.jumper;

import java.util.List;

import javax.microedition.khronos.opengles.GL10;

import com.badlogic.androidgames.framework.Game;
import com.badlogic.androidgames.framework.Input.TouchEvent;
import com.badlogic.androidgames.framework.gl.Camera2D;
import com.badlogic.androidgames.framework.gl.FPSCounter;
import com.badlogic.androidgames.framework.gl.SpriteBatcher;
import com.badlogic.androidgames.framework.impl.GLScreen;
import com.badlogic.androidgames.framework.math.OverlapTester;
import com.badlogic.androidgames.framework.math.Rectangle;
import com.badlogic.androidgames.framework.math.Vector2;
import com.badlogic.androidgames.jumper.World.WorldListener;

public class GameScreen extends GLScreen {
    static final int GAME_READY = 0;
    static final int GAME_RUNNING = 1;
    static final int GAME_PAUSED = 2;
    static final int GAME_LEVEL_END = 3;
    static final int GAME_OVER = 4;

    int state;
    Camera2D guiCam;
    Vector2 touchPoint;
    SpriteBatcher batcher;
    World world;
    WorldListener worldListener;
    WorldRenderer renderer;
    Rectangle pauseBounds;
    Rectangle resumeBounds;
    Rectangle quitBounds;
    int lastScore;
    String scoreString;
```

The class starts off with a couple of constants defining the five states of the screen. Next, we have the members. We have a camera for rendering the UI elements, as well as a vector so that we can transform touch coordinates to world coordinates (as in the other screens, to a view frustum of 320×480 units, our target resolution). Next, we have a SpriteBatcher, a World instance, and a WorldListener. The WorldRenderer class is something we'll look into in a minute. It basically just takes a World and renders it. Note that it takes a reference to the SpriteBatcher, as well as the World, as parameters of its constructors. This means that we'll use the same SpriteBatcher to render the UI elements of the screen, as well as the game world. The rest of the members are Rectangles for different UI elements (such as the RESUME and QUIT menu entries on the paused subscreen) and two members for keeping track of the current score. We want to avoid creating a new string every frame when rendering the score so that we make the garbage collector happy.

```java
public GameScreen(Game game) {
    super(game);
    state = GAME_READY;
    guiCam = new Camera2D(glGraphics, 320, 480);
    touchPoint = new Vector2();
    batcher = new SpriteBatcher(glGraphics, 1000);
    worldListener = new WorldListener() {
        @Override
        public void jump() {
            Assets.playSound(Assets.jumpSound);
        }

        @Override
        public void highJump() {
            Assets.playSound(Assets.highJumpSound);
        }

        @Override
        public void hit() {
            Assets.playSound(Assets.hitSound);
        }

        @Override
        public void coin() {
            Assets.playSound(Assets.coinSound);
        }
    };
    world = new World(worldListener);
    renderer = new WorldRenderer(glGraphics, batcher, world);
    pauseBounds = new Rectangle(320- 64, 480- 64, 64, 64);
    resumeBounds = new Rectangle(160 - 96, 240, 192, 36);
    quitBounds = new Rectangle(160 - 96, 240 - 36, 192, 36);
    lastScore = 0;
    scoreString = "score: 0";
}
```

In the constructor, we initialize all the member variables. The only interesting thing here is the WorldListener we implement as an anonymous inner class. It's registered with the World instance, and it will play back sound effects according to the event that gets reported to it.

Updating the GameScreen

Next we have the update methods, which will make sure any user input is processed correctly and will also update the World instance if necessary. Listing 9–20 shows the code.

Listing 9–20. *Excerpt from GameScreen.java: The Update Methods.*

```java
@Override
public void update(float deltaTime) {
    if(deltaTime > 0.1f)
        deltaTime = 0.1f;

    switch(state) {
```

```
        case GAME_READY:
            updateReady();
            break;
        case GAME_RUNNING:
            updateRunning(deltaTime);
            break;
        case GAME_PAUSED:
            updatePaused();
            break;
        case GAME_LEVEL_END:
            updateLevelEnd();
            break;
        case GAME_OVER:
            updateGameOver();
            break;
    }
}
```

We have the GLScreen.update() method as the master method again, which calls one of the other update methods depending on the current state of the screen. Note that we limit the delta time to 0.1 seconds. Why do we do that? In Chapter 6, we talked about a bug in the direct ByteBuffers in Android version 1.5, which generates garbage. We will have that problem in Super Jumper as well on Android 1.5 devices. Every now and then, our game will be interrupted for a couple of hundred milliseconds by the garbage collector. This would be reflected in a delta time of a couple of hundred milliseconds, which would make Bob sort of teleport from one place to another instead of smoothly moving there. That's annoying for the player, and it also has an effect on our collision detection. Bob could tunnel through a platform without ever overlapping with it, due to him moving a large distance in a single frame. By limiting the delta time to a sensible maximum value of 0.1 seconds, we can compensate for those effects.

```
private void updateReady() {
    if(game.getInput().getTouchEvents().size() > 0) {
        state = GAME_RUNNING;
    }
}
```

The updateReady() method is invoked in the paused subscreen. All it does is wait for a touch event, in which case it will change the state of the game screen to the GAME_RUNNING state.

```
private void updateRunning(float deltaTime) {
    List<TouchEvent> touchEvents = game.getInput().getTouchEvents();
    int len = touchEvents.size();
    for(int i = 0; i < len; i++) {
        TouchEvent event = touchEvents.get(i);
        if(event.type != TouchEvent.TOUCH_UP)
            continue;

        touchPoint.set(event.x, event.y);
        guiCam.touchToWorld(touchPoint);

        if(OverlapTester.pointInRectangle(pauseBounds, touchPoint)) {
            Assets.playSound(Assets.clickSound);
```

```
                state = GAME_PAUSED;
                return;
            }
        }

        world.update(deltaTime, game.getInput().getAccelX());
        if(world.score != lastScore) {
            lastScore = world.score;
            scoreString = "" + lastScore;
        }
        if(world.state == World.WORLD_STATE_NEXT_LEVEL) {
            state = GAME_LEVEL_END;
        }
        if(world.state == World.WORLD_STATE_GAME_OVER) {
            state = GAME_OVER;
            if(lastScore >= Settings.highscores[4])
                scoreString = "new highscore: " + lastScore;
            else
                scoreString = "score: " + lastScore;
            Settings.addScore(lastScore);
            Settings.save(game.getFileIO());
        }
    }
}
```

In the updateRunning() method, we first check whether the user touched the pause
button in the upper-right corner. If that's the case, then the game is put into the
GAME_PAUSED state. Otherwise, we update the World instance with the current delta time
and the x-axis value of the accelerometer, which are responsible for moving Bob
horizontally. After the world is updated, we check whether our score string needs
updating. We also check whether Bob has reached the castle, in which case we enter
the GAME_NEXT_LEVEL state, which will show the message in the top left screen in Figure
9–2 and will wait for a touch event to generate the next level. In case the game is over,
we set the score string to either score: #score or new highscore: #score, depending on
whether the score achieved is a new high score. We then add the score to the Settings
and tell it to save all the settings to the SD card. Additionally, we set the game screen to
the GAME_OVER state.

```
private void updatePaused() {
    List<TouchEvent> touchEvents = game.getInput().getTouchEvents();
    int len = touchEvents.size();
    for(int i = 0; i < len; i++) {
        TouchEvent event = touchEvents.get(i);
        if(event.type != TouchEvent.TOUCH_UP)
            continue;

        touchPoint.set(event.x, event.y);
        guiCam.touchToWorld(touchPoint);

        if(OverlapTester.pointInRectangle(resumeBounds, touchPoint)) {
            Assets.playSound(Assets.clickSound);
            state = GAME_RUNNING;
            return;
        }
```

```
            if(OverlapTester.pointInRectangle(quitBounds, touchPoint)) {
                Assets.playSound(Assets.clickSound);
                game.setScreen(new MainMenuScreen(game));
                return;
            }
        }
    }
}
```

In the updatePaused() method, we check whether the user has touched the RESUME or QUIT UI elements and react accordingly.

```
private void updateLevelEnd() {
    List<TouchEvent> touchEvents = game.getInput().getTouchEvents();
    int len = touchEvents.size();
    for(int i = 0; i < len; i++) {
        TouchEvent event = touchEvents.get(i);
        if(event.type != TouchEvent.TOUCH_UP)
            continue;
        world = new World(worldListener);
        renderer = new WorldRenderer(glGraphics, batcher, world);
        world.score = lastScore;
        state = GAME_READY;
    }
}
```

In the updateLevelEnd() method, we check for a touch-up event; if there has been one, we create a new World and WorldRenderer instance. We also tell the World to use the score achieved so far and set the game screen to the GAME_READY state, which will again wait for a touch event.

```
private void updateGameOver() {
    List<TouchEvent> touchEvents = game.getInput().getTouchEvents();
    int len = touchEvents.size();
    for(int i = 0; i < len; i++) {
        TouchEvent event = touchEvents.get(i);
        if(event.type != TouchEvent.TOUCH_UP)
            continue;
        game.setScreen(new MainMenuScreen(game));
    }
}
```

In the updateGameOver() method, we again just check for a touch event, in which case we simply transition back to the main menu as indicated in Figure 9–2.

Rendering the GameScreen

After all those updates, the game screen will be asked to render itself via a call to GameScreen.present(). Let's have a look at that method in Listing 9–21.

Listing 9–21. *Excerpt from GameScreen.java: The Rendering Methods*

```
@Override
public void present(float deltaTime) {
    GL10 gl = glGraphics.getGL();
    gl.glClear(GL10.GL_COLOR_BUFFER_BIT);
```

```
    gl.glEnable(GL10.GL_TEXTURE_2D);

    renderer.render();

    guiCam.setViewportAndMatrices();
    gl.glEnable(GL10.GL_BLEND);
    gl.glBlendFunc(GL10.GL_SRC_ALPHA, GL10.GL_ONE_MINUS_SRC_ALPHA);
    batcher.beginBatch(Assets.items);
    switch(state) {
    case GAME_READY:
        presentReady();
        break;
    case GAME_RUNNING:
        presentRunning();
        break;
    case GAME_PAUSED:
        presentPaused();
        break;
    case GAME_LEVEL_END:
        presentLevelEnd();
        break;
    case GAME_OVER:
        presentGameOver();
        break;
    }
    batcher.endBatch();
    gl.glDisable(GL10.GL_BLEND);
}
```

Rendering of the game screen is done in two steps. We first render the actual game
world via the WorldRenderer class, and then render all the UI elements on top of the
game world depending on the current state of the game screen. The render() method
does just that. As with our update methods, we again have a separate rendering method
for all the subscreens.

```
private void presentReady() {
    batcher.drawSprite(160, 240, 192, 32, Assets.ready);
}
```

The presentRunning() method just displays the pause button in the top-right corner, as
well as the score string in the top-left corner.

```
private void presentRunning() {
    batcher.drawSprite(320 - 32, 480 - 32, 64, 64, Assets.pause);
    Assets.font.drawText(batcher, scoreString, 16, 480-20);
}
```

In the presentRunning() method, we simply render the pause button and the current
score string.

```
private void presentPaused() {
    batcher.drawSprite(160, 240, 192, 96, Assets.pauseMenu);
```

```
        Assets.font.drawText(batcher, scoreString, 16, 480-20);
    }
```

The presentPaused() method displays the pause menu UI elements and the score
again.

```
private void presentLevelEnd() {
    String topText = "the princess is ...";
    String bottomText = "in another castle!";
    float topWidth = Assets.font.glyphWidth * topText.length();
    float bottomWidth = Assets.font.glyphWidth * bottomText.length();
    Assets.font.drawText(batcher, topText, 160 - topWidth / 2, 480 - 40);
    Assets.font.drawText(batcher, bottomText, 160 - bottomWidth / 2, 40);
}
```

The presentLevelEnd() method renders the string THE PRINCESS IS ... at the top of the
screen and the string IN ANOTHER CASTLE! at the bottom of the screen as shown in
Figure 9–2. We perform some calculations to center those strings horizontally.

```
private void presentGameOver() {
    batcher.drawSprite(160, 240, 160, 96, Assets.gameOver);
    float scoreWidth = Assets.font.glyphWidth * scoreString.length();
    Assets.font.drawText(batcher, scoreString, 160 - scoreWidth / 2, 480-20);
}
```

The presentGameOver() method displays the game-over UI element as well the score
string. Remember that the score screen is set in the updateRunning() method to either
score: #score or new highscore: #value.

Finishing Touches

That's basically our game screen class. The rest of its code is given in Listing 9–22.

Listing 9–22. *The Rest of GameScreen.java: The pause(), resume(), and dispose() Methods.*

```
    @Override
    public void pause() {
        if(state == GAME_RUNNING)
            state = GAME_PAUSED;
    }

    @Override
    public void resume() {
    }

    @Override
    public void dispose() {
    }
}
```

We just make sure our game screen is paused when the user decides to pause the
application.

The last thing we have to implement is the `WorldRenderer` class.

The WorldRenderer Class

This class should be no surprise. It simply uses the `SpriteBatcher` we pass to it in the constructor and renders the world accordingly. Listing 9–23 shows the beginning of the code.

Listing 9–23. *Excerpt from WorldRenderer.java: Constants, Members, and Constructor.*

```java
package com.badlogic.androidgames.jumper;

import javax.microedition.khronos.opengles.GL10;

import com.badlogic.androidgames.framework.gl.Animation;
import com.badlogic.androidgames.framework.gl.Camera2D;
import com.badlogic.androidgames.framework.gl.SpriteBatcher;
import com.badlogic.androidgames.framework.gl.TextureRegion;
import com.badlogic.androidgames.framework.impl.GLGraphics;

public class WorldRenderer {
    static final float FRUSTUM_WIDTH = 10;
    static final float FRUSTUM_HEIGHT = 15;
    GLGraphics glGraphics;
    World world;
    Camera2D cam;
    SpriteBatcher batcher;

    public WorldRenderer(GLGraphics glGraphics, SpriteBatcher batcher, World world) {
        this.glGraphics = glGraphics;
        this.world = world;
        this.cam = new Camera2D(glGraphics, FRUSTUM_WIDTH, FRUSTUM_HEIGHT);
        this.batcher = batcher;
    }
```

As always, we start off by defining some constants. In this case, it's the view frustum's width and height, which we define as 10 and 15 meters. We also have a couple of members—namely a `GLGraphics` instance, a camera, and the `SpriteBatcher` reference we get from the game screen.

The constructor takes a `GLGraphics` instance, a `SpriteBatcher`, and the `World` the `WorldRenderer` should draw as parameters. We set up all members accordingly. Listing 9–24 shows the actual rendering code.

Listing 9–24. *The Rest of WorldRenderer.java: The Actual Rendering Code*

```java
    public void render() {
        if(world.bob.position.y > cam.position.y )
            cam.position.y = world.bob.position.y;
        cam.setViewportAndMatrices();
        renderBackground();
        renderObjects();
    }
```

The render() method splits up rendering into two batches: one for the background image and another one for all the objects in the world. It also updates the camera position based on Bob's current y-coordinate. If he's above the camera's y-coordinate, the camera position is adjusted accordingly. Note that we use a camera that works in world units here. We only set up the matrices once for both the background and the objects.

```
public void renderBackground() {
    batcher.beginBatch(Assets.background);
    batcher.drawSprite(cam.position.x, cam.position.y,
                FRUSTUM_WIDTH, FRUSTUM_HEIGHT,
                Assets.backgroundRegion);
    batcher.endBatch();
}
```

The renderBackground() method simply renders the background so that it follows the camera. It does not scroll but instead is always rendered so that it fills the complete screen. We also don't use any blending for rendering the background so that we can squeeze out a little bit more performance.

```
public void renderObjects() {
    GL10 gl = glGraphics.getGL();
    gl.glEnable(GL10.GL_BLEND);
    gl.glBlendFunc(GL10.GL_SRC_ALPHA, GL10.GL_ONE_MINUS_SRC_ALPHA);

    batcher.beginBatch(Assets.items);
    renderBob();
    renderPlatforms();
    renderItems();
    renderSquirrels();
    renderCastle();
    batcher.endBatch();
    gl.glDisable(GL10.GL_BLEND);
}
```

The renderObjects() method is responsible for rendering the second batch. This time we use blending, as all our objects have transparent background pixels. All the objects are rendered in a single batch. Looking back at the constructor of GameScreen, we see that the SpriteBatcher we use can cope with 1,000 sprites in a single batch—more than enough for our world. For each object type, we have a separate rendering method.

```
private void renderBob() {
    TextureRegion keyFrame;
    switch(world.bob.state) {
    case Bob.BOB_STATE_FALL:
        keyFrame = Assets.bobFall.getKeyFrame(world.bob.stateTime,
Animation.ANIMATION_LOOPING);
        break;
    case Bob.BOB_STATE_JUMP:
        keyFrame = Assets.bobJump.getKeyFrame(world.bob.stateTime,
Animation.ANIMATION_LOOPING);
        break;
    case Bob.BOB_STATE_HIT:
    default:
        keyFrame = Assets.bobHit;
```

```
        }
        float side = world.bob.velocity.x < 0? -1: 1;
        batcher.drawSprite(world.bob.position.x, world.bob.position.y, side * 1, 1,
keyFrame);
    }
```

The method `renderBob()` is responsible for rendering Bob. Based on Bob's state and
state time, we select a keyframe out of the total of five keyframes we have for Bob (see
Figure 9–9 earlier in the chapter). Based on Bob's velocity's x-component, we also
determine which side Bob is facing. Based on that, we multiply by either 1 or –1 to flip
the texture region accordingly. Remember, we only have keyframes for a Bob looking to
the right. Note also that we don't use BOB_WIDTH or BOB_HEIGHT to specify the size of the
rectangle we draw for Bob. Those sizes are the sizes of the bounding shapes, which are
not necessarily the sizes of the rectangles we render. Instead we use our 1×1-meter-to-
32×32-pixel mapping. That's something we'll do for all sprite rendering; we'll either use
a 1×1 rectangle (Bob, coins, squirrels, springs), a 2×0.5 rectangle (platforms), or a 2×2
rectangle (castle).

```
    private void renderPlatforms() {
        int len = world.platforms.size();
        for(int i = 0; i < len; i++) {
            Platform platform = world.platforms.get(i);
            TextureRegion keyFrame = Assets.platform;
            if(platform.state == Platform.PLATFORM_STATE_PULVERIZING) {
                keyFrame = Assets.brakingPlatform.getKeyFrame(platform.stateTime,
Animation.ANIMATION_NONLOOPING);
            }

            batcher.drawSprite(platform.position.x, platform.position.y,
                                2, 0.5f, keyFrame);
        }
    }
```

The method `renderPlatforms()` loops through all the platforms in the world and selects
a TextureRegion based on the platform's state. A platform can either be pulverized or
not pulverized. In the latter case, we simply use the first keyframe; in the former case,
we fetch a keyframe from the pulverization animation based on the platform's state time.

```
    private void renderItems() {
        int len = world.springs.size();
        for(int i = 0; i < len; i++) {
            Spring spring = world.springs.get(i);
            batcher.drawSprite(spring.position.x, spring.position.y, 1, 1,
Assets.spring);
        }

        len = world.coins.size();
        for(int i = 0; i < len; i++) {
            Coin coin = world.coins.get(i);
            TextureRegion keyFrame = Assets.coinAnim.getKeyFrame(coin.stateTime,
Animation.ANIMATION_LOOPING);
            batcher.drawSprite(coin.position.x, coin.position.y, 1, 1, keyFrame);
        }
    }
```

The method `renderItems()` renders springs and coins. For springs, we just use the one `TextureRegion` we defined in `Assets`, and for coins we again select a keyframe from the animation based on a coin's state time.

```
private void renderSquirrels() {
    int len = world.squirrels.size();
    for(int i = 0; i < len; i++) {
        Squirrel squirrel = world.squirrels.get(i);
        TextureRegion keyFrame = Assets.squirrelFly.getKeyFrame(squirrel.stateTime,
Animation.ANIMATION_LOOPING);
        float side = squirrel.velocity.x < 0?-1:1;
        batcher.drawSprite(squirrel.position.x, squirrel.position.y, side * 1, 1,
keyFrame);
    }
}
```

The method `renderSquirrels()` renders squirrels. We again fetch a keyframe based on the squirrel's state time, figure out which direction it faces, and manipulate the width accordingly when rendering it with the `SpriteBatcher`. This is necessary since we only have a left-facing version of the squirrel in the texture atlas.

```
private void renderCastle() {
    Castle castle = world.castle;
    batcher.drawSprite(castle.position.x, castle.position.y, 2, 2, Assets.castle);
}
}
```

The last method is called `renderCastle()`, and simply draws the castle with the `TextureRegion` we defined in the `Assets` class.

That was pretty simple, wasn't it? We only have two batches to render: one for the background and one for the objects. Taking a step back, we see that we render a third batch for all the UI elements of the game screen as well. That's three texture changes and three times uploading new vertices to the GPU. We could theoretically merge the UI and object batches, but that would be cumbersome and would introduce some hacks into our code. According to our optimization guidelines from Chapter 6, we should have lightning-fast rendering. Let's see whether that's true.

We are finally done. Our second game, Super Jumper, is now ready to be played.

To Optimize or Not to Optimize

It's time to benchmark our new game. The only place we really need to deal with speed is the game screen. We simply placed an `FPSCounter` instance in the `GameScreen` class and called its `FPSCounter.logFrame()` method at the end of the `GameScreen.render()` method. Here are the results on a Hero, a Droid, and a Nexus One:

```
Hero (1.5):
01-02 20:58:06.417: DEBUG/FPSCounter(8251): fps: 57
01-02 20:58:07.427: DEBUG/FPSCounter(8251): fps: 57
01-02 20:58:08.447: DEBUG/FPSCounter(8251): fps: 57
01-02 20:58:09.447: DEBUG/FPSCounter(8251): fps: 56
```

```
Droid (2.1.1):
01-02 21:03:59.643: DEBUG/FPSCounter(1676): fps: 61
01-02 21:04:00.659: DEBUG/FPSCounter(1676): fps: 59
01-02 21:04:01.659: DEBUG/FPSCounter(1676): fps: 60
01-02 21:04:02.666: DEBUG/FPSCounter(1676): fps: 60

Nexus One (2.2.1):
01-02 20:54:05.263: DEBUG/FPSCounter(1393): fps: 61
01-02 20:54:06.273: DEBUG/FPSCounter(1393): fps: 61
01-02 20:54:07.273: DEBUG/FPSCounter(1393): fps: 60
01-02 20:54:08.283: DEBUG/FPSCounter(1393): fps: 61
```

Sixty frames per second out of the box is pretty good. The Hero struggles a little, of course, due to its less-than-stellar CPU. We could use the SpatialHashGrid to speed up the simulation of our world a little. We'll leave that as an exercise for you, dear reader. There's no real necessity for doing so, though, as the Hero will always be fraught with problems (as will any other 1.5 device, for that matter). What's worse are the hiccups due to garbage collection every now and then on the Hero. We know the reason (a bug in direct ByteBuffer), but we can't really do anything about it. Let's hope Android version 1.5 will die a quick death soon.

We took the preceding measurements with sound disabled in the main menu. Let's try it again with audio playback turned on:

```
Hero (1.5):
01-02 21:01:22.437: DEBUG/FPSCounter(8251): fps: 43
01-02 21:01:23.457: DEBUG/FPSCounter(8251): fps: 48
01-02 21:01:24.467: DEBUG/FPSCounter(8251): fps: 49
01-02 21:01:25.487: DEBUG/FPSCounter(8251): fps: 49

Droid (2.1.1):
01-02 21:10:49.979: DEBUG/FPSCounter(1676): fps: 54
01-02 21:10:50.979: DEBUG/FPSCounter(1676): fps: 56
01-02 21:10:51.987: DEBUG/FPSCounter(1676): fps: 54
01-02 21:10:52.987: DEBUG/FPSCounter(1676): fps: 56

Nexus One (2.2.1):
01-02 21:06:06.144: DEBUG/FPSCounter(1470): fps: 61
01-02 21:06:07.153: DEBUG/FPSCounter(1470): fps: 61
01-02 21:06:08.173: DEBUG/FPSCounter(1470): fps: 62
01-02 21:06:09.183: DEBUG/FPSCounter(1470): fps: 61
```

Ouch. The Hero has significantly lower performance when we play back our background music. The audio also takes its toll on the Droid. The Nexus One doesn't really care, though. What can we do about it? Nothing really. The big culprit is not so much the sound effects but the background music. Streaming and decoding an MP3 or OGG file takes away CPU cycles from our game; that's just how the world works. Just remember to factor that into your performance measurements.

Summary

We've created our second game with the power of OpenGL ES. Due to our nice framework, it was actually a breeze to implement. The use of a texture atlas and the

`SpriteBatcher` made for some very good performance. We also discussed how to render fixed-width ASCII bitmap fonts. Good initial design of our game mechanics and a clear definition of the relationship between world units and pixel units makes developing a game a lot easier. Imagine the nightmare we'd have if we tried to do everything in pixels. All our calculations would be riddled with divisions—something the CPUs of less-powerful Android devices don't like all that much. We also took great care to separate our logic from the presentation. All in all, Super Jumper is a success.

Now it's time to turn the knobs to 11. Let's get our feet wet with some 3D graphics programming.

Chapter 10

OpenGL ES: Going 3D

Super Jumper worked out rather well with the 2D OpenGL ES rendering engine. Now it's time to go full 3D. You've already worked in a 3D space when you defined your view frustum and the vertices of your sprites. In the latter case, the z-coordinate of each vertex was simply set to zero by default. The difference from 2D rendering really isn't all that big:

- Vertices not only have x- and y-coordinates, but they also have a z-coordinate.

- Instead of an orthographic projection, a perspective projection is used. Objects further away from the camera will appear smaller.

- Transformations, such as rotations, translations, and scales, have more degrees of freedom in 3D. Instead of just moving the vertices in the x-y plane, they can now be moved around freely on all 3 axes.

- A camera is defined with an arbitrary position and orientation in 3D space.

- The order in which you render the triangles of your objects is now important. Objects further away from the camera must be overlapped by objects that are closer to the camera.

The best thing is that you have already laid the groundwork for all of this in your framework. You just need to adjust a couple classes slightly to go 3D.

Before We Begin

As always, you'll write a couple of examples in this chapter. For this, you'll follow the same route as before by having a starter activity showing a list of examples. You'll reuse the entire framework created over the last couple chapters, including the GLGame, GLScreen, Texture, and Vertices classes.

The starter activity of this chapter is called GL3DBasicsStarter. You can reuse the code of the GLBasicsStarter from Chapter 6; you'll just change the package name for the example classes that are going to run to com.badlogic.androidgames.gl3d. You must also add each of the tests to the manifest in the form of <activity> elements again. All the tests will be run in fixed landscape orientation, which will be specified per <activity> element.

Each of the tests is an instance of the GLGame abstract class, and the actual test logic is implemented in the form of a GLScreen contained in the GLGame implementation of the test, as seen in previous chapters. You will only present the relevant portions of the GLScreen to conserve some pages. The naming conventions are again XXXTest and XXXScreen for the GLGame and GLScreen implementation of each test.

Vertices in 3D

In Chapter 7, you learned that a vertex has a few attributes:

- Position
- Color (optional)
- Texture coordinates (optional)
- You created a helper class called Vertices, which handles all the dirty details for you. You limited the vertex positions to have only x- and y-coordinates. All you need to do to go 3D is modify the Vertices class so that it supports 3D vertex positions.

Vertices3: Storing 3D Positions

Let's write a new class called Vertices3 to handle 3D vertices based on your original Vertices class. Listing 10–1 shows the code.

Listing 10–1. *Vertices3.java, Now with More Coordinates.*

```
package com.badlogic.androidgames.framework.gl;

import java.nio.ByteBuffer;
import java.nio.ByteOrder;
import java.nio.IntBuffer;
import java.nio.ShortBuffer;

import javax.microedition.khronos.opengles.GL10;

import com.badlogic.androidgames.framework.impl.GLGraphics;

public class Vertices3 {
    final GLGraphics glGraphics;
    final boolean hasColor;
    final boolean hasTexCoords;
    final int vertexSize;
    final IntBuffer vertices;
```

```java
    final int[] tmpBuffer;
    final ShortBuffer indices;

    public Vertices3(GLGraphics glGraphics, int maxVertices, int maxIndices,
            boolean hasColor, boolean hasTexCoords) {
        this.glGraphics = glGraphics;
        this.hasColor = hasColor;
        this.hasTexCoords = hasTexCoords;
        this.vertexSize = (3 + (hasColor ? 4 : 0) + (hasTexCoords ? 2 : 0)) * 4;
        this.tmpBuffer = new int[maxVertices * vertexSize / 4];

        ByteBuffer buffer = ByteBuffer.allocateDirect(maxVertices * vertexSize);
        buffer.order(ByteOrder.nativeOrder());
        vertices = buffer.asIntBuffer();

        if (maxIndices > 0) {
            buffer = ByteBuffer.allocateDirect(maxIndices * Short.SIZE / 8);
            buffer.order(ByteOrder.nativeOrder());
            indices = buffer.asShortBuffer();
        } else {
            indices = null;
        }
    }

    public void setVertices(float[] vertices, int offset, int length) {
        this.vertices.clear();
        int len = offset + length;
        for (int i = offset, j = 0; i < len; i++, j++)
            tmpBuffer[j] = Float.floatToRawIntBits(vertices[i]);
        this.vertices.put(tmpBuffer, 0, length);
        this.vertices.flip();
    }

    public void setIndices(short[] indices, int offset, int length) {
        this.indices.clear();
        this.indices.put(indices, offset, length);
        this.indices.flip();
    }

    public void bind() {
        GL10 gl = glGraphics.getGL();

        gl.glEnableClientState(GL10.GL_VERTEX_ARRAY);
        vertices.position(0);
        gl.glVertexPointer(3, GL10.GL_FLOAT, vertexSize, vertices);

        if (hasColor) {
            gl.glEnableClientState(GL10.GL_COLOR_ARRAY);
            vertices.position(3);
            gl.glColorPointer(4, GL10.GL_FLOAT, vertexSize, vertices);
        }

        if (hasTexCoords) {
            gl.glEnableClientState(GL10.GL_TEXTURE_COORD_ARRAY);
            vertices.position(hasColor ? 7 : 3);
            gl.glTexCoordPointer(2, GL10.GL_FLOAT, vertexSize, vertices);
```

```
        }
    }

    public void draw(int primitiveType, int offset, int numVertices) {
        GL10 gl = glGraphics.getGL();

        if (indices != null) {
            indices.position(offset);
            gl.glDrawElements(primitiveType, numVertices,
                    GL10.GL_UNSIGNED_SHORT, indices);
        } else {
            gl.glDrawArrays(primitiveType, offset, numVertices);
        }
    }

    public void unbind() {
        GL10 gl = glGraphics.getGL();
        if (hasTexCoords)
            gl.glDisableClientState(GL10.GL_TEXTURE_COORD_ARRAY);

        if (hasColor)
            gl.glDisableClientState(GL10.GL_COLOR_ARRAY);
    }
}
```

Everything stays the same compared to Vertices, except for a few small things:

- In the constructor, you calculate vertexSize differently since the vertex position takes three instead of two floats now.

- In the bind() method, you tell OpenGL ES that your vertices have three rather than two coordinates in the call to glVertexPointer() (first argument).

- You also have to adjust the offsets that you set in the calls to vertices.position() for the optional color and texture coordinate components.

That's all you need to do. Using the Vertices3 class, you now have to specify the x-, y-, and z-coordinates for each vertex when you call the Vertices3.setVertices() method. Everything else stays the same in terms of usage. You can have per-vertex colors, texture coordinates, indices, and so on.

An Example

Let's write a simple example called Vertices3Test. You want to draw two triangles, one with z being –3 for each vertex and one with z being –5 for each vertex. You'll also use per-vertex color. Since we haven't discussed how to use a perspective projection, you'll just use an orthographic projection with appropriate near and far clipping planes so that the triangles are in the view frustum (that is, near is 10 and far is –10). Figure 10–1 shows the scene.

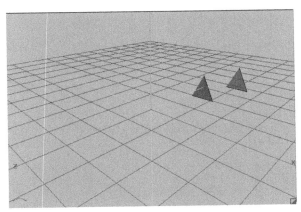

Figure 10-1. *A red triangle (front) and a green triangle (back) in 3D space.*

The red triangle is in front of the green triangle. It is possible to say "in front" because the camera is located at the origin looking down the negative z-axis by default in OpenGL ES (which actually doesn't have the notation of a camera). The green triangle is also shifted a little to the right so that we can see a portion of it when viewed from the front. It should be overlapped by the red triangle for the most part. Listing 10-2 shows the code for rendering this scene.

Listing 10-2. *Vertices3Test.java: Drawing Two Triangles.*

```
package com.badlogic.androidgames.gl3d;

import javax.microedition.khronos.opengles.GL10;

import com.badlogic.androidgames.framework.Game;
import com.badlogic.androidgames.framework.Screen;
import com.badlogic.androidgames.framework.gl.Vertices3;
import com.badlogic.androidgames.framework.impl.GLGame;
import com.badlogic.androidgames.framework.impl.GLScreen;

public class Vertices3Test extends GLGame {

    @Override
    public Screen getStartScreen() {
        return new Vertices3Screen(this);
    }

    class Vertices3Screen extends GLScreen {
        Vertices3 vertices;

        public Vertices3Screen(Game game) {
            super(game);

            vertices = new Vertices3(glGraphics, 6, 0, true, false);
            vertices.setVertices(new float[] { -0.5f, -0.5f, -3, 1, 0, 0, 1,
                                                0.5f, -0.5f, -3, 1, 0, 0, 1,
                                                0.0f,  0.5f, -3, 1, 0, 0, 1,
```

```
                                             0.0f,  -0.5f, -5, 0, 1, 0, 1,
                                             1.0f,  -0.5f, -5, 0, 1, 0, 1,
        }                                    0.5f,   0.5f, -5, 0, 1, 0, 1}, 0, 7 * 6);

        @Override
        public void present(float deltaTime) {
            GL10 gl = glGraphics.getGL();
            gl.glClear(GL10.GL_COLOR_BUFFER_BIT);
            gl.glViewport(0, 0, glGraphics.getWidth(), glGraphics.getHeight());
            gl.glMatrixMode(GL10.GL_PROJECTION);
            gl.glLoadIdentity();
            gl.glOrthof(-1, 1, -1, 1, 10, -10);
            gl.glMatrixMode(GL10.GL_MODELVIEW);
            gl.glLoadIdentity();
            vertices.bind();
            vertices.draw(GL10.GL_TRIANGLES, 0, 6);
            vertices.unbind();
        }

        @Override
        public void update(float deltaTime) {
        }

        @Override
        public void pause() {
        }

        @Override
        public void resume() {
        }

        @Override
        public void dispose() {
        }
    }
}
```

As you can see, this is the complete source file. The following examples will only show the relevant portions since the rest stays mostly the same, apart from the class names.

There is a Vertices3 member in Vertices3Screen, which is initialized in the constructor. There are six vertices in total, a color per vertex, and no texture coordinates. Since neither triangle shares vertices with the other, you don't use indexed geometry. This information is passed to the Vertices3 constructor. Next, you set the actual vertices with a call to Vertices3.setVertices(). The first three lines specify the red triangle in the front, and the other three lines specify the green triangle in the back, slightly offset to the right by 0.5 units. The third float on each line is the z-coordinate of the respective vertex.

In the present() method, you must first clear the screen and set the viewport, as always. Next, load an orthographic projection matrix, setting up a view frustum big enough to show your entire scene. Finally, just render the two triangles contained within the Vertices3 instance. Figure 10–2 shows the output of this program.

Figure 10–2. *The two triangles—but something's wrong.*

Now that is strange. According to our theory, the red triangle (in the middle) should be in front of the green triangle. The camera is located at the origin looking down the negative z-axis, and from Figure 10–1 you can see that the red triangle is closer to the origin than the green triangle. What's happening here?

OpenGL ES will render the triangles in the order in which you specify them in the Vertices3 instance. Since you specified the red triangle first, it will get drawn first. You could change the order of the triangles to fix this. But what if your camera wasn't looking down the negative z-axis, but was looking from behind? You'd again have to sort the triangles before rendering according to their distance from the camera. That can't be the solution. And it isn't. We'll fix this in a minute. Let's first get rid of this orthographic projection and use a perspective one instead.

A note on coordinate systems: You may notice that, in our examples, we start by looking down the Z-Axis, where if Z increases towards us, X increases to the right and Y increases up. This is called the "Right Hand Rule," and it is what OpenGL uses as the standard coordinate system. If your thumb represents the X-axis, then your first finger pointed straight out will be Y and your middle finger sticking down from your palm will represent Z. See Figure 10–3 for an example. Sometimes you will have to flip your hand around a little and think hard about it, but if you ever get confused, just remember this rule and it will eventually come quite naturally to you.

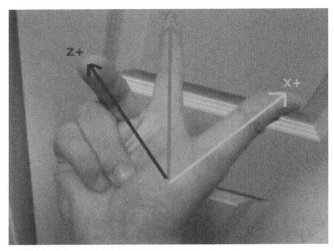

Figure 10–3. *The Right Hand Rule.*

Perspective Projection: The Closer, the Bigger

Until now, we have always used an orthographic projection, meaning that no matter how far an object is from the near clipping plane, it will always have the same size on the screen. Our eyes show us a different picture of the world. The further away an object is, the smaller it appears to us. This is called perspective projection, which was discussed a little in Chapter 4.

The difference between an orthographic projection and a perspective projection can be explained by the shape of the view frustum. In an orthographic projection, there is a box. In a perspective projection, there is a pyramid with a cut-off top as the near clipping plane, the pyramid's base as the far clipping plane, and its sides as the left, right, top, and bottom clipping planes. Figure 10–4 shows a perspective view frustum through which you can view your scene.

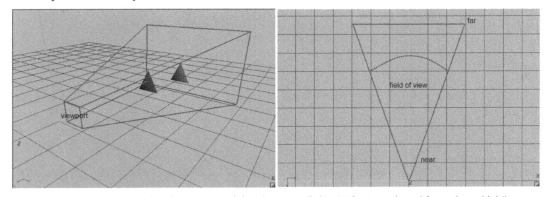

Figure 10–4. *A perspective view frustum containing the scene (left); the frustum viewed from above (right).*

The perspective view frustum is defined by four parameters:

1. The distance from the camera to the near clipping plane

2. The distance from the camera to the far clipping plane

3. The aspect ratio of the viewport, which is embedded in the near clipping plane given by viewport width divided by viewport height

4. The field of view, specifying how wide the view frustum is, and therefore, how much of the scene it shows

While we've talked about a camera, there's no such concept involved here yet. Just pretend that there is a camera sitting fixed at the origin looking down the negative z-axis, as shown in Figure 10–3.

The near and far clipping plane distances are no strangers to us. You just need to set them up so that the complete scene is contained in the view frustum. The field of view is also easily understandable when looking at the right image in Figure 10–4.

The aspect ratio of the viewport is a little less intuitive. Why is it needed? It ensures that your world doesn't get stretched in case the screen to which you render has an aspect ratio that's not equal to 1.

Previously, you used gl0rthof() to specify the orthographic view frustum in the form of a projection matrix. For the perspective view frustum, you could use a method called glFrustumf(). However, there's an easier way.

Traditionally, OpenGL comes with a utility library called GLU. It contains a couple helper functions for things like setting up projection matrices and implementing camera systems. That library is also available on Android in the form of a class called GLU. It features a few static methods we can invoke without needing a GLU instance. The method in which we are interested is called gluPerspective():

```
GLU.gluPerspective(GL10 gl, float fieldOfView, float aspectRatio, float near, float
far);
```

This method will multiply the currently active matrix (that is, projection or model-view matrix) with a perspective projection matrix, similar to gl0rthof(). The first parameter is an instance of GL10, usually the one used for all other OpenGL ES-related business. The second parameter is the field of view given in angles; the third parameter is the aspect ratio of the viewport, and the last two parameters specify the distance of the near and far clipping plane from the camera position. Since there is no a camera yet, those values are given relative to the origin of the world, forcing us to look down the negative z-axis, as shown in Figure 10–4. That's totally fine at the moment; you will make sure that all the objects you render stay within this fixed and immovable view frustum. As long as you only use gluPerspective(), you can't change the position or orientation of your virtual camera. You will always only see a portion of the world looking down the negative z-axis.

Let's modify the last example so that it uses perspective projection. You just copied over all code from Vertices3Test to a new class called PerspectiveTest, and you also renamed Vertices3Screen to PerspectiveScreen. The only thing you need to change is the present() method. Listing 10–3 shows the code.

Listing 10–3. *Excerpt from PerspectiveTest.java: Perspective Projection.*

```
@Override
public void present(float deltaTime) {
    GL10 gl = glGraphics.getGL();
    gl.glClear(GL10.GL_COLOR_BUFFER_BIT);
    gl.glViewport(0, 0, glGraphics.getWidth(), glGraphics.getHeight());
    gl.glMatrixMode(GL10.GL_PROJECTION);
    gl.glLoadIdentity();
    GLU.gluPerspective(gl, 67,
                       glGraphics.getWidth() / (float)glGraphics.getHeight(),
                       0.1f, 10f);
    gl.glMatrixMode(GL10.GL_MODELVIEW);
    gl.glLoadIdentity();
    vertices.bind();
    vertices.draw(GL10.GL_TRIANGLES, 0, 6);
    vertices.unbind();
}
```

The only difference from the previous present() method is that you are now using GLU.gluPerspective() instead of glOrtho(). The field of view is 67 degrees, which is close to the average human field of view. By increasing or decreasing this value, you can see more or less to the left and right. The next thing specified is the aspect ratio, which is the screen's width divided by its height. Note that this will be a floating-point number, so you have to cast one of the values to a float before dividing. The final arguments are the near and far clipping plane distance. Given that the virtual camera is located at the origin looking down the negative z-axis, anything with a z-value smaller than –0.1 and bigger than –10 will be between the near and far clipping planes, and thus be potentially visible. Figure 10–5 shows the output of this example.

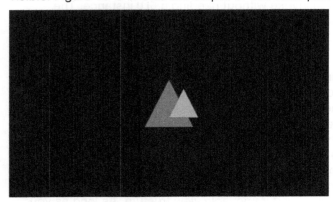

Figure 10–5. *Perspective (mostly correct).*

Now you are actually doing proper 3D graphics. As you can see, there is still a problem with the rendering order of our triangles. That can be fixed by using the almighty z-buffer.

Z-buffer: Bringing Order into Chaos

What is a z-buffer? In Chapter 4, we discussed the framebuffer. It stores the color for each pixel on the screen. When OpenGL ES renders a triangle to the framebuffer, it just changes the color of the pixels that make up that triangle.

The z-buffer is very similar to the framebuffer in that it also has a storage location for each pixel on the screen. Instead of storing colors, it stores depth values. The depth value of a pixel is roughly the normalized distance of the corresponding point in 3D to the near clipping plane of the view frustum.

OpenGL ES will write a depth value for each pixel of a triangle to the z-buffer by default (if a z-buffer was created alongside the framebuffer). All you have to tell OpenGL ES is to use this information to decide whether a pixel being drawn is closer to the near clipping plane than the one that's currently there. For this, you just need to call glEnable() with an appropriate parameter:

```
GL10.glEnable(GL10.GL_DEPTH_TEST);
```

That's all you need to do. OpenGL ES will then compare the incoming pixel depth with the pixel depth that's already in the z-buffer. If it is smaller, it is also closer to the near clipping plane and thus in front of the pixel that's already in the frame- and z-buffer.

Figure 10–5 illustrates the process. The z-buffer starts off with all values set to infinity (or a very high number). When you render the first triangle, compare each of its pixels' depth values to the value of the pixel in the z-buffer. If the depth value of a pixel is smaller than the value in the z-buffer, it passes the so-called *depth test*, or *z-test*. The pixel's color will be written to the framebuffer, and its depth will overwrite the corresponding value in the z-buffer. If it fails the test, neither the pixel's color nor the depth value will be written to the buffers. This is shown in Figure 10–6, where the second triangle is rendered. Some of the pixels have smaller depth values and thus get rendered; other pixels don't pass the test.

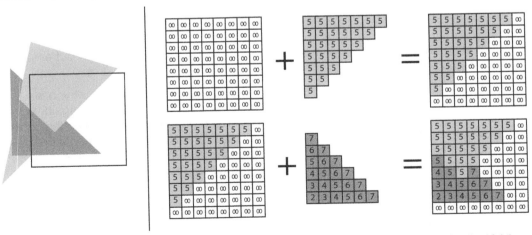

Figure 10–6. *Image in the framebuffer (left); z-buffer contents after rendering each of the two triangles (right).*

As with the framebuffer, we also have to clear the z-buffer for each frame, otherwise the depth values from the last frame would still be in there. To do this, call glClear(), as per the following:

```
gl.glClear(GL10.GL_COLOR_BUFFER_BIT | GL10.GL_DEPTH_BUFFER_BIT);
```

This will clear the framebuffer (or colorbuffer) as well as the z-buffer (or depthbuffer), all in one go.

Fixing the Last Example

Let's fix the last example's problems by using the z-buffer. You just copied all the code over to a new class called ZBufferTest, and you modified the present() method of the new ZBufferScreen class, as shown in Listing 10–4.

Listing 10–4. *Excerpt from ZBufferTest.java: Using the Z-buffer.*

```
@Override
public void present(float deltaTime) {
    GL10 gl = glGraphics.getGL();
    gl.glClear(GL10.GL_COLOR_BUFFER_BIT | GL10.GL_DEPTH_BUFFER_BIT);
    gl.glViewport(0, 0, glGraphics.getWidth(), glGraphics.getHeight());
    gl.glMatrixMode(GL10.GL_PROJECTION);
    gl.glLoadIdentity();
    GLU.gluPerspective(gl, 67,
            glGraphics.getWidth() / (float)glGraphics.getHeight(),
            0.1f, 10f);
    gl.glMatrixMode(GL10.GL_MODELVIEW);
    gl.glLoadIdentity();

    gl.glEnable(GL10.GL_DEPTH_TEST);

    vertices.bind();
    vertices.draw(GL10.GL_TRIANGLES, 0, 6);
    vertices.unbind();

    gl.glDisable(GL10.GL_DEPTH_TEST);
}
```

The first thing changed is the arguments to the call to glClear(). Now both buffers are cleared instead of just the framebuffer.

You must also enable depth-testing before rendering the two triangles. After you are done with rendering all of the 3D geometry, you must disable depth-testing again. Why? Imagine that you want to render 2D UI elements on top of your 3D scene, like the current score or buttons. Since you'd use the SpriteBatcher for this, which only works in 2D, you wouldn't have any meaningful z-coordinates for the vertices of the 2D elements. You wouldn't need depth-testing either, since you would explicitly specify the order in which you want the vertices to be drawn to the screen.

The output of this example, shown in Figure 10–7, looks as expected now.

Figure 10–7. *The z-buffer in action, making the rendering order-independent.*

Finally, the green triangle in the middle is rendered correctly behind the red triangle, thanks to our new best friend, the z-buffer. As with most friends, however, there are times when your friendship suffers a little from minor issues. Let's examine some caveats when using the z-buffer.

Blending: There's Nothing Behind You

Assume that you want to enable blending for the red triangle at z = –3 in your scene. Say you set each vertex color's alpha component to 0.5f, so that anything behind the triangle shines through. In this case, the green triangle at z = –5 should shine through. Let's think about what OpenGL ES will do and what else will happen:

- OpenGL ES will render the first triangle to the z-buffer and colorbuffer.

- Next OpenGL ES will render the green triangle because it comes after the red triangle in our Vertices3 instance.

- The portion of the green triangle behind the red triangle will not get shown on the screen due to the pixels being rejected by the depth test.

- Nothing will shine through the red triangle in the front since nothing was there to shine through when it was rendered.

When using blending in combination with the z-buffer, you have to make sure that all transparent objects are sorted by increasing the distance from the camera position and rendering them back to front. All opaque objects must be rendered before any transparent objects. The opaque objects don't have to be sorted, though.

Let's write a simple example that demonstrates this. Keep your current scene composed of two triangles and set the alpha component of the vertex colors of the first triangle (z = –3) to 0.5f. According to our rule, you have to first render the opaque objects—in this case the green triangle (z = –5)—and then all the transparent objects, from furthest to closest. In this scene, there's only one transparent object: the red triangle.

Copy over all the code from the last example to a new class called ZBlendingTest and rename the contained ZBufferScreen to ZBlendingScreen. All you need to do is change are the vertex colors of the first triangle, and enable blending and rendering the two triangles in order in the present() method. Listing 10–5 shows the two relevant methods.

Listing 10–5. *Excerpt from ZBlendingTest.java: Blending with the Z-buffer Enabled.*

```
public ZBlendingScreen(Game game) {
    super(game);

    vertices = new Vertices3(glGraphics, 6, 0, true, false);
    vertices.setVertices(new float[] { -0.5f, -0.5f, -3, 1, 0, 0, 0.5f,
                                        0.5f, -0.5f, -3, 1, 0, 0, 0.5f,
                                        0.0f,  0.5f, -3, 1, 0, 0, 0.5f,
                                        0.0f, -0.5f, -5, 0, 1, 0, 1,
                                        1.0f, -0.5f, -5, 0, 1, 0, 1,
                                        0.5f,  0.5f, -5, 0, 1, 0, 1}, 0, 7 * 6);
}

@Override
public void present(float deltaTime) {
    GL10 gl = glGraphics.getGL();
    gl.glClear(GL10.GL_COLOR_BUFFER_BIT | GL10.GL_DEPTH_BUFFER_BIT);
    gl.glViewport(0, 0, glGraphics.getWidth(), glGraphics.getHeight());
    gl.glMatrixMode(GL10.GL_PROJECTION);
    gl.glLoadIdentity();
    GLU.gluPerspective(gl, 67,
            glGraphics.getWidth() / (float)glGraphics.getHeight(),
            0.1f, 10f);
    gl.glMatrixMode(GL10.GL_MODELVIEW);
    gl.glLoadIdentity();

    gl.glEnable(GL10.GL_DEPTH_TEST);
    gl.glEnable(GL10.GL_BLEND);
    gl.glBlendFunc(GL10.GL_SRC_ALPHA, GL10.GL_ONE_MINUS_SRC_ALPHA);

    vertices.bind();
    vertices.draw(GL10.GL_TRIANGLES, 3, 3);
    vertices.draw(GL10.GL_TRIANGLES, 0, 3);
    vertices.unbind();

    gl.glDisable(GL10.GL_BLEND);
    gl.glDisable(GL10.GL_DEPTH_TEST);
}
```

In the constructor of the ZBlendingScreen class, you only change the alpha components of the vertex colors of the first triangle to 0.5. This will make the first triangle transparent. In the present() method, you do the usual things like clearing the buffers and setting up the matrices. You must also enable blending and set a proper blending function. The interesting bit is how to render the two triangles now. You first render the green triangle, which is the second triangle in the Vertices3 instance, as it is opaque. All opaque objects must be rendered before any transparent objects are rendered. Next, render the transparent triangle, which is the first triangle in the Vertices3 instance. For both drawing calls, simply use proper offsets and vertex counts as the second and third arguments to the vertices.draw() method. Figure 10–8 shows the output of this program.

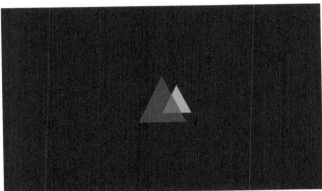

Figure 10–8. *Blending with the z-buffer enabled.*

Let's reverse the order in which you draw the two triangles as follows:

```
vertices.draw(GL10.GL_TRIANGLES, 0, 3);
vertices.draw(GL10.GL_TRIANGLES, 3, 3);
```

So you first draw the triangle starting from vertex 0 and then draw the second triangle starting from vertex 3. This will render the red triangle in the front first and the green triangle in the back second. Figure 10–9 shows the outcome.

Figure 10–9. *Blending done wrong; the triangle in the back should shine through.*

The objects only consist of triangles so far, which is of course a little bit simplistic. We'll revisit blending in conjunction with the z-buffer again when we render more complex shapes. For now, let's summarize how to handle blending in 3D:

1. Render all opaque objects.

2. Sort all transparent objects in increasing distance from the camera (furthest to closest).

3.   Render all transparent objects in the sorted order, furthest to closest.

The sorting can be based on the object center's distance from the camera in most cases. You'll run into problems if one of your objects is large and can span multiple objects. Without advanced tricks, it is not possible to work around that issue. There are a couple of bulletproof solutions that work great with the desktop variant of OpenGL, but they can't be implemented on most Android devices due to their limited GPU functionality. Luckily, this is very rare, and you can almost always stick to simple center-based sorting.

Z-buffer Precision and Z-fighting

It's always tempting to abuse the near and far clipping planes to show as much of your awesome scene as possible. You've put a lot of effort into adding a ton of objects to your world, after all, and that effort should be visible. The only problem with this is that the z-buffer has a limited precision. On most Android devices, each depth value stored in the z-buffer has no more than 16 bits; that's 65,535 different depth values at most. Thus, instead of setting the near clipping plane distance to 0.00001 and the far clipping plane distance to 1000000, you should stick to more reasonable values. Otherwise, you'll soon find out what nice artifacts an improperly configured view frustum can produce in combination with the z-buffer.

What is the problem? Imagine you set your near and far clipping planes as just mentioned. A pixel's depth value is more or less its distance from the near clipping plane—the closer it is, the smaller its depth value. With a 16-bit depth buffer, you'd quantize the near-to-far-clipping-plane depth value internally into 65,535 segments; each segment takes up 1000000 / 65535 = 15 units in your world. If you choose your units to be meters and have objects of usual sizes like 1×2×1 meters, all within the same segment, the z-buffer won't help you a lot as all the pixels will get the same depth value.

> **NOTE:** Depth values in the z-buffer are actually not linear, but the general idea is still true.

Another related problem when using the z-buffer is so-called z-fighting. Figure 10–10 illustrates the problem.

Figure 10–10. *Z-fighting in action.*

The two rectangles in Figure 10–10 are *coplanar*; that is, they are embedded in the same plane. Since they overlap, they also share some pixels, which should have the same depth values. However, due to limited floating-point precision, the GPU might not arrive at the same depth values for pixels that overlap. Which pixel passes the depth test is then a sort of lottery. This can usually be resolved by pushing one of the two coplanar objects away from the other object by a small amount. The value of this offset is dependent on a few factors, so it's usually best to experiment. To summarize,

- Do not use values that are too small or large for your near and far clipping plane distances.

- Avoid coplanar objects by offsetting them a little.

Defining 3D Meshes

So far, you've only used a couple of triangles as placeholders for objects in your worlds. What about more complex objects?

We already talked about how the GPU is just a big, mean triangle-rendering machine. All the 3D objects, therefore, have to be composed of triangles as well. In the previous chapters, two triangles were used to represent a flat rectangle. The principles used there, like vertex positioning, colors, texturing, and vertex indexing, are exactly the same in 3D. The triangles are just not limited to lie in the x-y plane anymore; you can freely specify each vertex's position in 3D space.

How do you go about creating such soups of triangles that make up a 3D object? You can do that programmatically, as you've done for the rectangles of your sprites. You could also use software that lets you sculpture 3D objects in a WYSIWYG fashion. There are various paradigms used in those applications, ranging from manipulating separate triangles to just specifying a few parameters that output a so-called *triangle mesh* (a fancy name for a list of triangles that you'll adopt).

Prominent software packages like Blender, 3ds Max, ZBrush, and Wings 3D provide users with tons of functionality for creating 3D objects. Some of them are free (such as Blender and Wings 3D) and some are commercial (for example, 3ds Max and ZBrush). It's not within the scope of this book to teach you how to use one of these programs, so we'll do something else instead. All these programs can save the 3D models to different file formats. The Web is also full of free-to-use 3D models. In the next chapter, you'll write a loader for one of the simplest and most common file formats in use.

In this chapter, you'll do everything programmatically. Let's create one of the simplest 3D objects possible: a cube.

A Cube: Hello World in 3D

In the last couple chapters, you've made heavy use of the concept of model space. It's the space in which to define models; it's completely unrelated to the world space. You must use the convention of constructing all objects around the model space's origin so that an object's center coincides with that origin. Such a model can then be reused for rendering multiple objects at different locations and with different orientations in world space, just as in the massive BobTest example in Chapter 7.

The first thing you need to figure out for your cube is its corner points. Figure 10–11 shows a cube with a side length of 1 unit (for example, 1 meter). We also exploded the cube a little so that you can see the separate sides made up of two triangles each. In reality, the sides would all meet at the edges and corner points, of course.

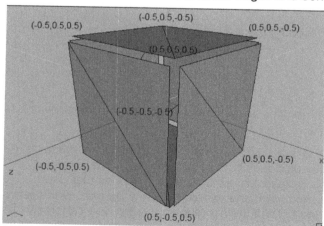

Figure 10–11. *A cube and its corner points.*

A cube has six sides, and each side is made up of two triangles. The two triangles of each side share two vertices. For the front side of the cube, the vertices at (–0.5,0.5,0.5) and (0.5,–0.5,0.5) are shared. You only need four vertices per side; for a complete cube, that's 6 × 4 = 24 vertices in total. However, you do need to specify 36 indices, not just 24. That's because there are 6 × 2 triangles, each using 3 out of your 24 vertices. You can create a mesh for this cube using vertex indexing, as follows:

```
float[] vertices = { -0.5f, -0.5f,  0.5f,
                      0.5f, -0.5f,  0.5f,
                      0.5f,  0.5f,  0.5f,
                     -0.5f,  0.5f,  0.5f,

                      0.5f, -0.5f,  0.5f,
                      0.5f, -0.5f, -0.5f,
                      0.5f,  0.5f, -0.5f,
                      0.5f,  0.5f,  0.5f,

                      0.5f, -0.5f, -0.5f,
                     -0.5f, -0.5f, -0.5f,
                     -0.5f,  0.5f, -0.5f,
                      0.5f,  0.5f, -0.5f,

                     -0.5f, -0.5f, -0.5f,
                     -0.5f, -0.5f,  0.5f,
                     -0.5f,  0.5f,  0.5f,
                     -0.5f,  0.5f, -0.5f,

                     -0.5f,  0.5f,  0.5f,
                      0.5f,  0.5f,  0.5f,
                      0.5f,  0.5f, -0.5f,
                     -0.5f,  0.5f, -0.5f,

                     -0.5f, -0.5f,  0.5f,
                      0.5f, -0.5f,  0.5f,
                      0.5f, -0.5f, -0.5f,
                     -0.5f, -0.5f, -0.5f
};

short[] indices = { 0, 1, 3, 1, 2, 3,
                    4, 5, 7, 5, 6, 7,
                    8, 9, 11, 9, 10, 11,
                    12, 13, 15, 13, 14, 15,
                    16, 17, 19, 17, 18, 19,
                    20, 21, 23, 21, 22, 23,
};

Vertices3 cube = new Vertices3(glGraphics, 24, 36, false, false);
cube.setVertices(vertices, 0, vertices.length);
cube.setIndices(indices, 0, indices.length);
```

You are only specifying vertex positions in this code. Start with the front side and its bottom-left vertex at (–0.5,–0.5,0.5). Then specify the next three vertices of that side, going counterclockwise. The next side is the right side of the cube, followed by the back side, the left side, the top side, and the bottom side—all following the same pattern. Compare the vertex definitions with Figure 10–10.

Next define the indices. There are a total of 36 indices—each line in the preceding code defines two triangles made up of three vertices each. The indices (0, 1, 3, 1, 2, 3) define the front side of the cube, the next three indices define the left side, and so on. Compare these indices with the vertices given in the preceding code, as well as with Figure 10–10 again.

Once all vertices and indices are defined, store them in a `Vertices3` instance for rendering, which you do in the last couple of lines of this snippet.

What about texture coordinates? Easy, just add them to the vertex definitions. Let's say there is a 128×128 texture containing the image of one side of a crate. We want each side of the cube to be textured with this image. Figure 10–12 shows how you can do this.

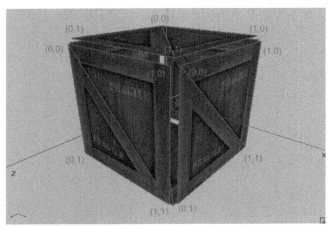

Figure 10–12. *Texture coordinates for each of the vertices of the front, left, and top sides. (This is the same for the other sides as well.)*

Adding texture coordinates to the front side of the cube would then look like the following in code:

```
float[] vertices = { -0.5f, -0.5f,  0.5f, 0, 1,
                      0.5f, -0.5f,  0.5f, 1, 1,
                      0.5f,  0.5f,  0.5f, 1, 0,
                     -0.5f,  0.5f,  0.5f, 0, 0,
                     // rest is analogous
```

Of course, you also need to tell the `Vertices3` instance that it contains texture coordinates as well:

```
Vertices3 cube = new Vertices3(glGraphics, 24, 36, false, true);
```

All that's left is loading the texture itself, enabling texture mapping with `glEnable()`, and binding the texture with `Texture.bind()`. Let's write an example.

An Example

You want to create a cube mesh, as shown in the preceding snippets, with the crate texture applied. Since you model the cube in model space around the origin, you have to use `glTranslatef()` to move it into world space, much like you did with Bob's model in the `BobTest` example. You also want your cube to spin around the y-axis, which you can achieve by using glRotatef(), again like in the BobTest example. Listing 10–6 shows the complete code of the CubeScreen class contained in a CubeTest class.

Listing 10–6. *Excerpt from CubeTest.java: Rendering a Texture Cube.*

```java
class CubeScreen extends GLScreen {
    Vertices3 cube;
    Texture texture;
    float angle = 0;

    public CubeScreen(Game game) {
        super(game);
        cube = createCube();
        texture = new Texture(glGame, "crate.png");
    }

    private Vertices3 createCube() {
        float[] vertices = { -0.5f, -0.5f,  0.5f, 0, 1,
                              0.5f, -0.5f,  0.5f, 1, 1,
                              0.5f,  0.5f,  0.5f, 1, 0,
                             -0.5f,  0.5f,  0.5f, 0, 0,

                              0.5f, -0.5f,  0.5f, 0, 1,
                              0.5f, -0.5f, -0.5f, 1, 1,
                              0.5f,  0.5f, -0.5f, 1, 0,
                              0.5f,  0.5f,  0.5f, 0, 0,

                              0.5f, -0.5f, -0.5f, 0, 1,
                             -0.5f, -0.5f, -0.5f, 1, 1,
                             -0.5f,  0.5f, -0.5f, 1, 0,
                              0.5f,  0.5f, -0.5f, 0, 0,

                             -0.5f, -0.5f, -0.5f, 0, 1,
                             -0.5f, -0.5f,  0.5f, 1, 1,
                             -0.5f,  0.5f,  0.5f, 1, 0,
                             -0.5f,  0.5f, -0.5f, 0, 0,

                             -0.5f,  0.5f,  0.5f, 0, 1,
                              0.5f,  0.5f,  0.5f, 1, 1,
                              0.5f,  0.5f, -0.5f, 1, 0,
                             -0.5f,  0.5f, -0.5f, 0, 0,

                             -0.5f, -0.5f,  0.5f, 0, 1,
                              0.5f, -0.5f,  0.5f, 1, 1,
                              0.5f, -0.5f, -0.5f, 1, 0,
                             -0.5f, -0.5f, -0.5f, 0, 0
        };

        short[] indices = { 0, 1, 3, 1, 2, 3,
                            4, 5, 7, 5, 6, 7,
                            8, 9, 11, 9, 10, 11,
                            12, 13, 15, 13, 14, 15,
                            16, 17, 19, 17, 18, 19,
                            20, 21, 23, 21, 22, 23,
        };

        Vertices3 cube = new Vertices3(glGraphics, 24, 36, false, true);
```

```
            cube.setVertices(vertices, 0, vertices.length);
            cube.setIndices(indices, 0, indices.length);
            return cube;
    }

    @Override
    public void resume() {
        texture.reload();
    }

    @Override
    public void update(float deltaTime) {
        angle += 45 * deltaTime;
    }

    @Override
    public void present(float deltaTime) {
        GL10 gl = glGraphics.getGL();
        gl.glViewport(0, 0, glGraphics.getWidth(), glGraphics.getHeight());
        gl.glClear(GL10.GL_COLOR_BUFFER_BIT | GL10.GL_DEPTH_BUFFER_BIT);
        gl.glMatrixMode(GL10.GL_PROJECTION);
        gl.glLoadIdentity();
        GLU.gluPerspective(gl, 67,
                           glGraphics.getWidth() / (float) glGraphics.getHeight(),
                           0.1f, 10.0f);
        gl.glMatrixMode(GL10.GL_MODELVIEW);
        gl.glLoadIdentity();

        gl.glEnable(GL10.GL_DEPTH_TEST);
        gl.glEnable(GL10.GL_TEXTURE_2D);
        texture.bind();
        cube.bind();
        gl.glTranslatef(0,0,-3);
        gl.glRotatef(angle, 0, 1, 0);
        cube.draw(GL10.GL_TRIANGLES, 0, 36);
        cube.unbind();
        gl.glDisable(GL10.GL_TEXTURE_2D);
        gl.glDisable(GL10.GL_DEPTH_TEST);
    }

    @Override
    public void pause() {
    }

    @Override
    public void dispose() {
    }
}
```

There is a field to store the cube's mesh, a Texture instance, and a float to in which to store the current rotation angle. In the constructor, create the cube mesh and load the texture from an asset file called crate.png, a 128×128-pixel image of one side of a crate.

The cube creation code is located in the createCube() method. It just sets up the vertices and indices, and creates a Vertices3 instance from them. Each vertex has a 3D position and texture coordinates.

The `resume()` method just tells the texture to reload it. Remember, textures must be reloaded after an OpenGL ES context loss.

The `update()` method just increases the rotation angle by which you'll rotate the cube around the y-axis.

The `present()` method first sets the viewport and clears the framebuffer and depthbuffer. Next set up a perspective projection and load an identity matrix to the model-view matrix of OpenGL ES. Enable depth testing and texturing, and bind the texture as well as the cube mesh. Then use `glTranslatef()` to move the cube to the position (0,0,–3) in world space. With `glRotatef()`, rotate the cube in model space around the y-axis. Remember that the order in which these transformations get applied to the mesh is reversed. The cube will first be rotated (in model space), and then the rotated version will be positioned in world space. Finally, draw the cube, unbind the mesh, and disable depth-testing and texturing. You don't need to disable those states; that is put in in case you are going to render 2D elements on top of the 3D scene. Figure 10–13 shows the output of the first real 3D program.

Figure 10–13. *A spinning texture cube in 3D.*

Matrices and Transformations Again

In Chapter 6, you learned a little bit about matrices. Let's summarize some of their properties as a little refresher:

- A matrix translates points (or vertices in our case) to a new position. This is achieved by multiplying the matrix with the point's position.
- A matrix can translate points on each axis by some amount.
- A matrix can scale points, meaning that it multiplies each coordinate of a point by some constant.
- A matrix can rotate a point around an axis.
- Multiplying an identity matrix with a point has no effect on that point.

- Multiplying one matrix with another matrix results in a new matrix. Multiplying a point with this new matrix will apply both transformations encoded in the original matrices to that point.

- Multiplying a matrix with an identity matrix has no effect on the matrix.

OpenGL ES provides us with three types of matrices:

- *Projection matrix*: This is used to set up the view frustum's shape and size, which governs the type of projection and how much of the world is shown.

- *Model-view matrix*: This is used to transform the models in model space and to place a model in world space.

- *Texture matrix*: This is broken on many devices.

Now that you are working in 3D, you have more options at your disposal. You can, for example, not only rotate a model around the z-axis, you we did with Bob, but around any arbitrary axis. The only thing that really changes, though, is the additional z-axis you can now use to place your objects. You were actually already working in 3D when you rendered Bob back in Chapter 6; you just ignored the z-axis. But there's more that can be done.

The Matrix Stack

Up until now, you have used matrices like this with OpenGL ES:

```
gl.glMatrixMode(GL10.GL_PROJECTION);
gl.glLoadIdentity();
gl.glOrthof(-1, 1, -1, 1, -10, 10);
```

The first statement sets the currently active matrix. All subsequent matrix operations will be executed on that matrix. In this case, you set the active matrix to an identity matrix and then multiply it by an orthographic projection matrix. You did something similar with the model-view matrix:

```
gl.glMatrixMode(GL10.GL_MODELVIEW);
gl.glLoadIdentity();
gl.glTranslatef(0, 0, -10);
gl.glRotate(45, 0, 1, 0);
```

This snippet manipulates the model-view matrix. It first loads an identity matrix to clear whatever was in the model-view matrix before that call. Next it multiplies the matrix with a translation matrix and a rotation matrix. This order of multiplication is important as it defines in what order these transformations get applied to the vertices of the meshes. The last transformation specified will be the first to be applied to the vertices. In the preceding case, you first rotated each vertex by 45 degrees around the y-axis. Then you moved each vertex by –10 units along the z-axis.

In both cases, all the transformations are encoded in a single matrix, in either the OpenGL ES projection or model-view matrix. But it turns out that for each matrix type, there's actually a stack of matrices at your disposal.

For now, you're only using a single slot in this stack: the top of the stack (TOS). The TOS of a matrix stack is the one actually used by OpenGL ES to transform the vertices, be it with the projection or model-view matrix. Any matrix below the TOS on the stack just sits there idly, waiting to become the new TOS. So how can you manipulate this stack?

OpenGL ES has two methods you can use to push and pop the current TOS:

```
GL10.glPushMatrix();
GL10.glPopMatrix();
```

Like glTranslatef() and consorts, these methods always work on the currently active matrix stack that you set via glMatrixMode().

The glPushMatrix() method takes the current TOS, makes a copy of it, and pushes it on the stack. The glPopMatrix() method takes the current TOS and pops it from the stack so that the element below it becomes the new TOS. Let's work through a little example:

```
gl.glMatrixMode(GL10.GL_MODELVIEW);
gl.glLoadIdentity();
gl.glTranslate(0,0,-10);
```

Up until this point, there has only been a single matrix on the model-view matrix stack. "Save" this matrix:

```
gl.glPushMatrix();
```

Now you've made a copy of the current TOS and pushed down the old TOS. You have two matrices on the stack now, each encoding a translation on the z-axis by −10 units.

```
gl.glRotatef(45, 0, 1, 0);
gl.glScalef(1, 2, 1);
```

Since matrix operations always work on the TOS, you now have a scaling operation, a rotation, and a translation encoded in the top matrix. The matrix you pushed still only contains a translation. When you now render a mesh given in model space, like your cube, it will first be scaled on the y-axis, then rotated around the y-axis, and then translated by −10 units on the z-axis. Now, pop the TOS:

```
gl.glPopMatrix();
```

This will remove the TOS and make the matrix below it the new TOS. In your example, that's the original translation matrix. After this call, there's only one matrix on the stack again—the one initialized in the beginning of the example. If you render an object now, it will only be translated by −10 units on the z-axis. The matrix containing the scaling, rotation, and translation is gone because it was popped from the stack. Figure 10–14 shows what happens to the matrix stack when you execute the preceding code.

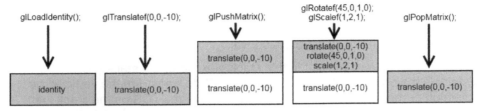

Figure 10-14. *Manipulating the matrix stack.*

So what's this good for? The first thing you can use it for is to remember transformations that should be applied to all the objects in your world. Say you want all objects in your world to be offset by 10 units on each axis, you could do the following:

```
gl.glMatrixMode(GL10.GL_MODELVIEW);
gl.glLoadIdentity();
gl.glTranslatef(10, 10, 10);
for( MyObject obj: myObjects) {
    gl.glPushMatrix();
    gl.glTranslatef(obj.x, obj.y, obj.z);
    gl.glRotatef(obj.angle, 0, 1, 0);
    // render model of object given in model space, e.g., the cube
    gl.glPopMatrix();
}
```

This pattern will be used later on when discussing how to create a camera system in 3D. The camera position and orientation is usually encoded as a matrix. You will load this camera matrix, which will transform all objects in such a way that you see them from the camera's point of view. There's something even better for which you can use the matrix stack, though.

Hierarchical Systems with the Matrix Stack

What's a hierarchical system? Our solar system is an example of one. In the center is the sun. Around the sun are the planets orbiting it at certain distances. Around some planets are moons that orbit the planet itself. The sun, the planets, and the moons all rotate around their own centers (sort of). You can build such a system with the matrix stack.

The sun has a position in our world and rotates around itself. All planets move with the sun, so if the sun changes position, the planets must change position as well. You can use glTranslatef() to position the sun and glRotatef() to let it rotate around itself.

The planets have a position relative to the sun and rotate around themselves as well as around the sun. Rotating the planet around itself can be done via glRotatef(), and rotating it around the sun can be done using glTranslatef() and glRotatef(). Letting the planet move with the sun can be done by an additional glTranslatef().

The moons have a position relative to the planet they orbit and rotate around themselves as well as around their planet. Rotating the moon around itself can be done via glRotatef(), and rotating it around the planet can be done by glTranslatef() and `glRotatef()`. Letting the moon move with the planet can be done by `glTranslatef()`. Since the planet moves with the sun, the moon must also move with the sun, which can again be done via a call to `glTranslatef()`.

There are so-called parent/child relationships here. The sun is a parent of each planet, and each planet is a parent of each moon. Each planet is a child of the sun, and each moon is a child of its planet. This means that the position of a child is always given relative to its parent, not relative to the world's origin.

The sun has no parent, so its position is indeed given relative to the world's origin. A planet is a child of the sun, so its position is given relative to the sun, and a moon is a child of a planet, so its position is given relative to the planet. You can think of each parent's center being the origin of the coordinate system in which you specify a parent's children.

The self-rotation of each of the objects in the system is independent of its parent. The same would be true if you wanted to scale an object. These things are given relative to their center. This is essentially the same as the model space.

A Simple Crate Solar System

Let's create a little example, a very simple crate solar system. There is one crate in the center of the system located at (0,0,5) in the world's coordinate system. Around this "sun" crate, you want to have a "planet" crate orbiting that sun at a distance of 3 units. The planet crate should also be smaller than the sun crate; scale it down to 0.2 units. Around the planet crate, you want to have a "moon" crate. The distance between the planet crate and the moon crate should be 1 unit, and the moon crate will also be scaled down, say to 0.1 units. All the objects rotate around their respective parent in the x-z plane and also around their own y-axes. Figure 10–15 shows the basic setup of the scene.

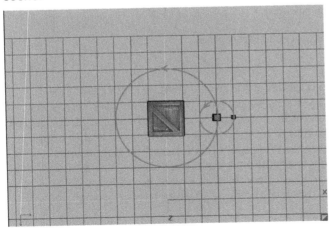

Figure 10–15. *The crate system.*

The HierarchicalObject Class

Let's define a simple class that can encode a generic solar system object with the following properties:

- A position relative to its parent's center.
- A rotation angle around the parent.
- A rotation angle around its own y-axis.
- A scale.
- A list of children.
- A reference to a Vertices3 instance to be rendered.

The HierarchicalObject should update its rotation angles and its children, and render itself and all its children. This is a recursive process since each child will render its own children. Use glPushMatrix() and glPopMatrix() to save a parent's transformations so that children will move along with the parent. Listing 10–7 shows the code.

Listing 10–7. *HierarchicalObject.java, Representing an Object in the Crate System.*

```
package com.badlogic.androidgames.gl3d;

import java.util.ArrayList;
import java.util.List;

import javax.microedition.khronos.opengles.GL10;

import com.badlogic.androidgames.framework.gl.Vertices3;

public class HierarchicalObject {
    public float x, y, z;
    public float scale = 1;
    public float rotationY, rotationParent;
    public boolean hasParent;
    public final List<HierarchicalObject> children = new
ArrayList<HierarchicalObject>();
    public final Vertices3 mesh;
```

The first three members encode the position of the object relative to its parent (or relative to the world's origin if the object has no parent). The next member stores the scale of the object. The rotationY member stores the rotation of the object around itself, and the rotationParent member stores the rotation angle around the parent's center. The hasParent member indicates whether this object has a parent or not. In case it doesn't, then you don't have to apply the rotation around the parent. This is true for the "sun" in your system. Finally, there is a list of children as well as a reference to a Vertices3 instance, which holds the mesh of the cube you use to render each object.

```
    public HierarchicalObject(Vertices3 mesh, boolean hasParent) {
        this.mesh = mesh;
        this.hasParent = hasParent;
    }
```

The constructor just takes a `Vertices3` instance and a Boolean indicating whether this object has a parent or not.

```
public void update(float deltaTime) {
    rotationY += 45 * deltaTime;
    rotationParent += 20 * deltaTime;
    int len = children.size();
    for (int i = 0; i < len; i++) {
        children.get(i).update(deltaTime);
    }
}
```

In the update() method, first update the `rotationY` and `rotationParent` members. Each object will rotate by 45 degrees per second around itself and by 20 degrees per second around its parent. You also call the update() method recursively for each child of the object.

```
public void render(GL10 gl) {
    gl.glPushMatrix();
    if (hasParent)
        gl.glRotatef(rotationParent, 0, 1, 0);
    gl.glTranslatef(x, y, z);
    gl.glPushMatrix();
    gl.glRotatef(rotationY, 0, 1, 0);
    gl.glScalef(scale, scale, scale);
    mesh.draw(GL10.GL_TRIANGLES, 0, 36);
    gl.glPopMatrix();

    int len = children.size();
    for (int i = 0; i < len; i++) {
        children.get(i).render(gl);
    }
    gl.glPopMatrix();
}
```

The render() method is where it gets interesting. The first thing you do is push the current TOS of the model-view matrix, which will be set active outside of the object. Since this method is recursive, you save the parent's transformations by this.

Next, apply the transformations that rotate the object around the parent and place it relative to the parent's center. Remember that transformations are executed in reverse order, so you actually first place the object relative to the parent and then rotate it around the parent. The rotation is only executed in case the object actually has a parent. The sun crate doesn't have a parent, so you don't rotate it. These are transformations that are relative to the parent of the object and will also apply to the children of the object. Moving a planet around the sun also moves the "attached" moon.

The next thing you do is push the TOS again. Up until this point, it has contained the parent's transformation and the object's transformation relative to the parent. You need to save this matrix since it's also going to be applied to the object's children. The self-rotation of the object and its scaling do not apply to the children, and that's why you perform this operation on a copy of the TOS (which is created by pushing the TOS). After applying the self-rotation and the scaling transformation, render this object with the crate mesh to which it stores a reference. Let's think about what will happen to the vertices given in model space due to the TOS matrix. Remember the order in which transformations are applied: last to first.

The crate will be scaled to the appropriate size first. The next transformation that gets applied is the self-rotation. These two transformations are applied to the vertices in model space. Next the vertices will be translated to the position relative to the object's parent. If this object has no parent, you'll effectively translate the vertices to the world space. If it has a parent, you'll translate them to the parent's space, with the parent being at the origin. You will also rotate the object around the parent if it has one in parent space. If you unroll the recursion, you will see that you also apply the transformations of this object's parent, and so on. Through this mechanism, a moon will first be placed in a parent's coordinate system, and then into the sun's coordinate system, which is equivalent to world space.

When you are done rendering the current object, pop the TOS so that the new TOS only contains the transformation and rotation of the object relative to its parent. You don't want the children to also have the "local" transformations of the object applied to them (that is, rotation around the object's y-axis and object scale). All that's left is recursing into the children.

> **NOTE:** You should actually encode the position of the HierarchicalObject in the form of a vector so that you can work with it more easily. However, you have yet to write a Vector3 class. You will do that in the next chapter.

Putting It All Together

Let's use this HierarchicalObject class in a proper program. For this, simply copy over the code from the CubeTest, which also contains the createCube() method that we'll reuse. Rename the class HierarchyTest and also rename the CubeScreen to HierarchyScreen. All you need to do is create your object hierarchy and call the HierarchicalObject.update() and HierarchicalObject.render() methods in the appropriate place. Listing 10–8 shows the portions of HierarchyTest that are relevant.

Listing 10–8. *Excerpt from HierarchyTest.java: Implementing a Simple Hierarchical System.*

```
class HierarchyScreen extends GLScreen {
        Vertices3 cube;
        Texture texture;
        HierarchicalObject sun;
```

You've only added a single new member to the class, called sun. It represents the root of the object hierarchy. Since all other objects are stored as children inside this sun object, you don't need to store them explicitly.

```
    public HierarchyScreen(Game game) {
        super(game);
        cube = createCube();
```

```
                texture = new Texture(glGame, "crate.png");

                sun = new HierarchicalObject(cube, false);
                sun.z = -5;

                HierarchicalObject planet = new HierarchicalObject(cube, true);
                planet.x = 3;
                planet.scale = 0.2f;
                sun.children.add(planet);

                HierarchicalObject moon = new HierarchicalObject(cube, true);
                moon.x = 1;
                moon.scale = 0.1f;
                planet.children.add(moon);
        }
```

In the constructor, set up the hierarchical system. First, load the texture and create the cube mesh to be used by all the objects. Next, create the sun. It does not have a parent, and it is located at (0,0,–5) relative to the world's origin (where the virtual camera sits). Next, create the planet crate orbiting the sun. It's located at (0,0,3) relative to the sun, and it has a scale of 0.2. Since the crate has a side length of 1 in model space, this scaling factor will make it render with a side length of 0.2 units. The crucial step here is that you add the planet to the sun as a child. For the moon, you do something similar. It is located at (0,0,1) relative to the planet, and it has a scale of 0.1 units. Also add it as a child to the planet. Refer to Figure 10–14, which uses the same unit system to get a picture of the setup.

```
        @Override
        public void update(float deltaTime) {
                sun.update(deltaTime);
        }
```

In the update() method, simply tell the sun to update itself. It will recursively call the same methods of all its children, which in turn call the same methods of all their children, and so on. This will update the rotation angles of all objects in the hierarchy.

```
        @Override
        public void present(float deltaTime) {
                GL10 gl = glGraphics.getGL();
                gl.glViewport(0, 0, glGraphics.getWidth(), glGraphics.getHeight());
                gl.glClear(GL10.GL_COLOR_BUFFER_BIT | GL10.GL_DEPTH_BUFFER_BIT);
                gl.glMatrixMode(GL10.GL_PROJECTION);
                gl.glLoadIdentity();
                GLU.gluPerspective(gl, 67, glGraphics.getWidth()
                                / (float) glGraphics.getHeight(), 0.1f, 10.0f);
                gl.glMatrixMode(GL10.GL_MODELVIEW);
                gl.glLoadIdentity();
                gl.glTranslatef(0, -2, 0);

                gl.glEnable(GL10.GL_DEPTH_TEST);
                gl.glEnable(GL10.GL_TEXTURE_2D);
                texture.bind();
                cube.bind();

                sun.render(gl);
```

```
        cube.unbind();
        gl.glDisable(GL10.GL_TEXTURE_2D);
        gl.glDisable(GL10.GL_DEPTH_TEST);
    }
// rest as in CubeScreen
```

Finally, there is the render() method. Start off with the usual setting of the viewport and clearing of the framebuffer and depthbuffer. Also set up a perspective projection matrix and load an identity matrix to the model-view matrix of OpenGL ES. The call to glTranslatef() afterward is interesting: it will push the solar system down by 2 units on the y-axis. This way, you sort of look down on the system. This could be thought of as actually moving the camera up by 2 units on the y-axis. This interpretation is actually the key to a proper camera system, which we'll investigate in the next chapter.

Once you have all the basics set up, enable depth-testing and texturing, bind the texture and the cube mesh, and tell the sun to render itself. Since all the objects in the hierarchy use the same texture and mesh, you only need to bind these once. This call will render the sun and all of its children recursively, as outlined in the last section. Finally, disable depth-testing and texturing, just for fun. Figure 10–16 shows the output of this program.

Figure 10–16. *The crate solar system in action.*

Great, everything works as expected. The sun is rotating only around itself. The planet is orbiting the sun at a distance of 3 units. It is also rotating around itself and is 20 percent as big as the sun. The moon orbits the planet, but also moves along with it around the sun due to the use of the matrix stack. It also has local transformations in the form of self-rotation and scaling.

The HierarchicalObject class is generic enough that you can play around with it. Add more planets and moons, and maybe even moons of moons. Go crazy with the matrix stack until you get the hang of it. It's again something you can learn only through a lot of practice. You need to be able to visualize in your brain what's actually going on when combining all the transformations.

> **NOTE:** Don't go too crazy with the matrix stack. It has a maximum depth, usually between 16 and 32 entries, depending on the GPU/driver. Four hierarchy levels are the most we've ever had to use in an application.

A Simple Camera System

In the last example, you saw a hint of how you could implement a camera system in 3D. You used glTranslatef() to push down the complete world by 2 units on the y-axis. Since the camera is fixed to be at the origin, looking down the negative z-axis, this approach gives the impression that the camera itself was moved up by 2 units. All the objects are still defined with their y-coordinates set to zero.

It's like in the classic saying, "If the mountain will not come to the prophet, the prophet will go to the mountain." Instead of actually moving the camera, you need to move the world around. Say you want your camera to be at position (10,4,2). All you need to do is use glTranslatef() as follows:

```
gl.glTranslatef(-10,-4,-2);
```

If you wanted your camera to be rotated around its y-axis by 45 degrees, you could do the following:

```
gl.glRotatef(-45,0,1,0);
```

You can also combine these two steps, just as you do for "normal" objects:

```
gl.glTranslatef(-10,-4,-2);
gl.glRotatef(-45,0,1,0);
```

The secret is that you must invert the arguments to the transformation methods. Let's think about it using the preceding example. You know that the "real" camera is doomed to sit at the origin of the world looking down the z-axis. By applying inverse camera transformations, you bring the world into the camera's fixed view. Using a virtual camera rotated around the y-axis by 45 degrees is the same as fixing the camera and rotating the world around the camera by –45 degrees. The same is true for translation. Your virtual camera could be placed at (10,4,2). However, since your real camera is fixed at the origin of the world, you just need to translate all objects by the inverse of that position vector, which is (–10,–4,–2).

When you modify the following three lines of the last example's present() method,

```
gl.glMatrixMode(GL10.GL_MODELVIEW);
gl.glLoadIdentity();
gl.glTranslatef(0, -2, 0);
```

with these four lines,

```
gl.glMatrixMode(GL10.GL_MODELVIEW);
gl.glLoadIdentity();
gl.glTranslatef(0, -3, 0);
gl.glRotatef(45, 1, 0, 0);
```

you get the output in Figure 10–17.

Figure 10–17. *Looking down at the world from (0,3,0).*

Conceptually, the camera is now located at (0,3,0), and it looks down at your scene at a –45 degree angle (which is the same as rotating the camera by –45 degrees around the x-axis). Figure 10–18 shows the setup of your scene with the camera.

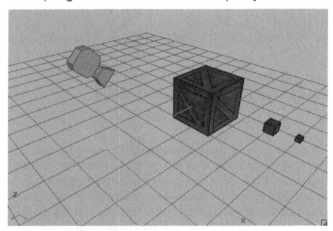

Figure 10–18. *How the camera is positioned and oriented in the scene.*

You could actually specify a very simple camera with four attributes:

- Its position in world space.

- Its rotation around its x-axis (pitch). This is equivalent to tilting your head up and down.

- Its rotation around its y-axis (yaw). This is equivalent to turning your head left and right.

- Its rotation around its z-axis (roll). This is equivalent to tilting your head to the left and right.

Given these attributes, you can use OpenGL ES methods to create a camera matrix. This is called a *Euler rotation* camera. Many first-person shooter games use this kind of camera to simulate the tilting of a head. Usually you'd leave out the roll and only apply the yaw and pitch. The order in which the rotations are applied is important. For a first-person shooter, you'd first apply the pitch rotation and then the yaw rotation:

```
gl.glTranslatef(-cam.x,- cam.y,-cam.z);
gl.glRotatef(cam.yaw, 0, 1, 0);
gl.glRotatef(cam.pitch, 1, 0, 0);
```

Many games still use this very simplistic camera model. If the roll rotation had been included, you might observe an effect called *gimbal lock*. This effect will cancel out one of the rotations given a certain configuration.

> **NOTE:** Explaining gimbal lock with text or even images is very difficult. Since you'll only use yaw and pitch, you won't have this problem. To get an idea of what gimbal lock actually is, look it up on your favorite video site on the Web. This problem can't be solved with Euler rotations. The actual solution is mathematically complex, and we won't go into that in this book.

A second approach to a very simple camera system is the use of the GLU.glLookAt() method.

```
GLU.gluLookAt(GL10 gl,
            float eyeX, float eyeY, float eyeZ,
            float centerX, float centerY, float centerZ,
            float upX, float upY, float upZ);
```

Like the GLU.gluPerspective() method, it will multiply the currently-active matrix with a transformation matrix. In this case, it's a camera matrix that will transform the world:

- gl is just the GL10 instance used throughout the rendering.

- eyex, eyey, and eyez specify the camera's position in the world.

- centerx, centery, and centerz specify a point in the world that the camera looks at.

- upX, upY, and upZ specify the so-called *up vector*. Think of it as an arrow coming out at the top of your skull pointing upward. Tilt your head to the left or right and the arrow will point in the same direction as the top of your head.

The up vector is usually set to (0,1,0), even if that's not entirely correct. The gluLookAt() method can renormalize this up vector in most cases. Figure 10–19 shows the scene with the camera at (3,3,0), looking at (0,0,–5), as well as its "real" up vector.

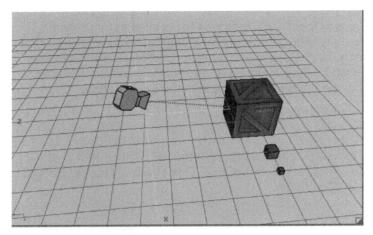

Figure 10–19. *A camera at position (3,3,0), looking at (0,0,–3).*

You can replace the code in the HierarchyScreen.present() method you changed before with the following code snippet:

```
gl.glMatrixMode(GL10.GL_MODELVIEW);
gl.glLoadIdentity();
GLU.gluLookAt(gl, 3, 3, 0, 0, 0, -5, 0, 1, 0);
```

This time, you also commented out the call to sun.update(), so the hierarchy will look like the one shown in Figure 10–19. Figure 10–20 shows the result of using the camera.

Figure 10–20. *The camera in action.*

This kind of camera is great when you want to follow a character or want better control over how you view the scene by only specifying the camera's position and look-at point. For now, that's all you need to know about cameras. In the next chapter, you'll write two simple classes for a first-person shooter–type camera and a look-at camera that can follow an object.

Summary

You should now know the basics of 3D graphics programming with OpenGL ES. You learned how to set up a perspective view frustum, how to specify 3D vertex positions, and what is the z-buffer. You also saw how the z-buffer can both be friend and foe, depending on whether it is used correctly. You created your first 3D object: a texture cube, which turned out to be really easy. Finally, you learned a little bit more about matrices and transformations, and created a hierarchical and very simple camera system. You'll be happy to know that this was not even the tip of the iceberg. In the next chapter, we'll revisit a couple of topics from Chapter 7 in the context of 3D graphics programming. We'll also introduce a few new tricks that will come in handy when you write your final game. We highly recommend playing around with the examples in this chapter. Create new shapes, and go crazy with transformations and the camera systems.

Chapter 11

3D Programming Tricks

3D programming is an incredibly wide and complex field. This chapter explores some topics that are the absolute minimum requirement to write a simple 3D game:

- We'll revisit our friend the vector and attach one more coordinate.

- Lighting is a vital part of any 3D game. We'll look at how to perform simple lighting with OpenGL ES.

- Defining objects programmatically is cumbersome. We'll look at a simple 3D file format so that we can load and render 3D models created with 3D modeling software.

- In Chapter 8, we discussed object representation and collision detection. We'll look at how to do the same in 3D.

- We'll also briefly revisit some of the physics concepts that we explored in Chapter 10—this time in a 3D context.

Let's start with 3D vectors.

Before We Begin

As always, we'll create a couple of simple example programs in this chapter. To do that, we just create a new project and copy over all of the source code of the framework we've developed so far.

As In previous chapters, we'll have a single test starter activity that presents us with the tests in the form of a list. We'll call it GLAdvancedStarter and make it our default activity. Simply copy over the GL3DBasicsStarter, and replace the class names of the tests. We also need to add each of the test activities to the manifest with a proper <activity>element.

Each of the tests will extend GLGame as usual; the actual code will be implemented as a GLScreen that we'll hook up with the GLGame instance. To conserve space, we'll only present you with the relevant portions of the GLScreen implementations. All of the tests and the starter activity reside within the package com.badlogic.androidgames.gladvanced. Some of the classes will be part of our framework and will go into the respective framework packages.

Vectors in 3D

In Chapter 8, we discussed vectors and their interpretation in 2D. As you might have guessed, all of the things we discussed there still hold in 3D space as well. All we need to do is to add one more coordinate to our vector, namely the z-coordinate.

The operations we looked at with vectors in 2D can be easily transferred to 3D space. We specify vectors in 3D with a statement like the following:

$v = (x, y, z)$

Addition in 3D is carried out as follows:

$c = a + b = (a.x, a.y, b.z) + (b.x, b.y, b.z) = (a.x + b.x, a.y + b.y, a.z + b.z)$

Subtraction works exactly the same way:

$c = a - b = (a.x, a.y, b.z) - (b.x, b.y, b.z) = (a.x - b.x, a.y - b.y, a.z - b.z)$

Multiplying a vector by a scalar works like this:

$a' = a \times scalar = (a.x \times scalar, a.y \times scalar, a.z \times scalar)$

Measuring the length of a vector in 3D is also quite simple; we just add the z-coordinate to the Pythagorean equation:

$|a| = sqrt(a.x \times a.x + a.y \times a.y + a.z \times a.z)$

Based on this, we can also normalize our vectors to unit length again:

$a' = (a.x\ /\ |a|, a.y\ /\ |a|, a.z\ /\ |a|)$

All of the interpretations of vectors we talked about in Chapter 8 hold in 3D as well:

- Positions are just denoted by a normal vector's x-, y- and z-coordinates.
- Velocities and accelerations can also be represented as 3D vectors. Each component then represents a certain quantity of the attribute on one axis, such as meters per second in the case of velocity or meters per second per second for acceleration.
- We can represent directions (or axes) as simple 3D unit vectors. We did that in Chapter 8 when we used the rotation facilities of OpenGL ES.
- We can measure distances by subtracting the starting vector from the end vector and measuring the resulting vector's length.

One more operation that can be rather useful is rotation of a 3D vector around a 3D axis. We used this principle earlier via the OpenGL ES glRotatef() method. However, we can't use it to rotate one of the vectors that we'll use to store positions or directions of our game objects, because it only works on vertices that we submit to the GPU. Luckily, there's a Matrix class in the Android API that allows us to emulate what OpenGL ES does on the GPU. Let's write a Vector3 class that implements all of these features. Listing 11–1 shows you the code, which we'll again explain along the way.

Listing 11–1. *Vector3.java, a Vector in 3D*

```
package com.badlogic.androidgames.framework.math;

import android.opengl.Matrix;
import android.util.FloatMath;

public class Vector3 {
    private static final float[] matrix = new float[16];
    private static final float[] inVec = new float[4];
    private static final float[] outVec = new float[4];
    public float x, y, z;
```

The class starts with a couple of private static final float arrays. We'll need them later on when we implement the new rotate() method of our Vector3 class. Just remember that the matrix member has 16 elements and the inVec and outVec each have 4 elements.

The x, y, and z members defined next should be self-explanatory. They store the actual components of the vector:

```
    public Vector3() {
    }

    public Vector3(float x, float y, float z) {
        this.x = x;
        this.y = y;
        this.z = z;
    }

    public Vector3(Vector3 other) {
        this.x = other.x;
        this.y = other.y;
        this.z = other.z;
    }

    public Vector3 cpy() {
    return new Vector3(x, y, z);
    }

    public Vector3 set(float x, float y, float z) {
        this.x = x;
        this.y = y;
        this.z = z;
        return this;
    }

    public Vector3 set(Vector3 other) {
        this.x = other.x;
        this.y = other.y;
        this.z = other.z;
        return this;
    }
```

Like Vector2, our Vector3 class has a couple of constructors and setters and a cpy() method, so that we can easily clone vectors or set them from components calculated in our program.

```java
public Vector3 add(float x, float y, float z) {
    this.x += x;
    this.y += y;
    this.z += z;
    return this;
}

public Vector3 add(Vector3 other) {
    this.x += other.x;
    this.y += other.y;
    this.z += other.z;
    return this;
}

public Vector3 sub(float x, float y, float z) {
    this.x -= x;
    this.y -= y;
    this.z -= z;
    return this;
}

public Vector3 sub(Vector3 other) {
    this.x -= other.x;
    this.y -= other.y;
    this.z -= other.z;
    return this;
}

public Vector3 mul(float scalar) {
    this.x *= scalar;
    this.y *= scalar;
    this.z *= scalar;
    return this;
}
```

The various add(), sub() and mul() methods are just an extension of what we had in our Vector2 class with an additional z-coordinate. They implement what we discussed a few pages ago. Straightforward, right?

```java
public float len() {
    return FloatMath.sqrt(x * x + y * y + z * z);
}

public Vector3 nor() {
    float len = len();
    if (len != 0) {
        this.x /= len;
        this.y /= len;
        this.z /= len;
    }
    return this;
}
```

The `len()` and `nor()` methods are also essentially the same as in the `Vector2` class. All we do is incorporate the new z-coordinate into the calculations.

```java
public Vector3 rotate(float angle, float axisX, float axisY, float axisZ) {
    inVec[0] = x;
    inVec[1] = y;
    inVec[2] = z;
    inVec[3] = 1;
    Matrix.setIdentityM(matrix, 0);
    Matrix.rotateM(matrix, 0, angle, axisX, axisY, axisZ);
    Matrix.multiplyMV(outVec, 0, matrix, 0, inVec, 0);
    x = outVec[0];
    y = outVec[1];
    z = outVec[2];
    return this;
}
```

And here's our new `rotate()` method. As indicated earlier, it makes use of Android's `Matrix` class. The `Matrix` class essentially consists of a couple of static methods, like `Matrix.setIdentityM()` or `Matrix.rotateM()`. These operate on float arrays, similar to the ones we defined earlier. A matrix is stored as 16 float values, and a vector is expected to have four elements. We won't go into detail about the inner workings of the class; all we need is a way to emulate the matrix capabilities of OpenGL ES on the Java side, and that's exactly what this class offers to us. All of the methods work on a matrix and operate in exactly the same way as `glRotatef()`, `glTranslatef()`, or `glIdentityf()` in OpenGL ES.

The method starts off by setting the vector's components to the `inVec` array we defined earlier. Next, we call `Matrix.setIdentityM()` on the matrix member of our class. This will "clear" the matrix. With OpenGL ES, we used `glIdentityf()` to do the same thing with matrices residing on the GPU. Next we call `Matrix.rotateM()`. It takes the float array holding the matrix, an offset into that array, the angle we want to rotate by in degrees, and the (unit length) axis we want to rotate around. This method is equivalent to `glRotatef()`. It will multiply the given matrix by a rotation matrix. Finally, we call `Matrix.multiplyMV()`, which will multiply our vector stored in `inVec` by the matrix. This applies all of the transformations stored in the matrix to the vector. The result will be output in `outVec`. The rest of the method just grabs the resulting new components from the `outVec` array and stores them in the `Vector3`'s members.

> **NOTE:** You can use the Matrix class to do a lot more than just rotating vectors. It operates in exactly the same way as OpenGL ES in its effects on the passed-in matrix.

```java
public float dist(Vector3 other) {
    float distX = this.x - other.x;
    float distY = this.y - other.y;
    float distZ = this.z - other.z;
    return FloatMath.sqrt(distX * distX + distY * distY + distZ * distZ);
}

public float dist(float x, float y, float z) {
```

```
            float distX = this.x - x;
            float distY = this.y - y;
            float distZ = this.z - z;
            return FloatMath.sqrt(distX * distX + distY * distY + distZ * distZ);
        }

    public float distSquared(Vector3 other) {
            float distX = this.x - other.x;
            float distY = this.y - other.y;
            float distZ = this.z - other.z;
            return distX * distX + distY * distY + distZ * distZ;
        }

    public float distSquared(float x, float y, float z) {
            float distX = this.x - x;
            float distY = this.y - y;
            float distZ = this.z - z;
            return distX * distX + distY * distY + distZ * distZ;
        }
}
```

Finally, we have the usual dist() and distSquared() methods to calculate the distance between two vectors in 3D.

Note that we left out the angle() method from Vector2. While it is possible to measure the angle between two vectors in 3D, that does not give us an angle in the range 0 to 360. Usually, we get away with just evaluating the angle between two vectors in the x/y, z/y, and x/z plane by using only two components of each vector and applying the Vector2.angle() method. We won't need this functionality until our last game, so we'll return to the topic at that point.

We think you'll agree that we don't need an explicit example of using this class. We can just invoke it the same way we did with the Vector2 class in Chapter 8. On to the next topic: lighting in OpenGL ES.

Lighting in OpenGL ES

Lighting in OpenGL ES is a useful feature that can give our 3D games a nice touch. To use this functionality, we have to have an idea of the OpenGL ES lighting model.

How Lighting Works

Let's think about how lighting works for a moment. The first thing we need is a light source to emit light. We also need an object that can be lit. Finally, we need a sensor, like our eyes or a camera, which will catch the photons that are sent out by the light source and reflected back by the object. Lighting changes the perceived color of an object depending on the following:

- The light source's type
- The light source's color or intensity

■   The light source's position and direction relative to the lit object

■   The object's material and texture

The intensity with which light is reflected by an object can depend on various factors. We are mostly concerned with the angle at which a light ray hits a surface. The more perpendicular a light ray is to a surface it hits, the greater the intensity of the light reflected by the surface. Figure 11–1 illustrates this point.

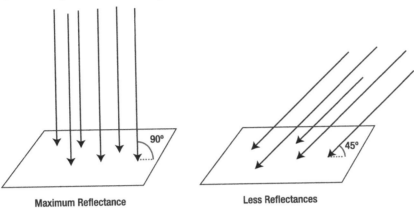

Figure 11–1. *The more perpendicular a light ray is to a surface, the greater the intensity of the reflected light.*

Once a light ray hits a surface, it is reflected in two different ways. Most of the light is reflected *diffusely*, which means that the reflected light rays are scattered randomly by irregularities of the object's surface. Some reflections are *specular*, which means that the light rays bounce back as if they had hit a perfect mirror. Figure 11–2 shows the difference between diffuse and specular reflection.

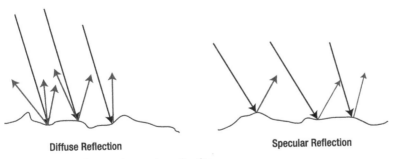

Figure 11–2. *Diffuse and specular reflection*

Specular reflection will manifest itself as highlights on objects. Whether an object will cast specular reflections depends on its material. Objects with rough or uneven surfaces, like skin or fabric, are unlikely to have specular highlights. Objects that have a smooth surface, like glass or a marble, do exhibit these lighting artifacts. Of course, glass or marble surfaces aren't really smooth in an absolute sense either. Relative to materials like wood or human skin, though, they are very smooth.

When light hits a surface, its reflection also changes color depending on the chemical constitution of the object it hits. The objects we see as red, for example, are those that reflect only the red portions of light. The object "swallows" all other wavelengths. A black object is one that swallows almost all of the light that is shone on it.

OpenGL ES allows us to simulate this real-world behavior by specifying light sources and materials of objects.

Light Sources

We are surrounded by all kind of light sources. The sun constantly throws photons at us. Our monitors emit light, surrounding us with that nice blue glow at night. Light bulbs and headlights keep us from bumping or driving into things in the dark. OpenGL ES allows you to create four types of light sources:

- **Ambient light**: Ambient light is not a light source *per se* but rather the result of photons coming from other light sources and bouncing around in our world. All of these stray photons combined make for a certain default level of illumination that is directionless and illuminates all objects equally.

- **Point lights**: These have a position in space and emit light in all directions. A light bulb is a point light, for example.

- **Directional lights**: These are expressed as directions in OpenGL ES and are assumed to be infinitely far away. The sun can be idealized as a directional light source. We can assume that the light rays coming from the sun all hit the earth at the same angle because of the distance between the earth and the sun.

- **Spotlights**: These are similar to point lights in that they have an explicit position in space. Additionally, they have a direction in which they shine and create a light cone that is limited to some radius. A street lamp is a spotlight.

We'll only look into ambient, point, and directional lights. Spotlights are often hard to get right with limited GPUs like those found on Android devices because of the way OpenGL ES calculates the lighting. You'll see why that is in a minute.

Besides a light source's position and direction, OpenGL ES lets us also specify the color or intensity of a light. This is expressed as an RGBA color. However, OpenGL ES requires us to specify four different colors per light source instead of just one.

- **Ambient**: This is the intensity/color that contributes to the overall shading of an object. An object will be uniformly lit with this color, no matter its position or orientation relative to the light source.

- **Diffuse**: This is the intensity/color with which an object will be lit when calculating the diffuse reflection. Sides of an object that do not face the light source won't be lit, just as in real life.

■ **Specular**: This intensity/color is similar to the diffuse color. However, it will only affect spots on the object that have a certain orientation toward the viewer and the light source.

■ **Emissive**: This is totally confusing and has very little use in real-word applications, so we won't go into it.

Usually, we'll only set the diffuse and specular intensities of a light source and leave the other two at their defaults. We'll also use the same RGBA color for both the diffuse and specular intensity most of the time.

Materials

Every object in our world has a material covering. The material defines how the light that is hitting an object will be reflected and it modifies the color of the reflected light. OpenGL ES lets us specify the same four RGBA colors for a material as we can for a light source:

■ **Ambient**: This is the color that's combined with the ambient color of any light source in the scene.

■ **Diffuse**: This is the color that's combined with the diffuse color of any light source.

■ **Specular**: This is the color that's combined with the specular color of any light source for specular highlight points on an object's surface.

■ **Emissive**: We again ignore this as it has little use in our context.

Figure 11–3 illustrates the first three types of material/light source properties: ambient, diffuse, and specular.

Figure 11–3. *Different material/light types. Left: ambient only. Center: Diffuse only. Right: Ambient and diffuse with specular highlight.*

In Figure 11–3, we can see the contributions of the different material and light properties. Ambient light illuminates the object uniformly. Diffuse light will be reflected depending on the angle that the light rays hit the object; areas that directly face the light source will be brighter, and areas that can't be reached by light rays are dark. In the right-most image we see the combination of ambient, diffuse, and specular light. The specular light manifests itself as a white highlight on the sphere.

How OpenGL ES Calculates Lighting: Vertex Normals

You know that the intensity of the reflected light bouncing back from an object depends on the angle it hits the surface of the object. OpenGL ES uses this fact to calculate lighting. It does so by using *vertex normals*, which we have to define in our code, just as we define texture coordinates or vertex colors. Figure 11–4 shows a sphere with its vertex normals.

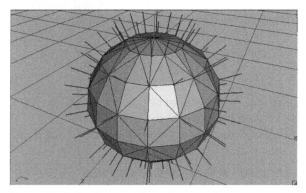

Figure 11–4. *A sphere and its vertex normals*

Normals are simply unit-length vectors that point in the direction a surface is facing. In our case, a surface is a triangle. Instead of specifying a surface normal, though, we have to specify a vertex normal. The difference between a surface normal and a vertex normal is that the vertex normal might not have to point in the same direction as the surface normal. We can clearly see this in Figure 11–4, where each vertex normal is actually the average of the normals of the triangles to which that vertex belongs. This averaging makes for a smooth shading of the object.

When we render an object with vertex normals and lighting enabled, OpenGL ES will determine the angle between each vertex and light source. With this angle, it can calculate the vertex's color based on the ambient, diffuse, and specular properties of the material of the object and the light source. The end result is a color for each vertex of an object that is then interpolated over each triangle in combination with the calculated colors of the other vertices. This interpolated color will then be combined with any texture maps we apply to the object.

This sounds scary, but it really isn't that bad. All we need to do is enable lighting and specify the light sources, the material for the object we want to render, and the vertex normals, in addition to the other vertex attributes we usually specify, like position or texture coordinates. Let's have a look at how to implement all of this with OpenGL ES.

In Practice

We'll now go through all of the necessary steps to get lighting to work with OpenGL ES. Along the way, we'll create a few little helper classes that make working with light sources a bit easier. We'll put those in the com.badlogic.androidgames.framework.gl package.

Enabling and Disabling Lighting

As with all OpenGL ES states, we first have to enable the functionality in question. We do that with this:

```
gl.glEnable(GL10.GL_LIGHTING);
```

Once enabled, lighting will be applied to all of the objects that we render. Of course, we'll have to specify the light sources and materials as well as the vertex normals to achieve meaningful results. Once we are done with rendering all of the objects that should be illuminated, we can disable lighting again:

```
gl.glDisable(GL10.GL_LIGHTING);
```

Specifying Light Sources

OpenGL ES offers us four types of light sources: ambient lights, point lights, directional lights, and spot lights. We'll take a look at how to define the first three. In order for spot lights to be effective and to look good, we'd need to have a very high triangle count for each of our objects' models. This is prohibitive on most current mobile devices.

OpenGL ES limits us to having a maximum of eight light sources in a scene, plus a global ambient light. Each of the eight light sources has an identifier, from GL10.GL_LIGHT0 up to GL10.GL_LIGHT7. If we want to manipulate the properties of one of these light sources, we do so by specifying the respective ID of that light source.

Light sources have to be enabled with this syntax:

```
gl.glEnable(GL10.GL_LIGHT0);
```

In this case, OpenGL ES will then take the properties of the light source with ID zero and apply it to all rendered objects accordingly. If we want to disable a light source, we can do it with a statement like this:

```
gl.glDisable(GL10.GL_LIGHT0);
```

Ambient light is a special case as it does not have an identifier. There is only one ambient light ever in an OpenGL ES scene. Let's have a look at that.

Ambient Light

Ambient light is a special type of light, as explained already. It has no position or direction, but only a color by which all objects in the scene will be uniformly lit. OpenGL ES lets us specify the global ambient light as follows:

```
float[] ambientColor = { 0.2f, 0.2f, 0.2f, 1.0f };
gl.glLightModelfv(GL10.GL_LIGHT_MODEL_AMBIENT, color, 0);
```

The ambientColor array holds the RGBA values of the ambient light's color encoded as floats in the range 0 to 1. The glLightModelfv() method takes a constant as the first parameter specifying that we want to set the ambient light's color, the float array holding the color and an offset into the float array from which the method should start reading the RGBA values. Let's put this into a lovely little class. Listing 11–2 shows the code.

Listing 11–2. *AmbientLight.java, a Simple Abstraction of OpenGL ES Global Ambient Light*

```
package com.badlogic.androidgames.framework.gl;

import javax.microedition.khronos.opengles.GL10;

public class AmbientLight {
    float[] color = {0.2f, 0.2f, 0.2f, 1};

    public void setColor(float r, float g, float b, float a) {
        color[0] = r;
        color[1] = g;
        color[2] = b;
        color[3] = a;
    }

    public void enable(GL10 gl) {
        gl.glLightModelfv(GL10.GL_LIGHT_MODEL_AMBIENT, color, 0);
    }
}
```

All we do is store the ambient light's color in a float array and then provide two methods: one to set the color and the other to make OpenGL ES use the ambient light color that we define. By default, we use a gray ambient light color.

Point Lights

Point lights have a position as well as an ambient, diffuse, and specular color/intensity (we leave out the emissive color/intensity). To specify the different colors, we can do the following:

```
gl.glLightfv(GL10.GL_LIGHT3, GL10.GL_AMBIENT, ambientColor, 0);
gl.glLightfv(GL10.GL_LIGHT3, GL10.GL_DIFFUSE, diffuseColor, 0);
gl.glLightfv(GL10.GL_LIGHT3, GL10.GL_SPECULAR, specularColor, 0);
```

The first parameter is the light identifier; in this case we use the fourth light. The next parameter specifies the attribute of the light we want to modify. The third parameter is again a float array that holds the RGBA values, and the final parameter is an offset into that array. Specifying the position is easy:

```
float[] position = {x, y, z, 1};
gl.glLightfv(GL10.GL_LIGHT3, GL10.GL_POSITION, position, 0);
```

We again specify the attribute we want to modify (in this case the position), along with a four-element array that stores the x-, y-, and z-coordinates of the light in our world. Note that the fourth element of the array must be set to 1 for a positional light source! Let's put this into a helper class. Listing 11–3 shows you the code.

Listing 11–3. *PointLight.java, a Simple Abstraction of OpenGL ES Point Lights*

```java
package com.badlogic.androidgames.framework.gl;

import javax.microedition.khronos.opengles.GL10;

public class PointLight {
    float[] ambient = { 0.2f, 0.2f, 0.2f, 1.0f };
    float[] diffuse = { 1.0f, 1.0f, 1.0f, 1.0f };
    float[] specular = { 0.0f, 0.0f, 0.0f, 1.0f };
    float[] position = { 0, 0, 0, 1 };
    int lastLightId = 0;

    public void setAmbient(float r, float g, float b, float a) {
        ambient[0] = r;
        ambient[1] = g;
        ambient[2] = b;
        ambient[3] = a;
    }

    public void setDiffuse(float r, float g, float b, float a) {
        diffuse[0] = r;
        diffuse[1] = g;
        diffuse[2] = b;
        diffuse[3] = a;
    }

    public void setSpecular(float r, float g, float b, float a) {
        specular[0] = r;
        specular[1] = g;
        specular[2] = b;
        specular[3] = a;
    }

    public void setPosition(float x, float y, float z) {
        position[0] = x;
        position[1] = y;
        position[2] = z;
    }

    public void enable(GL10 gl, int lightId) {
        gl.glEnable(lightId);
        gl.glLightfv(lightId, GL10.GL_AMBIENT, ambient, 0);
        gl.glLightfv(lightId, GL10.GL_DIFFUSE, diffuse, 0);
        gl.glLightfv(lightId, GL10.GL_SPECULAR, specular, 0);
        gl.glLightfv(lightId, GL10.GL_POSITION, position, 0);
        lastLightId = lightId;
    }

    public void disable(GL10 gl) {
        gl.glDisable(lastLightId);
    }
}
```

Our helper class stores the ambient, diffuse, and specular color components of the light as well as the position (with the fourth element set to 1). In addition, we store the last light identifier used for this light so that we can offer a disable() method that will turn off the light if necessary. For each light attribute, we have a nice setter method. We also have an enable() method, which takes a GL10 instance and a light identifier (like GL10.GL_LIGHT6). It enables the light, sets its attributes, and stores the light identifier used. The disable() method just disables the light using the lastLightId member set in enable().

We use sensible defaults for the ambient, diffuse, and specular colors in the initializers of the member arrays. The light will be white, and it will not produce any specular highlights because the specular color is black.

Directional Lights

A *directional light* is nearly identical to a point light. The only difference is that it has a direction instead of a position. The way the direction is expressed is somewhat confusing. Instead of using a direction vector, OpenGL ES expects us to define a point in the world. The direction is then calculated by taking the direction vector from that point to the origin of the world. The following snippet would produce a directional light that comes from the right side of the world:

```
float[] dirPos = {1, 0, 0, 0};
gl.glLightfv(GL10.GL_LIGHT0, GL10.GL_POSITION, dirPos, 0);
```

We can translate that to a direction vector:

```
dir = -dirPos = {-1, 0, 0, 0}
```

The rest of the attributes, like the ambient or diffuse color, are identical to those of a point light. Listing 11–4 shows you the code of a little helper class for diffuse lights.

Listing 11–4. *DirectionLight.java, a Simple Abstraction of OpenGL ES Directional Lights*

```java
package com.badlogic.androidgames.framework.gl;

import javax.microedition.khronos.opengles.GL10;

public class DirectionalLight {
    float[] ambient = { 0.2f, 0.2f, 0.2f, 1.0f };
    float[] diffuse = { 1.0f, 1.0f, 1.0f, 1.0f };
    float[] specular = { 0.0f, 0.0f, 0.0f, 1.0f };
    float[] direction = { 0, 0, -1, 0 };
    int lastLightId = 0;

    public void setAmbient(float r, float g, float b, float a) {
        ambient[0] = r;
        ambient[1] = g;
        ambient[2] = b;
        ambient[3] = a;
    }

    public void setDiffuse(float r, float g, float b, float a) {
        diffuse[0] = r;
        diffuse[1] = g;
        diffuse[2] = b;
```

```
        diffuse[3] = a;
    }

    public void setSpecular(float r, float g, float b, float a) {
        specular[0] = r;
        specular[1] = g;
        specular[2] = b;
        specular[3] = a;
    }

    public void setDirection(float x, float y, float z) {
        direction[0] = -x;
        direction[1] = -y;
        direction[2] = -z;
    }

    public void enable(GL10 gl, int lightId) {
        gl.glEnable(lightId);
        gl.glLightfv(lightId, GL10.GL_AMBIENT, ambient, 0);
        gl.glLightfv(lightId, GL10.GL_DIFFUSE, diffuse, 0);
        gl.glLightfv(lightId, GL10.GL_SPECULAR, specular, 0);
        gl.glLightfv(lightId, GL10.GL_POSITION, direction, 0);
        lastLightId = lightId;
    }

    public void disable(GL10 gl) {
        gl.glDisable(lastLightId);
    }
}
```

Our helper class is nearly identical to the PointLight class. The only difference is that the direction array has its fourth element set to 1. We also have a setDirection() method instead of a setPosition() method. The setDirection() method allows us to specify a direction, like (–1, 0, 0) so that the light comes from the right side. Inside the method, we just negate all of the vector components so that we transform the direction to the format that OpenGL ES expects from us.

Specifying Materials

A material is defined by a couple of attributes. As with anything in OpenGL ES, a material is a state and will be active until we change it again or the OpenGL ES context is lost. To set the currently active material attributes, we can do the following:

```
gl.glMaterialfv(GL10.GL_FRONT_AND_BACK, GL10.GL_AMBIENT, ambientColor, 0);
gl.glMaterialfv(GL10.GL_FRONT_AND_BACK, GL10.GL_DIFFUSE, diffuseColor, 0);
gl.glMaterialfv(GL10.GL_FRONT_AND_BACK, GL10.GL_SPECULAR, specularColor, 0);
```

As usual, we have an ambient, a diffuse, and a specular RGBA color to specify. This is again done via four-element float arrays, just as we did with the light source attributes. Putting this together into a little helper class is again very easy. Listing 11–5 shows you the code.

Listing 11–5. *Material.java, a Simple Abstraction of OpenGL ES Materials*

```java
package com.badlogic.androidgames.framework.gl;

import javax.microedition.khronos.opengles.GL10;

public class Material {
    float[] ambient = { 0.2f, 0.2f, 0.2f, 1.0f };
    float[] diffuse = { 1.0f, 1.0f, 1.0f, 1.0f };
    float[] specular = { 0.0f, 0.0f, 0.0f, 1.0f };

    public void setAmbient(float r, float g, float b, float a) {
        ambient[0] = r;
        ambient[1] = g;
        ambient[2] = b;
        ambient[3] = a;
    }

    public void setDiffuse(float r, float g, float b, float a) {
        diffuse[0] = r;
        diffuse[1] = g;
        diffuse[2] = b;
        diffuse[3] = a;
    }

    public void setSpecular(float r, float g, float b, float a) {
        specular[0] = r;
        specular[1] = g;
        specular[2] = b;
        specular[3] = a;
    }

    public void enable(GL10 gl) {
        gl.glMaterialfv(GL10.GL_FRONT_AND_BACK, GL10.GL_AMBIENT, ambient, 0);
        gl.glMaterialfv(GL10.GL_FRONT_AND_BACK, GL10.GL_DIFFUSE, diffuse, 0);
        gl.glMaterialfv(GL10.GL_FRONT_AND_BACK, GL10.GL_SPECULAR, specular, 0);
    }
}
```

There are no big surprises here, either. We just store the three components of the material and provide setters and an enable() method, which sets the material.

OpenGL ES has one more trick up its sleeve when it comes to materials. Usually one wouldn't use glMaterialfv(), but would instead choose something called *color material*. This means that instead of the ambient and diffuse color specified via glMaterialfv(), OpenGL ES will take the vertex color of our models as the ambient and diffuse material color. To enable this nice feature, we just have to call it:

```java
gl.glEnable(GL10.GL_COLOR_MATERIAL);
```

We usually use this instead of a full-blown material class, as shown earlier, because ambient and diffuse colors are often the same. Since we also don't use specular highlights in most of our demos and games, we can get away with just enabling color materials and not using any glMaterialfv() calls at all. The choice of using the Material class or color materials is totally up to you.

Specifying Normals

For lighting to work in OpenGL ES, we have to specify vertex normals for each vertex of a model. A vertex normal must be a unit length vector that points in the (average) facing direction of the surface(s) to which a vertex belongs. Figure 11–5 illustrates vertex normals for our cube.

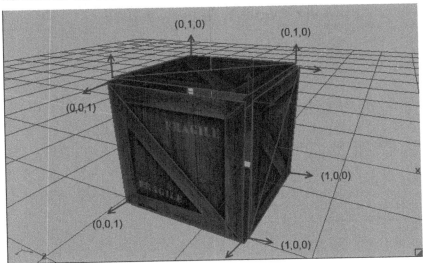

Figure 11–5. *Vertex normals for each vertex of our cube*

A vertex normal is just another vertex attribute, like position or color. In order to upload vertex normals, we have to modify our Vertices3 class one more time. To tell OpenGL ES where it can find the normals for each vertex, we use the glNormalPointer() method, just like we used the glVertexPointer() or glColorPointer() methods previously. Listing 11–6 shows our final revised Vertices3 class.

Listing 11–6. *Vertices3.java, the Final Version with Support for Normals*

```
package com.badlogic.androidgames.framework.gl;

import java.nio.ByteBuffer;
import java.nio.ByteOrder;
import java.nio.IntBuffer;
import java.nio.ShortBuffer;

import javax.microedition.khronos.opengles.GL10;

import com.badlogic.androidgames.framework.impl.GLGraphics;

public class Vertices3 {
    final GLGraphics glGraphics;
    final boolean hasColor;
    final boolean hasTexCoords;
    final boolean hasNormals;
    final int vertexSize;
```

```
final IntBuffer vertices;
final int[] tmpBuffer;
final ShortBuffer indices;
```

Among the members, the only new addition is the hasNormals Boolean, which keeps track of whether the vertices have normals or not.

```
public Vertices3(GLGraphics glGraphics, int maxVertices, int maxIndices,
        boolean hasColor, boolean hasTexCoords, boolean hasNormals) {
    this.glGraphics = glGraphics;
    this.hasColor = hasColor;
    this.hasTexCoords = hasTexCoords;
    this.hasNormals = hasNormals;
    this.vertexSize = (3 + (hasColor ? 4 : 0) + (hasTexCoords ? 2 : 0) + (hasNormals
? 3   : 0)) * 4;
    this.tmpBuffer = new int[maxVertices * vertexSize / 4];

    ByteBuffer buffer = ByteBuffer.allocateDirect(maxVertices * vertexSize);
    buffer.order(ByteOrder.nativeOrder());
    vertices = buffer.asIntBuffer();

    if (maxIndices > 0) {
        buffer = ByteBuffer.allocateDirect(maxIndices * Short.SIZE / 8);
        buffer.order(ByteOrder.nativeOrder());
        indices = buffer.asShortBuffer();
    } else {
        indices = null;
    }
}
```

In the constructor, we now also take a hasNormals parameter. We have to modify the calculation of the vertexSize member as well, adding three floats per vertex if normals are available.

```
public void setVertices(float[] vertices, int offset, int length) {
    this.vertices.clear();
    int len = offset + length;
    for (int i = offset, j = 0; i < len; i++, j++)
        tmpBuffer[j] = Float.floatToRawIntBits(vertices[i]);
    this.vertices.put(tmpBuffer, 0, length);
    this.vertices.flip();
}

public void setIndices(short[] indices, int offset, int length) {
    this.indices.clear();
    this.indices.put(indices, offset, length);
    this.indices.flip();
}
```

As you can see, the methods setVertices() and setIndices() stay the same.

```
public void bind() {
    GL10 gl = glGraphics.getGL();

    gl.glEnableClientState(GL10.GL_VERTEX_ARRAY);
    vertices.position(0);
    gl.glVertexPointer(3, GL10.GL_FLOAT, vertexSize, vertices);
```

```
        if (hasColor) {
            gl.glEnableClientState(GL10.GL_COLOR_ARRAY);
            vertices.position(3);
            gl.glColorPointer(4, GL10.GL_FLOAT, vertexSize, vertices);
        }

        if (hasTexCoords) {
            gl.glEnableClientState(GL10.GL_TEXTURE_COORD_ARRAY);
            vertices.position(hasColor ? 7 : 3);
            gl.glTexCoordPointer(2, GL10.GL_FLOAT, vertexSize, vertices);
        }

        if (hasNormals) {
            gl.glEnableClientState(GL10.GL_NORMAL_ARRAY);
            int offset = 3;
            if (hasColor)
                offset += 4;
            if (hasTexCoords)
                offset += 2;
            vertices.position(offset);
            gl.glNormalPointer(GL10.GL_FLOAT, vertexSize, vertices);
        }
    }
```

In the bind() method just shown, we do the usual ByteBuffer tricks, this time also incorporating normals via the glNormalPointer() method. To calculate the offset for the normal pointer, we have to take into account whether colors and texture coordinates are given.

```
    public void draw(int primitiveType, int offset, int numVertices) {
        GL10 gl = glGraphics.getGL();

        if (indices != null) {
            indices.position(offset);
            gl.glDrawElements(primitiveType, numVertices,
                    GL10.GL_UNSIGNED_SHORT, indices);
        } else {
            gl.glDrawArrays(primitiveType, offset, numVertices);
        }
    }
```

You can see that the draw() method is again unmodified; all of the magic happens in the bind() method.

```
    public void unbind() {
        GL10 gl = glGraphics.getGL();
        if (hasTexCoords)
            gl.glDisableClientState(GL10.GL_TEXTURE_COORD_ARRAY);

        if (hasColor)
            gl.glDisableClientState(GL10.GL_COLOR_ARRAY);

        if (hasNormals)
            gl.glDisableClientState(GL10.GL_NORMAL_ARRAY);
    }
}
```

Finally, we also modify the unbind() method slightly. We disable the normal pointer if normals were used, to clean up the OpenGL ES state properly.

Using this modified Vertices3 version is as easy as before. Here's a small example:

```
float[] vertices = { -0.5f, -0.5f, 0, 0, 0, 1,
                      0.5f, -0.5f, 0, 0, 0, 1,
                      0.0f,  0.5f, 0, 0, 0, 1 };
Vertices3 vertices = new Vertices3(glGraphics, 3, 0, false, false, true);
vertices.setVertices(vertices);
```

We create a float array to hold three vertices, each having a position (the first three floats on each line) and a normal (the last three floats on each line). In this case, we have a triangle in the x/y plane, with its normals pointing in the direction of the positive z-axis. All that's left to do is to create the Vertices3 instance and set the vertices. Easy, right? Binding, drawing, and unbinding work is exactly the same as with the old version. We can, of course, also add vertex colors and texture coordinates, as done previously.

Putting it All Together

Let's put all this together. We want to draw a scene with a global ambient light, a point light, and a directional light that all illuminate a cube centered at the origin. For good measure, we'll also throw in a call to gluLookAt() to position our camera in the world. Figure 11–6 shows the setup of our world.

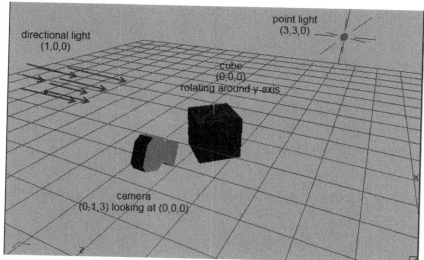

Figure 11–6. *Our first lit scene*

As with all of our examples, we create a class called LightTest, which extends GLGame as usual. It returns a new LightScreen instance from its getStartScreen() method. The LightScreen class extends GLScreen, and this is shown in Listing 11–7.

Listing 11–7. *Excerpt from LightTest.java, Lighting with OpenGL ES*

```
class LightScreen extends GLScreen {
    float angle;
    Vertices3 cube;
    Texture texture;
    AmbientLight ambientLight;
    PointLight pointLight;
    DirectionalLight directionalLight;
    Material material;
```

We start off with a couple of members. The angle member stores the current rotation of the cube around the y-axis. The Vertices3 member stores the vertices of the cube model, which we are going to define in a bit. In addition, we store an AmbientLight, PointLight, and DirectionalLight instance, as well as a Material.

```
    public LightScreen(Game game) {
        super(game);

        cube = createCube();
        texture = new Texture(glGame, "crate.png");
        ambientLight = new AmbientLight();
        ambientLight.setColor(0, 0.2f, 0, 1);
        pointLight = new PointLight();
        pointLight.setDiffuse(1, 0, 0, 1);
        pointLight.setPosition(3, 3, 0);
        directionalLight = new DirectionalLight();
        directionalLight.setDiffuse(0, 0, 1, 1);
        directionalLight.setDirection(1, 0, 0);
        material = new Material();
    }
```

Next is the constructor. Here we create the cube model's vertices and load the crate texture, just as we did in the previous chapter. We also instantiate all of the lights and the material and set their attributes. The ambient light color is a light green, and the point light is red and sits at (3,3,0) in our world. The directional light has a blue diffuse color and comes from the left. For the material, we use the default values (a little ambient, white for diffuse, and black for specular).

```
    @Override
    public void resume() {
        texture.reload();
    }
```

In the resume() method, we make sure that our texture is (re)loaded in case of a context loss.

```
    private Vertices3 createCube() {
        float[] vertices = { -0.5f, -0.5f, 0.5f, 0, 1, 0, 0, 1,
                              0.5f, -0.5f, 0.5f, 1, 1, 0, 0, 1,
                              0.5f,  0.5f, 0.5f, 1, 0, 0, 0, 1,
                             -0.5f,  0.5f, 0.5f, 0, 0, 0, 0, 1,

                              0.5f, -0.5f,  0.5f, 0, 1, 1, 0, 0,
                              0.5f, -0.5f, -0.5f, 1, 1, 1, 0, 0,
                              0.5f,  0.5f, -0.5f, 1, 0, 1, 0, 0,
```

```
                          0.5f,   0.5f,   0.5f, 0, 0, 1, 0, 0,

                          0.5f, -0.5f, -0.5f, 0, 1, 0, 0, -1,
                         -0.5f, -0.5f, -0.5f, 1, 1, 0, 0, -1,
                         -0.5f,  0.5f, -0.5f, 1, 0, 0, 0, -1,
                          0.5f,  0.5f, -0.5f, 0, 0, 0, 0, -1,

                         -0.5f, -0.5f, -0.5f, 0, 1, -1, 0, 0,
                         -0.5f, -0.5f,  0.5f, 1, 1, -1, 0, 0,
                         -0.5f,  0.5f,  0.5f, 1, 0, -1, 0, 0,
                         -0.5f,  0.5f, -0.5f, 0, 0, -1, 0, 0,

                         -0.5f,  0.5f,  0.5f, 0, 1, 0, 1, 0,
                          0.5f,  0.5f,  0.5f, 1, 1, 0, 1, 0,
                          0.5f,  0.5f, -0.5f, 1, 0, 0, 1, 0,
                         -0.5f,  0.5f, -0.5f, 0, 0, 0, 1, 0,

                         -0.5f, -0.5f, -0.5f, 0, 1, 0, -1, 0,
                          0.5f, -0.5f, -0.5f, 1, 1, 0, -1, 0,
                          0.5f, -0.5f,  0.5f, 1, 0, 0, -1, 0,
                         -0.5f, -0.5f,  0.5f, 0, 0, 0, -1, 0 };
        short[] indices = { 0, 1, 2, 2, 3, 0,
                            4, 5, 6, 6, 7, 4,
                            8, 9, 10, 10, 11, 8,
                            12, 13, 14, 14, 15, 12,
                            16, 17, 18, 18, 19, 16,
                            20, 21, 22, 22, 23, 20,
                            24, 25, 26, 26, 27, 24 };
        Vertices3 cube = new Vertices3(glGraphics, vertices.length / 8, indices.length,
    false, true, true);
        cube.setVertices(vertices, 0, vertices.length);
        cube.setIndices(indices, 0, indices.length);
        return cube;
    }
```

The createCube() method is mostly the same as the one we used in previous examples. This time, however, we add normals to each vertex, as shown in Figure 11–4. Apart from that, nothing has really changed.

```
    @Override
    public void update(float deltaTime) {
        angle += deltaTime * 20;
    }
```

In the update() method, we simply increase the rotation angle of the cube.

```
    @Override
    public void present(float deltaTime) {
        GL10 gl = glGraphics.getGL();
        gl.glClearColor(0.2f, 0.2f, 0.2f, 1.0f);
        gl.glClear(GL10.GL_COLOR_BUFFER_BIT | GL10.GL_DEPTH_BUFFER_BIT);
        gl.glEnable(GL10.GL_DEPTH_TEST);
        gl.glViewport(0, 0, glGraphics.getWidth(), glGraphics.getHeight());

        gl.glMatrixMode(GL10.GL_PROJECTION);
        gl.glLoadIdentity();
        GLU.gluPerspective(gl, 67, glGraphics.getWidth()
```

```
            / (float) glGraphics.getHeight(), 0.1f, 10f);
    gl.glMatrixMode(GL10.GL_MODELVIEW);
    gl.glLoadIdentity();
    GLU.gluLookAt(gl, 0, 1, 3, 0, 0, 0, 0, 1, 0);

    gl.glEnable(GL10.GL_LIGHTING);

    ambientLight.enable(gl);
    pointLight.enable(gl, GL10.GL_LIGHT0);
    directionalLight.enable(gl, GL10.GL_LIGHT1);
    material.enable(gl);

    gl.glEnable(GL10.GL_TEXTURE_2D);
    texture.bind();

    gl.glRotatef(angle, 0, 1, 0);
    cube.bind();
    cube.draw(GL10.GL_TRIANGLES, 0, 6 * 2 * 3);
    cube.unbind();

    pointLight.disable(gl);
    directionalLight.disable(gl);

    gl.glDisable(GL10.GL_TEXTURE_2D);
    gl.glDisable(GL10.GL_DEPTH_TEST);
}
```

Here it gets interesting. The first couple of lines are our boilerplate code for clearing the color and depth buffer—enabling depth testing and setting the viewport.

Next, we set the projection matrix to a perspective projection matrix via gluPerspective() and also use gluLookAt() for the model-view matrix, so that we have a camera setup as shown in Figure 11–6.

Next we enable lighting itself. At this point, no lights have yet been defined, so we do that in the next couple of lines by calling the enable() methods of the lights as well as the material.

As usual, we also enable texturing and bind our crate texture. Finally, we call glRotatef() to rotate our cube and then render its vertices with well-placed calls to the Vertices3 instance.

To round off the method, we disable the point and directional lights (remember, the ambient light is a global state) as well as texturing and depth testing. And that's all there is to lighting in OpenGL ES!

```
    @Override
    public void pause() {
    }

    @Override
    public void dispose() {
    }
}
```

The rest of the class is just empty; we don't have to do anything special in case of a pause.

Figure 11–7 shows you the output of our example.

Figure 11–7. *Our scene from Figure 11–6, rendered with OpenGL ES*

Some Notes on Lighting in OpenGL ES

While lighting can add some nice eye candy, it has its limits and pitfalls. Here are a few things you should take to heart.

- Lighting is expensive, especially on low-end devices. Use it with care. The more light sources you enable, the more computational power is required to render the scene.

- When specifying the position/direction of point/directional lights, you must do it after you have loaded the camera matrices and before you multiply the model-view matrix with any matrices to move and rotate objects around! This is crucial. If you don't follow this method, you will have some inexplicable lighting artifacts.

- When you use glScalef() to change the size of a model, its normals will also be scaled. This is bad because OpenGL ES expects unit-length normals. To work around this issue you can use the command glEnable(GL10.GL_NORMALIZE) or, in some circumstances, glEnable(GL10.GL_RESCALE_NORMAL). We'd suggest sticking to the former, as the latter has some restrictions and caveats. The problem is that normalizing or rescaling normals is computationally heavy. For optimum performance, it's best not to scale your lit objects.

Mipmapping

If you've played around with our previous examples and let the cube move further away from the camera, you might have noticed that the texture starts to looks grainy and full of little artifacts the smaller the cube gets. This effect is called *aliasing*, a prominent effect in all types of signal processing. Figure 11–8 shows you the effect on the right side and the result of applying a technique called *mipmapping* on the left side.

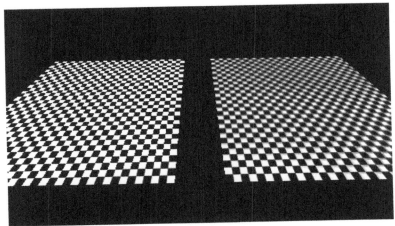

Figure 11–8. *Aliasing artifacts on the right;the results of mipmapping on the left*

We won't go into the details of why aliasing happens; all you need to know is how to make objects look better. That's where mipmapping comes in.

The key to fixing aliasing problems is to use lower-resolution images for parts of an object that are smaller on screen or further away from the view point. This is usually called a *mipmap pyramid* or *chain*. Given an image in its default resolution, say 256×256 pixels, we create smaller versions of it, dividing the sides by two for each level of the mipmap pyramid. Figure 11–9 shows the crate texture with various mipmap levels.

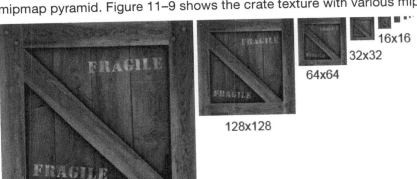

Figure 11–9. *A mipmap chain*

To make a texture mipmapped in OpenGL ES, we have to do two things:

- Set the minification filter to one of the GL_XXX_MIPMAP_XXX constants, usually GL_LINEAR_MIPMAP_NEAREST.

- Create the images for each mipmap chain level by resizing the original image and upload them to OpenGL ES. The mipmap chain is attached to a single texture, not multiple textures.

To resize the base image for the mipmap chain, we can simply use the Bitmap and Canvas classes that the Android API provides. Let's modify the Texture class a little. Listing 11–8 shows you the code.

Listing 11–8. *Texture.java, Our Final Version of the Texture Class*

```java
package com.badlogic.androidgames.framework.gl;

import java.io.IOException;
import java.io.InputStream;

import javax.microedition.khronos.opengles.GL10;

import android.graphics.Bitmap;
import android.graphics.BitmapFactory;
import android.graphics.Canvas;
import android.graphics.Rect;
import android.opengl.GLUtils;

import com.badlogic.androidgames.framework.FileIO;
import com.badlogic.androidgames.framework.impl.GLGame;
import com.badlogic.androidgames.framework.impl.GLGraphics;

public class Texture {
    GLGraphics glGraphics;
    FileIO fileIO;
    String fileName;
    int textureId;
    int minFilter;
    int magFilter;
    public int width;
    public int height;
    boolean mipmapped;
```

We add only one new member, called mipmapped, which stores whether the texture has a mipmap chain or not.

```java
    public Texture(GLGame glGame, String fileName) {
        this(glGame, fileName, false);
    }

    public Texture(GLGame glGame, String fileName, boolean mipmapped) {
        this.glGraphics = glGame.getGLGraphics();
        this.fileIO = glGame.getFileIO();
        this.fileName = fileName;
        this.mipmapped = mipmapped;
        load();
    }
```

For compatibility, we leave the old constructor in, which calls the new constructor. The new constructor takes a third argument that lets us specify whether we want the texture to be mipmapped.

```
private void load() {
    GL10 gl = glGraphics.getGL();
    int[] textureIds = new int[1];
    gl.glGenTextures(1, textureIds, 0);
    textureId = textureIds[0];

    InputStream in = null;
    try {
        in = fileIO.readAsset(fileName);
        Bitmap bitmap = BitmapFactory.decodeStream(in);
        if (mipmapped) {
            createMipmaps(gl, bitmap);
        } else {
            gl.glBindTexture(GL10.GL_TEXTURE_2D, textureId);
            GLUtils.texImage2D(GL10.GL_TEXTURE_2D, 0, bitmap, 0);
            setFilters(GL10.GL_NEAREST, GL10.GL_NEAREST);
            gl.glBindTexture(GL10.GL_TEXTURE_2D, 0);
            width = bitmap.getWidth();
            height = bitmap.getHeight();
            bitmap.recycle();
        }
    } catch (IOException e) {
        throw new RuntimeException("Couldn't load texture '" + fileName
                + "'", e);
    } finally {
        if (in != null)
            try {
                in.close();
            } catch (IOException e) {
            }
    }
}
```

The load() method stays essentially the same as well. The only addition is the call to createMipmaps() in case the texture should be mipmapped. Non-mipmapped Texture instances are created as before.

```
private void createMipmaps(GL10 gl, Bitmap bitmap) {
    gl.glBindTexture(GL10.GL_TEXTURE_2D, textureId);
    width = bitmap.getWidth();
    height = bitmap.getHeight();
    setFilters(GL10.GL_LINEAR_MIPMAP_NEAREST, GL10.GL_LINEAR);

    int level = 0;
    int newWidth = width;
    int newHeight = height;
    while (true) {
        GLUtils.texImage2D(GL10.GL_TEXTURE_2D, level, bitmap, 0);
        newWidth = newWidth / 2;
        newHeight = newHeight / 2;
        if (newWidth <= 0)
            break;
```

```
                    Bitmap newBitmap = Bitmap.createBitmap(newWidth, newHeight,
                            bitmap.getConfig());
                    Canvas canvas = new Canvas(newBitmap);
                    canvas.drawBitmap(bitmap,
                            new Rect(0, 0, bitmap.getWidth(), bitmap.getHeight()),
                            new Rect(0, 0, newWidth, newHeight), null);
                    bitmap.recycle();
                    bitmap = newBitmap;
                    level++;
            }

            gl.glBindTexture(GL10.GL_TEXTURE_2D, 0);
            bitmap.recycle();
        }
```

The createMipmaps() method is fairly straightforward. We start off by binding the texture so that we can manipulate its attributes. The first thing we do is to keep track of the bitmap's width and height and set the filters. Note that we use GL_LINEAR_MIPMAP_NEAREST for the minification filter. If we don't use that filter, mipmapping will not work and OpenGL ES will fall back to normal filtering, only using the base image.

The while loop is straightforward. We upload the current bitmap as the image for the current level. We start at level 0, the base level with the original image. Once the image for the current level is uploaded, we create a smaller version of it, dividing its width and height by 2. If the new width is less than or equal to zero, we can break out of the infinite loop, since we have uploaded an image for each mipmap level (the last image has a size of 1×1 pixels). We use the Canvas class to resize the image and to store the result in newBitmap. We then recycle the old bitmap so that we clean up any of the memory it used and set the newBitmap as the current bitmap. This process is repeated until the image is smaller than 1×1 pixels.

Finally, we unbind the texture and recycle the last bitmap that got created in the loop.

```
    public void reload() {
        load();
        bind();
        setFilters(minFilter, magFilter);
        glGraphics.getGL().glBindTexture(GL10.GL_TEXTURE_2D, 0);
    }

    public void setFilters(int minFilter, int magFilter) {
        this.minFilter = minFilter;
        this.magFilter = magFilter;
        GL10 gl = glGraphics.getGL();
        gl.glTexParameterf(GL10.GL_TEXTURE_2D, GL10.GL_TEXTURE_MIN_FILTER,
                minFilter);
        gl.glTexParameterf(GL10.GL_TEXTURE_2D, GL10.GL_TEXTURE_MAG_FILTER,
                magFilter);
    }

    public void bind() {
        GL10 gl = glGraphics.getGL();
        gl.glBindTexture(GL10.GL_TEXTURE_2D, textureId);
    }
```

```java
    public void dispose() {
        GL10 gl = glGraphics.getGL();
        gl.glBindTexture(GL10.GL_TEXTURE_2D, textureId);
        int[] textureIds = { textureId };
        gl.glDeleteTextures(1, textureIds, 0);
    }
}
```

The rest of the class is the same as in the previous version. The only difference in usage is how we call the constructor. Since this is perfectly simple, we won't write an example just for mipmapping. We'll use mipmapping on all of our textures that we used for 3D objects. In 2D, mipmapping is less useful. A few final notes on mipmapping:

- Mipmapping can increase performance quite a bit if the objects you draw using a mipmapped texture are small. The reason for this is that the GPU has to fetch fewer texels from smaller images in the mipmap pyramid. It's therefore wise to use mipmapped textures always on objects that might get small.

- A mipmapped texture takes up 33 percent more memory compared to an equivalent non-mipmapped version. This trade-off is usually fine.

- Mipmapping works only with square textures in OpenGL ES 1.x. This is crucial to remember. If your objects stay white even though they are textured with a nice image, you can be pretty sure that you forgot about this limitation.

> **NOTE:** Once again, because this is really important, remember that mipmapping will only work with square textures! A 512×256 pixel image will not work.

Simple Cameras

In the previous chapter, we talked about two ways to create a camera. The first one, the Euler camera, was similar to what is used in first-person shooters. The second one, the look-at camera, is used for cinematic camera work or for following an object. Let's create two helper classes that we can use in our games.

The First-Person or Euler Camera

The first-person or Euler camera is defined by the following attributes:

- The field of view in degrees.
- The viewport aspect ratio.
- The near and far clipping planes.
- A position in 3D space.
- An angle around the y-axis (yaw).
- An angle around the x-axis (pitch). This is limited to the range –90 to +90 degrees. Think how far you can tilt your own head and try to go beyond those angles! We are not responsible for any injuries.

The first three attributes are used to define the perspective projection matrix. We did this already with calls to `gluPerspective()` in all of your 3D examples.

The other three attributes define the position and orientation of the camera in our world. We will construct a matrix from this as outlined in the previous chapter. Let's put all this together into a simple class. Listing 11–9 shows you the code.

We also want to be able to move the camera in the direction that it is heading. For this, we need a unit length direction vector and we can add this to the position vector of the camera. We can create this type of a vector with the help of the `Matrix` class that the Android API offers us. Let's think about this for a moment.

In its default configuration, our camera will look down the negative z-axis, giving it a direction vector of (0, 0,–1). When we specify a yaw or pitch angle, this direction vector will be rotated accordingly. To figure out the direction vector, we just need to multiply it with a matrix that will rotate the default direction vector, just as OpenGL ES will rotate the vertices of our models.

Let's have a look at how all this works in code. Listing 11–9 shows you the `EulerCamera` class.

Listing 11–9. *EulerCamera.java, a Simple First Person Camera Based on Euler Angles Around the x- and y-Axes*

```java
package com.badlogic.androidgames.framework.gl;

import javax.microedition.khronos.opengles.GL10;

import android.opengl.GLU;
import android.opengl.Matrix;

import com.badlogic.androidgames.framework.math.Vector3;

public class EulerCamera {
    final Vector3 position = new Vector3();
    float yaw;
    float pitch;
    float fieldOfView;
```

```
float aspectRatio;
float near;
float far;
```

The first three members hold the position and rotation angles of the camera. The other four members hold the parameters used for calculating the perspective projection matrix. By default, our camera is located at the origin of the world, looking down the negative z-axis.

```
public EulerCamera(float fieldOfView, float aspectRatio, float near, float far){
    this.fieldOfView = fieldOfView;
    this.aspectRatio = aspectRatio;
    this.near = near;
    this.far = far;
}
```

The constructor takes four parameters that define the perspective projection. We leave the camera position and rotation angles as they are.

```
public Vector3 getPosition() {
    return position;
}
public float getYaw() {
    return yaw;
}

public float getPitch() {
    return pitch;
}
```

The getter methods just return the camera orientation and position.

```
public void setAngles(float yaw, float pitch) {
    if (pitch < -90)
        pitch = -90;
    if (pitch > 90)
        pitch = 90;
    this.yaw = yaw;
    this.pitch = pitch;
}

public void rotate(float yawInc, float pitchInc) {
    this.yaw += yawInc;
    this.pitch += pitchInc;
    if (pitch < -90)
        pitch = -90;
    if (pitch > 90)
        pitch = 90;
}
```

The setAngles() method allows us to specify the yaw and pitch of the camera directly. Note that we limit the pitch to be in the range of –90 to 90. We can't rotate our own head further than that, so our camera shouldn't be able to do that either.

The rotate() method is nearly identical to the setAngles() method. Instead of setting the angles, it increases them by the parameters. This will be useful when we implement a little touchscreen-based control scheme in the next example.

```
public void setMatrices(GL10 gl) {
    gl.glMatrixMode(GL10.GL_PROJECTION);
    gl.glLoadIdentity();
    GLU.gluPerspective(gl, fieldOfView, aspectRatio, near, far);
    gl.glMatrixMode(GL10.GL_MODELVIEW);
    gl.glLoadIdentity();
    gl.glRotatef(-pitch, 1, 0, 0);
    gl.glRotatef(-yaw, 0, 1, 0);
    gl.glTranslatef(-position.x, -position.y, -position.z);
}
```

The setMatrices() method just sets the projection and model-view matrices as discussed earlier. The projection matrix is set via gluPerspective() based on the parameters given to the camera in the constructor. The model-view matrix performs the "prophet-mountain" trick by applying a rotation around the x- and y-axes as well as a translation. All involved factors are negated to achieve the effect where the camera remains at the origin of the world, looking down the negative z-axis. We therefore rotate and translate the objects around the camera, not the other way around.

```
final float[] matrix = new float[16];
    final float[] inVec = { 0, 0, -1, 1 };
    final float[] outVec = new float[4];
    final Vector3 direction = new Vector3();

    public Vector3 getDirection() {
        Matrix.setIdentityM(matrix, 0);
        Matrix.rotateM(matrix, 0, yaw, 0, 1, 0);
        Matrix.rotateM(matrix, 0, pitch, 1, 0, 0);
        Matrix.multiplyMV(outVec, 0, matrix, 0, inVec, 0);
        direction.set(outVec[0], outVec[1], outVec[2]);
        return direction;
    }
}
```

Finally, we have the mysterious getDirection() method. It is accompanied by a couple of final members that we use for the calculations inside the method. We do this so that we don't allocate new float arrays and Vector3 instances each time the method is called. Consider those members to be temporary working variables.

Inside the method, we first set up a transformation matrix that contains the rotation around the x- and y-axes. We don't need to include the translation, since we only want a direction vector, not a position vector. The direction of the camera is independent of its location in the world. The Matrix methods we invoke should be self-explanatory. The only strange thing is that we actually apply them in reverse order, without negating the arguments. We do the opposite in the setMatrices() method. That's because we are now actually transforming a point in the same way that we'd transform our virtual camera, which does not have to be located at the origin or be oriented so that it looks down the negative z-axis. The vector we rotate is (0,0,–1), stored in inVec. That's the default direction of our camera if no rotation is applied. All that the matrix multiplications do is rotate this direction vector by the camera's pitch and roll so that it points in the direction that the camera is heading. The last thing we do is set a `Vector3` instance based on the result of the matrix-vector multiplication, and return that to the caller. We can use this unit-length direction vector later on to move the camera in the direction it is heading.

Equipped with this little helper class, we can write a tiny example program that allows us to move through a world of crates.

A Euler Camera Example

We now want to use the `EulerCamera` class in a little program. We want to be able to rotate it up and down and left and right, based on swiping the touchscreen with a finger. We also want it to move forward when a button is pressed. Our world should be populated by a couple of crates. Figure 11–10 shows you the initial setup of our scene.

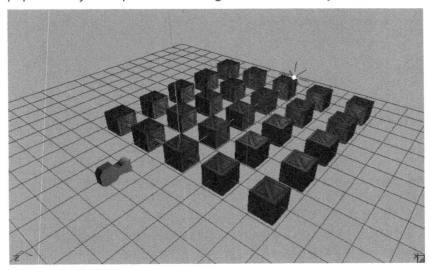

Figure 11–10. *A simple scene with 25 crates, a point light, and a Euler camera in its initial position and orientation*

The camera will be located at (0,1,3). We also have a white point light at (3,3,-3). The crates are positioned in a grid from -4 to 4 on the x-axis and from 0 to -8 on the z-axis, with a 2-unit distance between the centers.

How will we rotate the camera via swipes? We want the camera to rotate around the y-axis when we swipe horizontally. That is equivalent to turning our head left and right. We also want the camera to rotate around the x-axis when we swipe vertically. That's equivalent to tilting our head up and down. We also want to be able to combine these two swipe motions. The most straightforward way to achieve this is to check whether a finger is on the screen and, if so, to measure the difference on each axis to the last known position of that finger on the screen. We can then derive a change in rotation on both axes by using the difference in x for the y-axis rotation and the difference in y for the x-axis rotation.

We also want the camera to be able to move forward by pressing an on-screen button. That's simple; we just need to call `EulerCamera.getDirection()` and multiply its result by the speed we want the camera to move and the delta time, so that we once again perform time-based movement. The only thing that we need to do is draw the button (we decided to draw a 64×64 button in the bottom-left corner of the screen) and check whether it is currently touched by a finger.

To simplify our implementation, we'll only allow the user either to swipe-rotate or move. We could use the multitouch facilities for this, but that would complicate our implementation quite a bit.

With this plan of attack in place, let us look at `EulerCameraScreen`, a `GLScreen` implementation contained in a `GLGame` implementation called `EulerCameraTest` (just the usual test structure). Listing 11–10 shows the code.

Listing 11–10. *Excerpt from EulerCameraTest.java, the EulerCameraScreen*

```
class EulerCameraScreen extends GLScreen {
    Texture crateTexture;
    Vertices3 cube;
    PointLight light;
    EulerCamera camera;
    Texture buttonTexture;
    SpriteBatcher batcher;
    Camera2D guiCamera;
    TextureRegion buttonRegion;
    Vector2 touchPos;
    float lastX = -1;
    float lastY = -1;
```

We start off with a couple of members. The first two store the texture for the crate as well as the vertices of the texture cube. We'll generate the vertices with the `createCube()` method from the last example.

The next member is a `PointLight`, which we are already familiar with, as well as an instance of our new `EulerCamera` class.

Next up are a couple of members we need to render the button. We use a separate 64×64 image called `button.png` for that button. To render it, we also need a `SpriteBatcher` as well as a `Camera2D` instance and a `TextureRegion`. This means that we are going to combine 3D and 2D rendering in this example! The last three members are used to keep track of the current `touchPos` in the UI coordinate system (which is fixed to 480×320), as well as store the last known touch positions. We'll use the value −1 for `lastX` and `lastY` to indicate that no valid last touch position is known yet.

```
    public EulerCameraScreen(Game game) {
        super(game);

        crateTexture = new Texture(glGame, "crate.png", true);
        cube = createCube();
        light = new PointLight();
        light.setPosition(3, 3, -3);
        camera = new EulerCamera(67, glGraphics.getWidth() /
(float)glGraphics.getHeight(), 1, 100);
```

```
        camera.getPosition().set(0, 1, 3);

        buttonTexture = new Texture(glGame, "button.png");
        batcher = new SpriteBatcher(glGraphics, 1);
        guiCamera = new Camera2D(glGraphics, 480, 320);
        buttonRegion = new TextureRegion(buttonTexture, 0, 0, 64, 64);
        touchPos = new Vector2();
    }
```

In the constructor, we load the crate texture and create the cube vertices as we did in
the last example. We also create a PointLight and set its position to (3,3,–3). The
EulerCamera is created with the standard parameters, a 67-degree field of view, the
aspect ratio of the current screen resolution, a near clipping plane distance of 1, and a
far clipping plane distance of 100. Finally, we set the camera position to (0,1,3), as
shown in Figure 11–10.

In the rest of the constructor, we just load the button texture and create a
SpriteBatcher, a Camera2D, and TextureRegion instance needed for rendering the
button. Finally, we create a Vector2 instance so that we can transform real touch
coordinates to the coordinate system of the Camera2D that we use for UI rendering, just
as we did in Super Jumper in Chapter 9.

```
    private Vertices3 createCube() {
        // same as in previous example
    }

    @Override
    public void resume() {
        crateTexture.reload();
    }
```

The createCube() and resume() methods are exactly the same as in the previous
example, so all the code isn't repeated here.

```
    @Override
    public void update(float deltaTime) {
        game.getInput().getTouchEvents();
        float x = game.getInput().getTouchX(0);
        float y = game.getInput().getTouchY(0);
        guiCamera.touchToWorld(touchPos.set(x, y));


        if(game.getInput().isTouchDown(0)) {
            if(touchPos.x < 64 && touchPos.y < 64) {
                Vector3 direction = camera.getDirection();
                camera.getPosition().add(direction.mul(deltaTime));
            } else {
                if(lastX == -1) {
                    lastX = x;
                    lastY = y;
                } else {
                    camera.rotate((x - lastX) / 10, (y - lastY) / 10);
                    lastX = x;
                    lastY = y;
                }
```

```
            }
        } else {
            lastX = -1;
            lastY = -1;
        }
    }
```

The update() method is where all the swipe rotation and movement happens, based on touch events. The first thing we do is empty the touch event buffer via a call to Input.getTouchEvents(). Next, we fetch the current touch coordinates for the first finger on the screen. Note that if no finger is currently touching the screen, the methods we invoke will return the last known position of the finger with index zero. We also transform the real touch coordinates to the coordinate system of our 2D UI so that we can easily check whether the button in the bottom-left corner is pressed.

Equipped with all of these values, we then check whether a finger is actually touching the screen. If so, we first check whether it is touching the button, which spans the coordinates (0,0) to (64,64) in the 2D UI system. If that is the case, we fetch the current direction of the camera and add it to its position, multiplied by the current delta time. Since the direction vector is a unit-length vector, this means that the camera will move one unit per second.

If the button is not touched, we interpret the touch as a swipe gesture. For this to work, we need to have a valid last known touch coordinate. The first time the user puts his or her finger down, the lastX and lastY members will have a value of –1, indicating that we can't create a difference between the last and current touch coordinates since we only have a single data point. Therefore, we just store the current touch coordinates and return from the update() method. If we recorded touch coordinates the last time update() was invoked, we simply take the difference on the x- and y-axes between the current and the last touch coordinates. We directly translate these into increments of the rotation angles. To slow down the rotation a little, we divide the differences by 10. The only thing left is to call the EulerCamera.rotate() method, which will adjust the rotation angles accordingly.

Finally, if no finger is currently touching the screen, we set the lastX and lastY members to –1, to indicate that we have to await the first touch event before we can do any swipe gesture processing.

```
    @Override
    public void present(float deltaTime) {
        GL10 gl = glGraphics.getGL();
        gl.glClear(GL10.GL_COLOR_BUFFER_BIT | GL10.GL_DEPTH_BUFFER_BIT);
        gl.glViewport(0, 0, glGraphics.getWidth(), glGraphics.getHeight());

        camera.setMatrices(gl);

        gl.glEnable(GL10.GL_DEPTH_TEST);
        gl.glEnable(GL10.GL_TEXTURE_2D);
        gl.glEnable(GL10.GL_LIGHTING);

        crateTexture.bind();
        cube.bind();
        light.enable(gl, GL10.GL_LIGHT0);
```

```
    for(int z = 0; z >= -8; z-=2) {
        for(int x = -4; x <=4; x+=2 ) {
            gl.glPushMatrix();
            gl.glTranslatef(x, 0, z);
            cube.draw(GL10.GL_TRIANGLES, 0, 6 * 2 * 3);
            gl.glPopMatrix();
        }
    }

    cube.unbind();

    gl.glDisable(GL10.GL_LIGHTING);
    gl.glDisable(GL10.GL_DEPTH_TEST);

    gl.glEnable(GL10.GL_BLEND);
    gl.glBlendFunc(GL10.GL_SRC_ALPHA, GL10.GL_ONE_MINUS_SRC_ALPHA);

    guiCamera.setViewportAndMatrices();
    batcher.beginBatch(buttonTexture);
    batcher.drawSprite(32, 32, 64, 64, buttonRegion);
    batcher.endBatch();

    gl.glDisable(GL10.GL_BLEND);
    gl.glDisable(GL10.GL_TEXTURE_2D);
}
```

The present() method is surprisingly simple, thanks to the work we put into all of those little helper classes. We start off with the usual things like clearing the screen and setting the viewport. Next, we tell the EulerCamera to set the projection and model-view matrix. From this point on, we can render anything that should be 3D on screen. Before we do that, we enable depth testing, texturing, and lighting. Next, we bind the crate texture and the cube vertices and also enable the point light. Note that we bind the texture and cube vertices only once, since we are going to reuse them for all of the crates that we render. This is the same trick that we used in our BobTest in Chapter 8 when we wanted to speed up rendering by reducing state changes.

The next piece of code just draws the 25 cubes in a grid formation via a simple nested for loop. Since we have to multiply the model-view matrix with a translation matrix to put the cube vertices at a specific position, we must also use glPushMatrix() and glPopMatrix() so that we don't destroy the camera matrix that's also stored in the model-view matrix.

Once we are done with rendering our cubes, we unbind the cube vertices and disable lighting and depth testing. This is crucial, since we are now going to render the 2D UI overlay with the button. Since the button is actually circular, we also enable blending to make the edges of the texture transparent.

Rendering the button is done in the same way that we rendered the UI elements in Super Jumper. We tell the Camera2D to set the viewport and matrices (we wouldn't really need to set the viewport here again; feel free to "optimize" this method) and tell the SpriteBatcher that we are going to render a sprite. We render the complete button texture at (32,32) in our 480×320 coordinate system that we set up via the guiCamera.

Finally, we just disable the last few states we enabled previously, blending and texturing.

```
@Override
public void pause() {

}

@Override
public void dispose() {
}
}
```

The rest of the class is again just some stub methods for pause() and dispose(). Figure 11–11 shows the output of this little program.

Figure 11–11. *A simple example of first-person-shooter controls, without multitouch for simplicity*

Pretty nice, right? It also doesn't take a lot of code, either, thanks to the wonderful job our helper classes do for us. Now, adding multi-touch support would be awesome of course. Here's a hint: instead of using polling, as in the example just seen, use the actual touch events. On a "touch down" event, check whether the button was hit. If so, mark the pointer ID associated with it as not being able to produce swipe gestures until a corresponding "touch up" event is signaled. Touch events from all other pointer IDs can be interpreted as swipe gestures!

A Look-At Camera

The second type of camera usually found in games is a simple look-at camera. It is defined by the following:

- A position in space.

- An up vector. Think of this like an arrow that you would see if you slapped a "This Side Up" sticker on the back of the camera when your camera is sitting flat on a level surface.

- A look-at position in space or alternatively a direction vector. We'll use the former.

- A field of view in degrees.

- A viewport aspect ratio.

- A near and far clipping plane distance.

The only difference between a look-at camera and the Euler camera is the way we encode the orientation of the camera. In this case, we specify the orientation by the up vector and the look-at position. Let's write a helper class for this type of camera. Listing 11–11 shows you the code.

Listing 11–11. *LookAtCamera.java, a Simple Look-At Camera Without Bells and Whistles*

```java
package com.badlogic.androidgames.framework.gl;

import javax.microedition.khronos.opengles.GL10;

import android.opengl.GLU;

import com.badlogic.androidgames.framework.math.Vector3;

public class LookAtCamera {
    final Vector3 position;
    final Vector3 up;
    final Vector3 lookAt;
    float fieldOfView;
    float aspectRatio;
    float near;
    float far;

    public LookAtCamera(float fieldOfView, float aspectRatio, float near, float far) {
        this.fieldOfView = fieldOfView;
        this.aspectRatio = aspectRatio;
        this.near = near;
        this.far = far;

        position = new Vector3();
        up = new Vector3(0, 1, 0);
        lookAt = new Vector3(0,0,-1);
    }
```

```
    public Vector3 getPosition() {
        return position;
    }

    public Vector3 getUp() {
        return up;
    }

    public Vector3 getLookAt() {
        return lookAt;
    }

    public void setMatrices(GL10 gl) {
        gl.glMatrixMode(GL10.GL_PROJECTION);
        gl.glLoadIdentity();
        GLU.gluPerspective(gl, fieldOfView, aspectRatio, near, far);
        gl.glMatrixMode(GL10.GL_MODELVIEW);
        gl.glLoadIdentity();
        GLU.gluLookAt(gl, position.x, position.y, position.z, lookAt.x, lookAt.y,
lookAt.z, up.x, up.y, up.z);
    }
}
```

There are no real surprises here. We just store the position, up, and lookAt values as Vector3 instances, along with the perspective projection parameters we also had in the EulerCamera. In addition, we provide a couple of getters so that we can modify the attributes of the camera. The only interesting method is setMatrices(), but even that is old hat for us. We first set the projection matrix to a perspective projection matrix based on the field of view, aspect ratio, and near and far clipping plane distances. Then we set the model-view matrix to contain the camera position and orientation matrix via gluLookAt(), as discussed in the previous chapter. This will actually produce a matrix very similar to the matrix we "handcrafted" in the EulerCamera example. It will also rotate the objects around the camera, instead of the other way around. However, the nice interface of the gluLookAt() method shields us from all those silly things like inverting positions or angles.

We could, in fact, use this camera just like a EulerCamera. All we need to do is create a direction vector by subtracting the camera's position from its look-at point and normalizing it. Then we just rotate this direction vector by the yaw and pitch angles. Finally, we set the new look-at to the position of the camera and add the direction vector. Both methods would produce exactly the same transformation matrix. It's just two different ways to handle camera orientation.

We'll refrain from writing an explicit example for the LookAtCamera, since the interface is perfectly simple. We'll use it in our last game in this book, where we let it follow a neat little space ship! If you want to play around with it a little, add it to the LightTest we wrote earlier or modify the EulerCameraTest in such a way that the LookAtCamera can be used like a first-person-shooter camera, as outlined in the previous paragraph.

Loading Models

Defining models like our cube in code is very cumbersome, to say the least. A better way to create these types of models is to use special software that allows WYSIWYG creation of complex forms and objects. There's a plethora of software available for that task:

- *Blender*, an open source project used in many game and movie productions. Very capable and flexible, but also a little bit intimidating.

- *Wings3D*, our weapon of choice and also open-source. We use it for simple low-poly (read: not many triangles) modeling of static objects. It's very simplistic but gets the job done.

- *3D Studio Max*, one of the *de facto* standards in the industry. It's a commercial product, but there are student versions available.

- *Maya*, another industry favorite. It's also a commercial product but has some pricing options that might fit smaller purses.

That's just a selection of the more popular options out in the wild. Teaching you how to use one of these is well outside the scope of this book. However, no matter what software you use, at some point you will save your work to some kind of format. One such format is Wavefront OBJ, a very old plain-text format that can easily be parsed and translated to one of our Vertices3 instances.

The Wavefront OBJ Format

We will implement a loader for a subset of this format. Our loader will support models that are composed of triangles only and that optionally may contain texture coordinates and normals. The OBJ format also supports storage of arbitrary convex polygons, but we won't go into that. Whether you simply find an OBJ model or create your own, just make sure that it is triangulated—meaning that it's composed of triangles only.

The OBJ format is line based. Here are the parts of the syntax we are going to process:

- v x y z: The v indicates that the line encodes a vertex position, while x, y, and z are the coordinates encoded as floating-point numbers.

- vn i j k: The n indicates that the line encodes a vertex normal, with i, j, and k being the x-, y-, and z-components of the vertex normal.

- vt u v: The vt indicates that the line encodes a texture coordinate pair, with u and v being the texture coordinates.

- ▪ `f v1/vt1/vn1 v2/vt2/vn2 v3/vt3/vn3`: The f indicates that the line encodes a triangle. Each of the v/vt/vn blocks contains the indices of the position, texture coordinates, and vertex normal of a single vertex of the triangle. The indices are relative to the vertex positions, texture coordinates, and vertex normal defined previously by the other three line formats. The vt and vn indices can be left out, to indicate that there are no texture coordinates or normals for a specific vertex of a triangle.

We will ignore any line that does not start with v, vn, vt, or f; we will also output an error if any of the permissible lines don't follow the formatting just described. Items within a single line are delimited by whitespaces, which can include spaces, tabs, and so on.

> **NOTE:** The OBJ format can store a lot more information than we are going to parse here. We can get away with only parsing the syntax shown here, and ignoring anything else, as long as the models are triangulated and have normal and texture coordinates.

Here's a very simple example of a texture triangle with normals in OBJ format:

```
v -0.5 -0.5 0
v 0.5 -0.5 0
v 0 0.5 0
vn 0 0 1
vn 0 0 1
vn 0 0 1
vt 0 1
vt 1 1
vt 0.5 0
f 1/1/1 2/2/2 3/3/3
```

Note that the vertex positions, texture coordinates, and normals do not have to be defined in such a nice order. They could be intertwined if the software that saved the file chose to do so.

The indices given in an f statement are one based, rather than zero based (as in the case of a Java array). Some software even outputs negative indices at times. This is permitted by the OBJ format specification but is a major pain. We have to keep track of how many vertex positions, texture coordinates, or vertex normals we have loaded so far and then add that negative index to the respective number of positions, vertex coordinates, or normals, depending on what vertex attribute that index is indicating.

Implementing an OBJ Loader

Our plan of attack will be to load the file completely into memory and to create a string per line. We will also create temporary float arrays for all of the vertex positions, texture coordinates, and normals that we are going to load. Their size will be equal to the number of lines in the OBJ file times the number of components per attribute; that is, two for texture coordinates or three for normals. Doing this, we overshoot the necessary amount of memory needed to store the data, but that's still better than allocating new arrays every time we have filled them up.

We also do the same for the indices that define each triangle. While the OBJ format is indeed an indexed format, we can't use those indices directly with our Vertices3 class. The reason for this is that a vertex attribute might be reused by multiple vertices, so there's a one-to-many relationship that is not allowed in OpenGL ES. Therefore, we'll use a non-indexed Vertices3 instance and simply duplicate the vertices. For our needs, that's OK.

Let's see how we can implement all of this. Listing 11–12 shows the code.

Listing 11–12. *ObjLoader.java, a Simple Class for Loading a Subset of the OBJ Format*

```java
package com.badlogic.androidgames.framework.gl;

import java.io.BufferedReader;
import java.io.IOException;
import java.io.InputStream;
import java.io.InputStreamReader;
import java.util.ArrayList;
import java.util.List;

import com.badlogic.androidgames.framework.impl.GLGame;

public class ObjLoader {
    public static Vertices3 load(GLGame game, String file) {
        InputStream in = null;
        try {
            in = game.getFileIO().readAsset(file);
            List<String> lines = readLines(in);

            float[] vertices = new float[lines.size() * 3];
            float[] normals = new float[lines.size() * 3];
            float[] uv = new float[lines.size() * 2];

            int numVertices = 0;
            int numNormals = 0;
            int numUV = 0;
            int numFaces = 0;
```

The first thing we do is to open an InputStream to the asset file specified by the file parameter. We then read in all of the lines of that file using a method called readLines() (defined in the code that follows). Based on the number of lines, we allocate float arrays that will store the x-, y-, and z-coordinates of each vertex's position, the x-, y-, and z-component of each vertex's normal, and the u- and v-components of each vertex's texture coordinates. Since we don't know how many vertices there are in the file, we just allocate more space than needed for the arrays. Each vertex attribute is stored in subsequent elements of the three arrays. The position of the first read vertex is in vertices[0], vertices[1], and vertices[2], and so on. We also keep track of the indices in the triangle definitions for each of the three attributes of a vertex. In addition, we have a couple of counters to keep track of how many things we have already loaded.

```java
for (int i = 0; i < lines.size(); i++) {
    String line = lines.get(i);
```

Next we have a `for` loop that iterates through all the lines in the files.

```java
if (line.startsWith("v ")) {
    String[] tokens = line.split("[ ]+");
    vertices[vertexIndex] = Float.parseFloat(tokens[1]);
    vertices[vertexIndex + 1] = Float.parseFloat(tokens[2]);
    vertices[vertexIndex + 2] = Float.parseFloat(tokens[3]);
    vertexIndex += 3;
    numVertices++;
    continue;
}
```

If the current line is a vertex position definition, we split the line by whitespaces, read the x-, y-, and z-coordinates, and store it in the `vertices` array:

```java
if (line.startsWith("vn ")) {
    String[] tokens = line.split("[ ]+");
    normals[normalIndex] = Float.parseFloat(tokens[1]);
    normals[normalIndex + 1] = Float.parseFloat(tokens[2]);
    normals[normalIndex + 2] = Float.parseFloat(tokens[3]);
    normalIndex += 3;
    numNormals++;
    continue;
}

if (line.startsWith("vt")) {
    String[] tokens = line.split("[ ]+");
    uv[uvIndex] = Float.parseFloat(tokens[1]);
    uv[uvIndex + 1] = Float.parseFloat(tokens[2]);
    uvIndex += 2;
    numUV++;
    continue;
}
```

We do the same for the normals and texture coordinates:

```java
if (line.startsWith("f ")) {
    String[] tokens = line.split("[ ]+");

    String[] parts = tokens[1].split("/");
    facesVerts[faceIndex] = getIndex(parts[0], numVertices);
    if (parts.length > 2)
        facesNormals[faceIndex] = getIndex(parts[2], numNormals);
    if (parts.length > 1)
        facesUV[faceIndex] = getIndex(parts[1], numUV);
    faceIndex++;

    parts = tokens[2].split("/");
    facesVerts[faceIndex] = getIndex(parts[0], numVertices);
    if (parts.length > 2)
        facesNormals[faceIndex] = getIndex(parts[2], numNormals);
    if (parts.length > 1)
        facesUV[faceIndex] = getIndex(parts[1], numUV);
    faceIndex++;
```

```
                parts = tokens[3].split("/");
                facesVerts[faceIndex] = getIndex(parts[0], numVertices);
                if (parts.length > 2)
                    facesNormals[faceIndex] = getIndex(parts[2], numNormals);
                if (parts.length > 1)
                    facesUV[faceIndex] = getIndex(parts[1], numUV);
                faceIndex++;
                numFaces++;
                continue;
            }
        }
```

In this code, each vertex of a triangle (here called a *face*, as that is the term used in the OBJ format) is defined by a triplet of indices into the vertex position, texture coordinate, and normal arrays. The texture coordinate and normal indices can be omitted, so we keep track of this. The indices can also be negative, in which case we have to add them to the number of positions/texture coordinates/normals loaded so far. That's what the getIndex() method does for us.

```
            float[] verts = new float[(numFaces * 3)
                    * (3 + (numNormals > 0 ? 3 : 0) + (numUV > 0 ? 2 : 0))];
```

Once we have loaded all vertex positions, texture coordinates, normals, and triangles, we can start assembling a float array, holding the vertices in the format expected by a Vertices3 instance. The number of floats needed to store these vertices can easily be derived from the number of triangles we loaded and whether normal and texture coordinates are given.

```
            for (int i = 0, vi = 0; i < numFaces * 3; i++) {
                int vertexIdx = facesVerts[i] * 3;
                verts[vi++] = vertices[vertexIdx];
                verts[vi++] = vertices[vertexIdx + 1];
                verts[vi++] = vertices[vertexIdx + 2];

                if (numUV > 0) {
                    int uvIdx = facesUV[i] * 2;
                    verts[vi++] = uv[uvIdx];
                    verts[vi++] = 1 - uv[uvIdx + 1];
                }

                if (numNormals > 0) {
                    int normalIdx = facesNormals[i] * 3;
                    verts[vi++] = normals[normalIdx];
                    verts[vi++] = normals[normalIdx + 1];
                    verts[vi++] = normals[normalIdx + 2];
                }
            }
```

To fill the verts array, we just loop over all the triangles, fetch the vertex attribute for each vertex of a triangle, and put them into the verts array in the layout we usually use for a Vertices3 instance.

```
            Vertices3 model = new Vertices3(game.getGLGraphics(), numFaces * 3,
                    0, false, numUV > 0, numNormals > 0);
            model.setVertices(verts, 0, verts.length);
```

```
            return model;
```

The last thing we do is instantiate the Vertices3 instance and set the vertices.

```
        } catch (Exception ex) {
            throw new RuntimeException("couldn't load '" + file + "'", ex);
        } finally {
            if (in != null)
                try {
                    in.close();
                } catch (Exception ex) {

                }
        }
    }
```

The rest of the method just does some exception handling and closing of the InputStream.

```
    static int getIndex(String index, int size) {
        int idx = Integer.parseInt(index);
        if (idx < 0)
            return size + idx;
        else
            return idx - 1;
    }
```

The getIndex() method takes one of the indices given for an attribute of a vertex in a triangle definition, as well as the number of attributes loaded so far, and returns an index suitable to reference the attribute in one of our working arrays.

```
    static List<String> readLines(InputStream in) throws IOException {
        List<String> lines = new ArrayList<String>();

        BufferedReader reader = new BufferedReader(new InputStreamReader(in));
        String line = null;
        while ((line = reader.readLine()) != null)
            lines.add(line);
        return lines;
    }
}
```

Finally, there's the readLines() method, which just reads in each line of a file and returns all these lines as a List of strings.

To load an OBJ file from an asset, we can use the ObjLoader as follows:

```
Vertices3 model = ObjLoader.load(game, "mymodel.obj");
```

Pretty straightforward after all of this index juggling, right? To render this Vertices3 instance, we need to know how many vertices it has, though. Let's extend the Vertices3 class one more time, adding two methods to return the number of vertices as well as the number of indices currently defined in the instance. Listing 11–13 shows you the code.

Listing 11–13. *An excerpt from Vertices3.java, Fetching the Number of Vertices and Indices*

```
public int getNumIndices() {
    return indices.limit();
}

public int getNumVertices() {
    return vertices.limit() / (vertexSize / 4);
}
```

For the number of indices, we just return the limit of the ShortBuffer storing the indices. For the number of vertices, we do the same. However, since the limit is reported in the number of floats defined in the FloatBuffer, we have to divide it by the vertex size. Since we store that in number of bytes in vertexSize, we divide that member by 4.

Using the OBJ Loader

To demonstrate the OBJ loader, we've rewritten the last example and created a new test called ObjTest along with an ObjScreen. We copied over all the code from the previous example and only changed a single line in the constructor of ObjScreen:

```
cube = ObjLoader.load(glGame, "cube.obj");
```

Therefore, instead of using the createCube() method (which we removed), we are now directly loading a model from an OBJ file, called cube.obj. We created a replica of the cube we previously specified programmatically in createCube() in Wings3D. It has the same vertex positions, texture coordinates, and normals as the handcrafted version. It should come as no surprise that, when you run ObjTest, it will look exactly like our EulerCameraTest. We'll therefore spare you the obligatory screenshot.

Some Notes on Loading Models

For the game we are going to write in the next chapter, our loader is sufficient, but it is far from robust. There are some caveats:

- String processing in Android is inherently slow. The OBJ format is a plain-text format and, as such, it needs a lot of parsing. This will have a negative influence on load times. You can work around this issue by converting your OBJ models to a custom binary format. You could, for example, just serialize the verts array that we fill in the ObjLoader.load() method.

- The OBJ format has a lot more features that we don't exploit. If you want to extend our simple loader, look up the format specification on the Web. It should be easy to add more functionality.

■ An OBJ file is usually accompanied by what's called a *material file*. This file defines the colors and textures to be used by groups of vertices in the OBJ file. We will not need this functionality since we know which texture to use for a specific OBJ file. For a more robust loader, you'll want to look into the material file specification as well.

A Little Physics in 3D

In Chapter 8, we developed a very simple point-mass based physics model in 2D. Here's the good news: everything works the same in 3D!

■ Positions are now 3D vectors instead of 2D vectors. We just add a z-coordinate.

■ Velocities are still expressed in meters per second on each axis. We just add one more component for the z-axis!

■ Accelerations are also still expressed in meters per second squared on each axis. Again, we just add another coordinate.

The pseudocode in Chapter 8, where we described a physics simulation update, looked like this:

```
Vector2 position = new Vector2();
Vector2 velocity = new Vector2();
Vector2 acceleration = new Vector2(0, -10);
while(simulationRuns) {
   float deltaTime = getDeltaTime();
   velocity.add(acceleration.x * deltaTime, acceleration.y * deltaTime);
   position.add(velocity.x * deltaTime, velocity.y * deltaTime);
}
```

We can translate this into 3D space by simply exchanging the Vector2 instances with Vector3 instances:

```
Vector3 position = new Vector3();
Vector3 velocity = new Vector3();
Vector3 acceleration = new Vector3(0, -10, 0);
while(simulationRuns) {
   float deltaTime = getDeltaTime();
   velocity.add(acceleration.x * deltaTime, acceleration.y * deltaTime, acceleration.z *
deltaTime);
   position.add(velocity.x * deltaTime, velocity.y * deltaTime, velocity.z * deltaTime);
}
```

And that is all there is to it! This simple physics model is again sufficient for many simple 3D games. In the final game of this book, we will not even use any acceleration because of the nature of the objects in the game.

More complex physics in 3D (and 2D) are, of course, harder to implement. For this purpose, you'd usually use a third-party library instead of reinventing the wheel yourself. The problem on Android is that Java-based solutions will be much too slow, due to the heavy computations involved. There are some solutions for 2D physics for Android that wrap native C++ libraries like Box2D via the Java Native Interface (JNI), providing the native API to a Java application. For 3D physics, there's a library called Bullet. However, there aren't any usable JNI bindings for this library yet. Those topics are well outside of the scope of this book, though, and in many cases we don't need any sophisticated rigid-body physics.

Collision Detection and Object Representation in 3D

In Chapter 8, we discussed the relationship between object representation and collision detection. We strive to make our game-world objects as independent from their graphical representation as possible. Instead, we'd like to define them in terms of their bounding shape, position, and orientation. Position and orientation are not much of a problem: we can express the former as a Vector3 and the latter as the rotation around the x-, y-, and z-axes (minding the potential gimbal lock problem mentioned in the last chapter.) Let's take a look at bounding shapes.

Bounding Shapes in 3D

In terms of bounding shapes, we again have a ton of options. Figure 11–12 shows some of the more popular bounding shapes in 3D programming.

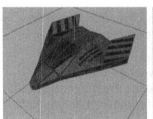 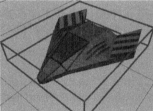 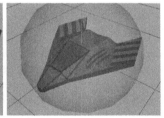

Figure 11–12. *Various bounding shapes. From left to right: triangle mesh, axis aligned bounding box, and bounding sphere*

- **Triangle Mesh:** This bounds the object as tightly as possible. However, colliding two objects based on their triangle meshes is computationally heavy.

- **Axis-Aligned Bounding Box:** This bounds the object loosely. It is a lot less computationally intensive than a triangle mesh.

- **Bounding Sphere:** This bounds the object even less well. It is the fastest way to check for collisions.

Another problem with triangle meshes and bounding boxes is that we have to reorient them whenever we rotate or scale the object, just as in 2D. Bounding spheres on the other hand don't need any modification if we rotate an object. If we scale an object, we just need to scale the radius of the sphere, which is a simple multiplication.

Bounding Sphere Overlap Testing

The mathematics of triangle mesh and bounding box collision detection can be pretty involved. For our next game, bounding spheres will do just fine. There's also a little trick we can apply, which we already used in Super Jumper: to make the bounding sphere fit a little better, we make it smaller than the graphical representation. Figure 11–13 shows you how that could look in case of the space ship.

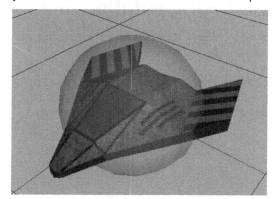

Figure 11–13. *Making the bounding sphere smaller to better fit an object*

That's, of course, a very cheap trick, but it turns out that, in many situations, it is more than sufficient to keep up the illusion of mostly correct collision detection.

So how do we collide two spheres with each other? Or rather, how do we test for overlap? It works exactly the same as in the case of circles! All we need to do is measure the distance from the center of one sphere to the center of the other sphere. If that distance is smaller than the two radii of the spheres added together, then we have a collision. Let's create a simple Sphere class. Listing 11–13 shows you the code.

Listing 11–13. *Sphere.java, a Simple Bounding Sphere*

```
package com.badlogic.androidgames.framework.math;

public class Sphere {
    public final Vector3 center = new Vector3();
    public float radius;

    public Sphere(float x, float y, float z, float radius) {
        this.center.set(x,y,z);
        this.radius = radius;
    }
}
```

That's the same code that we used in the Circle class. All we changed is the vector holding the center, which is now a Vector3 instead of a Vector2.

Let's also extend our OverlapTester class with methods to check for overlap of two spheres and to test whether a point is inside a sphere. Listing 11–14 shows the code.

Listing 11–14. *Excerpt from OverlapTester.java, Adding Sphere-Testing Methods*

```
public static boolean overlapSpheres(Sphere s1, Sphere s2) {
    float distance = s1.center.distSquared(s2.center);
    float radiusSum = s1.radius + s2.radius;
    return distance <= radiusSum * radiusSum;
}

public static boolean pointInSphere(Sphere c, Vector3 p) {
    return c.center.distSquared(p) < c.radius * c.radius;
}

public static boolean pointInSphere(Sphere c, float x, float y, float z) {
    return c.center.distSquared(x, y, z) < c.radius * c.radius;
}
```

That's again exactly the same code as in the case of Circle overlap testing. We just use the center of the spheres, which is a Vector3 instead of a Vector2, as in the case of a Circle.

> **NOTE:** Entire books have been filled on the topic of 3D collision detection. If you want to dive deep into that rather interesting world, we suggest the book *Real-time Collision Detection* by Christer Ericson (Morgan Kaufmann, 2005). It should be on the shelf of any self-respecting game developer!

GameObject3D and DynamicGameObject3D

Now that we have a nice bounding shape for our 3D objects, we can easily write the equivalent of the GameObject and DynamicGameObject classes we used in 2D. We just replace any Vector2 with a Vector3 instance and use the Sphere class instead of the Rectangle class. Listing 11–15 shows you the GameObject3D class.

Listing 11–15. *GameObject3D, Representing a Simple Object with a Position and Bounds*

```
package com.badlogic.androidgames.framework;

import com.badlogic.androidgames.framework.math.Sphere;
import com.badlogic.androidgames.framework.math.Vector3;

public class GameObject3D {
    public final Vector3 position;
    public final Sphere bounds;

    public GameObject3D(float x, float y, float z, float radius) {
        this.position = new Vector3(x,y,z);
        this.bounds = new Sphere(x, y, z, radius);
    }
}
```

This code is so trivial that you probably don't need any explanation. The only hitch is that we have to store the same position twice: once as the position member in the

GameObject3D class, and again within the position member of the Sphere instance that's contained in the GameObject3D class. This is somewhat ugly but, for the sake of clarity, we'll stick to it.

Deriving a DynamicGameObject3D class from this class is also simple. Listing 11–16 shows you the code.

Listing 11–16. *DynamicGameObject3D.java, the Dynamic Equivalent to GameObject3D*

```
package com.badlogic.androidgames.framework;

import com.badlogic.androidgames.framework.math.Vector3;

public class DynamicGameObject3D extends GameObject {
    public final Vector3 velocity;
    public final Vector3 accel;

    public DynamicGameObject3D(float x, float y, float z, float radius) {
        super(x, y, z, radius);
        velocity = new Vector3();
        accel = new Vector3();
    }
}
```

We again just replace any Vector2 with a Vector3 and smile happily.

In 2D, we had to think hard about the relationship between the graphical representation of our objects (given in pixels) and the units used within the model of our world. In 3D, we can break free from this! The vertices of our 3D models that we load from, say, an OBJ file can be defined in whatever unit system we want. We no longer need to transform pixels to world units and vice versa. This makes working in 3D a little easier. We just need to train our artist so that he or she provides us with models that are properly scaled to the unit system of our world.

Summary

Again, we have uncovered a lot of mysteries in the world of game programming. We talked a little bit about vectors in 3D, which turned out to be as simple to use as their 2D counterparts. The general theme is: Just add a z-coordinate! We also took a look at lighting in OpenGL ES. With the helper classes we wrote to represent materials and light sources; it is pretty simple to set up the lighting in a scene. For better performance and fewer graphical artifacts, we also implemented simple mipmapping as part of our Texture class. We also explored implementation of simple Euler and look-at cameras, using very little code and a little help from the Matrix class.

Since creation of 3D meshes by hand in code is tedious, we also looked at one of the simplest and most popular 3D file formats: Wavefront OBJ. We revisited our simple physics model and transferred it to the realm of 3D, which turned out to be as simple as creating 3D vectors.

The last point on our agenda was to figure out how to cope with bounding shapes and object representation in 3D. Given our modest needs, we arrived at very simple solutions for both problems, which are very similar or even identical to those we used in 2D.

While there is a lot more to 3D programming than we can present here, you now have a pretty good idea about what is needed to write a 3D game. The big realization is that there is indeed not a lot of difference between a 2D game and a 3D game (up to a certain degree of complexity, of course). We don't have to be afraid of 3D anymore! In Chapter 12, we'll use our new knowledge to write the final game of this book: Droid Invaders!

Droid Invaders: The Grand Finale

You are finally ready to create the last game for this book. This time you are going to develop a simple action/arcade game, adapting an old classic and giving it a nice 3D look, using the techniques discussed in the last two chapters.

Core Game Mechanics

As you might have guessed from the title of this chapter, you are about to implement a variation of Space Invaders, a 2D game in its original form (illustrated in Figure 12–1).

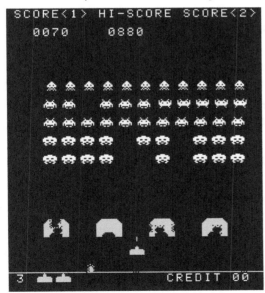

Figure 12–1. *The original Space Invaders arcade game*

Here's a little surprise: you'll continue to stay in 2D, for the most part. All of your objects will have 3D bounds in the form of bounding spheres and positions in 3D space. However, movement will only happen in the x/z plane, which makes certain things a little easier. Figure 12–2 shows the adapted 3D Space Invaders world. The mock-up was created with Wings3D.

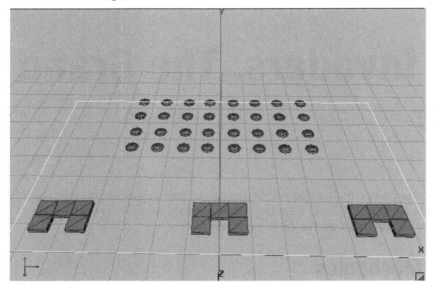

Figure 12–2. *The 3D game field mock-up*

Now to define the game mechanics:

- A ship is flying at the bottom of the playfield, capable of navigating only on the x-axis.

- The movement is limited to the boundaries of the playfield. When the ship reaches the left or right boundary of the game field, it simply stops moving.

- You want to give the player the option of using either the accelerometer to navigate the ship, or the on-screen buttons, for left and right movement.

- The ship can fire one shot per second. The player shoots by pressing an on-screen button.

- At the bottom of the game field, there are three shields, each composed of five cubes.

- Invaders start off with the configuration shown in Figure 12–2, and then they move to the left for some distance, and then they move some distance in the positive z-direction, and then to the right for some distance. There will be 32 invaders in total, making up four rows of eight invaders.

- Invaders will shoot randomly.

- When a shot hits the ship, the ship explodes and loses one life.

- When a shot hits a shield, the shield disappears permanently.

- When a shot hits an invader, the invader explodes and the score is increased by 10 points.

- When all invaders are destroyed, a new wave of invaders appears, moving slightly faster than the last wave.

- When an invader collides directly with a ship, the game is over.

- When the ship has lost all of its lives, the game is over.

That's not an overwhelming list, is it? All operations can essentially be performed in 2D (in the x/z plane instead of the x/y plane). You'll still use 3D bounding spheres, however. And maybe you'll want to extend the game to real 3D after you are done with the first iteration. And now? You can move on to the backstory.

A Backstory and Art Style

The game will be called Droid Invaders, in deference to Android and Space Invaders. That's cheap, but we don't plan on producing an AAA title yet. In the tradition of classic shooters, like Doom, the backstory will be minimal. It goes like this:

> *Invaders from outer space attack Earth. You are the sole person capable of fending off the evil forces.*

That was good enough for Doom and Quake, so it's good enough for Droid Invaders, too.

The art style will be a little retro when it comes to the GUI, using the same old-fashioned font you used in Chapter 9 for Super Jumper. The game world itself will be displayed in fancy 3D, with textured and lighted 3D models. Figure 12–3 shows what the game screen will look like.

Figure 12–3. *The Droid Invaders mockup. Fancy!*

The music will be a rock/metal mixture, and the sound effects will match the scenario.

Screens and Transitions

Since you have already implemented help screens and high-score screens twice, in Chapter 6's Mr. Nom and in Chapter 9's Super Jumper, you can refrain from doing so for Droid Invaders; it's always the same principle, and a player should immediately know what to do once he or she is presented with the game screen, anyway. Instead, add a settings screen that allows the player to select the type of input (multitouch or accelerometer) and to disable or enable sound. Here's the list of screens for Droid Invaders:

- A main screen with a logo and Play and Settings options.

- A game screen that will immediately start with the game (no more ready signal!) and also handle paused states, as well as display "Game Over" text once the ship has no more lives.

- A settings screen that displays three icons representing the configuration options (multitouch, accelerometer, and sound).

This is very similar to what you had in the previous two games. Figure 12–4 shows all the screens and transitions.

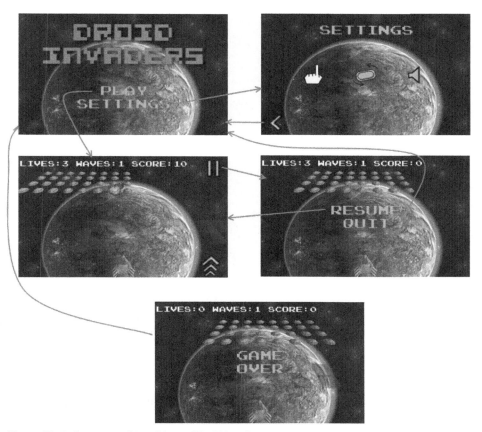

Figure 12–4. *Screens and transitions of Droid Invaders*

Defining the Game World

One of the joys of working in 3D is that you are free from the shackle of pixels. You can define your world in whatever units you want. The game mechanics that were outlined dictate a limited playing field, so start by defining that field. Figure 12–5 shows you the area of the playing field in the game's world.

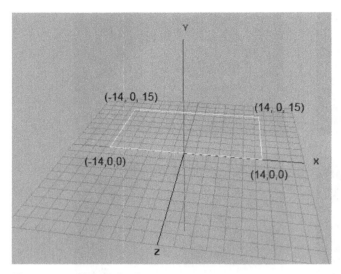

Figure 12–5. *The playing field*

Everything in the world will happen inside this boundary in the x/z plane. Coordinates will be limited on the x-axis from –14 to 14 and on the z-axis from 0 to –15. The ship will be able to move along the bottom edge of the playing field, from (–14,0,0) to (14,0,0).

Next, define the sizes of the objects in the world:

■ The ship will have a radius of 0.5 units.

■ The invaders will have a slightly larger radius of 0.75 units. This makes them easier to hit.

■ The shield blocks each have a radius of 0.5 units.

■ The shots each have a radius of 0.1 units.

How do you arrive at these values? Simply divide the game world up in cells of 1 unit by 1 unit and think about how big each game element has to be in relation to the size of the playing field. Usually, you arrive at these measurements through a little experimentation, or by using real-world units like meters. In Droid Invaders, don't use meters, use nameless units.

The radii just defined can be directly translated to bounding spheres, of course. In the case of the shield blocks and the ship, you can cheat a little, as those are clearly not spherical. Thanks to the 2D properties of the world, you can get away with this little trick. In the case of the invaders, the sphere is actually a pretty good approximation.

You also have to define the velocities of the moving objects:

■ The ship can move with a maximum velocity of 20 units per second. As in Super Jumper, you'll usually have a lower velocity, as it is dependent on the device's tilt.

- The invaders initially move 1 unit per second. Each wave will slightly increase this speed.

- The shots move at 10 units per second.

With these definitions, you can start implementing the logic of the game world. It turns out, however, that creating the assets is directly related to the defined units.

Creating the Assets

As in the previous games, you have two kinds of graphical assets: UI elements, such as logos or buttons, and the models for the different types of objects in the game.

The UI Assets

Create your UI assets relative to some target resolution. Your game will be run in landscape mode, so simply choose a target resolution of 480×320 pixels. The screens in Figure 12–4 already show the elements in your UI: a logo, different menu items, a couple of buttons, and some text. For the text, reuse the font from Super Jumper. You've already done the compositing for these in previous games, and you've learned that putting them into a texture atlas can be beneficial for performance. The texture atlas for Droid Invaders, containing all the UI elements (as well as the font for all the screens in the game), is shown in Figure 12–6.

Figure 12–6. *The UI element atlas, with buttons, logo, and font. It is stored in the file items.png, 512×512 pixels*

This is essentially the same concept used in Super Jumper. You also have a background that will be rendered in all screens. Figure 12–7 shows this image.

Figure 12–7. *The background stored in background.jpg. 512×512 pixels*

As you can see in Figure 12–4, you only need to use the top-left region of this image to render a full frame (480×320 pixels).

That's all the UI elements needed. Now you can look at your 3D models and their textures.

The Game Assets

As mentioned in Chapter 11, this book can't possibly go into detail on how to create 3D models with software like Wings3D. If you want to create your own models, choose an application to work with and plow through some tutorials, which are often freely available on the net. For the models of Droid Invaders, you can use Wings3D and simply export them to the OBJ format, which you can load with your framework. All models are composed of triangles only, and they have texture coordinates and normals. You won't need texture coordinates for some of them, but it doesn't hurt to have them.

The ship model and its texture are illustrated in Figure 12–8.

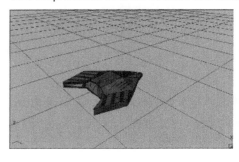

Figure 12–8. *The ship model in Wings3D (ship.obj) and its texture (ship.png, 256×256 pixels)*

The crucial thing is that the ship in Figure 12–8 has roughly the "radius" outlined in the previous section. You don't need to scale anything or transform sizes and positions from one coordinate system to the other. The ship's model is defined with the same units as its bounding sphere!

Figure 12–9 shows the invader model and its texture.

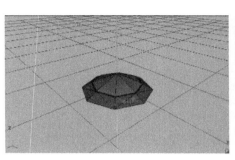 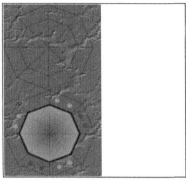

Figure 12–9. *The invader model (invader.obj) and its texture (invader.png, 256×256 pixels)*

The invader model follows the same principles as the ship model. Have one OBJ file store the vertex positions, texture coordinates, normals and faces, and a texture image.

The shield blocks and shots are modeled as cubes and are stored in the files shield.obj and shot.obj. Although they have texture coordinates assigned, don't actually use texture mapping when rendering them. Just draw them as (translucent) objects with a specific color (blue in the case of the shield blocks, yellow for the shots).

Finally, there are the explosions (see Figure 12–3 again). How do you model those? You don't. Do what you did in 2D and simply draw a rectangle with a proper z-position in the 3D world, texture mapping it with a frame from a texture image containing an explosion animation. It's the same principle you used for the animated objects in Super Jumper. The only difference is that you draw the rectangle at a z-position smaller than zero (wherever the exploding object is located). You can even abuse the SpriteBatcher class to do this! Hurray for OpenGL ES. Figure 12–10 shows you the texture.

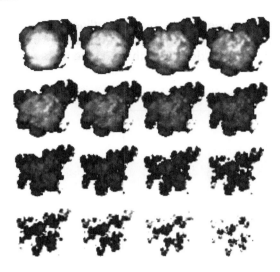

Figure 12–10. *The explosion animation texture (explode.png, 256×256 pixels)*

Each frame of the animation is 64×64 pixels in size. All you need to do is generate TextureRegions for each frame and put them into an Animation instance you can use to fetch the correct frame for a given animation time, just as you did for the squirrels or Bob in Super Jumper.

Sound and Music

For the sound effects, use sfxr again. Find the explosion sound effect on the Web. It's a public domain sound effect, so you can use it in Droid Invaders. For our own version of Droid Invaders, we recorded the music ourselves with real instruments. Yes—that's very old-school. Here's the list of audio files for Droid Invaders.

- click.ogg, a click sound used for the menu items/buttons
- shot.ogg, a shot sound
- explosion.ogg, an explosion
- music.mp3, the rock/metal song written for Droid Invaders

Plan of Attack

With your game mechanics, design, and assets in place, you can start coding. As usual, create a new project, copy over all of your framework code, ensure that you have a proper manifest and icons, and so on. By now, you should have a pretty good grasp of how to set things up. All the code of Droid Invaders will be placed in the package com.badlogic.androidgames.droidinvaders. The assets are stored in the assets/ directory of the Android project. Use the same general structure used in Super Jumper: a default activity deriving from GLGame, a couple of GLScreen instances implementing the different screens and transitions, as shown in Figure 12–4, classes for loading assets and storing settings, as well as the classes for the game objects, and a rendering class that can draw the game world in 3D. Start with the `Assets` class.

The Assets Class

Well, you've done this before, so don't expect any surprises. Listing 12–1 shows you the code of the `Assets` class.

Listing 12–1. *Assets.java, Loading and Storing Assets as Always*

```java
package com.badlogic.androidgames.droidinvaders;

import com.badlogic.androidgames.framework.Music;
import com.badlogic.androidgames.framework.Sound;
import com.badlogic.androidgames.framework.gl.Animation;
import com.badlogic.androidgames.framework.gl.Font;
import com.badlogic.androidgames.framework.gl.ObjLoader;
import com.badlogic.androidgames.framework.gl.Texture;
import com.badlogic.androidgames.framework.gl.TextureRegion;
import com.badlogic.androidgames.framework.gl.Vertices3;
import com.badlogic.androidgames.framework.impl.GLGame;

public class Assets {
    public static Texture background;
    public static TextureRegion backgroundRegion;
    public static Texture items;
    public static TextureRegion logoRegion;
    public static TextureRegion menuRegion;
    public static TextureRegion gameOverRegion;
    public static TextureRegion pauseRegion;
    public static TextureRegion settingsRegion;
    public static TextureRegion touchRegion;
    public static TextureRegion accelRegion;
    public static TextureRegion touchEnabledRegion;
    public static TextureRegion accelEnabledRegion;
    public static TextureRegion soundRegion;
    public static TextureRegion soundEnabledRegion;
    public static TextureRegion leftRegion;
    public static TextureRegion rightRegion;
    public static TextureRegion fireRegion;
    public static TextureRegion pauseButtonRegion;
    public static Font font;
```

Have a couple of members storing the texture of the UI elements, as well as the background image. Also, store a couple of TextureRegions, as well as a Font. This covers all of your UI needs.

```java
    public static Texture explosionTexture;
    public static Animation explosionAnim;
    public static Vertices3 shipModel;
    public static Texture shipTexture;
    public static Vertices3 invaderModel;
```

```
public static Texture invaderTexture;
public static Vertices3 shotModel;
public static Vertices3 shieldModel;
```

Use textures and Vertices3 instances to store the models and textures of the game's objects. An Animation instance can hold the frames of the explosion animation.

```
public static Music music;
public static Sound clickSound;
public static Sound explosionSound;
public static Sound shotSound;
```

Finally, a couple of Music and Sound instances can be used to store the game's audio.

```
public static void load(GLGame game) {
    background = new Texture(game, "background.jpg", true);
    backgroundRegion = new TextureRegion(background, 0, 0, 480, 320);
    items = new Texture(game, "items.png", true);
    logoRegion = new TextureRegion(items, 0, 256, 384, 128);
    menuRegion = new TextureRegion(items, 0, 128, 224, 64);
    gameOverRegion = new TextureRegion(items, 224, 128, 128, 64);
    pauseRegion = new TextureRegion(items, 0, 192, 160, 64);
    settingsRegion = new TextureRegion(items, 0, 160, 224, 32);
    touchRegion = new TextureRegion(items, 0, 384, 64, 64);
    accelRegion = new TextureRegion(items, 64, 384, 64, 64);
    touchEnabledRegion = new TextureRegion(items, 0, 448, 64, 64);
    accelEnabledRegion = new TextureRegion(items, 64, 448, 64, 64);
    soundRegion = new TextureRegion(items, 128, 384, 64, 64);
    soundEnabledRegion = new TextureRegion(items, 190, 384, 64, 64);
    leftRegion = new TextureRegion(items, 0, 0, 64, 64);
    rightRegion = new TextureRegion(items, 64, 0, 64, 64);
    fireRegion = new TextureRegion(items, 128, 0, 64, 64);
    pauseButtonRegion = new TextureRegion(items, 0, 64, 64, 64);
    font = new Font(items, 224, 0, 16, 16, 20);
```

The load() method starts off by creating the UI-related stuff. It's just some texture loading and region creation, as usual.

```
    explosionTexture = new Texture(game, "explode.png", true);
    TextureRegion[] keyFrames = new TextureRegion[16];
    int frame = 0;
    for (int y = 0; y < 256; y += 64) {
        for (int x = 0; x < 256; x += 64) {
            keyFrames[frame++] = new TextureRegion(explosionTexture, x, y, 64, 64);
        }
    }
    explosionAnim = new Animation(0.1f, keyFrames);
```

Next, create the Texture for the explosion animation, along with the TextureRegions for each frame and the Animation instance. Simply loop from the top left to the bottom right in 64-pixel increments, and create one TextureRegion per frame. All the regions are then fed to an Animation instance, whose frame duration is 0.1 second.

```
    shipTexture = new Texture(game, "ship.png", true);
    shipModel = ObjLoader.load(game, "ship.obj");
    invaderTexture = new Texture(game, "invader.png", true);
```

```
invaderModel = ObjLoader.load(game, "invader.obj");
shieldModel = ObjLoader.load(game, "shield.obj");
shotModel = ObjLoader.load(game, "shot.obj");
```

Next, load the models and textures for the ship, the invaders, the shield blocks, and the shots. This is pretty simple with your mighty ObjLoader, isn't it? Note that you use mipmapping for the Textures.

```
music = game.getAudio().newMusic("music.mp3");
music.setLooping(true);
music.setVolume(0.5f);
if (Settings.soundEnabled)
    music.play();

clickSound = game.getAudio().newSound("click.ogg");
explosionSound = game.getAudio().newSound("explosion.ogg");
shotSound = game.getAudio().newSound("shot.ogg");
}
```

Finally, load the music and sound effects for the game. You can see a reference to the Settings class, which is essentially the same as in Super Jumper and Mr. Nom. This method will be called once when your game is started in the DroidInvaders class that you'll implement in a minute. Once all assets are loaded, you can forget about most of them, except for the Textures, which you need to reload if the game is paused and then resumed.

```
public static void reload() {
    background.reload();
    items.reload();
    explosionTexture.reload();
    shipTexture.reload();
    invaderTexture.reload();
    if (Settings.soundEnabled)
        music.play();
}
```

That's where the reload() method comes in. Call this method in the DroidInvaders.onResume() method so that your textures will be reloaded and the music will be unpaused.

```
public static void playSound(Sound sound) {
    if (Settings.soundEnabled)
        sound.play(1);
}
}
```

Finally, the same convenience method you used in Super Jumper will ease the pain of playing back a sound effect. When the user disables sound, don't play anything in this method.

> **NOTE:** Although this method of loading and managing assets is easy to implement, it can become a mess if you have more than a handful of assets. Another issue is that sometimes not all assets will fit into the memory all at once. For simple games, like the ones you've developed from this book, the method is fine. We often use it in our games, as well. For larger games, you have to consider a more elaborate asset management strategy.

The Settings Class

As with the Assets class, you can again reuse what you wrote for the previous games, to some extent. You can now store an additional Boolean that tells you whether the user wants to use the touchscreen or the accelerometer for moving the ship. You can drop the high-score support, as you don't need to keep track of this. As an exercise, you can, of course, reintroduce both the high-score screen and the saving of these scores to the SD card. Listing 12–2 shows you the code.

Listing 12–2. *Settings.java, Same Old, Same Old*

```java
package com.badlogic.androidgames.droidinvaders;

import java.io.BufferedReader;
import java.io.BufferedWriter;
import java.io.IOException;
import java.io.InputStreamReader;
import java.io.OutputStreamWriter;

import com.badlogic.androidgames.framework.FileIO;

public class Settings {
    public static boolean soundEnabled = true;
    public static boolean touchEnabled = true;
    public final static String file = ".droidinvaders";
```

Store whether the sounds are enabled, as well as whether the user wants to use touch input to navigate the ship. The settings will be stored in the file droidinvaders on the SD card.

```java
    public static void load(FileIO files) {
        BufferedReader in = null;
        try {
            in = new BufferedReader(new InputStreamReader(files.readFile(file)));
            soundEnabled = Boolean.parseBoolean(in.readLine());
            touchEnabled = Boolean.parseBoolean(in.readLine());
        } catch (IOException e) {
            // :( It's ok we have defaults
        } catch (NumberFormatException e) {
            // :/ It's ok, defaults save our day
        } finally {
            try {
                if (in != null)
```

```
                in.close();
            } catch (IOException e) {
            }
        }
    }
```

There is nothing in this section that you need to go over, really; you've done this before. Try to read the two Booleans from the file on the SD card. If that fails, fall back to the default values.

```
    public static void save(FileIO files) {
        BufferedWriter out = null;
        try {
            out = new BufferedWriter(new OutputStreamWriter(
                    files.writeFile(file)));
            out.write(Boolean.toString(soundEnabled));
            out.write("\n");
            out.write(Boolean.toString(touchEnabled));
        } catch (IOException e) {
        } finally {
            try {
                if (out != null)
                    out.close();
            } catch (IOException e) {
            }
        }
    }
}
```

Saving is again very boring. Just store whatever you have, and if that fails, ignore the error. This is another good place for improvement, as you'll probably want to let the user know that something went wrong.

The Main Activity

As usual, have a main activity that derives from the GLGame class. It is responsible for loading the assets through a call to Assets.load() on startup, as well as pausing and resuming the music when the activity is paused or resumed. As the start screen, just return the MainMenuScreen, which you will implement shortly. One thing to remember is the definition of the activity in the manifest file. Make sure that you have the orientation set to landscape! Listing 12–3 shows you the code.

Listing 12–3. *DroidInvaders.java, the Main Activity*

```
package com.badlogic.androidgames.droidinvaders;

import javax.microedition.khronos.egl.EGLConfig;
import javax.microedition.khronos.opengles.GL10;

import com.badlogic.androidgames.framework.Screen;
import com.badlogic.androidgames.framework.impl.GLGame;

public class DroidInvaders extends GLGame {
    boolean firstTimeCreate = true;
```

```
@Override
public Screen getStartScreen() {
    return new MainMenuScreen(this);
}

@Override
public void onSurfaceCreated(GL10 gl, EGLConfig config) {
    super.onSurfaceCreated(gl, config);
    if (firstTimeCreate) {
        Settings.load(getFileIO());
        Assets.load(this);
        firstTimeCreate = false;
    } else {
        Assets.reload();
    }
}

@Override
public void onPause() {
    super.onPause();
    if (Settings.soundEnabled)
        Assets.music.pause();
}
}
```

This is exactly the same as in Super Jumper. On a call to getStartScreen(), return a new instance of the MainMenuScreen that you'll write next. In onSurfaceCreated(), make sure your assets are reloaded, and in onPause(), pause the music if it is playing.

As you can see, there are a lot of things that can be repeated once you have a good idea how to approach the implementation of a simple game. Think about how you could reduce the boilerplate code even more by moving things to the framework!

The Main Menu Screen

You've already written many trivial screens for the previous games. Droid Invaders also has some of these. The principle is always the same: offer some UI elements to click and trigger transitions or configuration changes, and display some information. The main menu screen presents only the logo and the Play and Settings options, as shown in Figure 12–4. Touching one of these buttons triggers a transition to the GameScreen or the SettingsScreen. Listing 12–4 shows the code.

Listing 12–4. *MainMenuScreen.java, the Main Menu Screen*

```
package com.badlogic.androidgames.droidinvaders;

import java.util.List;

import javax.microedition.khronos.opengles.GL10;

import com.badlogic.androidgames.framework.Game;
import com.badlogic.androidgames.framework.Input.TouchEvent;
```

```
import com.badlogic.androidgames.framework.gl.Camera2D;
import com.badlogic.androidgames.framework.gl.SpriteBatcher;
import com.badlogic.androidgames.framework.impl.GLScreen;
import com.badlogic.androidgames.framework.math.OverlapTester;
import com.badlogic.androidgames.framework.math.Rectangle;
import com.badlogic.androidgames.framework.math.Vector2;

public class MainMenuScreen extends GLScreen {
    Camera2D guiCam;
    SpriteBatcher batcher;
    Vector2 touchPoint;
    Rectangle playBounds;
    Rectangle settingsBounds;
```

As usual, you need a camera to set up your viewport and the virtual target resolution of 480×320 pixels. Use a SpriteBatcher to render the UI elements and background image. The Vector2 and Rectangle instances will help you decide whether a touch hit a button.

```
    public MainMenuScreen(Game game) {
        super(game);

        guiCam = new Camera2D(glGraphics, 480, 320);
        batcher = new SpriteBatcher(glGraphics, 10);
        touchPoint = new Vector2();
        playBounds = new Rectangle(240 - 112, 100, 224, 32);
        settingsBounds = new Rectangle(240 - 112, 100 - 32, 224, 32);
    }
```

In the constructor, set up the camera and the SpriteBatcher, as you always do. Instantiate the Vector2 and the Rectangles, using the position, width, and height of the two elements on screen, in your 480×320 target resolution.

```
    @Override
    public void update(float deltaTime) {
        List<TouchEvent> events = game.getInput().getTouchEvents();
        int len = events.size();
        for(int i = 0; i < len; i++) {
            TouchEvent event = events.get(i);
            if(event.type != TouchEvent.TOUCH_UP)
                continue;

            guiCam.touchToWorld(touchPoint.set(event.x, event.y));
            if(OverlapTester.pointInRectangle(playBounds, touchPoint)) {
                Assets.playSound(Assets.clickSound);
                game.setScreen(new GameScreen(game));
            }
            if(OverlapTester.pointInRectangle(settingsBounds, touchPoint)) {
                Assets.playSound(Assets.clickSound);
                game.setScreen(new SettingsScreen(game));
            }
        }
    }
```

In the update() method, fetch the touch events and check for "touch-up" events. If there is such an event, transform its real coordinates to the coordinate system the camera sets up. All that's left to do is to check the touch point against the two rectangles bounding the menu entries. If one of them is hit, play the click sound and transition to the respective screen.

```java
@Override
public void present(float deltaTime) {
    GL10 gl = glGraphics.getGL();
    gl.glClear(GL10.GL_COLOR_BUFFER_BIT);
    guiCam.setViewportAndMatrices();

    gl.glEnable(GL10.GL_TEXTURE_2D);

    batcher.beginBatch(Assets.background);
    batcher.drawSprite(240, 160, 480, 320, Assets.backgroundRegion);
    batcher.endBatch();

    gl.glEnable(GL10.GL_BLEND);
    gl.glBlendFunc(GL10.GL_SRC_ALPHA, GL10.GL_ONE_MINUS_SRC_ALPHA);

    batcher.beginBatch(Assets.items);
    batcher.drawSprite(240, 240, 384, 128, Assets.logoRegion);
    batcher.drawSprite(240, 100, 224, 64, Assets.menuRegion);
    batcher.endBatch();

    gl.glDisable(GL10.GL_BLEND);
    gl.glDisable(GL10.GL_TEXTURE_2D);
}
```

The present() method does the same thing it did in most of the screens for Super Jumper. Clear the screen and set up the projection matrix via your camera. Enable texturing and then immediately render the background via the SpriteBatcher and TextureRegion defined in the Assets class. The menu items have translucent areas, so enable blending before you render them.

```java
@Override
public void pause() {
}

@Override
public void resume() {
}

@Override
public void dispose() {
}
}
```

The rest of the class consists of boilerplate methods that don't do anything. Texture reloading is done in the DroidInvaders activity, so there isn't anything left to take care of in the MainMenuScreen.

The Settings Screen

The settings screen offers the player an option to change the input method, as well as enable or disable audio. Indicate this with three different icons (see Figure 12–4).

Touching either the hand or the tilted device will enable the respective input method. The icon for the currently active input method will have a gold color. For the audio icon, do the same as in the previous games.

The choices of the user are reflected by setting the respective Boolean values in the `Settings` class. Make sure these settings are instantly saved to the SD card each time one of them changes, via a call to `Settings.save()`. Listing 12–5 shows you the code.

Listing 12–5. *SettingsScreen.java, the Settings Screen*

```java
package com.badlogic.androidgames.droidinvaders;

import java.util.List;

import javax.microedition.khronos.opengles.GL10;

import com.badlogic.androidgames.framework.Game;
import com.badlogic.androidgames.framework.Input.TouchEvent;
import com.badlogic.androidgames.framework.gl.Camera2D;
import com.badlogic.androidgames.framework.gl.SpriteBatcher;
import com.badlogic.androidgames.framework.impl.GLScreen;
import com.badlogic.androidgames.framework.math.OverlapTester;
import com.badlogic.androidgames.framework.math.Rectangle;
import com.badlogic.androidgames.framework.math.Vector2;

public class SettingsScreen extends GLScreen {
    Camera2D guiCam;
    SpriteBatcher batcher;
    Vector2 touchPoint;
    Rectangle touchBounds;
    Rectangle accelBounds;
    Rectangle soundBounds;
    Rectangle backBounds;
```

As usual, have a camera and `SpriteBatcher` render your UI elements and the background. To check whether a touch event hit a button, store a vector and rectangles for the three buttons on screen.

```java
    public SettingsScreen(Game game) {
        super(game);
        guiCam = new Camera2D(glGraphics, 480, 320);
        batcher = new SpriteBatcher(glGraphics, 10);
        touchPoint = new Vector2();

        touchBounds = new Rectangle(120 - 32, 160 - 32, 64, 64);
        accelBounds = new Rectangle(240 - 32, 160 - 32, 64, 64);
        soundBounds = new Rectangle(360 - 32, 160 - 32, 64, 64);
        backBounds = new Rectangle(32, 32, 64, 64);
    }
```

In the constructor, set up all the members for the screen. No rocket science involved here.

```java
    @Override
    public void update(float deltaTime) {
        List<TouchEvent> events = game.getInput().getTouchEvents();
```

```
            int len = events.size();
            for (int i = 0; i < len; i++) {
                TouchEvent event = events.get(i);
                if (event.type != TouchEvent.TOUCH_UP)
                    continue;

                guiCam.touchToWorld(touchPoint.set(event.x, event.y));
                if (OverlapTester.pointInRectangle(touchBounds, touchPoint)) {
                    Assets.playSound(Assets.clickSound);
                    Settings.touchEnabled = true;
                    Settings.save(game.getFileIO());
                }
                if (OverlapTester.pointInRectangle(accelBounds, touchPoint)) {
                    Assets.playSound(Assets.clickSound);
                    Settings.touchEnabled = false;
                    Settings.save(game.getFileIO());
                }
                if (OverlapTester.pointInRectangle(soundBounds, touchPoint)) {
                    Assets.playSound(Assets.clickSound);
                    Settings.soundEnabled = !Settings.soundEnabled;
                    if (Settings.soundEnabled) {
                        Assets.music.play();
                    } else {
                        Assets.music.pause();
                    }
                    Settings.save(game.getFileIO());
                }
                if (OverlapTester.pointInRectangle(backBounds, touchPoint)) {
                    Assets.playSound(Assets.clickSound);
                    game.setScreen(new MainMenuScreen(game));
                }
            }
        }
    }
```

The update() method fetches the touch events and checks whether a "touch-up" event has been registered. If so, it transforms the touch coordinates to the camera's coordinate system. With these coordinates, it tests the various rectangles to decide what action to take.

```
    @Override
    public void present(float deltaTime) {
        GL10 gl = glGraphics.getGL();
        gl.glClear(GL10.GL_COLOR_BUFFER_BIT);
        guiCam.setViewportAndMatrices();

        gl.glEnable(GL10.GL_TEXTURE_2D);

        batcher.beginBatch(Assets.background);
        batcher.drawSprite(240, 160, 480, 320, Assets.backgroundRegion);
        batcher.endBatch();

        gl.glEnable(GL10.GL_BLEND);
        gl.glBlendFunc(GL10.GL_SRC_ALPHA, GL10.GL_ONE_MINUS_SRC_ALPHA);

        batcher.beginBatch(Assets.items);
        batcher.drawSprite(240, 280, 224, 32, Assets.settingsRegion);
```

```
        batcher.drawSprite(120, 160, 64, 64,
              Settings.touchEnabled ? Assets.touchEnabledRegion : Assets.touchRegion);
        batcher.drawSprite(240, 160, 64, 64,
              Settings.touchEnabled ? Assets.accelRegion
                     : Assets.accelEnabledRegion);
        batcher.drawSprite(360, 160, 64, 64,
              Settings.soundEnabled ? Assets.soundEnabledRegion : Assets.soundRegion);
        batcher.drawSprite(32, 32, 64, 64, Assets.leftRegion);
        batcher.endBatch();

        gl.glDisable(GL10.GL_BLEND);
        gl.glDisable(GL10.GL_TEXTURE_2D);
    }
```

The `render()` method does the same thing as the `MainMenuScreen.render()` method. Render the background and buttons with texturing and blending where needed. Based on the current settings, decide which `TextureRegion` to use to render the three settings buttons.

```
    @Override
    public void pause() {
    }

    @Override
    public void resume() {
    }

    @Override
    public void dispose() {
    }
}
```

The rest of the class is again composed of a few boilerplate methods with no functionality whatsoever.

Before you can create the `GameScreen`, you first have to implement the logic and rendering of your world. Model-View-Controller to the rescue!

The Simulation Classes

As usual, create a single class for each object in the world. You have the following:

- A ship
- Invaders
- Shots
- Shield Blocks

The orchestration is performed by an all-knowing `World` class. As you saw in the last chapter, there's really not such a huge difference between 2D and 3D when it comes to object representation. Instead of `GameObject` and `DynamicObject`, you can now use `GameObject3D` and `DynamicObject3D`. The only differences are that you use `Vector3` instances instead of `Vector2` instances to store positions, velocities, and accelerations, and you use bounding spheres instead of bounding rectangles to represent the shapes of the objects. All that's left to do is implement the behavior of the different objects in the world.

The Shield Class

From the game mechanics definition, you know the size and behavior of your shield blocks. They just sit there in the world at some location, waiting to be annihilated by a shot, either from the ship or an invader. There's not a lot of logic in them, so the code is rather concise. Listing 12–6 shows the internals of a shield block.

Listing 12–6. *Shield.java, the Shield Block Class*

```java
package com.badlogic.androidgames.droidinvaders;

import com.badlogic.androidgames.framework.GameObject3D;

public class Shield extends GameObject3D {
    static float SHIELD_RADIUS = 0.5f;

    public Shield(float x, float y, float z) {
        super(x, y, z, SHIELD_RADIUS);
    }
}
```

Define the shield's radius and initialize its position and bounding sphere according to the constructor parameters. That's all there is to it!

The Shot Class

The shot class is equally simple. It derives from DynamicGameObject3D, as it is actually moving. Listing 12–7 shows you the code.

Listing 12–7. *Shot.java, the Shot Class*

```java
package com.badlogic.androidgames.droidinvaders;

import com.badlogic.androidgames.framework.DynamicGameObject3D;

public class Shot extends DynamicGameObject3D {
    static float SHOT_VELOCITY = 10f;
    static float SHOT_RADIUS = 0.1f;

    public Shot(float x, float y, float z, float velocityZ) {
        super(x, y, z, SHOT_RADIUS);
        velocity.z = velocityZ;
    }

    public void update(float deltaTime) {
        position.z += velocity.z * deltaTime;
        bounds.center.set(position);
    }
}
```

You have to define some constants, namely the shot velocity and its radius. The constructor takes a shot's initial position, as well as its velocity on the z-axis. Wait, didn't you just define the velocity as a constant? Yes, but that would let your shot travel only in the direction of the positive z-axis. That's fine for shots fired by the invaders, but the shots from the ship must travel in the opposite direction. When you create a shot (outside of this class), you know the direction the shot should travel. So the shot has its velocity set by its creator.

The update() method just does the usual point-mass physics. There is no acceleration involved, and thus you only need to add the constant velocity, multiplied by the delta time, to the shot's position. The crucial part is that you also update the position of the bounding sphere's center in accordance with the shot's position. Otherwise, the bounding sphere would not move with the shot.

The Ship Class

The Ship class is responsible for updating the ship's position, keeping it within the bounds of the game field, and keeping track of the state it is in. It can either be alive or exploding. In both cases, keep track of the amount of time the ship has been in this state. The state time can then be used to do animations, for example, just as you did in Super Jumper and its WorldRenderer class. The ship will get its current velocity from the outside, based on the user input, either with accelerometer readings, as you did for Bob, or based on a constant, depending on what on-screen buttons are being pressed. Additionally, the ship will keep track of the number of lives it has, and offer us a way to tell it that it has been killed. Listing 12–8 shows you the code.

Listing 12–8. *Ship.java, the Ship Class*

```
package com.badlogic.androidgames.droidinvaders;

import com.badlogic.androidgames.framework.DynamicGameObject3D;

public class Ship extends DynamicGameObject3D {
    static float SHIP_VELOCITY = 20f;
    static int SHIP_ALIVE = 0;
    static int SHIP_EXPLODING = 1;
    static float SHIP_EXPLOSION_TIME = 1.6f;
    static float SHIP_RADIUS = 0.5f;
```

Start off with a couple of constants to define the maximum ship velocity, two states (alive and exploding), the amount of time it takes the ship to explode fully, and the ship's bounding sphere radius. Also, let the class derive from DynamicGameObject3D, since it has a position and bounding sphere, as well as a velocity. The acceleration vector stored in a DynamicGameObject3D will again be unused.

```
    int lives;
    int state;
    float stateTime = 0;
```

Next, you have the members, consisting of two integers, to keep track of the number of lives the ship has, as well as its state (either SHIP_ALIVE or SHIP_EXPLODING). The last member keeps track of how many seconds the ship has been in its current state.

```
public Ship(float x, float y, float z) {
    super(x, y, z, SHIP_RADIUS);
    lives = 3;
    state = SHIP_ALIVE;
}
```

The constructor performs the usual super class constructor call and initializes some of the members. The ship will have a total of three lives.

```
public void update(float deltaTime, float accelY) {
    if (state == SHIP_ALIVE) {
        velocity.set(accelY / 10 * SHIP_VELOCITY, 0, 0);
        position.add(velocity.x * deltaTime, 0, 0);
        if (position.x < World.WORLD_MIN_X)
            position.x = World.WORLD_MIN_X;
        if (position.x > World.WORLD_MAX_X)
            position.x = World.WORLD_MAX_X;
        bounds.center.set(position);
    } else {
        if (stateTime >= SHIP_EXPLOSION_TIME) {
            lives--;
            stateTime = 0;
            state = SHIP_ALIVE;
        }
    }
    stateTime += deltaTime;
}
```

The update() method is pretty simple. It takes the delta time, as well as the current accelerometer reading on the y-axis of the device (remember, you are in landscape mode, so the accelerometer y-axis is your screen's x-axis). If the ship is alive, set its velocity based on the accelerometer value (which will be in the range –10 to 10), just as you did for Bob in Super Jumper. Additionally, update its position based on the current velocity. Next, check whether the ship has left the boundaries of the playing field, using two constants that you'll define later on in your World class. When the position is fixed, update the center of the bounding sphere for the ship.

If the ship is exploding, check how long that's been the case. After 1.6 seconds in the exploding state, the ship is finished exploding, loses one life, and goes back to the alive state.

Finally, update the stateTime member based on the given delta time.

```
public void kill() {
    state = SHIP_EXPLODING;
    stateTime = 0;
    velocity.x = 0;
}
}
```

The last kill() method will be called by the World class if it determines a collision has occurred between the ship and either a shot or an invader. It will set the state to exploding, reset the state time, and make sure that the ship's velocity is zero on all axes (never set the y- and z-component of the velocity vector, since you only move on the x-axis).

The Invader Class

Invaders are simply floating in space according to a predefined pattern. Figure 12–11 shows you this pattern.

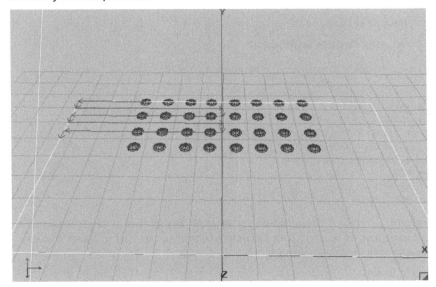

Figure 12–11. *Movement of the invaders. Left, down, right, down, left, down, right, down...*

An invader follows an extremely simplistic movement pattern. From its initial position, it first moves to the right for some distance. Next, it moves downward (which means in the direction of the positive z-axis on the playing field), again for a specified distance. Once it is done with that, it will start moving to the right, basically backtracking to the same x-coordinate where it was before it started moving left.

The left and right movement distances are always the same, except in the beginning. Figure 12–11 illustrates the movement of the top-left invader. Its first left movement is shorter than all subsequent movements to the left or right. The horizontal movement distance is half the playing field width, 14 units in this case. For the first horizontal movement, the distance an invader has to travel is half this, or 7 units.

What you have to do is keep track of the direction in which an invader is moving, and how far it has already moved in that direction. If it reaches the movement distance for the given movement state (14 units for horizontal movement, 1 unit for vertical movement), it switches to the next movement state. All invaders will initially have their movement distance set to half the playing field's width. Look again at Figure 12–11 to see why that works! This will make the invaders bounce off the edges of the playing field to the left and right.

Invaders also have a constant velocity. Well, the velocity will actually increase each time you generate a new wave of invaders if all the invaders from the current wave are dead. You can achieve this simply by multiplying this default velocity by some constant that is set from outside, namely the World class responsible for updating all invaders.

Finally, you have to keep track of the state of the invader, which can be alive or exploding. Use the same mechanism as in the case of the ship, with a state and a state time. Listing 12–9 shows you the code.

Listing 12–9. *Invader.java, the Invader Class*

```java
package com.badlogic.androidgames.droidinvaders;

import com.badlogic.androidgames.framework.DynamicGameObject3D;

public class Invader extends DynamicGameObject3D {
    static final int INVADER_ALIVE = 0;
    static final int INVADER_DEAD = 1;
    static final float INVADER_EXPLOSION_TIME = 1.6f;
    static final float INVADER_RADIUS = 0.75f;
    static final float INVADER_VELOCITY = 1;
    static final int MOVE_LEFT = 0;
    static final int MOVE_DOWN = 1;
    static final int MOVE_RIGHT = 2;
```

Start with some constants, defining the state of an invader, the duration of its explosion, its radius and default velocity, as well as three constants that allow you to keep track of the direction the invader is currently moving.

```java
    int state = INVADER_ALIVE;
    float stateTime = 0;
    int move = MOVE_LEFT;
    boolean wasLastStateLeft = true;
    float movedDistance = World.WORLD_MAX_X / 2;
```

Keep track of an invader's state, state time, movement direction, and movement distance, which should initially be set to half the playing field width. Keep track of whether the last horizontal movement was to the left or not. This allows you to decide in which direction the invader should go once it has finished its vertical movement on the z-axis.

```java
    public Invader(float x, float y, float z) {
        super(x, y, z, INVADER_RADIUS);
    }
```

The constructor performs the usual set up of the invader's position and bounding ship, via the super class constructor.

```java
    public void update(float deltaTime, float speedMultiplier) {
        if (state == INVADER_ALIVE) {
            movedDistance += deltaTime * INVADER_VELOCITY * speedMultiplier;
```

```
        if (move == MOVE_LEFT) {
            position.x -= deltaTime * INVADER_VELOCITY * speedMultiplier;
            if (movedDistance > World.WORLD_MAX_X) {
                move = MOVE_DOWN;
                movedDistance = 0;
                wasLastStateLeft = true;
            }
        }
        if (move == MOVE_RIGHT) {
            position.x += deltaTime * INVADER_VELOCITY * speedMultiplier;
            if (movedDistance > World.WORLD_MAX_X) {
                move = MOVE_DOWN;
                movedDistance = 0;
                wasLastStateLeft = false;
            }
        }
        if (move == MOVE_DOWN) {
            position.z += deltaTime * INVADER_VELOCITY * speedMultiplier;
            if (movedDistance > 1) {
                if (wasLastStateLeft)
                    move = MOVE_RIGHT;
                else
                    move = MOVE_LEFT;
                movedDistance = 0;
            }
        }

        bounds.center.set(position);
    }

    stateTime += deltaTime;
}
```

The update() method takes the current delta time and speed multiplier to make the new waves of invaders move faster. Only perform the movement if the invader is alive, of course.

Start off by calculating how many units the invader will travel in this update and increase the movedDistance member accordingly. If it moves to the left, update the position directly by subtracting the movement velocity to the x-coordinate of the position multiplied by the delta time and speed multiplier. If it has moved far enough, tell it to start moving vertically by setting the move member to MOVE_DOWN. Also, set the wasLastStateLeft to true, so that you know that, after the down movement is finished, you have to move to the right.

Do exactly the same for handling movement to the right. The only difference is that you subtract the movement velocity from the position's x-coordinate and set the wasLastStateLeft to false once the movement distance has been reached.

If you move downward, manipulate the z-coordinate of the invader's position and again check how far you've been moving in that direction. If you reached the movement distance for downward movement, switch the movement state either to MOVE_LEFT or MOVE_RIGHT, depending on the last horizontal movement direction encoded in the wasLastStateLeft member. Once you are done updating the invaders position, set the position of the bounding sphere, as you did for the ship. Finally, update the current state time and consider the update done.

```java
    public void kill() {
        state = INVADER_DEAD;
        stateTime = 0;
    }
}
```

The `kill()` method here serves the same purpose as the `kill()` method for the Ship class. It allows you to tell the invader that it should start dying. Set its state to `INVADER_DEAD` and reset its state time. The invader will then stop moving, and only update its state time based on the current delta time.

The World Class

The `World` class is the mastermind in all of this. It stores the ship, the invaders, and the shots, and it is responsible for updating them and checking on collisions. It's much the same as in Super Jumper, with a few minor differences. The initial placement of the shield blocks, as well as the invaders, is also a responsibility of the `World` class. Create a `WorldListener` interface to inform any outside parties of events within the world, such as an explosion or a shot that's been fired. This will allow you to play sound effects, just like in Super Jumper. It helps to go through the code one method at a time. Listing 12–10 shows you the code.

Listing 12–10. *World.java, the World Class, Tying Everything Together*

```java
package com.badlogic.androidgames.droidinvaders;

import java.util.ArrayList;
import java.util.List;
import java.util.Random;

import com.badlogic.androidgames.framework.math.OverlapTester;

public class World {
    public interface WorldListener {
        public void explosion();

        public void shot();
    }
```

You want outside parties to know when an explosion takes place or when a shot is fired. For this, define a listener interface, which you can implement and register with a World instance that will be called when one of these events happen. This is much like Super Jumper, just with different events.

```java
    final static float WORLD_MIN_X = -14;
    final static float WORLD_MAX_X = 14;
    final static float WORLD_MIN_Z = -15;
```

You should also have a couple of constants that define the extents of the world, as discussed in the "Defining the Game World" section.

```
WorldListener listener;
int waves = 1;
int score = 0;
float speedMultiplier = 1;
final List<Shot> shots = new ArrayList<Shot>();
final List<Invader> invaders = new ArrayList<Invader>();
final List<Shield> shields = new ArrayList<Shield>();
final Ship ship;
long lastShotTime;
Random random;
```

The world keeps track of a couple of things. You have a listener that you invoke when an explosion happens or a shot is fired. Also, keep track of how many waves of invaders the player has already destroyed. The score member keeps track of the current score, and the speedMultiplier allows you to speed up the movement of the invaders (remember the Invaders.update() method). Also, store lists of the shots, invaders, and shield blocks currently alive in the world. Finally, have an instance of a Ship, and store the last time a shot was fired by the ship. Store this time in nanoseconds, as returned by System.nanoTime()—hence the long data type. The Random instance will come in handy when you want to decide whether an invader should fire a shot or not.

```
public World() {
    ship = new Ship(0, 0, 0);
    generateInvaders();
    generateShields();
    lastShotTime = System.nanoTime();
    random = new Random();
}
```

In the constructor, create the Ship at its initial position, generate the invaders and shields, and initialize the rest of the members.

```
private void generateInvaders() {
    for (int row = 0; row < 4; row++) {
        for (int column = 0; column < 8; column++) {
            Invader invader = new Invader(-WORLD_MAX_X / 2 + column * 2f,
                    0, WORLD_MIN_Z + row * 2f);
            invaders.add(invader);
        }
    }
}
```

The generateInvaders() method simply creates a grid of invaders, eight by four, arranged as in Figure12–11.

```
private void generateShields() {
    for (int shield = 0; shield < 3; shield++) {
        shields.add(new Shield(-10 + shield * 10 - 1, 0, -3));
        shields.add(new Shield(-10 + shield * 10 + 0, 0, -3));
        shields.add(new Shield(-10 + shield * 10 + 1, 0, -3));
        shields.add(new Shield(-10 + shield * 10 - 1, 0, -2));
        shields.add(new Shield(-10 + shield * 10 + 1, 0, -2));
    }
}
```

The generateShields() class does pretty much the same: instantiating three shields composed of five shield blocks each, as laid out in Figure 12–2.

```
public void setWorldListener(WorldListener worldListener) {
    this.listener = worldListener;
}
```

A setter method can set the listener of the World.

```
public void update(float deltaTime, float accelX) {
    ship.update(deltaTime, accelX);
    updateInvaders(deltaTime);
    updateShots(deltaTime);

    checkShotCollisions();
    checkInvaderCollisions();

    if (invaders.size() == 0) {
        generateInvaders();
        waves++;
        speedMultiplier += 0.5f;
    }
}
```

The update() method is surprisingly simple. It uses the current delta time, as well as the reading on the accelerometer's y-axis, which you can pass to Ship.update(). Once the ship has updated, call updateInvaders() and updateShots(), which are responsible for updating these two types of objects. After all the objects in the world have been updated, start checking for a collision. The checkShotCollision() method will check collisions between any shots and the ship and/or invaders.

Finally, check whether the invaders are dead, and if they are you can generate a new wave of invaders. For love of the garbage collector, you could reuse the old Invader instances, for example via a Pool. However, to keep things simple, you can simply create new instances. The same is true for shots, by the way. Given the small number of objects you create in one game session, the GC is unlikely to fire. If you want to make the GC really happy, just use a Pool to reuse dead invaders and shots. Also, note that you increase the speed multiplier here!

```
private void updateInvaders(float deltaTime) {
    int len = invaders.size();
    for (int i = 0; i < len; i++) {
        Invader invader = invaders.get(i);
        invader.update(deltaTime, speedMultiplier);

        if (invader.state == Invader.INVADER_ALIVE) {
            if (random.nextFloat() < 0.001f) {
                Shot shot = new Shot(invader.position.x,
                        invader.position.y,
                                                invader.position.z,
                        Shot.SHOT_VELOCITY);
                shots.add(shot);
                listener.shot();
            }
        }
    }
```

```
        if (invader.state == Invader.INVADER_DEAD &&
                    invader.stateTime > Invader.INVADER_EXPLOSION_TIME) {
            invaders.remove(i);
            i--;
            len--;
        }
    }
}
```

The updateInvaders() method has a couple of responsibilities. It loops through all invaders and calls their update() method. Once an Invader instance is updated, check whether it is alive. In that case, give it a chance to fire a shot by generating a random number. If that number is below 0.001, a shot is fired. This means that each invader has a 0.1% chance of firing a shot each frame. If that happens, instantiate a new shot, set its velocity so that it moves in the direction of the positive z-axis, and inform the listener of that event. If the Invader is dead and has finished exploding, simply remove it from the current list of invaders.

```
private void updateShots(float deltaTime) {
    int len = shots.size();
    for (int i = 0; i < len; i++) {
        Shot shot = shots.get(i);
        shot.update(deltaTime);
        if (shot.position.z < WORLD_MIN_Z ||
            shot.position.z > 0) {
            shots.remove(i);
            i--;
            len--;
        }
    }
}
```

The updateShots() method is simple, as well. Loop through all shots, update them, and check whether each one has left the playing field, in which case remove it from the shots list.

```
private void checkInvaderCollisions() {
    if (ship.state == Ship.SHIP_EXPLODING)
        return;

    int len = invaders.size();
    for (int i = 0; i < len; i++) {
        Invader invader = invaders.get(i);
        if (OverlapTester.overlapSpheres(ship.bounds, invader.bounds)) {
            ship.lives = 1;
            ship.kill();
            return;
        }
    }
}
```

In the checkInvaderCollisions() method, check whether any of the invaders has collided with the ship. That's a pretty simple affair, since all you need to do is loop through all invaders and check for overlap between each invader's bounding sphere and the ship's bounding sphere. According to the game mechanics definition, the game ends if the ship collides with an invader. This is why you set the ship's lives to 1 before you call the Ship.kill() method. After that call, the ship's live member is set to 0, which you'll use in another method to check for the game-over state.

```
private void checkShotCollisions() {
    int len = shots.size();
    for (int i = 0; i < len; i++) {
        Shot shot = shots.get(i);
        boolean shotRemoved = false;

        int len2 = shields.size();
        for (int j = 0; j < len2; j++) {
            Shield shield = shields.get(j);
            if (OverlapTester.overlapSpheres(shield.bounds, shot.bounds)) {
                shields.remove(j);
                shots.remove(i);
                i--;
                len--;
                shotRemoved = true;
                break;
            }
        }
        if (shotRemoved)
            continue;

        if (shot.velocity.z < 0) {
            len2 = invaders.size();
            for (int j = 0; j < len2; j++) {
                Invader invader = invaders.get(j);
                if (OverlapTester.overlapSpheres(invader.bounds,
                        shot.bounds)
                        && invader.state == Invader.INVADER_ALIVE) {
                    invader.kill();
                    listener.explosion();
                    score += 10;
                    shots.remove(i);
                    i--;
                    len--;
                    break;
                }
            }
        } else {
            if (OverlapTester.overlapSpheres(shot.bounds, ship.bounds)
                    && ship.state == Ship.SHIP_ALIVE) {
                ship.kill();
                listener.explosion();
                shots.remove(i);
                i--;
                len--;
            }
        }
    }
}
```

The checkShotCollisions() method is a little bit more complex. It loops through each Shot instance and checks for overlap between it and a shield block, an invader, or the ship. Shield blocks can be hit by shots fired by the ship or by an invader. An invader can only be hit by a shot fired by the ship. And the ship can only be hit by a shot fired by an invader. To distinguish whether a shot was fired by a ship or an invader, all you need to do is look at its z-velocity. If it is positive, it moves toward the ship, and was therefore fired by an invader. If it is negative, it was fired by the ship.

```
public boolean isGameOver() {
    return ship.lives == 0;
}
```

The isGameOver() method simply tells an outside party if the ship has lost all its lives.

```
public void shoot() {
    if (ship.state == Ship.SHIP_EXPLODING)
        return;

    int friendlyShots = 0;
    int len = shots.size();
    for (int i = 0; i < len; i++) {
        if (shots.get(i).velocity.z < 0)
            friendlyShots++;
    }

    if (System.nanoTime() - lastShotTime > 1000000000 || friendlyShots == 0) {
        shots.add(new Shot(ship.position.x, ship.position.y,
                ship.position.z, -Shot.SHOT_VELOCITY));
        lastShotTime = System.nanoTime();
        listener.shot();
    }
}
```

Finally, there's the shoot() method. It will be called from outside each time the Fire button is pressed by the user. As noted in the game mechanics section, a shot can be fired by the ship every second, or it can be fired if there's no ship shot on the field yet. The ship can't fire if it explodes, of course, so that's the first thing you check. Next, run through all the Shots and check if one of them is a ship shot. If that's not the case, you can shoot immediately. Otherwise, check when the last shot was fired. If more than a second has passed since the last shot, fire a new one. This time, set the velocity to – Shot.SHOT_VELOCITY so that the shot moves in the direction of the negative z-axis toward the invaders. As always, invoke the listener to inform it of the event.

And that's all the classes that make up the game world! Compare that to what you had in Super Jumper. The principles are nearly the same, and the code looks quite similar. Droid Invaders is, of course, a very simple game, so you can get away with simple solutions, such as using bounding spheres for everything. For many simple 3D games, that's all you need. On to the last two parts of your game: the GameScreen and the WorldRenderer class!

The GameScreen Class

Once the game transitions to the GameScreen class, the player can immediately start playing without having to state that he or she is ready. The only states you have to care about for are these:

- The running state, where you render the background, the world, and the UI elements, as shown in Figure 12–4.

- The paused state, where you render the background, the world, and the paused menu, as shown in Figure 12–4.

- The game-over state, where you render pretty much the same thing.

Follow the same method used in Super Jumper, and have different update() and present() methods for each of the three states.

The only interesting part of this class is how you handle the user input to move the ship. You want your player to be able to control the ship with either on-screen buttons or the accelerometer. You can read the Settings.touchEnabled field to figure out what the user wants in regard to this. Depending on which input method is active, decide on whether to render the on-screen buttons or not, and pass the proper accelerometer values to the World.update() method to move the ship.

With the on-screen buttons, you don't need to use the accelerometer values; instead, just pass a constant artificial acceleration value to the World.update() method. It has to be in the range –10 (left) to 10 (right). After a little experimentation, you might arrive at a value of –5 for left movement and 5 for right movement via the on-screen buttons.

The last interesting for this class is the way you combine the rendering of the 3D game world and the 2D UI elements. Take a look at the code of the GameScreen class in Listing 12–11.

Listing 12–11. *GameScreen.java, the Game Screen*

```java
package com.badlogic.androidgames.droidinvaders;

import java.util.List;

import javax.microedition.khronos.opengles.GL10;

import com.badlogic.androidgames.droidinvaders.World.WorldListener;
import com.badlogic.androidgames.framework.Game;
import com.badlogic.androidgames.framework.Input.TouchEvent;
import com.badlogic.androidgames.framework.gl.Camera2D;
import com.badlogic.androidgames.framework.gl.FPSCounter;
import com.badlogic.androidgames.framework.gl.SpriteBatcher;
import com.badlogic.androidgames.framework.impl.GLScreen;
import com.badlogic.androidgames.framework.math.OverlapTester;
import com.badlogic.androidgames.framework.math.Rectangle;
import com.badlogic.androidgames.framework.math.Vector2;

public class GameScreen extends GLScreen {
    static final int GAME_RUNNING = 0;
```

```
static final int GAME_PAUSED = 1;
static final int GAME_OVER = 2;
```

As usual, you have a couple of constants for encoding the screen's current state.

```
int state;
Camera2D guiCam;
Vector2 touchPoint;
SpriteBatcher batcher;
World world;
WorldListener worldListener;
WorldRenderer renderer;
Rectangle pauseBounds;
Rectangle resumeBounds;
Rectangle quitBounds;
Rectangle leftBounds;
Rectangle rightBounds;
Rectangle shotBounds;
int lastScore;
int lastLives;
int lastWaves;
String scoreString;
FPSCounter fpsCounter;
```

The members of the GameScreen are business as usual. You have a member keeping track of the state, a camera, a vector for the touch point, a SpriteBatcher for rendering the 2D UI elements, the World instance, along with the WorldListener, the WorldRenderer (which you are going to write in a minute), and a couple of Rectangles for checking whether a UI element was touched. In addition, three integers keep track of the last number of lives, waves, and score, so that you don't have to update the scoreString each time in order to reduce GC activity. Finally, there is an FPSCounter, so that later on you can figure out how well the game performs.

```
public GameScreen(Game game) {
    super(game);

    state = GAME_RUNNING;
    guiCam = new Camera2D(glGraphics, 480, 320);
    touchPoint = new Vector2();
    batcher = new SpriteBatcher(glGraphics, 100);
    world = new World();
    worldListener = new WorldListener() {
        @Override
        public void shot() {
            Assets.playSound(Assets.shotSound);
        }

        @Override
        public void explosion() {
            Assets.playSound(Assets.explosionSound);
        }
    };
    world.setWorldListener(worldListener);
    renderer = new WorldRenderer(glGraphics);
    pauseBounds = new Rectangle(480 - 64, 320 - 64, 64, 64);
    resumeBounds = new Rectangle(240 - 80, 160, 160, 32);
```

```
        quitBounds = new Rectangle(240 - 80, 160 - 32, 160, 32);
        shotBounds = new Rectangle(480 - 64, 0, 64, 64);
        leftBounds = new Rectangle(0, 0, 64, 64);
        rightBounds = new Rectangle(64, 0, 64, 64);
        lastScore = 0;
        lastLives = world.ship.lives;
        lastWaves = world.waves;
        scoreString = "lives:" + lastLives + " waves:" + lastWaves + " score:"
                + lastScore;
        fpsCounter = new FPSCounter();
    }
```

In the constructor, set up all the members, as you are now accustomed to doing. The
WorldListener is responsible for playing the correct sound in the case of an event in the
world. The rest is the same as for Super Jumper, though adapted slightly for the
somewhat different UI elements.

```
    @Override
    public void update(float deltaTime) {
        switch (state) {
        case GAME_PAUSED:
            updatePaused();
            break;
        case GAME_RUNNING:
            updateRunning(deltaTime);
            break;
        case GAME_OVER:
            updateGameOver();
            break;
        }
    }
```

The update() method delegates the real updating to one of the other three update
methods, depending on the current state of the screen.

```
    private void updatePaused() {
        List<TouchEvent> events = game.getInput().getTouchEvents();
        int len = events.size();
        for (int i = 0; i < len; i++) {
            TouchEvent event = events.get(i);
            if (event.type != TouchEvent.TOUCH_UP)
                continue;

            guiCam.touchToWorld(touchPoint.set(event.x, event.y));
            if (OverlapTester.pointInRectangle(resumeBounds, touchPoint)) {
                Assets.playSound(Assets.clickSound);
                state = GAME_RUNNING;
            }

            if (OverlapTester.pointInRectangle(quitBounds, touchPoint)) {
                Assets.playSound(Assets.clickSound);
                game.setScreen(new MainMenuScreen(game));
            }
        }
    }
```

The updatePaused() method loops through any available touch events and checks whether one of the two menu entries was pressed (**Resume** or **Quit**). In each case, play the click sound. Nothing new here.

```
private void updateRunning(float deltaTime) {
    List<TouchEvent> events = game.getInput().getTouchEvents();
    int len = events.size();
    for (int i = 0; i < len; i++) {
        TouchEvent event = events.get(i);
        if (event.type != TouchEvent.TOUCH_DOWN)
            continue;

        guiCam.touchToWorld(touchPoint.set(event.x, event.y));

        if (OverlapTester.pointInRectangle(pauseBounds, touchPoint)) {
            Assets.playSound(Assets.clickSound);
            state = GAME_PAUSED;
        }
        if (OverlapTester.pointInRectangle(shotBounds, touchPoint)) {
            world.shot();
        }
    }

    world.update(deltaTime, calculateInputAcceleration());
    if (world.ship.lives != lastLives || world.score != lastScore
            || world.waves != lastWaves) {
        lastLives = world.ship.lives;
        lastScore = world.score;
        lastWaves = world.waves;
        scoreString = "lives:" + lastLives + " waves:" + lastWaves
                + " score:" + lastScore;
    }
    if (world.isGameOver()) {
        state = GAME_OVER;
    }
}
```

The updateRunning() method is responsible for two things: to check whether the pause button was pressed and react accordingly, and to update the world based on the user input. The first piece of the puzzle is trivial, so take a look at the world updating mechanism. As you can see, you delegate the acceleration value calculation to a method called calculateInputAcceleration(). Once the world is updated, check whether any of the three states (lives, waves, or score) have changed and update the scoreString accordingly. Finally, check whether the game is over, in which case enter the GameOver state.

```
private float calculateInputAcceleration() {
    float accelX = 0;
    if (Settings.touchEnabled) {
        for (int i = 0; i < 2; i++) {
            if (game.getInput().isTouchDown(i)) {
                guiCam.touchToWorld(touchPoint.set(game.getInput()
                        .getTouchX(i), game.getInput().getTouchY(i)));
                if (OverlapTester.pointInRectangle(leftBounds, touchPoint)) {
                    accelX = -Ship.SHIP_VELOCITY / 5;
```

```
            }
            if (OverlapTester.pointInRectangle(rightBounds, touchPoint)) {
                accelX = Ship.SHIP_VELOCITY / 5;
            }
        }
    }
} else {
    accelX = game.getInput().getAccelY();
}
return accelX;
}
```

The calculateInputAcceleration() is where you actually interpret the user input. If touch is enabled, check whether the left or right on-screen movement buttons were pressed and set the acceleration value accordingly to either –5 (left) or 5. If the accelerometer is used, simply return its current value on the y-axis (remember, you are in landscape mode).

```
private void updateGameOver() {
    List<TouchEvent> events = game.getInput().getTouchEvents();
    int len = events.size();
    for (int i = 0; i < len; i++) {
        TouchEvent event = events.get(i);
        if (event.type == TouchEvent.TOUCH_UP) {
            Assets.playSound(Assets.clickSound);
            game.setScreen(new MainMenuScreen(game));
        }
    }
}
```

The updateGameOver() method is again trivial and simply checks for a touch event, in which case you transition to the MainMenuScreen.

```
@Override
public void present(float deltaTime) {
    GL10 gl = glGraphics.getGL();
    gl.glClear(GL10.GL_COLOR_BUFFER_BIT | GL10.GL_DEPTH_BUFFER_BIT);
    guiCam.setViewportAndMatrices();

    gl.glEnable(GL10.GL_TEXTURE_2D);
    batcher.beginBatch(Assets.background);
    batcher.drawSprite(240, 160, 480, 320, Assets.backgroundRegion);
    batcher.endBatch();
    gl.glDisable(GL10.GL_TEXTURE_2D);

    renderer.render(world, deltaTime);

    switch (state) {
    case GAME_RUNNING:
        presentRunning();
        break;
    case GAME_PAUSED:
        presentPaused();
        break;
    case GAME_OVER:
        presentGameOver();
```

```
        }

        fpsCounter.logFrame();
    }
```

The present() method is actually pretty simple, as well. As always, start off by clearing the framebuffer. Also, clear the z-buffer, since you are going to render some 3D objects for which you need z-testing. Next, set up the projection matrix so that you can render your 2D background image, just as you did in the MainMenuScreen or SettingsScreen. Once that is done, tell the WorldRenderer to render the game world. Finally, delegate the rendering of the UI elements depending on the current state. Note that the WorldRenderer.render() method is responsible for setting up all things needed to render the 3D world!

```
    private void presentPaused() {
        GL10 gl = glGraphics.getGL();
        guiCam.setViewportAndMatrices();
        gl.glEnable(GL10.GL_BLEND);
        gl.glBlendFunc(GL10.GL_SRC_ALPHA, GL10.GL_ONE_MINUS_SRC_ALPHA);
        gl.glEnable(GL10.GL_TEXTURE_2D);

        batcher.beginBatch(Assets.items);
        Assets.font.drawText(batcher, scoreString, 10, 320-20);
        batcher.drawSprite(240, 160, 160, 64, Assets.pauseRegion);
        batcher.endBatch();

        gl.glDisable(GL10.GL_TEXTURE_2D);
        gl.glDisable(GL10.GL_BLEND);
    }
```

The presentPaused() method just renders the scoreString via the Font instance you stored in the Assets, as well as the Pause menu. Note that, at this point, you have already rendered the background image, as well as the 3D world. All the UI elements will thus overlay the 3D world.

```
    private void presentRunning() {
        GL10 gl = glGraphics.getGL();
        guiCam.setViewportAndMatrices();
        gl.glEnable(GL10.GL_BLEND);
        gl.glBlendFunc(GL10.GL_SRC_ALPHA, GL10.GL_ONE_MINUS_SRC_ALPHA);
        gl.glEnable(GL10.GL_TEXTURE_2D);

        batcher.beginBatch(Assets.items);
        batcher.drawSprite(480- 32, 320 - 32, 64, 64, Assets.pauseButtonRegion);
        Assets.font.drawText(batcher, scoreString, 10, 320-20);
        if(Settings.touchEnabled) {
            batcher.drawSprite(32, 32, 64, 64, Assets.leftRegion);
            batcher.drawSprite(96, 32, 64, 64, Assets.rightRegion);
        }
        batcher.drawSprite(480 - 40, 32, 64, 64, Assets.fireRegion);
        batcher.endBatch();

        gl.glDisable(GL10.GL_TEXTURE_2D);
        gl.glDisable(GL10.GL_BLEND);
    }
```

The presentRunning() method is also pretty straightforward. Render the scoreString first. If touch input is enabled, render the left and right movement buttons. Finally, render the Fire button and reset any OpenGL ES states you've changed (texturing and blending).

```
private void presentGameOver() {
    GL10 gl = glGraphics.getGL();
    guiCam.setViewportAndMatrices();
    gl.glEnable(GL10.GL_BLEND);
    gl.glBlendFunc(GL10.GL_SRC_ALPHA, GL10.GL_ONE_MINUS_SRC_ALPHA);
    gl.glEnable(GL10.GL_TEXTURE_2D);

    batcher.beginBatch(Assets.items);
    batcher.drawSprite(240, 160, 128, 64, Assets.gameOverRegion);
    Assets.font.drawText(batcher, scoreString, 10, 320-20);
    batcher.endBatch();

    gl.glDisable(GL10.GL_TEXTURE_2D);
    gl.glDisable(GL10.GL_BLEND);
}
```

The presentGameOver() method is more of the same—just some string and UI rendering.

```
@Override
public void pause() {
    state = GAME_PAUSED;
}
```

Finally, you have the pause() method, which simply puts the GameScreen into the paused state.

```
@Override
public void resume() {

}

@Override
public void dispose() {

}
}
```

The rest is just empty stubs so that you can fulfill the GLGame interface definition. On to your final class: the WorldRenderer!

The WorldRender Class

Recall what you have to render in 3D:

- The ship, using the ship model and texture, and applying lighting.

- The invaders, using the invader model and texture, again with lighting.

- Any shots on the playfield, based on the shot model, this time without texturing but with lighting.

■ The shield blocks, based on the shield block model, again without texturing, but with lighting and transparency (see Figure 12–3).

■ Explosions instead of the ship or invader model, in case the ship or invader is exploding. The explosion is not lit, of course.

You know how to code the first four items on this list. But what about the explosions?

It turns out that you can abuse the SpriteBatcher for this. Based on the state time of the exploding ship or invader, you can fetch a TextureRegion from the Animation instance holding the explosion animation (see Assets class). The SpriteBatcher can only render textured rectangles in the x/y plane, so you have to find a way to move such a rectangle to an arbitrary position in space (where the exploding ship or invader is located). You can easily achieve this by using glTranslatef() on the model-view matrix before rendering the rectangle via the SpriteBatcher!

The rendering setup for the other objects is pretty straightforward. You have a directional light coming from the top right, and an ambient light can light all the objects a little, no matter their orientation. The camera is located a little above and behind the ship, and it will look at a point a little ahead of the ship. Use your LookAtCamera for this. To let the camera follow the ship, keep the x-coordinate of its position and the look-at point in sync with the ship's x-coordinate.

For some extra eye candy, rotate the invaders around the y-axis. Also, rotate the ship around the z-axis based on its current velocity, so that it appears to be leaning in the direction it is moving.

Let's put this into code! Listing 12–12 shows you the final class of Droid Invaders.

Listing 12–12. *WorldRenderer.java, the World Renderer*

```
package com.badlogic.androidgames.droidinvaders;

import java.util.List;

import javax.microedition.khronos.opengles.GL10;

import com.badlogic.androidgames.framework.gl.AmbientLight;
import com.badlogic.androidgames.framework.gl.Animation;
import com.badlogic.androidgames.framework.gl.DirectionalLight;
import com.badlogic.androidgames.framework.gl.LookAtCamera;
import com.badlogic.androidgames.framework.gl.SpriteBatcher;
import com.badlogic.androidgames.framework.gl.TextureRegion;
import com.badlogic.androidgames.framework.impl.GLGraphics;
import com.badlogic.androidgames.framework.math.Vector3;

public class WorldRenderer {
    GLGraphics glGraphics;
    LookAtCamera camera;
    AmbientLight ambientLight;
    DirectionalLight directionalLight;
    SpriteBatcher batcher;
    float invaderAngle = 0;
```

The `WorldRenderer` keeps track of the `GLGraphics` instance from which you'll fetch the `GL10` instance. You also have a `LookAtCamera`, an `AmbientLight`, a `DirectionLight`, and a `SpriteBatcher`. Finally, use a member to keep track of the current rotation angle for all invaders.

```java
public WorldRenderer(GLGraphics glGraphics) {
    this.glGraphics = glGraphics;
    camera = new LookAtCamera(67, glGraphics.getWidth()
            / (float) glGraphics.getHeight(), 0.1f, 100);
    camera.getPosition().set(0, 6, 2);
    camera.getLookAt().set(0, 0, -4);
    ambientLight = new AmbientLight();
    ambientLight.setColor(0.2f, 0.2f, 0.2f, 1.0f);
    directionalLight = new DirectionalLight();
    directionalLight.setDirection(-1, -0.5f, 0);
    batcher = new SpriteBatcher(glGraphics, 10);
}
```

In the constructor, set up all members, as usual. The camera has a field of view of 67°, a near clipping plane distance of 0.1 units, and a far clipping plane distance of 100 units. The view frustum will thus easily contain the entire game world. Position it above and behind the ship, and let it look at (0,0,–4). The ambient light is just a faint gray, and the directional light is white and comes from the top-right side. Finally, instantiate the `SpriteBatcher` so that you can render the explosion rectangles.

```java
public void render(World world, float deltaTime) {
    GL10 gl = glGraphics.getGL();
    camera.getPosition().x = world.ship.position.x;
    camera.getLookAt().x = world.ship.position.x;
    camera.setMatrices(gl);

    gl.glEnable(GL10.GL_DEPTH_TEST);
    gl.glEnable(GL10.GL_TEXTURE_2D);
    gl.glEnable(GL10.GL_LIGHTING);
    gl.glEnable(GL10.GL_COLOR_MATERIAL);
    ambientLight.enable(gl);
    directionalLight.enable(gl, GL10.GL_LIGHT0);

    renderShip(gl, world.ship);
    renderInvaders(gl, world.invaders, deltaTime);

    gl.glDisable(GL10.GL_TEXTURE_2D);

    renderShields(gl, world.shields);
    renderShots(gl, world.shots);

    gl.glDisable(GL10.GL_COLOR_MATERIAL);
    gl.glDisable(GL10.GL_LIGHTING);
    gl.glDisable(GL10.GL_DEPTH_TEST);
}
```

In the `render()` method, start off by setting the camera's x-coordinate to the ship's x-coordinate. Of course, also set the x-coordinate of the camera's look-at point accordingly. This way, the camera will follow the ship. Once the position and look-at point are updated, set the projection and model-view matrix via a call to LookAtCamera.setMatrices().

Next, set up all the states that you need for rendering. You'll need depth-testing, texturing, lighting, and the color material functionality so that you don't have to specify a material for the objects via glMaterial(). The next two statements activate the ambient and directional light. With these calls, you have everything set up and you can start rendering the objects.

The first thing you render is the ship via a call to renderShip(). Next, render the invaders with a call to renderInvaders().

Since the shield blocks and shots don't need texturing, simply disable that to save some computations. Once texturing is turned off, render the shots and shields via calls to renderShots() and renderShields().

Finally, disable the other states you set so that you return a clean OpenGL ES state to whoever called you.

```
private void renderShip(GL10 gl, Ship ship) {
    if (ship.state == Ship.SHIP_EXPLODING) {
        gl.glDisable(GL10.GL_LIGHTING);
        renderExplosion(gl, ship.position, ship.stateTime);
        gl.glEnable(GL10.GL_LIGHTING);
    } else {
        Assets.shipTexture.bind();
        Assets.shipModel.bind();
        gl.glPushMatrix();
        gl.glTranslatef(ship.position.x, ship.position.y, ship.position.z);
        gl.glRotatef(ship.velocity.x / Ship.SHIP_VELOCITY * 90, 0, 0, -1);
        Assets.shipModel.draw(GL10.GL_TRIANGLES, 0,
                Assets.shipModel.getNumVertices());
        gl.glPopMatrix();
        Assets.shipModel.unbind();
    }
}
```

The renderShip() method starts off by checking the state of the ship. If it is exploding, disable lighting, call renderExplosion() to render an explosion at the position of the ship, and enable lighting again.

If the ship is alive, bind its texture and model, push the model-view matrix, move it to its position and rotate it around the z-axis based on its velocity, and draw its model. Finally, pop the model-view matrix again (leaving only the camera's view), and unbind the ship model's vertices.

```
private void renderInvaders(GL10 gl, List<Invader> invaders, float deltaTime) {
    invaderAngle += 45 * deltaTime;

    Assets.invaderTexture.bind();
    Assets.invaderModel.bind();
    int len = invaders.size();
    for (int i = 0; i < len; i++) {
        Invader invader = invaders.get(i);
        if (invader.state == Invader.INVADER_DEAD) {
```

```
            gl.glDisable(GL10.GL_LIGHTING);
            Assets.invaderModel.unbind();
            renderExplosion(gl, invader.position, invader.stateTime);
            Assets.invaderTexture.bind();
            Assets.invaderModel.bind();
            gl.glEnable(GL10.GL_LIGHTING);
        } else {
            gl.glPushMatrix();
            gl.glTranslatef(invader.position.x, invader.position.y,
                    invader.position.z);
            gl.glRotatef(invaderAngle, 0, 1, 0);
            Assets.invaderModel.draw(GL10.GL_TRIANGLES, 0,
                    Assets.invaderModel.getNumVertices());
            gl.glPopMatrix();
        }
    }
    Assets.invaderModel.unbind();
}
```

The renderInvaders() method is pretty much the same as the renderShip() method.
The only difference is that you loop through the list of invaders and bind the texture and
mesh before you do so. This considerably reduces the number of binds and speeds up
the rendering. For each invader, check its state again, and render either an explosion or
the normal invader model. Since you bind the model and texture outside the for loop,
you have to unbind and rebind them before you can render an explosion instead of an
invader.

```
private void renderShields(GL10 gl, List<Shield> shields) {
    gl.glEnable(GL10.GL_BLEND);
    gl.glBlendFunc(GL10.GL_SRC_ALPHA, GL10.GL_ONE_MINUS_SRC_ALPHA);
    gl.glColor4f(0, 0, 1, 0.4f);
    Assets.shieldModel.bind();
    int len = shields.size();
    for (int i = 0; i < len; i++) {
        Shield shield = shields.get(i);
        gl.glPushMatrix();
        gl.glTranslatef(shield.position.x, shield.position.y,
                shield.position.z);
        Assets.shieldModel.draw(GL10.GL_TRIANGLES, 0,
                Assets.shieldModel.getNumVertices());
        gl.glPopMatrix();
    }
    Assets.shieldModel.unbind();
    gl.glColor4f(1, 1, 1, 1f);
    gl.glDisable(GL10.GL_BLEND);
}
```

The renderShields() method renders, you guessed it, the shield blocks. Apply the same
principle as in the case of rendering invaders. You only bind the model once. Since you
have no texture, you don't need to bind one. However, you need to enable blending. Set
the global vertex color to blue, with the alpha component set to 0.4. This will make the
shield blocks a little transparent.

```
private void renderShots(GL10 gl, List<Shot> shots) {
    gl.glColor4f(1, 1, 0, 1);
    Assets.shotModel.bind();
```

```
        int len = shots.size();
        for (int i = 0; i < len; i++) {
            Shot shot = shots.get(i);
            gl.glPushMatrix();
            gl.glTranslatef(shot.position.x, shot.position.y, shot.position.z);
            Assets.shotModel.draw(GL10.GL_TRIANGLES, 0,
                    Assets.shotModel.getNumVertices());
            gl.glPopMatrix();
        }
        Assets.shotModel.unbind();
        gl.glColor4f(1, 1, 1, 1);
    }
```

Rendering the shots in renderShots() is the same as rendering the shields, except that you don't use blending and you use a different vertex color (yellow).

```
    private void renderExplosion(GL10 gl, Vector3 position, float stateTime) {
        TextureRegion frame = Assets.explosionAnim.getKeyFrame(stateTime,
                Animation.ANIMATION_NONLOOPING);

        gl.glEnable(GL10.GL_BLEND);
        gl.glPushMatrix();
        gl.glTranslatef(position.x, position.y, position.z);
        batcher.beginBatch(Assets.explosionTexture);
        batcher.drawSprite(0, 0, 2, 2, frame);
        batcher.endBatch();
        gl.glPopMatrix();
        gl.glDisable(GL10.GL_BLEND);
    }
}
```

Finally, the mysterious renderExplosion() method. Get the position at which you want to render the explosion, as well as the state time of the object that is exploding. The latter is used to fetch the correct TextureRegion from the explosion Animation, just as you did for Bob in Super Jumper.

The first thing you do is fetch the explosion animation frame based on the state time. Next, enable blending, since the explosion has transparent pixels that you don't want to render. Push the current model-view matrix and call glTranslatef() so that anything you render after that call will be positioned at the given location. Tell the SpriteBatcher that you are about to render a rectangle using the explosion texture.

The next call is where the magic happens. Tell the SpriteBatcher to render a rectangle at (0,0,0) (the z-coordinate is not given but implicitly zero, remember?), with a width and height of 2 units. Because you used glTranslatef(), that rectangle will not be centered around the origin, but rather around the position you specified to glTranslatef(), which is exactly the position of the ship or invader that exploded. Finally, pop the model-view matrix and disable blending again.

That's it. Twelve classes, forming a full 3D game, parroting the classic Space Invaders game. Try it out. When you come back, you can have a look at the performance characteristics.

Optimizations

Before you think about optimizing the game, you have to evaluate how well it performs. We put an FPSCounter in the GameScreen class, so let's look at its output on a Hero, a Droid, and a Nexus One.

```
Hero (Android 1.5):
02-17 00:59:04.180: DEBUG/FPSCounter(457): fps: 25
02-17 00:59:05.220: DEBUG/FPSCounter(457): fps: 26
02-17 00:59:06.260: DEBUG/FPSCounter(457): fps: 26
02-17 00:59:07.280: DEBUG/FPSCounter(457): fps: 26

Nexus One (Android 2.2.1):
02-17 01:05:40.679: DEBUG/FPSCounter(577): fps: 41
02-17 01:05:41.699: DEBUG/FPSCounter(577): fps: 41
02-17 01:05:42.729: DEBUG/FPSCounter(577): fps: 41
02-17 01:05:43.729: DEBUG/FPSCounter(577): fps: 40

Droid (Android 2.1.1):
02-17 01:47:44.096: DEBUG/FPSCounter(1758): fps: 47
02-17 01:47:45.112: DEBUG/FPSCounter(1758): fps: 47
02-17 01:47:46.127: DEBUG/FPSCounter(1758): fps: 47
02-17 01:47:47.135: DEBUG/FPSCounter(1758): fps: 46
```

The Hero struggles quite a bit, but the game is playable at 25 fps. The Nexus One achieves around 47 fps, and the Droid also reaches 47 fps, which is pretty playable. Can it get better?

In terms of state changes, this is not all that bad. You can reduce some redundant changes here and there, for example some glEnable()/glDisable() calls. But from previous optimization attempts, you know that that won't shave off a lot of overhead.

On the Hero, there's one thing you can do: disable lighting. Once you remove the respective glEnable()/glDisable() calls in WorldRenderer.render(), as well as WorldRenderer.renderShip() and WorldRenderer.renderInvaders(), the Hero achieves the following frame rate:

```
Hero (Android 1.5):
02-17 01:14:44.580: DEBUG/FPSCounter(618): fps: 31
02-17 01:14:45.600: DEBUG/FPSCounter(618): fps: 31
02-17 01:14:46.610: DEBUG/FPSCounter(618): fps: 31
02-17 01:14:47.630: DEBUG/FPSCounter(618): fps: 31
```

That's quite a bit of improvement, and all you have to do is turn off lighting. Special-casing the rendering code for a certain device is possible, but it's good to avoid that. Is there anything else you can do?

The way you render explosions is suboptimal in the case of an exploding invader. You can change the model and texture bindings in the middle of rendering all invaders, which will make the graphics pipeline a little unhappy. However, explosions don't happen often, and don't take a long time (1.6 seconds). The measurements just shown, however, were taken without any explosions on screen, so that's not the culprit.

The truth is that you are rendering too many objects per frame, causing significant call-overhead and stalling the pipeline a little. With your current knowledge of OpenGL ES, there's nothing much you can do about that. However, given that the game "feels" rather playable on all devices, it's not an absolute must to achieve 60 fps. The Droid and Nexus One have a notoriously hard time rendering even mildly complex 3D scenes at 60 frames per second. So, the final lesson to take away from this is: don't get crazy if your game doesn't run at 60 fps. If it is visually smooth and plays well, you can even make do with 30 fps.

> **NOTE:** Other common optimization strategies involve using culling, vertex buffer objects, and other more advanced topics that aren't discussed here. We tried adding these to our Droid Invaders—the effect: zero. None of these devices benefit from these optimizations. That does not mean these techniques are useless. That depends on a lot of factors and their side-effects, and it's hard to predict how certain configurations will behave. If you are interested, just search for those terms on the Web and try the techniques out yourself!

Summary

In this chapter, you completed your third game, a full-blown 3D Space Invaders clone. Yuu employed all the techniques and tricks you learned on your way through this book, and the final outcome is rather satisfying. Of course, these are not AAA games. In fact, none of these are enjoyable for a long period of time. That's where you come in. Get creative, extend these games, and make them fun! You have the tools at your disposal.

Chapter **13**

Publishing Your Game

The last step in becoming an Android game developer is getting your game to your players. There are two possible routes:

■ Take the APK file from your project's `bin/` folder, put it on the Web, and tell your friends to download it and install it on their devices.

■ Publish your application on the Android Market, like a real pro.

The first option is a great way to let other people test your application before you throw it on the market. All they need to do is get a hold of the APK file and install it on their devices. The real fun starts once your game is ready for prime time.

A Word on Testing

As we've seen in the previous chapters, there are various differences among devices. Before you publish your application, make sure it runs well on a couple of common devices and different Android versions. Sadly, there's no easy way to do that at this point. We were lucky enough to get a few phones, covering different device classes and generations, for testing. Depending on your budget, though, that might not be an option. You might have to rely on the emulator (but not too much, as it is indeed unreliable) or preferably on a couple of friends to help you out.

Another way to test your application is to put a beta version on the Android Market. You can clearly mark your application as beta in its title so that users know what to expect. Some users, of course, will gladly ignore all the warnings and still complain about the quality of your potentially unfinished application. That's just how life is, and you'll probably have to deal with negative and possibly unjustified comments. Remember, though: Your users are king. Don't get angry at them—try to figure out how to improve your application instead.

Here's a list of devices we commonly use for testing applications before release:

■ Samsung Galaxy Leo/I5801, 320×240-pixel screen

■ HTC Hero with Android 1.5, 480×320-pixel screen

- HTC G1 with Android 1.6, 480×320-pixel screen

- Motorola Milestone/Droid with Android 2.1, 854×480-pixel screen

- HTC Desire HD with Android 2.2, 800×480-pixel screen

- Nexus One with Android 2.3, 800×480-pixel screen

- Samsung Galaxy S with Android 2.3, 800×480-pixel screen

- Samsung Galaxy Tab 10.1 with Android 3.1, 1280×800-pixel screen

As you can see, we cover quite a range of screen sizes/resolutions and device generations. If you look for outside testers, make sure you get coverage of most of the device generations outlined here. Newer devices should, of course, also be on your list, but less for reasons of performance testing than for compatibility testing.

Finally, you have to accept the fact that you can't test your application on all the devices out there. You are likely to receive error reports that are inexplicable and might well stem from the fact that a user is running a custom rom that doesn't behave as expected. In any case, don't panic; this is normal to some extent. If the problem with errors goes overboard, though, you'll have to try to come up with a scheme to battle it. Luckily, the Android Market helps us out in that regard. We'll see how that works in a bit.

> **NOTE:** Apart from the Android Market's error reporting feature, there's another nice solution called ACRA (Application Crash Report for Android), which is an open-source library specifically designed to report all crashes of your Android application. It's available at `http://code.google.com/p/acra/` and is very easy to use. Just follow the guide on the Google Code page to integrate it into your application.

Becoming a Registered Developer

Google makes it really easy to publish your application on the official Android Market. All you have to do is register an Android developer account for a one-time fee of $25 USD. Depending on the country you live in, this account will allow you to put free and/or paid applications on the market. Google is working hard to expand the number of countries where you can sell your applications.

To register an account, visit `https://market.android.com/publish/signup` and follow the instructions given there.

In addition to your Android developer account, you will also need to register for a free Google Checkout merchant account if you want to sell your applications. You will have the option to do this during the developer account sign-up process. We're not lawyers, so we can't give you any legal advice at this point. Make sure you understand the legal implications of selling an application before you do so. If in doubt, consider consulting an expert on the matter. We don't mean to scare you off by this, as the process is pretty streamlined in general, but you should be prepared to keep your government's tax department apprised about what you are doing.

Google will take 30 percent of your hard-earned money for distributing your app and providing the infrastructure. That seems to be pretty much the standard cut taken by all the application stores on the various platforms.

Signing Your Game's APK

After you have successfully registered as an official Android developer, it's time to prepare your application for publishing. In order to publish your application, you have to sign the APK file. Before you do that, you should make sure everything is in place. Here's a laundry list of things to do before signing the application:

- Remove the `android:debuggable` attribute from the `<application>` tag in your manifest file.

- In the `<manifest>` tag, you'll find the `android:versionCode` and `android:versionName` attributes. If you have already published a previous version of your application, you must increase the `versionCode` attribute, and you should also change the `versionName`. The `versionCode` attribute has to be an integer; the `versionName` can be anything you like.

- If your build target is equal to or higher than SDK level 8 (Android 2.2), you should also make sure the `<manifest>` tag has the `android:installLocation` attribute set to `preferExternal` or `auto`. This will satisfy your users by ensuring that your application is installed on external storage if possible.

- Make sure you only specify the permissions that your game really needs. Users don't like to install applications that seem to demand unnecessary permissions. Check the `<uses-permission>` tags in your manifest file.

- Confirm that you set the `android:minSdkVersion` and `android:targetSdkVersion` correctly. Your application will only be visible in the Android Market on phones that run a version of Android equal to or higher than the specified SDK version.

Double-check all of these items. Once you are done, you can finally export a signed APK file that is ready to be uploaded to the market following these steps:

1. Right-click your project in the package explorer view and select **Android Tools ➤ Export Signed Application Package**. You'll be greeted with the dialog shown in Figure 13–1.

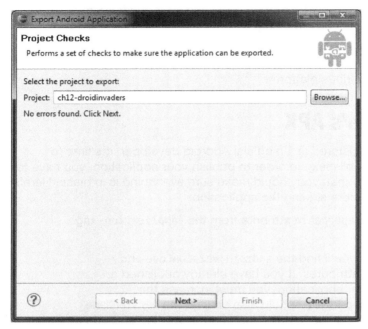

Figure 13–1. *The signed export dialog*

2. Click the Next button to bring up the dialog shown in Figure 13–2.

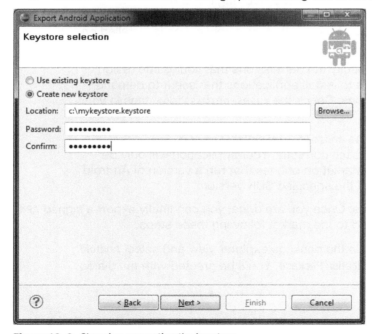

Figure 13–2. *Choosing or creating the keystore*

3. A *keystore* is a password-protected file that stores the key with which you sign your APK file. Since you haven't created one yet, you'll do so now in this dialog. Just provide the location of the keystore, along with the password that you will use to secure it. If you have already created a keystore (for example, if you're publishing a second version of your application), you can select the Use existing keystore radio button and simply provide the dialog with the location of the keystore file. Click the Next button to bring up the dialog shown in Figure 13–3.

Figure 13–3. *Creating the key for signing the* APK

4. To create a valid key, you have to fill out the alias, password, and validity in years, as well as a name in the First and Last Name field. The rest is optional, but it's a good idea to fill it out nevertheless. Another click on Next, and you are shown the final dialog (see Figure 13–4).

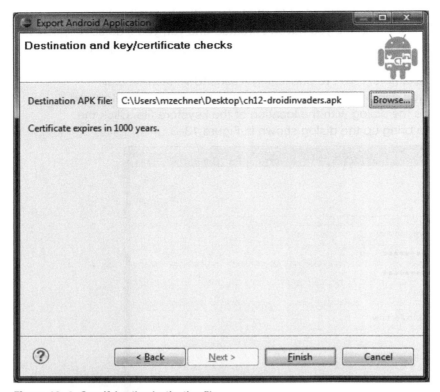

Figure 13–4. *Specifying the destination file*

5.   Now, you are basically done. Just specify where the exported APK file should be stored and remember the path. You'll need it later when you want to upload that APK to the market.

When you want to publish a new version of a previously-published application, you can just reuse the keystore you created the first time you went through the dialog. In the dialog shown in Figure 13–2, just select the keystore file you created previously and provide the password for the keystore. You'll then see the dialog in Figure 13–5.

Just select the key you created previously, provide the password for it, and proceed as before. In both cases, the result will be a signed APK file that is ready for upload to the Android Market.

NOTE: Once you upload a signed APK, you have to use the same key to sign any subsequent versions of the same application.

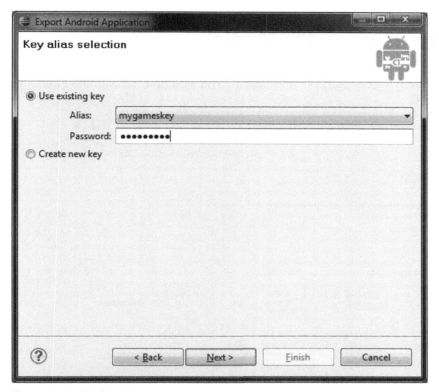

Figure 13–5. *Reusing a key*

So, you've created your first signed APK—congratulations! Now let's throw a wrench into the works, and inform you about the market's multiple APK support. For a single app, you can create multiple APKs that use device capability filtering to get the "best fit" for each user who installs your app. This is a great feature because it means you can do things like the following:

- Ship specific image sets that are compatible with specific GPUs.

- Have a limited feature set targeted for older versions of Android.

- Ship larger-scale graphics for larger screen sizes and regular-scale graphics for all others.

Google will surely add more filters as time goes by, but just the set outlined here enables you to really hone in on a target device (like tablets) without having to jump through too many hoops to keep the download at a reasonable size for first-generation device support.

Putting Your Game on the Market

It's time to log in to your developer account on the Android Market website. Just go to `http://market.android.com/publish` and sign in. You'll be greeted with the interface shown in Figure 13–6.

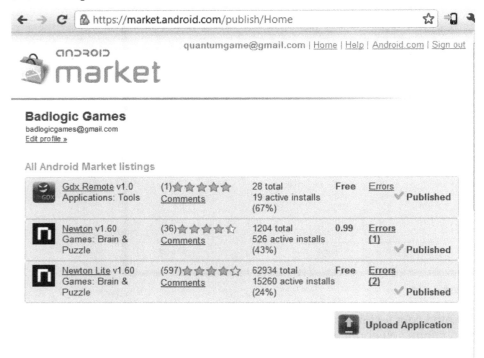

Figure 13–6. *Welcome to the Android Market, developer!*

This is what Android calls the *developer console*, which we'll talk about in a minute. For now, let's concentrate on publishing your app. The Upload Application button will let you do that. Let's go through some of the sections of the uploading page, the first of which is shown in Figure 13–7.

Figure 13–7. *Edit Application screen segment on the Android Developer console*

Uploading Assets

The first thing you have to specify is the APK file you just signed and exported. Just choose the file, and click the Upload button. You can proceed with uploading the rest of the assets in the meantime, as the APK will continue to upload in the background. The system checks the APK once it is uploaded and reports any errors to you on the same page.

You must also provide at least two screenshots of your application. They must be of a certain format (JPEG or PNG) and size (320×480, 480×800, 480×854, 1280×720, or 1280×800). These will display when a user views the details of your application on the Android Market (on the mobile app and on the official website at http://market.android.com).

Next, you have to upload a 512×512, high-resolution PNG or JPEG of your application's icon. At present, this is only shown when a user views your application on the Android Market website. Make it fancy.

The promo graphic (180×120, PNG or JPEG) and feature graphic (1024×500) show up on the Android Market if your game is featured. Being featured is a huge deal, as it means that your application will be the first thing users see when they open up the Android

Market on the mobile app or website. Who gets featured is up to Google, and only they know the basis for this decision.

Finally, you can provide a link to a promotional YouTube video of your application. This will appear on the Android Market website. Note that the Android Market developer interface is constantly changing and may include additional features not listed here.

Product Details

In the Product Details section, which will be displayed to users on the Android Market, you can specify the title (30 characters maximum) and the optional description (4000 characters maximum) of your app in multiple languages.

An additional 500 characters are available to notify users of recent changes in the latest version of your application. The promo text will only be used if your application gets featured.

Next, you have to specify your application's type and category. For each application type, there's a range of categories from which you can choose. For games, you can specify Arcade & Action, Brain & Puzzle, Cards & Casino, Casual, or Racing and Sports. The options make categorization a bit confusing (racing is not a sport?), and they could be better thought out. Here's hoping for some changes in the future.

Finally, you have to decide whether users will pay for your game or not. This decision is final. Once you implement one of the two options, you can't change it unless you publish your game anew, with a different key. If you do so, you'll lose any user reviews, and you'll also alienate your users a little. Think about the route you want to go with your game. We won't give you tips on pricing your game, as that depends on a variety of factors. A price of $0.99 USD seems to be the standard for most games, and users sort of expect it. However, there's nothing keeping you from experimenting a little here.

If you sell your game, make sure that you understand the legal issues involved in doing so.

Publishing Options

The Publishing Options panel lets you specify if you want to copy protect your application, its content rating, and the locations where you want it to be available.

The copy protection feature is pretty much useless, as it can be easily circumnavigated by following a couple of guides on the Internet. Google is going to deprecate this type of copy protection, which should prevent the user from copying your APK file from their device and offering it for free on the Web. Instead, Google now offers an API to integrate a licensing service into your application. This service is supposed to make it harder for users to pirate your game. Evaluating this service is out of scope of this book; we suggest heading over to the Android developer site if you are paranoid about pirates. As with many digital rights management (DRM) schemes, problems have been reported by users who can't run or install an app that uses the licensing service. Take this with a grain of salt, of course. It's the best option you currently have for DRM if you need it.

The content rating allows you to specify your target audience. There are guidelines for rating your own application, which you can find out about by clicking the `Learn More` link on the publishing page. Your application will be filtered by the market based on the content rating you give it. So, carefully evaluate the rating that fits your game.

Finally, you can choose the locations where your application will be available. Usually, you want it to be available everywhere, of course. However, though this is unlikely, there might be scenarios where you want to publish your application only in select locations, possibly for legal reasons.

Publish!

The last few things you will specify on the publishing page are your contact information, your agreement to the Android Content Guidelines (linked on the same page—read them), and confirmation that you agree with U.S. export laws, which you usually do. After providing all of that information, it's time to click the huge `Publish` button at the bottom of the page!

Your game will be instantaneously available to millions of people around the globe. On the Android Market, your application will enter the "Just In" category, making it discoverable for users for as long as it doesn't get pushed down the list by other new applications. Do not try to game the Just In mechanism; it won't work. Uploading a "new" version of your application every few hours will not result in your application bubbling up the Just In list.

Marketing

While it's way outside of our area of expertise, here are a few thoughts on marketing. There's a healthy ecosystem around the Android platform on the Web, consisting of news sites, blogs, forums, and so on. Most blogs and news sites are happy to report on new games, so try to get in touch with as many of them as possible. There are also game-specific Android sites, like `http://www.droidgamers.com`, that should be your number one target for getting the word out. Without a little marketing, your game is unlikely to get noticed, as the Just In list is highly dynamic. Marketing is part of the success of your game. Many thousands of books have been written on the topic, but we assume there's no magic formula. Make a great game, and let people know about it.

The Developer Console

Once your game is on the market, you will want to keep track of its status. How many people have downloaded it so far? Have there been crashes? What are the users saying? You can check all this out in the developer console (see Figure 13–6).

For each of your published applications, you can get a few pieces of information:

- Overall rating of your game and number of ratings

- Comments made by users (just click the Comments link for the respective application)

- Number of times your application has been installed

- Number of active installs of your application

- Error reports

The error reports are of special interest to us. Figure 13–8 shows the error reports received for the game Newton.

Figure 13–8. *Error Reports overview*

In total, there have been eight freezes and two crashes. Newton has been on the market for more than a year, so that's not bad. You can drill down further into the specific errors, of course. The error-reporting feature of the developer console will provide you with detailed information about the crashes and freezes, such as the device model on which the problem occurred, full stack traces, and so on. This can be of immense help when you're trying to figure out what's actually going wrong with your app. Comments on the market won't help for much more than general problem identification.

> **NOTE:** Error reporting is a device-side feature that is not supported on older Android versions. If you want to have full confidence that you are catching all problems, we suggest giving ACRA a look, as mentioned earlier.

Summary

Publishing your game on the market is a breeze, and it has a very low barrier of entry. The hard part is making people aware of your game, a task that we can't help you with. You now have all the knowledge necessary to design, implement, and publish your first game on Android. May the force be with you!

Chapter 14

What's Next?

We talked about a ton of stuff in this book, and there's still so much more to learn. If you feel comfortable with all of the material you've read in this book, you'll probably want to dig deeper. Here are a couple of ideas and directions for your journey.

Getting Social

One of the biggest trends in gaming in the last couple of years has been the integration with social media and services. Twitter, Facebook, and Reddit have become a part of many people's lives, and those people want their friends and family to participate with them in their games as well. What's cooler than having your dad beat you in the latest iteration of Zombie Shooter, right?

Both Twitter and Facebook provide APIs that let your games interact with their services. Want to give the user a way to tweet their latest high score? No problem—integrate the Twitter API, and away you go.

On a related note, there are two big services in the mobile space that make it their goal to connect gamers and let them discover new games easily: Scoreloop and OpenFeint. Each of these services provides an API for Android that lets players easily keep high scores, compare their achievements, and more online. Both APIs are pretty straightforward and come with good examples and documentation.

Location Awareness

We only briefly touched on this in Chapters 1 and 4, and we didn't exploit it in any of our games. All Android devices come with some type of sensor that lets you determine their location. An interesting enough feature in itself, using it in a game can make for some innovative and never-before-seen game mechanics. Most Android games hardly use this capability. Can you think of a fun way to use the GPS sensor in your game?

Multiplayer Functionality

This being a beginner's book, we haven't talked about how to create multiplayer games. Suffice it to say that Android provides you with the APIs to do just that. Depending on the type of game, the difficulty of implementing multiplayer functionality varies. Turn-based games, such as chess or card games, are pretty simple to implement. Fast-paced action games or real-time strategy games are a different matter altogether. In both cases, you need to have an understanding of network programming, a topic for which a lot of materials exist on the Web.

OpenGL ES 2.0 and More

So far, you've seen only half of OpenGL ES, so to speak. We used OpenGL ES 1.0 exclusively, because it is the most widely-supported version on Android at this point. Its fixed-function nature lends itself well to getting into 3D graphics programming. However, there's a newer, shinier version of OpenGL ES that enables you to code directly on the GPU. It's very different from what you have seen in this book in that you are responsible for all the nitty-gritty details, such as fetching a single texel from a texture or manually transforming the coordinates of a vertex, all directly on the GPU.

OpenGL ES 2.0 has a so-called "shader-based," or programmable, pipeline as opposed to the fixed-function pipeline of OpenGL ES 1.0 and 1.1. For many 3D (and 2D) games, OpenGL ES 1.x is more than sufficient. If you want to get fancy, though, you might want to consider checking out OpenGL ES 2.0! Don't be afraid—all the concepts you learned in this book are easily transferable to the programmable pipeline.

There is a Google-supported library for Android called RenderScript, which is a high-level interface for building flashy OpenGL ES 2.0–based effects without all of the pain of implementing them using its tedious API. Don't get us wrong—OpenGL ES 2.0 is great, and we have plenty of experience with it—but RenderScript certainly provides an easier way of creating many graphics effects, and it is at the heart of many of the default Live Wallpapers which ship with stock versions of Android.

We also haven't touched on topics such as animated 3D models and some more-advanced OpenGL ES 1.x concepts such as vertex buffer objects. As with OpenGL ES 2.0, you can find many resources on the Web, as well as in book form. You know the basics. Now it's time to learn even more!

Frameworks and Engines

If you bought this book with little prior game development knowledge, you may have wondered why we didn't choose to use one of the many pre-existing frameworks available for Android game development. Reinventing the wheel is bad, right? We want you to firmly understand the principles. Although learning them may be tedious at times, it will pay off in the end. It will be so much easier to pick up any precanned solution out there when you are armed with the knowledge you gained here, and it is our hope that you'll recognize the advantage that gives you.

For Android, several commercial and noncommercial open-source frameworks and engines exist. What's the difference between a framework and an engine?

- A framework gives you control over every aspect of your game development environment. This comes at the price of having to figure out your own way of doing things (for example, how you organize your game world, how you handle screens and transitions, and so on). In this book, we developed a very simple framework upon which we build our games.

- An engine, on the other hand, is more streamlined for specific tasks. It dictates how you should do things, giving you easy-to-use modules for common tasks and a general architecture for your game. The downside is that your game might not fit the precanned solutions the engine offers you. Oftentimes, you'll have to modify the engine itself to achieve your goals, which may or may not be possible depending on whether the source is available. Engines can greatly speed up initial development time, but they might slow it to a grinding halt if you encounter a problem for which the engine was not made.

In the end, it's a matter of personal taste, budget, and goals. As independent developers, we prefer frameworks because they are usually easier to understand and because they let us do things in the exact way we want them to be done.

With that said, choose your poison. Here's a list of frameworks and engines that can speed up your development process:

- *Unreal Development Kit* (www.udk.com): A commercial game engine running on a multitude of platforms, developed by Epic Games. Epic made games such as Unreal Tournament, so this engine is quality stuff. Uses its own scripting language.

- *Unity* (http://unity3d.com): Another commercial game engine with great tools and functionality. It, too, works on a multitude of platforms, including iOS and Android, or in the browser, and it is easy to learn. Allows a couple of languages for coding the game logic; Java is not among them.

- *jPCT-AE* (www.jpct.net/jpct-ae/): A port of the Java-based jPCT engine for Android, this has some great features with regard to 3D programming. Works on the desktop and on Android. Closed source.

- *Ardor3D* (www.ardor3d.com): A very powerful Java-based 3D engine. Works on Android and on the desktop, and is open source with great documentation.

- *libgdx* (http://code.google.com/p/libgdx/): An open-source Java-based game development framework by Mario Zechner for 2D and 3D games. Works on Windows, Linux, Mac OS X, and of course Android without any code modifications. You can develop and test on the desktop without needing to attach a device and upload you're APK file (or having to use the slow emulator). You'll probably feel right at home after having read this book—it's all part of our evil plan. Did you notice that this bullet point is just slightly bigger than the rest?

- *Slick-AE* (http://slick.cokeandcode.com): A port of the Java-based Slick framework to Android, built on top of libgdx. Tons of functionality and an easy-to-use API for 2D game development. Cross platform and open source, of course.

- *AndEngine* (www.andengine.org): A nice Java-based, Android-only 2D engine, partially based on libgdx code (open source for the win). Similar in concept to the famous cocos2d game development engine for iOS.

- *BatteryTech* (www.batterypoweredgames.com/batterytech): An open-source commercial library in C++ that supports cross-platform game code and officially supports Android, iOS, Windows, and OS X as build targets.

- *Moai* (http://getmoai.com): Another open-source commercial library in C++ that targets Android and iOS with cross-platform game code.

- *Papaya* (http://papayamobile.com/developer/engine): A free Android-exclusive 2D game engine that includes a physics API, OpenGL support, particle effects, and more.

More and more middleware, frameworks, and engines are showing up all the time, so this list is by no means exhaustive. We suggest giving these options a try at some point. They can help you speed up your game development quite a bit.

Resources on the Web

The Web is full of game development resources. In general, Google will be your best friend, but there are some special places that you should check out, including these:

- www.gamedev.net: One of the oldest game development sites on the Web, with a huge treasure trove of articles on all sorts of game development topics.

- www.gamasutra.com: Another old Goliath of game development. More industry-oriented, with lots of postmortems and insight into the professional game development world.

- www.gpwiki.org: A big wiki on game development, chock full of articles on game programming for different platforms, languages, and so on.

■ `www.flipcode.com/archives/`: The archives of the now-defunct flipcode site. Some pearls can be found here. Although slightly outdated at times, it is still an incredibly good resource.

■ `www.java-gaming.org`: The number one place to go for Java game developers. People such as Markus Persson of Minecraft fame have been known to frequent this place.

Closing Words

Many sleepless nights followed by days of bloodshot eyes went into the writing of this book, and let us say that, while there are few things in life that we enjoy more than building video games and spreading our knowledge to others, making it to the final few paragraphs of this project is certainly up there.

Writing this book was a joy (the mornings, not so much), and we hope we gave you what you came here for. There's so much more to discover, so many more techniques, algorithms, and ideas to explore. This is just the beginning for you. There's more to learn ahead.

We feel confident that, with the material we dissected and discussed, you have a solid foundation to build upon, which will enable you to grasp new ideas and concepts faster. There's no need to fall into the trap of copying and pasting code anymore. Even better, almost all the things we discussed will translate well to any other platform (give or take some language or API differences). We hope you can see the big picture, and that it will enable you to start building the games of your dreams.

Index

E

F

◼ H

writer.close( ) method, 156

X, Y

XML file, 110

CPSIA information can be obtained at www.ICGtesting.com
Printed in the USA
LVOW02s2152020913

350696LV00007B/135/P

9 781430 239871